FUNDAMENTAL RIGHTS AND THE LEGAL OBLIGATIONS OF BUSINESS

Corporations can significantly affect the fundamental rights of individuals. This book investigates how to determine the substantive content of their obligations that emanate from these rights. In doing so, it addresses important conceptual issues surrounding fundamental rights. From an investigation of existing legal models, a clear structural similarity surfaces in how courts make decisions about corporate obligations. The book seeks to systematise, justify and develop this emergent 'multi-factoral approach' through examining key factors for determining the substantive content of corporate obligations. The book defends the use of the proportionality test for ascertaining corporations' negative obligations and outlines a novel seven-step test for determining their positive obligations. The book finally proposes legal and institutional reforms – on both the national and international levels – designed to enhance the quality of decision-making surrounding corporate obligations, and embed fundamental rights within the corporate structure and the minds of key decision-makers.

DAVID BILCHITZ is Professor of Fundamental Rights and Constitutional Law, University of Johannesburg, South Africa and Professor of Law, University of Reading, United Kingdom. He is also Director of the South African Institute for Advanced Constitutional, Public, Human Rights and International Law. He is a member of the Academy of Science of South Africa and Vice-President of the International Association of Constitutional Law. He is the author of *Poverty and Fundamental Rights: the Justification and Enforcement of Socio-Economic Rights* (2007) and has published extensively in the area of business and human rights.

CAMBRIDGE STUDIES IN CONSTITUTIONAL LAW

The aim of this series is to produce leading monographs in constitutional law. All areas of constitutional law and public law fall within the ambit of the series, including human rights and civil liberties law, administrative law, as well as constitutional theory and the history of constitutional law. A wide variety of scholarly approaches is encouraged, with the governing criterion being simply that the work is of interest to an international audience. Thus, works concerned with only one jurisdiction will be included in the series as appropriate, while, at the same time, the series will include works which are explicitly comparative or theoretical - or both. The series editor likewise welcomes proposals that work at the intersection of constitutional and international law, or that seek to bridge the gaps between civil law systems, the US, and the common law jurisdictions of the Commonwealth.

Books in the Series

Courting Constitutionalism: The Politics of Public Law and Judicial Review in Pakistan Moeen Cheema

Ruling by Cheating: Governance in Illiberal Democracy András Sajó

Local Meanings of Proportionality Afroditi Marketou

Property Rights and Social Justice: Progressive Property in Action Rachael Walsh

Carl Schmitt's Early Legal-Theoretical Writings: Statute and Judgment and the Value of the State and the Significance of the Individual Lars Vinx and Samuel Garrett Zeitlin

Remedies for Human Rights Violations: A Two-Track Approach to Supra-national and National Law Kent Roach

A. W. Dicey and the Common Law Constitutional Tradition Mark D. Walters

Europe's Second Constitution: Crisis, Courts and Community Markus W. Gehring

A. V. Dicey and the Common Law Constitutional Tradition: A Legal Turn of Mind Mark D. Walters

Administrative Competence: Reimagining Administrative Law Elizabeth Fisher and Sidney A. Shapiro

Legal Sabotage: Ernst Fraenkel in Hitler's Germany Douglas Morris

Proportionality in Action: Comparative and Empirical Perspectives on the Judicial Practice Edited by Mordechai Kremnitzer, Tayla Steiner and Andrej Lang

Constitutional Dialogue: Democracy, Rights, Institutions Edited by Geoffrey Sigalet, Grégoire Webber and Rosalind Dixon

The Veiled Sceptre: Reserve Powers of Heads of State in Westminster Systems Anne Twomey

Vigilance and Restraint in the Common Law of Judicial Review Dean Knight

The Alchemists: Questioning Our Faith in Courts as Democracy-Builders Tom Gerald Daly

Australia's Constitution after Whitlam Brendan Lim

Building the Constitution: The Practice of Constitutional Interpretation in Post-Apartheid South Africa James Fowkes

Dimensions of Dignity: The Theory and Practice of Modern Constitutional Law Jacob Weinrib

Reason of State: Law, Prerogative, Empire Thomas Poole

Bills of Rights in the Common Law Robert Leckey

The Guardian of the Constitution: Hans Kelsen and Carl Schmitt on the Limits of Constitutional Law Translated by Lars Vinx, with an introduction and notes by Lars Vinx

Parliamentary Bills of Rights: The Experiences of New Zealand and the United Kingdom Janet L. Hiebert and James B. Kelly

Lawyering for the Rule of Law: Government Lawyers and the Rise of Judicial Power in Israel Yoav Dotan

Balancing Constitutional Rights: The Origins and Meanings of Postwar Legal Discourse Jacco Bomhoff

Judges on Trial: The Independence and Accountability of the English Judiciary Shimon Shetreet and Sophie Turenne

Proportionality and Constitutional Culture Moshe Cohen-Eliya and Iddo Porat

The Politics of Principle: The First South African Constitutional Court, 1995–2005 Theunis Roux

The New Commonwealth Model of Constitutionalism: Theory and Practice Stephen Gardbaum

Searching for the State in British Legal Thought: Competing Conceptions of the Public Sphere Janet McLean

Judging Social Rights Jeff King

Proportionality: Constitutional Rights and Their Limitations Aharon Barak

Parliamentary Sovereignty: Contemporary Debates Jeffrey Goldsworthy

FUNDAMENTAL RIGHTS AND THE LEGAL OBLIGATIONS OF BUSINESS

DAVID BILCHITZ
University of Johannesburg and University of Reading

CAMBRIDGE
UNIVERSITY PRESS

CAMBRIDGE
UNIVERSITY PRESS

Shaftesbury Road, Cambridge CB2 8EA, United Kingdom

One Liberty Plaza, 20th Floor, New York, NY 10006, USA

477 Williamstown Road, Port Melbourne, VIC 3207, Australia

314–321, 3rd Floor, Plot 3, Splendor Forum, Jasola District Centre, New Delhi – 110025, India

103 Penang Road, #05–06/07, Visioncrest Commercial, Singapore 238467

Cambridge University Press is part of Cambridge University Press & Assessment, a department of the University of Cambridge.

We share the University's mission to contribute to society through the pursuit of education, learning and research at the highest international levels of excellence.

www.cambridge.org
Information on this title: www.cambridge.org/9781108815314

DOI: 10.1017/9781108895224

First published 2022
First paperback edition 2023

A catalogue record for this publication is available from the British Library

Library of Congress Cataloging-in-Publication data
Names: Bilchitz, David, author.
Title: Fundamental rights and the legal obligations of business / David Bilchitz, University of Johannesburg.
Description: Cambridge, United Kingdom ; New York, NY : Cambridge University Press, 2021. | Series: Cambridge studies in constitutional law | Includes bibliographical references and index.
Identifiers: LCCN 2021028152 (print) | LCCN 2021028153 (ebook) | ISBN 9781108841948 (hardback) | ISBN 9781108815314 (paperback) | ISBN 9781108895224 (ebook)
Subjects: LCSH: Social responsibility of business – Law and legislation.
Classification: LCC K1329.5 .B553 2021 (print) | LCC K1329.5 (ebook) | DDC 346/.0664–dc23
LC record available at https://lccn.loc.gov/2021028152
LC ebook record available at https://lccn.loc.gov/2021028153

ISBN 978-1-108-84194-8 Hardback
ISBN 978-1-108-81531-4 Paperback

To Ruvi Ziegler
In love, companionship and a joint commitment to a better, rights-respecting world.

CONTENTS

FIGURES

TABLES

PREFACE

The finalisation of this manuscript has taken place in the shadow of the COVID-19 pandemic that has severely disrupted life across the globe and, sadly, led to millions of deaths. Whilst the origins of the virus in humans is still being researched, the current thinking has been that it emerged from a market for live animals – a place where abuse of sentient creatures is routine in the name of economic gain. Once the virus had started spreading, critical shortages of personal protective equipment arose: reports soon started emerging of workers in developing countries being forced to work long hours in unsafe conditions to ramp up production. Corporations in many countries were involved in the development of new mobile applications to trace people and their contacts. Early on, the search for a vaccine began: large pharmaceutical companies teamed up with universities and research institutes in a competitive race. The names of pharmaceutical corporations – Pfizer, AstraZeneca, Moderna, Novavax and Johnson & Johnson – have quickly become the subjects of daily conversation and synonymous with potential routes out of this dark period in world history. Their patent rights will allow them to profit from our common desperation and to place limits on who can manufacture the vaccine, thus restricting the use of any spare manufacturing capacity across the world to produce more vials of these life-saving injections.

The current role of corporations in the health crisis facing our world highlights the power they hold today both within states and internationally. They, at times, control whether we are able to live or die and, in many instances, affect our most basic interests – free speech, privacy, food and healthcare. They have the capacity profoundly to impact on our most precious entitlements – fundamental rights. It is, for this reason, there has been a growing discourse internationally around 'business and human rights': yet, in these debates, limited attention has been paid within legal discourse to the question of exactly how we are to determine the obligations of businesses – and corporations in particular – with respect to fundamental rights. Indeed, there has been a reluctance to engage with the exact implications of fundamental rights beyond the realm of state. The relative neglect of this question and the centrality of corporations both to constitutional orders and the international community is what motivated me to write this book. As will become evident from the argument, there is no simple formulaic answer: I grapple with the implications of fundamental rights for corporations and argue that we can identify an analytical framework for making decisions both in relation to their negative and positive obligations. That, in turn, requires changes to what we require of all decision-makers – both within corporations and outside of them – when they consider corporate obligations and, to this effect, I make proposals for law reform both at the national and international levels. I hope the book will help advance our understanding of what can be expected of corporations through identifying a structured process of reasoning for determining their obligations and thus, in turn, help advance the realisation of fundamental rights in our world.

I am deeply grateful, in the long shadow of our own mortality that COVID-19 has created, that I have been able to complete this book. It was a huge undertaking and represents a culmination of thinking that has developed since I first grappled with business and fundamental rights in 2008. I am grateful to Theunis Roux, the then director of the South African Institute for Advanced Constitutional, Public, Human Right and International Law (SAIFAC) (now a centre of the University of Johannesburg), for his encouragement and pressing on me the importance of these questions. Two wonderful collaborations with my esteemed colleague Surya Deva resulted in two edited collections seeking to engage with two of the most prominent developments at the international level – the 'United Nations Guiding Principles on Business and Human Rights' and the process for negotiating a 'Treaty on Business and Human Rights'. A co-authored article with Laura Ausserladscheider Jonas, an intern at SAIFAC at the time, started my thinking about the application of the proportionality test in the corporate sphere – I am grateful to Laura for her permission to draw on this prior work which I have sought to develop here. The book itself has taken around four years to complete since its origins in thinking of a larger project for my sabbatical leave in 2017–2018. I am deeply grateful to the University of Johannesburg for granting me a year of research leave, something sadly that is becoming increasingly rare and rendering it difficult for academics to embark upon extended projects such as this. I am grateful for the continuing support for my research and the institute I direct – SAIFAC – at the Faculty of

Law of the University of Johannesburg and wish to thank colleagues, both junior and senior. I am excited also to have recently joined part-time at the University of Reading and thank my colleagues there for a warm welcome.

I am also deeply grateful to the Von Humboldt Foundation for awarding me a Georg Forster Research Fellowship which enabled me to spend over a year in Germany conducting research for this book. I was based in Berlin as a visiting research professor at the Humboldt University – Philipp Dann was a generous and supportive host, and I am deeply grateful to him for his friendship, collegiality and creating the conductive conditions in which this work could progress. A public lecture he invited me to give proved a turning point in the genesis of this book: I am grateful for a question by Christian Schliemann (from the European Center for Constitutional and Human Rights) which prompted reflections that led the structure of the book to crystallise. I am also grateful to the Minerva Center for Human Rights at Tel Aviv University for hosting me for two months as a visiting professor during my sabbatical, as well as for inviting me to deliver a public lecture there which stimulated many wonderful conversations that helped develop the book. The Bonavero Institute for Human Rights at the University of Oxford very kindly hosted an online seminar on Chapter 9 of this book (the corporate law reform proposals). I am deeply grateful to Ekaterina Aristova for organising it as well as to Peter Muchlinski and John Armour for their thoughtful comments and deep engagement with my work – I could not have asked for better interrogators who have led me to revise earlier shortcomings.

I am also grateful to have had the research assistance of a number of excellent researchers. Simon Willaschek was a diligent, intelligent and attentive researcher in Berlin who has gone beyond the call of duty and, in particular, enabled me to grapple with the relevant German legal developments. I look forward to seeing his legal and academic career flourish in the future. Gonzalo Ramirez Cleves provided me with an initial steer in addressing Colombian cases. Rafael Andrés Gomez Campo has helped me improve my grasp of the relevant cases and to refine my understanding of the relevant principles – thank you to both of them! I am also grateful to a number of researchers at SAIFAC who have helped to find relevant sources: Raisa Cachalia, Robert Freeman, Nabeelah Mia and Ropafadzo Maphosa are all extremely talented, and I look forward to watching their stars rise. Naomi Hove deserves a special mention for her administrative excellence that has helped carve out time for me to focus on the book. The library staff at the University of

Johannesburg have been incredibly helpful in finding sources and, in particular, assisting me to access material that was not readily available online in recent months – for their friendliness and helpfulness, I would like to thank Lizette Van Zyl and, in particular on this project, Catrin ver Loren van Themaat for quickly responding to queries and Gerda Van der Berg for her help with interlibrary loans.

I am also grateful to the editor of this series, Professor David Dyzenhaus, for an enthusiastic response to the initial proposal and to reviewers at Cambridge University Press for their comments that led me to plug a number of gaps. I am grateful to Marianne Nield who has been a friendly and attentive commissioning editor. I also thank Finola O'Sullivan for her support of this project. The production of this book has been extremely smooth due to the excellent management skills of Laura Blake and Priyanka Durai to whom I am extremely grateful. I also deeply appreciate the conscientious copy-editing by Padma Priya Ranganathan. It was also a delight to work with Sanet le Roux who is a highly professional and talented indexer – thank you!

On a personal level, I am deeply fortunate to have a wonderful group of supportive friends, family and colleagues who have nurtured me during the writing of this book. My time in Berlin was incredible and so enriching partly because of many new friendships formed for which I am grateful. There was also a sense of historical justice in writing a book partially in a research office that faced Bebelplatz where the books of those who share my religion and sexual orientation were burnt on 10 May 1933.

My family has been a constant source of nourishment – it is a joy to see the development of my nephews Gavi and Shalev in the caring, warm home my brother, Leonard Bilchitz, and sister-in-law, Lara Cohen, have created. The love and support of my incredible parents – Ruven and Cynthia Bilchitz – has been the source from which all else emerged. Words cannot do justice to explain how grateful I am to them for nurturing my intellectual curiosity and providing me with the foundations upon which to flourish.

The period of writing this book also overlapped with the most significant development in my personal life – finding my husband, Dr Ruvi Ziegler, and our marriage. When COVID-19 unexpectedly forced us into sharing a small space, he gave up his own desk for me to work on finishing this book. He is a companion, confidante and colleague, all-in-one, always considerate, gentle and full of joie de vivre. He never fails to brighten my day and I love him dearly. This book is dedicated to him.

ACKNOWLEDGEMENTS

This book emerges from about thirteen years of reflections on questions relating to business and human rights. It inevitably draws from ideas developed in some of my prior work though it is a significant development thereon. I list here some of the prior works that have shaped my thinking and thank the publishers for permission to draw on elements thereof in certain segments of this book. I have indicated and referenced where I have done so at the relevant points in the book.

Bilchitz, D. I. 2007. *Poverty and Fundamental Rights*. Oxford: Oxford University Press. Permission granted from Oxford University Press.

2008. 'Corporate Law and the Constitution: Towards Binding Human Rights Responsibilities for Corporations'. *South African Law Journal* 124: 754–789. Permission granted by Juta.

2010a. 'Do Corporations Have Positive Fundamental Rights Obligations?' *Theoria* 125: 1–35. Permission granted by Berghahn Books.

2010b. 'The Ruggie Framework: An Adequate Rubric for Corporate Human Rights Obligations?' *SUR International Journal on Human Rights* 12: 199–229. Permission granted by Conectas.

2013. 'A Chasm Between "Is" and "Ought"? A Critique of the Normative Foundations of the SRSG's Framework and the Guiding Principles'. In S. Deva and D. Bilchitz (eds.) *Human Rights Obligations of Business: Beyond the Corporate Responsibility to Respect?* Cambridge: Cambridge University Press. Permission granted by Cambridge University Press.

2014. 'Necessity and Proportionality: Towards a Balanced Approach'. In L. Lazarus, C. McCrudden and N. Bowles (eds.). *Reasoning Rights* Oxford: Hart. Permission granted by Hart Publishing, an Imprint of Bloomsbury Publishing Plc.

2016a. 'Corporations and the Limits of State-Based Models for Protecting Fundamental Rights in International Law'. *Indiana Journal of Global Legal Studies* 23: 143–170. Permission granted by Indiana University Press.

2016b. 'The Necessity for a Business and Human Rights Treaty'. *Business and Human Rights Journal* 1: 203–227. Permission granted by Cambridge University Press.

Bilchitz, D. I. and Ausserladscheider Jonas, L. 2016. 'Proportionality, Fundamental Rights and the Duties of Directors'. *Oxford Journal of Legal Studies* 36: 828–854. Permission granted by Oxford University Press and my co-author, Laura Ausserladscheider Jonas.

Bilchitz, D. I. 2017a. 'Putting Flesh on the Bone: What Should a Business and Human Rights Treaty Look Like?' In S. Deva and D. Bilchitz (eds.). *Building a Treaty on Business and Human Rights: Context and Contours*. Cambridge: Cambridge University Press. Permission granted by Cambridge University Press.

2017b. 'Corporate Obligations and a Business and Human Rights Treaty: a Constitutional Law Model?'. In S. Deva and D. Bilchitz (eds.). *Building a Treaty on Business and Human Rights: Context and Contours*. Cambridge: Cambridge University Press. Permission granted by Cambridge University Press.

TABLE OF CASES

Introduction

The Question of Substantive Corporate Obligations for Fundamental Rights

Fundamental rights are, ultimately, about individuals and their lives. It is therefore fitting to begin this book with a concrete example that provides the background to the central problem that it attempts to address.

The Story of Herceptin and the Content of Corporate Obligations

Thandi is a healthy thirty-eight-year-old who lives with her partner and small children of five and three in Johannesburg, South Africa. She works hard as a domestic worker, scraping by each month to ensure her family can live decently. Sadly, in 2017, Thandi was diagnosed with metastatic breast cancer and, after doing tests, her doctors concluded that this disease is HER2-positive: this means that her breast cancer cells make too many copies of a particular gene known as HER2.[1] As a result, they recommend an effective drug known as Herceptin which can help stop the growth of her breast cancer. The drug is manufactured by the Swiss pharmaceutical company Roche which had a patent on it until 2019. In 2017, it retailed in the private sector for around R500,000 (USD40,000) a year.[2] Thandi is unable to afford this additional expenditure nor does she have access to private health insurance which might provide the drug. She is dependent upon the public health system: yet, the high cost of the drug meant, in 2017, that the government had only a limited supply available with 500 treatment spaces.[3] Thandi's doctor informs her that, for the foreseeable future, all the treatment spaces have been taken and so she will be unable to access the treatment. Thandi is in deep trauma as without this drug there is a significant chance that her cancer will be fatal.

[1] See www.breastcancer.org/treatment/targeted_therapies/herceptin/how_works

[2] See www.timeslive.co.za/news/south-africa/2017-06-14-11-things-you-need-to-know-about-the-half-a-million-rand-breast-cancer-drug/ (14 June 2017)

[3] See www.businesslive.co.za/bd/companies/healthcare/2017-08-29-roche-cuts-the-price-of-breast-cancer-drug/ (29 August 2017).

This emblematic scenario is indicative of real-life situations, which are replicated across the world. Famously, pharmaceutical companies had priced HIV/AIDS drugs at very high levels: in South Africa, for instance, only after significant public campaigning and the threat of legal action did the price come down significantly.[4] There are many other diseases – such as breast cancer – where there are highly priced treatments which have not attracted such a wide public campaign. The price and availability of COVID-19 vaccinations is, currently, raising serious concerns about its accessibility in the poorest countries. It is clear that a developing country like South Africa – with so many demands on the public purse – cannot have an unlimited budget for healthcare. The question thus arises: do corporations have an unlimited discretion to charge whatever they wish for life-saving drugs? Or, alternatively, do they have obligations to ensure the medicines they develop and manufacture are accessible to all who need them?

There have been recent reports that some directors of pharmaceutical corporations understand their responsibility in a narrow way. For instance, the former CEO of Valeant Pharmaceuticals is quoted as saying that if 'products are sort of mispriced and there's an opportunity, we will act appropriately in terms of doing what I assume our shareholders would like us to do'.[5] As part of this strategy, Valeant would buy up drugs and then raise the price, often beyond the ability of many people to afford. Of course, this approach would lead to serious conflicts between profit-making for the corporation and two very basic rights of individuals: the right to life and the right to health.

The ability to set prices at very high levels often derives from the system of intellectual property that has developed globally. In particular, patents often allow a corporation to have a monopoly over the production of a certain medicine (or other good) for a limited period of time. Given that monopoly and the desperate needs of many people for a drug (such as Thandi suffering from breast cancer), the corporation is able to price that drug very highly. The system is justified on the basis that there are significant research and development costs in finding successful medicine formulas such as Herceptin and, hence, as a reward for such expenditure, inventors of new drugs should be capable of exploiting them financially for a period. Seemingly, however, this patent system was developed without considering the costs to fundamental rights it would

4 For a recent account of this case and series of events, see Sundaram, 2018: 175–179.

5 See www.nytimes.com/2016/03/22/business/valeant-ackman-pearson-earnings.html

impose. There have been attempts by developing countries under the World Trade Organisation to mitigate the effects of this system through certain flexibilities in the TRIPS agreement though there have also been attempts to undermine their ability to utilise them, particularly by the United States.[6]

There are a number of issues that arise from the aforementioned example. First, there is a particular approach to the nature of the corporation that is in evidence. The former CEO of Valeant expresses a view that the corporation is simply a vehicle for individuals to utilise for their own economic gain. That, of course, allows it to operate without considering its obligations to others. An alternative view would see the corporation as being an entity fundamentally integrated into society, benefitting from society and so owing obligations to society. A corporation on this view could not claim to operate without considering the impact of its activities on others.

Secondly, in relation to fundamental rights, the question arises concerning the corporation's obligations. In this regard, it is important to distinguish between 'negative' and 'positive' obligations. 'Negative' obligations involve avoiding harm to others: for instance, a negative obligation flowing from the right to life would be not to shoot an individual. 'Positive' obligations, on the other hand, involve active duties to assist in the realisation of rights. In relation to the right to life, for instance, that might involve being required to provide an individual with life-saving medication to cure them of a fatal disease. Since negative obligations are associated with 'not' having to do anything and, usually involve, simply leaving individuals alone, they are often less controversial. This is particularly so in the context of an actor such as a corporation which is frequently considered to be part of the 'private' sphere and so, justifiably, focused on pursuing its own economic projects. Negative obligations, in this context, would not require a corporation to provide anything but simply amount to a duty not to harm individual rights in the course of conducting business. However, determining the substantive content of such 'negative' obligations is not as simple as it often seems: as will be argued, there is substantial complexity in understanding when negative impacts on rights translate into impermissible 'harms' or 'violations' thereof.

[6] For an account of the DOHA declaration, the flexibilities under TRIPS and the attempts to undermine them through bilateral and regional free trade agreements, see, for instance, Sundaram, 2018: 58–80.

Beyond that issue is the further question whether corporations have 'positive' obligations in relation to fundamental rights and how to determine them. In the example I have provided, it could persuasively be claimed that Roche is not violating any negative obligations to Thandi as the corporation did not cause her disease: she is just unfortunate to have breast cancer. Instead, what the example raises is the question whether corporations have a duty actively to contribute towards keeping her alive and maintaining her health. If they have such positive obligations, a further set of questions arise concerning the substantive content thereof: does Roche have a more onerous set of obligations given that it operates in the healthcare sector, which significantly affects the fundamental rights of individuals? Once it has developed the drug, must it provide it to all those who cannot afford that drug for free? If not, how far do its obligations extend and what are their limits?[7]

The Focus of This Book and the Question of Methodology

This example sets the scene for the two related questions which are the subject of this book. The first concerns whether corporations themselves have obligations that flow from fundamental rights;[8] and the second concerns, assuming an affirmative answer to the first question, how to understand the substantive content of those

[7] On top of these questions is the further question whether Thandi would have any legal redress in this situation. Could a court intervene to force Roche to provide such drugs at a reduced cost? How would it enforce such a judgment, particularly if Roche decides to leave the country upon receiving such a ruling?

[8] I generally utilise the locution 'fundamental rights' in this book to cover what are often referred to as 'human rights' in some international instruments and bills of rights. The locution 'human rights' is used when the context requires – such as when an instrument uses this term. The term 'fundamental rights' is foreign to neither international law nor domestic law: the European Union has, as a foundational normative document, a Charter of Fundamental Rights; the German Constitution speaks of 'Grundrechte'; and the Colombian Constitution of 'derechos fundamentales'. Apart from its usage in positive law, I believe this locution has much to commend it normatively. Firstly, it refers to the fact that these rights are 'constitutional essentials' for any society (Rawls, 1993: 227–230) and at its normative foundation. Secondly, the locution avoids the implication that it is only humans – as a species – that possess such rights. The claim that rights are only possessed by human beings is, I believe, a serious mistake which has caused significant harms to other creatures (see Bilchitz, 2009) and, consequently, it is best to shift our language in a more inclusive direction. Sadly, given space constraints, I am not able, in this work, to elaborate on the obligations of corporations in relation to the fundamental rights of non-human animals, which must await a future treatment.

obligations.[9] Much of the academic discussion in this area has become stuck on the first question with very limited consideration of the second question.[10] Whilst I shall address the first question and provide arguments for why it should be answered in the affirmative, the focus of this book will be on developing a general legal analytical framework for determining the content of corporate obligations in relation to fundamental rights. Such a framework is not focused simply on the level of concrete cases in concrete circumstances – though it must provide guidance for determining such cases. Nor is such a framework simply a matter of abstract high-level philosophical reasoning. The goal is to develop something in-between: a structured process of reasoning at an intermediate level of determinacy that can guide decision-making in concrete cases. That will, at times, involve moving between abstract, conceptual discussions and particular concrete cases.

In developing such a framework, I shall also not engage with many other important questions that arise in the burgeoning field of 'business and human rights' which range from procedural questions – such as, in cases with a global dimension, the jurisdiction in which a claim may be lodged – to substantive ones – such as which law is applicable where multiple jurisdictions are involved.[11] I shall also not engage with the much-discussed issue of the obligations of one corporation for the activities of another – whether that be in relation to the liability of parents for subsidiaries or across supply chains.[12] Instead, the focus is on the prior question: when the interests underlying a right are affected, how do we determine what the substantive obligations of corporations are? Clearly, any answers that emerge will need to be supplemented with an approach to apportioning liability in large groups and supply chains. Yet, often the 'obligations' question I focus on is glossed over in discussing the apportionment question. A project such as this thus seeks to advance thinking in an area that has only been engaged to a limited extent in existing legal

[9] In this book, I will, at times, simply refer to 'corporate obligations' as a shorthand for 'corporate obligations in relation to fundamental rights'. Clearly, corporations may have obligations beyond the sphere of fundamental rights, but the focus of this book is on fundamental rights obligations and hence to avoid unwieldiness and for the sake of brevity, the shorthand form is sometimes used.

[10] Muchlinski, 2010: 518 writes, in the context of multinational enterprises, that the precise content of their fundamental rights obligations 'is open to considerable speculation'.

[11] Each issue requires a detailed examination and it is not possible within the scope of one book to cover them all.

[12] See, for instance, Muchlinski, 2010: 317–326; Nolan, 2017.

literature. It is an ambitious project, but, humbly, I hope it will place the question of substantive obligations firmly on the research agenda and stimulate further contributions. This project also requires several methodological choices to be made concerning how I will approach it to which I now turn.

Obligations under International Law, Domestic Law or Both?

In approaching this question, the problem one immediately confronts is which jurisdiction is the particular target of the argument – a legal approach regarding corporate obligations can be developed for a particular territorial jurisdiction, a series of jurisdictions or for international law. Which of these is to be the focus of this book? Returning to the aforementioned example of Thandi, it is clear that the harms experienced by individuals that are caused by corporations – and the potential benefits of their activities – can arise within a particular jurisdiction such as South Africa: yet, the ability of particular states to address these legal difficulties cannot be considered in a vacuum as they are themselves affected by a number of international law rules and conventions. Sometimes, individual states are unable or unwilling to engage with corporate obligations, creating legal gaps which can render rights-holders unable to access remedies. Recognising an international dimension to this problem can provide a corrective to impunity at a domestic level. The legal problems experienced by individuals are also intensified when we consider the complex connections between businesses that cross borders and attempt some kind of cross-border accountability. Given this context and the deep interconnections between the local and the global, I have decided not to limit the focus of the book either to the sphere of international law or domestic law – I engage with both spheres, and the approach I propose is relevant to both. Such a methodology in my view is particularly apposite in the field of fundamental rights. I now wish briefly to provide several justifications for why this is so.[13]

First, let us consider the question of origins. Fundamental rights at the international level did not emerge from nowhere. Whilst I cannot provide a lengthy discussion of their history, clearly, they were initially moral

[13] There is an interesting literature which considers the development of a type of 'transnational human rights law', which has also been linked in some academic writing to the internationalization of constitutional law: see, for example, Besson, 2017; Gardbaum, 2008. Since this debate is not the focus of this book, I do not attempt to engage in detail with it but rather provide a justification – in the context of the goals of this book – for the approach I adopt.

concepts for which philosophers such as Locke and Rousseau provided philosophical foundations.[14] Nevertheless, their comprehensive presence in law originated at the domestic level with the enactment of the Declaration of the Rights of Man and of the Citizen after the French revolution in 1789. Shortly, thereafter, in 1791, the United States included a bill of rights in its Constitution with the various amendments. The idea that there were fundamental rights of individuals emerged in the international sphere after a history of inclusion in law in the domestic sphere: the first instrument in this regard was the 1948 Universal Declaration on Human Rights (UDHR), which was itself influenced by the French declaration as well as the constitutions that the negotiators were familiar with.[15] Subsequently, however, the development of a list of internationally accepted rights at the international level has influenced many modern constitutions which now regularly include a full panoply of rights.[16] These origins thus clearly suggest an interrelationship between the two spheres in the very etiology of rights.

Secondly, and unsurprisingly given this history, there are also clearly continuities of language between the two domains: the UDHR (1948), for instance, begins in article 1 by recognizing that '[a]ll human beings are born free and equal in dignity and rights'.[17] The French Declaration in its first article states that 'Men are born and remain free and equal in rights.'[18] Apart from this linguistic continuity, thirdly, there is also a conceptual relationship between rights in these two spheres. Fundamental rights at the domestic constitutional sphere are often rooted in notions of dignity, freedom and equality.[19] At the international level, dignity too is regarded as the foundation of fundamental rights and a notion of equality is centrally enshrined in international treaties protecting those rights.[20] As such, these clear similarities suggest a deep interconnection between how fundamental rights are conceived at the domestic and international levels.

[14] For a more detailed philosophical discussion on fundamental rights and their application to business, see Chapters 2 and 5.

[15] www.un.org/en/universal-declaration-human-rights/ and see Elkins, Ginsburg, and Simmons, 2013: 74 for the historical claim.

[16] See, for instance, Van Alstine, 2009. Elkins, Ginsburg, and Simmons, 2013 provide empirical evidence of this phenomenon.

[17] UDHR (note 15 earlier).

[18] There has clearly been a change since then to more inclusive and gender-neutral language.

[19] See, for instance, sections 1 and 7 of the South African Constitution available at www.gov.za/documents/constitution/chapter-2-bill-rights#7 and chapter one of Ecuador's Constitution available in English at http://pdba.georgetown.edu/Constitutions/Ecuador/english08.html

[20] See the UDHR (note 15 earlier) Preamble, Article 1 and 2; ICESCR Preamble.

Given this continuity, there has been and continues to be a two-way influence between the development of fundamental rights at the domestic constitutional level and at the international level. Domestic courts – even when they are not bound by the decisions of international courts and institutions – often take notice of developments at the international sphere. The South African Constitutional Court, for instance, is required to consider international law when interpreting fundamental rights in the South African Constitution, but is not bound by it.[21] In its *Glenister* judgment, dealing with whether the state has a duty to create an independent corruption authority, the court refers to and utilizes international law to interpret its own domestic bill of rights to generate such a duty.[22] On the other hand, the international law relating to fundamental rights can be influenced by developments at a domestic level. For instance, the Optional Protocol to the Convention on Economic, Social and Cultural Rights includes a provision[23] that appears to have been influenced by the formulation of certain socio-economic rights in the South African Constitution[24] and the jurisprudence of the South African Constitutional Court concerning the notion of 'reasonableness'.[25]

Whilst there are natural continuities between the international and domestic spheres in relation to fundamental rights, there is also a need for some caution in simply moving from one domain to the other. At the international level, standards relating to fundamental rights are applicable across the whole world, and their scope is literally universal. In a similar vein, international law in relation to fundamental rights has asserted that such rights can be claimed by all human beings simply by virtue of their dignity without any restrictions based on their nationalities.[26] At the domestic level, rights also apply usually only within the boundaries of the political community itself: whilst some may apply to non-citizens, certain rights are often reserved for citizens.[27]

[21] In terms of section 39(1)(b) of its Constitution.

[22] *Hugh Glenister* v. *the President of the Republic of South Africa* [2011] ZACC 6 paras 192–197.

[23] Article 8(4).

[24] For instance, sections 26(2) and 27(2) of the Constitution.

[25] See *Government of the Republic of South Africa* v. *Grootboom* [2000] ZACC 19 paras 39–44 and Liebenberg, 2020: 53.

[26] Gardbaum, 2008: 767 sees the fact that international human rights law can *only* be conceptualized to apply to all human beings as a significant contribution and particularity of the international sphere.

[27] As Gardbaum, ibid. points out, different countries adopt different rules in that regard, but, at the domestic level, membership of a political community often becomes of importance in determining the rights one may claim. See also Keitner, 2011: 113.

The difference in scope also may lead us to adopt different approaches to specifying and interpreting the rights in question. Since international standards apply across a range of contexts, it may be necessary to state them at a higher level of generality, whereas at the domestic level it is possible to state them at a greater level of particularity in a way that responds to the particular context. Consider the right to adequate housing: in a national community where the weather is largely cold, a standard may be developed whereby adequate housing involves modalities for heating interiors; in a community where there is sweltering heat, there may be a need for adequate ventilation or air conditioning. At the international level, it would be undesirable to specify the content of the right too narrowly and better to do so in a more general way that covers both countries with hot and cold climatic conditions: adequate housing, as an international standard, thus is better conceived of as involving protection from the elements.

Moreover, there also may be differences in the understanding of rights and their content given cultural or historical differences. For instance, the standards and tests around hate speech are stricter in Germany and South Africa than in the United States.[28] This variation may result from the particular historical circumstances of Nazism and Apartheid in the former countries as well as a historical commitment in the United States to very broad free speech protection. An international standard dealing with hate speech may thus involve a minimum common denominator across the world rather than addressing special contextual dimensions and factors that are applicable at the national level. Differences in norms, culture and context may also lead some countries to balance rights differently against other rights and the public interest.

These similarities and differences suggest the following approach: there is a clear interrelationship between norms at the national and international level yet caution must also be exercised when moving between the levels such that important differences are not obscured. For instance, even if there is greater particularity in the national domain, a particular norm such as the right to interior heating is still recognizable as being connected to the more general international norm (the right to adequate housing). Similarly, with cultural or historical differences, there must still be a capacity to provide a justification for the norms at the domestic level in terms that are recognizable to the international fundamental right. At the same time, if there is too much of a divergence

[28] Rosenfeld, 2002.

between the two, the national norm may well be seen to be inconsistent with the international norm or, indeed, fail really to be an expression of fundamental rights at all.[29] The same holds true with weighting: not any balancing exercise is acceptable and, as will be discussed, courts can strike down balancing exercises which are not properly justified and inconsistent with retaining respect for fundamental rights.[30] In this sense, the international realm adds an important external check on developments relating to fundamental rights at the national level which is 'not exclusively specified or enforced by the state itself'.[31]

In the context of this book particularly, there is good reason to consider both the national and international level when considering a legal approach to the obligations of corporations in relation to fundamental rights. The focus of this book is upon an agent – the corporation – that, generally, is formed at the national level and regulated at that level. Of course, the corporation also has the potential to operate across borders. The question concerning the obligations of this agent relating to fundamental rights is something that national legislatures and courts need to address. Yet, the concerns at this level are similar to those raised at the international level: how to ensure the rights of individuals are protected against the power of corporations. An approach needs to be developed that can speak to both levels concerning the obligations of such a particular actor – even though there may be some differences between the level of specification at the different levels. The international level raises a number of further complications concerning the operation of these entities in different countries and their obligations to distant others. Yet, ultimately, the central question of the legal manner in which to approach constructing their obligations is conceptually similar.

Moreover, Besson provides an 'epistemic' justification for engaging with both the domestic and international spheres. She provides reasons for thinking that examining critically the different approaches adopted by various jurisdictions as well as those within international law can offer us the best epistemic basis for developing the most desirable approach to particular legal questions.[32] As will be explored further later in this introductory chapter, the goal in this book is to connect the normative

[29] In a sense, this is an important function of the international realm in placing constraints on what is permissible at the domestic level.

[30] For instance, see Chapter 2 for a discussion of the European Court of Human Rights' ruling in the *Von Hannover* case.

[31] Gardbaum, 2008: 766.

[32] Besson, 2017: 239–240.

and descriptive and develop what I take to be the most desirable doctrine for determining the legal obligations of corporations in relation to fundamental rights. Understanding and engaging with the different approaches at different levels can aid in this process and, consequently, I will proceed along the route of dealing with both levels as the argument unfolds in the book. If the legal analytical framework I develop is adopted by decision-makers, differences between the various levels should be considered when applying it.

Overlapping Disciplines within Law

The aforementioned issues relating to business and fundamental rights cannot easily be confined to one of the traditional disciplines within law and rather straddle the boundaries between what have been regarded traditionally as separate areas of law. A claim for damages for harm caused to an individual traditionally would be formulated within the domain of tort law – traditionally, one of the core areas of 'private' law. The wrong that is complained of, in the context of this book, however, is one that is characteristically associated with constitutional or public law: a violation of fundamental rights. Given that we are dealing with a corporation and its liability, in determining its obligations in relation to fundamental rights, it is necessary to consider the nature of this agent, which is formed and regulated according to the principles of corporate law. Moreover, when we are dealing with cases that cross borders and where the national legal system is inhospitable to such claims, we are immediately catapulted into the domain of international law. Certain facets of such claims – such as questions relating to jurisdiction, applicable law and the recognition of judgments – are usually included within the domain of private international law. The substance of these claims – which, in the context of this book, is centred on the violation of international human rights law – falls within the traditional domain of public international law. The focus of this book is, as has been mentioned earlier, on the obligations of corporations in respect of fundamental rights and will thus require concentrating on those areas of law that are most relevant. Inevitably, the questions engaged will require breaking down the traditional silos of law and considering both traditional 'private' and 'public' law dimensions of the problem both at the domestic and international levels.[33]

[33] For a historical justification for this overlap, see Lustig, 2020: 3.

Linking with Disciplines beyond the Legal Domain

The questions involved in this book also naturally lend themselves to moving beyond the traditional boundaries of law itself. Determining the substantive content of the moral obligations of corporate actors that flow from fundamental rights is a matter that has attracted some detailed attention and debate within philosophical and business ethics literature.[34] It is clear that, whilst there are differences between moral and legal approaches to such obligations, it is of importance to consider these philosophical discussions in developing a legal framework for determining their substantive content.

Determining the obligations of corporations will, of necessity, also require taking a view about the nature of the corporate agent. Ratner, for instance, writes that when determining such obligations, 'we need to take into account the differences between corporations and the state'.[35] Debates surrounding the nature of the corporate entity have been conducted in a range of disciplines such as economics, political science and law. Whilst the corporation is itself a legal entity and thus law in this work is primary, it is necessary also to consider relevant aspects of these debates and, where necessary, I will attempt to do so within the limits of what is possible within one monograph.

The Normative and the Descriptive

This book is not simply an exercise in abstract philosophy, seeking to determine the moral obligations of corporations a priori though the reasoning in this field is relevant. This work rather develops an analytical framework for determining the obligations of corporations in relation to fundamental rights in the realm of *law*. To do so, it is necessary to adopt methods of reasoning that are characteristic of law itself. I am influenced in this respect by the work of Ronald Dworkin on the distinctive modalities of legal reasoning. Dworkin recognises that there are twin pulls within law: on the one hand, there is the relationship with sources that have a certain authority – the constitution, statute, case law (Dworkin terms this the dimension of 'fit'); whilst on the other hand, there is the need to realise certain substantive values, and, ultimately, to do justice both generally and in particular cases (Dworkin terms this the dimension

[34] See, for example, Donaldson, 1989; Hsieh, 2004; O'Neill, 2004; Young, 2006; Wettstein, 2009; Santoro, 2010.

[35] Ratner, 2001: 513.

of 'justice' or 'value').[36] Moral and political philosophy operate purely in the domain of values and reasoning without reference to authoritative sources; on the other hand, a slavish following of the existing sources would never allow for legal development or addressing injustices in the status quo. Legal sources also have some claim to serious consideration: they often exemplify both social values but also some of the collective distilled wisdom regarding questions of justice that has accrued over time. Developing a legal approach, in my view, requires engaging with both these dimensions, though, ultimately, the normative will need to guide the authority-based dimension.[37]

The subject of fundamental rights in law requires a mixed approach too. I have argued in the past that fundamental rights 'are best conceived of as a bridge between morality and law: they are moral entities whose inherent nature creates a push towards legal institutionalisation and social realization'.[38] As such, when engaging with the obligations of corporations in relation to fundamental rights in law, we will of necessity have to engage with both questions of what those 'obligations' ought to be, and what legal developments have already taken place in relation to their institutionalisation.

The exact nature of my approach will become clearer when explaining the structure of the book and the argument in the next section. At this point, I wish to highlight that this book is not about attempting exhaustively to examine all the case law that is relevant and describe the existing doctrine. It also is not simply an attempt to reason philosophically about what the legal position should be. Instead, it systematises and analyses critically existing and leading legal sources and approaches together with relevant argumentation from disciplines such as political philosophy to provide an argument for what the best legal doctrinal approach to determining corporate obligations in relation to fundamental rights is. Along the way, the contours of the doctrinal approach are developed and refined.[39] The recognition that there is an ineliminable degree of judgement in any determination of the content of these obligations then places

[36] Dworkin, 1986: 254–258.

[37] Dworkin, ibid: 257–258 also essentially sees the value dimension as guiding the fit dimension.

[38] Bilchitz, 2018: 128.

[39] There are similarities and differences to the 'reconstructive approach' adopted by Möller, 2012: 20; as Möller does, I do not adopt simply an abstract philosophical approach and take case law seriously. The goal, however, is to draw out and develop not simply a coherent legal approach but also one that is morally the best that it can be.

a focus on designing optimal legal institutional structures to ensure such judgments are exercised in the best epistemic manner they can be. The book thus draws out an approach that is latent within existing sources, and both helps provide a normatively desirable development and clarification thereof. Readers should thus expect a combination of the normative and descriptive in this work, reflecting what I take to be an attractive methodology for conducting legal research which does not aim simply to capture the existing state of law but to argue for its advancement.

The Structure and Outline of the Argument in This Book

Seeing that this book focuses on the obligations of corporations in relation to fundamental rights, it is necessary to begin – in Chapter 1 – with an understanding of the nature of the corporation itself. After outlining some of the key legal characteristics of the corporation, I focus on two critical questions for determining its obligations. The first concerns the relationship between the corporate structure and the individuals underlying it. I argue for what I term a 'supervenience model' of the corporation: this means that the legal corporation is not reducible to the individuals underlying it yet remains dependent upon those individuals. The second issue I focus on concerns the purpose of the corporate entity. I argue for what I term a 'socio-liberal' conception of the corporation, which involves an understanding that it has a complex character. On the one hand, I contend that its very raison d'être is to achieve a range of social benefits; yet, on the other hand, it is designed to enable individuals to achieve their economic goals through a structure that is advantageous to them. The conception of the corporation I articulate is of great importance for the rest of the book in providing a persuasive view of corporate obligations in relation to fundamental rights.

Part I: Legal Doctrinal Models for Addressing the Substantive Obligations of Non-State Actors for Fundamental Rights

With this conception of the corporation in mind, I turn to consider the series of legal doctrinal responses that have been adopted to address the fact that corporations have serious potential impacts on fundamental rights. Chapters 2–4 focus on approaches that regard the state as being the primary entity that can have obligations flowing from fundamental rights. In evaluating these doctrines, I do not seek simply to re-hash old debates but have two key goals in mind. The first is to examine the coherence and justifiability of approaches that focus only on the state as the locus of fundamental rights obligations. Here, I deliberately broaden the discussion to include case law that implicates non-state actors beyond the corporate form itself – such as individuals, partnerships, religious organisations, non-governmental organisations and the like.

Whilst the focus of this work is on corporations,[40] in academic discussions and case law, it is common to engage with the obligations of this larger group of non-state actors rather than focusing only on one particular type of entity. There is also a limited number of cases that focus solely on corporations and, if we are able to gain guidance from cases relating to other non-state actors, that could of course be useful and illuminating. Adopting this approach is justifiable because these actors have in common the fact that they are not usually part of the state[41] and, as Chapters 2–4 show, many legal systems have sought to confine obligations in relation to fundamental rights to state entities. All non-state actors raise a similar conceptual question of whether one can extend the realm of obligations in relation to fundamental rights beyond the state and what the nature of their obligations are. If we can extend the bearers of obligations beyond the state, it is, of course, possible to argue that only a particular subset of agents do in fact have such obligations. Yet, by considering a range of actors which are distinct from the state, it is possible to consider what the grounds are for imposing obligations on such actors and which characteristics of agents affect the nature of those obligations. For these reasons, the discussions in Chapters 2–4 will include the various legal doctrines that have developed to address the obligations of non-state actors in relation to fundamental rights more generally. In later chapters, this analysis will be narrowed to engage with the specificities of corporate agents. Of course, future work should engage with other non-state actors and how their specificities impact on their fundamental rights obligations.

40 Chapter 1 also details the particular nature of the corporate form and its prevalence, which provides a justification for this focus.

41 In recent years, states have sought to conduct various activities through setting up corporate structures. Those that are wholly owned by the state clearly must have a public purpose at their heart and raise different considerations from corporations that are privately owned, which are the focus of this book. Some decent engagements on the topic of state-owned enterprises include Ng, 2019; Barnes, 2018; Backer, 2017.

The second goal is to show that, in each of the state-focused approaches I analyse in Chapters 2–4 and despite ostensibly avoiding the need to do so, the courts do in fact have to engage with the task of determining the obligations of non-state actors in relation to fundamental rights. Given that they unavoidably have to perform this task, I seek to understand the principles upon which the content of those obligations have been determined under these doctrines. As was discussed earlier in connection with the distinctiveness of legal methodology, this can be understood as a type of 'inductive' approach whereby I attempt to understand and draw out how courts in various jurisdictions – at both national and international levels – have thus far sought to determine corporate obligations.

In Chapter 2, I begin the analysis with international law and a central tension that arises between the traditional notion that only states have binding obligations and the idea of fundamental rights – which I seek to show requires obligations to be imposed on both state and non-state actors. To square the circle, the 'state duty to protect' model has been developed which is the focus of this chapter. It involves imposing obligations upon the state to ensure non-state actors do not harm the fundamental rights of individuals. I seek to show both theoretical and practical drawbacks of this model: in particular, I highlight conceptually why the doctrine is fundamentally incomplete and parasitic on having an idea of what the state must protect individuals against – which requires a construction of the obligations of non-state actors. Through a qualitative analysis of particular cases decided by the European Court of Human Rights, I also seek to understand the structure of the court's reasoning about the content of the obligations of non-state actors and the factors that it takes into account in making its decisions in this regard.

Chapter 3 turns to the realm of constitutional law and the parallel doctrine in the domestic sphere that fundamental rights only 'indirectly' impose obligations on non-state actors, which I term the 'indirect application model'. Its conceptual underpinning are, I argue, unpersuasive and, ultimately, it collapses into a form of direct obligation model since it cannot avoid requiring courts to develop a conception of the obligations of non-state actors which flow from fundamental rights. In the second half of this chapter, I seek to demonstrate this point through an analysis of seminal cases in Germany and South Africa, which I then analyse through a different lens: namely, seeing how these courts have sought to construct the content of the obligations of non-state actors.

Chapter 4 turns to what I term the 'expanding the state model' in which courts utilize an expansive conception of what constitutes the state to extend fundamental rights obligations to certain non-state actors. Conceptually, I argue this approach undesirably elides the distinction between different types of agents: by rendering private bodies 'public', it can fail adequately to recognize the distinctive character of non-state agents. It is also premised on developing a coherent understanding of what is, ultimately, private and what is public. Through an analysis of seminal cases in the United States, Germany and South Africa, I seek to show how, in drawing these distinctions, courts in fact outline a series of factors on the basis of which they determine the obligations of non-state actors.

Unlike the last three approaches, Chapter 5 focuses on what I term the 'direct obligations model', which recognizes that non-state actors and, corporations in particular, have direct fundamental rights obligations. Building on the arguments provided in the prior chapters, I defend conceptually the recognition that non-state actors have fundamental rights obligations. I then turn to consider the nature of those obligations and the inadequacies of two existing models for determining direct obligations proposed in the international sphere. The last part of the chapter examines qualitatively the reasoning employed in determining the substantive content of these direct obligations in a number of cases in two domestic jurisdictions – South Africa and Colombia – where direct obligations have already been recognized as applying to corporations.

Part II: Towards a Multi-Factoral Approach for Determining the Substantive Content of Corporate Obligations

What emerges from the analysis in the first part of the book is that there is an interesting convergence in the approach utilized by courts to determine the substantive content of the obligations of non-state actors. This second part of the book attempts to recognize that there is a 'multi-factoral approach' that has emerged and seeks to justify, systematise and develop an understanding of its contours. I also seek to defend the emergent approach not just as descriptive of existing practice but also as having a deeper normative justification. This part of the book also moves from identifying this general model, which is relevant to all non-state actors, to engage with its application in the context of the particularities of the corporation.

Chapter 6 provides a justification for why a 'multi-factoral approach' is both suitable and desirable for determining corporate obligations. I suggest there is a need to identify clearly the relevant factors, understand their normative underpinnings and how they condition obligations, and attempt to develop certain presumptions that flow from each factor.

Two sets of factors are identified: 'beneficiary-orientated factors' and 'agent-relative ones'. The former include the interests protected by the right; the vulnerability of the individual to the exercise of corporate power; and the concrete impact on the beneficiary. Agent-relative factors include the capacity of a corporate agent to harm fundamental rights, their general and specific function and the value to be accorded to autonomy in their decision-making. A key argument of this chapter is that no one factor is normatively sufficient as a basis for determining the obligations of corporations (or, indeed, other non-state actors). Given that these factors can pull in different directions, the question then arises as to how to reach a final determination of what must be done in particular circumstances.

Chapter 7 grapples with the question of how to structure the balancing enquiry that must inevitably take place, and I argue, in relation to negative obligations, for the usefulness of the proportionality test in this regard. Conceptually, I contend proportionality is well-suited as a structured reasoning process to address conflicts of normative considerations that arise between corporations and individuals and is not only applicable in relations between the state and the individual. The second part of this chapter considers in detail the complexities and adaptations required when applying each stage of the proportionality analysis to corporations given their dual nature outlined in Chapter 1. I conclude the chapter by providing an outline of the structured reasoning process that decision-makers should undertake in determining corporate 'negative' obligations and how the factors identified in Chapter 6 enter into this evaluation.

The focus of Chapters 6 and 7 is on negative obligations, and Chapter 8 explicitly considers what I term the 'negative obligations model' adopted by some courts that limits the obligations of non-state actors only to obligations not to harm individuals. I provide several arguments challenging this model and justify imposing positive obligations on corporations. I then seek to show the justifiability of utilizing a modified multi-factoral model for determining the substantive content of these obligations: in doing so, I consider the application of the factors in this context (including the need for an additional factor that considers the role of other actors who can contribute towards the realization of rights) and also propose a novel seven-step test for reaching final determinations about the content of such obligations. The last part of the chapter considers the practical meaning of this discussion through a concrete engagement with case law and legislation relating to the positive obligations of non-state actors in South Africa and India. I seek to show how the multi-factoral model can assist in strengthening both the case law and legislation in this regard.

Part III: The Institutional Implications of the Multi-Factoral Approach

The multi-factoral approach, ultimately, requires the exercise of significant judgement in determining the content of corporate obligations. The last part of this book considers what processes and structures need to be put in place – including reforming existing law and institutional structures – to ensure that any judgments concerning corporate obligations are exercised in a diligent and justifiable manner. I argue that a multi-pronged approach is necessary, which includes a variety of institutional structures and decision-makers that together can ensure corporations adequately address their obligations. In a sense, this section of the book considers the institutions and processes necessary to give effect to the multi-factoral model and translate an analytical framework of factors into substantive obligations in concrete circumstances.

Chapter 9 identifies the aim as being to embed fundamental rights within the corporate structure and enhance decision-making concerning corporate obligations in this regard. In order to accomplish this aim, it argues for the need to consider all aspects of the corporate structure and to adopt significant reforms to domestic corporate law across the world. Such measures require attending to the make-up and particularities of the decision-makers within a corporation, their legal duties and accountability. It also requires developing forms of accountability to external mechanisms, which include oversight by corporate regulators and the ability for courts to review corporate decision-making with respect to fundamental rights.

Chapter 10 moves from the national sphere to the international and investigates the potential contribution global structures and mechanisms can make to enhancing corporate decision-making surrounding their obligations, providing guidance on corporate obligations and in bolstering accountability. I look towards the future and consider possible institutional reforms at the international level that could both enhance corporate decision-making surrounding fundamental rights as well as develop a better global understanding of corporate obligations in relation to fundamental rights. The multi-factoral model, I argue, can help in this regard through providing a common analytical framework that through the dynamic interplay between decision-making both at the domestic and global levels can help provide greater certainty about and concretise fundamental rights obligations in specific sets of circumstances.

I began this chapter with a concrete example of where business has a large impact on fundamental rights. On the basis of understanding the problems an example such as this one raises, the book attempts to provide an analytical framework for determining the legal obligations of corporations as well as considering the institutional changes required to give effect to the framework and render it meaningful. There is here a union of substance, process and institutional design. It is hoped that the model and proposed institutional changes will generate an impetus for engaging more deeply with the substantive content of corporate obligations in respect of fundamental rights. I also hope that this book contributes to enhancing decision-making both within the corporation and without in this regard and, in so doing, helps to advance fundamental rights realisation across the world today which is so deeply dependent on the activities of corporations.

1

The Nature and Purpose of the Corporation in Law

1.1 The Dominance of the Corporate Form

Business can be conducted in a variety of ways. Its origins, arguably, lie in the simple desire of individuals to trade with one another and, through doing so, to enhance their well-being. These humble origins, however, quickly led to the development of co-operative networks through which people trade. The partnership is perhaps the simplest business form that expresses the desire of individuals to work together for common goals, but it has a number of drawbacks. As a result, over time, the limited liability corporation has emerged as the dominant structure for conducting business.[1]

This chapter focuses on attempting to understand, in more detail, the legal nature of the corporation. Two main issues will be addressed in this regard: first, I shall consider the relationship between a corporation and the individuals underlying it; secondly, I shall consider the very purpose of forming a corporate entity. The latter question is often framed in terms of whether a corporation should be conceived of as 'public' or 'private' in nature. These questions will involve considerations surrounding the function of corporations in society and their capacity to affect individuals. These reflections on the nature of the corporate form – as will be seen later in this book – are of importance to explicating the obligations such entities have that flow from fundamental rights.

[1] Bottomley, 2007: 18–19 outlines the success of the corporate form as well as its significant social impact today.

1.2 The Legal Characteristics of the Corporation

The corporation has a certain complexity in that it can be formed by one individual acting alone or involve hundreds, if not thousands, of individuals in various capacities. To understand this entity, it is useful to start with a short history.

1.2.1 *Brief History*

There is a long history in which human beings have grouped together in seeking to advance their business interests. Business organisations can be traced to forms existing in classical antiquity such as the *societas* in Roman law: yet, these entities, whereby individuals worked together for an aim and pooled resources accordingly, also retained the personal liability of investors for debts incurred by the *societas*.[2] If the *societas* went bankrupt, every individual involved risked serious consequences including imprisonment and being sold into slavery.[3] A variety of forms developed in the Middle Ages and the Renaissance due to these inherent drawbacks.[4]

One of the earliest ancestors of the business corporation was formed in Britain, known as the 'regulated company', a corporation that was formed by the grant of a charter specifically by the Crown.[5] These companies were initially granted monopolies over trading rights in certain areas. Individuals, however, could still trade in their own right under the umbrella of the corporation. Since 1692, individuals were prohibited from trading in these areas with corporations given the exclusive rights to do so. In contrast, 'joint stock companies' were not originally corporations but similar to partnerships. Members would provide capital to a common fund which was then handled by a group of managers: the member's interest could be bought and sold.[6]

The first corporations were often set up by states to advance their interests – such as the East India Company – and were granted monopolies on trade in parts of the world. Such companies were deeply connected to furthering the colonial interests of the states from which they

[2] Baskin and Miranti, 1997: 38.
[3] Ibid.
[4] Ibid: 38ff.
[5] Nicholls, 2005: 9.
[6] Ibid: 11–12.

emerged. The close connection with the public realm was indicated by their being incorporated specifically by public statutes.[7]

This short early history, importantly, highlights the fact that the present legal contours of the corporation are relatively recent and cannot be regarded as some kind of natural form that has always existed. At the same time, the underlying impetus behind the corporation can be discerned: to create a co-operative mechanism for pursuing business through enabling the pooling of capital; the pursuit of specialisation; the taking of risk and the coordination of multiple persons. We can already see in these early precursors tendencies for concentrated power in the monopolisation of trading rights in an area and the desire for restricted responsibility.

In the nineteenth century, we see the modern corporation being developed with some of its specific features emerging that we regard today as being characteristic of the form. The lines between the regulated company and joint stock company began to blur and led to legislative reform.[8] Importantly, these changes attempted to de-link the corporation from explicit state purposes, with the form being recognised by the late 1800s as suitable for ordinary day-to-day business.[9] From having an explicitly public purpose, the corporation becomes a vehicle for giving expression to the interests of individuals who simply wish to conduct business for their own advancement. What then were the features of this entity that were developed in law and that made it so attractive?

1.2.2 The Characteristic Features of a Corporation

Ultimately, the corporation has a central feature known as *separate legal personality*. This idea is a legal fiction but essentially involves recognising that there is an entity that is a separate legal person from those human individuals who own it, control it or work in it. The notion of separate legal personality thus provides some separation between the corporation and the individuals who make decisions on its behalf and benefit from its existence. The notion in its fundamental form raises questions

[7] Pahuja and Saunders, 2019: 144; Bakan, 2004: 6–16; Ciepley, 2013: 141.

[8] See, for instance, the Joint Stock Companies Registration and Regulation Act of 1844 (Joint Stock Companies Act). An amendment to this act in 1855 in England created limited liability.

[9] Lustig, 2020: 15-16 – Lustig, in her recent book, provides an historical account where she fascinatingly traces the rise of the corporation and considers its relationship to developing international law and power relations.

concerning the relationship between the overarching entity and the individuals underlying it, as well as the reasons for allowing the construction of such an entity.

Before exploring these issues, it is important to understand some of the key features that render separate legal personality attractive and are responsible for the corporation becoming the dominant business form in the world today. The first dimension thereof is the notion of *limited liability*:[10] given the fact that the corporation is separate from the individuals underlying it, such individuals cannot be held responsible for the corporation's debts or actions.[11] Thus, if the corporation goes insolvent, individuals may lose the money they invested in it, but the rest of their personal wealth will remain untouched.[12] This is extremely attractive for individuals and has a number of distinct advantages. Business by its nature can be risky: individuals may wish to invest in a new product in the hope that it would prove to be successful, yet there is no guarantee that this will happen. If there is no limited liability, taking such a risk could not just be disappointing but personally devastating in that individuals could become destitute in having to pay off these debts. Moreover, individuals may at a certain point succeed in business but years later demand for those products or services takes a downturn. Limited liability limits the economic harm that individual owners (or part-owners) can suffer to what they invest in the corporation. It thus encourages individuals to invest in a business with the security that if it fails, not all will be lost.

The corporate form thus encourages individuals to take risks. Risk-taking can have a number of positive social effects: individuals will be willing to invest in new products and technologies, for instance, many of which may not prove popular or fail. Yet some – like the mobile phone or computer – will succeed and have the possibility of transforming and improving individual lives.[13] It could also be that limited liability enables more competition: where there may be one large company that is dominant in an industry and sets prices too high, individuals may be

[10] As Stephens, 2002: 54–55 points out, limited liability only became widespread in the early nineteenth century in the United States and some fifty years later in England but is currently seen to be a 'core element of the corporate form'.

[11] Hudson, 2017: 17.

[12] This is generally true but, put simply, if the corporate form were abused as a 'device' or 'sham', it is possible for the corporate veil to be 'pierced' and the individuals sued who lie behind the corporate form. This is a relatively rare occurrence in order to gain the benefits of separate personality which would be lost if 'piercing' happened too often.

[13] Robins, 2006: 24.

encouraged to create rival businesses where the consequences of doing so are not devastating for them personally.

Importantly, one of the major attractions of limited liability is the desire of individuals to protect their most fundamental interests and ensure they are not harmed by risky ventures. In other words, part of the very motivation for limited liability lies in individuals wishing to avoid economic destitution and ensure that the losses that could affect the very foundations of their existence are restricted. Those foundational interests are the very ground of certain fundamental rights claims: indeed, part of the underpinnings of fundamental rights lie in attempting to set a minimum baseline of entitlements that protect the most important interests of individuals. Thus, it would not be inaccurate to say that a corporation is precisely set up so individuals can pursue their business goals without the fear of risking threats to some of their most basic interests they value (which are protected by fundamental rights). Acknowledging this point is important because it underlines the fact that the very motivation for the formation of the corporation includes a recognition of the value of fundamental rights for those investing in businesses. Since rights are possessed equally by all who have these entitlements, the corporate form must then not be allowed to undermine the fundamental rights of any other individuals who are not owners or investors. Of course, the corporation may insulate interests that are less foundational from risk too, but the stake individuals have in limited liability becomes particularly pronounced when there are serious threats to their most important individual interests.

The separate legal personality of corporations also has another major benefit, known as 'perpetual succession'. The corporation is not linked to any particular individual underlying it and thus continues in operation no matter if some individuals leave the enterprise or die. Perpetual succession allows for the mobility of individuals underlying the corporation who need not commit forever to an enterprise. The underlying make-up of the corporation may be fluid, and this principle allows for complex trading in the shareholding of such an entity. It also allows for a certain stability in the entity itself: if individuals pass away, the entity itself remains and can continue operating. A sole proprietorship would clearly end on the death of the individual who conducts its business; in law, a partnership usually has to be dissolved and reconstituted in such a scenario.[14]

[14] See, for example, the position articulated in the context of South Africa in Davis et al., 2019: 425.

These features also have a number of important consequences. The corporation changes the normal rules of property and corporate property is not reducible to that of the individuals who invest in it. Investors cannot simply pull out their initial investment, as the property in question has transformed to become that of the 'corporation'. This legal position lowers capital costs given that lenders need not fear that investors will suddenly withdraw.[15] The corporation can also use its assets for production and for specialised purposes without the fear that investors will withdraw. Ciepley calls this dimension of the corporation 'asset lock-in'. The transformation of those assets into company property also means that they are not available to personal creditors of shareholders should they go bankrupt. Ciepley terms this 'strong entity shielding'. This, together with 'asset lock-in', creates 'the protection from liquidation that allows corporations to specialize their assets and that boosts their credit'.[16] Strong entity shielding may also be seen as the converse of limited liability: restricting the liability of the company for the debts of its investors. These two dimensions also enable shares to be 'tradable' as they allow investors to 'draw out the value of their shares, provided they can find buyers for them'.[17] The separation of investors from the company and tradability in turn enables the corporation to 'combine the capital, and thus the economic power, of unlimited numbers of people'.[18]

The attractiveness of these ideas for conducting business has led vastly different legal systems to recognise similar features of the corporation. Armour et al. attempt to specify the common underlying structural characteristics of corporations across the world and suggest they share five core principles: (1) separate legal personality, (2) limited liability, (3) transferable shares (allowing underlying ownership to change whilst the operations remain the same), (4) centralised management under a board structure (allowing decisions to be taken that are not dependent upon the underlying owners' agreement) and (5) shared ownership by contributors of equity capital (the right to control and receive net earnings proportional to contribution).[19]

The discussion thus far has highlighted the fact that the corporation is itself a creature of law that has evolved in particular ways and provided an understanding of some of the unique features of its structure. Whilst

[15] Blair, 2003: 427.
[16] Ciepley, 2013: 144.
[17] Ibid.
[18] Bakan, 2004: 8.
[19] Armour et al., 2017a: 5–15.

these features are commonly recognised, several disputes have arisen surrounding a number of issues related to the corporate form. The first question I shall deal with concerns the relation between the corporation and the individuals underlying it. The second question relates to the purpose of the corporation. My goal in exploring these issues is to examine key conceptual positions relating to the nature of the corporation which are essential in determining its obligations in relation to fundamental rights. The position I eventually articulate is one I hope that draws on the insights of the contrasting perspectives I engage with and provides a reasonable normative basis for making progress concerning the nature of its obligations.[20]

1.3 The Corporation and the Individuals Underlying It

In the aforementioned description, I considered the general form the corporation takes in law in multiple jurisdictions. One key question that has arisen concerns the relationship between the corporation as a 'separate legal person' and the individuals underlying it. The question matters for a range of reasons for our purposes: amongst other matters, it affects how we conceptualise whether corporations have rights, its justification for limiting the rights of other individuals and whether the corporation can be regarded as responsible for particular actions.

1.3.1 The Aggregate View

Two main approaches exist. The first approach is what we might term the 'aggregate' theory: a corporation is a legal fiction, and it is ultimately reducible to the individuals underlying it. A second approach might be termed the 'irreducibility' theory: a corporation cannot simply be reduced to the individuals underlying it.

The aggregate theory doctrine was given clear expression in the *Citizens United* case in a concurring opinion by Justice Scalia. The case

[20] The ideal would be to articulate a type of 'thin theory' of the corporation that could be the subject of broad-based agreement amongst reasonable persons. The idea of a 'thin theory' is drawn from the work of John Rawls, who seeks to avoid overly controversial assumptions about the human good and articulate only that which is necessary for developing a theory of justice: see Rawls, 1999: 348ff. Given the strong differences in this area, and also the strong self-interest some have in perpetuating particular theoretical perspectives that are profitable to them, a broad-based consensus may prove elusive and so the best that can be achieved is providing a conception of the corporate structure that all who are reasonable can and should accept.

dealt with whether protections for freedom of expression in the First Amendment of the United States Constitution applied to corporations. Justice Scalia stated that '[a]ll the provisions of the Bill of Rights set forth the rights of individual men and women – not, for example, of trees or polar bears. But the individual person's right to speak includes the right to speak *in association with other individual persons*'.[21] He then went on to consider the protections for speech in political parties such as the Republican Party or Democratic Party which, he states, 'is the speech of many individual Americans, who have associated in a common cause, giving the leadership of the party the right to speak on their behalf'.[22] He continues, making a vital analogy which expresses the aggregate approach: 'the association of individuals in a business corporation is no different.'[23] In other words, a business corporation is to be understood as simply an association of individuals for common ends: free speech rights therefore transfer from the individual to the corporation.

Similar views have been advocated generally by a libertarian school of economists and thinkers. Milton Friedman, in arguing against wider social responsibilities being placed upon corporations states that '[o]nly people can have responsibilities. A corporation is an artificial person and in this sense may have artificial responsibilities.'[24] Ultimately, the corporation is understood by him as a collective grouping of individuals who use it for their own purposes. These individuals have property rights in the corporation and are entitled to use their property to achieve greater wealth. If corporate executives spend the money of the corporation on social issues, they are essentially 'spending someone else's money for a general social interest'.[25] Importantly, Friedman's argument thus largely ignores the particularity of the corporate form itself but rather understands it as an expression of the individual economic interests of those who invest in it.

A slightly more sophisticated version of the latter group of ideas has been advanced in economic theory which holds that the corporation is itself simply 'a legal fiction that serves as a nexus for contracting relationships and which is also characterized by the existence of divisible residual claims on the assets and cash flows of the organization which can

[21] *Citizens United* v. *Federal Election Commission* 558 US 310 (2010) at 391–392 (emphasis in original).
[22] Ibid.
[23] Ibid.
[24] Friedman, 1970: 51.
[25] Ibid: 53.

generally be sold without permission of the other contracting individuals'.[26] The corporation here is simply a 'nexus' for a range of individual contracting relationships. Easterbrook and Fischel develop this view into a full conception of corporate law. They contend that the

> 'personhood' of a corporation is a matter of convenience rather than reality, however: we also treat the executor of an estate as a legal entity without submerging the fact the executor is a stand-in for other people. It is meaningful to speak of the legislative branch of the U.S Government, or Congress, of the House, or of a committee of the Senate, or of members of the Congress, depending on context, but it would be misleading to think of Congress – an entity with a name – only as an entity, or to believe that its status as an entity is the most significant thing about the institution. 'Congress' is a collective noun for a group of independent political actors and their employees, and it acts as an entity only when certain forms have been followed (such as majority approval in each house). So too with corporations. … So we often speak of the corporation as a 'nexus of contracts' or a set of implicit or explicit contracts. This reference, too, is shorthand for the complex arrangements of many sorts that those who associate voluntarily in the corporation will work out among themselves. The form of reference is a reminder that the corporation is a voluntary adventure, and that we must always examine the terms on which real people have agreed to participate.[27]

It is important to try and understand the core components of this view. These include the idea that the corporation is not really a special entity created by law: it is rather something that human beings could form naturally with one another. There is no such entity in reality, but the corporation is simply a placeholder for a group of relations that exist between persons. The work that the corporate form does is not essential as it could be replaced by a network of contracts which could accomplish the same legal effect. The corporate form is simply a 'convenience' which essentially saves the transaction costs that would be necessary to achieve similar results through contract.[28]

This aggregate view of the corporation purports to offer an explanation and account of the entity that is simple and intuitive. There are strands of truth within it which render it seemingly attractive. Yet, conceptually, there are a number of difficulties with it which are necessary to identify in order to attain a more defensible view of the corporation and one which

[26] Jensen and Meckling, 1976: 311.
[27] Easterbrook and Fischel, 1991: 12.
[28] This line of thought can be traced to a seminal article by Coase, 1937.

can assist in properly conceiving of corporate obligations in relation to fundamental rights.

1.3.2 *A Critique of the Aggregate View*

In analysing the difficulties with this view, I will focus on the understanding of the corporation as a 'nexus of contracts' and examine the two critical components in this conception, namely, the notions of 'nexus' and 'contracts'. First, what exactly does it mean to say that the corporation is a 'nexus' of contracts? Bratton pointed out that the notion is itself vague and metaphorical.[29] Is the nexus itself an entity of some kind constructed by the intersection of multiple contracts? If so, what is the nature of that intersection itself?

If one individual supplier contracts with another individual customer, then they are subject to the terms of the contract between them. That individual supplier may create an employment contract with two employees to provide labour to fulfil aspects of the contract. In such a situation, there is nothing over and above the individual contracts: the nexus which exists (the fact that the two employees are necessary to supply the goods) does not give rise to any additional institution or entity.

Yet, in law, there is a difference between a situation where the individual supplier remains an individual or forms a corporation to engage in these transactions. As we saw, the corporation is granted by law an agency to make contracts and enter into relations that are separate from the individuals underlying it. That agency is operative not only in relation to those with whom there are contractual relations but also in relation to those without any such ties. This cannot be described simply as an intersection between different contracts: there is rather the formation of a separate entity. The nexus becomes an empowered agent with respect to the whole of society and even globally. It is entirely unclear how such a result could come from individual contracting alone: why should anyone accept that there exists an entity separate from any individual other than through societal recognition? The law of the jurisdiction in which a corporation is incorporated provides that recognition.[30]

[29] Bratton, 1989: 410.

[30] Ibid: 429. Bratton proceeds to highlight how there is a failure in the 'nexus' theory fully to succeed in dispensing with the 'entity' in question.

Indeed, the examples given as analogies in the quotation by Easterbrook and Fischel earlier actually help advance the opposite case. An executor is an *office* which one or perhaps several people inhabit. Whilst there are people behind the decisions, the executor is recognised as behaving on behalf of the estate of a deceased person in an independent capacity. No matter what the will of an individual contains, the only way that could be accepted as legitimate is for the law to provide rules in that regard.

Congress, on the other hand, is a *collective body* made up of multiple individuals. Yet the acts of individuals are not automatically acts of Congress – they are transformed into the acts of a collective by agreed rules. The force of an act of Congress is not equivalent simply to the force of the majority who support it: it takes on a life of its own as the rules are binding on the whole country.

A number of authors point to other limitations of the 'nexus of contracts' theory in accounting for the key characteristics of the corporation. Hansmann and Kraakmann argue that the essential role of organisational law is 'to provide for the creation of a pattern of creditors' rights – a form of "asset partitioning" – that could not practicably be established otherwise'.[31] It is not clear how one could, for instance, on the aggregate view limit the liability of individuals involved in a business for harms caused to third parties *outside* the realm of those with whom they contract (where clearly liability could be excluded by a contractual device). Moreover, Hansmann and Kraakmann argue that the most difficult feat to achieve in the absence of corporate law would be the shielding of the entity from the claims of the creditors of its owners and managers (entity shielding). Several authors such as Parkinson thus conclude that the attributes of the corporation are 'beyond the reach of private agreement'.[32] Ciepley, similarly, states that

> [t]he inescapable fact is that corporations rely on government to override the normal market rules of property and liability and reordain which assets bond which creditors. Indeed, asset lock-in, entity shielding, and limited liability together create the very distinction between corporate assets and personal assets . . . [G]overnment intervention in the market is what begets the corporate 'person'.[33]

[31] Hansmann and Kraakmann, 2000: 390.
[32] Parkinson, 1993: 32.
[33] Ciepley, 2013: 145. This conclusion challenges the most extreme statements by aggregate theorists: some indeed moderate their claims and accept that the very purpose of

Furthermore, even if one accepts for purposes of argument that a corporation could be created by contract, the reality is that nowhere is this done today. The corporation is treated as being a separate entity formed in terms of relevant corporate laws that has contractual agency in its own right.

For the purposes of this chapter, the aforementioned arguments are sufficient to establish the irreducibility of the corporate form. Yet, there is a further flaw in the 'nexus of contracts' view that is of importance to this book, namely whether a corporation should be thought of fundamentally as an entity that is constructed through a process of 'contracting'? There are two main problems with this idea. Firstly, the relationships which form around the corporation cannot easily be reduced to an idealised vision of the contract, which usually is understood to involve free and voluntary agreement. The reality is that contracts – and the wider relationships surrounding the corporation – are entered into in situations where there is often a lack of equal power: consider, for instance, an individual contracting with a major mobile phone business which can set the terms of any business engagement without any negotiation. Similarly, employees may enter into a labour contract with a business given the lack of job opportunities even though they are deeply unhappy with its terms. The vision of a realm of free, independent, symmetrical voluntary relationships does not conform to reality. It would be better then to see the corporation as involved in a multiplicity of relationships, where the free, voluntary contract is only one form of relation the corporation enters into.[34] This leads to the next point.

The 'contractual' approach over-stresses the degree to which the corporation is itself consented to and acts with the voluntary agreement of others. Unlike sole proprietorships or partnerships, corporations are not simply forms that can (or did) come about in a state of nature without governmental recognition. Corporations have always been constructs of law. This feature of corporations automatically means that there is a degree of coercion – a core feature of law – in their very set-up. One may be a radical sceptic about the corporate form and deny that Microsoft really exists, but the law will treat it as if it does and provide it with numerous protections. It is thus simply false to assert that the

corporate law is to attain the benefits of reduced transaction costs through the particularities the law attributes to the corporate entity – see Easterbrook and Fischel, 1991: 48.

34 This is a central dimension of the stakeholder approach to the corporation: see Freeman et al., 2010: 24–26. The key insight here is that those who have a stake in the corporation are not only those who voluntarily engage in relations with it.

entity is just an expression of voluntary agreement. Moreover, that founding act of incorporation leads to a whole range of other consequences which may not be voluntarily consented to. This is most important when we consider that the corporation impacts upon those with whom it has no contractual relationship. A community suffering from environmental pollution caused by a corporation may well have no contractual relationship with it yet be seriously affected by its behaviour. It has in many jurisdictions no choice to sue the individual director who they know made a fateful decision as he is often protected by the separate legal personality of the corporation. It is hard to understand what the implications are of the view that the corporation just is a nexus of contracts for those who do not stand in contractual relations with it. A view founded in contract is thus not adequate to capture the legal reality of the corporate form or the multiple relationships that it forms.[35]

1.3.3 *The Irreducibility of the Legal Corporation*

A key point that has emerged concerns the degree to which the corporation is treated as being irreducible to the individuals underlying it.[36] No matter what hypothetically might be the case, the reality is that the law recognises corporations as distinct persons who can act on their own and hold their own property. The fact that the law treats the corporation as irreducible to the individuals underlying it is supported by a number of the features of corporate personality in law and how the corporation functions in practice. Firstly, as was mentioned earlier, the identity of the corporation is not affected by changes in the individuals who lie behind it: one of its key advantages is the fact of perpetual succession. The corporation cannot therefore be reducible simply to any one individual or, in fact, many individuals.

Secondly, individuals who lie behind the corporation may bear responsibility only for those particular decisions that they take or are involved with (where such responsibility exists). If a director could not reasonably be expected to have known about a decision taken by another director, she will often not bear any personal responsibility for it (and liability, where it exists in law). The corporation, however, bears responsibility and liability for all decisions by individuals empowered to act on its

[35] For further limitations to the notion of 'contract' when applied to corporations, see Bottomley, 2007: 40–43.

[36] This section contains some of the arguments made in Bilchitz, 2010a: 8–9.

behalf. In many legal systems, corporations may thus bear independent civil and/or criminal liability for acts that are attributed to it.[37] The liability of the corporation is thus distinct from that of any particular individual or group of individuals who are empowered to act on its behalf.

A third and related point involves the difficulty of attributing particular actions to individuals. In the case of corporations with a simple structure, it may be easier to identify the individuals responsible for a particular decision. Even here, however, individuals may claim that the very purpose of the entity and the expectations it creates involves recognising that acts they perform for the sake of the corporation should not be attributed to them in their personal capacities. In corporations with more complex decision-making structures, the collective nature of the enterprise may render it extremely difficult to attribute particular actions to specific individuals or to decide upon whom individual responsibility is to be pinned.[38]

Fourthly, the corporation may, as a separate entity, wield more power than the individuals who make it up do collectively. For instance, a large multinational corporation when it lobbies a government to adopt a particular position may have more bargaining power than the individuals who form it do even when they act together. For instance, often the claim that Microsoft or Apple support a particular goal is perceived to have greater significance than simply if the collection of individuals who lie behind these corporations expressed support for it. Separate legal personality thus amplifies the voice of the individuals who own or manage a corporation.[39]

Lastly, as we saw, the separate legal personality of a corporation also enables the entity to acquire resources in its own right. These resources become the property of the corporation. The collective efforts that underpin corporate structures often lead to wealth being concentrated in its hands. Corporations also are taxed at different rates to the individuals underlying them and are able to utilise separate legal personality to

[37] See, for instance, in South Africa, section 332 of the Criminal Procedure Act 51 of 1977 in relation to the possibility of criminal liability for corporations.

[38] This is precisely part of the reason for the evolution of liability (of various forms) on the part of the corporation where it is difficult to trace accountability to particular individuals: see, for instance, Coleman, 1975: 922; Slye, 2008: 962–963.

[39] Peritz, 1996: 253 writes that '[f]rom the political perspective, corporate speech can be seen as amplified voice in a political sphere whose most effective arenas – large metropolitan newspapers and radio and television broadcast media – often require the purchase of expensive amplification'.

create complex structures through which this wealth is diffused (and often avoid paying tax). The property holdings of a corporation thus become separate and are not entirely traceable to the individuals underlying it.

This section has sought to highlight the various respects in which a corporation is treated in law as not being reducible to the individuals underlying it. At the same time, it is important not to take this argument too far.[40] Clearly, the notion of separate legal personality in some sense is a construct: the corporation cannot in reality act other than through individuals who are the intelligent entities behind it. Every decision taken will be a decision of an individual or a collection of individuals who are tasked with representing the corporation through a specific decision structure.[41] The property holdings of a corporation will, when it is founded, be invested by the individuals who form the company. Whilst corporate activity may build upon such resources in various ways and the ownership be diffused (through a listing on a stock exchange), ultimately, it will be individuals with a shareholding in the corporation who are entitled to the profits from its activities. These considerations taken together point to the fact that the very legal nature of the corporation requires us to adopt a nuanced position, recognising that, ultimately, the corporation is an entity that has a complex relationship to the individuals underlying it. It cannot be reduced to those very individuals whilst in some sense being fundamentally dependent upon them.

1.3.4 A Supervenience Model

How then can we capture the relationship between corporations and the individuals underlying them? This takes us into complex territory about an entity that is essentially a legal construction. The corporation could be viewed as a type of 'collective structure' like

[40] This is partly why I am unconvinced by Keay's entity maximisation and sustainability model of the corporation which focuses on maximising the interests of the entity itself and ensuring its sustainability (Keay, 2011: chapter 4). The corporation is itself a legal construction and the 'interests' of the entity are not ethically foundational. Entity maximisation and sustainability, it seems, must be defended in some sense in relation to the interest of those who lie behind the corporation. That, in turn, challenges the attempt to create an absolutely strict separation between the entity itself and the interests of those who lie behind it, which Keay seeks to accomplish.

[41] This fact raises the complex question of corporate agency: see, for a useful overview, Moore, 1999. The classic defence of corporate agency was put forward by French, 1979 and French, 1995. See important revisions to his view in French, 1996 and Arnold, 2006.

a university;[42] yet, a corporation can also be formed with only one individual shareholder which counts against this idea. The part–whole relation too does not seem adequate to capture the relationship between an individual and the corporation: a small corporation that insulates one individual from liability does not appear to be much more than the sum of its individual parts. What transforms it into a corporation is not a relation of part to whole but the operation of law.

I would suggest that we investigate rather the applicability of the notion of 'supervenience' that has been utilised in other areas of philosophy to give expression to the legal relationship in question, at least in relation to corporate activities. The supervenience relation states that 'a set of properties A supervenes upon another set B just in case no two things can differ with respect to A-properties without also differing with respect to their B-properties'.[43] The supervenience relation has been used in philosophy, for instance, to capture the relationship between the mind and the body. Thus, there can be no change in mental properties (say, my feeling sad or happy) without a change in underlying physical properties (neurons firing in particular ways). At the same time, this does not mean a mental property (such as feeling sad) is reducible to particular physical properties (a particular neuron firing given that the same feeling could be produced by a different configuration of neurons firing).

Similarly, it could be said, at least, that corporate actions are supervenient on the actions of the individual human beings underlying them. In other words, there can be no corporate action without the action of an individual (or individuals). That does not mean that the same individual must act every time a corporation acts or that similar actions are always performed by the same individuals – and so corporate actions are not reducible to the actions of particular individuals. This idea can help capture the notion that there can be complex chains of activity underlying any action attributable to the corporation whilst recognising that there are always individuals who act in these circumstances. This conception of corporate activity can thus be of importance in both understanding the respect in which it is dependent upon and different from the

[42] This could also be question-begging as a university could be considered a type of corporate structure.

[43] See B. Mclaughlin and K. Bennett, 'Supervenience', the Stanford Encyclopaedia of Philosophy (Winter 2018 Edition) Edward N Zalta ed. Available at https://plato.stanford.edu/cgi-bin/encyclopedia/archinfo.cgi?entry=supervenience. See, for a more detailed discussion, Kim, 1984.

behaviour of individuals.[44] The supervenience relation would mean that any action of a corporation can be traced ultimately to a set of actions of individuals even if those are difficult to specify (as a feeling like happiness is difficult to specify in relation to neurons firing). That would provide reasons, at times, for instance, to recognise corporate liability for certain wrongs. It would also though require us to attend to individual decision-making and liability for corporate actions where that can be traced and so prevent wholesale individual impunity.[45] The supervenience relation may also be interesting in capturing the broader relationship between the corporation and the physical properties that underlie it (which includes human action but also land and property) though it is not clear exactly what turns upon this.

The discussion thus far aims to provide an approach to the relationship between the corporation and the individuals underlying it that is justifiable and should be capable of garnering the agreement of reasonable persons. It does not reify the corporation whilst recognising the distinctness it holds in law. It also provides an account of the crucial role individuals play in the corporate structure.

1.4 Determining the Corporate Purpose

Having understood some of the key features that have come to characterise the corporation in law as well as engaging with its nature, what then is the purpose of creating such an entity? This question is also particularly important in understanding whether the corporation is essentially part of the 'private' or the 'public' realm. In turn, understanding these issues becomes of great importance when we come to specify its obligations.

1.4.1 The Libertarian Conception of the Corporation: The Primacy of the Individual Perspective

In general, it is possible to discern three distinct positions concerning the purpose of a corporation. The first is what I term the *libertarian conception of the corporation.* This vision conceives of the corporation as essentially an expression of the private interests underlying it. Corporations are essentially part of the 'private' realm, and individuals

44 Whilst not engaging with the notion of supervenience, Keay, 2011: 183 also recognises the corporation as an entity that 'is independent from, but dependent on, its members'.

45 For the need for both corporate and individualised responsibility, see Garrett, 1989.

when investing in a corporation have a fundamental economic aim, which is to maximise profit whilst limiting their own risk. Perhaps, most famously, this view was articulated by Friedman when he said: 'there is one and only one social responsibility of business – to use its resources and engage in activities designed to increase its profits so long as it stays within the rules of the game, which is to say, engages in open and free competition, without deception or fraud.'[46]

The libertarian vision of the corporation thus conceives of it ultimately as a vehicle designed to enable individuals to express their economic interests in conducting business profitably. This view is often linked with the problematic conception of the nature of a corporation – as being wholly reducible to the individuals underlying it – I discussed earlier. Yet, the flaws of this conception run even deeper.[47] The major question that remains unanswered is why should a law-making body – usually the legislature in modern societies – create an entity to further the interests of only the individuals who are involved in creating corporate structures? Libertarianism generally is interested in the state leaving people alone freely to conduct their activities. Individuals are not prevented from conducting business by failing to have the option of forming a corporation. It is unclear therefore what positive reasons a proponent of this conception could give for why the state should legislate specifically to create the corporate form for particular individuals to benefit from.

As we saw, proponents of the 'aggregate' theory discussed earlier may wish to deny the fact that state recognition is necessary for the construction of the corporate form and assert that it could be formed contractually. Yet, they tend to admit that the state does become involved in enabling the construction of the form essentially to save transaction costs.[48] That saving is a great benefit for the individuals forming a corporation. Yet, what is not clear with this justification is why the state should intervene in the first place to serve particular individuals' interests if there is no wider social benefit for all. There thus remains a need to provide an explanation for why the state should intervene in this area and enable the construction of the corporate form. As I shall argue later in this chapter, such a justification, inevitably, will require reference to a societal perspective as to why the corporation as a form is

[46] Friedman, 1970: 55.

[47] For a detailed critique of the 'shareholder value myth' and the harm it causes to shareholders as well as other stakeholders, see Stout, 2012.

[48] See note 33.

designed to achieve social benefits and must be consistent with ensuring the treatment of every individual with equal importance.

1.4.2 *The Corporation as Wholly Public: A Quasi-Governmental Institution?*

If the corporation then is not entirely about the private domain of individuals simply exercising their own freedom to conduct business, it seems we must recognise a fundamental public dimension to this entity: can we not then conceive of the corporation as essentially public in nature?

An alternative approach diametrically opposed to the libertarian vision conceives of the corporation as no longer a private entity at all but rather as a quasi-governmental institution. This view may be termed the 'political conception of the corporation'. One of the most prominent defenders of this view has been Florian Wettstein, and I shall consider his approach in some detail.[49]

1.4.2.1 Wettstein's Analysis of the Nature of the Corporation

In the section of his book dealing with the nature of the corporation,[50] Wettstein seeks to demonstrate the growth in the power of corporations over time. He also, ultimately, seeks to show that corporations today wield a form of public power and have concomitant obligations. He starts his account with the proposition that 'the large multinational corporation is acting in an increasingly dominant societal position'.[51]

Wettstein argues that there is a central paradox that has emerged in recent years: namely, that with the consignment of corporations to the 'private' sphere and increasing deregulation, its role in society and influence has increased. Their factual control of the economic sphere has led them to have de facto political powers. Wettstein terms this 'implicit politicisation': it involves 'a shift of influence on the constitution of the society and its will-formation processes to multinational corporations'.[52]

Wettstein's view is rooted in a conception of power which, he claims, is inherently public and relational. Power he defines 'as the ability of an actor to achieve desired outcomes, possibly but not necessarily by

[49] Wettstein, 2009. For a similar approach, see also Valentini, 2017.
[50] His focus is on the multinational corporation which may also explain certain aspects of his analysis.
[51] Wettstein, 2009: 168.
[52] Ibid: 178. See also Bottomley, 2007: 18.

influencing the behavior of other individuals'.[53] Drawing from the work of Susan Strange, he contends that corporate political power is conceptualised as the 'capability to determine outcomes by controlling, shaping and influencing the structures of the global political economy'.[54] This power does not only arise from their general control over production processes but also their ability to utilise their dominant positions to gain a number of advantages from states. Corporate power is thus both structural and concrete.

Wettstein charts the rise of the multinational corporation, which has become the dominant player in the global economy. This has gone together, he claims, with an ability to influence states to advance the preferences of multinationals and so to improve their position. If a country fails to bend to the demands of multinationals, it risks becoming uncompetitive and corporations may threaten to move their investments elsewhere. Moreover, corporations are attaining control over one of the most significant dimensions of the economy: knowledge.[55] Internet companies control the flow of information, and large media conglomerates control what people hear and see. International trade agreements have allowed corporations to gain monopolies over life-saving drugs and even new life forms. Control of knowledge helps to shape individual beliefs, principles and morals and so the very foundations of democratic life.

These points are important for Wettstein, as he wishes to show that corporations are not only secondary agents of justice but primary agents too. The distinction emerges from the work of Onora O'Neill, who argues that primary agents of justice effectively set up the framework within which other agents operate. Primary agents have the ability to regulate, define and allocate the contributions of other agents, who operate within those terms; secondary agents of justice are those who simply comply with the obligations established by those frameworks.[56] Wettstein aims to show that corporations today often have the power not simply to act within existing frameworks but to determine those frameworks themselves.[57]

53 Wettstein, ibid: 189.
54 Ibid: 195.
55 Ibid: 201.
56 O'Neill, 2004: 242.
57 Wettstein, 2009: 162–164. For another similar and wide-ranging analysis of corporate power in the economic realm, see Parkinson, 1993: 8–21.

He thus sets about demonstrating how corporations today exercise governmental functions over a range of actors. In relation to people, he examines how corporations not only exercise significant power as employers and as producers of the most basic goods that we need but actively seek to shape individuals' very preferences. Corporations, he argues, 'have relentlessly fostered a culture of materialism and consumerism'.[58] Corporations also organise within networks of subsidiaries and subcontractors such that they increase their influence. A small number of companies also dominate whole industries, which are thus far from the perfect competitive markets advocated for by capitalist economics. Multinational corporations, he writes, are 'now the dominant institutional form in the global market. They control large parts of the world's resources, hold a quarter of the world's productive assets and determine the market's structure and outcomes. They have become major determinants of the location of industries and services, trade flows and technological development, as well as major sources of capital and market access'.[59] Multinational corporations, he concludes, in many ways have succeeded in controlling global markets.

Given their economic role, they also wield significant power over governments, the traditional locus of public authority. In large measure, Wettstein attributes this to the forces of globalisation, which has meant increasing rewards for being investor-friendly (through greater corporate investment); but, that itself, has meant decreasing the role of the state in the regulation of corporations. The influence of corporations on the political sphere, he contends, can be traced to three main forces. First, given that production is mobile and states want to remain competitive, corporations have the capacity to exit (or threaten to exit) from states that do not comply with their wishes around, for instance, granting them tax exemptions or limiting regulation. Secondly, increasingly states have privatised significant parts of the public domain, such as security and services – for example, electricity and water – and thus have transferred significant public power to corporations. Lastly, corporations often directly seek to lobby public officials and engage in political processes – such as through funding particular candidates – in order to advance their ends and limit countervailing forces. These forces enable them to have an influence over the regulations that they are subject to and so strongly to determine their own governance. They are also increasingly involved in

[58] Wettstein, 2009: 217.
[59] Ibid: 225.

voluntary initiatives to self-regulate around the social and environmental impacts of their activities: self-regulation, by its very name, allows them to determine the standards they are subject to as well as to be in charge of monitoring, even though that involves a conflict of interests.

Wettstein concludes after this empirical analysis of their power that corporations are indeed primary agents of justice who are involved in determining the very background rules in terms of which they and other agents operate. As such, they are not simply the subjects of regulation but exercise a form of political power and authority that are regarded generally as the preserve of governments. The corporation has thus become a 'quasi-governmental institution'. Since their evolution has led the corporation itself to act in a fundamentally public manner, its obligations are conceptualised through taking account of this dimension of its nature.

1.4.2.2 A Critique of Wettstein's Approach

There is much that is meritorious in Wettstein's analysis: its attempt deeply to conceptualise the power of the corporation today and the manner in which it has transformed is impressive. Yet, there are a number of limitations on its ability to provide an adequate general conception of the corporation for purposes of specifying its obligations. At the outset, it is important to recognise the nature of Wettstein's claims: they are, it seems, tied to an understanding of the empirical evolution of corporate power. Wettstein could well argue that this is entirely appropriate given that the corporation is an entity whose contours are constructed by law. Determining what it 'is' fundamentally requires understanding how it operates in reality. On several occasions, Wettstein has recourse to the idea of 'de facto' power: the corporation here may have the capacity to act and influence in certain ways which has developed beyond ordinary conceptions of what it *should* do.

This idea is important as it highlights the fact that the corporation may have grown to exercise powers that were never part of what it was designed to accomplish. Distinguishing between the actual power it exercises and the purpose and role it should have is important as it allows us to argue for a reversion to a position that it actually should occupy in law. An analogy can help to explain this point. A dictator – let us say Kim Jong-un – may well exercise absolute power and invest all the trappings of the state in himself. Yet, we might well still say that Kim Jong-un has no right to exercise that role and, in fact, there is a mistake in conflating the notion of the state itself with the interests of one individual (or a family). Similarly, we might recognise that corporations do exercise the de facto power Wettstein identifies without accepting they normatively have a right to do so or, indeed, that they were designed to do so. This distinction allows us to recognise the pathologies in the status quo and to create a strategy to align its current power better with the normative nature of the entities concerned.

Indeed, Wettstein uses the example of thirty pharmaceutical companies in South Africa who sought to challenge the regulations promulgated in the country to alleviate some of the hardship caused by their monopolistic production of certain life-saving drugs. That monopoly enabled them to price those drugs beyond the reach of most people and the public healthcare sector.[60] The companies went to court and sought to lobby the government to change its position, so attempting to structure the rules of the marketplace to meet their interests irrespective of the great human cost their prevailing pricing policies were causing. Yet, there was a massive backlash by civil society in South Africa and across the world, leading the corporations to withdraw their challenge. The overreach in their power and their failure to recognise the most vital interests of individuals led to the strengthening of the recognition that they were the subjects of regulation not the creators of it. Moreover, the example also fundamentally highlights, in some sense, the weakness of multinational corporations in the face of concerted public action. It also draws attention to the specific individual interests they represent, which were recognised as not being furthered in the wider interests of society itself. That recognition provided the basis for massive protests and their eventual limited acquiescence.

Indeed, Wettstein argues from the power the corporation has to a conception of its obligations. Yet, it can be countered that the power the corporation has today exceeds what it is designed to do or what is normatively justifiable. Part of the problem is to square this power with a nature that is not suited for its exercise. What corporations must do is to act within the domain of what they have been designed to accomplish: that gives us an indication of what constitutes the rightful exercise of their power.

Wettstein essentially argues that the empirical developments he charts are a given and have come to define the very nature of the corporation as a quasi-governmental institution. He need not – and could not – have argued that the corporation was designed to be such an institution. The

[60] Ibid: 204.

manner in which the purpose of a corporation is construed is of great importance as it affects the rules and make-up of how it is constructed in law and its obligations. As I shall argue later in this chapter, the corporation should be conceived of as having a public purpose – of seeking to enhance public welfare – that is realised through harnessing the power of private individuals' motivation to advance their own economic interests.

It is thus important to resist the conflation of the purpose of the entity with the power that it comes to exercise. The corporation was not designed to be a branch of the government: it is designed – at least partially – to be a space for individuals optimally to structure their economic activity. As such, if we simply co-opt it into the space of governance, we fail to capture one aspect of its essential nature. Whereas the libertarian picture overreached in the direction of reducing the corporation to the individuals who lie behind it, Wettstein's picture overreaches in failing adequately to capture the role of individuals and protecting the space for the exercise of their own autonomy within the corporation itself. That, in turn, can lead us to fail adequately to capture the normative questions involved when seeking to specify its obligations.[61]

Indeed, if corporations are simply a part of the state, then they may be subject to all the obligations that the state has: in a sense they become nationalised. Thus, we can legitimately ask the question whether corporations would have duties to provide the infrastructure for voting, to ensure an effective criminal justice system and to provide healthcare for all.[62] It may be responded that such obligations would not necessarily be entailed by recognising corporations as part of the state: just as different parts of the state have different functions and obligations, so too could corporations and their distinctness be captured in this way.[63] Yet, clearly, such a view would require an account of why corporations have certain state obligations and not others. Conceiving of them as entirely public in nature causes particular problems for this project: one of the key distinctions between corporations and the state is that corporations are entitled to act in a partial way to further their own interests (and those of the individuals underlying them) as opposed to

[61] A further exploration of this question will be undertaken in Chapters 6–8.

[62] See this worry articulated in Ruggie, 2013: 51.

[63] One of the worries here is that the blurring could lead the state to attempt to avoid realising its own obligations and seek to transfer them to the corporate sphere undermining 'domestic political incentives to make governments more responsive and responsible to their own citizenry' (Ruggie, ibid: 52).

always acting in the general interest.[64] Whilst constraints may be placed upon the extent to which the corporation can act in its self-interest and it may be required as well to contribute to the general weal, one of the key reasons for the creation of the corporation is to try and enable the furtherance of the individual interests underlying it – as we will see, ultimately, for the purpose of achieving social benefits. To conceptualise the corporation as ultimately public in nature fails to capture the fact that its very existence is due to the powerful manner in which private motives can create public benefits.[65]

Moreover, part of the reason for distinguishing between the public and the private in liberal political theory lies in the idea that the private sphere is one in which individuals may have a certain level of autonomy to determine the course of their own lives. Individuals may legitimately pursue their own ends (within certain constraints) and this is understood to be the hallmark of a free society.[66] They need not always operate neutrally, impartially or with a public purpose in mind (which are characteristics only of the public sphere). The corporation was set up as a vehicle for individuals to pursue their business interests, which would otherwise have been conducted in other forms (as sole proprietors or partnerships). Its very success – as is acknowledged by Wettstein – lies in the particular advantages it offers individuals in their entrepreneurial activities. It is possible to recognise the fact that the corporation itself is created through law which renders it more public in nature than some of the other forms of business enterprise: at the same time, it does not fundamentally lose its character as an entity which individuals employ to express their autonomy in the sphere of business. As such, space must be preserved for the exercise of this autonomy separate from collective and public goals: to collapse the public and private spheres would be to subsume the individual into the collective rather than preserving the complex interplay between the two, which is characteristic of the corporate entity.

[64] Smith, 2013: 10–11.

[65] Capitalist economic theory suggests that a market consisting of rational and self-interested individuals and an adequate level competition will naturally allocate resources efficiently. Effectively, a competitive market will ensure that capital will be directed to those enterprises which produce products for which there is public demand. In this way, the public benefits by being able to purchase desired products at the lowest possible price whilst ensuring that producers remain profitable. See Begg et al., 2005: 261.

[66] Rawls, 1993: 30.

If we accept this analysis, however, Wettstein's approach still poses the difficult question of what to do where the de facto power of an entity exceeds the power it should exercise.[67] To utilise the analogy again, Kim Jong-un's power may well be illegitimate and based on an incorrect view of the state, but unseating him remains terribly difficult. Wettstein might argue that we need to emphasise Kim Jong-un's obligations that flow from assuming this significant power. Yet, given the real Kim Jong-un seems rather unconcerned with his people's plight and is focused rather on amassing nuclear weapons that could threaten world peace, it is not clear such a strategy will succeed where the nature of the person is fundamentally at odds with the obligations they are to assume.

Similarly, the corporation is itself not set up as an organ of governance with the institutional structure and checks and balances that would be required for exercising truly public functions. Accepting that it is such an organ would necessitate developing these dimensions, which entails effectively acknowledging the legitimacy of its being an essentially public entity. Instead of doing so, an alternative approach involves recognising that the corporation's role is a more complex one: whilst it was set up to create social benefits, it does so through enabling individual interests to be furthered. Such an alternative view may well acknowledge that the corporation has come to exercise significant public power that exceeds the design and purpose of this entity – as is well-documented by Wettstein. Instead of accepting this overreach, the approach seeks to consider how to control such public exercises of power rather than to accept the legitimacy of the corporation doing so. The corporation, for instance, fundamentally overreaches where it seeks to determine the rules of the game: this was even recognised by Milton Friedman, who stated that the corporation has to operate within the 'rules of the game'.[68] To the extent that corporations are today determining those rules, they exercise power that is inconsistent with their nature and so need to be placed back in their role as secondary rather than primary agents.

Interestingly, there is a similarity between the libertarian view and Wettstein's approach in their scepticism about the role of law in constraining corporations. The libertarian view sees law as inessential in the formation of the corporation, which could be formed naturally by individuals through contract and is fundamentally part of the private

[67] Wettstein, 2009: 146 contends that his view is rooted in the reality of corporate power today.

[68] See note 46.

domain. As we saw, this view underestimates the difficulty – if not impossibility – of achieving the core characteristics and benefits of the modern corporation without the use of law. On Wettstein's view, the corporation is fundamentally a primary agent of justice which today determines the very regulatory structures in which it operates. Law here is given a very limited role too as his approach suggests the futility of attempting to constrain the very overreach of the corporate structure through law.

1.4.3 *The Socio-Liberal Approach to the Purpose of the Corporation*

In contrast to the two aforementioned approaches, the approach I develop emphasises the fact that the corporation is a structure that is created by law in order to attain a proper understanding of the purpose of the corporation.[69] Two important elements must be kept in mind when seeking to understand its purpose. The first element involves examining the reasons for creating a structure in law with the characteristic features of the corporation; the second element involves adequately taking account of the important role individuals play within the structure of the corporation. When seeking to understand the purpose of a corporation, it is thus critical to distinguish between two perspectives: the point of view of the collective social structures (and particularly the lawmakers) that enable the creation of a corporation in law (I shall refer to this as the societal point of view), and the point of view of the individuals underlying the corporation.

The traditional focus has been on the individuals who wish to create the corporate form and usually have a calculated economic motivation in forming a corporation. They may prefer the corporate structure, for instance, because it offers the advantages of limited liability and perpetual succession. Whilst the corporation is clearly advantageous to individuals, why should any lawmaker accede to the demand to create such an entity?

The perspective from which law is created is not equivalent to the perspective of any particular individual. Indeed, one of the key purposes of a state and its laws is to move beyond the realm of destructive self-interest to a realm of impartiality. Quite different social contract theorists, for instance, such as Hobbes and Locke, converge on this point: part of the problem with the state of nature that leads to the need for a sovereign is the very partiality of individuals to their own interests.

[69] In this section, I draw on and develop the approach first outlined in Bilchitz, 2010a: 9–11.

For Hobbes, this is a fundamental condition of human nature; for Locke, the lack of an impartial body to judge disputes between people is likely to lead to a descent into conflict.[70]

A legislative assembly in the ideal sense is tasked with passing laws that are general in nature: doing so requires lawmakers to adopt a more impersonal perspective that seeks to advance the interests of the society as a whole.[71] In doing so, a legislature cannot simply seek to do the will of any particular individual – rather, it can only act legitimately if, in its deliberations, it acts impartially. To do so, it must treat all individuals as being of equal importance.[72] Of course, often individual legislators act in the interests of what they regard as politically expedient – sometimes, acting to please particularly powerful supporters – which is often not in the greater social interest. Yet, normatively, it is hard to understand why any particular individual in a society should accept a law that lacks a general justification and was made for the purposes of another individual. Indeed, Rawls gives expression to this point when he writes that 'our exercise of political power is fully proper only when it is exercised in accordance with a constitution the essentials of which all citizens as free and equal may reasonably be expected to endorse in the light of principles and ideals acceptable to their common human reason'.[73] Thus, in deciding whether to pass a law that brings corporations into legal existence, lawmakers must seek to determine whether that very structure has a justification that all citizens as free and equal could reasonably endorse. To meet the terms of that test, any law could not simply be partisan and in the interests of particular individuals, but would have to be shown to have benefits for all members of society. For all individuals to be capable of endorsing it, any such law would also have to be one that would not strike at the foundational commitment that all individuals are to be treated with equal importance.

This wider 'societal' perspective gives us a clear reason to reject the notion that the purpose of the corporation solely involves the maximisation of profit.[74] For any lawmaker would need to ask the further question:

[70] Hobbes, 1996: 86–89 and 117–121; Locke, 1988: 350–353.

[71] Locke, 1988: 353 writes, for instance, that 'the power of society or [l]egislative constituted by them, can never be suppos'd to extend farther than the common good'.

[72] Dworkin, 2000: 1 sees this as the key 'sovereign virtue'. I have attempted to expand on why this is central to the perspective from which social rules are constructed in Bilchitz, 2007: 57–62.

[73] Rawls, 1993: 137.

[74] Importantly, this argument is not one that seeks to show that maximising profit is self-defeating or that 'profitable firms have a purpose and values beyond profit maximization'

why would an entity focused purely on the maximisation of profit alone be beneficial to society and be consistent with treating every individual as being of equal importance? Even if one can find an answer to this question, the mere fact of having to ask it runs contrary to the libertarian vision. For the maximisation of profit cannot be an end in itself from the societal perspective; rather, the justification for the corporate structure must be rooted in the social advantages it would bring about.[75] It must also, to meet the requirement of impartiality, be a structure that is consistent with the central legislative goal of ensuring respect for the equal importance of individuals.

Traditionally, there is indeed a capitalist justification for the corporate structure that makes reference to the social benefits of its creation. The limited liability offered by the corporation to the individuals who invest in it can be said, for instance, to encourage people to take more risk, stimulate innovation and provide a catalyst for greater competition.[76] These benefits in turn often lead to the stimulation of growth in the economy and thus greater wealth in the society, creating more jobs and thus, ultimately, leading to an improvement in the quality of life for individuals. It is a structure that can also encourage the pooling of resources[77] and efforts[78] – without major worries about what happens when individuals die or wish to leave the endeavour – and thus it has the ability to develop more complex operations and enhance specialisation of both capital and labour. That too can be socially efficient, encourage innovation and expansion of existing initiatives and so has the potential to enhance the lives of individuals.

(Freeman et al., 2010: 12). That of course would provide further support for the argument but my contention goes to the very legitimate basis for the creation of a corporate entity by a legislature. The question of legitimacy is also raised centrally by Parkinson, 1993: 31–32 though his focus is on the legitimate basis for the exercise of private power by a corporation rather than on the foundational basis upon which the legislature can legitimately create such an entity in the first place.

75 This is recognised even by senior corporate law academics: see Armour et al., 2017a: 22–23.

76 This view of the function of business and corporations is linked to the broader justification concerning the benefits arising from free market capitalism and private property: see, for instance, Nozick 1972: 177. In relation to the rationale behind limited liability, in particular, see Easterbrook and Fischel 1985: 93–97. I am not seeking to engage in depth with the various arguments concerning the social benefits of capitalist structures but simply to outline in broad terms the way in which such arguments could be made.

77 Dine and Koutsias, 2005: 1–3; Keay, 2011: 15.

78 Blair and Stout, 1999: 265–271 emphasise the co-operative dimension of the corporate structure which they see as being about 'team production' and see corporate law as attempting to address the associated problems that flow from it.

Importantly, many of these advantages are only achievable if corporate structures are designed by lawmakers with a recognition of the particular perspective of individuals who seek to invest in the corporation – namely, that it is a structure that can allow them to structure their relations in a manner that is commercially advantageous and enables them to achieve profit.[79] Indeed, the focus of corporate law has been on the owners and shareholders and the social benefits that arise from insulating them from risk (for instance). Yet, it is also unclear why these are the only individuals who should be considered in determining the social benefits of a corporation. There are many individuals who are involved with the corporation itself: they range from shareholders, directors, employees, customers and those in the various communities affected by its operations.[80] When we consider the perspective of individuals underlying the corporation, it is not possible simply to consider the perspective of 'shareholders'[81] – that would be to fail to treat other individuals whose lives are connected to the corporation as having equal importance. We also need to consider the benefits to these other individuals that the form would create: if, for instance, the form does contribute to sustained social innovation, it could be shown to hold out benefits for everyone involved with the structure. Such an argument may, however, only be justifiable if it can be shown that the benefits of such a form do in fact accrue to other individuals in society.[82] The key point at this stage of the argument is that there are important reasons for lawmakers from their societal perspective to adopt an understanding of the purpose of a corporation that also takes into consideration the perspective of the *range* of various individuals who will utilise and connect with the corporate structure.

The corporation being a structure that is both irreducible to the individuals underlying it and fundamentally dependent upon them thus must be considered from two perspectives: of the individuals who are connected with a corporation; and from the perspective of society (acting through its lawmakers) that enables such a structure to exist. The

[79] Davis, 1977:40 argues that when directors take decisions focused on achieving success for the company in a manner that benefits shareholders, social benefits arise as well. See also, Armour et al., 2017a: 23, who view shareholder theory in this way.

[80] This is a key insight of the stakeholder approach to business, which recognises the fact that it is embedded in a series of relationships with a range of different stakeholders who have a 'stake' in the business: See Freeman et al., 2010: 24–29.

[81] Stout, 2012: 9 and 102 shows how shareholders are not a uniform group and have diverse needs and interests as well.

[82] We will see later in Chapter 8 how this reasoning impacts upon the need to place positive obligations on corporations for the realisation of fundamental rights.

'individual' perspective becomes a complex one once we move beyond the realm of a focus on shareholders (or owners) alone.[83] Indeed, shareholders no doubt will be concerned with whether the vehicle is fit for their purposes of creating more wealth for themselves (and perhaps making a social contribution when we consider a less reductionist approach to their motivations); employees will be concerned with whether the corporate structure is likely to have any impact on their working conditions and security of employment; suppliers will be interested in the stability of the form such that their contracts are not harmed; and individuals in communities may have a range of interests ranging from whether the corporate structure has an effect on employment creation, the environment in which they live and whether the innovation that results will improve their lives. Whilst we should not reduce the individual perspective to one of narrow self-interest alone – given that human motivations are complex – it can be said that this perspective would largely focus on the advantages to be gained from the perspective of various individuals through the creation of the corporate form.[84]

The social perspective, on the other hand, does not proceed from the interests of specific individuals or groups but considers overall what benefits the creation of such a form can have. Importantly, the social perspective will need to recognise and create place for the capitalist justification that the corporate form usually seeks to achieve social benefits in an indirect manner: in other words, the goal of the form would be to achieve social aims through harnessing the individual advantages that various stakeholders gain from the corporation. The classical

[83] Blair and Stout, 1999: 275–6 view the corporate form as emerging from the desire for co-operation amongst a range of individuals who form a 'team', each seeking advantages for themselves and bringing specific skills. The corporation has a 'mediating' function between these interests and establishes a governing hierarchy – expressed through the board of directors - aimed at addressing problems such as shirking and rent-seeking that arise in team production contexts. Their approach clearly extends beyond shareholders alone but still largely focuses on 'internal' stakeholders within the corporation – this book, whilst addressing the fundamental rights of such persons, is also concerned about the rights of those beyond the corporate 'team' upon which the corporation can have an impact. Their view also places strong emphasis on the role and power of directors: the law reforms proposed in Chapter 9 take that role seriously but recognise the need to ensure not just social but legal constraints on the exercise of their powers. These involve the need to guide the exercise of their discretion when fundamental rights are at stake and provide for their legal accountability to stakeholders, particularly those outside the corporate 'team'.

[84] Individuals who are altruistic might find those advantages are captured by the social benefits created by the form even if they do not benefit directly: nevertheless, given they value such benefits, it is still an advantage to them.

focus of this argument has been on the utility of the form for shareholders and involves the contention that the social benefits of the form can be achieved through harnessing the power of the individual profit motive to achieve social aims.[85] Recognising the wider range of individuals with a stake in the corporation does not necessarily change this point, namely, that the social benefits of the form may eventuate through the manner in which individuals utilise it to achieve the advantages they see it as embodying from their own perspectives. The corporation thus has a complex aim: its ultimate goal is the enhancement of overall well-being adjudged from an impartial perspective but the achievement of this goal is designed to occur through a structure that enables individuals to advance their own interests through it. I term this conception the 'socio-liberal conception of the corporation'.

Keeping track of the different perspectives involved in capturing the corporate purpose will be significant in determining a viable approach to the obligations of corporations.[86] The difficulty often lies in the tension between the perspectives in relation to its purpose: creating a structure such as a corporation has often allowed individual self-interest and greed to run amok, causing great social harms. Clearly, a structure designed for social benefits, ultimately, cannot be allowed to generate such harms. A major question since the original creation of the modern corporate form has been how to acquire the benefits of the structure without the harms. Whilst the separate legal personality of a corporation has clear advantages and is responsible for the popularity of this modality of conducting business, it also is evident that it creates clear risks. The corporation, as has been mentioned, is essentially a fictional entity created by law and dependent upon individuals to act on its behalf. The individuals who act on its behalf are essentially immunised in most cases from bearing full responsibility and accountability for their behaviour. Indeed, the corporation is specifically designed to enable risks to be taken: yet, some risks may be foolish, reckless and create major social

[85] See Parkinson, 1993: 41–43 for an articulation of this view in relation to wealth maximisation and the limits thereof.

[86] In this respect, the argument here is different to that of Bottomley, 2007: 63, who claims that the justification for the state's role in regulating corporations arises 'not from the state grant of corporate powers and attributes . . . but from the potential for the accumulation of private power created by those powers and attributes'. Whilst the latter is no doubt relevant, the argument I have made focuses on the very reasons for the creation of the corporate form which must lie in a conception of social benefit. The state creates the entity for these reasons and may also regulate to ensure the goals of its creation are achieved and not hindered.

harms. If done in the name of the corporation, individuals may also bear no liability for a failed investment, and they may also be able to avoid personal responsibility for their actions. Separate personality thus can allow individuals to hide behind the corporate veil and thus avoid responsibility for their actions. It is for this reason that Bakan terms the structure 'pathological' in the pursuit of profit.[87] Ciepley writes: 'The corporate form separates ownership and control; thus, corporate managers, like socialist managers, do not own the assets they control and do not bear the direct consequences of their control. Without supplemental devices to align incentives, a corporate economy is, literally an institutionalization of individual economic *ir*responsibility.'[88]

The focus usually within corporate law has been on some of the difficulties with regulating the structure in relation to its financial operations: the risks, for instance, caused by the separation of ownership by the shareholders and control of the corporation which vests in the directors.[89] More recently, this question has been raised in the context of wider social harms that the corporation has created and its potential to violate the fundamental rights of individuals. The question of the harm corporations can cause to fundamental rights and developing a legal analytical framework for determining the negative obligations that this entity has will be dealt with in some depth in Chapters 6 and 7.

If we accept the argument that the corporation was designed to create social benefits, then a further question concerns how to ensure an alignment between individual benefits and benefits to society overall from corporate activities. Thus, the creation of the structure may well lead to high levels of individual enrichment, but the wider social benefits may not eventuate. Given that the corporation is meant, at least partially, to harness the individual profit motive (or wider motives for individual advantages) for social ends and thus is not meant directly to focus on social benefits, the question remains as to how to ensure an alignment between the benefits for some individuals and the benefits for all (or society as a whole). This question raises firmly the issue of the positive obligations of corporations and will be dealt with in Chapter 8.

[87] Bakan, 2004: 56–57.

[88] Ciepley, 2013: 147.

[89] For a classic statement of the problem, see Berle and Means, 1932: 7 and 66–82. The relationship between shareholders and directors – and the internal processes of governance – is also at the heart of some more recent work on the corporate form such as that of Bottomley, 2007.

The socio-liberal conception of the corporation challenges both the libertarian and political conception thereof. The libertarian conception, importantly, seeks to cast the corporation largely within the realm of private relations. Yet, the socio-liberal conception recognises the ineradicable role of law in the formation of the corporation, and thus an essentially public dimension to its character. The movement of an individual or collection of individuals into a corporate form only happens through an act of public recognition. This public establishment also, as we have seen, conditions its purpose. The law intervenes here not only to regulate private relations but also to construct a particular vehicle through which individuals can conduct business. Thus, the corporation is neither wholly public nor wholly private: it straddles the boundary between these realms.[90]

The public dimension of the corporation is also highlighted by a number of other features it exhibits. In relation even to the smallest corporate entity, separate legal personality separates out the individual from the corporate entity and does so through a public act. That feature applies in relation to all actors that interact with the entity. However, whilst one individual can form a corporation, as we saw, one of its key benefits is its ability to serve as a vehicle for multiple individuals to pool their assets. The corporation thus often involves the exercise by a collection of individuals of their common interests in a co-operative structure. As such, it too develops a wider collective and thus public dimension.

[90] My view is similar in this regard to Bottomley, 2007: 61, who argues that the 'corporation is an institution in which public and private interests and values meet'. On this basis, he argues that corporations are 'political institutions' (60) of a type and thus it is necessary to attend carefully to the rules that govern them and their decision-making structures. Given their political nature, Bottomley argues for the application of a notion of constitutionalism to corporate structures and identifies a set of principles which are applicable to their internal governance (which is his focus). Some of these proposals are relevant to the discussion in Chapter 9. He does also recognise that corporations are actors within a wider context and have an impact on the rest of society. Their accumulation of power forms the justification for state regulation thereof. However, the external bonds of the corporation to the rest of society are not the focus of his work, nor is their potential impact on fundamental rights. This book can be seen to be consonant with the constitutional perspective outlined by Bottomley – except that it aims to explore the implications of fundamental rights usually contained in a country's constitution (or international law) for corporations. It thus can be understood to expand upon and develop an analytical framework for examining a particular foundational dimension of what it means to 'constitutionalise' the corporation.

At the same time, the corporation does not become wholly public as the political conception would advocate. As we saw, its purpose is not to create another branch of government or a regulatory structure but rather to serve as an enabling vehicle for business to be conducted and for individuals connected therewith to attain a variety of advantages. The structure ideally seeks to harness individual self-seeking behaviour for social ends that promise benefits for everyone. As such, it requires allowing a space for the exercise of individual autonomy (within constraints), a dimension that would usually be regarded as part of the private rather than the public sphere.

1.5 Conclusion: Neither Fish Nor Fowl

This chapter was concerned with understanding the limited liability corporation, the dominant form of conducting business today. The brief history I offered of the corporation sought to show that the particular manner in which it has been constructed is itself contingent and based on particular historical choices which were seen to be advantageous (sometimes for society and sometimes for individuals). This point is important as it highlights that the exact form of the corporation is not naturally constructed: as such, it is fundamentally dependent on existing law for the manner in which it is designed. The potential is thus opened for us to shift the current structure of and rules surrounding the corporation where they are not socially optimal.

I turned then to consider two questions that have arisen in trying to conceive of the type of entity that a corporation is: the first was the relationship between the corporate entity and the individuals underlying it. I argued that the relationship between the corporate structure and individuals was best captured by a 'supervenience relation': recognising that the corporation itself was not reducible to but dependent upon the individuals underlying it. That relationship can help us understand what is meant by its agency and provide us with a good grounding for engaging with a number of legal doctrinal questions.

This discussion set the scene for an engagement with the very purpose of setting up a corporate entity. The ineliminability of law provided the grounds for recognising that there must be a justification for its creation rooted in impartial and wider social benefits that are to be achieved through its creation. The corporation though, it was argued, is not an entity that then becomes simply another structure of the government. Indeed, the particular nature of the corporation lies in the fact that it is a structure designed to harness the expression of individual economic interests for social benefits. That complex duality cannot be lost without losing the distinctiveness of the corporate entity. As Ciepley writes, 'corporations are neither wholly private nor wholly public, but amphibian, incorporating properties and exhibiting additional properties unique to themselves'.[91]

The questions dealt with in this chapter are of great importance to determining the obligations of the corporation in relation to fundamental rights and how both corporate law and fundamental rights law should develop in this regard. To do justice to these questions must involve developing an understanding of the nature and purpose of this agent. Accepting the complexity I have outlined will, it is hoped, provide us with a view that is not only true in capturing the essence of the entity but also capable of commanding a fair degree of agreement amongst reasonable persons when they contemplate the nature of this entity. I now turn in the next part of the book to examine the legal doctrinal approaches through which courts have sought to address cases where non-state actors and corporations, in particular, have had an impact on fundamental rights and so begin the exploration of how to determine their obligations.

[91] Ciepley, 2013: 156.

PART I

Legal Doctrinal Models for Addressing the Substantive Obligations of Non-State Actors for Fundamental Rights

2

The State Duty to Protect Model

2.1 Introduction

International law, as traditionally understood, is a system set up by states to regulate the affairs between them. Since the Second World War, states have committed themselves in a variety of international instruments to ensuring that the fundamental rights of individuals are realised.[1] This has led to an understanding that individuals are the bearers of rights, and that states are the agents required to assume the obligations that flow from these entitlements.

This traditional understanding of the state's role in relation to fundamental rights has been challenged in this globalised world by the growth of a range of non-state actors with the capacity to impact significantly upon fundamental rights. These include multinational corporations, non-governmental organisations (NGOs) and groups fighting in armed conflicts. These non-state actors create a number of difficulties for the traditional view that states are the sole agents bound by fundamental rights obligations. If the traditional view is correct, then the discourse of fundamental rights should simply be inapplicable to non-state actors such as corporations.

Yet, as I seek to show in the first segment of this chapter, the legal normative foundations of fundamental rights challenge the idea that the state alone has obligations in relation to these entitlements. This raises the question of how international law has sought to reconcile this foundational dimension of rights reasoning with the traditional state-centric approach. The state duty to protect doctrine has become the dominant approach which attempts to extend the state-based model to cover non-state actors in an indirect manner: the state remains the primary duty-bearer but is under

[1] See, for instance, UN Charter art. 1, para 3; UDHR; ICCPR; ICESCR.

an obligation to protect individuals against harms by non-state actors such as corporations and so must itself 'create' the obligations of such actors.

The key focus of this chapter is on this doctrine and I provide a detailed critique thereof, showing, in particular, how conceptualising the state as the 'originator' of fundamental rights obligations between non-state actors, clashes with the nature of fundamental rights and the character of the state (as expressed in leading social contract theories). Apart from serious practical drawbacks, I focus on a key conceptual problem – that the state duty to protect model is parasitic on having an idea of what the state must protect individuals against. That, in turn, requires a construction of the obligations of non-state actors such as corporations in relation to fundamental rights.

The last part of this chapter considers how this theoretical critique applies in practice through a qualitative analysis of a few cases decided by the European Court of Human Rights (ECHR) which adopts this doctrine, many of which importantly involve corporations. This discussion highlights the manner in which the ECHR is, unavoidably, occupied with the construction of the obligations of non-state actors such as corporations vis-à-vis one another. It goes further though and attempts to understand the structure of the ECHR's reasoning about the content of such obligations and the factors that it takes into account in making such decisions. We will see in later chapters how its analysis is similar to that adopted by various domestic courts and so displays an interesting convergence on what I shall term the 'multi-factoral' approach.

2.2 The Legal Normative Foundations of Fundamental Rights

The language and concept of fundamental rights emerged importantly in the international sphere at the end of the Second World War, but it had precursors at the national level.[2] Though the notion had been discussed philosophically for centuries, the first major legal document at a national level incorporating a range of fundamental rights was the Declaration of the Rights of Man and of the Citizen enacted at the start of the French Revolution.[3] The document recognises certain 'natural and imprescriptible rights of man' which include 'liberty, property, security and resistance to oppression'.[4] Importantly, it also guarantees freedom of expression. In the

[2] See, for instance, Cruft et al., 2015: 1–2; Ishay, 2004; and for a challenge to the continuity, Moyn, 2010.

[3] See the Declaration of the Rights of Man and of the Citizen, 1789.

[4] Ibid: art. 2.

eighteenth century, this was a matter of deep concern, in that state power could be used to restrict the ability of individuals to express themselves with the threat of serious punitive consequences. This remained a concern at the origins of the international human rights regime: consequently, article 19 of the Universal Declaration of Human Rights recognises that 'everyone has the right to freedom of opinion and expression'[5] and article 19 of the International Covenant on Civil and Political Rights recognises that '[e] veryone shall have the right to freedom of expression'.[6] The concern about state interference with freedom of expression, of course, continues to be important in many parts of the world today.

Yet, what happens when that very liberty to express oneself is threatened not by the state but by another powerful non-state actor? Consider, for example, a situation where a large number of transnational corporations implement a policy that requires employees never to express their opinions without permission from the directors of the company, on pain of dismissal. The strong niche position of the companies in the marketplace and their being significant employers in each of the societies in which they operate mean that employees in this industry have limited opportunities to find work elsewhere. Such a policy would pose a direct threat to the liberty of individuals to express themselves, which is not caused by state interference. It thus raises the fundamental question as to whether the right to freedom of expression places obligations not only on the state but also on non-state entities such as these corporations.

This question raises a foundational normative issue as to why fundamental rights are important and what the point of protecting them is. Whilst I shall not provide an exhaustive discussion of various philosophical theories of fundamental rights, it is important to recognise that within legal documents and discourse, these rights are usually understood to flow from the foundational dignity or worth of individuals.[7] Thus, under international law, as is well known, 'they are the rights that one has simply because one is human'.[8] The International Covenant on Civil and Political

[5] See UDHR.

[6] See ICCPR.

[7] I first outlined this argument in Bilchitz, 2013. More recently, a similar argument has been expressed by Carrillo-Santarelli, 2018: 41.

[8] Donnelly, 1998: 18. I express here the generally accepted understanding of the foundation of these rights as is expressed in the treaties themselves though I do not, as was explained in the Introduction fn 8, endorse the fact that fundamental rights protection should only cover human beings. On the arbitrariness of locating the justification for fundamental rights in an assumption of human superiority (often couched in terms of dignity), see Beyleveld and Brownsword, 2001: 22–23.

Rights (ICCPR) and International Covenant on Economic, Social and Cultural Rights (ICESCR) recognise this idea in their Preamble where they state that the rights contained therein 'derive from the inherent dignity of the human person'.[9] Dignity involves the idea that every human being has a special worth or value. That, in turn, requires treatment in accordance with the value and respect individuals are to be afforded. What then must this treatment comprise? The fundamental rights in the Universal Declaration and various treaties enumerate upon the various dimensions of what is required to respect individuals. An understanding of what is required to respect an individual derives from the fact that individuals themselves have certain foundational interests in liberty (for instance, of expression, association and movement) and well-being (for instance, in having adequate housing, food and healthcare) that rights safeguard.[10]

From this foundation, two further important principles are derived. If rights flow from the inherent dignity of human beings, then they must apply equally to all human beings and are thus universal in nature.[11] The derivation of fundamental rights from human dignity also means that they cannot be 'renounced, lost, or forfeited, human rights are inalienable'.[12] Given these principles, it is clear that the idea of fundamental rights in international law ensures protection for each individual's fundamental interests simply as a result of their having dignity.[13] The underpinnings of fundamental rights in many national constitutions is similar.[14]

Importantly for our purposes, the fundamental deontic structure of fundamental rights means that they are themselves agnostic as to the agents who must realise them.[15] Rights are articulated from the perspective of the beneficiary of the right: the *rights-bearer* is the normative focus.[16] Naomi is entitled to freedom of expression; Lebogang is entitled

[9] See the Preamble of the ICCPR and ICESCR.

[10] See, for instance, Gewirth, 1978: 63; and the list of capabilities in Nussbaum, 2000: 78–80, which covers similar ground.

[11] Donnelly, 1998: 18. See also, Dicke, 2002: 118 who argues that human dignity provides the basis for claims as to the universality of fundamental rights.

[12] Donnelly, ibid: 18.

[13] See *Velasquez Rodriguez* v. *Honduras*: para 144, where it was stated that fundamental rights are 'higher values that "are not derived from the fact that (an individual) is a national of a certain state, but are based upon attributes of his human personality"'. For a justification of rights rooted in the fundamental interests of individuals, see Bilchitz, 2007: 6–101.

[14] In South Africa, for instance, see *Dawood* v. *Minister of Home Affairs*: para 35.

[15] Raz, 1986: 184 states, for instance: '[O]ne may know of the existence of a right . . . without knowing who is bound by duties based on it or what precisely are these duties.'

[16] This feature has been the basis of criticism of rights discourse. See O'Neill, 1996: 133–135, who criticises rights discourse and proposes a moral perspective focused on obligations

to have access to food. The entitlements themselves do not inherently tell us who must realise them.

To understand this point better, consider freedom of expression. This right protects the important interest of individuals in being able to express their views freely.[17] To prevent them from doing so is to demonstrate disrespect for the worth or dignity of the person: that explains why it is troubling for the state to wield its power to silence individuals. If that is so, however, then what matters is that the individual interest underlying the right to freedom of expression is protected: namely, being able to express their views freely. If then a non-state actor such as a military grouping, a corporation or an NGO fails to respect the ability of individuals to express themselves, they demonstrate the same lack of regard for individuals and their dignity. If dignity is the foundation of fundamental rights, then these forms of behaviour by non-state actors must also be prohibited: what matters is respect for these fundamental interests, not the identity of the agents who threaten such interests.[18]

This understanding of rights renders it in fact incoherent to suggest that only states are bound not to violate fundamental rights and all other entities may violate them at will.[19] If non-state actors can impact upon fundamental rights, then such guarantees potentially prima facie require such agents to take certain actions and refrain from others. Different types of agents may in fact have distinctive obligations and various considerations must be canvassed in allocating obligations.[20] Yet, in determining the obligations of agents, the focus on the rights-bearer remains primary.

After the Second World War, fundamental rights, as we saw, became a fundamental pillar of international law. States accepted a foundational notion – fundamental rights – that in its very logic, as we have seen, requires recognition of the fact that all agents, whether they be state or non-state actors, can be bound by the obligations they impose. Yet, international law has also traditionally been understood to be a system focused on states as the key agents. In turn, that understanding has been regarded as implying that it is only states that can be the subject of

rather than rights; and the response by Bilchitz, 2007: 72–74 that '[t]alk of duties alone fails to indicate that it is our connection to others who have interests that is of critical importance and which imposes obligations upon us'.

17 Freedom of expression in turn may be defended for both instrumental and intrinsic reasons: see generally, Mill, 1859.

18 See Dafel, 2015: 63.

19 See Ratner, 2001: 472 – '[i]f human rights are aimed at the protection of human dignity, the law needs to respond to abuses that do not implicate the state directly'.

20 See López Latorre, 2020: 79–80.

international fundamental rights obligations.[21] There is thus an awkward coexistence that has developed between an idea that is not state-centric (fundamental rights) within a state-focused system (international law).[22] How then can this tension be addressed? In section 2.3, I discuss the leading legal doctrine, which has sought to square this circle: the 'state duty to protect' model.

2.3 The State Duty to Protect Model and Its Shortcomings

2.3.1 The Indirect Duty Model

The traditional doctrinal response to the problem that non-state actors can impact upon fundamental rights is to find a way to hold them accountable without giving up on the idea that the state is the primary agent bound by fundamental rights obligations. The method of doing so involves expanding the scope of the state's obligations in relation to fundamental rights. The state not only assumes an obligation not to violate rights itself (the duty to respect) and to provide concrete goods itself (the duty to fulfil), but it is also required to ensure that non-state actors do not imperil the interests protected by fundamental rights (the duty to protect).[23] The state is thus responsible for imposing obligations on non-state actors that they would otherwise not have in relation to fundamental rights and creating enforcement mechanisms to ensure those obligations are realised.[24] The contours of this duty are famously outlined in *Velasquez Rodriguez* v. *Honduras*:

> An illegal act which violates human rights and which is initially not directly imputable to a State (for example, because it is the act of a private person or because the person responsible has not been identified) can lead to international responsibility of the State, not because of the act itself, but because of the lack of due diligence to prevent the violation or to respond to it as required by the Convention. . . . The State has a legal duty to take reasonable steps to prevent human rights violations and to use the

[21] See Zerk, 2006: 73, who argues that 'it was generally believed that only states could be "subjects" of international law'.

[22] I initially examined this problem in Bilchitz, 2016a, and sections 2.2 and 2.3 of this chapter are, in part, drawn from that exploration with some modifications and developments.

[23] See Kinley and Tadaki, 2004: 937.

[24] See Emedi, 2011: 629, who argues that the state, despite the growing size and power of multinational corporations, still remains as the 'actor that needs to be targeted to stop [multinational corporations] from violating human rights'; and Nolan, 2009: 225, who investigates the state's obligation to protect economic and social rights against third-party actors as interpreted by four different regional bodies.

> means at its disposal to carry out a serious investigation of violations committed within its jurisdiction, to identify those responsible, to impose the appropriate punishment and to ensure the victim adequate compensation.[25]

This idea has been adopted by other regional human rights institutions and within the international treaty system.[26] The state duty to protect, as understood in these international law instruments, appears to comprise several elements. The traditional doctrine that states are the sole subjects or addressees of international law seems to imply that a non-state actor such as a corporation would not have any obligations imposed by international human rights treaties. This appears to create a lacuna, in that non-state actors may then face no consequences for the severe harms they cause to the interests of individuals which are protected by fundamental rights. To address this problem, the duty to protect requires states to take reasonable steps to ensure that non-state actors do not violate such rights. The state effectively has a positive obligation which is focused upon preventing harm to individuals by non-state actors.

It should be recognised that this is an 'indirect' method of imposing obligations on non-state actors (and hence, at times, I refer to it as the 'indirect duty' view or model): whilst corporations, for instance, have no direct duties in relation to fundamental rights flowing from international law, they do have such duties indirectly through the state's realisation of its own obligations to develop a framework of laws and regulations which protect such rights. The state's first duty is thus to set up the legal framework and regulatory structures that create obligations for non-state actors such as corporations in relation to such rights. It must then adopt all the measures necessary to ensure enforcement of these laws and regulations, which must include an investigation and an enforcement system. The state is thus, under this conception, both the sole 'originator' of obligations for non-state actors (the 'binding agent') and the main 'enforcer' of those obligations (the 'enforcement agent'). The individual has no claim on a private actor, such as a corporation, outside the terms of

[25] *Velásquez Rodríguez* v. *Honduras*: paras 172 and 174.

[26] See *Social and Economic Rights Action Centre (SERAC) and Another* v. *Nigeria* in which it was stated that '[g]overnments have a duty to protect their citizens, not only through appropriate legislation and effective enforcement, but also by protecting them from damaging acts that may be perpetrated by private parties'; and *X and Y* v. *Netherlands* regarding the position of the European Court of Human Rights (which is discussed in more detail below). See, for the position, for instance, within the United Nations Committee on Economic, Social and Cultural Rights, General Comment No. 15 on the Right to Water paras 23 and 24.

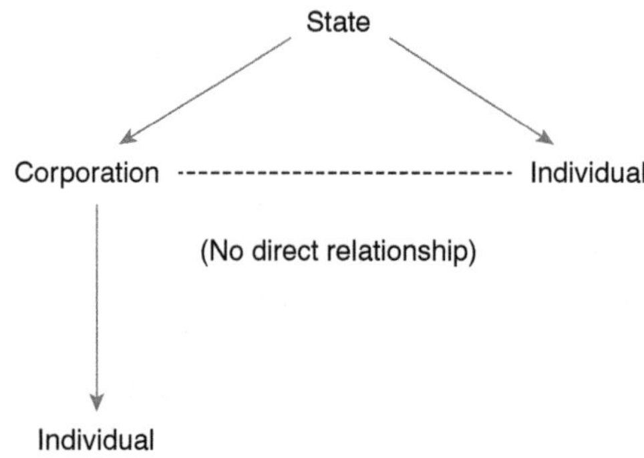

Figure 2.1 The state duty to protect model.

a framework set up and established by the state. This model can be illustrated as shown in Figure 2.1.

2.3.2 The Justification and Critique of the Indirect Duty Model

The indirect duty view flows from particular assumptions about the need to regulate the impact non-state actors can have on fundamental rights whilst retaining a state-based conception of international law. In engaging critically with it, I shall focus particularly on the idea that the state should be conceptualised as the 'originator' of fundamental rights obligations between non-state actors.

2.3.2.1 Logic of Fundamental Rights Challenges Indirect Approach

First, let us turn to internal problems in the very logic of the case for the indirect duty view.[27] States are tasked by international human rights treaties to create the laws and regulatory frameworks that bind non-state actors in relation to fundamental rights. The question that arises is why states should bear any responsibility for regulating the behaviour of such actors who are agents separate from the state. It is readily understandable why the state can have legal obligations for its own actions in relation to individuals, but why must it assume some responsibility for what others do or fail to do?

There are two types of answers that can be given in this regard: the first flows from the importance and nature of fundamental rights, and

[27] In the next few paragraphs, I attempt to elaborate and develop upon an argument made much more briefly in Bilchitz, 2013: 111–113.

the second from the very character and justification of the state itself. As we have seen, in relation to the first answer, individuals, corporations, and NGOs all have the potential to affect the individual interests protected by fundamental rights in serious ways. Since rights-bearers and their interests are primary, a system concerned with the protection of rights must potentially place obligations on any actor who has the capacity to imperil or affect the realisation of those rights. In a system focused on the obligations of states, the state duty to protect is one way of achieving this end, by requiring the state to create binding legal frameworks that place obligations upon non-state actors in relation to fundamental rights.

However, what is unclear is why we should follow an indirect route at all to recognise that all agents have binding obligations flowing from fundamental rights. If the goal of rights protection is to ensure the realisation of rights, and multiple actors can impact upon such rights, why then not simply recognise that all actors who have the capacity to affect their realisation are under direct obligations in this regard? The indirect duty approach places the state between the individual rights-bearer and other non-state actors, but it is simply unclear why this is necessary conceptually, efficient practically or desirable normatively. The problem with the indirect duty view, then, is to see why it does not collapse into a direct duty view: if protecting the fundamental interests of individuals is the goal of rights protection (as a condition of respect for their dignity), then that proposition would seem adequate to justify placing direct obligations on corporations and other non-state actors. The doctrinal commitment to states as the sole subjects of obligations flowing from fundamental rights appears rigid, unjustified and unconnected to the very normative underpinnings of fundamental rights.

Moreover, it is hard to see why the state should have such a duty to protect at all, unless there is some pre-existing reason to believe that non-state actors are not entitled to violate the fundamental rights of individuals at will. If a concern to protect rights-bearers and their interests is at the foundation of fundamental-rights protection, then the reason for the state's involvement in this area must be the fact that powerful non-state actors can significantly affect the fundamental interests of other individuals. If that is the case, however, it is unclear why this fact does not in itself provide a sufficient reason for recognising obligations upon those powerful non-state actors in relation to other individuals.

Moreover, this point becomes particularly important when we attempt to understand 'what' the content is of the obligations the state must impose on non-state actors. The state cannot simply impose obligations arbitrarily – what then can the normative foundation for those obligations be? Ultimately, the starting point in fundamental rights discourse must again lie in a focus on what duties are necessary to ensure the rights of individuals are realised. As we will see, other factors, such as the nature of an agent – for example, a corporation – and the strength of their own claim to fundamental rights may play a role too. In all this, the content of the obligations of non-state actors is determined by factors relating to the subjects of rights protection and the nature of the duty-bearers. The state's role may be to enshrine these obligations in law and to enforce them but, in determining what they are, the state ultimately is eliminable – it must have reference to obligations that arise by virtue simply of the relationship between the rights-holder and the non-state duty-bearer.

This reasoning challenges the notion that the state should be recognised as the 'originator' of the fundamental rights obligations of non-state actors. If the normative core of fundamental rights is the protection of individuals and their fundamental interests, then those rights are not created by the state but rather arise independently of the existence of the state. States themselves recognise these pre-existing moral rights in positive law (international or domestic), develop detailed regulations around them and help develop institutional mechanisms to give effect to them. They, however, create neither the rights themselves nor the obligations flowing from them. Importantly, states – by signing the international treaties that protect fundamental rights – provide legal recognition for pre-existing moral rights, which they then undertake to give effect to in their national systems and in their actions of an international character.

2.3.2.2 Non-State Actor Obligations Precede the State

A similar argument can be made by going back to some of the theory connected with the justification of the state itself. There are a range of variants of such theories and I shall focus on the social contract tradition which roots the state's legitimacy in a voluntary agreement between individuals. Historical contractarian theories usually begin by an account of human nature together with the identification of problems with a 'pre-political' state of affairs that lead individuals to agree to the existence of a sovereign power. The justification of the sovereign lies in remedying the problems with that pre-political state of affairs. The accounts of the key theorists differ as to how they conceptualise the realm of the 'pre-political', the problems therein and consequently the reasons for the emergence of a sovereign power. I will focus briefly on two of the most famous of such justifications provided by Thomas Hobbes and John Locke. A key theme I wish to highlight in this analysis is that, on both accounts, the very reason for the existence of the state lies in attempting to ensure enforcement of the obligations individuals already owe one another.

2.3.2.2.1 Hobbes Hobbes conceives of human beings as individuals concerned to achieve the goals that they value and with no natural constraints on what they may do to attain them. Whilst there may be differences in physical strength, roughly, Hobbes is of the view that 'when all is reckoned together, the difference between man, and man is not so considerable'.[28] With our roughly equal abilities, Hobbes believes that individuals also develop an 'equality of hope in the attaining of our Ends'.[29] This leads to a conflict: if we both want the same thing and there are limited numbers of these things, we need to find a way to assert our will over others which may involve seeking to subdue them. Thus, competition between people leads them continually to try to gain the best for themselves, which might involve individuals forcibly preventing other individuals from accomplishing the same goals. That leads to a condition Hobbes describes as a war of all against all:[30] where all are willing to utilise whatever means necessary to achieve their will. In such a situation, no one is secure and people live in continual fear: he famously stated that the life of human beings in the state of nature is 'solitary, poore, nasty, brutish and short'.[31]

To address this situation, which is to the benefit of nobody, reason counsels human beings to give up their unlimited powers of attaining their ends through whichever means they wish and to seek peace. They must renounce their absolute liberty to do as they wish in their own interests and only take on as much freedom as they are willing that others have too.[32] In other words, at the very least, they must acknowledge obligations not to harm the fundamental interests of others (which are protected today by fundamental rights).[33] The problem, however, is that such a renunciation has no power to enforce itself. Hobbes, being sceptical about the goodness of human nature, is not convinced that human individuals will, in and of

[28] Hobbes, 1996: 87.
[29] Ibid.
[30] Ibid: 91.
[31] Ibid: 89.
[32] Ibid: 92.
[33] Accounting for the binding force of such obligations is one of the difficulties that faces Hobbes' account: see Ryan, 1999: 226–227.

themselves, follow the dictates of reason where disputes arise and passions become inflamed. He writes that: '[f]or the Lawes of Nature . . .of themselves, without the terrour of some power, to cause them to be observed, are contrary to our naturall Passions, that carry us to Partiality, Pride, Revenge, and the like'.[34] People might attempt to reach agreements with one another to a similar effect by clearly renouncing their rights to harm others. Yet, such agreements without an enforcement power are 'but Words, and of no strength to secure a man at all'.[35] In such a situation, people require a common power that can enforce their observance of these covenants. The only way to establish such a power is for all people to give up their unlimited natural rights to a sovereign power whose task it is to maintain peace amongst its members and defend them against external threats.[36]

For our purposes, what is of importance to emphasise is that it is the threat – the capacity to harm – posed in the sphere of private relations between individuals and groupings thereof that potentially can lead to a descent into a state of war. The solution is for every individual to recognise obligations not to harm the fundamental interests of others. Yet, for Hobbes such responsibilities are weak without an enforcement power.[37] The need for obligations between private parties and the nature thereof pre-date the state.[38] The sovereign, however, by virtue of its enforcement power translates them into strong legal obligations that have not only binding force but consequences for failing to meet them. Thus, the state – on the Hobbesian account – is in fact the necessary condition for strong binding obligations to arise between private parties; yet, the necessity for and content of those obligations are already recognised in the state of nature. Consequently, part of the very goal of the state for Hobbes is to enforce the pre-existing obligations that are only weakly enforceable between private parties in the absence of the state.

2.3.2.2.2 Locke Locke's approach to justifying the state follows a similar structure to that of Hobbes; however, the details of his account differ. The view Locke articulates of the state of nature is much more sanguine. It is a space of liberty to do what one wishes within the confines of what he terms the law of nature. This law of nature essentially flows from reason, predates the state, and teaches that 'no one ought to harm

[34] Ibid: 117.
[35] Ibid.
[36] Ibid: 121.
[37] See Ryan, 1999.
[38] See Gert, 2010: 119.

another in his Life, Health, Liberty or Possessions'.[39] This law of nature clearly establishes negative obligations between private individuals to respect basic fundamental rights. The state of nature is also a space of deep equality between persons without 'subordination or subjection'[40] and can ground certain positive obligations too.[41]

Locke has a less bleak view of human beings than Hobbes and believes that humans are capable of following the laws of nature.[42] Since these laws, however, require enforcement, anyone breaking their terms may be disciplined by anyone else as there is no centralised authority in the state of nature. Locke has three concerns about allowing every person a power of enforcement over the law of nature. Firstly, since human beings are biased in favour of their own interests, they make mistakes in the application of the law of nature to particular cases – there is thus the need for a set of clearer, more specific laws. Secondly, without an impartial judge, individuals enforcing matters in their own cases are likely to go too far and, on occasion, act disproportionately. Thirdly, there is also the problem that any punishment for those offending the laws of nature needs to be executed: if there is no impartial authority, enforcement can well be dangerous for those attempting it and lead to outbreaks of physical violence.[43]

To avert these problems, it is rational for people, according to Locke, to give up two things: they agree to be bound by the laws of society which, in some respects, restrict their natural liberties; and they give up their power of punishing others for infractions of the law of nature and hand this over to the sovereign.[44] The express intention of their acceptance of such a sovereign is thus to preserve their liberty and property in a better manner.[45] This sets both the purpose and the limits of the power of the sovereign: it is set up to address the three defects of the state of nature and

[39] Locke, 1988: 271. See also, Pyle, 2013: 154.
[40] Locke, ibid: 269.
[41] Locke, ibid: 271 writes: '[S]o, by the like reason when his own Preservation comes not in competition, ought he, as much as he can, to preserve the rest of Mankind.' His theory on property (290–291) also provides a ground for positive obligations. Arguments for and against corporations having positive obligations will be dealt with in Chapter 8.
[42] See Ashcraft, 1994: 238–240, who interprets this view as relating to Locke's religious understanding of what God created human beings to be.
[43] Locke, 1988: 351.
[44] The nature and manner of their agreement is a difficulty for Locke, who articulates a much criticised view that people tacitly consent to the exercise of sovereign authority: see Pyle, 2013: 157–158.
[45] Locke, 1988: 353.

thus requires the enactment of clear laws, the appointment of impartial judges, and the impartial execution of the laws.

Importantly, then, for our purposes, for Locke, there exists in the state of nature binding claims individuals can make against each other. These rights flow from an intrinsic worth we have (in Locke's view this was sourced in our being creatures of a sovereign G-d)[46] together with our possessing similar 'Faculties'.[47] This early conception of rights is justified as flowing not from the fact that we are weak and need protection from powerful others but rather from the idea that, as beings with intrinsic worth, we are entitled to certain kinds of treatment from all other agents. From these rights thus flow direct obligations all agents have to individuals with intrinsic worth. Institutional structures set up by the state have important roles in clarifying the nature of these obligations, making judgments about them and exercising enforcement powers in that regard. What is clear for Locke is that binding obligations between private parties precede the state, and their content can be determined independently of the state. The legitimate role of the state for Locke lies in impartially enforcing those direct obligations of individuals and entities in the private sphere.

2.3.2.2.3 The Focus of the State Duty to Protect and Its Limitations

What both these approaches have in common is that part of the very justification for the state itself is the state's power to ensure that the relationships between private parties do not violate the fundamental interests of others, conform to certain basic standards, and do not imperil the material well-being of other individuals.[48] Since we know that fundamental rights protect the fundamental interests of individuals, we can reformulate this idea by pointing out that, on these accounts, individuals grant the state the powers of regulation and enforcement to ensure the realisation of their fundamental rights. The state's very *raison d'être* involves regulating the relationship between private parties inter se to ensure that they live together in such a way that the rights of each are realised (to the extent possible).

[46] For an exploration of the connection between Locke's thought and Christianity, see Waldron, 2002: 78–82.

[47] Ibid. This will be discussed further later in relation to the impartiality rationale.

[48] It should be recognised that neither of these social contract theories supports the idea that states should simply abstain, in general, from interfering with private parties, as some recent libertarian theorists argue. The very reason for the existence of the state provides grounds for the prevention of harm, but also for protecting individuals from private violence and ensuring that individuals have a certain level of material well-being, which may itself require interference with the property rights of others: see West, 2003: 84–85.

This reasoning has important implications for fundamental rights and the role of the state. It is evident from the social contract theory I have engaged that the state is not the 'originator' of obligations in relation to fundamental rights. On the contrary, concerns about the enforcement of such obligations are its very reason for coming into being. Central to this argument is the idea that the state is an entity that is wholly public in nature: its foundation and legitimacy lie in its impartiality and its fair and equal treatment of each individual. As such, the state is not meant to disclose preferences for the interests of particular persons, nor display favouritism or bias to any individual. In this way, the state can achieve the goals social contract theorists had in mind for it: preserving the peace between people and creating an impartial enforcement arm to adjudicate disputes between persons.[49]

Importantly, then, the focus of the state duty to protect is on ensuring an impartial enforcement power of already existing obligations between non-state parties. In fact, that duty to protect arises from the breakdown in the *enforcement* of those obligations that is likely in a state of nature – those obligations, however, precede the state. The state is thus not the originator of those obligations: if we are to understand what they are – and, consequently, which obligations the state must enforce – we need to understand how to ascertain the content of those obligations from an account of the duties that flow from fundamental rights and which are owed to individuals by non-state actors. We will see that this analytical point is borne out precisely when considering the case law of the ECHR later in this chapter.

2.3.2.3 Multiple Undesirable Implications that Flow from the State Duty to Protect Model

The notion that the state is the 'originator' of obligations for non-state actors also has a number of further undesirable implications. Firstly, the idea places the state in an extremely powerful position and suggests that it, in some sense, lies within its discretion as to whether to impose fundamental rights obligations on non-state actors.[50] The only reason the state is required to do so is the international obligations it voluntarily

[49] As we have seen, these represent the views of Hobbes and Locke, respectively, discussed earlier.

[50] For a philosophical tradition that suggests this notion, see Bentham, 1987: 46, 69 (accepting only legal positive rights recognised by the state and contending that natural rights make no sense – 'from real laws come real rights'). It is quite unclear why Bentham objects to moral rights if they are understood as the claim that an individual 'ought' to have certain legal rights: see Waldron, 1987: 39–45; see also Sen, 2004: 324–328.

assumes in relation to other states. Yet, given the sovereign equality of states, it may (at least theoretically) withdraw from these obligations. If the state is the 'originator' of fundamental rights obligations for non-state actors, then it may refuse to create them. This state of affairs then leaves non-state actors to violate rights as they wish in the absence of state action.

It also raises the question as to the source of the very obligations of the state itself in relation to fundamental rights. Is the state the 'originator' not only of the obligations of non-state actors but also of its own obligations? In what sense are its own obligations binding in this regard? Such obligations would stand on shaky ground if their only basis were the voluntary commitment of the state itself. As we saw from a brief consideration of social contract justifications for the state, such obligations provide some of the very reasons for the existence of the state and thus are preconditions for its legitimacy – they cannot therefore simply be voluntarily adopted by states.

This idea is also at odds with the recognition that it would be important to protect fundamental rights even if the state refused to bind itself to international treaties. As we have seen, the very idea of fundamental rights arises from the dignity or worth that is attached to individuals and the need to respect that worth through protecting their fundamental interests. Those interests exist prior to the state recognition thereof, and, as we have seen in the discussion of the justification of the state, individuals' desire to have these rights protected is part of their very reason for accepting state authority to begin with.[51] Recognition of these rights, therefore, is not a choice of the state; rather, its normative legitimacy depends upon recognising and giving effect to them.[52] The state should thus not be understood to be the 'originator' of fundamental rights obligations which set the very goals of and constraints upon legitimate state action.

A second major set of problems arises from the idea of the state as an 'originator' of fundamental rights obligations. If the state fails to implement a legal framework that binds non-state actors, then the inference would be that corporations and other non-state actors lack any obligations in relation to fundamental rights (recognised at an international level). There are many parts of the world today where states are weak, or otherwise fail adequately to give effect to their duty to protect. In these parts of the world where there is a lack of regulation, and if the aforementioned logic is accepted, then,

[51] In addition to the discussion of Hobbes and Locke above, see also Rousseau, 1947: 27–30.
[52] Michelman, 2008b: 675–6.

powerful non-state actors are under no obligation in relation to the fundamental rights of other individuals which are enshrined in international treaties and customary international law. Yet, once again, this is simply wrong if such rights attach to rights-bearers because of their inherent worth and dignity, and protect their significant interests – irrespective of state recognition thereof. Part of the very point of international fundamental rights is to recognise their application in contexts where states fail to acknowledge or give effect to them.

Indeed, the idea of the state as the 'originator' of fundamental rights obligations undermines another key feature of fundamental rights: the fact that they universally apply to all individuals who have those interests.[53] If the state were the 'originator' of fundamental rights obligations, such obligations might well fail to be recognised and realised universally where states do not fulfil their duties to do so. Such a doctrine would also preclude liability before any national or international tribunal for violations of fundamental rights by non-state actors who acted in jurisdictions that failed to impose fundamental rights obligations on them. The universality of rights protection is also undermined by this idea in that different states create different legal frameworks that impose different obligations on non-state actors. Such a scenario would be undesirable in that it would lead to a situation in which non-state actors such as corporations would have certain fundamental rights obligations in some states and not others. In some cases, this would lead to a situation in which non-state actors lack important obligations, placing rights in jeopardy. That would fail to address the key goal of fundamental rights protection outlined earlier, namely, to ensure protection for the fundamental interests of individuals.

Indeed, this is not just a theoretical problem that could arise.[54] With the advent of globalisation, many corporations shifted their manufacturing operations to countries (such as China) and regions (such as Southeast Asia) where minimum labour rights and standards were not incorporated into labour laws. The lack of these protections has led to exploitation and misery for many workers.[55] Yet, the multinational corporations in question might argue that, since these countries have not created labour protections for their workers, they have done nothing wrong and have not violated any fundamental rights, as they lack any obligations in the absence of state regulation. An understanding of the impact of their activities and

[53] Donnelly, 1998: 18.
[54] Ratner, 2001: 463.
[55] See, generally, Wu and Zheng, 2008.

conditions of work on the fundamental interests of workers would, however, testify otherwise. The universality of international fundamental rights thus requires acknowledging that there are common standards applicable across the globe, and that international fundamental rights can be violated by corporations even in circumstances where states have failed to implement adequate national legal frameworks to grant them recognition.[56]

A variant of this problem arises from the manner in which the duty to protect has been conceptualised in international law. The duty requires the state, when setting up legal frameworks and enforcement mechanisms, to exercise reasonable due diligence to ensure that non-state actors do not violate the rights of individuals. State liability is thus not absolute in relation to non-state actors, as seems fair: the state cannot completely control the actions of all those actors. Moreover, if the state were the originator of such obligations, it would need to establish a rather exhaustive set of requirements for such actors if it is to exercise its powers effectively. The possibility, however, exists that a corporation, for instance, will violate rights in a new and unexpected manner, despite the reasonable actions of the state in developing a legal framework to regulate corporate behaviour. Indeed, with the explosion of technology, the fourth industrial revolution and vast changes in our world, such situations have become increasingly likely. In such a scenario, victims of these rights violations may not be able to show that the state has been unreasonable in its actions. However, on the state duty to protect doctrine, if the corporate behaviour has not been proscribed by existing legal regulations, then it could also not be challenged, as the corporation lacks any direct obligations other than the ones imposed by the state. The only way to solve this problem is to avoid conceptualising state action as being the 'originator' of corporate obligations in the first place, and to recognise that fundamental rights at the international level already place obligations upon corporations which are amenable to being applied in new scenarios where the underlying interests they protect are affected.

A further undesirable implication of the state duty to protect doctrine arises from the important relationship between a normative obligation and the right to an effective remedy. The right to a remedy is recognised as a self-standing right in international human rights law.[57] At the same time, the right to a remedy is in some sense derived from a prior recognition of obligation: one can only acquire a remedy if a prior duty

[56] For a similar call in the context of the discussions around a Treaty on Business and Human Rights, see López Latorre, 2020: 71.

[57] UDHR article 8; ICCPR article 2(3).

has been breached. The duty to protect once again suggests that the only remedies that lie against corporations for wrongs they commit in relation to fundamental rights can arise from obligations that particular states have created in their laws and regulatory frameworks. The ability to access a remedy thus becomes contingent upon the relative strength of the laws in particular states. Scant possibilities for a remedy are offered to victims of rights violations living in states that have not recognised corporate obligations for rights violations.

Indeed, this lacuna exists within the United Nations Guiding Principles on Business and Human Rights ('UNGPs'). The UNGPs rest on three pillars: the state's duty to protect individuals from rights violations by corporations; the corporate responsibility to respect and avoid harm to the rights of individuals; and the importance of having access to a remedy for victims of rights violations. The corporate responsibility to respect, however, is expressly understood in the document as not being a legal responsibility.[58] Yet, the access-to-remedy pillar recognises the importance of legal remedies where the rights of victims have been violated. The framework thus operates as follows: since corporations have no direct legal obligations to individuals, no legal remedy can be claimed against them unless the state has created obligations for corporations and these obligations have been breached. Once again, this leaves individuals without a remedy against the perpetrator of the violations in circumstances where the state fails to create such obligations.

I have thus argued that there is good reason to jettison the idea underlying the indirect duty model that states are the 'originators' of the obligations of non-state actors in relation to fundamental rights. This argument should not be misconstrued as an argument against the need for states to develop detailed positive laws and regulations governing the relationship between non-state actors – such as corporations – and individuals. It simply means that corporate obligations in relation to fundamental rights precede and must guide such laws and regulations. The moral character of fundamental rights predates the state, and creates a demand for institutionalisation in the laws of the state.[59] As a result, it is no accident that most countries in the world include fundamental rights in their bill of rights. The legal normativity of such rights flows from the

[58] UNGPs: Commentary to GP 12, which states that '[t]he responsibility of business enterprises to respect human rights is distinct from issues of legal liability and enforcement, which remain defined largely by national law provisions in relevant jurisdictions'.

[59] See Bilchitz, 2018: 128.

nearly universal recognition of fundamental rights both in domestic bills of rights and at the international level by states as forming the normative legal foundations of the post-Second World War world order.

2.4 The State Duty to Protect and Corporate Obligations: An Unavoidable Reality

Thus far, I have provided a range of arguments that demonstrate the conceptual and practical weaknesses of the state duty to protect model. The key conceptual point, for our purposes in this book, concerns the fact that the state duty to protect model is incomplete as it requires answering the question what the state must protect individuals against. When attempting to provide an answer to that question, unavoidably, there is a need to determine what non-state actors must or must not do – with their obligations to individuals being determined independently of the state's obligations.

Importantly, the state duty to protect model is not simply a theoretical construct: it is in fact the dominant model adopted at the international level for holding non-state actors to account despite its weakness. It is thus important actually to engage with case law that draws on the model which can help illustrate some of the points that have been made on a theoretical level. To do so, I focus on the jurisprudence of the ECHR, which has expressly drawn on the state duty to protect model. The ECHR is a regional court which may only receive applications by individuals who claim to be victims of fundamental rights violations by the states which are signatories to the European Convention on Human Rights.[60] As such, it is required to focus its analysis on the obligations of state parties but has also often had to deal with cases where the interference with rights emerges from non-state actors. To address these cases, it has developed the doctrine that state parties have positive obligations to protect individuals from violations by non-state actors. In analysing these situations, the court often evaluates the reasoning of domestic courts and whether they correctly capture the obligations of non-state actors. Given its role as a regional court, it often exercises a degree of deference – or what it terms a 'margin of appreciation' – to the decisions of domestic courts and other governmental authorities. There are many cases which engage this area but, as has been noted, I wish to engage qualitatively with the reasoning of the court and so will focus on a few

[60] Article 34 of the European Convention on Human Rights.

cases which illustrate important points concerning the obligations of the non-state actors concerned (with a particular focus on corporations).

2.4.1 *Craxi (no. 2) v. Italy:*[61] Displacing the Responsibility of Non-State Actors

The case concerned a former prime minister of Italy – a Mr Craxi – who was prosecuted on corruption charges in 1993. In 1995, the public prosecutor gained an order from an Italian court, allowing for the interception of telephone calls for three months between his home in Tunisia – where he went into exile – and Italy for purposes of gaining evidence in the case. The interceptions were filed with the registry of the court as is required in terms of Italian law. Though this information was confidential, the press somehow gained access to it and published a range of damning stories concerning Mr Craxi. No one took responsibility for the leaks to the press.

The ECHR held that telephone conversations were covered within the ambit of the protections afforded by article 8 of the European Convention on Human Rights, which provides that 'everyone has the right to respect for his private and family life, his home and his correspondence'. Exposing such conversations will violate such a right unless there is a justification in terms of the categories recognised in the convention and, doing so, is 'necessary in a democratic society'.[62] The court then proceeds to evaluate whether there was such a justification.

It starts by recalling the vital importance in a democracy of both freedom of expression and safeguards to protect the press. Reporting of matters relating to a criminal trial, the court holds, indeed, is part of the public nature of such a trial. The press has an important social function to report on the proceedings, with the public having a right to receive such information.[63] This is more pronounced in the case of public figures who, in a sense, consent to opening themselves up to the public. Nevertheless, public figures are also entitled to respect for their privacy and the public interest only covers receiving information relating to the criminal charges in the trial. The court states the following:

> This must be borne in mind by journalists when reporting on pending criminal proceedings, and the press should abstain from publishing

[61] *Craxi* (no. 2) v. *Italy* (First Section Chamber) (17 July 2003).
[62] Ibid: para 58.
[63] Ibid: para 64.

> information which are likely to prejudice, whether intentionally or not, the right to respect for the private life and correspondence of the accused persons . . .[64]

The court found that much of what was published did not relate to the trial and was of a purely private nature, relating to the relationships of Mr Craxi with his wife and other friends. The publication thus did not correspond to a pressing social need and, consequently, neither conformed to a legitimate aim nor was 'necessary' in a democratic society.

In the aforementioned reasoning, it is quite clear that the court is constructing the obligations of the press in relation to other individuals. It does so by reference to factors such as the need to protect the privacy of telephonic communications, and the social function of the press. It then effectively applies the proportionality enquiry to the private relationship in question, finding that the purely private interests of the press (as opposed to an important public interest) cannot outweigh the right of individuals to privacy.

However, the majority of the court then has to consider, given the limitations of the reach of the Convention, whether the state had breached any of its obligations. The court recognises that Italy had positive obligations to protect Mr Craxi's right to his private life and proceeds to analyse whether the state had taken effective steps to secure respect for his right. Positive measures require appropriate safeguards to be put in place as well as efforts to remedy the situation in the event of a leak. The press appeared to have acquired the information through a malfunction in the registry or through one of the parties. Italy here had failed, the majority of the court finds, to safeguard the privacy of the information concerned. It had also not conducted any investigation into how the leak happened, nor did it seek to sanction those responsible. Consequently, it failed to meet its duty to protect Mr Craxi's right to privacy against the violation thereof by the press. The court decided as a result to award small amounts of damages to each of his heirs (given the applicant had passed away in the interim).[65]

The problem the majority of the court faced, in this instance, was that it was not in fact clear that there had been any wrongdoing on the part of the state or its agents in releasing the information to the press. In fact, it could equally have been Mr Craxi's lawyers or someone from his side who did so. There was a failure here but could it be placed at the door of

[64] Ibid: para 65.

[65] A separate violation found by the court which I do not consider in detail here (given its lack of relevance here) related to the reading out of a part of the transcripts in open court.

the state? Since it was not open to provide redress against the press, and there was a sense in which a wrong was done, the majority constructs the state's duty to protect as being highly onerous. Adequate safeguards, in this case, seem to require almost perfect systems; and the court creates a new duty to investigate such a leak.

It is these features that are objected to in an interesting dissent by Justice Zagrebelsky. He recognises that the imposition of a duty to conduct an effective investigation is a new dimension of the state duty to protect particularly in relation to article 8 of the Convention. Whilst he is not convinced that such a duty should be imposed in relation to article 8 rights, he also questions what the court would see as an effective investigation. In this case, the president of the court had tried to find out who was responsible for the leak but failed. In trying to imagine what else would be required, Zagrebelsky contends that the only effective methods would be to compel journalists to reveal their sources or intercept their communications – and these methods would be in violation of the Convention itself. He concludes that the court has now placed upon States 'an arduous, if not impossible, task to fulfill. In so doing, the judgment concludes by imposing on the state a kind of objective responsibility'.[66]

The debate between the majority of the court and the dissent is of relevance to and illustrates the conceptual points made in section 2.3.2.3 of this chapter, concerning the state duty to protect. That state duty has not generally been conceived of as an absolute one: it is rather a duty to take reasonable measures to protect individuals against harm from other non-state actors.[67] The doctrine, however, creates a major problem in circumstances where there is a clear wrong that was done by a non-state actor but the state appears to have been reasonable in the measures that it has taken. In such an instance, liability can be imposed upon no one and the beneficiary of fundamental rights goes uncompensated for the harm. To address this problem within the confines of the state duty to protect doctrine, it is not possible to impose liability on the non-state party for its violation – indeed, in this case, the locus of responsibility should have been the press's failure to meet its obligations (as recognised by the court) and, consequently, it should have paid damages. Yet, given the rigidity of the *state*-based doctrine, such a holding is not possible: consequently, if the victim is to be compensated, then the state must be held liable. To do

66 Dissenting judgment.

67 A similar point is made in the case of *Valiulene* v. *Lithuania* (dealing with domestic violence) and recognising that the state duty to protect is not absolute but requires the taking of 'practical and effective' measures (para 75).

so, one has to generate increasingly onerous duties on the state to take responsibility for the behaviour of non-state actors. At times, this will of necessity come close to imposing absolute liability in order to compensate the victim. The *Craxi* case provides an example of the strengthening of such a state duty in order to compensate an individual for the wrongs committed by a non-state actor.

Doing so is undesirable too: essentially, it requires the state to take responsibility for unacceptable actions of non-state actors and allows them to deflect responsibility away from their own behaviour to that of the state. An ECHR judgment such as this is no doubt a victory for errant corporate press actors: they can say that the state failed in its duty to protect individuals. Yet, the primary agent responsible for that failure was the press itself. The state duty to protect doctrine thus has a significant ability to deflect attention and sanctions away from non-state actors to the state. This is both unfair – with the political community having to bear such a cost – and has perverse consequences that can immunise non-state actors from bearing responsibility. States indeed have an incentive to change this situation.

2.4.2 *Von Hannover v. Germany*[68]: The Necessity of Constructing the Obligations of Non-State Actors

This case concerned the publication of photographs concerning the private life of Princess Caroline of Hannover. These included photographs with her children, photographs on a skiing holiday, photographs in a restaurant, and those when she was on a horse. In a range of cases, the Princess attempted to interdict such publication. In the first set of cases, and after going through the German courts, the German Constitutional Court found that she had to tolerate publication of pictures of herself when she entered public spaces (even if she were conducting private activities such as shopping), but the court refused to allow the publication of photographs that included her children.[69] The case was appealed to the ECHR and the court essentially overturned the ruling of the German Constitutional Court. The court found that the right to privacy of public personalities also applies when they conduct private activities in the public sphere. She was therefore entitled to stop the publication of such intrusive photographs. Since the reasoning is central to this discussion, I now examine it in more detail.

[68] *Von Hannover* v. *Germany* (Third Section Chamber) (24 September 2004).

[69] A fuller discussion of the German decision will be conducted in section 3.3.1.3 of Chapter 3.

The court begins by considering article 8 of the Convention – the right to respect for private and family life – and found that the notion of 'private life' includes one's name or image. It is designed to secure a person's physical or psychological integrity as well as enable the development of an individual's own personality (without outside interference).[70] The court concludes that these considerations mean that the right to respect for private life includes within its scope a concern for the publication of one's image when going about daily business.[71]

The court then has to deal with the problem that the party infringing on the rights of Princess Caroline was a newspaper corporation and not the state. The Convention, the court reiterates, places positive obligations on the signatory states to adopt measures 'to secure respect for private life even in the sphere of the relations of individuals between themselves'.[72] This also applies to protection by the state for individuals against the abuse of their images by others. The court states that the boundary between positive and negative obligations does not admit of 'precise definition' but requires striking a 'fair balance' between the individual and the community as a whole.[73] This statement is misleadingly framed, however, given that the balance here needed to be achieved between two non-state actors rather than between an individual and the community as a whole.

It is important in this case to recognise that the court is not evaluating whether there is a gap in the legislative framework of Germany or failure by its executive to take action. Instead, it is evaluating the decisions of the courts in Germany concerning whether their judgments adequately protect the fundamental rights of Princess Caroline. In so doing, the ECHR, of necessity, evaluates the reasoning process of the domestic courts in deciding on the obligations of the newspapers in relation to the rights of Princess Caroline. As such, it is not clear what the difference is between saying that the role of the ECHR is to evaluate whether the state (the domestic courts in this instance) had offered adequate protection for the rights of Princess Caroline or that its role is to determine whether the obligations of the non-state actors in question were constructed correctly (by the domestic courts). The ECHR, in effect, is analysing whether the German courts were right about what the newspapers were required to do in these circumstances with respect to fundamental rights.

70 *Von Hannover*: para 50.
71 Ibid: para 53.
72 Ibid: para 57.
73 Ibid.

The main right to be balanced with Caroline's privacy in this context was the freedom of expression of the press. The court proceeds to outline its view that the press has 'an essential role in a democratic society'.[74] The court states that:

> Although it must not overstep certain bounds, in particular in respect of the reputation and rights of others, its duty is nevertheless to impart – in a manner consistent with its obligations and responsibilities – information and ideas on all matters of public interest.[75]

Here the court outlines a conception of the role and purpose of the press which imposes certain obligations and responsibilities. It also delineates the principled limits of the press's power which must be exercised with respect for the rights and reputation of others – that proviso takes on a particular importance when the publication of photos is concerned. It acknowledges that photos appearing in the tabloid press often do so in a climate of 'continual harassment which induces in the person concerned a very strong sense of intrusion into their private life or even persecution'.[76] Importantly, here we see the court taking account of the particular capacity of the press to harm the private life of individuals.

Having articulated the two sides of what is at stake, the court attempts to balance these different considerations through what appears to be a form of proportionality analysis. On the one hand, it considers whether the press's publication has a 'general' or 'public' dimension to it: if it does, it will be more likely that its decision to publish will pass muster. In this particular case, it focuses on the fact that the pictures are taken of Princess Caroline whilst she is conducting private activities. The court stresses the fundamental distinction between reporting facts about politicians who are exercising public functions and covering the private life of an individual who is not exercising such a function. In the former case, the press expresses its social function of being a 'watchdog' in a democracy, whilst it cannot claim to be doing so in the latter case. The court essentially states here that there is no strong rationale – that is connected with the notion of free speech itself – for the limitation of the right of Princess Caroline to her private life.

On the other hand, the interests of Princess Caroline against publication are strong: they take place in a context of harassment and continued surveillance. Current technology also allows increasing interference with

[74] Ibid: para 58.
[75] Ibid.
[76] Ibid: para 59.

the private life of individuals. Consequently, when balancing the two rights against one another, the privacy right of Caroline had to win out. The court makes it clear that the core reason in this regard was the weakness of the 'general interest' in the publication of the photos particularly given the subject (who had no official functions) and the nature of the photos (which related to her private life). The court also recognises the commercial interest of magazines in publishing these photos but holds that must yield to the effective protection of the private life of Caroline.[77]

The court in this case focuses on whether the state has positive obligations to protect an individual's fundamental right to respect for their private life. Yet, what must the state protect Princess Caroline from? In answering this question, the court is required to construct the ambit of the obligations of the press in relation to Princess Caroline. In doing so, the court begins by considering factors that relate to Princess Caroline (what we may term 'beneficiary-orientated factors'): in particular, it focuses on her interest (protected by a right) in not having her image disseminated without her consent. Interestingly, that interest the court recognises is not just one that applies against the state, but it is an entitlement that must be taken account of in understanding what other non-state actors may do too. The court then turns to the particularities of the agent that imperils Princess Caroline's interest – what we may term 'agent-relative' factors. In doing so, it considers the social function of the 'press', its commercial interests, and its capacity to harm the rights of individuals.

Having done so, it proceeds to engage in a balancing process: the balancing essentially involves considering the deeper rationales for the protection of freedom of expression on the part of the press as against the right to privacy of individuals. Given the low weight the court attributes to a general prurient curiosity in the private lives of others, it finds that the right to privacy of Caroline must take precedence. Interestingly, in this process, the closer the press's rationale relates simply to self-interest – either commercial or satisfying people's curiosity – the less strength it has in providing a justification for infringing an individual's fundamental rights. On the other hand, the greater it realises a genuine public interest in a democratic community, the more likely that a restriction on privacy could be justified. As we will see, this understanding is helpful in addressing the balance to be achieved between non-state actors' rights.

77 Ibid: para 77.

In deciding what the state must allow or prohibit, the court thus unavoidably needs to specify the obligations of the non-state actors in question vis-à-vis one another. In a later case with similar facts, the court expressly states that:

> journalists enjoy the freedom to choose, from the news items that come to them, which they will deal with and how they will do so. This freedom, however, is not devoid of responsibilities. Wherever information bringing into play the private life of another person is in issue, journalists are required to take into account, in so far as possible, the impact of the information and pictures to be published prior to their dissemination.[78]

Interestingly enough, the court in the *Von Hannover* case does not expressly examine the make-up of the press or recognise its control by private corporations. The fact that the focus is on the state arguably leads the court – at times – to leave out a detailed consideration of the non-state actors in question and the potential nature, for example, of the asymmetry between a powerful media giant and a princess. Nor does it analyse whether corporate entities – in which form most media houses are incorporated – as opposed to individuals may claim the protections afforded by the right to freedom of expression. It is plausible to argue that the single-minded focus on the state's duties in a sense obscures these questions.

We see in this case, however, that in constructing the obligations of non-state actors (which the state must ensure are realised), the court nascently begins to have reference to a variety of factors. I now turn to a later case also dealing with the obligations of the press, where it explicitly adopts such a multi-factoral approach.

2.4.3 *Axel Springer v. Germany:*[79] Balancing through a Multi-Factoral Approach

This Grand Chamber judgment dealt with the publication by a newspaper (owned by a public company) of two articles concerning a well-known television actor who had played the part of a police superintendent in a popular television series. The actor was arrested at a popular beer festival in Munich for the possession of cocaine. The actor applied to court to interdict the publication of the articles on the grounds that they represented a serious interference with his

[78] *Couderc and Hachette Filipacchi Associes* v. *France* paras 139–140.

[79] *Axel Springer* v. *Germany* (Grand Chamber) (7 February 2012).

right to a reputation. The German courts issued the injunction and imposed a penalty for any further publication of the article.

In a Grand Chamber judgment, it was found that the injunction constituted a prima facie interference with the company's freedom of expression. It emphasised the essential role of the press in a democratic society and, in fact, recognised that it had a duty to impart 'information and ideas on all matters of public interest'.[80] The public, the court found, also have the right to receive information on such matters and this included reporting on criminal trials.

Consequently, there was a need to justify such interference with the company's freedom of expression and consider whether it was proportionate to the harm caused to the right to reputation of others (protected by article 8 of the Convention and a recognised ground for limiting freedom of expression in terms of article 10(2)). In considering this, the court affirmed that the media had duties and responsibilities when their reporting could harm the reputation of a particular individual. Courts in these cases, it was held, had to strike a fair balance between the two rights protected by the Convention.

The court identifies six criteria through which it effected the balance between these two rights. The first concerns the 'contribution' by an article in a newspaper to a debate of general interest; the second related to how well-known the person concerned was who was the subject of the report; the third engaged with the prior conduct of the person concerned, which indicated a willingness (or otherwise) to allow details of their private lives to be exposed in the press; the fourth involved the methods utilised by the newspaper in obtaining the information and its veracity; the fifth encompassed the content, form, and consequences of the publication; and the last criterion dealt with the nature and severity of the sanction imposed upon a newspaper for publication. Considering the fact that the actor had been charged criminally, was a public persona, the information was received by the reporter from the authorities, and that the reports were largely factual, the court found that the injunction and penalties did not constitute a proportional restriction on the free speech of the company.

As with the *Von Hannover* case, the ECHR is focused here on deciding whether the German courts established the correct balance between freedom of expression and the right to reputation. In doing so, it unavoidably – as I have argued – strays into the territory of constructing the obligations of the corporate entity vis-à-vis individuals. The Grand

[80] Ibid: para 79.

Chamber explicitly, in this case, references the duties and responsibilities of the press (perhaps echoing the Convention) but also, interestingly, went beyond that. Its discussion of the criteria it utilises in balancing clearly envisage concomitant obligations on the press: for instance, its recognition of the role of the press in reporting on matters of public interest entails that it has duties in this area but also implies that it must not report on purely private matters. The press clearly has duties to act in 'good faith and on an accurate factual basis and provide "reliable and precise" information in accordance with the ethics of journalism'.[81] Moreover, in addressing the application of one of the factors, the Grand Chamber spoke about the finding of the domestic courts that the company had a 'duty to balance its interest in publishing the information against X's right to respect for his private life'.[82] Clearly, the Grand Chamber approves of the existence of such a duty when it states that 'there is nothing to suggest that such a balancing exercise was not undertaken'.[83]

One interesting feature of this case is the fact that the press corporation brought the claim to defend its freedom of expression. There is strangely no discussion by the court about whether a corporation can claim such protection. Indeed, the court can be criticised for failing to distinguish between its treatment of the corporation and individuals. Indeed, in an important statement in the case, the court held that the outcome of a court case should not vary whether the case was lodged by the publishing company (protecting freedom of expression) or the person whose reputation is at stake (the actor in this case).[84] The court is correct to assert the lack of priority of one right over another in the abstract – yet it seems incorrect to suggest that the claim for protection by a corporation is equivalent to the claim for protection by an individual.[85] Rights protection is primarily aimed at individuals; moreover, it is necessary for courts to bear in mind the nature of the agents involved and whether there is any asymmetry in the relations between the parties whose rights are affected. There should be a higher burden of justification placed upon a powerful agent in society that wishes to restrict the rights of a less powerful individual. The framing of the court's enquiry around the positive duties to protect of the state

[81] Ibid: para 93.
[82] Ibid: para 106.
[83] Ibid: para 107.
[84] Ibid: para 87.
[85] Here, I depart from Voorhoof, 2017: 164.

perhaps leads it to consider all other agents as being equivalent – which is a mistake.

The court proceeds to outline a range of criteria through which it balances these rights. This is a welcome development that helps provide greater guidance and coherence to the manner in which the ECHR balances rights in such cases.[86] At the same time, there appears to be no particular attempt to explain why these factors are relevant or to show how they function together as a coherent whole. Whilst it is useful to have these fine-grained factors in decision-making, it is also important to understand their normative significance.

In attempting to systematise and deepen our understanding of what the court is doing, in a similar vein to *Von Hannover*, I would suggest the analysis can be broken down into beneficiary-orientated factors, agent-relative factors, and a balancing exercise that draws on both of these. Consistent with the view I have articulated earlier that takes account of power relations, I shall regard the beneficiary as the individual – or less powerful entity – whose rights are affected and the agent-relative factors as relating to the more powerful entity – the media corporation in this case.[87] The beneficiary-orientated factors such as the 'content, form and consequences of the publication' attempt to ascertain the impact of publication on the right to reputation of an individual. Prior conduct too raises questions about the degree to which the beneficiary can be said to be harmed. Agent-relative factors engage the role and particularities of the more powerful agent and its interests. Two central issues can be discerned in this regard from factors such as whether the article 'contributes to the public interest', the method of obtaining information and its veracity, whether it relates to a public personality and the severity of the sanction involved: namely, the function of the press in society, and the extent of the autonomy it should be entitled to exercise. Once these various factors are identified, it is necessary to reach a conclusion about how they are to be balanced in relation to one another – the Grand Chamber sadly does not really specify how it utilises them to reach the conclusion it does concerning proportionality. Nevertheless, the judgment remains significant for offering greater specificity about the factors that guided the court in reaching its conclusion and, thus, offers a clear articulation of what may

[86] The court has been criticised for vague and inadequately justified uses of balancing – some authors argue that the antidote is a more structured balancing test that identifies relevant reasons or criteria on the basis of which decisions are made. See Smet, 2017: 40–49; and Voorhoof, 2017: 157.

[87] I shall justify this in more detail in section 6.3 of Chapter 6.

be termed a nascent 'multi-factoral approach' in addressing the rights and obligations of non-state parties.

2.4.4 *Eweida v. United Kingdom:*[88] Blurring the Boundary between State and Non-State Actors

This judgment of the Fourth Section of the ECHR dealt with the decision of a staff member of British Airways to wear a cross openly on her neck as a sign of her commitment to her religious beliefs. British Airways had strict regulations concerning the uniform of its employees that dealt with the general public, which prohibited openly wearing religious symbols. When Ms Eweida refused to hide the cross she wore, she was sent home without pay. She was then offered administrative work which did not require contact with customers, which she refused. Her case led British Airways to review its policy on visible religious symbols, and Ms Eweida was allowed to return to work several months later with permission to wear her cross visibly. The company, however, refused to compensate her for lost earnings during the time she did not come to work, which became the subject of Ms Eweida's legal action which reached the ECHR after exhausting domestic remedies in the United Kingdom.

The court began by affirming that Ms Eweida's desire to wear a cross was protected by article 9 of the Convention and that the refusal by British Airways to allow her to wear it visibly 'amounted to an interference with her right to manifest her religion'.[89] Given the interference was by a private company, it needed to consider whether the state had met its positive obligations to protect her rights within the domestic order and to strike a fair balance with the rights of others.

On the one side of the matter, the court considered the importance to democratic societies of sustaining pluralism and diversity and also the significance to Ms Eweida of being able to communicate a central tenet of her religious belief and identity to others. On the other side of the equation was the airline's desire to project a certain corporate image which the court found to be a legitimate goal but accorded too much weight by the courts in the United Kingdom. The court then applied proportionality-style reasoning to balance these interests. It found there to be no clear rational relationship between the prohibition on wearing visible religious symbols and the goal of the corporation: Ms Eweida's cross, the court found, was

[88] *Eweida* v. *United Kingdom* (Fourth Section Chamber) (15 January 2013).
[89] Ibid: para 91.

discreet and there was little evidence to show the wearing of religious symbols negatively impacted on the image of the brand. The necessity of the prohibition to achieve the goal was also placed in question by the very quick change in the airline's policy. Since there was no clear countervailing interest on the part of British Airways, there were no good grounds for the infringement of Ms Eweida's religious freedom and it was found that domestic authorities failed sufficiently to protect her rights.

The case was conjoined with three other cases dealing with employment conditions and circumstances which clashed with the religious convictions of particular individuals. The case of *Chaplin* dealt with a nurse who wished to wear a cross whilst performing her duties for a public hospital, which claimed that to do so posed health and safety risks. The *Ladele* case dealt with an employee of a local public authority in London who refused – on the basis of her religious beliefs – to conduct same-sex civil partnerships. The last case of *McFarlane* dealt with an individual employed by a private company offering sex and relationship counselling services who – on the basis of genuine religious beliefs – refused to offer such counselling services to gay, lesbian, and bisexual clients of the company in violation of its equal opportunities policy.

The rest of the applicants were not successful in their claims. These conjoined cases are interesting because they offer an opportunity to consider how the court reasons when faced with similar interferences with rights by non-state actors and state parties. In the *Chaplin* case, the court explicitly takes into account the fact that the employer was a public authority and considers the nature and function of that authority – a hospital. Ultimately, the court deferred to the judgment of those managing this institution that a cross might pose a health and safety risk. In *Ladele* too, the fact that public authorities were seeking to comply with their duty not to discriminate played an important role in the court's refusal to interfere with their decision. In the case of public authorities, and where there are strong reasons for their decisions which are designed to secure the rights of others, the ECHR is unwilling to interfere.

In relation to *McFarlane*, similar reasoning was used in relation to a private company. In addition to the fact that he voluntarily joined the company knowing about its equal opportunities policy, the court stated that the most important factor in its assessment was that the 'employer's action was intended to secure the implementation of its policy of providing a service without discrimination'.[90] Given its compliance with its own obligations in relation to equality, the court held that the state then benefits from a wide discretion as to how to balance religious freedom with the employer's commitment to non-discrimination. In *Eweida*, British Airways, on the other hand, was seeking to protect its own corporate interests and was willing to restrict religious freedom in the process for no good reason. Without a justification centred on realising the rights of others, its weak commercial interest was not sufficient to override the fundamental rights of Eweida, and the state failed to meet its obligations to protect her religious freedom. What the state must do, therefore, is contingent upon whether the private employer fulfils its obligations or not – thus, highlighting the manner in which the state duty to protect is parasitic on a conception of the obligations of non-state parties.

Whilst the court is clear that formally the reasoning processes should differ, what appears notable from these cases is the fact that the court applies similar tests and reasoning both to state and non-state actors. The rather sparse reasoning of the court does not explicitly consider whether the nature of the agent should affect their obligations. Yet, in fact, the nature of the agents and their function in the society do appear, upon deeper analysis of the judgments, to link to the legitimacy of the purposes for which they act and the weight to be accorded to them.

2.4.5 *Appleby v. United Kingdom:*[91] Prioritising Corporations over Individuals

This case concerned three residents of a town called Washington (Tyne and Wear) in the United Kingdom who wished to distribute information and protest a new development by their local Council and the reduction in consequent public space. They set up their stands at the centre of the town, which was a shopping mall known as the Galleries, owned by a company called Postel. Security guards employed by the shopping centre refused to allow them to set up their stand there. A request to protest sent by a resident to the management of the shopping centre was declined. The residents contended that their rights to freedom of expression (article 10) and freedom of association (article 11) in terms of the European Convention were violated by these actions and that the state had a duty to protect their rights and ensure they

[90] Ibid: para 109.
[91] *Appleby* v. *United Kingdom* (Fourth Section Chamber) (6 May 2003).

could distribute information and protest within these spaces which were 'quasi-public'.

The majority of the court reiterates the importance of freedom of expression as well as the duty of the state to take positive measures to protect it even in the sphere of private relations. The expression of the residents was recognised as being designed to alert fellow residents to a matter of public concern: the development of a public field and the consequent reduction of public space. The court though states that whilst the right to freedom of expression is important, it is not unlimited and the court needs to have regard to the countervailing right to property of the 'owner of the shopping centre'.[92] The court then turns to consider the agent that was implicated in the alleged violation and considers the argument made that the social function of shopping centres is changing. Whilst they are regarded as being primarily aimed at the 'pursuit of private commercial interests', increasingly they are also being designed to be spaces in which people gather and hold events. The court writes:

> Frequently, individuals are not merely invited to shop but encouraged to linger and participate in a wide range of activities – from entertainment to community, educational and charitable events. Such shopping centres may assume the characteristics of the traditional town centre and indeed, in this case, the Galleries is labelled on maps as the town centre and either contains, or is close to, public services and facilities.[93]

The shopping centre therefore has taken on a character not simply of a private space but a public one too. Given that fact, the residents argued that they had a right to exercise free speech in a reasonable manner in these contexts.

The court makes no definite finding on this argument and, instead, moves to another point, claiming that the right to freedom of expression does not guarantee one the right to any particular forum for that expression. It is only where

> the bar on access to property has the effect of preventing any effective exercise of freedom of expression or it can be said that the essence of the right has been destroyed, the Court would not exclude that a positive obligation could arise for the State to protect the enjoyment of the Convention rights by regulating property rights. A corporate town where the entire municipality is controlled by a private body might be an example.[94]

[92] Ibid: para 43.
[93] Ibid: para 44.
[94] Ibid: para 47.

The court though finds that, in this case, the residents had the opportunity to communicate their views in spaces outside the shopping centre. The restriction on their rights in the context of the shopping centre did not provide a complete bar to the exercise of their freedom of expression and, consequently, there was no violation of article 10.

The reasoning of the court is troubling for several reasons. Firstly, its framing of the issue around positive obligations in some ways distorts the questions that lie before it. This can be seen for instance in its statement – meant to be a general principle – that in determining whether positive obligations of the state exist, the court's task is to balance the general interests of the community with the interests of individuals. This initial framing by the court simply restates the balancing question that relates to the relationship between the state and individuals: yet, that is distinct from the function the state performs when it balances between individuals and other actors (or individuals) in the non-state sphere. In fact, in a case such as this one, the court needed to determine the balance to be struck between the rights of the residents to freedom of expression and that of the corporation owning the shopping centre to restrict those rights in furtherance of its right to property. The formulation by the court also obscures the manner in which the balancing should take place.

Furthermore, we see, in this case, a disturbing approach to such balancing. After briefly recounting the importance of freedom of expression, the court proceeds to reference the property rights of the owners. It, however, does not accord any priority to the freedom of expression of the residents in its reasoning as would have been expected if it had utilised a proper proportionality enquiry. If it had done so, it should then have evaluated whether there was a legitimate purpose of the corporation in restricting the speech in question. The court could also then have considered whether there was a rational relationship between the restrictions and that purpose; whether there was an alternative to the approach adopted by the shopping centre that would have achieved its purpose but had a lesser impact on the rights of the residents; and whether the restriction on the rights of residents was proportional to the benefits for the shopping centre. The court did none of this and, in fact, in its main reasoning appears to have reversed the burden of justification.

Instead of placing the residents at the centre of its enquiry, it effectively asked whether there were good reasons to restrict the rights of the shopping centre to prevent the speech in question. The residents may have had a legitimate aim to reach other members of their local community in an easy and effective way. Yet, the court finds two problems with this: on the one hand, it is not clear that they needed to protest at the shopping centre to reach other members of their community; and, on the other hand, there are alternatives which can sufficiently realise their purpose and not restrict the rights of the owners of the shopping centre. When it comes to balancing, therefore, the property rights of the owners trump the right to freedom of expression of the residents.

Some of these flaws are called out by the dissenting judgment of Judge Maruste. He contends that 'the property rights of the owner of the shopping mall were unnecessarily given priority over the applicants' freedom of expression'.[95] Judge Maruste acknowledges that the town centre was originally planned by a public agency and later privatised. It was also a huge area that had been privatised, and its central location meant it was, of necessity, connected to many public features of the city such as the library, police station, and health centre. The space was, according to Judge Maruste, therefore clearly a 'quasi-public' space. Public interests and money were and are involved in the area. The residents therefore had justified expectations to be able to protest in the area and inform other members of the community of their views. They also did so in relation to a question of public import and in a manner that respected the boundaries of free speech.

Judge Maruste goes on to say that privatisation cannot mean that public authorities only have the responsibility to protect property rights. Importantly, he states that it is in the public interest to enable the exercise of freedom of expression in quasi-public spaces such as this. What in fact occurred is that the public authorities affirmed the rights of the shopping centre to deprive the residents of access without any consideration of the reasonableness of their requests. Consequently, the state failed in its duty to protect articles 10 and 11.

Judge Maruste's opinion helps to provide support for my argument that the vagueness of the balancing exercise in this case in fact reversed the process that should have occurred in relation to a fundamental rights violation. The weaker parties who complained of the violation of their fundamental rights were required to explain why they should not interfere with the rights of the stronger party, the corporation which owned a large piece of land in the centre of the city. The failure to engage adequately with the nature of the agents in question – and to recognise the power of corporations and their distinct capacity to harm fundamental rights – allowed the majority to conduct some kind of detached balancing exercise and place the burden of justification in the wrong place. This decision

[95] Dissenting opinion of Judge Maruste.

raises the question of how we frame and engage with balancing in the private sphere, a matter I deal with in more detail in Chapter 7.

Whilst I have drawn attention to some of the shortcomings of the court's reasoning in this case, it is also useful to consider some of the factors that it employs in its judgment. In particular, in an important paragraph, the majority accepts that a corporation that controlled a whole town, for instance, might well be found to have obligations to allow a protest. Here, it references essentially two important factors: firstly, it highlights the capacity of the corporation to affect the fundamental right; secondly, it considers the social function of the corporation – if such an entity essentially assumed the role of the state in a particular community, then its function changes from private to public and so do its consequent obligations. Although the court does not make a finding in this regard, it does recognise the substantial changes occurring in the social function of shopping centres and how that may in fact modify the obligations of corporations that own them over time (or, in its formulation, the states' positive obligations in relation to such corporations).

Judge Maruste, too, in his opinion, references three important dimensions. Firstly, there is the size of the space that is privately owned which relates to its capacity to impact on individuals. Secondly, he considers the relationship between public services and the private space which could have an impact on the obligations of the non-state entity, for instance, not to impede access to the public. Finally, he highlights the importance of the history and financing of a development which, if public planning and funds are involved, could also play a role in its designation as 'quasi-public'. Clearly, a major question raised by this judgment is whether the function of a corporation or the powers it exercises are conceptualised as being 'public' or 'private': as we will see in Chapter 4, that itself is an important question which is at the foundation of another model for determining the obligations of non-state actors.

2.5 Conclusion

This chapter has considered a central tension that arises in international law between the state-centric nature of the system and its acceptance of a notion – fundamental rights – that is not fundamentally tied to the state. International lawyers have attempted to resolve this tension primarily through adopting a state duty to protect model which essentially imposes responsibility on states for the actions of non-state actors.[96] This type of 'indirect' approach to responsibility has numerous shortcomings on both theoretical and practical levels, which I have attempted to identify. In particular, and most importantly for purposes of this book, I have sought to show that the state duty to protect model is parasitic on having an idea of what the state must protect individuals against. That, in turn, requires an understanding of and construction of the legally enforceable obligations of non-state actors, a matter that takes us beyond the conceptual resources of the state duty to protect doctrine as it has been developed thus far. That very problem also is indicative of the state's role in the fundamental rights sphere, which, I have argued, should be conceived of as an enforcer of fundamental rights obligations rather than being an 'originator' thereof.

Through a detailed analysis of several cases from the ECHR, it was possible to see how the court purportedly is constructing the obligations of the state – yet, unavoidably, is required to engage in the construction of the obligations of non-state actors vis-à-vis one another. In the process, it was instructive to consider in some detail how the court reasons – though its justifications are often spartan in this context. I have attempted to systematise the analysis by recognising a number of central factors utilised by the court in constructing the obligations of non-state actors vis-à-vis individuals as well as the outlines of a doctrinal approach. The court identifies firstly 'beneficiary-orientated factors' which focus on the impact of any interference on an individual whose fundamental rights are affected. Secondly, the court engages with a number of 'agent-relative factors' which relate to the non-state actors causing the interference and include the social role or function of this non-state actor as well as its capacity to cause the interference. Finally, in reaching a final conclusion, the court usually engages in balancing the respective rights and interests, though that is often done in an unstructured and amorphous way. As we will see in the coming chapters, this nascent approach is mirrored in the case law of many national jurisdictions faced with the task of determining the obligations of non-state actors.

The chapter also highlighted in the ECHR case law some of the distortions caused by the state duty to protect doctrine. The failure to reason directly about the obligations of non-state parties can often lead to an imposition of near-absolute duties on the state to compensate for the inability directly to hold non-state actors to account. Perhaps the largest

96 In section 5.3 of Chapter 5, I will engage with alternative international law approaches which have been suggested for dealing with this conundrum, which, on the whole, as I will demonstrate there, are underdeveloped.

difficulty which emerges from the analysis is the failure by the court often to acknowledge the distinct nature of different non-state actors. The court tends to regard any non-state actor as being symmetrically situated with respect to other non-state actors: in doing so, it fails to recognise the divergences in the nature of different agents, their asymmetrical power, and their differential capacities to harm fundamental rights. In so doing, it has, at times, overemphasised the rights and interests of corporations and failed to accord priority to individuals whom fundamental rights are ultimately designed to protect.

From the international law context, I turn now to consider the key doctrinal approaches adopted in national jurisdictions when confronting the impact non-state actors can have upon fundamental rights.

3

The Indirect Application Model

3.1 Introduction

Most national jurisdictions today include a bill of rights in their constitutions.[1] In many of these, the understanding has developed that fundamental rights are designed to apply to the relationship between the state and individuals. As was discussed in Chapter 2, the origins of fundamental rights in law are often traced to the struggle to challenge the exercise of tyrannical power by the state over individuals.

Nevertheless, national jurisdictions too are confronted by the fact that the interests protected by fundamental rights can be seriously affected by non-state actors. The power and influence of these actors – and particularly the corporate sphere – have increased vastly and are continually expanding. This situation is often particularly pronounced in contexts of historical injustice where the private sphere as much as the public sphere needs to be reconstructed on the basis of principles of justice.

The question then becomes how do courts tasked with interpreting bills of rights take account of the impact non-state actors have upon fundamental rights within a paradigm that has largely focused only upon the obligations of the state in relation to the individual. Three approaches can be discerned. The first is similar to the 'state duty to protect' model discussed in Chapter 2.[2] It maintains the traditional view that only the state is subject to direct obligations in relation to fundamental rights but recognises the state's duty to ensure non-state actors do not harm individual rights – as such, fundamental rights apply in an 'indirect' manner to non-state actors

[1] See Elkins et al., 2013 for a description and exploration of the growth of fundamental rights in domestic constitutions.

[2] See Brinktrine, 2001: 426.

through state regulation and changes to existing private law. This indirect application model has been influential and will be the subject of the present chapter. The next chapter will consider the second approach, which retains the view that only the state can be bound by fundamental rights obligations but expands the conception of what constitutes the state. The last approach rejects the foundational assumption that fundamental rights only place obligations on the state and proceeds to recognise 'direct' obligations upon non-state actors – that will be the subject of Chapter 5.

The first part of this chapter is more theoretical: I first attempt to describe the indirect application model and understand the reasons that have been provided for it. I then turn to key criticisms of it, which focus upon its vagueness as well as its lack of articulation of a clear methodology through which fundamental rights influence other areas of the law. Indeed, I shall argue that the indirect application model really collapses into a form of direct application model: it ultimately cannot avoid requiring courts to develop a conception of the obligations of the non-state actors which flow from fundamental rights. This analysis demonstrates that, substantively, the model is an 'emperor with no clothes', failing actually to offer any alternative – at least in the conceptualisation of the obligations of non-state actors – to the direct model.[3]

Once we recognise this, it is then possible to view the case law that has adopted the doctrine through a different lens: of seeing how courts have in fact sought to construct the content of the obligations of non-state actors. I thus turn in the second part of the chapter to an analysis of a few seminal cases which have adopted this approach which deal with corporations, in the main, given the focus of this book. The starting point is with the case law of the German Constitutional Court which first outlined this doctrine. Its influence has also extended to other countries like South Africa – whose Constitutional Court despite having direct application available to it, has, at times, applied the indirect application model. The analysis will demonstrate some of the theoretical points made in the first part of the chapter but also seeks to understand the reasoning process the courts have employed surrounding the obligations of non-state actors. The analysis highlights a number of factors or principles which guide the determination of those obligations. The courts also explicitly recognise the need for balancing, though, that is often conducted in an amorphous manner without any structure. The analysis also highlights some of the deficits in reasoning that

[3] The reasons for its adoption must thus be found elsewhere – which I will suggest really lie in institutional considerations I elaborate upon later.

indirect approaches are often prone to. Interestingly though, a pattern starts to emerge of the overlap between the reasoning of the courts in this chapter and Chapter 2. As we will see, that overlap continues in the next two chapters and provides the contours of the multi-factoral approach I seek to systematise, develop, and justify in the second part of this book.

3.2 The Indirect Application Model

3.2.1 The Contours of the Model

The indirect application model was first developed by the German Constitutional Court in the seminal *Lüth* case, which outlines the contours of the model.[4] The court claims that the main purpose of fundamental rights is 'to protect the individual's sphere of freedom against incursions by public authority'.[5] It thus emphasises that their primary sphere of application is in relation to the obligations of the state vis-à-vis individuals.

The court does not, however, stop there and goes on to say that 'basic rights norms contain not only defensive subjective rights for the individual but embody at the same time an objective value system which, as a fundamental constitutional value for all areas of the law, acts as a guiding principle and stimulus for the legislature, executive and the judiciary'.[6] The Constitution thus establishes an objective system of values which must affect private law – and, consequently, non-state actors – as well. Private law rules must be constructed in light of the fundamental rights in the Constitution: '[j]ust as new law must conform to the value system of fundamental rights, so must existing older law be reoriented in its contents towards this value system. From it, the law derives a specifically constitutional element, which thereafter determines its interpretation'.[7] The court refers to the 'radiating effect' of such rights[8] but that constitutes the extent of its methodology through which this evaluation and development of private law is to be accomplished.

The Constitutional Court in Germany thus appears to accept that fundamental rights must have implications for the sphere of relations between non-state actors. Nevertheless, its approach of indirect

4 BVerfGE 7, 198. The case will be analysed, in more detail, in section 3.3.1.1.

5 Ibid: 204. Given flaws in some existing translations, I am grateful for the assistance of Simon Willaschek in helping to improve the accuracy and coherence of the translations I utilise in the text.

6 BverfGE 7, 198: 205.

7 Ibid.

8 Ibid: 207.

application means that an individual cannot obtain a remedy against a non-state actor simply on the basis of a violation of fundamental rights which do not create their own self-standing remedies. Instead, if individuals complain of a fundamental rights violation by a non-state actor, they need to utilise the remedies available within existing private law. If the current state of such law is inhospitable to a claim that a non-state actor has seriously impacted upon fundamental rights, it can be developed by considering the implications of the objective values underpinning fundamental rights for the private law. Often, such development takes place through the interpretation of 'general clauses'[9] in private law such as notions of 'good faith' in contract[10] and 'public policy' in tort.[11] In constructing what constitutes good faith or public policy, the values underpinning fundamental rights play a role and can have an effect. Private law ultimately thus becomes 'an expression of the constitutional human rights of private individuals in their relationships with other individuals'.[12]

We can visually represent this model using Figure 3.1.

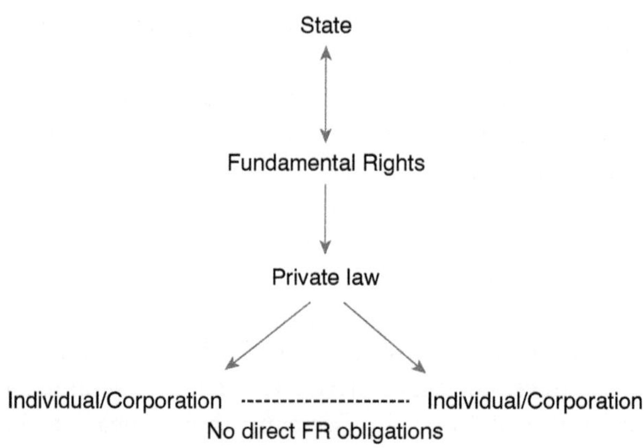

Figure 3.1 The indirect application model.

[9] Ibid: 206.

[10] See, for instance, §242 of the BGB and its relevance for indirect application in BVerfGE 89, 214, 229.

[11] A similar notion is found in §826 of the BGB, which was the subject of interpretation in the *Lüth* case, BVerfGE 7, 198: 206.

[12] Barak, 2001: 31.

Robert Alexy attempts to understand more precisely what is meant by asserting that fundamental rights give expression to an objective, normative value system. He suggests that the best way to understand this idea is that it involves abstracting from a rights claim which is usually understood as an entitlement of a particular individual against a particular entity to a concrete mode of treatment. Instead, the court asserts a simple statement that a certain value is good.[13] Thus, the right to freedom of expression, for example, would usually involve, at least, the entitlement of Janet not to have her speech censored with the corresponding obligation upon the state not to do so. The objective value derived from this right is simply the stark statement that freedom of expression is an important value in the legal system. Alexy refers to these as 'principles at the highest level of abstraction'.[14] Such principles could form the starting point for a justification that existing private law is inadequate[15] or perhaps suggest that perhaps some additional weight is to be attached to freedom of expression when balancing it against other considerations when applying or giving content to private law doctrines.[16] The difficulty, of course, is that this notion is incomplete and raises the challenge of how we move analytically from this very abstract level to derive more concrete implications.[17]

Indeed, the central question that arises in relation to the indirect application model for our purposes concerns understanding in what way the objective values underlying fundamental rights influence the obligations of non-state actors in other branches of the law. Clearly, an assumption of this reasoning is that freedom of expression does not simply apply in the relations between individuals and the state and has implications for the relations between individuals (and other non-state actors too). When determining whether a non-state actor has committed a wrong in tort, for instance, it is commonly thought that one needs to have reference to ideas of public policy and the legal convictions of the community.[18] The indirect application model essentially suggests that fundamental rights in the private context require a court to consider a broad value say of 'freedom of expression' when determining what public policy requires of a non-state actor.

13 Alexy, 2002: 353–4.
14 Ibid: 354.
15 Ibid.
16 Barak, 2001: 22.
17 Alexy, 2002: 354.
18 In the South African context, for instance, see *Loureiro* v. *Imvula Quality Protection* para 53, where the Constitutional Court held that '[t]he wrongfulness enquiry focuses on the conduct and goes to whether the policy and legal convictions of the community, constitutionally understood, regard it as acceptable'.

Several questions arise in this regard: firstly, is there a persuasive justification for courts having adopted an indirect application model rather than a model that directly considers the implications of constitutional rights for non-state actors? Secondly, if there is such a justification, how do we determine the implications of the notion that 'freedom of expression is of value' for the obligations of non-state actors? Given the paucity of an articulated methodology in this regard, that question is intimately tied to considering the drawbacks of the indirect application model and whether they can be overcome.

3.2.2 *Justifications for the Indirect Application Model*

What then lies behind the indirect application model? A first line of defence could be that it seeks to preserve the idea that fundamental rights apply only between the state and the individual. The German Constitutional Court justifies its claim in this regard with three arguments, each of which can be challenged. Firstly, it references intellectual and political history as supporting this claim.[19] I have already engaged with this point in Chapter 2: in short, it is possible to show that fundamental rights arose philosophically both in relation to the importance of controlling state power as well as the need to address the harms individuals can cause each other. Moreover, even if we were to accept for purposes of argument that the historical origins of this idea were connected to the struggle against the tyranny of the state, that does not preclude the recognition that its logic extends beyond the realm of the state.[20]

Secondly, the court suggests that its claim concerning the primary application of fundamental rights as lying in the state–individual relationship is supported by the positioning of human dignity in the first section of the Constitution and the express recognition that state authority specifically is bound by it. The inviolability of dignity, however, could also be regarded as binding non-state actors:[21] indeed, as was also argued in Chapter 2, the notion that individuals have worth appears to require respect for that worth by all agents and not only the state.

Lastly, the court refers to the fact that the special constitutional complaint mechanism contained in the Constitution only applies in relation to actions of the state and not in relation to non-state actors.

[19] This argument has been influential: see Lübbe-Wolf, 1988: 160.
[20] For this argument in the German debate, see Leisner, 1960: 312.
[21] See, for example, Zippelius, 2018: 20–21.

There are indeed restrictions of language in the German Constitution[22] relating to the use of that mechanism which could justify the court's approach: it is important to recognise though that this is a procedural justification for its method of proceeding relating to specific constitutional provisions and does not provide a substantive justification for limiting the application of fundamental rights to the relationship between individuals and the state.

Given its conception that the focus of fundamental rights is on the state–individual relationship, the court goes on to emphasise that it is through the mediation of state law that the relations between individuals are governed. Ultimately, in an analogue of the approach adopted in Chapter 2, this doctrine essentially places a duty on the state – through the mediation of the legislature and courts – to ensure the private law realises the objective values underlying fundamental rights.

Yet, in understanding the court's argument, it is important to appreciate that the objective values underlying fundamental rights themselves are considered to have implications for how private law constructs the relations between and obligations of individuals. Yet, if the values underlying fundamental rights have implications for the obligations of individuals between themselves, then it is unclear why it is necessary – other than for procedural reasons – to retain an 'indirect' view at all: why not simply reason from those values to the obligations of individuals? It is thus not really possible to say that fundamental rights do not apply to or bind non-state actors but have implications for their relationships. If they have such implications, then determining those implications will of necessity involve considering their application to non-state actors. When it comes to determining the implications of fundamental rights for non-state actors, the indirect view in a sense collapses into the direct view. I hope to illustrate this point in the case discussions of this chapter: there is actually no clear-cut methodology adopted for how the indirect application of fundamental rights occurs other than a refuge into vagueness. When we try and reconstruct the reasoning (where it exists), it essentially mirrors what applies in relation to a direct approach.[23] It is for this reason that some authors contend that the

[22] Article 93(1)(4a) of the Basic Law provides that the constitutional claim can only be raised against actions of a 'public authority'. This is generally interpreted to mean the legislature, executive, and the judiciary. For an extensive analysis, see Zuck, 2017: 186–201.

[23] Bearing this point out, some German academic literature argues that when civil cases do reach the Constitutional Court, they are subject to the same level of scrutiny as in other constitutional or administrative law cases. See Schlaich and Korioth, 2015: 206; Poscher, 2003: 268–272; Ruffert, 2001: 135.

choice between indirect and direct application models is in fact 'outcome-neutral'.[24]

If this is so, what then are other possible justifications for an indirect model? A further reason for the adoption of the doctrine may be said to be jurisdictional:[25] as developed by the Federal Constitutional Court in Germany, it helps to preserve the distinction between the jurisdiction of the civil courts and the Constitutional Court.[26] Whilst the doctrine requires civil courts to consider the application of fundamental rights in their domain, the Constitutional Court makes it clear that it will only intervene where the other courts have failed rather blatantly to capture the implications of fundamental rights for non-state actors.[27] A direct application model would likely have required the court to have been involved in a greater number of such cases. Consequently, the indirect application model helps to preserve the domains of the different courts and ensures the Constitutional Court is not swamped by ordinary civil cases.[28]

Whilst this gate-keeping function may be understandable pragmatically, there is a wider conceptual worry of the need to distinguish procedural and substantive questions: it is not clear that questions of court jurisdiction should be determining the issue of whether or not fundamental rights apply directly to non-state actors or not. Indeed, the conceptual issues are distinct. Moreover, given the exceptional nature of the cases coming before the Constitutional Court, it may be said that its influence over civil law is likely to be limited.[29] Indeed, the court seems to be particularly concerned with trying to prevent the broadening of its jurisdiction to embrace the transformation of the whole of German law: '[i]t is not the Constitutional Court's responsibility to review the civil

[24] Alexy, 2001: 357. See also Kumm and Comella, 2005: 243–244; Michelman, 2008a: 18.

[25] Kumm and Comella, 2005: 244 refer to these doctrines as being primarily 'about institutional and procedural questions'. See also the argument I contended had merit about the application of the constitutional complaint mechanism only to actions brought by individuals against the state.

[26] For a similar set of issues in the context of South Korea and the tension between courts there, see Yune, 2015: 137–138.

[27] The court has repeatedly stressed the exceptionality of the constitutional claim, which allows it to review other court's decisions, to differentiate it from other legal remedies (see e.g. BVerfGE 18, 315, 325). See Brinktrine, 2001: 429 outlining the criteria the court has developed for intervening.

[28] See Taylor, 2002: 214; Schlaich and Koriath, 2015: 204–205.

[29] See Tushnet, 2003: 87. This point is borne out by the evidence: in 2016, there were 1,020,966 cases before courts of first instance in civil matters. Of these, only 2,072 constitutional claims reached the Federal Constitutional Court regarding civil court decisions.

court's judgments to their full extent . . .'.[30] It is arguable that a stronger role may have been normatively required particularly in light of the need to reconstruct the German legal system – both private and public – in the wake of the Nazi era.

A further justification I will consider – and perhaps the most compelling – for the indirect application model lies in its mediation of fundamental rights thinking through the structures of private law. Indeed, instead of reasoning directly from fundamental rights as a self-standing branch of law to particular legal rules, the indirect approach begins with existing current private law rules and reconsiders them in light of fundamental rights.[31] Why is this important?

The core argument would focus on the fact that fundamental rights are stated at a highly abstract level and, whilst they might have implications for other branches of law, they do not themselves require a replacement of other legal rules. In fact, Beever argues that private law predated the modern legal focus on fundamental rights and, in a sense, is more foundational in providing the necessary legal basis for the emergence of such rights.[32] It also addresses many of the issues such as protection for bodily integrity that fundamental rights attempt to cover.[33] In response to this historical claim, I would contend that whilst the express language of fundamental rights is relatively modern, the interests and normative values protected by such rights predate the use of such express language. Indeed, the potential harm individuals can do to one another's fundamental rights has lain at the foundation of the earliest legal systems and rules that have developed to protect individuals from such harms.[34] Indeed, as we have seen in Chapter 2, philosophically, a core purpose of the state is to provide protection for individuals against one another and mediate their disputes. Consequently, the interests underlying fundamental rights have in the past – as now – been central to legal systems and provided a grounding for the private law that has developed.

Thus, private law arose specifically to address the very foundational interests that fundamental rights protect – consequently, fundamental

[30] BVerfGE 7, 198: 207.

[31] Barak, 2001: 29ff defends a version of this approach in this way.

[32] Social contract theories, for instance, such as that of Hobbes rest upon the notion that there are binding obligations to obey contracts even in the state of nature: see Beever, 2011: 73.

[33] Ibid: 84.

[34] See Chapter 2 and ibid: 80 – it is not clear to me that Beever would fundamentally disagree with this as he writes that the foundational nature of private law may in fact emerge from the fact that it deals with the interaction between individuals.

rights can be understood to be deeply foundational for all other law. At the same time, this does not mean we can dispense with the need for particular rules and simply have a legal system that is governed by abstract ideas such as fundamental rights.[35] Even fundamental rights law itself needs to concretise over time and doctrines develop concerning how we understand particular rights and their implications. This very book can be seen as an attempt to comprehend how we move from the deep abstract principles surrounding fundamental rights to develop a more concrete understanding of the obligations of corporations. Private law has developed a range of rules and principles that help us understand the grounds, for instance, for holding someone responsible for harm to fundamental rights such as bodily integrity or privacy: these include detailed doctrines of causation and intention. Private law thus provides a collective store of human wisdom that cannot simply be replaced with an injunction to respect fundamental rights even though reasoning relating to these rights may require a reconsideration of aspects of these doctrines.[36] It would be foolhardy simply to discard all this collective wisdom gathered in legal systems over time and supplant that simply with a doctrine that focuses on the abstract principles surrounding fundamental rights.[37] Moreover, even if one could do so, it seems likely that many of the existing principles would be retained as they are wholly compatible with fundamental rights and in fact give expression to modalities for their protection.

If fundamental rights do not replace existing private law, then what is their role?[38] In determining this, it is necessary to refer back to the basic theory underlying fundamental rights outlined in Chapter 2. Fundamental rights are rooted in a notion of individual worth which, if it is to be respected, requires protection for the foundational interests of individuals. Such interests can broadly be captured under the notions of 'freedom' (civil and political rights), and 'wellbeing' (economic, social, and cultural rights).[39] The role of fundamental rights in a legal system is foundational and thus involves ensuring that all areas of the law provide protection for

[35] Barak, 2001: 29.

[36] See, for instance, *Lee* v. *Minister of Correctional Services* [2012] ZACC 30 para 65, where the Constitutional Court of South Africa effectively considered the implications of fundamental rights for the doctrine of factual causation. For a critique, see Fagan, 2013.

[37] Alexy, 2002: 364; Taylor, 2002: 209 take similar views.

[38] Clearly, this is a fascinating question which could itself be the subject of more extensive writing. Given the need to deal with this question but also the focus of the book lying elsewhere, I here can only sketch an answer.

[39] See section 2.2 of Chapter 2 and section 6.3.1.1 of Chapter 6.

these interests.[40] Realising such interests, however, requires not just state action but also the action of non-state actors: attending to fundamental rights thus requires understanding what these rights require of non-state actors and then enshrining that understanding in the rules of the legal system itself.[41] Whether this can be done through using 'general clauses' of private law (such as good faith or public policy) or whether new rules need to be developed may depend on what is required and the flexibility of the legal system in question. Nevertheless, what is indispensable is an understanding of the obligations these rights impose on non-state actors and their consequent implications for existing law. Our grasp of these obligations and their implications also advances over time. The indirect application model appears to entail a different modality of influence – for instance, using general clauses of private law – rather than offering any different methodology for determining the obligations of non-state actors. In doing so, it has several drawbacks – which I will articulate later – in contrast with a direct model which would consider directly the obligations of non-state actors and their implications for private law.

An additional defence of the indirect application model could be that it is more 'democratic' than direct application in that it works through the modality of already-legislated law.[42] It thus allows the legislature the first attempt at balancing private interests against one another. A wholly direct system would amplify the role of the judiciary in such a balancing exercise.[43] This argument is one that emerges particularly from civil law countries with codified laws rather than common law countries which are accustomed to judge-made rules that develop over time. Nevertheless, even in civil law countries, the argument is not convincing. Where fundamental rights apply indirectly, it is recognised that judges must utilise these rights in making sense of general clauses such as 'good faith' or 'wrongfulness'. The judge, essentially, still has to determine what the implications of fundamental rights are for the obligations of non-state parties. Yet, these clauses are so vague and broad that it remains hard to see that there is much constraint placed upon the exercise of judicial

[40] The explicit engagement with and normative priority accorded to these fundamental interests is perhaps the important contribution of fundamental rights law given the fact that, as Beever, 2001: 83 admits, 'few modern lawyers think there is anything fundamental about private law'.

[41] The aforementioned argument provides a response to Barak's contention that '[h]uman rights in relations between private parties require no special constitutional protection, because regular legislation or common law suffices' (2001: 17).

[42] See Nolan, 2014: 64–65, who defends direct horizontal application against this charge.

[43] See, for instance, Taylor, 2002: 192–195; Barak, 2001: 17.

discretion in this regard. It is possible of course to argue that judges should not have a role in applying fundamental rights to non-state parties as occurs in some jurisdictions: if they do, however, it is hard to see that much is gained for the separation of powers from an indirect over a direct approach. Furthermore, it is also unclear that their task of balancing is significantly different from what they ordinarily need to do in applying legal rules. If the worry is to control their discretion, then what is necessary is a clear analytical framework and reasoning process according to which such balancing takes place – which this book seeks to provide.

The last justification I shall consider involves the argument that the indirect application model is meant to guarantee the 'autonomy' of the individual that is protected in private law. Direct application, it is contended, would lead to an impermissible limitation of such autonomy.[44] Autonomy though is central to many fundamental rights. Importantly, autonomy is also not absolute and may be limited in any legal system.[45] Both private law and public law place restrictions on what may be done to others in the name of autonomy.[46] Essentially, the application of fundamental rights to non-state actors requires engaging with the limits of autonomy, a matter we will see emerges from an analysis of the case law. It is not clear what is gained by an indirect approach over a direct approach in this regard: both will require the balancing of autonomy against other pressing concerns.

Having outlined what is meant by the indirect application model and provided a critical discussion of the justifications offered for it, I turn to a consideration of some of its drawbacks in determining the obligations of non-state actors.

3.2.3 *The Drawbacks of the Indirect Application Model*

As we saw, the indirect application model essentially works with the notion of the 'objective values' underlying fundamental rights influencing private law and our understanding of the obligations of non-state actors in relation to fundamental rights. There are at least three major drawbacks to the approach. Firstly, as we saw in Alexy's attempt to explain the doctrine of 'objective values', it appears that it involves a pure statement that a value such as 'freedom of expression' is important in the relations between individuals. Rendering fundamental rights abstract 'value' claims

44 See Alexy, 2002: 363.
45 Alexy, 2002: 363; Nolan, 2014: 70–71.
46 Barak, 2001: 35–36.

diminishes their normative force by reducing them to one value amongst many others that courts have to consider and take into account. Such values have no normative priority over any other value that may exist in the private law. In contrast, if someone has a fundamental right, then there is a strong presumption in favour of realising the right and a strong justification is required to defeat that presumption. If Su-Yen has a right to freedom of expression, unless there are very strong reasons to the contrary, the interests freedom of expression protects must be realised in law. The objective values approach reduces the entitlement dimension of rights – and their normative priority – to simply one value to be considered and weighed amongst many.[47]

Secondly, the approach, as we saw in Alexy's analysis thereof, essentially abstracts from the rights-holders and the agents who are required to realise rights.[48] In doing so, the approach structurally removes from view a range of factors which are of central importance in constructing the obligations of non-state actors. As I demonstrate in this book, the nature of rights-holders and their particular vulnerability affect the obligations that result from a fundamental right. Similarly, the capacity of a particular agent to harm rights and their social function are critical factors in determining the obligations they have. By focusing on objective values, the indirect application model de-emphasises these critical normative dimensions of fundamental rights – and, in the process, thus increases the risk that the reasoning of courts surrounding the obligations of non-state actors will not be adequate.

Finally, the indirect application model also provides no structured reasoning process which determines the manner in which fundamental rights may or may not be limited. The reasoning process in relation to these 'objective values' appears to be entirely open, offering no clear guidance as to how to address conflicts between important values. It thus simply leaves this process at the mercy of an unguided judicial (or legislative) discretion.[49] In contrast, where reasoning directly engages with fundamental rights, courts have developed a structured proportionality test for determining when rights can be limited.

These drawbacks render it likely that judges, when reasoning about the obligations of non-state actors, will omit to consider relevant factors or

47 A similar critique is made in the context of the proportionality enquiry: see Meyerson, 2009: 809–817.

48 Alexy, 2002: 353–354.

49 Woolman, 2007: 763.

balance in an unstructured manner.[50] As such, the model will, at best, lead to inadequately reasoned judgments and, at worst, to poorer outcomes than an alternative model that engages the relevant factors directly. These conceptual points thus challenge the claim mentioned earlier that the indirect and direct application models will be 'outcome-neutral'.[51] In terms of outcomes, Alexy writes, 'it is not the construction but the evaluation with which it is combined which is the decisive issue'.[52] The difficulty with the indirect application model is its potential to obscure central factors and reasoning processes in any such evaluation.

If we are to give fundamental rights the respect they deserve, then these defects of 'vagueness' need to be remedied: firstly, we need to ensure that rights themselves are given the priority they deserve in any reasoning process which determines the obligations of non-state actors; secondly, we need to ensure that factors relevant to the particular beneficiaries and agents are adequately taken into account in the reasoning determining their obligations; and, finally, we need to ensure there is a structured reasoning process to address how to balance competing normative considerations and limit rights. The indirect application model in its pure form, for the reasons provided, is not well-suited to addressing these issues. Where it has worked to create positive results, courts in their decision-making have often sought to plug the gaps described by reasoning clearly about the specific issues I have identified.[53] I now turn to consider how these issues have played out in two jurisdictions – Germany and South Africa – when applying the indirect application model. The discussion is not meant to be exhaustive and the focus will be on a qualitative analysis of the reasoning of the courts in the construction of the obligations of non-state actors (with a particular focus on corporations).

[50] I cannot take the matter further empirically here in detail (apart from the qualitative analysis of certain cases below). An interesting research project would be to consider whether the indirect model does bear out these weaknesses across the world and, if not, what strategies have been adopted to remedy its conceptual weaknesses: see also Michelman, 2008a: 40.

[51] See fn 24.

[52] Ibid: 358.

[53] Michelman, 2008a: 9 suggests its use is compatible with a deep engagement with rights in the bill of rights: that would nevertheless bear out my point that this model does require an engagement with the obligations of non-state actors that flow from fundamental rights.

3.3 The Indirect Application Model in Practice

3.3.1 *Germany*

The dominant approach in Germany towards applying its bill of rights to non-state actors has been that of indirect application or what is known as mittelbare Drittwirkung (mediated third-party effect). Germany, after the Second World War, faced a serious problem that the private sphere had itself been severely infused by Nazism after twelve years of Nazi rule and that there was a need to reconstruct it in light of modern constitutional values. Yet, despite some early differences amongst the German courts,[54] the judges of the Constitutional Court decided against applying the bill of rights directly to the private sphere and, instead, outlined the indirect application model with its emphasis on objective values and the 'radiating' effect thereof upon private law. This language, as we saw, is vague[55] and it is worth investigating how the courts actually utilise the approach in practice.

3.3.1.1 *Lüth:* The Intimations of a Multi-Factoral Approach

The famous *Lüth* case, early in the German Constitutional Court's jurisprudence, essentially dealt with the need to reconstruct an aspect of private law which placed a serious restriction on freedom of expression and, essentially, hindered the attempt to rid Germany of its fascist past. It dealt with a Mr Lüth, an official spokesperson for the City of Hamburg, who called for a boycott of a movie that was directed by Veit Harlan, who had made notorious anti-semitic films for the Nazis. An injunction was obtained against him in the lower courts by the film distributors, preventing him from calling for such a boycott on pain of criminal sanction. Mr Lüth submitted a constitutional complaint to the Constitutional Court against the lower court's verdict, claiming that the injunction infringed his right to freedom of expression.

I have already described in section 3.2.1 how the Constitutional Court used the opportunity to outline the indirect application model for determining the impact of fundamental rights on private law. I thus turn to consider its decision on the specific facts of the case where the Constitutional Court had to interrogate whether the civil courts had adequately considered the implications of the right to freedom of expression

[54] The Federal Labor Court held in a 1955 decision that at least some fundamental rights had a direct horizontal effect (BAGE 1, 258, 262). The Bundesgerichtshof had reached the same result regarding the right of personality in 1954 (BGHZ 13, 334, 338).

[55] See also Burkiczak, 2014: 119 for whom mittelbare Drittwirkung ultimately remains 'diffuse'.

for the private law. In doing so, it started off by recognising the value and importance of free speech as a central right of the new democratic order in Germany.[56] Whilst Harlan and the distributors had a countervailing right, 'the civil judge too has to weigh the importance of the fundamental right against the value of the legal right protected in the "general law" for the person allegedly injured by the statement.'[57] The private law allowed such a balancing of interests to take place through a 'general clause' – damages could only be claimed where the conduct which harmed another was 'contrary to public policy'.[58] The court ruled that this notion needed to be interpreted with reference to the constitutional right to freedom of expression suitably balanced against countervailing considerations.

In making its findings, the court considered the fact that Lüth spoke in his capacity as a private person and not as a representative of the state. It also stated that the 'motive, goals and purpose' of the statements had to be considered when determining whether the tort in question had been committed.[59] The court finds that Lüth was not motivated by economic interests – such as seeking to harm a competitor in the same industry – which would have rendered the reasons for his speech being protected less compelling.[60] Lüth's goals were instead connected with his political and cultural endeavours: in making it clear, Germany had moved on from national socialism and was truly contrite about its persecution of the Jews. That, in turn, was connected to an important national interest: in helping Germany regain its reputation in the world. Lüth was himself also deeply involved in improving German–Jewish relationships and saw Harlan's reappearance in the public sphere as a threat to this work: in a sense, then, his actions were not simply an unprovoked attack but a defensive posture to ensure the continuation of his work on German–Jewish reconciliation.[61]

Lüth's call for a boycott was intimately connected with these goals and so, if permissible, had the potential to affect Harlan. The court proceeded to consider the impact of a call for a boycott on Harlan's right to free development of his personality, his artistic freedom, and his future ability to work. It was also claimed that Harlan was acquitted of crimes against humanity and, consequently, should not be subjected to continual criticism for his role in directing anti-semitic

[56] BVerfGE 7, 198: 208.
[57] Ibid: 212.
[58] BGB § 826.
[59] BVerfGE 7, 198: 215.
[60] Ibid: 216.
[61] Ibid: 218.

films.[62] The court emphasised that, whilst these were important interests, Lüth was not seeking to exercise any formal power of the state to enforce the boycott he called for. Instead, his call for a boycott flowed from a moral stance: indeed, he claimed that whilst Harlan was legally acquitted on grounds that he had to submit to the orders of Goebbels on pain of possible imprisonment or death, the judgment recognised his complicity in crimes against humanity and represented a form of moral damnation.[63] Such a moral view about Harlan's conduct was a legitimate one within a democracy and to stop it from being expressed would be severely to limit freedom of expression.[64] Lüth's opinions were also not his alone: they were shared more widely in society and had been expressed by others, including a group of university professors and a member of parliament.[65]

The court also accepted that Lüth's statement could cause the distributing companies economic loss: that, however, had to be accorded less weight than the intrusive effects on free speech of preventing Lüth's expression of his opinion. Moreover, the court, interestingly, took into account the fact that these companies had publicly advertised that Harlan was the director of the films.[66] Entering the public sphere in this way was not guaranteed only to have benefits for a corporation: it also came with the concomitant risks of criticism. As such, the corporations could not at the same time enter the public sphere and then complain about public criticism. Having considered these various factors, the court reached the conclusion that '. . . the Landgericht [regional court] . . . failed to recognize the particular importance which must be accorded to the fundamental right to freedom of expression where it comes into conflict with the private interests of others.'[67]

The *Lüth* case is the central case that outlined the German Constitutional Court's approach to the application of constitutional rights to the private sphere. The court refers to the Constitution's enshrining of an objective, normative value system and, in rather mystical terms, to the 'radiating' effect of the values thereof on the private law. Yet, the central question remains as to how this radiating effect works in practice. I have considered the court's application of its approach to the factual complex of

[62] Ibid: 219.
[63] Ibid: 221.
[64] Ibid: 227.
[65] Ibid: 229.
[66] Ibid: 228.
[67] BVerfGE 7, 198: 230.

this case in order to analyse a little more closely what it is in fact doing. A number of important points emerge in this regard.

Firstly, as we saw, the court's approach required it to apply the values underlying fundamental rights through an assessment of whether Lüth's conduct was 'contrary to public policy'. In doing so, the court ultimately has to decide whether Lüth is entitled to call for a boycott of Harlan's films or not, thus constructing his obligations vis-à-vis another individual. In doing so, as we saw, the court engages with constitutionally relevant factors and attempts to achieve a balancing of the two interests. The process of reasoning focuses really on the constitutionally relevant dimensions of the situation and it is not clear that it in any significant way differs from what would have been required if it directly applied the Constitution to the case at hand. This bears out the point that, though the methodology appears different, in substance there is a convergence between the enquiries that are required.

Secondly, one fascinating difficulty when considering cases where there is a conflict of rights between non-state actors is the question of how to conduct the enquiry and whether there is a presumption in favour of a particular right. In *Lüth*, the lower courts focused their enquiry on the infringement of Harlan's rights (and that of the distributor companies) and whether there was a justification for Lüth's behaviour – by analysing the matter in this way, a priority was accorded to Harlan's rights and the finding, unsurprisingly, was against Lüth. The Constitutional Court case was framed differently with Lüth claiming that his right to freedom of expression was violated by the court order preventing him from calling for a boycott on pain of criminal sanction. In this construction, Lüth's right to freedom of expression received a degree of normative priority and the question arose whether there was a justification for restricting that right to protect the entitlements of Harlan and the distributor corporations. Interestingly, this framing leads the Constitutional Court to find in favour of Lüth and that insufficient attention had been paid to his right to freedom of expression. As we saw, one of the worries with the indirect application model is the reduction of rights to values and, consequently, a lack of clarity on where the normative priority should lie. In this regard, one important factor relates to whether one of the parties has greater power or influence than another (a matter that will become of central importance in the *Blinkfüer* case considered next in this chapter). The Constitutional Court alludes to this when recognising that Lüth was not seeking to act in a public capacity but a private one and so was not exercising significantly more power than an ordinary individual can. The power dimension is also in evidence in its reasoning surrounding the distributor corporation's advertising in the public sphere and its consequent need to accept public criticism.

Thirdly, when we analyse the reasoning of the court more closely, we see that it references a number of factors it considers relevant to reach its conclusion. We saw the worry that an approach purely focused on 'objective values' would abstract from the parties to a relationship where fundamental rights are at issue. The court, arguably, does not fall into this trap because it considers in some detail the effects on both parties to the relationship – its reasoning actually considers the rights of both parties rather than simply the values that are at stake and so again actually mirrors what a direct application process would entail.

The factors it considers can be grouped as including at least the severity of the interference with the autonomy of both parties – the freedom of expression of Lüth and the right to free development of the personality of Harlan; the social function of Lüth's speech and that it was directed at a valuable purpose; the capacity of Lüth to harm Harlan's rights (and that of the company); and whether there was prior conduct on the part of Harlan and the distributor companies which rendered any interference with their rights justifiable. Interestingly, we see the court accords relatively low weight to economic interests in contrast with political and moral concerns.

Having outlined these factors, ultimately, the court is required to balance these interests to reach a conclusion. One problem in the *Lüth* case is the lack of any clear methodology for doing so. The court did not explain how it saw the relationship between and relative importance of these factors. The vague concept of 'radiating effect' cannot disguise the need for a systematic approach to such balancing.

The *Lüth* case thus demonstrates how the indirect application model cannot but avoid a construction of the obligations of non-state actors vis-à-vis one another. We can also discern a nascent multi-factoral approach in the court's analysis and the need for a structured reasoning process to determine, ultimately, the obligations of the parties.

3.3.1.2 *Blinkfüer*: The Relevance of Power

An important case which also concerned non-state actors and developed the case law relating to boycotts was *Blinkfüer*.[68] The case took place just after the East German government decided to block its residents from being able freely to move to the West – which eventually led to the construction of

[68] BVerfGE 25, 256.

the Berlin Wall. Several powerful publishing companies such as Axel Springer took the view that it was their duty to stop the publication of East German radio and television schedules ostensibly to reduce the effectiveness of East German propaganda. They called on sellers of newspapers not to distribute any publications which did so and threatened to end their business relationships with those that refused to comply.[69] These measures were found essentially to constitute a call on the part of these publishing companies for a boycott by sellers of newspapers of any publication that continued to publish these schedules. The publisher and editor in chief of one of the magazines – *Blinkfüer* – that continued to publish these schedules were dependent on these sellers for the distribution of their publication. They sued Axel Springer and the other publishing houses (in what follows, 'the publishing houses') that had joined the call to boycott for damages, claiming unfair competition.[70] The Bundesgerichtshof did not regard the unfair competition claim as justified and held that the publishing houses were not acting from economic motives but were entitled to take these measures in furtherance of their constitutionally protected right to freedom of expression. A constitutional complaint was lodged by *Blinkfüer's* publisher with the Constitutional Court, on the grounds that the right to freedom of the press – of publications that wished to continue publishing these schedules – had been violated by the Bundesgerichtshof's decision.[71]

Following its approach in *Lüth*, the Constitutional Court finds that the dispute must be decided under private law, which must be infused with the objective values underlying fundamental rights. In this case, fundamental rights were relevant in determining whether the actions of the publishing companies were unlawful.

The Constitutional Court finds that an appeal for a boycott that forms a means of achieving political, economic, social, or cultural interests is, generally, protected by freedom of speech. This can also be the case if the appeal is made by a party that is in competition with the object of the boycott provided it is focused on an intellectual clash of opinions.[72] Nevertheless, a call for a boycott is not protected if it uses a range of illegitimate means to force the boycotter's opinion on others such that they cannot exercise their own freedom to decide whether to support it or not. Such means would include threats of serious disadvantages – often financial – for those refusing

[69] Ibid: 257–258.
[70] Ibid: 259.
[71] Ibid: 261.
[72] Ibid: 264.

to adhere to the boycott; and the exploitation of the socio-economic vulnerability of another entity/individual. The court thus proscribes the use of serious economic pressure which would violate the equality of individuals to hold their own opinions and undermine the fundamental basis of free speech, which is to allow for a contestation of opinions.[73]

The court held that the publishing companies could well have used their own publications to express their views surrounding the need for a boycott of publications that continued to print East German media schedules. That exercise of freedom of expression would have been similar to what occurred in the *Lüth* case and protected. However, they went further: they threatened the very economic basis for the sale of the offending publications – namely, their distribution by newspaper sellers upon which the publications were economically or legally dependent.[74] The publishing companies also bore a dominant position in the magazine market and, thus, the weight of their threat to news-sellers who refused to comply was a severe one. In *Lüth*, the call for a boycott was simply addressed to other people's sense of moral responsibility and it was up to them to decide whether to accept or reject the call. In contrast, in *Blinkfüer*, massive economic pressure was brought to bear in favour of the boycott: this was due to the market-dominant position of the publishing companies calling for the boycott and the dependence of the complainants upon being sold and distributed by news-sellers who in turn needed a business relationship with the powerful publishing houses.

The court went on to hold that the *Blinkfüer* magazine had its own right to freedom of the press. Freedom of the press was of critical importance in protecting free intellectual activity and opinion-formation in a democracy. Importantly, the court found that 'in order to protect the institution of the free press, the independence of its publications from interference by economic pressure groups must … be secured'.[75] That would entail ensuring the protection of a diversity of opinions and to prevent economic pressure from being utilised to limit what may be said. The court, consequently, held that the Bundesgerichtshof had failed to take account adequately of the violation

[73] Ibid: 268.

[74] The court has since affirmed its position that the means by which a boycott is executed determines its legitimacy: see BVerfGE 62, 230: 245–246. For an analysis of this matter, see Menzel and Müller-Terpitz, 2017: 180–182.

[75] BVerfGE 25, 256: 268. Poscher, 2003: 241–242 contends that the court's wording in this passage implies a direct effect.

of the right to freedom of the press of *Blinkfüer* and had extended the scope of the freedom of expression of the publishing houses too far in enabling them to use their economic power to support their call for a boycott.

This case is interesting for our purposes for a number of reasons. Firstly, the dispute arose initially in private law. Yet, in its reasoning, the court appears to leave behind the private law virtually completely and engages with the freedom of expression of the large publishing houses and how that is to be balanced against the freedom of press claim of the complainant. The court thus focuses its judgment on the relevant constitutional rights and their implications for the behaviour of the non-state actors.[76] Whilst ostensibly an exercise of indirect application, the court in fact appears to consider the direct implications of constitutional rights for the non-state actors.[77]

Secondly, the court's analysis essentially involves constructing the obligations and entitlements of the powerful publishing houses in respect of the publisher of *Blinkfüer*. Strangely, there is no discussion about whether fundamental rights actually can be claimed by juristic persons, which is simply assumed to be the case.

Thirdly, the court's analysis in reaching its conclusions draws on a number of important factors. The key factor relating to the beneficiary of the right is economic vulnerability and a recognition that the ability to speak freely can be infringed seriously as a result of economic pressure. The court also considers, importantly, the relationship between the parties and, in particular, whether there is a dependency of one upon another. It is to be commended in this regard for recognising the dimension of power that can be significantly asymmetrical in the private sphere. In doing so, it also considers a factor that arises on the other side of the relationship, namely, the manner in which a non-state actor has the capacity to infringe on the fundamental rights of another non-state actor. Here, it is necessary to take account of the dominance of an economic actor in the market and their ability to influence others to follow their views on pain of severe economic consequences.[78]

[76] This has become common practice for the court. See, for example, also BVerfGE 90, 27: 33, where the court also moves quickly beyond engaging with the interpretation and application of private law to focus its argumentation on the relevant fundamental rights. See Barczak, 2017: 94.

[77] Gardbaum, 2003: 443 suggests that the court in this case analytically crossed 'the clear line between indirect and direct horizontal effect'. See also Quint, 1989: 275–277.

[78] We will see this dimension resurface expressly again in the judgments of the Colombian Constitutional Court discussed in section 5.4.2 of Chapter 5.

Finally, the question arises as to what reasoning process the court utilises to reach a final conclusion concerning the balance between the rights of the publishing houses and that of *Blinkfüer*. Though there is clearly a need to balance in this context, the court does not do so through any structured process. The court rules that the freedom of the press requires being free from economic coercion. It does not investigate how that connects with the other publishing houses' right to express themselves and how these conflicting entitlements could be balanced against each other. What the court seems to be saying is that the publishing houses may express their views and even openly call for a boycott but they must not use their economic power to impose their view: thus, there are less restrictive means that could be employed to preserve the rights of *Blinkfuer's* publisher and staff whilst still preserving their freedom of expression. Though the court does not expressly say so, its reasoning here is suggestive of the necessity component of the proportionality enquiry.

3.3.1.3 *Von Hannover*: Failing to Accord Normative Priority to Individual Rights

A very interesting series of cases in Germany concerned Princess Caroline von Hannover of Monaco.[79] The case arose when a German magazine published private photographs of her in domestic settings and whilst she was going about everyday chores without her permission. They also published pictures of her daily life with her young children. The existing German law did not, in general, allow publication of photos without permission. Consent was, however, not necessary to publish photos of people 'from the realm of contemporary history' provided they did not violate the 'legitimate interests' of such a person.[80] Princess Caroline argued that her fundamental right to the free development of her personality (read with her fundamental human dignity) gave her a legitimate interest in having a space of privacy free from cameras and also in being able to control the dissemination of her image.[81] Two clashing rights, once again, existed in this case: Princess Caroline's right to control the dissemination of her photograph (essentially a dimension of the right to privacy) and the magazine's right to freedom of the press. The court considers the implications of these fundamental rights through their impact on interpreting the existing statutory law and such notions as 'legitimate interest'. It

[79] We will consider BVerfGE 101, 361. We encountered an appeal to the ECHR against the German case in section 2.4.2 of Chapter 2.

[80] Ibid: 364–365.

[81] Ibid: 371–372.

finds the existing law to strike an adequate balance between these competing rights. It also finds that courts must draw on the interests protected by these fundamental rights in applying the law to particular factual circumstances. In doing so, the court divides its analysis essentially into two parts.

The first considers the rights of Princess Caroline as a beneficiary of the right to free development of her personality and, in particular, the dimension of privacy. The court recognises an important interest of individuals to be able to withdraw from the public sphere without the constant sense of others watching them. Celebrities and other individuals who play a role in public life, the court held, are also entitled to withdraw into a private sphere which clearly involves the home but extends beyond it.[82] Nevertheless, an individual cannot claim that spaces where there are many people constitute the private sphere. Moreover, individuals may consent to aspects of their private life being made public – such prior conduct will affect the court's assessment of how strong their privacy interests are when reporting takes place about their private lives in other contexts. The private sphere is also more strongly protected when children are involved: since their personality interests are more vulnerable, heightened protections will be provided to cover instances where parents are interacting with their children.[83]

On the other hand, the court found that the freedom of the press must include a broad ability to determine the content and appearance of a publication which includes photographs. In doing so, it recognised the important social function of the media, which it described as serving an important role in the development of individuals and in the formation of public opinion.[84] The court argues that entertainment and politics often go together and the line between them has become increasingly blurred. It goes further, however, to hold that even pure entertainment is protected under 'freedom of the press'.[85] This is because entertainment often engages and reflects attitudes to life, values, and behavioural patterns. That also applies, the court finds, to news reports about people who often stand for certain values, provide role models and examples of lifestyles against which individuals compare their own lives. As such, the public interest in persons who are 'from the realm of contemporaneous history' must play an important role in determining the permissibility of publications about

[82] Ibid: 382–383.
[83] Ibid: 385.
[84] Ibid: 389.
[85] Ibid: 390.

them. That can also apply to people – such as the Princess – who attract public attention by virtue of their status. Moreover, the press is also not limited to showing photographs about them when they exercise their purely public functions but also in other contexts. In a very permissive statement, the court holds that 'it is central to the freedoms of press and of opinion that the press is granted a sufficient margin under the law to decide, according to journalistic criteria, what demands public attention'.[86] In balancing the two rights, the court finds that the press is entitled to report on the ordinary life of an individual when they are in public – in this area freedom of the press can take precedence over the right to privacy. Moreover, in effecting the balance, the court places strong weight on the method utilised to obtain the picture – obtaining photos by secrecy or surprise will tend towards their being legally unacceptable. Given these principles, the court finds that most of the pictures published by the magazine were taken in the public sphere and were therefore constitutionally acceptable. Those photographs, however, which showed the Princess with her children, were in all likelihood not consistent with the heightened protection to be provided to children and were consequently sent back for a different determination to be made by the lower civil court.

The court in this case applies the indirect application model by utilising fundamental rights to interpret existing statutory law. Whilst it does engage briefly with the statute, the judgment is notable for its extensive consideration of the competing rights of the parties. Ultimately, the court's reasoning substantively involves deciding whether the magazine in question was entitled to publish the photos and constructing its obligations in respect of Princess Caroline and her family. Whilst ostensibly filtered through statute, in fact, the clear burden of analysis lies in the constitutional rights at stake, highlighting once again the effective collapse of indirect into direct application.

In its reasoning, the language of 'values' is less pronounced, which perhaps is why the court engages in some depth as to what falls within the domain of each of the clashing rights. Nevertheless, some of the drawbacks of the indirect application model are also in evidence, which may in fact have impacted on the result of the case. The court does, on the one hand, consider the right of Princess Caroline to a private sphere: yet, unlike in *Blinkfüer*, its reasoning fails to engage in any detail with her vulnerability to the potential intrusiveness of the press into her private life. It only does so in respect of her children. On the other hand, the

[86] Ibid: 392.

court considers press freedom and its crucial function in society. Yet it pays very little attention, again, unlike in *Blinkfüer*, to the capacity of the press to harm the right to privacy of individuals. Its reasoning in this respect focuses on the important social function of the press in a very abstract way as well as its autonomy to decide on what should or should not be published. The lack of a clear methodology and relevant considerations relating to the relationship between the parties, arguably, leads the court to leave out central factors that could have led it to decide differently.

This reasoning of the court also, as is evident from the above analysis, does not take into account the relative power of the parties in *structuring* its opinion. Instead, the rights of Princess Caroline appear to be placed on the same level in the analysis as the freedom of the press – the court essentially constructs the right to personality of Princess Caroline through examining what the right to freedom of the press entails. Yet, without any normative priority accorded to the rights of the more vulnerable party, this approach can easily be seen to weaken an individual's rights substantially through determining the rights of a beneficiary in relation to the rights of the violator. Arguably, given the power disparity, the court should have started with considering the infringement of Princess Caroline's rights and then whether the press had provided an adequate justification for doing so. A proportionality analysis could then have been conducted to help determine what a fair balance in these circumstances would be. It is quite possible if this power imbalance were to have been given greater prominence, the court's approach would have been different: indeed, the court's reasoning is perhaps least persuasive when it seeks to allow the press to interfere with the privacy of individuals for entertainment purposes where the public interest is particularly weak. Such a wide latitude to press freedom appears to place little weight on the privacy interests of the individuals in question.

This is perhaps why the decision was overturned by the European Court of Human Rights (ECHR) – which was analysed in Chapter 2. The ECHR more closely tracks a reasoning structure that can better capture the normative importance of Princess Caroline's right to privacy. When considering whether there was a justification for the interference with the right, the ECHR was clearly able to see the weakness of the press's claim in circumstances which focused purely on the private life of individuals like Princess Caroline. The ECHR court also expressly dealt with the dimension of power and the vulnerability of celebrities to the intrusive interference by the press which affected its assessment.

The two judgments are thus fascinating to consider against one another and suggest the importance of the reasoning structure in affecting the outcomes of rights decision-making and adjudication. It is strongly arguable that the very limited protection for Princess Caroline's privacy rights afforded in the German Constitutional Court is a consequence of a very vague and loose structure for balancing individual rights against each other brought about through employing the indirect application model.

3.3.2 *South Africa*

When apartheid ended, South Africa, like Germany, was faced with the challenge of transforming its legal system which had been seriously compromised through the utilisation of the law to entrench racialised (and other) inequalities. If the values of a new society were to take root, it was not only the sphere of public authority that had to be changed.[87] Non-state actors were themselves deeply implicated in the entrenchment of injustice and it was necessary to ensure that the Constitution reached this sphere as well. There was a debate that ensued concerning how this was to be accomplished. During the period of the interim Constitution, the majority of the Constitutional Court, perhaps under the influence of the German approach, expressed a preference for an indirect application model.[88]

The Final Constitution, however, appeared to change the position: section 8(2) provided that 'a provision of the Bill of Rights binds a natural or juristic person if, and to the extent that, it is applicable, taking into account the nature of the right and the nature of any duty imposed by the right': this suggested the possibility of direct binding obligations upon corporations and other non-state actors.[89] Section 8(3), however, muddied the waters somewhat: it provides

> [w]hen applying a provision of the Bill of Rights to a natural or juristic person in terms of subsection (2), a court a. in order to give effect to a right in the Bill, must apply, or if necessary develop, the common law to the extent that legislation does not give effect to that right; and b. may develop

[87] Madlanga, 2018: 367–368.

[88] *Du Plessis* v. *De Klerk*: paras 60–62.

[89] I will analyse the court's use of the direct model in section 5.4.1 of Chapter 5 and section 8.4.1 of Chapter 8.

> rules of the common law to limit the right, provided that the limitation is in accordance with section 36(1).

This suggested that the application of the bill of rights to non-state actors would occur through existing common law, suggestive of the indirect application model. Moreover, section 39(2) of the Constitution provides that '[w]hen interpreting any legislation and when developing the common law or customary law, every court, tribunal or forum must promote the spirit, purport and objects of the Bill of Rights'. The language of 'spirit, purport and objects' has similarities to the 'objective values' of the German approach. These provisions have led to a debate as to the exact manner in which the Final Constitution applies to non-state actors and existing common law more generally.[90] In a series of cases, the majority of the Constitutional Court has, when it comes to applying the Constitution to the existing common law, exhibited a preference for indirect application.[91] In what follows, I consider a qualitative analysis of the reasoning in two of these important cases.

3.3.2.1 *Barkuizen* v. *Napier*:[92] The Deleterious Effects of Reducing Rights to Values

This case is a seminal one in the area of contract law. The applicant entered into an insurance contract with a syndicate of Lloyd's Underwriters in London for the insurance of his motor car. After having an accident, the car was damaged beyond repair and a claim was lodged. The claim was repudiated by the insurer who claimed that the car was used for 'business' and not 'private' purposes. Two years later, a claim was lodged in court against the insurer for the economic value of the car. The insurer, however, objected to the claim based on a standard clause in its contract with the claimant requiring summons to be served within ninety days of the repudiation of a claim. The applicant argued that this clause provided an unreasonably short time to institute an action and thus violated his right of access to courts.

The majority of the court – per Ngcobo J – held against an approach that would evaluate contractual terms directly against the fundamental rights in the Constitution. Instead, the court held there is a general principle in contract law that no contract may be incompatible with public policy.

[90] For a small sample, see Woolman, 2007; Klare and Davis, 2010; Friedman, 2014.
[91] Chirwa, 2006: 42–43 and Dafel, 2015: 62–64 provide an explanation for this preference.
[92] [2007] ZACC 5.

> What public policy is and whether a term in a contract is contrary to public policy must now be determined by reference to the values that underlie our constitutional democracy as given expression by the provisions of the Bill of Rights. Thus a term in a contract that is inimical to the values enshrined in our Constitution is contrary to public policy, and is, therefore, unenforceable.[93]

Turning to the particular circumstances of the case, the majority held that the right of access to courts reflects a fundamental value of South African society, which must, as a result, be regarded as an important prong of public policy. As such, any contractual term that deprived an individual of such access would be unacceptable. The question, however, was whether time limitation clauses for instituting legal claims were compatible with public policy. On the one hand, they denied people legal redress if they did not institute a claim within a specified period. On the other hand, the court found that there were good reasons for having time limitation clauses – such as ensuring claims are processed quickly and that sources of evidence to establish a claim remain available. Such clauses were thus not per se unconstitutional but subject to the tests of 'reasonableness and fairness'.[94] To determine this, the court referred to the general test utilised in relation to time limitation clauses imposed by the state: namely, whether the time limitation clause could provide the claimant with an 'adequate and fair opportunity to seek judicial redress'.[95] This test was held to be compatible with the requirements of fairness and justice inherent in public policy and thus could apply to testing such clauses within the context of a contract.

The court found there to be two dimensions to determining fairness. The first requires a balancing of two competing values: the first value is freedom of contract, which requires parties to comply with the contractual obligations they have freely undertaken. That value flows from the autonomy and dignity of persons to make decisions for themselves; in deciding on the weight to be attached to this, the court held it is necessary to determine the extent to which a contract was freely and voluntarily entered into. The second competing value would naturally be 'that all persons have a right to seek judicial redress'.[96] This determination requires assessing also the relative position of the contracting parties, including the degree to which their bargaining position is equal.[97] It was also necessary to consider

[93] Ibid: para 29.
[94] Ibid: para 48.
[95] Ibid: para 51.
[96] Ibid: para 57.
[97] Ibid: para 60.

whether such a clause allows a party enough time to lodge a claim: the court recognises it is possible for a period to be so short – 24 hours, for instance – such that its unfairness is manifest. The second dimension of fairness involves considering whether or not the time limitation clause should be enforced through considering the circumstances which prevented non-compliance. It could be impossible for a person to comply – for instance, a person in a coma – and then it would be unreasonable to insist on the term in such circumstances. The onus of proof, the court held, is on the party seeking to avoid compliance with the time limitation clause.

On the facts of this case, the court held that the applicant had not provided a good factual basis as to why he did not comply with the time limitation clause. He knew his cause of action, the identity of the defendant, and the amount of his claim. The time period also was not 'manifestly unfair'. The court found there was no evidence to show that the applicant had not entered into the contract freely, fully aware of its terms and with equal bargaining power. Simply to allow the claimant not to comply, the court found, would go against the principle that contracts were generally to be honoured and thus be unfair to the opposing party. The court thus found against the claimant and in favour of the insurer.

The *Barkhuizen* case is a clear exemplar of an indirect application model which utilises the values underlying constitutional rights to fill out 'general clauses' – such as public policy – in other areas of the law. In determining whether an insurer may include a restrictive time limitation clause in its contracts, the court examines its existing jurisprudence on the right of access to courts and applies – in the context of relations between non-state parties – the same test as it had developed for the relations between individuals and the state.[98] Effectively, the court recognises that insurers have an obligation to ensure individuals have an adequate and fair opportunity to seek judicial redress. The indirect application model thus requires having reference directly to the substantive content of the fundamental right at stake and, effectively, applies it directly to determine the obligations of non-state actors.[99] It is likely for this reason that Langa CJ holds in a concurring judgment that the distinction between direct and indirect application will – when pure substance is considered – seldom be 'outcome-determinative'.[100]

[98] See Woolman, 2007: 778.

[99] Woolman, ibid. writes that '[o]ne can be forgiven for thinking that we are directly applying a specific substantive provision of the Bill of Rights'.

[100] *Barkhuizen*: para 186.

It is not clear that Langa CJ is correct about this: the problems with the indirect application model arise in the reasoning processes it encourages, which may lead to different outcomes. Indeed, the difficulty arises with the reduction of rights simply to values which can, as we have seen, affect the normative priority they should have when considered in relation to other values. This is illustrated in this judgment too as one of the disturbing features of the majority judgment is the lop-sided focus on the conduct of the applicant who had claimed that his right to have access to courts was violated. The conclusion about the reasonableness of the ninety-day period is reached without considering at all whether there was any hardship caused to the insurer if a longer period were to be given or its own ability to deal with claims over a longer period. The majority of the court thus focuses all its energies on the conduct of the party who claimed his rights were violated (the beneficiary) and not on the party that was claimed to have violated those rights. That is the opposite of the process that is usually required when it is claimed a right is infringed in the South African bill of rights – where the agent responsible for infringing a right has to justify his or her actions in terms of the limitations clause.[101] As Woolman has argued, the indirect application model appears to lose the clarity of the reasoning structure generally involved in considering fundamental rights claims,[102] which is designed to ensure rights are given the priority they deserve.

Moreover, the vague reasoning engendered by the indirect application model also, as we saw in the German cases, leads courts to situate non-state actors symmetrically even when there are significant power disparities between them. Despite its recognition that power was a factor to be considered, the court, in *Barkhuizen*, bizarrely reaches the conclusion that 'there is nothing to suggest that the contract was not freely concluded between persons of equal bargaining power or that the applicant was not aware of the clause'.[103] It is hard indeed to see how an individual signing up for an insurance contract can be regarded as having equal bargaining power to an insurance company of the magnitude of Lloyd's.

The minority judgments highlight some of these defects. Moseneke DCJ recognises that there is no reciprocity in the contract given that there is no time-bar on the right of the insurer to repudiate the claim. He thus highlights the disparity in the power between the parties. Moreover, he wonders why there is a need for such a tight time limitation and

[101] Woolman and Botha, 2006: 34-3 to 34-6.
[102] See Woolman, 2007: 763.
[103] *Barkhuizen*: para 66.

concludes that 'the prejudice that the clause visits on claimants is disproportionate to the conceivable benefits that it confers on the insurance company'.[104] In this statement, he references albeit briefly the notion of proportionality, suggesting the need for a proper balancing to take place between the relevant considerations.

Justice Sachs too, in his judgment, focuses on the fact that the time limitation clause was part of a standard-form agreement which essentially imposes terms on individuals by powerful companies. In his judgment, he acknowledges the clear need individuals have for insurance, rendering them vulnerable to the exercise of power by insurance companies. Sachs J also highlights an important dimension that was left out by the majority, namely, the social function of insurance companies.[105]

3.3.2.2 *NM* v. *Smith*:[106] A Multi-Factoral Approach in Development?

This case concerned the publication of a biography of a well-known politician in South Africa, Patricia De Lille. In the course of describing her work in dealing with HIV/AIDS, the HIV status and names of three women who were living with the disease were disclosed. The women claimed that their names and status were published without their consent, which violated their rights to privacy, dignity, and psychological integrity. The claim was made in terms of the common law of tort, which includes a prohibition on wrongfully and intentionally impairing the privacy rights of another. The Constitutional Court found that the precepts of the Constitution needed to 'inform the application of the common law'.[107] In doing so, the court needed to consider, in terms of the existing law, whether the author and publisher had demonstrated the intention to act wrongfully. If not, the question arose whether it was necessary to extend the civil law to cover the negligent disclosure of private information. There were several judgments in this case: the majority – per Madala J – found that there was the requisite intention to disclose wrongful information and awarded damages. Langa CJ found that there was no such intention; he, however, held that the negligent disclosure of private information was actionable in the constitutional order and found such negligence to have been present. O'Regan J agreed with Langa CJ on the need to extend the civil law to cover negligent disclosure but found that negligence was not present in this case.

[104] Ibid: para 113.
[105] Ibid: para 144.
[106] [2007] ZACC 6.
[107] Ibid: para 28.

The reasoning of the judges and the dispute between them is cloaked in an analysis of the question of intention in tort; yet, substantively, it involved deciding on what obligations the constitutional rights to dignity and privacy imposed on non-state actors in relation to the disclosure of personal information of other individuals. Indeed, Sachs J, in his judgment, states that the case was about 'defining the appropriate journalistic and publishing standards in a murky and undeveloped area of our law'.[108] Considering this issue, I will focus on the way in which the various judgments outline a range of factors to arrive at their conclusions in this regard. They also rather obliquely reference the question of balancing.

The majority judgment can be seen to engage with the following factors in reaching its conclusion that there was an intentional and wrongful invasion of privacy. Firstly, it considers a range of issues relating to the beneficiaries of the rights – namely, the women whose private information was disclosed. The court engages with the question of prior conduct and waiver: had the women already by their actions shown an intention to disclose their identity and status which would have absolved the author and publisher from attaining consent? The court found that they had not. Secondly, the court considers the nature and importance for individuals of the right to control sensitive medical information. It does this with reference specifically to the South African context where there was serious stigma and discrimination around HIV/AIDs. The court considered how the women had suffered as a result – one, for instance, had her shack burnt down and her boyfriend broke up with her. Thirdly, the court places specific emphasis when considering the violation of dignity on the vulnerability of the individuals concerned: the court says that 'because of their disadvantaged circumstances their case should have been treated with more than ordinary sensitivity'.[109]

In relation to the agents who caused the harm – the author and publisher – it was accepted that they were themselves involved in an activist manner with addressing HIV/AIDS in South Africa. That, in part, added to their obligations given they knew the serious impact disclosing sensitive information surrounding HIV/AIDS could have on the women concerned. The court also found that there was no time pressure that would have prevented them from gaining the express informed consent of the women. The author had gone ahead with the publication of the names for purposes of 'authenticity' despite knowing of the possibility of using

[108] Ibid: para 240.
[109] Ibid: para 53.

pseudonyms.[110] Whilst this was a deliberate authorial choice, the court found that 'the public's interest in authenticity does not outweigh the public's interest in maintaining the confidentiality of private medical facts as well as the right to privacy and dignity that everybody should enjoy'.[111] The court here effectively engages in a balancing of interests and finds, ultimately, that the author and publisher must, at least, have foreseen the possibility of a lack of consent, which was sufficient to establish intention.

Langa CJ, on the other hand, disagreed with the view that the author and publisher had the requisite intention; however, he found that the civil law needed to be extended in light of fundamental rights to cover the negligent disclosure of private information by the media. Langa focuses a lot of his attention on the agent who causes harm. He references the fact that the media – as a result of its power – bears a special responsibility to ensure its exercise of freedom of expression does not violate the constitutional rights of others. This duty arises from a number of features of the media: firstly, they are experts in their field of publication; secondly, they routinely distribute information to vast numbers of people; thirdly, they have an air of authority; and, finally, they do so for commercial gain. Langa CJ expressly states that these factors impose higher standards of responsibility upon the media than they do in relation to ordinary individuals.

O'Regan J agrees with Langa CJ that the common law should be developed to recognise negligent disclosure. She states that the law should reflect a balance to be achieved between the importance both of privacy and freedom of expression. She too considers the power and capacity of the media to cause harm to individuals, which is particularly true in light of modern electronic media.[112] The potential scale of the damage in this regard provides the justification for special obligations being placed upon the media. Such entities also have the ability and systems to ensure there are no unlawful disclosures. The social function of professional and commercial purveyors of information also provides strong reasons to impose a higher standard on them than would be required from ordinary citizens.[113] An appropriate balance can be attained by the media having to show that their publication of the material was reasonable.

Lastly, Sachs J, in his judgment, adds his view that the way to resolve the tension between freedom of expression and privacy in this case is

[110] Michelman, 2008a: 33 highlights how weak this justification in fact was.
[111] *NM v Smith*: para 61.
[112] Ibid: para 177.
[113] Ibid: paras 181–182.

through an approach that prioritises 'context, balance and proportionality'. In so doing, the following rule of thumb can be perceived, which has similarities at least with the ECHR ruling in *von Hannover*:

> The more private the matter, the greater the call for caution on the part of the media, while conversely, the more profound the public interest, the more heavily will it weigh in the scales.[114]

We thus see in this judgment how the indirect application model of fundamental rights, through the prism of tort law, essentially requires substantively a consideration of the implications of such rights for the obligations of non-state actors in relation to confidential information. The court, interestingly, in this case references the rights rather than the values underlying such rights, and in deciding the case engages a range of factors and principles. The majority places greater emphasis on beneficiary-orientated factors such as the impact of the disclosure on the women and their vulnerability. In making findings extending the obligations of authors and publishers in terms of the common law to cover negligent disclosures, we see both Langa CJ and O'Regan J referencing the particular nature of the agent that causes the harm, its function in society, together with its capacity to impact on the fundamental rights of others. There is also no clear methodology articulated for how the rights finally influence the common law obligations[115] – the various judgments, at several points, suggest the need for balancing though no structured process is evident for doing so.

3.4 Conclusion: The Indirect Application Model and the Obligations of Non-State Actors

The indirect application model attempts to preserve the idea that fundamental rights apply only between the state and individuals – at the same time, it recognises that fundamental rights must have implications for the relations between non-state actors and their obligations. It attempts to square the circle through contending that fundamental rights do not apply 'directly' to the relations between individuals but that they nevertheless

114 Ibid: para 204.

115 This is a source of criticism by Woolman, 2007: 781 who suggests that the fact that 'the Constitution actually contains a right to privacy and a right to dignity is entirely epiphenomenal'. For an attempt to reconstruct the reasoning of the majority in a way that draws on fundamental rights in its application of the 'intention' test, see Michelman, 2008a: 34 and 40–42.

influence the content of the private law legal rules that apply between non-state actors. The legal rules though articulate the obligations of non-state actors and, if fundamental rights affect those rules, they of course affect the obligations of those actors. To decide on the content of those obligations, courts therefore need to reason 'directly' about what substantively they should be. Consequently, we saw both theoretically and, through the analysis of cases, that courts must, unavoidably, in utilising the model construct the obligations of non-state parties that flow from fundamental rights. The claims of this book, which focus on the reasoning process to determine the obligations of a particular non-state party, the corporation, are thus clearly of relevance to jurisdictions which apply the indirect application model.

We saw various procedural and jurisdictional reasons why courts (and some academics) prefer the indirect model but, ultimately, substantively there is no difference between the task direct and indirect application models set for courts. There is also no clarity in the indirect application model as to how the process of application of rights happens with vague, magical language such as their 'radiating effect' on legal rules being used. That results in a lack of clarity concerning whether the reasoning should create a presumption in favour of a particular right, the factors involved in determining obligations, and the balancing process that takes place between the parties. There appear often to be times though where these drawbacks are not in evidence as strongly: where that occurs, we see usually that the courts reason directly about the obligations of the parties.

In cases where they do so, we see that the courts tend to apply an approach that references a number of relevant factors in deciding the cases. On the beneficiary side of rights, the key factor that emerged was individuals' vulnerability to the other non-state actor in the dispute, who potentially can harm their rights. In relation to the latter, we saw the courts identify the power wielded by such an agent over the beneficiary as a critical factor which demonstrates their capacity to imperil the rights of another. The function of that agent in society was also engaged with by the courts in several cases. We also see the language of balancing utilised although often the structure by which that takes place is not as transparent as cases involving the direct application of fundamental rights. Similarities have already emerged between the model adopted in this chapter and Chapter 2: as we will see, these factors together with balancing also emerge from an analysis of the 'expanding the state model', which is the subject of the next chapter.

4

The Expanding the State Model

4.1 Introduction

A number of jurisdictions still struggle with the notion that fundamental rights apply at all beyond the state. In some – such as the United States – there has been a denial that fundamental rights apply to relations between non-state actors; rather it is only when 'state action' is at issue that these rights are implicated. The fact remains, however, in these systems that non-state actors have the capacity seriously to affect fundamental rights. That creates a pressure to extend the notion of what constitutes 'state action'. The 'expanding the state' model involves reclassifying non-state actors as being part of the state, or recognising, at least, that in certain respects they can be regarded as entities within an enlarged ambit of the state. Doing so then allows them to be bound by obligations flowing from fundamental rights.

Yet, of course, this model fundamentally raises the question of what constitutes part of the state or not. This question is often formulated in terms of the public/private divide: when does an actor cross over from being 'private' to being 'public'? That question itself is extremely interesting for our purposes because, in a number of jurisdictions, it represents the shift between entities that have no obligations flowing from fundamental rights and those that do. Given this sharp divide, the factors that courts use in determining when an entity moves from being private to public are instructive in understanding what determines whether they have obligations in relation to fundamental rights.[1]

[1] They also may affect the content of these obligations, as we shall see.

This chapter proceeds as follows. Firstly, I attempt to outline the expanding the state model through a particular focus on the 'state action' doctrine in its pure form in the United States and the immediate problem that it raises. Theoretically, the only way to proceed with imposing obligations upon non-state entities is to re-classify them as being part of the state. I consider a prominent philosophical justification for this model to understand its underpinnings better. I then turn to a critical evaluation of the model and its drawbacks. I shall argue that it, ultimately, requires a sharp line to be drawn between state and non-state actors where in fact there is a continuum. Moreover, it places at the centre of legal analysis the wrong issue: a 'who' question – which agents are part of the state or not – rather than a 'what' question – the factors that are relevant to determining the nature of the obligations of differing entities.

The second part of this chapter turns to the case law of three jurisdictions to demonstrate the operation of the model in practice. I start with the United States and chart how its courts, for a period, sought to expand what constituted the state and the concomitant obligations of non-state actors. The 'expanding the state' model has, interestingly, been utilised not only in jurisdictions that reject the application of rights to non-state parties such as the United States. Judges appear cautious about applying fundamental rights to non-state parties – even when legal doctrine allows them to do so – and, consequently, they often prefer to impose obligations on non-state actors by re-classifying them as part of the state. Courts, in Germany, for instance – where, as we saw in Chapter 3, indirect application is available – have in a series of interesting cases expanded on the obligations of certain non-state actors through drawing them within the sphere of state activity. South Africa too – which has both direct and indirect application available – has seen the Constitutional Court determine the responsibility of certain non-state actors through drawing them within the realm of the state.

In engaging with this case law, I will be particularly concerned about the factors the courts employ to determine whether an entity or function it exercises is public in nature and how they reason about the concomitant obligations of these entities. As we shall see, interestingly, many of these factors overlap with those identified in Chapters 2 and 3 – that not only confirms the relevance of these factors but also the artificiality of attempting to preserve the application of fundamental rights only within the domain of the state.

4.2 The Expanding the State Model

4.2.1 *The Contours of the Model*

The historical origins of fundamental rights, as we saw in Chapters 2 and 3, have led to the view that they are designed to govern the actions of the state in relation to individuals (what are often referred to as 'vertical' relations). This conception has most famously been entrenched in the United States with its 'state action' doctrine, which was clearly established in the aftermath of the American civil war in cases that arose concerning racial discrimination in private inns and theatres.[2] The power of Congress to utilise the 14th Amendment of the Constitution (passed in the wake of the American civil war) in order to enact a law prohibiting racial discrimination in private spaces was challenged. The relevant portion of the 14th Amendment reads:

> No State shall make or enforce any law which shall abridge the privileges or immunities of citizens of the United States; nor shall any State deprive any person of life, liberty, or property, without due process of law; nor deny to any person within its jurisdiction the equal protection of the laws.[3]

In a troubling judgment declaring the non-discrimination law to be unconstitutional, Justice Bradley held for the majority of the Supreme Court that Congress only had the power to make laws to counteract its own discriminatory actions but not that of non-state actors. Expounding on the meaning of the 14th Amendment, he wrote in a classic exposition of this doctrine: '[i]t is state action of a particular character that is prohibited. Individual invasion of individual rights is not the subject matter of the amendment'.[4]

As understood in this way, then, the prohibition on discriminatory treatment applies to the state and it may take all measures necessary to prevent any of its organs from violating this prohibition. However, individuals are not bound by this prohibition and so the private sphere is left unregulated in that regard. The federal legislature has only limited powers derived from fundamental rights to protect individuals from discrimination caused by other individuals or non-state actors.[5] Fundamental rights,

[2] Though established, it has attracted voluminous criticism from academics: for a summary of some key positions until 1967, see Black, 1967: 91–95. I will only engage the literature in so far as is relevant to the purposes of this chapter and book.

[3] See www.law.cornell.edu/constitution/amendmentxiv.

[4] *The Civil Rights Cases* 109 US 3 (1883). Already, at the same time, the insufficiency of this approach was seen by Justice Harlan in his ringing and impressive dissent.

[5] This was affirmed by the majority of Supreme Court in the context of domestic violence in *US* v. *Morrison* 529 US 598 (2000).

on this account, thus do not aim at addressing and improving a state of affairs that individuals find themselves in and wish to avoid; rather, they are only concerned with the behaviour of a particular entity – the state – and its relationship with the individuals in its domain.[6]

The account, however, raises the question of what forms part of the state and why only such an entity can be bound by obligations flowing from fundamental rights. In his dissent, amongst other challenges, Harlan J considers the nature of the spaces in which the racial discrimination in question was challenged: public conveyances, inns, and places of public amusement. In terms of railways and highways, Harlan holds these are the essence of public spaces as they fundamentally affect the ability of individuals to move around.[7] Stopping people from utilising such services on grounds of race deprives them of 'the most essential means of existence'.[8] Inns were distinguished from public guesthouses and regulated by law to provide accommodation to travellers. Harlan finds that in relation to innkeepers, '[t]he law gives him special privileges and he is charged with certain duties and responsibilities to the public'. [9] In relation to public places of amusement, Harlan contends that the ability to operate them flows from a licence granted in terms of the law. The authority and ability to create and operate them, therefore, comes from the public and is subject to a principle of non-discrimination on grounds of race. He also argues that property could be regulated when it affects the community at large and there is a public interest in it. The law may therefore regulate these spaces as they cannot be regarded as being simply private in nature.[10]

In this reasoning, Harlan highlights the idea that the realm of the public does not extend only to what is regarded formally as being part of the state. Instead, an entity may be regarded as having a public or quasi-public dimension for a number of reasons: for instance, if it has the ability to have a major impact on other individuals or the community as a whole. This idea provides the basis for the expanding the state model: it essentially involves extending the realm of the state to include entities and individuals which either become part of the state in some way or exercise powers or functions which are 'state-like' (or public) in some manner.[11]

[6] It is founded thus on a strict separation between the public and private spheres: see *Harvard Law* Review, 2010: 1257.

[7] *The Civil Rights Cases*: 39.

[8] Ibid: 40.

[9] Ibid: 41.

[10] Ibid: 42.

[11] Quint, 1989: 339.

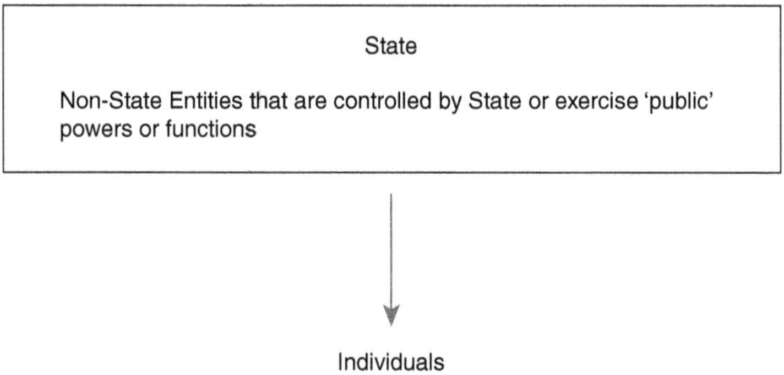

Figure 4.1 The expanding the state model.

Where that is the case, there is then a justification also for imposing obligations usually reserved for the state on entities that possess these powers or functions. In the words of the US Supreme Court, '[c]onduct that is formally "private" may become so entertwined with governmental policies or so impregnated with a governmental character as to become subject to the constitutional limitations placed upon state action'.[12]

This model can be represented in a simplified form as shown in Figure 4.1.

4.2.2 *The Justification for the Model*

The model appears to have two components which require justification: the first involves limiting the bindingness of fundamental rights to the vertical relationship between the state and individuals; and the second involves a move to adopt a more expansive interpretation of what constitutes the state. On what basis could such an approach be justified?

A recent chapter by Valentini provides just such an account. She defends a 'political' view of fundamental rights – the idea that fundamental rights are conceptually tied to public political actors and only they bear primary responsibility for the duties that flow from fundamental rights.[13] In doing so, Valentini argues that there are three criteria that should be utilised in determining who are the bearers of fundamental rights responsibility. They are, firstly, the satisfaction of the 'ought-implies-can' principle – in other words, that the agent in question has the capacity to fulfil the responsibility

[12] See *Evans* v. *Newton* 382 US 296 (1966) at 299.
[13] Valentini, 2017: 168. A similar approach is examined and defended by Karp, 2014: 116ff.

imposed upon it; secondly, she claims it is necessary to be able to account for the distinctiveness of fundamental rights violations which involves a particular kind of affront to dignity; and, finally, that fundamental rights violations are of such a nature that they require particular responses and, in particular, trigger international concern.[14] These criteria are drawn from general constraints on the imposition of duties such as the 'ought-implies-can' principle and from the general judgments we make about fundamental rights.

States, Valentini argues, meet these criteria. In relation to the ought-implies-can criterion, we regard the state as generally responsible to secure fundamental rights for those who live within its territory. She recognises, however, that a wealthy individual or corporation may also have the capacity to provide certain fundamental rights to persons – such as food or housing – yet she claims that we do not ordinarily think that they are under a general duty to provide for the people in a country. What explains the difference?

According to Valentini, it is what she terms the 'authority-plus-sovereignty' package of the state.[15] States, she claims, have de facto authority over those within their territory, which includes a socially accepted right to rule over them and for them to obey it (this is the 'authority' dimension). At the same time, states are also entitled to act within their domain and not to be interfered with by external agents (this is the 'sovereignty' dimension).[16] These facets of the state, however, are only legitimate if the state exercises them with respect for the fundamental rights of those within their domain. The 'authority-plus-sovereignty' package helps to explain why, on the political view, the state is the primary duty-bearer in respect of fundamental rights.

Returning to her second criterion, Valentini argues that the state is capable of causing distinctive harms to individuals. In illustrating this point, she asks us to consider whether there is a distinction between the murder by an individual of a fellow citizen and the official state execution of a political protester. Whilst any murder deprives a person of their life, we do not on that basis alone, she claims, regard it as a fundamental rights violation. The murder of the protestor becomes such a violation when perpetrated by the state because it violates certain special duties the state has to individuals. The 'authority' dimension of the state means that there is

[14] Valentini, ibid: 171.
[15] Ibid: 172.
[16] Ibid.

a distinctive harm to the dignity of individuals when the state is the violator itself – the agent that is supposed to act on behalf of individuals and protect them fails to do so.[17] Furthermore, fundamental rights violations trigger international concern because they are linked to state sovereignty – since the state is no longer performing its centrally important protective functions, it loses its claim to non-interference and outside intervention becomes permissible.[18]

Valentini recognises that there is an undesirable consequence of a strict interpretation of this view since it would entail that where the state lacks the capacity to provide for the fundamental rights of its members, no one else has such responsibilities, including powerful non-state actors such as transnational corporations (TNCs).[19] In such circumstances, TNCs can act in ways that seriously impact on the rights of individuals without governments having the ability to constrain them. Moreover, they may have the substantial capacity to assist in the realisation of rights without any obligation to do so. If we recognise that such TNCs have the capacity to affect fundamental rights in both positive and negative ways, the problem becomes, on her account, that they do not prima facie appear to exhibit the authority-plus-sovereignty elements.[20]

In responding to this problem, Valentini attempts to provide an argument for why TNCs can, in certain circumstances, be considered to have the authority-plus-sovereignty dimensions that are necessary, on her account, for having fundamental rights responsibilities. She argues that, in weak governance areas, TNCs can become ruling institutions, setting the ground rules for the existence of those who work for them. In particular, they can define a number of the features of workers' lives and often enforce company rules as well. Following Wettstein,[21] Valentini acknowledges that a TNC can have a de facto state-like authority and its failure to discharge its responsibilities 'conveys a systematic lack of recognition of its subjects' humanity'.[22] Moreover, such authority is not simply voluntarily acquired, in many cases, given that those who are weak and poor are often forced into employment – or other – relationships with these entities. Such authority also has a de facto sovereignty dimension in that these TNCs are immune from external interference by the state in which they operate (due to its weakness).

[17] Ibid: 172–173.
[18] Ibid: 173.
[19] Ibid: 175.
[20] Ibid: 176.
[21] See Chapter 1 section 4.2.1.
[22] Valentini, 2017: 177.

Valentini concludes: 'In sum, whenever TNCs are functionally sufficiently state-like, their *de facto* authority and sovereignty, just like those of states, can only be legitimate if they are accompanied by primary human-rights responsibilities. And TNCs' violations of human rights both carry a special harm to dignity and appropriately generate international concern.'[23]

Valentini's account thus exemplifies the expanding the state model and provides a justification for it. It first provides reasons for why fundamental rights usually only generate binding obligations between the state and individuals which are rooted in certain particular features that the state exhibits – yet, crucially, which are not simply definitional of the state itself. She then argues that this justification would also support extending such obligations to non-state actors when they share these features. Such a justification, of course, leads to the conclusion that it is not the agent per se but these features that determine the presence or absence of the obligations in question. In Valentini's account, for instance, these are understood largely in terms of possessing strong asymmetrical power to affect individuals' most basic interests and the autonomy to act within a certain sphere without external interference.[24]

The expanding the state model can also be defended as an attempt to limit the obligations fundamental rights place upon non-state actors so as to preserve their liberty to act as they wish in the private sphere.[25] Individuals may, for instance, discriminate in relation to whom they wish to marry, contract with or invite to a dinner party whilst the state must always treat individuals equally.[26] Even though the model expands the sphere of the state, it does so in a way that limits binding obligations to a class of actors that has 'state-like' features. As such, it could be argued that it preserves the greatest amount of liberty for those entities that lack these features. This justification has been prominent in the academic literature that engages with the state action doctrine in the United States[27] and some of the cases as will be seen later.[28]

A last defence of the model could be as an attempt to prevent the state from engaging non-state actors to violate rights on its behalf. In

[23] Ibid: 178.
[24] For a similar and more expansive account of what state-like features involve, see Karp, 2014: 116–151.
[25] Tushnet, 2003: 89–90.
[26] Taylor, 2002: 200.
[27] See, for instance, Henkin, 1962: 475; Black, 1967: 101.
[28] See the *Fraport* case in section 4.3.2.1 later.

such circumstances, the model recognises those non-state actors will be acting in a 'state-like' capacity. It can thus be viewed as a 'necessary device to prevent circumvention by the state of constitutional limitations'.[29]

4.2.3 *The Drawbacks of the Model*

Importantly, the deficiencies of this account in a sense begin to emerge from the very justifications offered earlier. As we saw, it is possible to try and hold the line that fundamental rights obligations only apply to state–individual relationships. That approach leads clearly to undesirable implications – it, for instance, allows naked discrimination between private persons to take place and, at its extreme, appears not even to allow the state to protect individuals against such discrimination[30] or violence.[31] If fundamental rights are rooted in dignity, as was argued in Chapter 2, then certain forms of treatment are impermissible, no matter whether enacted by state or non-state actors. Moreover, this account is also in need of a justification for what constitutes the special domain of the state and why it is uniquely bound by fundamental rights obligations.

These deficits lead theorists such as Valentini to begin their accounts by admitting that there is something fetishistic about focusing on the state alone and that an account that is unable to include powerful non-state actors within its ambit is somehow deficient.[32] They attempt, however, to understand what it is about the state that uniquely gives rise to obligations in relation to fundamental rights. In doing so, it is necessary to consider which features of the state matter in determining that it possesses fundamental rights obligations. Central to these accounts, however, is a recognition that it is these *features* that are critical and not the fact that there is a particular agent involved. As such, once those features are present, even actors that are not traditionally considered part of the state may also have those fundamental rights obligations.

[29] Quint, 1989: 340. This argument is also presented by the German Constitutional Court in the *Fraport* decision BVerfGE 128, 22: 245.

[30] Black, 1967: 70 in the foreword on the 'state action' doctrine recognises that the state action doctrine shields racial injustice from being adequately dealt with by governmental authorities.

[31] Feminist scholars have drawn attention to how a strict public–private divide can fail to protect women, for instance, against rape and domestic violence: see, for instance, West, 1990: 67.

[32] Valentini, 2017: 175–176.

The key move is from a particular agent – the state – to the features that are constitutive of what it is to exercise 'state-like' functions or powers. The model, thus, essentially admits that obligations for fundamental rights extend to agents beyond the state – what matters is the presence of certain 'state-like' features. It is thus not clear why it is necessary to retain a focus on categorising whether an agent forms part of the state or not.[33] Indeed, the importance of these features suggests that a better approach would be to consider directly the relationship between an agent, its possession of the relevant features either wholly or in part, and their obligations flowing from fundamental rights. Why is this preferable?

The focus on the entity – particularly on those that look in many respects like they are non-state actors – may obscure an investigation of whether it in fact possesses the relevant features for having fundamental rights obligations. This is problematic for several reasons. On the one hand, the question concerning the nature of the 'entity' suggests that it either fits within the state or does not. Yet an entity may, in some respects, have features that are 'state-like' and in other respects be more private in nature.[34] The entity itself may also be constituted as a private company, for instance, but exercise functions that are public in nature. There is thus in fact a continuum today between the private and the public.[35] If we accept that entities may have both public and private dimensions and exercise public and private functions, then to classify them as one or the other will fail adequately to do justice to their nature – and, consequently, their obligations. We saw in Chapter 1 precisely how the corporation is in fact a hybrid between the public and the private, and we need to grapple with this complexity in order to arrive at a reasonable view concerning its obligations. Categorical thinking thus tends to require a classification where the lines may in fact be blurred.[36]

[33] See also Tushnet, 2009: 70, who argues in the context of the state action doctrine in the United States that it distracts us from 'paying attention to what truly matters' and Quint, 1989: 342–43.

[34] See Karp, 2014: 138–142; and Dafel, 2015: 79–80, who discusses the difficulty of classifying a political party as either public or private.

[35] See Hoexter, 2018: 150, who suggests determining whether an entity or power is public or private is 'too much a matter of feel' (169). See also the statement by Justice Cameron in the *AMCU* decision discussed later at para 68.

[36] There is also a more subtle but different point that such categorical thinking often obscures the serious influence non-state entities have on the exercise of public functions by the state and vice versa – the salaries offered in the non-state sector may in fact prevent the public sector from being able to hire enough lawyers to represent poorer clients, for instance. This is an issue I will engage with further in Chapter 8 concerning a justification for the positive obligations of corporations.

The continuum difficulty also highlights the fact that the approach tends to conflate two different types of questions: 'who' has obligations with 'what' those obligations are. The 'expanding the state model' focuses on a threshold question: is one part of the state or not? If one is, one has obligations, and if not, one lacks obligations. Both sides of this equation are problematic: if one is part of the state, then this model suggests that one must have all the obligations of the state. Where an entity is not ordinarily considered part of the state – such as a corporation exercising a public function – normatively, it would appear to be unfair to impose all the responsibilities of the state on an entity formed to conduct business activities. Moreover, where such entities have obligations, it would seem to absolve traditional organs of the state from their obligations – it may, for instance, reduce the incentive or ability of weak states to provide for their populations where such provision is taken over by powerful TNCs.[37] On the other side of the equation, if one is classified as not being part of the state, then one lacks any obligations flowing from fundamental rights. That appears to be undesirable given that an agent may have the significant capacity to impact on the fundamental rights of individuals.[38]

A focus on the 'who' question obscures the 'what' question concerning the nature of the obligations of an entity. If we accept there is a continuum between the private and the public, then having obligations is not an all-or-nothing matter: entities may have some of the obligations of the state but not all of them.[39] This is essentially the response of Valentini to the worry that her view would lead to overdemanding consequences for TNCs – she claims that their responsibilities will be proportional to the degree to which they have features that are 'state-like' in nature.[40] This response effectively admits that these entities are, in considerable respects, not part of the state and so what matters are the relevant factors that determine the nature of their obligations in relation to rights (the 'what' question) rather than 'who' they are.

Valentini also struggles with the second problem outlined earlier of imposing obligations on entities that may not, for instance, exercise state-like authority over individuals (that are not their employees for instance) but have a significant capacity to impact upon their lives. Her account suggests that such non-state actors lack the prerequisites for having binding obligations even though they may have the significant capacity to affect the fundamental rights of these people. It is this latter proposition – focusing

[37] Valentini, 2017: 179; SRSG 2010 Report: para 64.
[38] Valentini, ibid: 180.
[39] Finn, 2015a: 651–654; Valentini, 2017: 179.
[40] Valentini, ibid.

on state-like authority as being a prerequisite for obligations – which is unconvincing. Valentini correctly recognises that, where an individual or corporation has a claim to a protected sphere of autonomy, this does affect our ability to translate their capacity to impact upon rights into binding obligations *automatically*.[41] Capacity may, nevertheless, prima facie support the recognition of some obligations – the degree to which autonomy is of importance may modulate and affect 'what' obligations one has. The state which lacks such autonomy interests and has a particular role in addressing the distribution of resources in a society will have the full range of obligations flowing from fundamental rights. Other agents may also have obligations but the nature and extent thereof will depend on the strength and importance of their autonomy interests and the nature and function of those agents in society even if they are not clearly 'state-like'. Continuously having to analogise corporate power to that of the state can lead to mistaken conclusions:[42] the fact, for instance, that a corporation only has direct authority or enforcement powers over employees does not mean that it lacks a significant ability to affect individuals in a nearby community through, for instance, monopolising the production of certain goods, or effectively dominating the economic activity in a particular area. A view focused on the relevant features of agents rather than their identity – being part of the state or not – thus allows for capturing better the nature and content of the obligations of different entities.

Moreover, the categorical reasoning involved in the model, as the last paragraph highlights, does not adequately lay bare the need for balancing the different interests that are at stake.[43] One of the central questions that arises concerns the degree to which the autonomy interests, for instance, of a non-state actor should be taken into account and what weight to afford them. The point is that a private or partially private entity will often have interests that need accounting for and provide countervailing normative reasons from those related to the beneficiary of rights. To reach an adequate account of obligations, it is necessary to balance these interests against one another.[44] The problem with this model is not only

[41] Ibid: 176.

[42] See Hoexter, 2018: 159 for an example and the importance of distinguishing narrower 'governmental' features of an entity from wider 'public' ones.

[43] See also Harvard Law Review, 2010: 1313 on the failures of a bright line rule adequately to balance competing claims and Taylor, 2002: 211.

[44] This offers a response to the concern that binding obligations would harm the liberty and privacy of individuals – ultimately, these interests must be balanced. See, in this regard, Henkin, 1962: 491–496.

that it may conflate different interests but also that it may obscure the need to balance. In the worst cases, this could land up subsuming private interests to the collective or vice versa and fail adequately to give expression to the normative dimensions of a situation.

I now turn to a qualitative analysis of some case law in the second part of this chapter that applies this model. As we will see, the cases tend to emphasise certain features which render a non-state actor 'state-like' in order to reach the conclusion that they also have obligations flowing from fundamental rights. I am particularly interested in what these features are which, on this model, are prerequisites for having obligations but also can, as we shall see, offer us insights into the factors that are relevant for the determination of these obligations. Where in evidence, I also highlight the drawbacks of the model which I have already identified.

4.3 The Expanding the State Model in Law

4.3.1 The United States

Of the jurisdictions I analyse, the United States is traditionally presented as exhibiting the most extreme version of a state action doctrine whereby the rights in the bill of rights – apart from the 13th Amendment – are only applicable to the state–individual relationship.[45] Where there are impacts upon fundamental rights caused by non-state actors that courts wish to proscribe, they are forced into finding alternative doctrinal methods to do so.[46] One approach was adopted in the case of *Shelley* v. *Kraemer*:[47] that case dealt with contracts between private parties that prohibited the sale or lease of property to African Americans. The Supreme Court held that there was no ground to prohibit these agreements as violative of fundamental rights given they did not constitute state action. However, state action was involved in the *enforcement* of these agreements by courts – given that they

[45] See Hunt, 1998: 427 but, also see Gardbaum, 2003, who accepts that whilst this is the traditional view (at 395), it is mistaken. Gardbaum presents an alternative account of the US jurisprudence, suggesting it is more similar to the indirect application model (at 414ff). Whilst he provides a persuasive account of the jurisprudence, it does not detract from my concern in this chapter, which is to explore the contours, limitations, and application of the expanding the state model, which has been expressly utilised in the United States in several cases.

[46] This has resulted in severe criticism leading Chemerinsky, 1985: 505 to claim it is incoherent and that it 'never could be rationally or consistently applied'.

[47] 334 US 1 (1948).

were discriminatory, courts were thus not entitled to enforce such agreements. Action by non-state actors essentially became public through reliance on state enforcement mechanisms.

This approach has parallels to the state duty to protect model though it is weaker by focusing less on positive action by the state to protect individuals from harms but rather on a negative duty not to participate in such harms.[48] It has some peculiarities: whilst ostensibly preserving a private space in which individuals may act contrary to the rights of others, it denies any ability to enforce these actions. As such, either it leads to a situation where individuals or communities will rely on self-help to enforce their wishes or it renders that space incapable of being given effect to. No doubt the court would not have sanctioned the former and desired the latter: the reality is that, in effect, the court's decision does, by default, limit what non-state actors may do. In deciding what is impermissible, this approach will also inevitably impose obligations flowing from fundamental rights that apply to state actors upon non-state actors in deciding what may or may not be enforced.[49]

The approach in *Shelley* has largely been abandoned.[50] An alternative expanding the state model was also developed by the Supreme Court, which, as we saw, widens the ambit of who is bound by fundamental rights through extending the conception of what constitutes the state. State action has been found where two circumstances are present: either there is significant state involvement or a private actor performs what is understood to be a 'public' function (the latter series of cases are the focus given they are more interesting for our purposes).[51] The willingness to extend the state has tracked a range of factors,[52] including the political nature of the Supreme Court: we see between the 1940s and 1960s – where liberal justices were in the ascendance – a willingness to apply fundamental rights to non-state actors to an extent when they exercised public functions or powers. With the conservative turn of the court in the 1970s, there has been less willingness to find state action in the activities

[48] See Quint, 1989: 281.

[49] That has been the basis upon which it has been subject to severe criticism in the United States on the ground that it may involve impermissible interventions in the private sphere: see, for instance, Wechsler, 1959: 29–30.

[50] It was the subject of much critical scholarly engagement: see Gardbaum, 2003: 414 and Peretti, 2010: 281 and the court has, largely, avoided engaging with it in subsequent cases – see, for instance, *Evans* v. *Abney* 396 US 435 (1970).

[51] Peretti, ibid: 276.

[52] Peretti, ibid: 288ff argues that the attitudes of the judges are only a partial explanation of the changes in approach.

of non-state actors.[53] For the purposes of this chapter, I will examine three cases from the liberal period exploring how the court expanded the realm of the state and the factors it considered in doing so.

4.3.1.1 *Marsh* v. *Alabama*:[54] Corporate Authority over a Town

This case (*Marsh*) dealt with a woman, a member of the Jehovah's witnesses, who sought to distribute leaflets in a town – called Chickasaw – which was owned by a company, namely, the Gulf Shipbuilding Corporation. The town was, for all intents and purposes, similar to other towns apart from the fact that the property thereof belonged to a company. The management of the company required an individual to receive a permit before they would be allowed to distribute pamphlets or solicit in any other way. The woman in question was told to stop by security guards yet persisted in her claim that she was entitled in terms of her constitutional rights to distribute her leaflets. She was then arrested, charged with trespassing and convicted.

The majority judgment (penned by Black J) reasoned that it was quite clear that a public municipality could not constitutionally prohibit an individual from distributing religious literature on grounds of trespassing – any such attempt would fail due to the rights of the individual to free expression and religious liberty (protected in the 1st Amendment). Moreover, the people of this particular town, the court held, could not have set up a local government to prohibit the distribution of religious literature. The question was therefore whether matters were different because a private company owned the property of the town?

Property interests were found not to settle the issue. The court held that 'the more an owner, for his own advantage, opens up his property for the use of the public in general, the more do his rights become circumscribed by the statutory and constitutional rights of those who use it'.[55] Thus, the owners of bridges, ferries, highways, and railways are more restricted in what they may do than a farmer who operates a farm for her own benefit. The reason for this distinction lies in the fact that the former constitute facilities and infrastructure designed to benefit the public and, thus, involve the exercise of a public function. In a similar vein, the court found there was little difference between these

[53] Ibid: 277 and 281–2 and see, for instance, *Morrison*, note 5 earlier.

[54] 326 US 501 (1946).

[55] Ibid: 506.

cases and circumstances where the state allowed a corporation to run a town. 'Whether a corporation or a municipality owns or possesses the town, the public in either case has an identical interest in the functioning of the community in such manner that the channels of communication remain free'.[56]

Chickasaw did not function differently from other towns and all the privately owned areas remained open and freely accessible to the public. Consequently, the managers of the corporation it was held are not permitted to violate the freedom of speech and religion of individuals; and the state may not enforce such actions. The people of Chickasaw have no lesser rights than others in the United States and have the same interests in speech and religion. The court also recognised the need to balance the property rights of the owners of the corporation against the freedom of speech and religion of the individuals in the town. The latter rights, the court held, occupy a preferred position, and the balance must tilt in favour of the liberty of the individual.

This case is extremely interesting to analyse in relation to its reasoning concerning the relationship between state and non-state action. The court was faced with two actions here: on the one hand, there was state action enforcing a criminal statute against trespassing. The second action was the decision by the company not to allow the distribution of leaflets and to activate law enforcement. The state action though depended upon the decision of the company not to allow the distribution of leaflets. The problem, of course, arose from the fact that, technically, fundamental rights do not apply to the company under the state action doctrine. The case, in some sense, foreshadows the approach adopted in *Shelley* (decided two years later) in asking whether the state was violating fundamental rights by enforcing a company decision that did so. Yet, in answering this question, the court clearly had to consider the effect of the company's decision on fundamental rights, and the function it was performing in the town. The reasoning of the majority focuses in several paragraphs on the similarity between the town of Chickasaw – owned by the private company – and other towns – controlled by a municipality. The function of managing and controlling a town is similar and the situation of individuals vis-à-vis the authorities was also found to be so. As such, the court recognises that private managers of towns – just like those individuals that own or manage bridges and highways – have obligations to respect the rights of individuals. Whilst the court does not classify these companies as

[56] Ibid: 507.

being part of the state, its reasoning exemplifies the expanding the state model. The justification for the extension of obligations to these corporations lies in the features they share with the state. What then are those features?

The focus of the court's reasoning is on factors that relate to the agent in question and, in particular, the extent to which it exercises a public function. That public nature is determined by the following dimensions: firstly, it is recognised that a corporation which owns a town has a tremendous capacity to restrict the rights of individuals subject to their power. A corollary of this dimension lies in the interests of members of this community to be able to express themselves freely and to exercise their religious liberty. The court insists that their rights are no less important than people living in other towns. Secondly, the court mentions the fact that these corporations deliberately keep the town open to members of the public and passers-by: this consideration suggests that, though, privately owned, in significant respects, these spaces mimic aspects of the public sphere – and, so, must be subject to similar obligations. Thirdly, the court considers the fact that the function of running a town is closely tied to the welfare and interests of the community as a whole. Lastly, the court also examines whether the fact that the property is owned by non-state actors provides them with the autonomy to make decisions concerning it which affect others.

The court also does expressly utilise the language of balancing but does not really provide any structure to doing so other than to assert a hierarchy of free expression/religious liberty rights over property rights. The dissent issued by Justice Reed, interestingly, balances in a different way. Strong emphasis is placed on the property rights of the corporations pursuant to their ownership of towns which are regarded as primary. A key dimension of his reasoning is the contention that the applicant could have distributed her leaflets near the corporate-owned town on a public highway rather than in it. As such, there were effectively less restrictive means available to her and, consequently, no need to restrict the right to private property of the company.[57]

The case thus illustrates the connection between the functions of a corporation that are 'state-like' in nature and their being bound by fundamental rights obligations. The authority the corporation exercised here appeared very similar to state control over a town, more generally, and went to the core of governmental activity. Ultimately, the court recognises in this case that the corporation is not part of the state but

[57] Ibid: 514.

what matters are the functions it exercises – which, significantly, extends the boundaries of the state action doctrine.

4.3.1.2 *Evans* v. *Newton*:[58] Corporate Authority over a Public Amenity

A US senator left a tract of land in his will to the City of Macon, Georgia, which he specified was to be utilised as a park for white people only. In his will, he stated that the park was to be managed by a board of seven white managers. The city kept the park segregated but eventually allowed African Americans to use it on the basis that it could not constitutionally enforce the racial segregation of a public amenity. Individual members of the board, as a result, sought to have the city removed from the board and new individual board members appointed. Several African American interveners in the case argued that these racial limitations were against the laws of the United States and asked the court to refuse to appoint alternative trustees. The city then resigned its place on the board. The courts in Georgia accepted its resignation and appointed other individual trustees, and this decision was then taken on appeal to the Supreme Court.

The majority of the Supreme Court (per Douglas J) recognised that the case concerned a clash between two principles: the first was the freedom to associate with whom one wishes, and the second was the right to equality and to be free from racial discrimination. The balance here the court held will be drawn differently between the public and private spheres. Yet, it held that 'what is "private action" and what is "state action" is not always easy to determine'.[59] After analysing prior cases such as *Marsh*, the court summarised the principle that emerges as follows: 'when private individuals or groups are endowed by the State with powers or functions governmental in nature, they become agencies or instrumentalities of the State and subject to its constitutional limitations'.[60] What then about the park?

To arrive at its conclusion, the court considered two important factors. Firstly, the court took into account how the municipality had been integrally involved in the maintenance and running of the park. The substitution of new trustees, it held, did not change the matter substantially. If the municipality is entwined in the control and upkeep of the park, then it will be subject to constitutional limitations.

[58] 382 US 296 (1966).
[59] Ibid: 299.
[60] Ibid.

Secondly, the court considered the nature of the service rendered, which it found to be 'municipal' in character.[61] It held that a park is less like a private club and more like 'a fire department or police station that traditionally serves the community'.[62] The character and purpose of a park, the court held, is thus fundamentally 'public' in nature and so subject to the obligations imposed by the 14th Amendment. A park, therefore, even if in private ownership, may not be operated on a segregated basis.

The court, interestingly, in this case takes a step beyond *Marsh,* where a corporation controlled an entire town. In contrast, in this case, we have a part of a city which is privately controlled and which is subject to rules issued by a private individual (who is now deceased). In considering whether such a segment of the city could be open only to one race, the court expressly acknowledges that the line between state and private action is not sharp. On the one hand, the two are often intertwined, which can implicate the state in private action. On the other hand, and perhaps the most significant holding of the case, is the recognition that a non-state actor may perform a public function which subjects it to the realm of rules applicable to the public sphere. What constitutes a public function is determined by whether it 'serves the community'.[63] Its being open to use by individuals and usually being regarded as being in the public domain are also referenced as an indication thereof. The majority of the court here goes beyond a simple focus on the identity of an actor – namely, is the entity part of the state or not? Instead, the question becomes, is the function over which it exercises authority 'public' or 'governmental' in nature? This opens the door to holding that non-state actors have binding obligations in relation to fundamental rights that usually only apply to the state.

The dissent by Harlan J objects to this holding based on the potentially wide application such a principle could have in the future:

> While this process of analogy might be spun out to reach privately owned orphanages, libraries, garbage collection companies, detective agencies, and a host of other functions commonly regarded as nongovernmental though paralleling fields of governmental activity, the example of schools is, I think sufficient to indicate the pervasive potentialities of this "public function" theory of state action.[64]

[61] Ibid: 301.
[62] Ibid: 302.
[63] Ibid: 302.
[64] Ibid: 322.

Harlan's argument highlights the potential reach of the expanding the state model but fails to be persuasive if there is no good reason to object to such a wide conception of the 'public' realm to which fundamental rights obligations apply. It does, perhaps, suggest the artificiality of attempting to expand the domain of actors who have fundamental rights obligations on the basis of their engaging in forms of 'state action' given the potentially wide group of non-state actors – and activities – that could include. The next case pushes the doctrine even further to apply to private property that 'looks' similar to public property and which, predominantly, relates to the business purposes of a corporation.

4.3.1.3 *Amalgamated Food Employees Union Local* v. *Logan Valley Plaza:*[65] Corporate Property as 'Public'?

This case ('*Logan*') concerned the right of union members to picket outside a private shopping centre – Logan Valley Plaza – in the large parking spaces which surrounded the centre and were owned by it. The centre was reached by a network of highways and quite isolated from other areas of the city of Altoona in Pennsylvania. A supermarket company – Weis Markets – was one of the two businesses in the shopping centre and employed only non-union staff. It posted a sign prohibiting trespassing or soliciting by anyone in the parking lots. Union members disregarded the notice and protested outside, claiming that Weis's employees were not receiving union wages and benefits. Weis, together with the shopping centre, applied for an interdict to stop the protest on grounds that it involved the union members trespassing on private property – which was granted in the lower courts.

On appeal, the majority of the Supreme Court began its reasoning by holding that 'peaceful picketing carried on in a location open generally to the public is … protected by the First Amendment'.[66] It then recognised that such picketing could not have been prohibited if the parking lot were owned by the municipality. The question thus arose whether the fact that it was privately owned changed matters. The court refers to *Marsh* and its summary of the holding in that matter expressly adopts the expanding the state model: it states that 'under some circumstances property that is privately owned may, at least for First Amendment purposes, be treated as though it were publicly held'.[67] The court found the similarities between

[65] 391 US 308 (1968).
[66] Ibid: 313.
[67] Ibid: 316.

the cases to be striking and that the shopping centre was the 'functional equivalent' of the business district of Chickasaw.[68] The court recognised that the powers of the corporation in *Marsh* were more extensive given it owned an entire town and provided services for it. Nevertheless, the focus of the case was on whether an individual could hand out leaflets in a commercial district which was similar to the issue in the present case. It found that the streets and sidewalks surrounding the shopping centre were the functional equivalent of streets and sidewalks in a normal town. Furthermore, '[t]the shopping center premises are open to the public to the same extent as the commercial center of a normal town'.[69]

Given these features, the court found that the state trespass laws could not be used by corporations to prevent pickets which did not significantly affect its ability to enjoy its property. The court did recognise, however, that a private owner may impose reasonable restrictions on the exercise of a right to protest on its premises. Indeed, the court accepts that these rights do confer a distinctive autonomy on owners 'to limit the use of that property by members of the public in a manner that would not be permissible were the property owned by a municipality'.[70] Nevertheless, the prohibitions it expressly mentions appear to track the kind of proportional restriction that the state may impose to ensure safety and the protection of the rights of others to use the sidewalks.

The court proceeds to consider the effect on the rights of protestors by requiring them to confine themselves to picketing outside the premises of the shopping centre. It finds that such a restriction would be very burdensome and, in effect, make it much harder for protestors to communicate their messages and place them at some personal risk. The protestors were also not interfering with the rights of shoppers or the ability of Weis to conduct its business. The only ground on which the companies assert that they can prohibit speech in this case was their naked title to the property which they claimed provided them with an absolute right to determine what occurs on their property. In deciding on this assertion, the court, interestingly, considers the growth and function of shopping centres in the United States at the time. It notes the movement of retail businesses out of city centres to shopping complexes in the suburbs. These changes make it much harder for protestors to criticise businesses: in city centres,

[68] Ibid: 318.
[69] Ibid: 319.
[70] Ibid.

they could utilise public space to do so. On the other hand, 'businesses situated in the suburbs could largely immunize themselves from similar criticism by creating a *cordon sanitaire* of parking lots around their stores'.[71] The court sees the tremendous threat this would pose to free speech rights. In reaching its conclusion that shopping centres be treated as a 'business block' for 1st Amendment purposes, the court repeats the principle in *Marsh* that the more an owner opens up his property to the public for his advantage, the more his rights become circumscribed by the statutory and constitutional rights of those who use it.

The court in *Marsh* dealt with a business which, relatively clearly, exercised a form of governmental authority through controlling a town. In *Logan*, the corporation only controlled its own (rather extensive) property and the surrounding parking lots. As such, it was not obvious that it exercised governmental authority over a traditionally 'public' domain. The majority of the court, nevertheless, found that features of its control over these areas were *sufficiently similar* to spaces that were regarded as 'public' in nature to warrant obligations on the shopping centre to allow picketing. The domain of the public – and consequent obligations – thus were extended to much more core areas of what would traditionally be considered private ownership.

This extension led to a deep disagreement between the majority and two dissenting judges as to what features were constitutive of the domain of the public. The reasoning of the majority focuses on the fact that the shopping centre functionally resembles the business area of a municipality: public highways exist around the mall, which lead into clearly-marked roads for vehicular traffic; there are sidewalks for car owners to walk to the mall; and the public has an unrestricted right of access to the mall. These are similar features to those that exist within a normal town.

Justice Black's dissent challenges these claims and contends that parking lots and pickup areas – that are closely associated with shopping activities – are fundamentally part of the private property rights of a corporation over which it has the autonomy to make decisions.[72] It is similar, in his view, to check-out counters or bagging areas and, so, he writes that 'I cannot conceive how such a pickup zone … could ever be considered dedicated to the public or to pickets'.[73] *Marsh* is distinguishable as there is little resemblance between a shopping centre and a town: '[t]here are no homes,

[71] Ibid: 325.
[72] Ibid: 328–330.
[73] Ibid: 328.

there is no sewage disposal plant, there is not even a post office on this private property . . . '.[74] For property to be treated as public, Black J reads *Marsh* to require it to have all the attributes of a town – having one of these attributes, such as a business district does, is not sufficient. White J, in his dissent, agrees with this reasoning and finds that the shopping centre is simply a collection of stores and individuals are invited to come there for the purpose of shopping – 'it is a place for shopping and not a place for picketing'.[75] Moreover, 'the "streets" of Logal Valley Plaza are not like public streets; they are not used as thoroughfares for general travel from point to point, for general parking, for meetings, or for Easter parades'.[76]

The disagreement between the judges suggests different conceptions concerning when a non-state actor is acting in a 'state-like' manner. The dissenting judges adopt a narrower conception of the domain of the state: only where a corporation exercises effectively *all* state functions over an area – such as the provision of public utilities – would it have the obligations of a state.[77] The majority, however, adopts a wider view, in which some functional similarities with the state – such as openness to the public and the provision of service-roads and sidewalks – are sufficient for the imposition of fundamental rights obligations. The dispute – and difficulty of adjudicating clearly between these views – highlights the complexity of drawing an exact boundary between the domain of the public and private and supports the existence of a continuum between them.

The disagreement about the nature of these spaces also, importantly, leads to different normative evaluations.[78] The dissenting judgments through classifying the parking lots as private place the normative priority on the property rights of the corporations and then consider whether there is a justification to interfere with those entitlements – ultimately, finding none to be present. The majority, on the other hand, starts its judgment with the 1st Amendment rights of those wishing to picket. It also recognises the severity of the restrictions on those rights and how they render the pickets virtually meaningless if individuals would be confined to public spaces around the shopping centres. The private property rights of the

[74] Ibid: 331.
[75] Ibid: 338.
[76] Ibid: 340.
[77] This view was largely adopted by the court in *Lloyd Corp* v. *Tanner* 407 US 551 (1972) at 569.
[78] See Harvard Law Review, 2010: 1310–11, which makes this point in relation to the divergence between the case law in California (which, largely, follows the majority in *Logan*) and the Supreme Court's express reversal of its approach to follow the *Logan* minority in *Hudgens* v. *National Labour Relations Board* 424 US 507 (1976).

corporations are considered but in the context of whether they can justify the serious limitations placed on the freedom to picket. The majority of the court thus appears to engage in a rudimentary balancing process: its conception of the parking lots as more 'public' in nature and akin to spaces over which the state exercises authority appears to tip the balance – and normative priority of their rights – in favour of the protestors.

The dissenting judges, in my view, have a point that parking lot spaces in shopping centre districts are not equivalent to the control over a town such as in *Marsh*.[79] The majority appears forced by the strictures of the state action doctrine into a rather tenuous analogy between control over a town and a parking lot. Its reasoning is most persuasive if understood to focus on the features of the situation and the competing rights at stake: the majority can be read to preserve the power and importance of the 1st Amendment rights of the protestors in the face of the significant financial power of corporations to immunise themselves from criticism and restrict those very rights. The focus on the 'publicity' or otherwise of the parking lots thus has an aura of artificiality about it and could easily have led to the wrong result. The relevant normative considerations in this case thus should have been the focus rather than whether the parking lot was sufficiently 'state-like' or 'private', a framing forced on the court by a prior commitment to a restrictive state action doctrine.

4.3.2 Germany

Germany, as we saw in Chapter 3, is able to apply the fundamental rights in its bill of rights to non-state actors through the indirect application model. Yet, at times, the courts have appeared to favour a more direct approach without departing from their prior doctrine. To do so, therefore, they have sought to expand the notion of what constitutes the state. There is a clear trend, in the decisions of the German Constitutional Court, thus towards imposing direct obligations upon non-state parties that act in a 'state-like' manner.[80] Once again, understanding in what way the court determines what it is to operate in such a manner is instructive.

[79] This is part of the grounds on which the majority holding was expressly overruled in *Hudgens* ibid.

[80] See Barczak, 2017: 113–114, who see the indirect application model as having been rendered partially obsolete by the *Fraport* and *Bierdosen* decisions.

4.3.2.1 *Fraport:*[81] Blurring the Boundaries between the Public and Private

This case dealt with an individual who together with five other activists distributed leaflets at Frankfurt airport protesting against deportations. She was stopped from doing so by employees of the company which owned the airport – Fraport. She was then given a notice by Fraport that threatened her with criminal proceedings should she ever attempt to protest or distribute leaflets again at the airport. As a result, she brought an action seeking to overturn the ban on her ability to protest freely at the airport rooted in her fundamental rights to freedom of expression[82] and freedom of assembly.[83] After being unsuccessful in the lower courts, she brought a constitutional complaint against their decisions before the Constitutional Court.

The court first addressed the question of whether Fraport was bound directly by the bill of rights. To do so, it needed to determine whether it was a public entity – in which case it would be subject to direct application – or a private entity – where the indirect application model would be utilised. In deciding this question, the court focused on the ownership of Fraport and found that fundamental rights could bind corporations directly not only where they are wholly publicly owned but also where they are jointly owned by private shareholders and the state, provided that the state had a 'controlling influence'.[84] Such an influence would generally be present when a majority of shares were owned by a public entity. At the time of this airport 'ban', 70 per cent of Fraport's shares were owned by the Federal Government, the State of Hesse, and the City of Frankfurt, respectively. The Federal Government later sold its shares, at which point 52 per cent of the shares were owned by the other two public entities. Consequently, the court found that public entities had a 'controlling influence' on Fraport and the bill of rights applied directly to the dispute.

Following the expanding the state model, the court, on the one hand, emphasises that the state is distinct from non-state bodies in that it 'assumes its responsibilities in a fiduciary capacity on behalf of the citizens and is accountable to them'.[85] In relation to private parties, it holds that each party has its own sphere of autonomy and rights which need to be balanced against one another. On the other hand, the court also, in certain

[81] BVerfGE 128, 226.
[82] Article 5.1 of the German Basic Law.
[83] Article 8.1 of the German Basic Law.
[84] BVerfGE 128, 226: 246.
[85] Ibid: 245.

statements, minimises the difference between these types of entity at least when the non-state body acts in a 'state-like' manner. It writes:

> Conversely, this does not, however, exclude the possibility of private persons being burdened similarly or to exactly the same degree through the indirect application of the fundamental rights, irrespective of their own fundamental rights, in particular, if they come to acquire in practice comparable positions as duty holders or guarantors as the state.[86]

The court then goes on to find a violation of the protesters' freedom of assembly rights. It holds that the right does not envisage protests being allowed at any location: but, for the right to be meaningfully exercised, assemblies must be capable of being held in spaces open to the general public.[87] Whilst such a right was traditionally exercised in the public street, there are spaces today which have taken on an equivalent function, such as shopping centres and malls.[88] The court considers the idea of a 'public forum' to be helpful, which it defines as being 'characterised by the fact that it can be used to pursue a variety of different activities and concerns leading to the development of a varied and open communications network'.[89] Such mixed-use spaces are inherently 'public' and cannot exclude political activity. Since the airport in question had large areas which 'are places of general traffic for communicative purposes'[90] (including large shopping areas), it, in principle, also was a space in which protest had to be allowed.[91] The court does recognise that Fraport may restrict the exercise of this right to protest for legitimate purposes relating to the public good – which, in relation to an airport, would primarily relate to the security of passengers and the functioning of airport operations.[92] These purposes have significant weight, the court holds, but nevertheless any restrictions on the right to protest must also be suitable, necessary, and proportionate – i.e. consistent with the proportionality test. Fraport could, legitimately, have placed limits on the number of protestors in an airport or confined them to a specific area[93] – its measures though had to be narrowly tailored to meet specific public purposes such as ensuring the security of air travellers or the functioning

[86] Ibid: 248.
[87] Ibid: 251.
[88] Ibid: 252.
[89] Ibid: 253.
[90] Ibid: 254.
[91] Ibid.
[92] Ibid: 259.
[93] Ibid: 261 and 262.

of baggage collection. The total nature of the ban and existence of less restrictive means led the court to the conclusion that the ban was disproportionate and, consequently, unconstitutional.[94]

The court was confronted in the *Fraport* case with a question concerning an entity and a space which did not neatly conform to the public–private divide. Given the fact that the direct application of constitutional rights applies in German constitutional law only to public entities, the court was forced to categorise on which side of the divide Fraport sat. The majority ultimately focuses on whether public entities have a majority stake in a company to determine whether it is public and subject to the direct application of fundamental rights. The dissenting judgment (per Schluckebier J), interestingly, challenges the sufficiency of this reasoning and, in particular, whether two distinct minority governmental shareholders whose share collectively adds up to 52 per cent can render such a company 'public'.[95] He recognises that ownership of shares in companies can be parcelled in different ways and contends that, in order for the interest of the state to be aggregated in this way, there needs to be some clear coordination between the different public bodies.[96] If that is not the case, then there is no obvious majority of public bodies given the interests of these bodies may diverge. This reasoning points to the complexity of ownership in modern companies and that this dimension may, therefore, not offer a clear criterion for determining the 'public' or 'private' nature of an entity. We can also add to these difficulties the separation of ownership and control in modern companies, which would render it problematic to infer control automatically from who owns the shares.[97] The composition of shareholders of mixed public–private company may thus be diffuse and their ability to influence the entity vary with a range of factors.

It is perhaps for this reason that the majority of the court is clearly uncomfortable with utilising such a categorisation as the basis for determining the obligations of an entity. It thus appears to water down the effects of any such categorisation in statements such as the following: '[d]epending on the content of the guarantee and the circumstances of the case, the indirect binding force of the fundamental rights on private persons may instead come closer to or even be the same as the binding force of the fundamental rights on the state'.[98] The court appears to suggest

[94] Ibid: 263.
[95] Ibid: 271.
[96] Ibid: 270.
[97] See also Kater, 2016: 68.
[98] BVerfGE 128, 226: 249.

here that what matters are the normative factors which condition obligations rather than whether the entity is classified as 'public' or 'private'.

In outlining which factors count, the court engages closely with the necessary conditions for the exercise of a right to protest effectively from the perspective of a rights-holder – which, inevitably, it finds must involve open access to the public sphere. This leads the majority to engage with the question of when a space is to be regarded as 'public' or 'private'. In determining this question, of clear importance is the 'communicative' function of open spaces, which can be gleaned from whether they are open to the public and can be utilised for multiple purposes. That may be so even if they are privately owned – and the court recognises the growth in spaces such as shopping centres which are 'public' in nature but privately owned. In this regard, the court adopts similar positions to those of the US Supreme Court discussed earlier.[99] The majority recognises the mixed uses of airports – particularly those that include large shopping centres – and contends they are essentially 'public' spaces akin to public streets. The dissent challenges this view of airports and argues that the purpose of an airport is primarily to check-in passengers and ensure they can depart and arrive efficiently – shopping is really a secondary function.[100] The disagreement highlights, once again, the difficulty of attaining a sharp categorisation of a mixed-use space as 'public' or 'private' or serving one function alone. It does though indicate that the 'function' of an entity or space is a crucial dimension in determining its obligations.

Indeed, in this regard, if a space is 'private', then the court recognises the significance of the 'autonomy' of the non-state actor in deciding on restrictions that apply over areas where they are in control: though not unlimited, greater weight will be accorded to their decisions in such spaces. Where a space is 'public' in nature, there may still be permissible restrictions but they cannot be justified based on the autonomy of the decision-maker to generate rules governing the spaces they control. Ultimately, in relation to both types of spaces, a form of balancing is required and the majority recognises the value of the proportionality test in assessing the ban on protests by Fraport – even in circumstances of an entity with complex shareholding exercising control over a mixed-use space that is not easily classified. Once again, the line between 'public' and 'private' was not sharp in the proportionality assessment as the court found, effectively, that Fraport's ability to regulate its property overlapped with the general principles for

[99] See Schaefer, 2012: 268.
[100] BVerfGE 128, 226: 273.

determining the constitutional limits on assemblies applicable to the state more generally.[101]

The approach adopted in *Fraport* has become important in later jurisprudence in continuing the erosion of the strict separation between the realm of the public and private, and, consequently, the realm of direct and indirect application. The *Bierdosen*[102] case saw the application of similar principles to a gathering in a square owned by a private corporation that was at the centre of the city of Passau. In a preliminary injunction, the Constitutional Court overturned a ban placed by the corporation on the gathering. Here, the court, giving expression to the expanding the state model, recognised that this was a private corporation yet

> [d]epending on the content of the guarantee and the circumstances of the case, the indirect binding force of the fundamental rights on private persons may come closer to or even be the same as the binding force of the fundamental rights on the state. This is relevant to the protection of communications, in particular when private enterprises themselves take over the provision of public communications and thus assume functions which were previously de facto only allocated to the state.[103]

Though, unlike *Fraport*, it was evident in this case that the court was dealing with a private entity, the crucial question concerned the function the entity exercised in the city and its capacity to impact on the fundamental rights of individuals. The line between public and private functions was blurred and so the private entity was subject to stronger obligations in relation to the fundamental right of assembly. The most recent case of interest in relation to this model highlights another critical factor in determining the 'public' nature of the function, namely, the power relations between the parties.

4.3.2.2 *Stadium Ban*:[104] The Relevance of Power

This case dealt with a football fan of Bayern Munich who had been involved in hurling verbal abuse at and engaging in physical attacks on fans from a rival club. As a result, the fan was banned by the German football associations from entering any stadium in the country for around two years, exercising their powers to enforce 'house rules'. Even though the criminal investigation against the fan was later dropped, the

[101] Ibid: 258.
[102] Neue Juristische Wochenschrift (NJW) 2015: 2485.
[103] Ibid: 2486.
[104] BVerfGE 148, 267.

football clubs kept in place the ban and he was expelled from his membership in Bayern Munich. The complainant sought to have the stadium ban on him declared unlawful.

The Constitutional Court used the decision to help clarify the application of fundamental rights in the private sphere. It reiterated its support for the indirect application model that was discussed in Chapter 3 and stated that in this sphere, it needed to achieve a balance between the freedom of various rights-holders.[105] In doing so, the court stated that '[d]ecisive factors may include the inevitable consequences resulting from certain situations, the disparity between opposing parties, the importance attached to certain services in society, or the social position of power held by one of the parties'.[106] The court then proceeded to look at the specific rights implicated in this case and held that individuals cannot, generally, limit the property rights of another based on the general right to liberty contained in article 2(1) of the Constitution. Nevertheless, 'where a particular heavy burden is imposed' and 'where one contracting party is at a structural disadvantage', such freedom rights could be applied to private relations.[107] A similar point is made in relation to equality in that this right does not generally limit how individuals may use their property or the contracts they may enter into. Nevertheless, in specific circumstances such as the present case, these rights do apply. The court states:

> The indirect horizontal effect of the requirement of equal treatment comes into play here because the stadium ban imposes – based on the right to enforce house rules – a one-sided exclusion from events, which the organisers, of their own volition, had opened up to a large audience without distinguishing between individual persons, and this ban has a considerable impact on the ability of the persons concerned to participate in social life.[108]

Through organising events such as this, the football associations assume a special responsibility under constitutional law which resulted from their right to enforce house rules. The court states that similar grounds for such a responsibility would be where a non-state actor has a monopoly or particular structural advantage.[109] These special responsibilities lead to heightened obligations. Stadium bans, the court holds,

[105] Ibid: 280, 281.
[106] Ibid: 281.
[107] Ibid: 282.
[108] Ibid: 283, 284.
[109] Ibid: 284.

must not be arbitrarily applied but be based on particular factual reasons. These could include the fact that there is a reasonable suspicion that individuals would cause a disturbance. This requirement, in turn, entails certain procedural obligations: those imposing a ban have a duty to investigate the facts of the case which would generally entail granting an individual a hearing. The football associations would also need to provide reasons for their decisions. The court recognises that such procedural obligations would not generally apply in relations between private persons. They arise in this case given that decisions concerning the enforcement of house rules have a 'factually punitive effect': as a result, individuals must be given the opportunity to address the allegations against them.[110] The court found that, in the circumstances of this case, the factual reasons for the imposition of a stadium ban had been justified and refused to overturn it.

On its face, the court claims to be applying the indirect application model to the obligations of a non-state entity – the football associations – towards a specific individual. Yet, this case clearly emphasises that, in deciding on the binding nature of fundamental rights obligations on non-state entities, the court will consider a range of factors relating to the nature of the function exercised by the entity concerned as well as its capacity to impact on fundamental rights. In considering the football associations' decision, the court is persuaded that the relevant function was its ability to impose punitive measures – which is usually the preserve of the state. The football associations, therefore, in some sense, came to exercise 'public power'. That public power is indicated largely by the asymmetrical relations that exist between a particular non-state actor – in this case, the football associations – and others. The court, interestingly, recognises such a punitive capacity as similar, in other contexts, to having a monopoly or other structural advantage. Other factors that are highlighted as being of relevance concern the openness of the activity to the general public as well as the capacity to impact on an individual's ability to participate in social life. Here, the court clearly is concerned with impact of the exercise of the power of a non-state entity on beneficiaries of rights.

With powers similar to those of the state, similar obligations follow.[111] The court, again, in this judgment, accepts that the 'autonomy' of non-state actors must be considered when determining their obligations.

[110] Ibid: 286.

[111] Hoexter, 2018: 159–163 demonstrates a similar trajectory in South Africa where at least sporting regulatory bodies have been recognised to exercise public rather than private power with the consequence that administrative law duties apply to them.

Nevertheless, in circumstances where they exercise functions that are state-like, heightened obligations – such as duties to hear an aggrieved party – will apply (even though they are not generally applicable to such entities). Those obligations, nevertheless, do not automatically assist the football fan: rather, the legitimate interests of the football clubs must also be considered. They do have an interest in preserving the safety of football matches and in ensuring that they are not disrupted. The court expressly accepts the need to balance competing rights in its reasoning.[112] How then does it do so? The court recognises, essentially, that not any arbitrary exercise of power on the part of the stadium owners will be acceptable: that power must relate to the threat posed and, hence, there is a need for each individual set of circumstances to be treated on its own merits. Adequate information needs to be garnered and decisions need to be reasoned. The court effectively imposes obligations consistent with the outcomes of a proportionality test on these non-state actors: the measures they take must still be connected to the reasons for the exercise of their powers (suitability), not be overly intrusive (necessity) and be proportional. Given the particular powers these non-state actors have, the enquiry determining their fundamental rights obligations thus comes to mirror the tests applicable in determining state obligations.

4.3.3 South Africa

As we saw in Chapter 3, and will analyse in more depth in the next chapter, the South African Constitution includes the possibility of the direct horizontal effect of fundamental rights. Yet, we saw too in Chapter 3 how courts have been rather reluctant to apply constitutional rights directly when developing the private law and have employed modes of reasoning that resemble the indirect application model. Despite the ability to apply fundamental rights beyond the realm of the state, the courts have also, at times, utilised an expanding the state model to include non-state actors within the broad category of the state and determine their fundamental rights obligations accordingly.[113] This approach has been facilitated by a rather expansive definition of an 'organ of state' within the South African Constitution.[114] Section 239(b) includes in this designation

112 BVerfGE 148, 267: 285.

113 Woolman, 2006: 31–106 predicted this development. For a critical assessment, see Finn, 2015a.

114 See Mdumbe, 2005 for an examination of the various dimensions thereof.

functionaries or institutions exercising a public power or function in terms of the Constitution or legislation.[115] As Woolman writes, '[t]hese institutions and individuals need not be an 'intrinsic part' of what we commonly or historically considered to be the 'government''.[116] The two cases discussed in the following section, interestingly, are helpful in highlighting the assumption of public functions that go beyond the spatial dimension, which is pronounced in the US and German examples discussed earlier.

4.3.3.1 *AllPay*:[117] Blurring the Entity/Function Distinction

In the *AllPay* case, the South African Social Security Agency (SASSA) issued a tender for a corporation to take over the payment of social grants across the country. These grants are relied upon by over fifteen million people in South Africa, many of whom are extremely vulnerable, in order to subsist. Cash Paymaster Services (CPS) was awarded the grant and began to deliver the services. A rival and unsuccessful tenderer, AllPay Consolidated Holdings (AllPay), challenged the tender award based on various irregularities in the tender process. The Constitutional Court found that these irregularities rendered the award of the tender to CPS invalid.[118] This decision entailed that there was no valid agreement between SASSA and CPS in terms of which CPS could continue paying social grants to the beneficiaries. If CPS's services were to have been terminated, however, millions of people could have been placed at risk of not receiving their social grants. The court ultimately decided that, despite the invalidity of the tender process and subsequent agreement, CPS was under an obligation to continue to provide the payment services it offered.

The court went on to reason that whilst CPS was a private company and not under the control of SASSA, 'the function that it performs – the country-wide administration of the payment of social grants – is fundamentally public in nature'.[119] This function was derived from the constitutional right to social assistance together with legislation imposing upon SASSA the

115 See Hoexter, 2018: 151–154 for an overview of the implications of being classified an organ of state.

116 Woolman, 2006: 31–105. See also Dafel, 2015: 79–81.

117 There were two judgments in this case. See *AllPay Consolidated. Investment Holdings* v. *Chief Executive Officer of the South African Social Security Agency* [2013] ZACC 42 (dealing with validity of the tender itself); and *AllPay Consolidated. Investment Holdings* v. *Chief Executive Officer of the South African Social Security Agency* [2014] ZACC 12 (dealing with the appropriate remedy). The focus will be on the latter case and references are to it.

118 Ibid: para 1.

119 Ibid: para 52.

obligation to pay social grants. That legislation also allowed for the outsourcing of the actual implementation of such an obligation to a private body. In undertaking to provide these services, CPS essentially performed a role as the 'gatekeeper of the right to social security'[120] and 'is not only the face, but also the operational arm'[121] of the government. As such, for purposes of the contract, it effectively became an organ of state. That meant it had constitutional – and not simply contractual – obligations.[122] The court writes that '[w]hen Cash Paymaster concluded the contract for the rendering of public services, it too became accountable to the people of South Africa in relation to the public power it acquired and the public function it performs'.[123] These constitutional functions it had assumed reduced the relevance of CPS's private autonomy. Nevertheless, the court went on to say that '[t]his does not mean that its entire commercial operation suddenly becomes open to public scrutiny. But the commercial part dependent on, or derived from, the performance of public functions is subject to public scrutiny, both in its operational and financial aspects'.[124]

What then did this mean practically? The court outlined three main implications of its holding: firstly, given CPS's obligations were constitutional and not simply contractual, it could not simply walk away from the provision of the payment services as it would be allowed to do if this were simply a private matter. Secondly, it is not required to make a loss in terms of the functions it performs but neither could it profit from an unlawful contract.[125] Lastly, its assumption of public power means that it is required to disclose financial information concerning the contract and it may be held publicly accountable in this regard.[126]

The Constitutional Court was faced in this case with a corporation whose activities had a significant impact upon the lives of millions. The fact that it performed a public function – even in the absence of a valid contract – was a crucial basis for imposing 'state-like' obligations upon this company. Central to this holding must be an understanding then of what constitutes a public function. Three main criteria can be discerned from the judgment. The first involves whether the functions flow directly from the

[120] Ibid: para 55.
[121] Ibid.
[122] Ibid: 56.
[123] Ibid: para 59.
[124] Ibid.
[125] This dimension was brought out in a subsequent case *Black Sash Trust* v. *Minister of Social Development* [2017] ZACC 8.
[126] *Allpay*: 66–67.

Constitution and relate to a fundamental right: in this case, CPS performed activities centrally connected to section 27(1)(c) of the Constitution.[127] The second concerns whether the functions in question flow from legislation – in this case, it was the Social Assistance Act. In relation to both the first and second 'source-based' criteria, the court appears to reason that these obligations will usually be the preserve of the state. Where, however, they are assumed by a non-state entity, they are effectively being delegated these powers by the state.[128] As such, they remain 'public' functions which attract 'state-like' obligations. The court does appear, however, also to suggest a substantive criterion that involves considering whether a non-state actor has the capacity significantly to affect an individual's access to basic interests or entitlements – it recognises that CPS 'effectively controls beneficiaries' access to social assistance'[129] and that 'grant beneficiaries would have become increasingly dependent on Cash Paymaster fulfilling its constitutional obligations'.[130] The latter criterion again seems to mirror the dimension of vulnerability to the exercise of asymmetrical power that we saw emerge from the German cases. Unlike the US and German cases, however, the *AllPay* case does not concern a function relating to control over a specific space such as an airport, park, shopping centre, or football stadium: it is rather control over access to critical resources that matters.

The reasoning in this case, confusingly, at times seems to elide the boundary between the nature of the entity and the functions that it exercises. On the one hand, the court states that CPS is an organ of state for purposes of the impugned contract.[131] The very nature of the entity is affected by the function it performs. The performance of a public function reduces significantly the importance of the normative consideration of respect for its private autonomy[132] and its ability, for instance, to evade public scrutiny. Yet, it is hard to see how an entity which is formed as a private corporation becomes entirely public simply through taking on public obligations. This leads the court to step back from the full implications of its holding, which would, logically, impose on CPS all the obligations of the state – effectively nationalising the entity. Instead, the

127 See Finn, 2015b: 265–266.

128 The court has held in *AAA Investments* v. *Micro Finance Regulatory Council* [2006] ZACC 9 at para 40 that the government 'cannot be released from its human rights and rule of law obligations simply because it employs the strategy of delegating its functions to another entity'.

129 *AllPay*: para 55.

130 Ibid: 66.

131 Ibid: 52.

132 Ibid: 66.

court states that '[t]his does not mean that its entirely commercial operation suddenly becomes open to public scrutiny'[133] – only that part related to its public functions does. Furthermore, it is not required to make a loss from the services it provides. Performing a public function thus does not completely eliminate the fact that this remains a non-state entity. The performance of a particular *function* is thus not a complete guide to the nature of an *entity*: in *AllPay*, we essentially had a situation in which the lines between the 'public' and the 'private' became blurred.[134] Importantly, the case thus demonstrates that determining the substantive content of fundamental rights obligations requires referencing the relevant normative factors flowing from both these dimensions – such as the capacity to affect significant interests, and the weight of autonomy interests – and is not solved simply by a classification as 'public' or 'private'.

4.3.3.2 *AMCU*:[135] Asymmetry Revisited

A further scenario where non-state entities were alleged to be performing public functions came before the South African Constitutional Court in the *AMCU* case, which dealt with an important question of labour law. The case concerned whether workers belonging to a minority trade union (AMCU) retained the right to strike when unions representing a majority of workers had reached an agreement with the employers (in this case an association of mines) which prohibited strike action. The prevailing statute – the Labour Relations Act – bound the workers of the minority union to the collective agreement reached by the unions representing the majority of workers. AMCU challenged the constitutionality of these provisions on several grounds. The relevant discussion in the judgment for this chapter concerns whether the extension of a collective agreement to workers who had not agreed to it involved an exercise of public power by non-state actors (the mines). The legislation did not provide expressly for any constraints on the exercise of this power and, hence, AMCU claimed that it allowed for this power to be exercised in a potentially arbitrary manner which violated the foundational constitutional principle that all exercises of public power must be rational in order to be lawful. The possibility for the judicial review of such agreements, the

[133] Ibid: 69.

[134] Finn, 2015a: 645–46 exposes some of the confusion in the judgment surrounding when CPS 'is bound by its contract, and when instead by virtue of being an organ of state' (645).

[135] *Association of Mineworkers and Construction Union* v. *Chamber of Mines South Africa* [2017] ZACC 3 ('*AMCU*').

court found, offered sufficient protection that any such agreements would be rational – and, hence, the schema established by the legislation was found to be constitutional.

For our purposes, of interest is the court's discussion of how to determine what constitutes an exercise of 'public' power. The court started by recognising that there was 'no impenetrable wall between the public and the private'.[136] Non-state actors could exercise public power within the South African constitutional schema. Determining whether public power is exercised, is really a function of its 'nature': '[t]he question is not so much, who exercises the power, nor even, where does the power come from: but what does the power look and feel like? What does it do?'[137] In elaborating upon this enquiry, the court adopts a multi-factoral approach which requires consideration of the source of the power, its nature, its subject matter, and whether it involves the exercise of a public duty.[138] It references prior case law to include further factors such as whether there was a relationship of coercion or power that an actor has in its capacity as a public institution; the impact of a decision on the public; whether there is a need for the decision to be exercised in the public interest; whether a decision being made was coercive in effect; and whether the decision emerges from a clear legislative framework.[139]

These factors were then applied to the circumstances of the case with the court finding that the extension of a collective agreement to non-parties was an exercise of public power. The following factors pointed in this direction: this extension has a coercive effect on non-parties without their consent across an entire industry; it has significant implications for members of the public; it is rooted in a clear legislative framework; and the rationale for the extension is the goal of improving the conditions of workers through strengthening collective bargaining processes. This conclusion in turn had the consequence that there was an obligation on the non-state actors that exercised this power to comply with the principle of legality and not exercise their authority in a manner that was arbitrary or capricious.

This judgment, interestingly, does not concern the execution by non-state actors of state functions such as in *AllPay*. Instead, it addresses a power conferred on employers specifically that regulates the relationships between the mining companies, the different unions in the sector, and the underlying employees. The application of the expanding the state model is

136 Ibid: para 68.
137 Ibid: para 74.
138 Ibid.
139 Ibid: paras 75 and 77 quoting prior judgments.

thus less obvious and leads the court expressly to recognise that a non-state *entity* may, nevertheless, exercise a public *function*.[140] Even then, the court essentially recognises that there is a continuum between the exercise of public and private power.[141] That recognition, perhaps, renders the judgment all the more puzzling in still attempting such a categorisation, particularly given the recognition in South Africa that non-state actors may, nevertheless, have binding fundamental rights obligations.[142]

The factors identified by the court in determining what constitutes a public power vary in their usefulness. Some appear to be circular – it seems to beg the question to determine what is a public power by whether 'it involves the exercise of a public duty'[143] or a 'need for the decision to be exercised in the public interest'.[144] Nevertheless, there are a few substantive criteria which overlap substantially with those already identified in the US and German cases. In particular, of interest are three considerations: firstly, there is the recognition that the impact of a decision on the public matters – this concerns both the capacity of non-state actors and their potential to affect the interests of beneficiaries of rights. Secondly, there is the emphasis on the source of any power and whether it is rooted in a legislative framework. Lastly, the court identified the importance of considering the power relationships between the parties and the degree to which non-state actors could enforce their will upon other individuals. The court recognised the market dominance of the chamber of mines and how it employed most of the workers in the industry. To grant them the power to impose an agreement on those who did not consent to it involved a significant exercise of control over them which could potentially become oppressive. This is perhaps why the court accepted the need for the principles of legality to apply and judicial review to be possible of any such collective agreements. The case can, in some ways, be seen to be a parallel to the *Stadium Ban* case in Germany which also saw non-state entities exercising coercive powers in relation to individuals. The findings are also similar – that various procedural safeguards usually only applicable to the state are extended to the realm of non-state actors.

[140] The express recognition of this point takes place at ibid: para 82.
[141] Ibid: paras 68 and 76.
[142] The court also recognises this at ibid: para 69. See Finn, 2015b: 271.
[143] *AMCU*: para 74.
[144] Ibid: para 75 quoting Justice Langa.

4.4 Conclusion

The expanding the state model seeks to preserve the idea that fundamental rights obligations only apply to the relationship between the state and individuals. It attempts to address at least some of the impacts non-state actors have upon fundamental rights by including them within the domain of the state. The central question for this model thus is to determine what forms part of the 'state' or realm of the 'public'. Usually, as we have seen, courts recognise in these cases that they are not dealing with traditional parts of the state and so the lines cannot be drawn sharply between these spheres. That very lack of distinctness of the boundaries between the two domains highlights one of the major drawbacks of the approach, which still insists on classifying an entity or function as 'public' as a precondition for having fundamental rights obligations. Given that this is required, however, then leads us to analyse what courts consider to be characteristic of the 'public' as opposed to 'private' spheres. Their reasoning in this regard provides us with insights into their understanding of the determinants for possessing fundamental rights obligations and, often, what is relevant to articulating the substantive content thereof.

Given that this model focuses on the agent who impacts upon fundamental rights, the emphasis is unsurprisingly on 'agent-relative' factors. We see an important tension lies in some of the jurisprudence between whether to focus on the nature of the *entity* itself or the *functions* it exercises. Whilst, in some cases, the ownership or control of the entity remains important, the trend is to focus on the 'public' or 'private' functions that it exercises. In determining what constitutes a public function, the cases analysed referred to *source-based* factors – such as whether the non-state actor exercises a function delegated from the state – but also a number of *substantive* characteristics thereof. These include, importantly, the capacity to impact upon the fundamental rights of individuals as well as the extent to which there is an asymmetrical power relationship at play. At this point, courts often also consider beneficiary-orientated factors such as the interests protected by the right and the vulnerability of rights-holders to violations by the agent given the functions it exercises.

Once a court has determined that an entity exercises a 'state-like' function, it usually follows that it has some fundamental rights obligations. However, many of the judgments analysed also usually include a recognition that non-state entities are not wholly incorporated within the realm of the state and thus are not subject to *all* its obligations. When supporting this conclusion, courts often accept that such non-state actors retain important autonomy interests of their own that cannot be subsumed fully within the realm of the public. Such an acknowledgment does, at times, lead courts to engage in a balancing process and, in some instances, expressly to invoke the proportionality test. One of the downsides of this model though remains its focus on the classification of an entity or function as 'public' or 'private', which is supposed automatically to result in certain conclusions regarding obligations – as a consequence, the balancing of interests is often not conducted explicitly or performed in a relatively cursory manner.

It is already possible to note a convergence between the factors identified in Chapters 2 and 3 for determining the substantive content of the obligations of non-state actors and those analysed in this chapter. Courts, despite the doctrinal differences they employ, ultimately appear to recognise that what conditions the imposition of obligations on non-state actors and the substantive content thereof are a range of specific normative factors. The next chapter turns to consider jurisprudential models in both international and domestic law that allow for the direct application of fundamental rights to non-state actors – and, particularly, corporations.

5

The Direct Obligations Model

5.1 Introduction

In Chapters 2–4, we have engaged with approaches at both the international and national levels that consider fundamental rights as, in some sense, essentially tied to the state. All these approaches thus attempt to avoid recognising direct obligations of non-state actors flowing from fundamental rights; yet, at the same time, they acknowledge the power of non-state actors, at least in certain circumstances, to impact significantly on fundamental rights. Various legal 'models' have thus been developed to offer protection for individuals against these harms.

This chapter is fundamentally different in that it examines an approach which recognises that non-state actors themselves – and corporations, in particular – have obligations in relation to fundamental rights. After briefly outlining the contours of this model and its justification (which has to an extent already been covered in Chapter 2), I consider one important theoretical challenge which has not been dealt with in prior chapters – namely, whether recognising the direct obligations of non-state actors entails that they can claim the protection of fundamental rights. Once the notion of direct obligations of non-state actors is accepted, however, the next challenge that is raised is how to determine their substantive content.

The second half of this chapter will first consider two approaches that have emerged at the international level concerning the obligations of corporations. The 'sphere of influence' model contains a large degree of vagueness and to be useful requires understanding the factors that are involved in determining the sphere of influence of a corporation. Once this is done, this approach becomes a form of multi-factoral approach which is defended in detail in Chapter 6. The 'due diligence' approach adopted in the United Nations Guiding Principles on Business and Human Rights ('UNGPs') is also an instance of a direct approach and has sought to provide practical guidance about what corporations must do to meet their 'responsibility to respect'. Yet, it fails to provide an answer to the substantive content of corporate obligations and actually is parasitic upon developing an approach in this regard.

The third part of this chapter focuses on certain facets of how the direct obligations model is operationalised in two domestic jurisdictions where it has been accepted – South Africa and Colombia. In this qualitative analysis of some of the case law, I attempt to understand the principles that have been utilised by these courts to determine the substantive content of the obligations of non-state actors – and corporations in particular – flowing from fundamental rights. Though there is a lack of articulation of a clear analytical framework for finally determining those obligations, what emerges are a range of relevant normative considerations which can form the building blocks of a more systematic approach developed in the following chapters.

5.2 The Direct Obligations Model

5.2.1 The Contours of the Model

The central feature of the direct obligations model is the notion that fundamental rights impose binding obligations on non-state actors directly. That idea does not specify the exact nature, type, or extent of the obligations – it means, at the very least, that non-state actors have legal obligations flowing from such rights.[1] These could involve negative obligations not to harm rights,[2] and also positive obligations actively to advance the realisation of rights.

The fact that non-state actors may have obligations flowing from fundamental rights can also have varying consequences for a legal system. It is important, in this regard, to distinguish between the question of the existence of direct obligations and the question of where they may be enforced.[3] At the international level, direct obligations may mean that fundamental rights can be invoked in international

[1] See Gardbaum, 2003: 395–396; Dafel, 2015: 61.

[2] Thus, the *Urbaser* arbitral decision recognises at para 1199 that there is an obligation on both public and private parties 'not to engage in activity aimed at destroying such rights'.

[3] Clapham, 2006: 267.

fora even when particular states fail to enact laws protecting individual rights.[4] On the other hand, there may be a lack of international enforcement mechanisms but, nevertheless, direct obligations under international law could be enforced within domestic jurisdictions.[5] Indeed, this is particularly important where such jurisdictions may lack clear laws and the international legally binding obligations can themselves be the foundation of a cause of action.

At the national level, direct obligations could also involve the introduction of specific remedies to enforce these obligations.[6] The 1991 Colombian Constitution, for instance, created a specific remedy which allows, in certain circumstances, direct appeal to constitutional rights where they are violated by non-state actors.[7] Yet, direct obligations do not automatically entail that private law is suddenly superseded by constitutional law. In Colombia, for instance, the courts have introduced principles for determining when direct constitutional actions apply and when ordinary private law applies. In general, if there is a private law remedy, it must be utilised unless it is not suitable and effective in the circumstances to protect the fundamental rights of vulnerable persons or an urgent remedy is required to avert irreparable harm to fundamental rights.[8] These rules, of course, allow some porousness between the two domains – nevertheless, they avoid a situation where all the rules of private law are simply replaced by constitutional actions.[9]

Whilst constitutional law cannot and should not replace the whole edifice of private law fields such as contract or tort, a direct obligations model can also require a reconsideration of these areas of law in light of whether they adequately capture the interests underlying fundamental rights.[10] Since those rights are the most basic norms of the legal system in liberal democratic constitutional systems, it is necessary to ensure they are given expression to in other areas of the law. That may involve considering

4 Ibid: 29–32. The converse is also true: the failure to recognise direct obligations can lead to a lack of accountability in the international sphere – see Kinley and Tadaki, 2004: 935.

5 Indeed, this is the model effectively proposed in the 2nd Revised Draft Treaty. For a discussion, see Skogly, 2017.

6 See Gardbaum, 2003: 397–398.

7 Article 86 of the Constitution provides for this and is discussed in section 5.4.2 of this chapter.

8 See *T-583 of 2017* para 10.

9 These points are articulated in a range of cases: see, for instance, *T-1236 of 2000* para 3; *T-258 of 2018* para 2.4; *T-404 of 2018* para 2.4.

10 Nolan, 2014: 79 refers to this as 'direct-indirect horizontal application or direct-mediated horizontal application'. See also, Woolman, 2006: 31–46; 31–66.

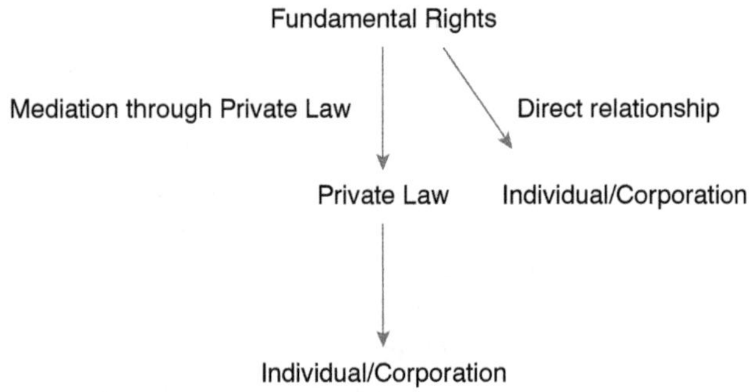

Figure 5.1 The direct obligations model.

whether they are offered adequate protection as well as whether a justifiable balancing of interests is achieved in these other areas of the law.

Understanding this means that its differences from the indirect application model considered in Chapter 3 are not as great as is often stated given that many of the obligations of non-state actors relating to fundamental rights will be given expression to in the existing legal rules of private law.[11] The central difference is the willingness to acknowledge openly that fundamental rights do impose obligations on non-state actors even if such obligations are given expression to through other bodies of law.[12] The possibility, as we saw, usually also exists in jurisdictions which accept direct obligations for some kind of direct constitutional action if private law is wholly inadequate. Figure 5.1 shows a diagrammatic representation of this model.

5.2.2 The Justification of the Model

The direct obligations model requires a justification for why fundamental rights impose binding obligations on non-state actors. In Chapter 2, when outlining the legal grounding of fundamental rights, I provided an understanding of the conceptual and normative basis for such an approach. In brief, the justification begins with a recognition of the foundational dignity

[11] I have discussed this point in greater detail at section 3.2.2 in Chapter 3.

[12] A ground-breaking example is the recognition by the Hague District Court in the Netherlands in *Vereniging Milieudefensie v Royal Dutch Shell PLC* – through an interpretation of a standard of care drawn from the Dutch Civil Code – of a direct obligation on Royal Dutch Shell and its subsidiaries to reduce CO2 emissions by 45% by 2030 (relative to 2019 levels).

(or worth) of every individual. This, in turn, requires that individuals be treated as beings with worth: to do so requires offering protection for their most foundational interests. Fundamental rights to speech, association, food, and water, amongst others, offer protection for these interests and thus represent the necessary conditions for being treated as an individual with dignity. Importantly, such rights are articulated in this justification from the perspective of the beneficiaries of the rights who have entitlements to have their foundational interests protected. There are no specific agents to which these rights are addressed: ultimately, they assert that the interests of these individuals must be realised and protected by whomever is in a position to do so. It follows from this reasoning that, conceptually, there is no good reason to tie obligations flowing from fundamental rights only to the state.

Given there are multiple agents who can affect rights, the question that then arises is whether we have reasons to allocate particular obligations to particular agents. This question of allocation is important given that there may be different ways in which different agents can affect rights and we also do not want multiple agents duplicating efforts for no good reason. Consequently, we need to develop principles for determining which obligations fall upon which agents.

Many of the reasons for imposing direct obligations have already emerged in the critiques of the doctrines outlined in the previous three chapters. I will not seek to repeat these arguments but briefly summarise the key points in what follows and provide some additional reasons that can provide a grounding for this model.

5.2.2.1 The International Sphere

The direct obligations model at the international level clearly has the advantage that obligations for non-state actors are not dependent on whether states enact laws imposing such obligations. Given the existence of states that are either too weak in governance to enact adequate laws protecting rights as well as those that deliberately refuse to do so, this facet of a direct approach is a major advantage.[13] Moreover, if direct obligations flow from fundamental rights already enacted at the international level, then they will apply universally, no matter the regulatory framework of particular states.

Furthermore, a corporation may, for instance, seek to take advantage of the lack of a decent fundamental rights framework within a state and

[13] See Kinley and Tadaki, 2004: 938.

claim they cannot be subject to any remedial action. Practically, a direct obligations approach can allow for such entities to be held to account in other states or in front of relevant international tribunals[14] given that the cause of action flows from a direct violation of international fundamental rights.[15] This model thus does not deny a remedy to victims of fundamental rights violations by non-state actors simply because they live in a state that is a serial fundamental rights abuser or lacks the capacity to enact and enforce adequate safeguards for such rights. Such an approach would also ensure that there is a remedy in cases where the state has taken all reasonable measures but could not have foreseen a particular violation. In the case of new technologies, for instance, fundamental rights can provide a framework of accountability for non-state actors even when developments outpace domestic or international regulation.[16]

It may be contended that it remains difficult to prosecute cases against corporations, for instance, in countries where the violation of rights did not take place. Further, there is a general lack of international tribunals in which to do so.[17] Whilst that statement of the current position is true, direct obligations leave open the possibility of liability under international law given they do not condition obligations on the enactment of a domestic legal framework.

Moreover, there is an important further benefit of the direct obligations approach: its 'expressive effect'. Cass Sunstein has explored the way in which law not only controls behaviour directly but also makes clear statements about particular issues and so, potentially, can affect social norms.[18] Recognising direct obligations of non-state actors sends out a clear message that violating fundamental rights is unacceptable no matter who commits the violation. Whether or not legal consequences follow, that expressive effect allows for strong social sanctions against violators, including potentially consumer boycotts and harm to the brand of a corporation. These social effects matter and offer non-governmental organisations an effective approach for holding corporations to account for their behaviour even in the absence of clear legal remedies.

[14] See Vázquez, 2005: 937.

[15] Whether such a cause of action is available will depend on whether international law directly applies within these jurisdictions as well as whether they procedurally and substantively allow for such actions. In principle, the direct obligations model allows for such accountability, whereas the state duty to protect model does not.

[16] See the discussion in Chapter 2 at section 2.3.2.3.

[17] These problems, which are explored by Kinley and Tadaki, 2004, remain relevant.

[18] Sunstein, 1996b: 2025–2026.

5.2.2.2 The National Sphere

Within the national sphere, a direct obligations model recognises overtly that non-state actors can, and indeed do, violate fundamental rights and that, in these situations, there is a need for a legal remedy. The great benefit of this approach, consequently, is that there is no need for subterfuge:[19] the implications of fundamental rights for non-state actors can be considered directly. That can avoid courts from focusing, at times, on largely irrelevant questions for determining the liability of non-state actors such as whether they can be classified as 'public' or 'private'.[20] It also means that courts must follow the general reasoning structures relating to fundamental rights: these entail giving normative priority to fundamental rights and requiring a strong justification for any infringement thereof. Courts can draw on all factors that are relevant to both the beneficiaries of rights and the agents who are required to realise them. When balancing, they also can understand clearly the relevance to their reasoning of structured justificatory processes such as the proportionality enquiry. A direct obligations model, of course, does not guarantee that courts will reason well but it means that they acknowledge overtly the need for a fundamental rights analysis when determining the obligations of non-state actors. That may take the form of examining existing private law for its consistency with fundamental rights, or it could involve the creation of new constitutional remedies where existing law cannot adequately address such rights.

In relation to the former possibility, the direct model has the benefit that private law and fundamental rights law are not seen as fundamental opposites: instead, they are required continually to interact and engage. Disputes between non-state actors are not automatically regarded as private law matters alone but can also implicate public law.[21] That would have the benefit that ordinary civil courts which consider most private law matters would, generally, need to reconsider their role and recognise the relevance of fundamental rights considerations for their judgments. The indirect application model and direct obligations model may well not diverge significantly here except that the former would – in a system such as Germany – theoretically only allow for rare interventions by a Constitutional Court when civil courts make significant mistakes in failing to integrate fundamental rights into their approach to

[19] Barak, 2001: 15.
[20] See Nolan, 2014: 72.
[21] See, for instance, the statement in *Kwazulu-Natal Joint Liaison Committee* v. *MEC Department of Education, Kwazulu-Natal* [2013] ZACC 10 para 92 that 'the divide between public and private law is more diffuse'.

private law.[22] The direct obligations model, which accepts more strongly the idea of a single system of law, would theoretically allow for more frequent interventions and, thus potentially, increase the influence of fundamental rights law on civil law.[23]

A direct obligations model also allows for an action – such as the tutela in Colombia – where individuals may approach courts concerning direct violations of their fundamental rights by non-state actors.[24] Such actions may plug gaps in existing law but may also help ameliorate many of the existing inequities within current legal systems: courts are often not easily accessible to the poorer and weaker segments of the population, rendering them vulnerable to the economic and social power of non-state actors such as corporations. Allowing a speedy, direct constitutional action against non-state actors, such as the tutela, can help correct for imbalances in the legal system, enabling effective remedies to be attained quickly to protect fundamental rights against powerful non-state actors.[25] They can also guard against irreparable damage in the interim whilst a case makes its way through the ordinary courts.

The direct obligations model also has an important procedural side effect. Systems that recognise direct obligations would enable state institutions concerned with fundamental rights outside the courts – such as human rights commissions and ombudspersons – legitimately to consider the impacts of non-state actors in relation to fundamental rights. This potentially includes a wider set of institutional actors in monitoring and responding to such violations by non-state actors.

5.2.3 *Objections to Direct Obligations*

The question of direct obligations of non-state actors often raises a number of objections.[26] At times, these arise from an unjustifiable dogma that fundamental rights obligations can only fall upon the state, which is a mantra often repeated by some lawyers and in some legal

22 See the discussion and references at section 3.2.2 in Chapter 3.

23 The possibility of a greater number of cases before constitutional courts, in this regard, may in some systems be seen to be a drawback of the direct obligations model.

24 Some countries such as Ireland have, on the basis of direct horizontality, developed a constitutional tort which can be claimed when other parts of the law fail to protect constitutional rights adequately: see Nolan, 2014: 74.

25 See Merhof, 2015: 719–721; Landau, 2012: 205–206.

26 Not all of these can be addressed here nor are they all apposite to the focus of this book. I have attempted to respond to certain other objections in Bilchitz, 2013. See also Nolan, 2014 for a response to certain objections.

systems. Some of these objections have already been discussed in other chapters.[27] I will focus here on responding to an objection – raised, particularly, in the context of corporations – which concerns the relationship between obligations and rights and is, consequently, of significance for the argument of this book.

5.2.3.1 Do Direct Obligations for Corporations Entail They Have Rights?

One worry that has been expressed is that a recognition of corporate obligations in relation to fundamental rights will necessarily have to be conjoined with the recognition that corporations themselves are entitled to claim fundamental rights.[28] According to this view, that would render symbolically the powerful language of rights – usually only applicable to individuals – at the service of corporations.[29] Doing so can also have concrete legal effects: recognising corporations have rights could well lead them to be accorded stronger procedural protections of due process which could enhance their power vis-à-vis the state.[30] It could also lead to enhanced substantive protections and a potential shift in the very meaning of certain fundamental rights.[31] Moreover, the normative weight of corporate claims would be strengthened and, in balancing, often lead to a defeat or weakening of individual entitlements. Apart from these concrete legal effects, it could also be argued that it is a philosophical mistake to accord fundamental rights which are entitlements of corporeal individuals with particular needs and interests – such as in having access to food, housing, and fundamental freedoms – to an entity that is a creation of law.[32] For these reasons, it is argued that corporations should not be able to claim that they have fundamental rights or utilise these entitlements as the basis for their own legal actions. Since it is contended that the recognition of direct obligations for corporations will

[27] See in particular the discussion around the justifications and drawbacks of the models in Chapters 2, 3, and 4.

[28] Werhane, 2016: 5–6 expresses this as an entailment – which I argue later in the chapter is mistaken.

[29] Alvarez, 2011: 28 discusses this as a potential result of recognising corporations as full 'persons' or 'subjects' of international law. He argues within the context of bilateral investment agreements that this is likely to 'enhance the rights of the investor – not *humans'* rights as traditionally construed' (emphasis in original).

[30] Ibid.

[31] Ibid: 27–29; Werhane, 2016: 6. For this worry in the context of bilateral investment treaties, see Muchlinski, 2017: 363.

[32] See Grear, 2010: 32.

be conjoined with a recognition of their rights, taking that step should be resisted.[33]

There are a number of important issues raised by this objection, yet, ultimately, it is, in my view, misconceived. The major flaw is the contention that recognising an entity has obligations is tantamount to accepting it has rights. Indeed, as we have seen, in both international law and domestic constitutional systems, the main duty-bearer for obligations flowing from fundamental rights is the state. Yet, the state itself cannot claim fundamental rights. Moreover, in the private sphere, we may set up a voluntary association which has the obligation to defend the rights of refugees without having any claims on those refugees itself. Further, consider a parent who is regarded as having obligations to a newly born infant without any right to claim anything from that infant. It is thus possible for an entity to have obligations without being able to claim corresponding rights.[34]

The reason that this is possible flows from an important conceptual feature of fundamental rights. Such rights are entitlements of those who are vulnerable to the exercise of power by another entity:[35] there is, consequently, a lack of symmetry between the position of the rights-holder and the duty-bearer. The duty-bearer may be capable of affecting fundamental rights in a manner it is obliged to address – but, the rights-bearer may lack a similar capacity. As a result, one party can have an obligation, whilst the other has a right.

A deeper question surrounds the features of an entity that may render it capable of having obligations and/or rights. The aforementioned example of the infant suggests that one requires a certain level of decision-making capacity and intentionality in order to have obligations; yet, the child may be a rights-holder given it is a corporeal entity with a fundamental interest, amongst others, in being free from being subjected to pain or abuse. It is also possible that one is an agent with the requisite ability to make decisions without having the fundamental interests required to be protected by rights. The state is regarded as being capable of having

[33] López Latorre, 2020: 67 states that 'one can neither have rights without obligations nor obligations without rights'. I take issue with both parts of this claim: as I will argue, correlativity does not imply that an individual or entity who has rights must have obligations or vice versa. López Latorre appears to qualify and reduce the scope of his claim but his broad statement above represents a common misunderstanding and is incorrect as stated.

[34] See Grear, 2010: 38. The converse is also possible: an infant may have rights but no duties.

[35] For further elaboration, see the discussion of vulnerability in Chapter 6 at section 6.3.1.2 and in the case law of the Colombian Constitutional Court later in this chapter.

obligations: yet, its very corporate nature and function render it unable to claim fundamental rights in its own right. What then about corporations?

As was discussed in Chapter 1, corporations are regarded as having the agency necessary to be the subject of obligations.[36] It does, however, not automatically follow that they are therefore entitled to claim fundamental rights. As we saw, there is no automatic relationship between being the subject of obligations and the subject of rights. Of course, the lack of such an entailment still poses the question whether corporations should be entitled to claim such rights. This question requires us to return to the nature of the corporation as was discussed in Chapter 1. In and of its own right, the corporation is an entity which is not sentient and which lacks a corporeality that is usually required for the possession of fundamental rights. In and of itself, it lacks the dignity and worth required for the attribution of rights. However, as I argued, the corporation is supervenient upon the interests of the corporeal individuals underlying it – it is thus intimately connected to their interests though not reducible to them. The structure is thus constituted partly to advance the economic interests that corporeal individuals have. We might then say that to the extent that the corporation affects the interests of corporeal individuals that are protected by fundamental rights, it may come to be seen to possess certain fundamental rights *derivatively*.[37]

This position has in fact been adopted in South African law in cases relating to the rights to privacy and property. The Constitutional Court has stated clearly that '[j]uristic persons are not the bearers of human dignity'.[38] As such, it recognised a fundamental difference between juristic persons and other natural persons. Yet, it also articulates reasons to find that they possess rights derivatively.[39] In a case concerning whether the state could search the premises of a motor-vehicle corporation, the court was worried about granting carte blanche to the state which it found would lead to 'grave disruptions and would undermine the very fabric of our democratic state'.[40] It found that '[j]uristic persons therefore do enjoy the right to privacy although not to the same extent as natural persons'.[41] Consistent with this holding, the court also suggested

[36] See Chapter 1 footnote 41 and surrounding text.
[37] Addo, 1999: 188–192.
[38] *The Investigating Directorate: Serious Economic Offences* v. *Hyundai Motor Distributors (Pty) Ltd* [2000] ZACC 12 para 18.
[39] Werhane, 2016: 15–17 argues for a similar view.
[40] *Hyundai*: para 18.
[41] Ibid.

that the burden of justification for infringing upon the right to privacy of corporations may be less onerous.

The court reaches a similar conclusion in a case concerning the right to property.[42] It finds that natural persons form companies for a range of 'legitimate purposes, including earning a livelihood, making investments and for structuring a pension scheme'.[43] The court acknowledges that there would be a terrible impact on the business world if property rights were not extended to companies. Its focus though is clearly on the primacy of the natural persons underlying the corporation who are shareholders: '[t]he property rights of natural persons can only be fully and properly realized if such rights are afforded to companies as well as natural persons'.[44] This reasoning about the derivative nature of corporate rights also, nicely, gives us an argument for the recognition of corporate obligations: if our primary concern is with protecting the fundamental rights of natural persons, then we must recognise corporations have certain obligations not to harm these rights and to help realise them to the extent that is reasonable.[45]

The South African approach is nuanced and, in my view, attractive given its recognition that corporations may be able to claim certain rights derivatively but that a lesser weight will be attached to those claims. However, this approach is far from universal and, in many legal systems today, the situation in fact reflects the converse problem: namely that corporations are regarded as having significant rights *without* corresponding obligations.[46] A further response to the objection being discussed is to acknowledge the reality that corporations have in fact been granted significant rights in legal systems without clear corresponding obligations.[47] Consequently, there is no basis for the concern that their legal position will be strengthened – the recognition that they bear obligations is simply a corrective to the imbalance that already exists and will, consequently, strengthen the position of individuals.

This case can be made out briefly by considering two arenas where this is true. In the United States, the Supreme Court considered the constitutionality of a law which banned direct corporate expenditure on political

42 *First National Bank of SA Limited t/a Wesbank* v. *Commissioner for the South African Revenue Services; First National Bank of SA Limited of SA Limited t/a Wesbank* v. *Minister of Finance* [2002] ZACC 5.

43 Ibid: para 44.

44 Ibid: para 45.

45 I first made this argument in Bilchitz, 2008: 775.

46 Vázquez, 2005: 932.

47 Ratner, 2001: 488.

campaigning relating to elections for or against particular candidates.[48] The majority of the Supreme Court confirmed that the 1st Amendment protections for free speech extended not only to individuals but also to corporations.[49] As such, corporations could claim the protection of these rights and, consequently, restrictions on their 'political speech' were found by the majority to be unconstitutional. In direct contrast, the Supreme Court has been reluctant to recognise obligations of corporations in relation to fundamental rights. As has already been discussed in Chapter 4, in relation to domestic companies in the United States, the state action doctrine prevents the application of fundamental rights directly to most non-state entities. In the case of *Jesner* v. *Arab Bank*,[50] the majority of the court, whilst acknowledging the power of corporations to violate fundamental rights in terrible ways and commit international crimes, doubted whether international law had evolved to embrace their liability for such harms.[51] The Supreme Court has thus recognised and, in fact, expanded upon the rights of corporations whilst refusing to accept they are bound by obligations flowing directly from fundamental rights either in domestic or international law.

A similar state of affairs has characterised bilateral investment agreements at the international level.[52] The nature of these agreements has, until recently, been a one-way street whereby states provide guarantees that the rights of corporations will be respected – for instance, that their property will not be nationalised – but impose no obligations upon those corporations.[53] Consequently, corporations have been able to sue states for the protection of their rights but have not, themselves, been the subject of claims by states.[54] An important corrective has been the *Urbaser* arbitral decision which found that corporations indeed have binding negative obligations not to harm fundamental rights when they go about their activities in terms of these agreements.[55]

These examples suggest that the fear of empowering the corporation through recognising their rights is misplaced. Whilst a recognition of their obligations does not automatically involve a recognition of their rights, in fact, corporations are already widely acknowledged to have

48 *Citizens United* v. *Federal Election Commission* 558 US 310 (2010).
49 Ibid: 342–3.
50 584 US _ 2018.
51 Ibid: 18.
52 López Latorre, 2020: 64.
53 Alvarez, 2011: 19–20.
54 See Blair et al., 2018: 405–6. For a review of certain key decisions, see Muchlinski, 2017: 349–362.
55 *Urbaser* arbitral decision paras 1199 and 1210.

rights – even if that is a debatable proposition normatively. The crucial step is actively to advance the recognition that they also have obligations in relation to fundamental rights. With that view increasingly being embraced, the next challenge becomes the need to articulate an approach to determining what the substantive content of those obligations are. I thus now turn to an engagement with this question through an examination, firstly, of two approaches at the international level towards direct obligations and, secondly, of some case law in two national jurisdictions which have adopted the direct obligations model.

5.3 The Direct Obligations Model in International Law

Since the 1970s, there has been a discussion of developing an international law framework to govern the activities of corporations. At first, the concerns were focused on the challenges corporations posed to the very sovereignty and autonomy of many newly decolonised states.[56] Over time, the discourse has shifted to highlight the impact corporations have on the fundamental rights of individuals.[57] Whilst much of the legal discourse has concentrated on the duty to protect of states (dealt with in Chapter 2), there have been some attempts to go beyond that framework. Those approaches that effectively recognise corporate obligations also provide certain conceptual resources that can be understood as a basis for determining the substantive content of those obligations. I will focus on two of these and their shortcomings: the 'sphere of influence' approach and the 'due diligence' approach.

5.3.1 The 'Sphere of Influence' Approach[58]

The release of the Draft Norms on the Responsibilities of Transnational Corporations and Other Business Enterprises with Regard to Human Rights represented an important step in the attempt to codify and to develop progressively the international law relating to corporate obligations. This document emerged from an expert working group appointed by the Sub-Commission on the Promotion and Protection of Human Rights. The Sub-Commission approved the Norms but, unfortunately, they attracted much criticism and eventually were declared by the

[56] Ramasastry, 2015: 240–241; Bilchitz and Deva, 2013: 5–6.

[57] For an account of this trajectory, see Ramasastry, ibid: 239–248.

[58] In this section, I draw from the discussion in Bilchitz, 2017b: 189–197.

Commission on Human Rights to have 'no legal standing'.[59] Whilst they were never formally adopted by the Commission, the approach adopted by the group of experts to the obligations of business and the criticism thereof is worth considering.

The Draft Norms begin in their preamble to recognise that 'transnational corporations and other business enterprises, their officers, and their workers have, inter alia, human rights obligations and responsibilities'.[60] They go on to elaborate the approach towards such obligations as follows:

> States have the primary responsibility to promote, secure the fulfilment of, respect, ensure respect of, and protect human rights recognised in international as well as national law, including assuring that transnational corporations and other business enterprises respect human rights. Within their respective spheres of activity and influence, transnational corporations and other business enterprises have the obligation to promote, secure the fulfilment of, respect, ensure respect of, and protect human rights recognized in international as well as national law.[61]

This key provision does a number of things. Firstly, it recognises that states have the *primary* obligations to ensure fundamental rights are realised, which includes a duty to protect individuals against violations by corporations. We can call this 'the primacy principle'.[62] Secondly, it acknowledges that transnational corporations and other business enterprises have the obligations – subject to the limitations discussed below – to 'promote, secure the fulfilment of, respect, ensure respect of, and protect' human rights.[63] These words include both negative and positive obligations under international human rights law.[64] Finally, the provision contains a key limiting principle in relation to the obligations of corporations: their obligations are said to apply only within their respective 'spheres of activity and influence'. This idea is meant to provide a basis to distinguish the obligations of corporations from those of the state. I now consider critically the adequacy of this concept for determining corporate obligations. In doing so, I use the shorthand notion of

59 Commission on Human Rights, 2004: para (c).
60 Draft Norms, 2003: Preamble.
61 Ibid: para 1.
62 For a critique of the primacy principle, see Bilchitz, 2017b: 192–194.
63 The notion of human rights is defined expansively in article 23 of the Draft Norms.
64 State actors are generally understood to have a combination of negative and positive duties arising from fundamental rights which include duties to respect, protect, and fulfil fundamental rights. This language reflected developments in the understanding of fundamental rights obligations flowing from the work of Shue, 1980.

'sphere of influence' given that the sphere of activity clearly is included within the domain of a corporation's influence.

5.3.1.1 The Notion of the 'Sphere of Influence'

The idea of a 'sphere of influence' had already become influential within the domain of corporate social responsibility when it was included in the Draft Norms.[65] It involves a spatial metaphor which conditions corporate responsibility on the extent of its activities and influence.[66] It is perhaps an analogue of an attempt to define the 'jurisdiction' of a corporation: the state's jurisdiction lies, mostly, within its territorial borders; the jurisdiction of a corporation lies within its 'sphere of influence'.[67] The problem is that the notion of 'sphere of influence' has much greater vagueness than the territorial boundaries of the state and the question is whether that can be remedied.[68]

The core idea behind this approach appears to be that the greater the activities of a corporation or its influence in an area, the more responsibility it has. The idea can be linked up with developments in the realm of stakeholder theory which contends that a corporation should be understood not merely as a vehicle for the shareholders who invest in it to achieve economic returns, but in relation to its effect on all stakeholders upon whom it has an impact.[69] A number of stakeholders are identified who are affected by company activities: these include employees, customers, shareholders, contractors, investors, and members of local communities. The 'sphere of influence' approach could be understood to determine the obligations of a corporation in accordance with the intensity of the relationship it has with particular stakeholders. Those obligations would be more intense where its sphere of influence is stronger and less intense as it wanes.

The 'sphere of influence' notion does seem to include a number of features which are normatively significant. The first is that the impact of the corporation on fundamental rights needs to be considered when determining its obligations. The second feature is that there may be a continuum of obligations: the more intrusive the impact upon

[65] Draft Norms, 2003: para A(1).

[66] UN Framework, 2008: para 66. For a visual representation, see Sphere of Influence Report, 2008: para 8.

[67] Sphere of Influence Report, 2008: para 10.

[68] Though the territory of a state is usually pretty clear and defined, its influence beyond its borders and the extent of its consequent extraterritorial obligations perhaps also raise similar difficulties.

[69] For the definition of a stakeholder, see Freeman, 2010: 46; Freeman et al., 2010: 28.

fundamental interests, the more extensive the obligations of particular agents must be.[70] Finally, the notion of 'sphere of influence' seems to embody the idea that there must be a limit to corporate obligations and there is a point at which it is not fair to hold them accountable for wrongs that occur.

Despite these attractive features, the concept has come in for detailed criticism which has highlighted several of its shortcomings.[71] The first critique concerns what is meant by 'influence'. Lehr and Jenkins, for instance, claim that the idea lumps together many disparate ideas such as 'proximity, impact, control, benefit and political influence'.[72] The notion is thus dependent, they claim, upon a range of underlying normative ideas and, in itself, it is irredeemably vague. Thus, it is necessary to disentangle these various concepts to arrive at a clearer basis for determining corporate obligations. Importantly, this critique suggests the inability to identify one single factor that determines corporate obligations; rather, there are several that are relevant in this regard. The 'sphere of influence' approach thus really reduces to a multi-factoral approach that recognises multiple determinants for the substantive content of corporate obligations. The approach is not helpful without an analysis of these underlying factors and how they each condition and determine the substantive content of corporate obligations.

The 'sphere of influence' approach does not provide guidance in this regard. Firstly, the stakeholder theory interpretation thereof would suggest that if, in general, a corporation is understood to have a greater influence on its employees, then it must have more extensive obligations towards them. However, in some cases, it can have an equal or even greater effect on another set of stakeholders such as a local community: consider the effect of a mining corporation on members of a nearby community who are not employed by it but significantly affected by the pollutants it releases into the environment. The idea, on this understanding, appears to be too rigid if, in advance, it identifies certain stakeholders – such as employees – upon whom a corporation is regarded as invariably having the greatest influence. It would be better to focus upon the impact of particular

[70] Such a principle has, for instance, been articulated by the South African Constitutional Court in relation to the right to privacy where intrusions into the domain of the home – where an individual can expect the greatest privacy – will require a greater level of justification than intrusions into privacy at the workplace. See *Bernstein* v. *Bester* [1996] ZACC 2 para 67.

[71] See Sphere of Influence Report, 2008; Macdonald, 2011: 555–556; Wood, 2012: 73.

[72] Lehr and Jenkins, 2007.

activities the corporation undertakes on the interests of differing rights-holders and thus determine their obligations accordingly.

Secondly, and more generally, the 'sphere of influence' idea, as I have mentioned, appears to be jurisdictional in seeking to determine that corporations have obligations *in some spheres and not others*. Yet, the concept in itself lacks the resources to determine what those obligations are *within* its sphere of influence. For instance, consider whether a corporation may view the personal communications of employees on office computers provided to them for performing their work. On the one hand, the 'sphere of influence' notion may require a high level of protection for the right to privacy of employees given the strong impact the corporation can have on their lives in this area. On the other hand, given the very close nature of its relationship with employees, the company may also have the greatest justifiable claim in these circumstances to monitor their communications (something a person, for instance, with a more distant relationship would lack). How does the 'sphere of influence' idea help determine the specific obligations of corporations in this case? In a sense, the notion simply expresses and, in some cases, amplifies the normative conflict involved without providing any means to resolve it.

An analogy can help strengthen this point: asserting that states have obligations flowing from fundamental rights within their territory in no way helps determine what the content of the obligations of the state are *within* that territory. The 'sphere of influence' concept aims to demarcate a domain in which corporations have obligations[73] but it fails to provide an adequate basis for determining the nature of those obligations *within* that domain. It is thus not a fit conceptual frame for the purpose of adequately determining the substantive content of corporate obligations.

5.3.2 The United Nations Guiding Principles and the 'Due Diligence' Approach

Unlike the Draft Norms, the United Nations Guiding Principles on Business and Human Rights (UNGPs)[74] were adopted in 2011 unanimously by the member states of the United Nations Human Rights Council. They have also garnered much corporate support and represent

[73] It is not clear as mentioned that it succeeds in doing this either.
[74] UNGPs available at www.ohchr.org/documents/publications/GuidingprinciplesBusinesshr_eN.pdf.

a significant development in the business and human rights field with other initiatives in this area being aligned with them. The question for our purposes concerns the approach of the UNGPs towards the obligations of corporations with respect to fundamental rights.[75]

The first important point to recognise is that the word 'obligation' is not used by the UNGPs – rather the word 'responsibility' is. The difference in locution is deliberate and designed to demarcate the difference between state and corporate responsibility.[76] The UNGPs were based on the prior work of the Special Representative of the Secretary General's (SRSG) mandate which maintained that states have binding obligations in international law to protect individuals from harms caused by corporations but that corporations in general lack binding international obligations flowing from fundamental rights.[77] The UNGPs explicitly state that they do not create any new international legal obligations.[78] The UNGPs thus see the corporate responsibility to respect not as an international legal obligation but as 'a global standard of expected conduct for all business enterprises'.[79] The UNGPs also do not purport to be purely voluntary: they articulate a vague notion of 'social bindingness' which arises as a result of social expectations.[80] I have in past work criticised this idea given the vagueness of what constitute social expectations and how we determine them.[81] It is also troubling to see international human rights being reduced simply to 'expected standards of conduct' rather than law.

With this caveat in mind, the UNGPs nevertheless articulate the view that businesses, importantly, have a responsibility to respect internationally recognised human rights. This is explicated as meaning that 'they should avoid infringing on the human rights of others and should address adverse human rights impacts with which they are involved'.[82] Importantly, this view of business responsibility is focused on avoiding harm to rights and largely releases them from any positive obligations

[75] The UNGPs use the word 'businesses' rather than 'corporations' though the latter is a subset of the former. Since the focus of this book is on corporations, I generally utilise the latter locution in the discussion below.

[76] Ruggie, 2011: 129–130 and Deva, 2013: 93–95.

[77] SRSG 2006 Interim Report: paras 64–65.

[78] UNGPs: General Principles.

[79] UNGPs: Commentary on GP 11.

[80] This initial idea builds upon the notion of a 'social license to operate' referenced in the UN Framework para 54.

[81] Bilchitz, 2013: 118–124.

[82] UNGPs: GP 11.

they may have actively to advance the realisation of fundamental rights (which will be addressed in Chapter 8).

Here, I want to focus on whether the UNGPs really provide us with an approach to determining the substantive content of the negative obligations of corporations flowing from fundamental rights. If we look at the second half of Guiding Principle 11, there is a responsibility imposed to address 'adverse human rights impacts' – but what is an 'impact', and does any 'impact' trigger a corporate responsibility? The notion of impact suggests that one can move directly from a corporation's capacity to cause a negative effect upon a right to an obligation upon that corporation to avoid causing that effect. Yet, that is a leap which obscures a whole lot of important issues.[83] To understand this, consider the fact that virtually all employers would restrict the freedom of movement of employees during work-time and, generally, place some restrictions on what they may say when they represent the corporation. These restrictions would have an adverse impact on the freedom of movement and expression of individuals – yet, they would, generally, be regarded as permissible. This example illustrates the point that not every negative impact on a fundamental right by a corporation automatically translates into an obligation. The crucial question then becomes what translates a permissible impact into an impermissible one that gives rise to a negative obligation of a corporation?[84] In Chapters 6 and 7, I attempt to grapple with this question and suggest an approach to answering it. Yet, what this discussion highlights is that the UNGPs do not address this central question for determining the substantive content of the obligations of corporations.

Moreover, it is not possible simply to derive what constitutes an impermissible corporate violation from a consideration of state violations.[85] Guiding Principle 12 states that businesses have responsibilities in relation to all 'internationally recognized human rights' and provides an understanding of what, at a minimum, this list of rights involves.[86] Yet, it does not provide an understanding of how we determine what the obligations of corporations are in relation to this list – this

[83] Deva, 2013: 97–98.

[84] Leader, 2017: 87 also recognises the importance of this distinction.

[85] The reasons are provided in the text and flow both from the normative gap identified and the differences between state and corporate obligations. I therefore disagree with Mccorquodale and Smit 2017a: 224–225 that the notion of human rights impact in the UNGPs should be read as equivalent to the notion of human rights violations. There are many indications that this is also not what the SRSG intended. For a strong and detailed rejoinder, see Birchall, 2019: 132–144.

[86] UNGPs: GP 12.

Guiding Principle suggests rather simplistically that corporate obligations can somehow be read off directly from these instruments.[87] Yet, if the responsibilities of corporations are indeed differentiated from those of the state – as the UNGPs themselves proclaim and the prior UN Framework articulates more clearly[88] – then we cannot simply translate the normative understanding of what constitutes the obligations of states into a guide to the obligations of corporations.[89]

Perhaps the most enduring contribution of the UNGPs in relation to business responsibility is the notion that they have a duty to carry out 'human rights due diligence' (HRDD) processes. Can this help in demarcating corporate responsibilities? This HRDD process is defined to involve 'assessing actual and potential human rights impacts, integrating and acting upon findings, tracking responses, and communicating how impacts are addressed'.[90] HRDD is focused on engaging with all the adverse impacts the business may cause through its own activities as well as through its business relationships with other entities – which raises the critical issue of the responsibilities of one business for the actions of its subsidiaries and subcontractors.[91] The UNGPs also require a consideration of risks to fundamental rights and thus potential human rights impacts. Once all potential effects on fundamental rights are understood, the business must take steps to prevent and mitigate potential impacts[92] and remediate actual harms.[93] It must then track the effectiveness of its responses to potential harms that occur[94] as well as communicate how it is addressing its human rights impacts.[95]

87 Deva, 2013: 87–88 suggests the avoidance of a complex issue such as this was deliberate in developing consensus surrounding the UNGPs.

88 See UNGPs: General Principles and UN Framework 2008: para 53: '[w]hile corporations may be considered "organs of society", they are specialized economic organs, not democratic public institutions. As such, their responsibilities cannot and should not simply mirror the duties of the State'.

89 Ratner, 2001: 493–4.

90 UNGPs: GP 17.

91 This question is, of course, critical in the context of globalisation and the complex structures and supply chains of businesses. As indicated in the introduction of this book, I have bracketed this question given the need to focus on trying to develop an analytical framework for determining the substantive content of corporate obligations in relation to fundamental rights.

92 UNGPs: GP 19.

93 UNGPs: GP 22.

94 UNGPs: GP 20.

95 UNGPs: GP 21.

The due diligence process has many positive sides to it: clearly, the UNGPs took a risk-management notion that businesses are familiar with – the due diligence process in the context of mergers and acquisitions, for instance – and applied it to the fundamental rights context.[96] Moreover, importantly, the HRDD process can require decision-makers in a corporation to plot their impacts in relation to fundamental rights and so understand their effects thereon.[97] The problem lies in the fact that the process, once again, has the normative gap articulated above at its core. Ultimately, due diligence needs to be exercised in relation to certain fundamental rights standards: the process itself does not determine the standards. The fundamental question a corporation must ask is 'in relation to what, must we exercise due diligence?' The answer of the UNGPs is that all adverse impacts upon rights must be identified and then action taken to prevent or mitigate potential effects (and remediate where those have already caused harm). Charting all impacts may be useful, but to understand what obligations corporations have to act, we need to understand when an impact turns into an impermissible impact or violation. The due diligence process, as articulated in the UNGPs, replicates and instantiates the problem of simplistically suggesting we can understand obligations directly from impacts as well as reading off the obligations of businesses directly from human rights instruments (where most of the normative work there has been done in relation to state obligations).[98] There is thus a missing step in the current due diligence process.

That gap also affects the ability to develop a clear understanding of what the corporation must do in response to finding that it has an impact on a fundamental right: the notions of prevention and mitigation, for instance, are distinct but they are run together in the UNGPs. Prevention will be appropriate where the corporation is proscribed from infringing on the right absolutely. Mitigation, on the other hand, may be apposite where there is a permissible impact on the right but the least restrictive means need to be adopted. Remediation will also require an understanding of where the corporation has impermissibly infringed on rights.

Without an understanding of the content of corporate obligations, identifying impacts fails to result in clear prescriptions of what must be

[96] See Muchlinski, 2012: 156 as well as Mccorquodale and Smit, 2017a: 220ff, who identify the origins of the notion and argue that it includes two elements: a 'process' and 'standard of conduct' dimension.

[97] For the transformative potential of this process, see Birchall, 2019: 144–146.

[98] Deva, 2013: 98 also recognises this gap.

done by the corporation.[99] In the next two chapters, I discuss the normative work necessary to fill this gap in relation to negative obligations, and in Chapter 10, I will make a practical proposal of how the UNGPs should be reformed to address this gap. I now turn to consider how two domestic jurisdictions have given effect to a direct obligations model.

5.4 The Direct Obligations Model in National Jurisdictions

It is perhaps notable that, despite the wide-ranging effects non-state actors have on fundamental rights, there are relatively few jurisdictions that have recognised obligations upon such actors flowing directly from fundamental rights. The constitutional systems that do so tend to be those that are of a more recent vintage – from the flurry of constitution-making in the early 1990s. A general reason for this development was perhaps a recognition of the massive growth in the power of non-state actors such as the corporation with globalisation and a willingness of emerging democracies to depart from established orthodoxies in constitutional theory. I now turn to consider certain key cases and, through a qualitative analysis, examine how the courts have sought to determine the substantive content of the obligations of non-state actors.

5.4.1 Direct Obligations in South Africa

South Africa had an important reason relating to its own historical context for placing obligations on non-state actors in relation to fundamental rights. As has been explained in Chapter 3, it was not only the public sphere that had been affected by the policy of apartheid and had entrenched a system of institutionalised discrimination on the basis of race. The private sphere too had internalised many of these norms:[100] corporations, for instance, had included differential pay schemes for black and white people and black people were not promoted beyond a certain level. Certain churches had implemented separate seating for black and white congregants and entrenched voting and other privileges for white members and

[99] As will be discussed in Chapter 10, the United Nations Working Group on Business and Human Rights in its reports on HRDD appears not to have properly recognised this normative gap and failed adequately to suggest how it can be plugged.

[100] See *Du Plessis* v. *De Klerk* (Kriegler dissenting para 145; and Madala dissenting para 163); Woolman and Davis, 1996: 403–404; Moseneke, 2009: 4–5; Friedman, 2014: 67; Madlanga, 2018: 368.

clergy.[101] The divisions and prejudicial attitudes were all-pervasive. The question was, of course, how the drafters of a new constitution could seek to address this legacy of past injustice and transform the society.

The drafters of the Final Constitution expressly made it clear that the fundamental rights therein could impose direct obligations on non-state actors.[102] As we saw in the previous two chapters, the Constitutional Court has also utilised, at times, an indirect application model[103] as well an expanding the state model.[104] It does though have the possibility of imposing direct obligations on non-state actors and I will focus in this chapter on the key provision – section 8(2).[105] It reads as follows: 'A provision of the Bill of Rights binds a natural or a juristic person if, and to the extent that, it is applicable, taking into account the nature of the right and the nature of any duty imposed by the right'.

It is important briefly to reflect on the radical nature of this provision. What it suggests is that neither a corporation nor a church nor an individual is outside the ambit of being bound by fundamental rights.[106] Rights become the foundational bond that connects all these different parts of society together in subscribing to common values and sharing common obligations. Fundamental rights are consequently the glue that binds all entities in South Africa together and that must be reflected in their relationships with one another.[107] Practically, direct obligations envisaged by this provision ensure that there will always be an effective remedy available for an individual where their rights are violated by a non-state actor.[108]

Clearly, section 8(2) contemplates direct obligations for non-state actors though, unlike in relation to the public sphere, such agents will only be bound when the relevant provision of the bill of rights is 'applicable'.[109] This phrasing is unfortunate and leads to circularity – it effectively says it applies when it is applicable. Nevertheless, we can

[101] See Randall 1972: 36–44 and a brief outline of the history in Bilchitz, 2011: 237–239.
[102] I explained in section 3.2.2 of Chapter 3 how sections 8(3) and 39(2) have muddied the waters surrounding how the Constitution applies to non-state actors.
[103] Moseneke, 2009: 8.
[104] Dafel, 2015: 62–64 provides an explanation why that has occurred.
[105] The Constitutional Court signalled in *AB* v. *Pridwin Preparatory School* [2020] ZACC 17 para 130 that it may be willing to utilise direct application more in the future.
[106] Friedman, 2014: 68.
[107] Meyersfeld, 2020: 458 argues that the section places a legal requirement on individuals and juristic persons 'to participate in the restorative project of healing fractured interpersonal relations'.
[108] Moseneke, 2009: 12.
[109] Friedman, 2014: 68. In the *Pridwin* case (note 105 earlier): para 186, the Constitutional Court incorrectly leaps from the possibility of obligations to their existence.

understand it to mean that there are three scenarios which are possible in relation to non-state actors: a right could be applicable, partially applicable, or not applicable at all.[110] There are two determinants of whether and the degree to which rights apply: the 'nature of the rights' and the 'nature of any duty imposed by the right'. The latter locution suggests that the type of obligation imposed may render a right applicable or not to non-state actors. Flowing from this idea, the Constitutional Court has a small and interesting body of jurisprudence that considers whether rights may only impose negative obligations upon non-state actors – which I shall discuss in Chapter 8. Here I will consider the former determinant of applicability – the 'nature of the rights' – and how it has been given effect to in a seminal case by the Constitutional Court.

5.4.1.1 *Khumalo* v. *Holomisa*:[111] Towards a Multi-Factoral Approach

This case dealt with a defamation action by a well-known politician (Bantu Holomisa) against editors and two publishing companies relating to a claim in a publication that Holomisa was part of a gang of bank robbers and was under police investigation in that regard. After a plaintiff had shown that a defamatory statement was made, the existing common law of defamation required the defendant(s) to bear the burden of proving that the statements were 'true and in the public benefit'. The applicants (originally the defendants) – the editors and publishing companies – sought to argue that the constitutionally entrenched right to freedom of expression required the existing common law to change to become less restrictive on speech through shifting the burden of proof onto the plaintiff to demonstrate that a published statement was false. The Constitutional Court, ultimately, found that the common law did need to be developed though not through a shift in the burden of proof but rather through the recognition of a new defence of 'reasonable publication' in defamation law. This defence means that a publisher only has the burden to demonstrate that their decision to publish information was reasonable – once they have done so, they will not be liable for defamation even if it turns out that the information they published was not true.[112] I will now focus on two elements of the reasoning in this case: horizontal application and its determinants, and the approach to balancing of the court.

[110] Bilchitz, 2008: 775.
[111] [2002] ZACC 12.
[112] Ibid: para 43. The Constitutional Court here essentially affirmed the decision of the Supreme Court of Appeal in *National Media Ltd* v. *Bogoshi* [1998] ZASCA 94.

5.4.1.1.1 Determining Horizontal Application: Relevant Factors This case dealt with a constitutional challenge to the existing common law – as such it looks very similar to some of the cases discussed in Chapter 3 relating to the indirect application model.[113] Justice O'Regan, who wrote the judgment, however, formulated the question being raised by the applicants as 'asserting that the right to freedom of expression in section 16 is directly applicable in this case despite the fact that the litigation does not involve the state or any organs of state'.[114] She also states later that the 'applicants' exception relies directly on section 16 of the Constitution, despite the fact that none of the parties to the defamation action is the state, or any organ of state'.[115] The court outlines a two-step approach when dealing with a constitutional challenge to the common law relating to non-state actors. The first step, in any such challenge, will be to consider the constitutional implications of fundamental rights – their 'applicability' – for the obligations of non-state actors in the circumstances. The second step would then be to examine whether the common law – in this case defamation law – needed to be changed in any way.[116] The approach of the South African Constitutional Court is thus refreshing in its willingness to engage directly with the question of what fundamental rights require in relation to non-state actors when determining how the common law should develop.

How then are we to understand what the implications are of fundamental rights for non-state actors? In a crucial paragraph,[117] the court firstly accepts that the 'applicants are members of the media who are expressly identified as bearers of the constitutional right to freedom of expression'.[118] It then recognises the potential of the law of defamation to impact upon freedom of expression. The court then goes on to say:

> Given the intensity of the constitutional right in question, coupled with the potential invasion of that right which could be occasioned by persons other than the state or organs of state, it is clear that the right to freedom of expression is of direct horizontal application in this case as contemplated by section 8(2) of the Constitution.

[113] Some writers thus see it as an example of strong, indirect horizontal application: see Dafel, 2015: 67–70.

[114] *Khumalo*: para 4.

[115] Ibid: para 29.

[116] Friedman, 2014: 69–70 and 72 expands on these two steps. Woolman, 2006: 31–45 appears to concur with this reading of the judgment albeit offering a preferred reading of the constitutional provisions.

[117] *Khumalo*: para 33.

[118] Ibid.

The court in this paragraph identifies two factors that are of importance for determining whether a right has direct application in relation to non-state actors. Firstly, the court references the 'intensity of the right', whose meaning is not completely clear. It would appear that this dimension requires an understanding of the right's importance in developing the society envisaged by the Constitution as well as the reasons lying behind its protection.[119] The court, earlier in the judgment, provides an understanding of the crucial role freedom of expression plays in a democracy.[120] This is a significant starting point as it requires ascertaining the individual's (or entity's) interest at stake in a particular context that requires protection against invasion.

The court then identifies the potential invasion upon a right by persons other than the state as a significant factor in its decision. This is obviously significant in the context of horizontality as it requires an understanding of the capacity of a non-state actor to affect a fundamental right. The difficulty here is that it is not clear how far the notion of 'potential' extends: clearly, any actual impact will need to be considered but it might be unfair to extend the obligations of non-state actors to impacts that are very unlikely or too remote.[121] Nevertheless, I would suggest that any foreseeable potential impact should be included in an examination of the obligations of a non-state actor.[122]

The case illustrates, however, that not every impact will necessarily translate into an obligation to avoid that effect – the court, in this case, accepted that existing defamation law had a 'chilling' effect on newspapers. Yet, it also recognises the potential of the media negatively to harm the significant reputational interests of others which are protected by the fundamental right to have one's dignity respected. In examining how the law should adapt, the court thus did not only consider the rights of the media to freedom of expression but also their obligations. In doing so, the court reflected, importantly, on the nature and function of the media within a constitutional democracy and how it could contribute

[119] I have previously made this point in Bilchitz, 2008: 776 and Bilchitz, 2017: 206. See also Nolan, 2014: 84.

[120] *Khumalo*: para 33. See also Currie and De Waal, 2013: 48 who suggest that this phrase is opaque but probably relates to the 'scope of the right'.

[121] See Bilchitz, 2008: 777 and Bilchitz, 2017: 206.

[122] As Woolman, 2006: 31–63 points out, these two steps require some interpretation of the content of the right to determine their application to non-state actors. This book recognises that application is already happening and the fascinating questions concern what the substantive content of the obligations of non-state actors are rather than whether they have any such obligations in the first place.

to the development of a democratic culture.[123] Though the media is often run by private corporations, the court thus found that it has significant 'public' effects on the political community. It also found that the media's role was of 'undeniable importance'[124] in providing 'citizens both with information and with a platform for the exchange of ideas'.[125] The media's function in this regard confers on it significant power in the society which justifies the imposition on it of duties to act with 'vigour, courage, integrity and responsibility'.[126] Here in evidence is the relationship between power, the capacity to impact upon rights, and concomitant obligations. The approach adopted by the court could also help allay the fears of those concerned with recognising corporate rights – the objection discussed in section 5.2.3.1 – since it shows how any such entitlements should be limited by an understanding of their obligations towards others.

5.4.1.1.2 Approach to Balancing The media thus was entitled to claim fundamental rights protection but was also a bearer of obligations in relation to the fundamental rights of others. To determine how the law should adapt, the court proposes an approach based on 'the need to establish an appropriate constitutional balance between freedom of expression and human dignity'.[127] The court does not elaborate on exactly what this balancing process entails: nevertheless, its practical resolution of the case provides some clues in this regard. I would suggest that the court applies a central dimension of the well-known proportionality test – namely, the necessity enquiry – to achieve the result it does. The court accepts that existing defamation law has a 'chilling effect' on the right to freedom of expression of the media given the difficulty, at times, of proving the truth of a statement. At the same time, there is a legitimate purpose in restricting that right in order to protect the reputation of individuals (and their concomitant right to dignity). The court, however, seeks to consider if there is an alternative which could still sufficiently protect the interest in reputation whilst having a lesser impact on the freedom of expression rights of the media.[128] The court identifies just such an alternative in its

[123] *Khumalo*: para 24.
[124] Ibid.
[125] Ibid.
[126] Ibid.
[127] Ibid: para 42.
[128] I defend this formulation in Bilchitz, 2014: 61–62, which has been adopted by the Indian Supreme Court in *Justice KS Putaswamy* v. *Union of India* paras 126 and 446.

'reasonable publication' defence and seeks to demonstrate how it still requires attention to be paid to reputational interests whilst not making it unduly difficult for publishers and editors to release stories.[129]

In summary, the court's reasoning in *Khumalo* recognises that, in the context of the horizontal application of constitutional rights, determining what an entity or individual can claim in law will be limited by their obligations towards others.[130] The court first engages with 'beneficiary-orientated' considerations which focus on understanding the interests of an individual or entity underlying a right and the potential impact of the impugned law or activity upon that right. In considering the obligations of a non-state actor towards others, the court references 'agent-relative considerations', which include the nature and function of that agent in society and its power to harm the rights of others. In reaching a conclusion on the practical outcome of the case and the obligations of the actors vis-à-vis one another, the court seeks to balance the interests and rights of those concerned. A central feature of the reasoning that has been identified is the search for 'less restrictive means', which gives expression to the 'necessity' component of the proportionality enquiry. I now turn to another jurisdiction in which the direct obligations of non-state actors are accepted, namely Colombia, and I examine the approach adopted there to determining their obligations.

5.4.2 *The Colombian Jurisprudence: Relationality and Vulnerability*

The Colombian Constitution was drafted against the backdrop of an attempt to solve the history of violence that has plagued the country.[131] These conflicts were rooted in socio-economic injustice as well as a sense of political exclusion.[132] The Colombian Constitution of 1991 thus also has transformative aims[133] and, consequently, provides for a wide range of both civil and political as well as socio-economic rights.[134] Whilst civil and political rights were clearly justiciable on the face of the Constitution, court jurisprudence has established that socio-economic rights too are

[129] Ibid: para 43.

[130] One can also put this the other way round: the obligations of an entity in the law require having reference both to its effect on the fundamental rights of others as well as its own claims to fundamental rights protection.

[131] Palacios, 2006: 246–247; Rios-Figueroa, 2012: 278.

[132] Cepeda-Espinosa, 2004: 533–534.

[133] Ariza, 2013: 135.

[134] Itturalde, 2013: 369.

similarly justiciable.[135] Importantly, the source of conflict in Colombian society has often been non-state actors such as powerful wealthy landowners and drug lords,[136] as well as guerilla movements.[137] It was thus necessary for fundamental rights not simply to be applicable against the state but against non-state actors too.

One of the important innovations of the Constitution was the creation of the 'tutela' action in article 86.[138] This article provides that individuals may claim legal protection from a judge through a speedy procedure to protect their fundamental constitutional rights when they fear that these rights may be harmed or threatened by any action or omission of a public authority. Important for our purposes is the last paragraph of the article, which extends the tutela to apply against non-state actors.[139] It provides as follows:

> The law will establish the cases in which the order of protection should apply to individuals entrusted with providing a public service or whose conduct may seriously and directly affect the collective interest or in respect of whom the applicant may find himself/herself in a state of subordination or vulnerability.[140]

Importantly, for our purposes, it has been clearly held by the court that the reference in article 86 to individuals includes legal entities.[141] The quoted segment from article 86 has also been understood to outline three alternate requirements for the tutela to be used to protect individual rights against infringements by non-state actors. I will focus on the Constitutional Court's jurisprudence in relation to the third requirement – subordination or vulnerability – given that this is of particular interest to the enquiry of this book. The first requirement – where individuals or legal entities are entrusted with providing a public service – demonstrates the adoption in these cases of the expanding the state model in Colombian law, which was discussed in Chapter 4.[142] The second requirement envisioned in this article is less interesting for our purposes where the focus is on individual rights.

[135] For an account of this development, see Cepeda-Espinosa, 2004: 616–620; Ariza, 2013: 137–140.

[136] Palacios, 2006: 242.

[137] Ibid: 256–257; Rios-Figueroa, 2012: 278.

[138] Available in English translation at www.constituteproject.org/constitution/Colombia_2005.pdf. The tutela has had widespread success in widening access to justice in Colombia: see Itturalde, 2013: 372–382; Pérez, 2012: 324.

[139] See Müller-Hoff, 2012: 336.

[140] See Colombian Constitution note 138 earlier. The 'tutela' is further regulated in the Decree No.2591 of 1991.

[141] See, for instance, *T-909 of 2011* and *T-738 of 2011*.

[142] For an example, see Müller-Hoff, 2012: 337–340.

The Colombian jurisprudence[143] is one of the clearest examples of the direct obligations model where remedies flow for individuals directly from the obligations of other non-state actors in relation to fundamental rights. Whilst the use of the tutela remedy is supposedly exceptional for claims against non-state actors – to avoid replacing other legal remedies – there are multiple cases that have been decided in this regard. I have chosen three which broadly reflect the approach of the court and allow for an understanding of what considerations it takes into account in determining the content of the obligations of non-state actors and, particularly, corporations.

5.4.2.1 *T-1236 of 2000*: A Focus on the Vulnerability of Rights-Holders

This case related to a driver who had been employed by a corporation – namely, Gustava Hernandez & Cia Ltda – for almost twenty years. The employer only registered him officially with the Institute for Social Security (ISS) eight years after he started working. Given he had already reached fifty-five, the ISS refused to recognise his entitlement to a pension as he was too old when his registration was effected. The employer also refused to provide him with a retirement pension. The driver was also owed nineteen months of wages as well as certain bonuses. The case raised the question whether an individual can utilise the tutela action for the protection of this kind of right against a private company.

The Constitutional Court answered the question in the affirmative. In doing so, it sought to interpret the third requirement in article 86 of the Constitution concerning what constituted a condition of subordination or vulnerability. Following from prior decisions, it held that the question of vulnerability arises when an individual lacks the physical or legal means to prevent or repel a threat to an actual violation of her fundamental right(s).[144] The court, following previous precedent, stressed that the decision about whether such a state existed ultimately rested upon whether a person was in a vulnerable or dependent relationship with another: such a state flowed from the particular relationships that existed between persons. Each individual circumstance would have to be judged on its merits as to whether a high degree of vulnerability was present that warranted the use of the tutela.[145]

[143] In engaging with the Colombian jurisprudence, I am grateful to Rafael Andrés Gomez Campo for his research assistance and help with translation.

[144] *T-1236 of 2000*: section III.2.

[145] Ibid.

The court then proceeded to evaluate whether such a condition existed in the case before it. It found that the driver was seventy years old and, being elderly, part of one of the groups with a particular vulnerability recognised in the Constitution. The work performed by the plaintiff – as a driver – indicated he was socio-economically vulnerable and, as a result, the lack of payment could have resulted in his being deprived of even the most basic social minimum level of resources necessary to exist with dignity. The fact that he also lacked access to social security in the form of healthcare and a pension was particularly concerning to the court given that he was advanced in age and could have required additional medical care. All these features of his situation led the court to conclude that he was no doubt in a position of vulnerability.

The court also raised the problem that labour claims should usually be addressed through other judicial remedies. It, however, found that the tutela can be used exceptionally in labour cases where there is a need to protect the fundamental rights of an individual and, specifically, in circumstances where such violations would threaten the basic minimum conditions of an individual's life and that of his family.[146]

The court then affirmed the relationship between earning a wage and being able to have access to a basic minimum condition of living. It also held that the payment of wages by both public and private entities was a very serious obligation which must be met even when these entities are going through financial difficulties. Moreover, it also affirmed the important obligation upon an employer to make social security payments. Based on these findings, the court ordered the company to pay all outstanding wages to the individual concerned, plus catching up on social security payments. Until this was done, the company had to pay for all medical expenses of the driver or pay for his enrolment in a medical insurance of his choosing.

This case, importantly, illustrates how fundamental rights place obligations directly upon non-state parties and how remedies emerge from these rights. Whilst this is clear from the Constitution, the court helpfully elaborates upon how to understand the terms 'subordination' and 'vulnerability', which is crucial for understanding the court's jurisprudence in this area.

'Subordination' specifically involves the existence of a 'legal relationship of dependency' such as exists between employers and employees; teachers and students; and parents and children. It essentially involves

[146] See also more recently *T-404 of 2018*, where the court was prepared to hear a tutela of an elderly person denied his proper pension payout. See also *T-258 of 2018*.

a pre-existing set of general relationships which create such dependency. Vulnerability, on the other hand, also involves dependency but it arises from situations in which the person factually or legally lacks the ability to respond effectively to a violation or threat to his or her fundamental rights. This notion takes account of difficulties faced by individuals in gaining access, for instance, to ordinary remedies in the legal system as well as their own personal circumstances.[147] Thus, the court almost automatically can assume a situation of subordination where particular legal relationships exist. In cases of vulnerability, it is necessary to show that it exists in the circumstances of the case.[148]

In developing these concepts, the Constitutional Court essentially holds that the core reason for the application of constitutional rights to non-state actors lies in the potential asymmetrical power relations that exist between the non-state actor and the individual whose rights are affected. That asymmetry arises given that some are accorded particular power and social status through the law and, in other cases, may de facto exercise such power. Abuses of power by stronger parties in the private sphere are thus analogous to the concerns about the exercise of state power:[149]

> The law establishes that the background of the tutela action against individuals lies in their relative superiority or their forgetting of the social purpose of their functions, which renders the remaining members of the community vulnerable to violations of their fundamental rights (CP art. 86). The idea that inspires the tutela action, which is none other than control over the abuse of power, is predicated on the individuals who exercise it arbitrarily.[150]

One notable feature about the court's approach in this case is the focus almost exclusively on beneficiary-orientated factors: from these, it moves very quickly to the obligations of the company. On the one hand, it is impressive to see a Constitutional Court deeply concerned to vindicate the rights of poor and elderly individuals such as Mr Zabala. On the other hand, it is not clear that it is fair to make Mr Zabala's vulnerability the *sole* basis for determining the obligations of the corporation. For instance, it is not clear why a lack of resources – due, for instance, to the company suffering from a serious fall in its income – does not provide a justification for being unable fully to pay wages or social security:

[147] This is seemingly what it means by legal barriers in the test for vulnerability: see *T- 351 of 1997*.

[148] For these principles, see, for instance, *T-179 of 2009*; *T-909 of 2011* para 6; *T-694 of 2013*.

[149] *T-100 of 1997*.

[150] *T-251 of 1993*: para 9. The paragraph has been translated to capture the sense thereof rather than purely literally.

practically, how is an individual corporation which lacks such resources to succeed in meeting its obligations to its employees? Clearly, employees cannot work for no pay, but in cases of serious temporary reductions in turnover or cash-flow, there have, for instance, been cases where companies reach agreements with employees to reduce their pay for a limited period of time. Such an arrangement seems preferable to large-scale retrenchments. This discussion suggests that the capacity of a corporation to pay employees must be factored into a realistic determination of the substantive content of its obligations towards them. The movement from the beneficiary's vulnerability to an immediate obligation on a non-state party is too quick and ignores relevant factors relating to the corporate agent itself.

The court also does not really articulate any framework for deciding what constitutes a fair outcome in relation to *both* parties: the focus of the court's decision is on the beneficiary of the right; whilst there is no doubt this should play a major role, it is not fair to the other party if the reasons for the infringement are not properly considered. A framework for balancing interests thus appears to be lacking from the analysis in this case.

5.4.2.2 *T-909 of 2011*: Towards a More Balanced Approach

This tutela action dealt with a situation in which two same-sex partners were asked to stop making overt expressions of affection towards one another in a shopping centre by security guards. These personnel were employed by a security company that was contracted to provide services by the privately-owned shopping centre. The claimant alleged in the tutela a violation of his right to dignity, free development of his personality, privacy, and equality. He requested an apology and that a human rights training programme be instituted by the shopping centre in question, educating employees and subcontractors not to discriminate on grounds of sexual orientation and to respect the liberty rights of those passing through its premises.

In granting the tutela, the court deals with a number of important issues. It acknowledges firstly that the tutela provides a remedy for rights violations by non-state actors as they can 'exercise power over other people'.[151] The court repeats the principles discussed above concerning subordination and vulnerability as a basis for utilising the tutela. Gay persons, the court finds, were historically marginalised and are subjected to continuing social stigma – as such, they are entitled to special protection and fall within the category of being 'vulnerable' to the negative

[151] *T-909 of 2011*: para 6.

exercise of power by other non-state actors.[152] Secondly, it affirms that obligations for non-state actors also arise due to the 'effective process of privatization of public areas of the lives of individuals'.[153] The blurring of the boundaries between the public and private has also resulted in the need to protect individuals against private exercises of social power.[154] The court also recognises, importantly, that the horizontal effect of fundamental rights is of particular significance in relation to legal entities such as corporations which 'have an increasing capacity to influence the lives of individuals and the exercise of their freedoms and rights'.[155]

The court considers an argument as to whether owners of property may restrict the freedom of others on the basis of their right to property. That right, the court acknowledges, does grant an owner some autonomy to control what happens on their property but that freedom cannot deny the fundamental rights of others.[156] Once again, as in *Khumalo*, the fundamental right is not considered to be absolute but must be considered in light of the owners' obligations. That is the case, a fortiori, in relation to shopping centres given the specific function they have come to play in human life. No longer, the court holds, can such spaces be conceived of as purely private, performing only a commercial function.[157] This change towards a more public function increases the owners' responsibilities to respect the fundamental rights of individuals within these domains.[158]

That also entailed direct responsibility by the shopping centre for the actions of those who are connected with it and act on its behalf.[159] The shopping centre, the court finds, therefore, was responsible for the actions of the security guards. The security company was also responsible in this case as its employees exercised power over what people did in the shopping space.[160] The court also, interestingly, includes a discussion of the nature and function of private security services which it holds involves monitoring citizens for purposes of preventing 'acts that threaten life,

152 Another interesting case where the court offers strong protection to pregnant women against employers on grounds of historic discrimination is *T-583 of 2017*.
153 *T-909 of 2011*: para 8.
154 Ibid.
155 Ibid: para 9.
156 Ibid: para 41.
157 Ibid: para 42.
158 Ibid: para 91. The court's holding here clearly goes against the US Supreme Court's current position and is more consonant with the progressive line of cases in the United States discussed in section 4.3.1 of Chapter 4.
159 Ibid: para 93.
160 Ibid: para 95.

physical integrity, the property of the subject... and, where appropriate, the commission of a crime'.[161] Importantly, such entities and the individuals working for them should not be restricting the freedom of individuals or be taking over the functions of the police.[162] They are also duty-bound to respect the Constitution and act in conformity with its tenets.[163]

Having outlined its jurisprudence relating to liberty rights as well as the prohibition against discrimination on grounds of sexual orientation, the court concluded that the legislature had not restricted kissing or expressions of affection between persons of the same sex. As such, it did not lie within the power of the shopping centre to violate individual freedom in this way.[164] Nor, the court held, may property rights be used to place arbitrary restrictions on people's freedom.[165] It also found a violation of the prohibition against non-discrimination on grounds of sexual orientation.[166] Its order included an apology to be made to the couple, and, as was requested, for the shopping centre and security company to develop a programme to train their employees in respect for freedom and the principle of non-discrimination on grounds of sexual orientation.

The judgment is important for its vigorous defence of the fundamental rights of individuals and its imposition on a corporation of an obligation to respect these rights. The court, in its order, effectively finds that this obligation requires the corporation to take active steps to address the impugned discrimination.[167] In deciding on the scope of the obligations of corporations, in this context, the court engages in a more complex discussion than was evident in T-1236 of 2000. It continues to display a deep sensitivity to beneficiary-orientated factors, speaking eloquently about the impact of the violation on the freedom and equality of the young couple – including the harm to their dignity and the potential to entrench prejudice. However, the court also considers significant agent-relative factors in this case: in particular, it discusses the role and function of shopping centres and security companies within society. In doing so, it also develops an understanding of the capacity these entities have within the context of daily life in Colombia to affect the fundamental rights of individuals. It also brings into consideration an understanding of how shopping centres today can be understood to

[161] Ibid: para 37.
[162] Ibid.
[163] Ibid.
[164] Ibid: para 100.
[165] Ibid: para 103.
[166] Ibid: para 106.
[167] This is in line with the position in UN Framework 2008: para 55.

exercise a form of 'public' power over those who enter them. That understanding forms the context in which the court considers the autonomy rights of shopping centres to control what happens on their property – which, given their function and capacity to harm rights, are highly restricted. The court thus focuses particularly on the rights of the beneficiaries but also, interestingly, considers factors relating to the corporations in question in determining their obligations. The judgment, ultimately, constructs the rights of the corporation in light of their obligations towards others – it appears to lack any express balancing discussion, perhaps because the violation by the security guards was so clearly unacceptable.

5.4.2.3 *T-694 of 2013*: The Impact of Autonomy on Obligations

In this case, the applicant, a Mr Alvarez, applied for a job at a mixed state-private company known as Ecopetrol. He went through various stages of a selection process but, ultimately, was informed that the company had decided not to employ him. The company refused to provide him with reasons concerning their decision and maintained they had a degree of discretion concerning who to employ. Mr Alvarez claimed the refusal to provide reasons was a violation of his right to due process, his right to work, and his right to equality and, therefore, instituted a tutela action.

After having reiterated its jurisprudence on subordination and vulnerability, the court, interestingly, finds that the rationale for allowing tutelas between private persons is to 'balance out those relationships that arise from situations of inequality between the parties'.[168] The court then goes on to hold that due process rights are applicable not only to the state but also to private sector companies when conducting labour relations. Its justification for doing so is that a 'social state of law must guarantee in every legal relationship minimum parameters that protect people from arbitrary and unjustifiable actions which violate the fundamental rights of individuals'.[169]

In applying its reasoning to the concrete case, the court attempts to understand the nature of Ecopetrol, which it describes as a 'mixed economy' company.[170] The court had previously held that its links to the state – through the investment of state capital, for instance – were sufficient to give it a public character; yet, at the same time, in relation

[168] *T-694 of 2013*: section 2.3.3.
[169] Ibid: section 2.4.5.
[170] Ibid: section 2.5.2.2.3.

to matters such as employment, it held that it should be considered to be a non-state actor. An employment relationship usually, in Colombian law, gives rise to a recognition that the employee is subordinate to the employer: the court extends its understanding of subordination to apply to an aspiring employee who is in a selection process. Perhaps out of a sense of ambivalence about whether the category of 'subordination' applies where there was no contract of employment, the court also finds that an applicant for a job is in a factual situation of 'vulnerability' and lacks any other means to defend himself against a violation of his rights.

In analysing the case, the court outlined a clear principle that corporations do have a sphere of autonomy and discretion as to how to conduct their business relations.[171] This includes who they appoint as employees: they are able to evaluate whether any individual is best suited for their purposes. That autonomy, however, has to be exercised within constitutional limits.[172] These include making it clear publicly what is required for the position, and keeping the potential employee informed about the process. A company also must give some reasons to any unsuccessful applicants about why they chose not to employ them.[173] On the facts of the case, the court found that the company had complied with its obligations to Mr Alvarez. It had kept him informed and provided an objective reason which was not discriminatory on any protected ground – concerning his undergoing criminal proceedings for fraud – as to why it did not appoint him. The court therefore dismissed this application.

Unlike the other two decisions discussed, the court, here, finds in favour of the corporation that had been charged with violating fundamental rights. In doing so, it affirms both that the corporation has some obligations to applicants for jobs but also places some limits on those obligations. The finding that corporations have certain obligations of due process is itself significant given these are often seen as the preserve of the state.[174] Its reasoning in that regard is not altogether clear but the principle seems to be that when a non-state entity has a large amount of power over another (through a disciplinary process), it has a duty to conduct its affairs with a degree of procedural fairness. Even though such an entity is not required to be impartial in the same way the state is, its exercise of power must be controlled given its capacity to affect the

[171] Ibid: section 2.5.9.
[172] Ibid: section 2.5.5.
[173] Ibid: section 2.5.7.
[174] As such, it is interesting to compare this case to the *Stadium Ban* decision of the German Constitutional Court (section 4.3.2.2) discussed in Chapter 4.

fundamental rights of individuals. The de facto vulnerability of a job applicant is also a central feature of the court's finding in this regard.

This is not the end of the story, however. The court emphasises the critical role of preserving a space of autonomy and discretion concerning who companies employ, which is central to the realisation of their business purposes. That freedom is not absolute but, nevertheless, must be factored into a proper capturing of their obligations to others and reduces the scope of what they must do. Whilst in relation to public sector employers there is a more detailed duty to justify a selection, in relation to non-state actors, the obligation is less onerous. The nature and function of an entity thus help determine its obligations – a 'mixed economy' company may have certain heightened obligations to respect fundamental rights but also retains significant discretion concerning who it wishes to employ. Ultimately, this 'autonomy' dimension of the company was determinative given that the court found it had been reasonable in how it behaved towards the applicant and complied with its obligations to provide reasons.

Although the court elucidated the key factors, it is not entirely clear how it arrived at a final conclusion concerning the scope of corporate due process obligations. The vulnerability of a job applicant argues in favour of more stringent obligations; the autonomy of the company against. The court, in this case, finds the latter determinative but, to be fully justified, it appears to need a reasoning process that can evaluate properly the different normative considerations against one another.

5.5 Conclusion: The Need for an Analytical Framework for Determining Corporate Obligations

This chapter considered the direct obligations model which accepts that fundamental rights can impose binding obligations upon non-state actors. After considering the case for the model as well as a prominent criticism, I turned to examine leading approaches to determining the substantive content of these obligations both at the international and national levels.

Given the dominance of the state duty to protect model in international law, there have been limited attempts to consider how to translate the obligations flowing from international fundamental rights from the realm of the state to the context of non-state actors. The 'sphere of influence' notion is normatively flawed and irredeemably vague: to be defended, it will require translation into a form of multi-factoral approach that will be discussed in the next part of this book. The UNGPs, we saw, appear to assume that one can simply read off what a responsibility to respect entails for corporations from understanding their impact on internationally recognised fundamental rights. Yet, that assumes incorrectly that one can move directly from understanding the impact of an activity on a right to an obligation to prevent that impact. As the next two chapters will highlight, the real normative work lies in deciding what constitutes an impermissible impact on a right by a corporation.

Given their need to decide concrete cases, unsurprisingly, more guidance is to be gained from the jurisprudence of courts in domestic jurisdictions which have applied the direct obligations model. Both South Africa and Colombia have shown the possibilities the direct obligations model holds for applying fundamental rights directly to non-state actors. The South African Constitutional Court's approach could be described perhaps as more individualistic: it strongly separates out the interests of the beneficiary of a right and the agent who has the potential to harm a right which, in turn, requires a subsequent balancing process.[175] The Colombian Constitutional Court's approach challenges this by being more relational in nature: it suggests that each of the parties cannot be considered entirely separately and emphasises how relationships in society *between* the parties to a dispute – and, their respective power and vulnerability – affect fundamental rights. This approach highlights our embeddedness in various forms of social connections; yet, it also has the potential to lose sight of the distinctness of individual interests.[176] That is in evidence, at times, where there is a failure to consider countervailing considerations and engage in a structured reasoning process to balance competing normative claims.

Despite showing promise and highlighting a number of relevant factors, neither jurisdiction has articulated a clear analytical legal framework for determining the substantive content of corporate obligations in relation to fundamental rights. Without that, the decisions, at times, appear rather ad hoc and may lose sight of important normative considerations. Drawing on the insights from the jurisprudence in both jurisdictions can address their respective deficiencies and assist in developing a more optimal approach. The next three chapters draw

[175] Nolan, 2014: 90 also seems to recognise this and calls for a corrective that is similar to that of the Colombian Court's relational approach.

[176] I do not here suggest the approach is utilitarian which it is not but the insight of Rawls, 1999: 24 that we must preserve an understanding of the distinctness between persons comes to mind as a potential concern with this approach.

together what we have learnt from the articulation and analysis of the various models that have been identified in Part 1 of this book and take up the challenge of systematising, developing and justifying an analytical legal framework for determining the substantive content of corporate obligations in relation to fundamental rights.

PART II

Towards a Multi-Factoral Approach for Determining the Substantive Content of Corporate Obligations

6

The Justification for and Contours of a Multi-Factoral Approach

6.1 Towards an Analytical Framework for Corporate Obligations

As the previous four chapters have demonstrated, it is undeniable that the interests protected by fundamental rights can be seriously impacted upon by non-state actors. The previous four chapters have also identified four 'models' which have been adopted in various legal regimes for addressing this problem. The first three models essentially attempt to retain the notion that it is only – or primarily – the state that has fundamental rights obligations. Yet, as I sought to show through a qualitative analysis of case law from these jurisdictions, in implementing these models, courts do in fact have to grapple with the question of the substantive content of non-state actors' obligations. The state duty to protect model needed to answer the question: what must the state protect individuals against? The indirect application model essentially required a construction of non-state actors' obligations even though this is often done through the interpretation of 'general clauses' in private law. The expanding the state model needs an understanding of the factors that establish when a non-state entity is part of the 'state' or public sphere which, in turn, are relevant to determining the substantive content of its obligations.

What these chapters consequently show is that there is no circumventing the need to determine legally what the obligations of non-state actors are. It could not in fact be otherwise given, as I argued in Chapter 2, that a central role of the state is precisely to address the relationships between non-state actors. Since there is no alternative to engaging with the question of how to construct the obligations of non-state actors in relation to fundamental rights, the matter must be tackled head-on.[1] As we saw, that is one of the core advantages of the last model I considered – the direct obligations model – which avoids any legal subterfuges. At the same time, the analysis in this chapter does not presume all states will adopt such a direct model given the diverse legal traditions and doctrines across the world. The forthcoming discussion thus retains its relevance for all jurisdictions that are confronted with the question of determining non-state actors' obligations – even though the doctrinal modalities through which this question will be addressed may differ.

Apart from the necessity of addressing the obligations of non-state actors, what has also emerged fascinatingly is a convergence across the various models and jurisdictions considered in addressing the 'substantive content' question: what are the obligations of non-state actors with respect to fundamental rights? Whilst there has generally been limited attention paid to developing a systematic approach in this regard, the cases analysed exhibit a similar pattern.

In the next two chapters, I shall attempt to systematise what emerges from these judgments into an analytical legal framework for determining the obligations of non-state actors which I shall term a 'multi-factoral approach'. At the outset, it should be recognised that the convergence of the cases already analysed across multiple jurisdictions provides strong support in favour of the multi-factoral approach. Yet, given the infancy of this jurisprudence and its incremental development, it is necessary to go beyond this practice both explicitly to define and explore the contours of the multi-factoral approach better as well as to consider its normative justifiability.

A multi-factoral approach utilises a range of determinants to reach final decisions in an area of law, which, in this book, relates to ascertaining the obligations of non-state actors and, particularly, corporations. These determinants, I suggest, can be classed into two major sets of factors: beneficiary-oriented factors and agent-relative ones. In turn, it is possible to identify the key factors in each set. In reaching final determinations concerning the obligations of non-state actors, we saw that courts engage in a balancing exercise.

The task of this chapter is threefold. In the first part of this chapter, I attempt to show why multi-factoral approaches arise and how they can be justified. In response to valid concerns about their drawbacks, I argue that the strongest articulation of such an approach should include the following aspects: it must specify the relevant factors, consider their

[1] For a similar view, see Dafel, 2015: 73–75.

normative grounding, develop a set of presumptions that can be used by decision-makers, and propose a structured reasoning process to balance competing principles.

The second half of this chapter attempts to accomplish the first three of these dimensions, identifying and engaging with the key beneficiary-orientated and agent-relative factors that have emerged from the analysis of court judgments in the previous four chapters. I seek to understand the normative importance of each one but I also argue that no one factor alone is sufficient to determine corporate obligations. That, in itself, provides an important justification for the multi-factoral approach. The next chapter will consider the last aspect of an attractive multi-factoral approach, namely, the balancing enquiry and how to reach final decisions concerning the substantive content of corporate obligations where competing factors are involved. It will also consider the place of each factor within the proposed legal reasoning structure.

Finally, the multi-factoral approach will apply generally to all non-state actors. Given the relevance of agent-relative considerations, it is necessary to examine each agent's particularities and ability to affect fundamental rights separately. This book focuses on the corporation and, consequently, in the analysis of each factor I consider its applicability to the context of the corporation specifically. The focus of this chapter is also, largely, on the negative obligations of corporations – Chapter 8 will consider the adaptations that are required to this model when determining the substantive content of the positive obligations of corporations.

6.2 Justifying a Multi-Factoral Approach

6.2.1 The Contours of a Multi-Factoral Approach

A multi-factoral approach means that there is no single criterion on the basis of which to reach a legal conclusion. In the context of this book, that would mean there is no one normative consideration – or factor – that alone determines the obligations of corporations. In other words, we cannot say simply that if X factor is present, then Y obligation flows. Instead, determining the substantive content of the obligation is a function of multiple considerations. Courts identify features of a situation that are relevant to specifying an obligation – where none are determinative – and then utilise a decision procedure such as 'balancing' to arrive at a conclusion. Such a multi-factoral approach can, of course, result over time in context-sensitive rules: it becomes known in a legal system, for instance, that where there is a particular constellation of factors, particular obligations flow.

Indeed, the idea of a multi-factoral approach connects in many ways with philosophical discussions concerning the nature of law and, in particular, the distinction, developed by Ronald Dworkin, between principles and rules. Rules, he contends, either apply in a situation or not: if it is clear a legal situation falls under a rule, then the legal consequences must follow.[2] In cases where rules conflict, one of them must be abandoned.[3] On the other hand, a principle is a 'reason that argues in one direction, but does not necessitate a particular decision'.[4] In each situation, a decision-maker has to weigh up how strong a weight to assign to a principle in the face of competing principles. If the principle does not prevail in a particular circumstance, it is not invalid but simply gives way to a stronger principle.[5]

Robert Alexy draws on these ideas for a similar distinction in his seminal work on constitutional rights. He describes principles as 'optimisation requirements', which are 'characterised by the fact that they can be satisfied to varying degrees, and that the appropriate degree of satisfaction depends not only on what is factually possible but also what is legally possible. The scope of the legally possible is determined by opposing principles and rules'.[6] Rules, for Alexy, are norms that are either fulfilled or not and require action strictly in conformity with their requirements. Fundamental rights in constitutions are, for Alexy, principles which need to be considered in light of the factual and legal possibilities to arrive at concrete consequences. Alexy seeks to demonstrate that once we have examined the weight of the principles at play in a particular context, and after balancing them and making a determination, then a rule results.[7] Thus, over time, the way in which principles interrelate and apply becomes clearer and they harden into rules.

A multi-factoral approach can be seen essentially to give expression to the idea that there are several principles at play when determining corporate obligations.[8] Whilst I have adopted the language of factors

2 Dworkin, 1977: 40–41.

3 Ibid: 43.

4 Ibid: 42.

5 Ibid.

6 Alexy, 2002: 48. I have provided a critique of the notion that principles should be understood as optimisation requirements in Bilchitz, 2014.

7 Alexy, ibid: 83.

8 For another example of a multi-factoral approach in the area of determining corporate obligations, see Dahan, Lerner and Sivan, 2011: 137–141, who outline several principles upon which the (shared) responsibility for labour violations should be decided. The

from courts, the language of principles could equally be used. This discussion has also highlighted that a multi-factoral approach is widely used in law, and specifically, in relation to fundamental rights and thus is not particular to the realm of determining corporate obligations in relation to those rights. The question we are concerned with is thus really a subspecies of a wider approach that is central to the determination of the obligations flowing from fundamental rights more generally. Indeed, it is interesting to consider the fact that one source of tension in this field relates to fact that the corporation straddles the boundary between private law and public law. Private law is often regarded as a domain in which there are stronger and clearer rules,[9] whilst public law is one where there are less definite principles at its core. It may be disputed whether this binary opposition is ever correct:[10] yet, part of the difficulty and the resistance encountered, practically, may be in advancing the utilisation of reasoning more associated with fundamental rights in the corporate context, a matter I shall address in Chapter 9. I now turn to consider, in a little more detail, the justification for multi-factoral approaches in fundamental rights decision-making and their particular relevance to the context of determining the obligations of corporations with respect to fundamental rights.

6.2.2 *The Justification for a Multi-Factoral Approach*

6.2.2.1 Normative Complexity and Context Sensitivity

In general, multi-factoral approaches are adopted where there is normative complexity. This means that there is no one reason which can alone justifiably determine the legal position in the context – surrounding, for instance, obligations or remedies – where other reasons operate too. It is potentially also possible that two legal principles, both with normative weight, conflict and the question arises as to how to resolve this conflict. A multi-factoral approach identifies the relevant (and, sometimes,

approach I adopt is wider in seeking to apply beyond labour rights to the full range of fundamental rights affected by corporate activity. It also is one that emerges from a consideration of case law and is thus rooted in aiming to provide a legal analytical framework for making decisions rather than simply a political philosophical one. The additional factors they propose also could be integrated into the multi-factoral model I propose where they are relevant.

9 That is more of an ideal than the reality for private law too with Dworkin, 1977: 45, arguing convincingly that his approach is in fact characteristic of the whole field of law.

10 Dworkin uses examples illustrating the distinction between principles and rules that are drawn from private law: see Dworkin, ibid: 39–40.

conflicting) normative principles that apply to the situation. To arrive at a concrete outcome, it is necessary to have a substantive method of evaluating the weight to be accorded to these factors vis-à-vis one another plus a decision procedure. The resulting decision often establishes a context-sensitive rule that in X circumstances, with Y constellation of factors, a certain set of Z obligations will follow.

Consider again the case of *Khumalo* v. *Holomisa,* discussed in the previous chapter, which dealt with the rights and obligations of publishing houses in contexts where they wish to publish material that can harm the reputations of individuals. If the legal position is solely determined by the right to free speech of publishing houses, they would be entitled to publish whatever they wish. Yet, such a position would show no respect for the right to dignity – which includes the right to reputation – of individuals. Given their power to disseminate information, and their role in the political community, the harm to individual reputations could be severe. On the other hand, it could also be possible to determine the legal position on the basis of the right to dignity and forbid publishing houses from publishing any material that could harm the reputation of individuals. Such a holding would impose a severe restriction on free speech, have a serious 'chilling effect', and potentially undermine the function of the media in providing crucial information to individuals on the basis of which they make both life and political choices.

Consequently, giving either right absolute weight in these circumstances has unacceptable consequences: it is thus necessary to recognise the normative relevance of both rights. Once that is done, it is necessary to ascertain whether there are any reasons why, in the particular circumstances of the case, one right should be accorded more weight than another. A method must then be sought of honouring both rights as far as is possible in the context: courts often use the metaphor of 'balancing' to do so. Balancing results in a legal conclusion and, as a result, a new rule may be crystallised. The *Khumalo* case is an example of where such an evaluation led to the recognition of a new legal rule: a defence of 'reasonable publication' in a defamation action, which both affirms the existence of a duty of care on publishers in relation to what they publish concerning others and seeks to uphold their right to free speech.

Such normative complexity as has just been articulated is an inevitable dimension of adjudicating on questions concerning fundamental rights. Even in the context of state obligations, competing normative considerations arise.[11] Yet, when it comes to non-state actors, a range of other considerations come into play too: our focus shall be on corporations which, as we saw in Chapter 1, have been designed specifically with a function that straddles the boundary between the public and private. Competing normative considerations may thus come into play in relation to the very interests of the entity itself and its internal decision-making but also in relation to its effect on others. Clearly, the impact on and relation it has to individual beneficiaries of fundamental rights will be of importance in determining its obligations. Yet, by virtue of its 'private' dimension, competing principles – such as its own 'autonomy' and business interests – also have normative validity. What is needed is a method of addressing this normative conflict: to find the means to soften it and to respect both sets of rights and interests. The argument for a multi-factoral approach is that it is capable of capturing the normative complexity involved in determining the fundamental rights obligations of corporations where alternatives cannot do so. Attempts to establish hard rules before balancing a range of factors would fail to be sufficiently sensitive to the nature of the corporation and the competing normative considerations involved in determining its obligations. Clarity can only be attained at the cost of sacrificing complexity and, as a result, fairness.

6.2.2.2 Incrementalism: One Case at a Time

Another argument for a multi-factoral approach can also be a certain judicious caution around decision-making. It could well be argued that, in complex and changing circumstances, decision-makers may not know in advance the full consequences of laying down firm rules.[12] To avoid deleterious consequences, as a result, they outline the principles that influence their decision-making and how they are balanced in a particular context. That, then, allows for a different result to be reached in a different context where the weighting of principles is different.[13]

Whilst I have shown in the previous four chapters that there is some discussion in case law surrounding corporate obligations, it also became

[11] The existence of limitations clauses in many constitutions and international instruments provide clear evidence of this point as does the widespread use of proportionality.

[12] Sunstein, 1996a: 18 argues for narrower, 'minimalist' decisions to be made by judges to avoid 'the costs of mistaken judgments as they affect the social and legal system as a whole'. I do not endorse 'minimalism' as he articulates it but rather make the argument for why uncertainty and complexity provide support for a multi-factoral approach to legal decision-making.

[13] Alexy, 2002: 52 describes this as establishing a 'conditional relation of precedence' between competing principles based on their weight in specific circumstances.

evident that there is little in the way of a systematic understanding of how the substantive content of those obligations should be determined. It is fair to say that, unfortunately, and despite their power, the discourse surrounding corporate obligations in relation to fundamental rights is in its infancy. Consequently, adopting blanket rule-based approaches to determining their obligations is not only normatively problematic but also unwise. Instead of jumping in and fearlessly creating legal rules which may not be optimal, a multi-factoral approach allows decision-makers – and particularly judges – to have reference to a range of factors which can help them reach decisions in particular contexts without making precedential determinations they may regret. Doing so also allows decision-makers to modify the rules and outcomes in these cases over time should alternatives be seen better to address the normative conflicts at stake. A certain flexibility is thus intrinsic to the multi-factoral approach, allowing decision-makers to depart from prior holdings in circumstances that warrant doing so. Such flexibility is particularly defensible in the context of a cutting-edge area of law where matters are still unfolding.[14] Over time, the substantive content of corporate obligations will be clarified – with a greater number of rules being developed – but the multi-factoral approach enables this to happen incrementally and, in a way, that can guide the modification and future development of those rules. As we have seen, the conversation surrounding corporate obligations is a global one that affects both constitutional and international law. A multi-factoral approach also allows for learning to take place between these various disciplines with a common understanding of the key normative factors driving outcomes.

6.2.2.3 Context Sensitivity

Multi-factoral approaches also have the great benefit that they identify a range of factors that may have differing degrees of relevance in differing circumstances. They thus determine obligations in a way that is especially sensitive to specific contexts.[15] This is particularly important in relation to entities and domains where there is a high degree of variation in the circumstances of specific cases.[16]

[14] King, 2012: 264 makes the case for flexibility in the context of a similar area of unfolding norms, namely, social rights adjudication.

[15] See Roux, 2009: 133–136 who provides a justification that is more political in nature for the use of this legal method by the Constitutional Court of South Africa, arguing that it allows the court the flexibility to navigate the tension between legal principle and building its own institutional security.

[16] Cragg, 2010: 290–292.

As such, a multi-factoral approach is well-suited to determining corporate obligations in relation to fundamental rights. Corporations have a range of differing impacts on fundamental rights and those effects can vary depending on the specific situation of individuals and the communities in which they live. Moreover, corporations themselves differ significantly – ranging from small operations to large multi-nationals. They also operate within multiple differing domains – for instance, jewellery, publishing, the production of pharmaceuticals, and so many others. It is entirely conceivable – and likely – that the obligations of corporations in these spheres will vary in relation to a range of factors that include the function of the corporation within that specific domain. A multi-factoral approach identifies the factors that apply but allows for the implications thereof to vary with the nature of the specific agent and the context in which they operate.

6.2.2.4 Judgement and Responsibility

A multi-factoral approach also requires judgement on the part of those utilising it. Whilst this can be a source of critique, it is also potentially a strength. Such an approach requires individuals to understand the relevant factors applicable to the context in which they operate and to take responsibility for – and be able to justify – the decisions that they make. This is particularly important in the context of the corporation, where it is necessary to ensure that an understanding of their obligations in relation to rights is embedded in the very decision-making processes of the corporation itself. A rules-based approach could lead simply to a mechanical box-ticking exercise which is externally imposed and not internalised, ultimately, having a lesser effect on corporate behaviour. I shall address these matters in more detail in Chapter 9, where I argue that the need for judgement by decision-makers in a corporation concerning their obligations has the potential to embed fundamental rights more firmly within corporate culture itself.

6.2.3 *The Drawbacks of a Multi-Factoral Approach*

Having sought to canvass reasons that can be provided for multi-factoral approaches, I now turn to consider criticisms thereof which have been raised in other contexts, for instance, concerning the application of the principle of proportionality and relating to legal doctrines for determining the substantive content of socio-economic rights. It is necessary to address these critiques given that they also raise difficulties in our context for determining corporate obligations in relation to fundamental rights.

6.2.3.1 Lack of Clarity

A multi-factoral approach outlines a range of factors for determining obligations, some of which pull in different directions. An important charge that can be made against such an approach is that what it does is simply to outline the relevance of particular factors without indicating their weight nor how they are to be assessed in relation to one another.[17] As a result, the approach leads to the exercise on the part of decision-makers of a wide and relatively uncontrolled discretion.[18] Flexibility is achieved through obfuscation and unclarity.[19] Flowing from this unclarity, there will inevitably be a lack of legal certainty concerning the applicable rules.

It could be argued that such an approach is particularly inapposite in the commercial context in which corporations require clear rules concerning what they are required to do in order to operate efficiently. A multi-factoral approach identifies the relevant factors but still leaves significant discretion and unclarity as to the exact content of corporate obligations. Doing so creates problems concerning commercial and other expectations and provides no unequivocal guidance to directors who are ultimately responsible in a corporation for taking decisions in this regard. A multi-factoral approach also renders it unclear to individuals and communities what they may expect of corporations.

6.2.3.2 Contributing to the Weakening of Fundamental Rights

A multi-factoral approach, it could be argued, is particularly bad in relation to fundamental rights which are meant to be strong entitlements that individuals can expect to be realised. If corporate obligations are determined through reference to a range of factors, it will not be clear what individuals may claim. Moreover, it will open the door for a range of justifications to be offered for abrogating these rights on the basis of a range of factors. The concern is that doing so would contribute to reducing the normative strength of these crucial entitlements. This concern parallels a worry that has arisen in the literature surrounding proportionality which, it has been claimed, reduces the priority afforded to strong fundamental rights to render them simply one normative consideration to be taken into account amongst many others.[20]

[17] Some argue, in the context of proportionality, that many of these considerations are incommensurable: see Endicott, 2014: 316; but, see, Da Silva, 2011 for a response.
[18] For this critique in the context of proportionality, see Urbina, 2012: 80.
[19] For this challenge in the context of socio-economic rights, see Bilchitz, 2007: 176.
[20] Meyerson, 2007: 809–817; Webber, 2010: 202.

Ensuring rights have greater normative strength, it could be contended, requires an approach that provides more definite normative guidance.[21]

This concern is particularly acute, it could be argued, in the corporate context where there are a range of competing pressures and interests. The dominant focus of decision-makers in this sphere is on whether their decisions enhance the profit of shareholders and that goal will tend to displace significant attention being paid to the serious interests of other stakeholders that are protected by fundamental rights. If rights are simply one consideration to be taken into account amongst many others, this criticism suggests that they will, at best, have little influence on corporate behaviour and, at worst, be ignored.

6.2.3.3 Corporate Capture

One further worry concerns whether a multi-factoral approach enhances the power of corporations to affect the substantive content of their obligations. Given the vast number of corporations and their wide-ranging role in society, arguably, their influence is strong. A multi-factoral approach to determining corporate obligations would allow for corporate influence in the process of deciding what they must do in relation to fundamental rights. That may initially seem to be a benefit – it involves decision-makers in reflecting on fundamental rights and enables those closest to the decisions to have a say in determining their obligations. However, the concern would be that the vagueness of the approach allows for corporate decision-makers to place disproportionate emphasis on commercial interests in comparison to the pressing concerns relating to fundamental rights.[22] Their initial decision-making might then be deferred to or influence the decision that a reviewing body such as a court eventually reaches in disputed matters. An approach that does not outline clear hard rules applicable to corporations can also provide them with an opportunity to assert the importance of countervailing considerations where there either are none or they lack sufficient weight. This concern extends

[21] As Webber, ibid: 199 argues, proportionality denies 'categorical answers to rights-claims'. A defender of proportionality would contend that no such categorical answers are generally possible. In the context of the plea for more content to be given to socio-economic rights beyond the vague notion of reasonableness, see Bilchitz, 2007: 155–157; Liebenberg, 2010: 183.

[22] A similar concern is articulated in the context of a systematic bias of judges and state officials towards what are said to be pressing matters of public interest like national security: see Meyerson, 2007: 817.

beyond decision-making within the corporate sphere itself given the weight that is afforded in societies today to the interests of business. Thus, for instance, where a multi-factoral approach is utilised to determine statutory legal rules, it could be argued that it could also provide the basis for legislatures to accord too much weight to the interests of business.[23]

6.2.4 A Strengthened Multi-Factoral Approach

These critiques raise important issues but, in my view, are not determinative against utilising a multi-factoral approach. It might be easier to pretend that the world does not contain normative complexity but it does. Where normative complexity exists, therefore, it would simply be wrong to assert that one principle is absolute with respect to another, where in fact there is a conflict of normative considerations. In such circumstances, both sets of principles must be considered and affect the outcome of any decision-making process. Serious mistakes may also eventuate through attempting to specify a set of rules to govern a particular area where there has been no long-standing experience in doing so. If in determining the substantive content of corporate obligations we are in the domain of normative complexity, the approach we adopt must reflect that reality: this is precisely what a multi-factoral approach does. Despite the desirability perhaps of simpler, bright-line rules, that is neither possible nor desirable in certain domains and, in particular, the one with which we are concerned in this book – determining corporate obligations in relation to fundamental rights.

These arguments do not mean that the concerns raised in the critiques should not be considered or an attempt made to respond to them. The fact that decision-making is normatively complex is not a ground upon which to abdicate responsibility for determining outcomes rationally. It also does not mean that any decision is as good as any other and that there are no correct outcomes. To achieve better decision-making in normatively complex areas, it is necessary to create an analytical framework that is, epistemologically, likely to lead to the appropriate evaluations of competing normative factors. It is clear that a decision where there is overt bias will be suboptimal. A failure to take account of all relevant considerations will affect the quality of decision-making. Consequently, it is necessary to consider how to strengthen reasoning processes that give effect to multi-factoral approaches in order to achieve

[23] On corporate influence in the legislative sphere, see Miller and Harkins, 2010: 568ff.

the best possible decisions, a task I shall now embark on. Doing so can help mitigate the problems of clarity, normative weakness, and corporate capture.

6.2.4.1 Identifying the Relevant Factors

The starting point is to develop an understanding of the relevant normative factors that arise in decisions within a certain domain. The qualitative analysis of existing case law in the last four chapters has identified two sets of factors for determining non-state actors' obligations in relation to fundamental rights: there are 'beneficiary-orientated' factors – which are concerned with the fundamental interests of the *rights-holder* – and 'agent-relative' factors – which are concerned with the *agent* that has the capacity to affect the fundamental rights of the rights-holder and upon whom concomitant obligations will fall. It is possible to discern a number of particular factors in each of these categories that are usually relevant to a determination of the obligations of non-state actors in relation to fundamental rights. These factors are not a closed list and it is possible others will become evident over time. Moreover, decision-makers need to be alert to consider which factors apply in specific contexts.[24] The starting point thus in a multi-factoral approach is for courts and other decision-makers to identify and consider the applicability of each factor in the particular circumstances.

6.2.4.2 Factors and Prima Facie Obligations

In attaining better decision-making, it is important though to move beyond a simple identification of the factors to have clarity about the normative grounding of each factor as well as its particular relevance to the context under discussion – in relation to this book, the determination of corporate obligations. On the basis of that analysis, it thus becomes possible to understand how each factor prima facie conditions obligations and thus, potentially, to develop a series of presumptive principles.

For instance, there may be a presumption that the larger the capacity of a corporate entity to harm a particular right, the more extensive will be its obligations to ensure it avoids harming the right. This presumption cannot alone determine obligations without considering other factors that are normatively relevant; yet, it provides some guidance concerning the relationship between capacity and obligation. Moreover, it also provides an indication of 'weight' in any balancing process: it suggests that

[24] My analysis focuses on what I take to be the key factors emerging from the case law but does not preclude the identification of others.

the larger the capacity of a corporation, the more weight will be attached to the need for it to avoid negative impacts on the fundamental rights of others. In this way, significant guidance can be offered to decision-makers concerning how particular factors should be taken into account in any decision-making process. The second part of this chapter will focus on examining the key factors I have identified and illustrating broadly their normative relevance for determining the substantive content of corporate obligations.

6.2.4.3 Balancing and Final Obligations

In some cases, the strong weights attached to particular factors will be determinative and almost invariably lead to the assumption of specific obligations with there being no significant countervailing factors – these circumstances will be normatively clearer and lead to the identification of specific rules. In other more normatively complex situations, matters will be less evident and a balancing process will need to be undertaken. In the latter set of circumstances, there is a need, of course, to consider not just each factor individually but how to make decisions where several are present and pull in different directions. That will allow for the determination of a final or all-things-considered obligation. In situations where balancing will be required, the question that arises concerns what is involved in doing so. If balancing simply involves decision-makers exercising an unconstrained judgement, the critiques outlined earlier are magnified. If, however, balancing can be understood to involve a relatively structured reasoning process, then that may improve decision-making and mitigate some of the critiques. The proportionality test has been developed, partly, for this purpose and to discipline the reasoning of decision-makers when weighing up competing normative principles.[25] I argue in the next chapter for utilising the proportionality test in the corporate sphere.[26]

6.2.4.4 The Decision-Maker and Decision-Making Processes

Ultimately, the argument presented here is that where normative complexity exists, judgement by a decision-maker will be ineliminable. Whilst in some cases outcomes may be straightforward, in others they will not be. As such, what become particularly important are the decision-making processes: we need to understand who makes the

[25] Kumm, 2010: 162 also sees the proportionality test as helping to guard against corporate capture.

[26] Some of the challenges discussed earlier have also been lodged against proportionality itself: for a response to some of them, see Alexy, 2002: 405; Bilchitz, 2011b: 430–433.

decisions, their potential for institutional/structural bias, and finding institutional correctives to these problems. Doing so can allow us to develop structures and processes that would be likely to lead to the optimal decision-making in this area. Chapters 9 and 10 of this book propose institutional and legal reforms that are necessary to improve decision-making concerning corporate obligations.

6.2.4.5 The Emergence of Rules

The argument presented here does not deny the desirability, in many instances, that clear legal rules will emerge from the reasoning processes I have outlined. At the same time, those rules must be based on some foundation and, it is suggested, that the aforementioned reasoning process constitutes that basis. Legislators may wish to pass legislation covering certain areas – they will need, in doing so, to utilise the analytical framework I identify. In the development of casuistic jurisprudence, this analytical framework can help judges develop rules in concrete circumstances. Over time, the rules governing a particular area or cluster of cases – such as the rules governing the press – will become more firmly established and clearer in legal systems. The movement from flexible principles to established rules will take place in this area as it does in other fields that implicate fundamental rights.[27]

6.3 Exploring the Factors that Determine the Obligations of Corporations

Flowing from this analysis, in giving effect to the strengthened multi-factoral approach, it is thus necessary to examine in more detail the key factors that determine the obligations of corporations. In doing so, it is important to consider the normative grounding of the factors, the way in which they affect obligations and the particular context of corporate actors. As has been explained in section 6.2.4.1, I divide these factors into two sets: 'beneficiary-orientated' factors and 'agent-relative' factors. It is also necessary to consider the relationship between these factors, which is integrated into the analysis in the following sections. This discussion will also offer a further defence of the multi-factoral approach, demonstrating why it is impossible for one factor alone to determine the substantive content of

[27] Alexy, ibid: 83 shows how this dynamic is foundational to adjudication relating to fundamental rights.

corporate obligations, and thus suggesting the unavailability of a viable alternative.

6.3.1 *Beneficiary-Orientated Factors*

Beneficiary-orientated factors refer to those which relate to the holder or subject of a right. In order to understand the obligations of particular agents such as corporations flowing from fundamental rights, the starting point must be an understanding of the normative underpinnings of fundamental rights and what they protect. Three factors are relevant here: identifying the interests affected and their urgency; examining the vulnerability of the individual; and, finally, understanding the impact of an infringement on the individual. These considerations are, however, not sufficient to reach conclusions about the final obligations of particular agents: for that, agent-relative factors will need to be considered as well.

6.3.1.1 The Interests Protected by the Right

In determining the obligations flowing from a right, the first step must be to understand what the right protects. Let us consider, for instance, the right contained in article 19 of the Universal Declaration of Human Rights: 'everyone has the right to freedom of opinion and expression'. This entitlement is stated at a very abstract level and it is not entirely clear exactly what is included within its scope. To determine its substantive content and implications, it is necessary to consider why such an entitlement is protected in law.

A range of justifications have been given but I will focus on the compelling idea that this right is based on the fact that individuals value having the freedom or autonomy to determine their own thoughts and to express them.[28] We could say, instead, that individuals have an 'interest' in such freedom. Individuals would have similar 'interests' in other freedoms (such as the freedom to associate with whom they wish) and in resources (such as food and housing) that represent the necessary conditions for them to flourish.[29] What then does it mean to say individuals have 'interests'?

[28] See, for instance, Scanlon, 1972: 215–216.

[29] Raz, 1986: 166 sees an interest as an aspect of an individual's well-being, which 'is a sufficient reason for holding some other person to be under a duty'.

An interest that grounds a fundamental right is not a purely subjective notion such as a preference. Preferences are multiple and relate to aspects of our lives that are both important and, relatively, trivial. I may, for instance, have a strong preference for a private swimming pool and even have a self-interest in having one – yet, no one would claim I have a right to a private swimming pool. There needs thus to be some way of judging which preferences are truly important and deserve translation into rights. Preferences also are 'adaptive' in that they change according to the circumstances in which I find myself.[30] Those with too little food to nourish them may lack the desire for more as they have become accustomed to being malnourished.[31] On the other hand, those with a large amount of wealth may find it hard to do without a private swimming pool. The adaptive nature of preferences means that they cannot provide a reliable guide as to what truly matters for individuals. Subjective preferences, for these reasons, cannot alone provide a guide to what is most fundamental in our lives. The notion of 'interests' must therefore include an objective dimension – what basis then is there for concluding something is objectively fundamental to individual lives?

In answering this question, the focus in a theory of fundamental rights must be on attempting to capture what is, in truth, foundationally important (or of value) to individuals. A decent theory, in this regard, should be capable of commanding widespread assent from diverse individuals – in doing so, it should identify matters that reasonable individuals can agree upon. Thus, a view that is dependent on adopting a particular ideology, say of Catholicism or Islam, would be undesirable – too specific or detailed an approach can fall into a similar trap. The key is to adopt cross-cutting, general understandings of value that even the holders of diverse ideologies could assent to: for instance, both Catholics and Muslims can agree on the importance of having the freedom to believe and practice their respective religions. Thus, a more general and abstract understanding of value that cuts across diverse ideologies is preferable in this context – this is often referred to as a 'thin' theory of the good.[32] In arriving at such a thin theory, we need to have regard to a range of sources, including objective knowledge of human needs, as well as common human judgements about what is of importance to individuals.[33]

30 See, for instance, Elster, 1982: 219ff and the wider notion of Nussbaum, 2000: 136ff.

31 See the example in Nussbaum, ibid: 113–114.

32 Rawls, 1999: 348.

33 Clearly, inter-subjective consensus could provide clear evidence that an interest is objectively important. On the other hand, it is not determinative given that it is possible

The purpose of this book is not to discuss in depth the justification for fundamental rights and so I draw on my past work to outline the contours of such a theory that is reasonable and can hopefully command widespread assent. Value, I suggest, lies in two features of individual lives.[34] The first is our experiences of the world as sentient creatures: being in constant state of pain will be a condition that individuals usually regard as negatively affecting their lives; experiencing pleasure and joy will no doubt contribute to the positive assessment of their lives.[35] The second dimension involves the achievement of our purposes as agents: for all beings capable of acting in the world, the inability to achieve our purposes is frustrating and regarded negatively whilst the achievement thereof is fulfilling and viewed positively.[36]

To generate an understanding of the most significant objective fundamental interests in individual lives, we need to ask ourselves: what are the general necessary conditions for living lives in which these sources of value are present? We know, for instance, that not having sufficient food is a general condition that gives rise to negative experiences and frustrates the realisation of individual purposes. Individuals can, therefore, be said to have an objective interest in having sufficient food. Similarly, in totalitarian societies, individuals are often unable to express their opinions, which generates anger and frustration, and inhibits their purposes from being achieved. We can thus say that individuals have an objective interest in being able to express their opinions freely.

A further important point to recognise is that interests may be realised to a greater or lesser degree: the greater the impact the lack of one of these conditions has upon the sources of value – experience and purpose – the greater the priority or importance that must be given to them.[37] Where the denial threatens life, we can speak of the most 'urgent' level at which such an interest can be imperilled and requires realisation.[38] The complete denial of food threatens survival without which there would be no experiences or purposes. Thus, it is a priority that the interest of individuals in having sufficient food is at least realised to the point where they

that many people believe something to be a fundamental interest but it is not – such as occurred in relation to patriarchal assumptions about the specific interests and roles of the sexes in the past. See Bilchitz, 2007: 15–16.

[34] Bilchitz, 2007: 23–27.

[35] This feature of the theory of value thus draws on the utilitarian insight about the importance of experience in determining quality of life: see Mill, 1863: chapter 2.

[36] Gewirth, 1978: 49–52.

[37] Bilchitz, 2007: 39.

[38] For the notion of urgency, see Scanlon, 1975: 660.

can survive: I have in the past referred to this as the 'minimum core', linking this analysis with a concept initially introduced by the United Nations Committee on Economic, Social and Cultural Rights.[39] Survival alone, however, is not sufficient to live lives rich in positive experiences and realised purposes. Consequently, in ordinary circumstances, it is important that individuals have their interest in sufficient food met at a level beyond survival – for instance, that they have sufficient food to live healthy lives that enable them to realise their purposes more generally:[40] I refer to this as the 'sufficiency threshold'.

The degree to which an interest is realised or harmed is important and, in any evaluation, may affect the weight to be accorded to the interest in question. Thus, an infringement of a fundamental interest in having sufficient food that relates to the very ability of individuals to survive – for instance, the poisoning of agricultural land by a corporation in a subsistence society – will have a greater degree of seriousness than a more limited infringement – for instance, where supply chains fail for a month to provide healthy food to supermarkets. Such an understanding of 'weight' will be of importance in the balancing of interests (and, consequently, rights).[41] This discussion can lead us to recognise a presumptive principle relating to the obligations flowing from rights that protect such interests: **the greater the degree of the interference with a fundamental interest in the lives of individuals, the stronger will be the claim that an agent – with the capacity to affect that interest – has an obligation not to harm the interest or assist in its realisation.**

The aforementioned discussion raises the question of how we move from a theory of the 'good' (what interests individuals have) to a claim that an individual has a fundamental right relating to those interests which places obligations on other agents. This is of course a large question, and here I chart two brief answers to supplement the discussion in Chapter 2. The first argument is Hobbesian in character. It is rooted in the idea that the fundamental interests of individuals are so important that, if they are not guaranteed in some way, individuals will continually clash, which will have deleterious consequences for everyone (leading to a state of war of 'every man against every man').[42] It is thus in the self-interest of individuals – even in the absence of a state-like authority – to respect the most fundamental interests of others and endeavour to create

[39] General Comment 3: para 10.
[40] Bilchitz, 2007: 40–45.
[41] See Alexy, 2002: 402.
[42] See Hobbes, 1996: 88 (gendered language is from the original).

a state of peace with them.[43] However, as a result of the attempts to achieve short-term self-interested gains, for instance, individuals may well fail to recognise the terrible consequences that could flow for them and others from not respecting the fundamental interests of others. There is thus a need for a 'sovereign' that through its monopoly of force provides guarantees that individuals will respect each other's fundamental interests.[44] The sovereign (or, in more modern terms, the 'state') comes into existence precisely for the purpose of ensuring individuals meet their obligations not to harm others' fundamental rights and to ensure no one is in a condition of utter destitution that threatens their survival.[45]

The second argument for fundamental rights is rooted in the idea that every individual has value (or what is often referred to as dignity).[46] As I have argued, that value lies in the two core features of an individual's life: experience and purpose. Yet, when we join together in society, every individual regards themselves as having value. There is no good reason why, from a societal perspective (which abstracts from the individual perspective), any one person should be preferred over anyone else. That societal perspective is the foundation upon which law is constructed. As such, law should be grounded in the normative view that every individual with these characteristics – the capacity to have experiences and purposes – has an equal value. That, in turn, requires every individual to be *treated* in accordance with that value. Since the individual value we have is connected to the two sources of value, treating someone with dignity means having respect for their fundamental interests – the necessary conditions for living lives rich in those sources of value. Broadly, we can conceive of these interests as being grouped under 'liberty' interests (freedom of speech/religion and others) and 'well-being' interests (food/housing and others). If, as a fundamental principle of our legal systems, we are then to treat individuals with respect for their value (or dignity), we must protect all their important interests in 'liberty' and 'well-being'. We do this, in domestic constitutional law and international law, through recognising that individuals have both civil-political and socio-economic rights which protect these fundamental interests of individuals.[47]

[43] Ibid: 91–92.
[44] Ibid: 120.
[45] I have engaged with this point in more detail in section 2.3.2.2 of Chapter 2.
[46] I use value here but, as explained in Chapter 2, this links up with the legal discussion through the notion of 'dignity'.
[47] For a more in-depth version of this argument, see Bilchitz, 2007: 57–65.

Understanding that fundamental rights protect fundamental interests helps us to translate the abstract expression of fundamental rights in legal documents into concrete implications for particular circumstances. Having a right to freedom of expression, for instance, does not automatically inform Magdalena if she can scrawl graffiti across the walls of the local cinema. Courts are usually given the task in concrete cases of determining the meaning of the abstract right for a particular case, a process often referred to as 'interpretation'. Does, for instance, the word 'expression' in article 19 of the ICCPR cover graffiti? A pure analysis of the words alone is not usually adequate in relation to fundamental rights: graffiti may be understood by some as an act of artistic expression but others could see it as worthless and destructive scrawling that expresses nothing. To adjudicate the verbal dispute, it is necessary to consider whether a case such as this falls within the broad normative protection offered by the right. To determine that, one needs to understand the interests the right protects and then consider whether the specific case is encompassed by those protected interests.[48]

It might be contended, for instance, that freedom of expression is designed to express the interest of individuals to form their own opinions, and give expression to them. Pictorial graffiti with no words attached would not clearly constitute 'expressing an opinion'. Freedom of expression, on the other hand, might be understood to protect individual self-expression in whatever form it takes, even if visual or lacking a clear meaning. Both approaches are possible understandings and, to adjudicate between them, we need to have reference to the fundamental interests lying behind this right. It seems true to assert, more generally, that individuals do not only have an interest in conveying opinions that signify meaning but also in giving expression to their emotions and artistic talents in a variety of ways. Since this interest constitutes part of their freedom to decide how to live and make meaning in their lives, freedom of expression can thus best be understood to include protecting pictorial expressions – such as graffiti – that communicate an individual's emotions or artistic intentions.[49]

I have elaborated upon this example as it is not possible to determine the obligations of any agent in society without an understanding of which fundamental interests the right protects. Understanding those interests, however, is not sufficient alone to determine the obligations of an agent

[48] This 'purposive' approach is adopted in many jurisdictions, including Canada (*R* v. *Big M Drug Mart Ltd* para 116) and South Africa (*S* v. *Makwanyane* para 9).

[49] One fascinating question is how we determine which specific rights provide protections for which fundamental interests – or how to 'individuate' rights: I engage with this issue in Bilchitz, 2021.

that flow from the right. Indeed, the rights of one person may be capable of being limited when considered in light of the rights of others or other pressing social goals. If the local cinema is privately owned, the right to property of the owners may entail preventing the graffiti artist from spray-painting the building. If it is publicly owned and many individuals in the community find graffiti harms their enjoyment of the facility, there will be a question of how to balance the interests of the individual in freedom of expression against the aesthetic preferences of the majority of the community.

In all the cases I have analysed in previous chapters, the courts have had to engage with the fundamental rights of beneficiaries and the interests they protect and then balance them against other interests. Two examples can suffice in this context: the ECHR in *Von Hannover* recognises the vital importance of privacy for a person's physical and psychological integrity and the development of their personality.[50] The same court in *Eweida* finds that freedom of religion protects the freedom to 'manifest one's belief, alone and in private but also to practice in community with others and in public'.[51] These rights were then weighed against countervailing factors (discussed later) to arrive at a conclusion.

It is thus clear, in summary, that when applying these ideas to determining the obligations of corporations, we need first to identify the interests protected by the right which will always require a justification where they are interfered with. The degree of 'urgency' attached to the realisation of that interest will also, as discussed earlier, affect the weight to be accorded to the interest in any balancing process.

6.3.1.2 Vulnerability

As we saw in Chapter 5, the Colombian Constitutional Court places great emphasis on the vulnerability of individuals in deciding on the obligations of non-state actors. This section will explore the notion of vulnerability and its implications for the obligations of non-state actors.

In the last section, we saw that fundamental rights protect the fundamental interests of individuals. Yet, importantly, those interests exist irrespective of what others can do to them. This fact raises the challenge about how to conceive of obligations flowing from fundamental rights where the fundamental interests of mine are imperilled not by another individual or institution but by a particular state of affairs. Consider, for

50 *Von Hannover*: para 50.
51 *Eweida*: para 80.

instance, a situation where my freedom of movement to shop at a supermarket is restricted by hurricane-force winds. My goal here is frustrated and I am not able to do what I wish to, nor is any current human intervention likely to assist me in this situation: is a fundamental right of mine violated in these circumstances? Similarly, imagine that a graffiti artist is unable to continue to work because of contracting a serious disease which currently cannot be treated. Important freedom interests are affected in these cases but can one claim a right to be free from interference from the weather or a virus?

These states of affairs are indeed undesirable and seriously impair the fundamental interests of individuals. Yet, the weather and a virus are simply features of the world that are not capable of responding to any claims against them.[52] Having one's fundamental interests affected alone, therefore, is not sufficient for having fundamental rights. It must be possible to claim a right and, to do so, requires an addressee who is capable of responding to such a claim.[53] Inherent in the notion of a right is, therefore, the idea that a particular form of relationship must exist:[54] between the holder of the claim and the addressee of the claim. The holder of the claim must have certain interests that are fundamental, which require protection. Those interests, when directed at agents capable of responding to those claims and with the ability to direct their behaviour according to reasons, generate entitlements on the part of the rights-holder and concomitant obligations on the part of the addressee(s) of the claim.[55]

A further interesting question arises from this analysis: does the possession of a right necessarily go along with the idea that the addressee (B) is capable of harming (or helping the rights-holder (A) achieve) her interests? In other words, let us imagine that there is a rational human being who understands and is capable of acting upon reasons. She is mentally agile but

[52] Fineman, 2013: 20 recognises that individual vulnerability often extends to forces beyond human control.

[53] Feinberg, 1980: 154. It may, of course, be that obligations exist upon the parties capable of responding to fundamental rights claims – such as the state – to develop warning systems for hurricanes and investing research in cures for diseases but these obligations will be circumscribed by the domain of the possible. Fineman, ibid: 22–24 recognises society cannot eradicate vulnerability but lessen its impact and produce resilience.

[54] Nedelsky, 1993: 13–19, importantly, places emphasis on the idea that a significant feature of rights involves structuring and constructing the relationships between individuals. Theories of fundamental rights drawn from African philosophy also place strong emphasis on the nature of the relationships between parties: see Metz, 2011: 539. I attempt to show how this is in fact a necessary conceptual feature of rights.

[55] Feinberg, 1980: 148.

Table 6.1 *Some conceptual conditions for the possession of a right.*

The holder of a right (A)	→	The addressee of the claim (B)
Possesses interests		Capability to respond to the claim: rational agent
Potential vulnerability		Ability or power to harm or help

locked into her body without the ability to express her thoughts in words or action. Could one hold a right against such an individual? For all practical purposes, holding a right against such a person is useless. She can neither harm nor help the holder of a right. A right is fundamentally a practical notion in that it involves an injunction either not to interfere with or to aid a holder in realising certain interests. Consequently, there is no point in holding a right against someone entirely without the capability to harm or help. A right therefore is a concept that applies only in relation to an agent who has the ability (or power) to harm or help the rights-holder. The converse implication of this idea is that rights only exist in circumstances where the holder of a right is in some sense potentially vulnerable to the exercise of power by another agent. A right thus gives expression foundationally to a relationship between rights-holders who have potential vulnerabilities and other agents who have the power to exploit or ameliorate them.[56] Vulnerability thus requires that we pay attention to any exercise of power by an agent in relation to the fundamental interests of others and to the justifications for such an exercise (see Table 6.1).

This analysis, however, does not mean that the holder of a right may not also be the addressee of a claim and vice versa. It may well be that B (the addressee of the claim in the aforementioned example) is also the holder of a right against A and that B is vulnerable to A in the same way that A is to B. Such a situation is what I term 'symmetrical situatedness': this exists where both A and B are holders of rights and duties, and possess a roughly equal ability to affect the fundamental interests of one another. Equal ability can be understood not just to mean 'physical capacity' but also

[56] Grear, 2010: 156–161 argues that fundamental rights presuppose the existence of a vulnerable living body and at the core of international human rights protection lies the goal of protecting human embodied vulnerability.

'mental skill'.[57] On the other hand, asymmetrical situatedness may exist in two situations. The first relates to where both A and B are holders of rights and duties but the power of B to affect the interests of A is much greater than the power of A to affect the interests of B. A second situation may exist where A is a holder of a right and only B an addressee – for instance, A may not be capable of being an addressee given a lack of the rational agency required for obligations such as exists in the case of a young child or animal.[58] Conceptually, obligations can emerge in situations both of symmetrical and asymmetrical situatedness: reciprocity is unnecessary for the possession of rights or obligations.[59]

Goodin, who has written a book on the notion of vulnerability, defines it as 'essentially a matter of being under threat of harm'.[60] He suggests this idea is fundamentally relational and helps us to allocate responsibility: '[s]aying that *A* is particularly vulnerable to *B* with respect to *X* clearly fingers *B* as the agent who should be particularly responsible for seeing to it that *A*'s interests in *X* are protected'.[61] In addition, Goodin contends that 'the strength of this responsibility depends strictly upon the degree to which *B* can affect *A*'s interests'.[62] In relation to fundamental rights, this would translate into a principle that **where A is vulnerable to B in relation to A's fundamental rights, prima facie, there is an obligation on B not to harm those rights (and potentially to help realise them)**. The weight accorded to the rights of A in balancing increases in proportion to A's vulnerability. However, vulnerability alone is not sufficient to determine obligations: a more powerful agent may have a perfectly reasonable justification for the exercise of its power which compromises the fundamental interests of a beneficiary.

This analysis is not simply theoretical but has important practical implications. The vulnerability dimension in any concrete analysis requires an understanding, from the rights-holder's perspective, of their relationship with the agent against whom a rights-claim is being made and their particular susceptibilities to having their fundamental interests impacted upon by that agent.[63] The Colombian Constitutional

57 Hobbes, 1996: 87.
58 Feinberg, 1980: 162–167.
59 I already addressed the objection about the relationship between obligations and rights in Chapter 5, section 2.3.
60 Goodin, 1985: 110.
61 Ibid: 118.
62 Ibid.
63 Fineman, 2013: 21 recognises that vulnerability is 'particular, varied and unique on the individual level'. See also, Grear, 2013: 49.

Court has given practical expression to these ideas through its jurisprudence, which identifies certain social relationships as always involving vulnerability, whereas some arise because of the factual circumstances of the particular situation.[64] The German Constitutional Court has also, for instance, in *Blinkfüer* and *Stadium Ban*, recognised the importance of identifying an asymmetry of power which then has an important effect on determining the resultant obligations of non-state actors.[65]

In the context of corporations, we have seen in Chapter 1 how the law creates major advantages for these entities. Let us take the extreme case where there is only one individual shareholder in a corporation who is also the main director. The notion of separate legal personality allows that individual to shield herself in most respects from bearing full responsibility for the activities of the corporate entity itself. Limited liability, as we saw, was particularly valuable because it also protects such an individual from having her fundamental rights imperilled through possible economic destitution.[66] The corporate form also enables individuals to create a separate personality that endures even beyond the life-time of its founding members. These are benefits that no individual alone can achieve and thus, any corporation, in a sense, is cloaked in law with powers that extend beyond the individuals that lie behind it.

It thus becomes important to recognise that when we think of the actions of such a small corporation against another individual, the situation should not be conceptualised as simply being one individual acting in relation to another. Instead, the relationship between them is now mediated through an entity whose very construction is designed to enable the individual behind the corporation to limit her responsibility for her own actions. By cloaking an individual in the form of a corporation, she transforms her relationship with other individuals and gains significant power which translates into concomitant vulnerabilities. This situation is magnified, of course, as the number of shareholders, directors, and employees lying behind the corporation increases, and it is not possible in any straightforward way to trace the actions of a corporation to any particular individual. Corporations also often involve and enable agglomerations of multiple individuals and are designed as co-operative structures which can contain collectivities: this facet increases their power. As such, from the perspective of individual

[64] See Chapter 5, section 5.4.2.

[65] In addition, for the usage of the notion of vulnerability in the case law of the ECHR, see Peroni and Timmer, 2013.

[66] See the discussion Chapter 1, section 1.2.2.

rights-holders, there will always be an asymmetrical relationship when we are concerned with their relationship with a corporation. It will also be important, in concrete cases, to analyse the particular vulnerabilities or power relationships that exist.

From this analysis, the following guidelines can be developed in relation to determining the obligations of corporations. Firstly, corporations are understood to be in an asymmetrical power relationship with individuals in all circumstances where they impact upon fundamental rights. Secondly, particular vulnerabilities must be examined in particular circumstances taking account of economic and structural factors. Thirdly, the particular vulnerability of an individual and their fundamental rights to corporate power will help determine the content and strength of its obligations towards that individual (or group of individuals). Finally, the particular vulnerability of an individual's fundamental rights to corporate power will affect the strength of the justification that must be provided by corporations for interfering with such rights.[67]

6.3.1.3 Impact

The last crucial dimension from the perspective of a beneficiary in determining obligations in relation to fundamental rights relates to what can be termed the 'impact' on the right: what are the effects on the fundamental interests of individuals of any interferences or omissions which are complained of in a concrete situation? This enquiry involves trying to detail the manner and extent to which the identified interests are affected.[68] The *Von Hannover* case, once again, in the ECHR is an example: the court does not simply refer to the general interests protected by the privacy right in question but tries to understand (albeit briefly) the impact on Princess Caroline of stalking photographers even when she is in private spaces with her children.[69] Similarly, in the *NM* case, the majority of the South African Constitutional Court specifically considers the serious impacts on the women concerned flowing from the violation of their right to privacy when their HIV-positive status was disclosed: these included one woman's shack being burnt down by her boyfriend, social ostracism, and depression.[70]

[67] On vulnerability in the proportionality enquiry of the ECHR, see Timmer, 2013: 164–165.

[68] The UNGPs place charting and responding to corporate impacts on fundamental rights at the heart of the fundamental responsibility of corporations to undergo a human rights due diligence process (GP 17).

[69] See, for instance, *Von Hannover*: paras 68 and 74.

[70] *NM*: para 63.

This enquiry draws on the other two dimensions: the interest underlying the impugned fundamental right must be identified, and an understanding developed of the specific vulnerabilities of individuals to an exercise of power in the concrete circumstances. The important point here is that the impact upon fundamental interests is a matter of degree. For instance, a corporation may have a policy that requires its employees not to make any public statements on any platform without its express permission. Such a policy has a severe impact on its employee's right to freedom of expression. A different policy – that simply requires an employee not to issue personal statements from the corporation's social media account – would have a lesser impact on that right. In determining obligations, it is necessary to consider the extent and degree of interference with the rights-holder's interests. It will be easier for a corporation to justify less severe impacts on fundamental rights – such as the less restrictive free speech policy mentioned earlier.[71] The lesser the impact, it is also likely, the less onerous any concomitant obligations would be.

Importantly, within this 'impact' enquiry, the question is not about the capacity of an agent to affect a fundamental interest (which we will consider further next in this chapter) but the extent to which the beneficiary's interests underlying rights are affected. When determining impact, it is necessary to distinguish two possible approaches. On the one hand, there is a 'subjective' approach: this means that the degree of impact is understood along the lines of what an individual considers to be the extent of the impact. An objective view attempts to provide some criteria external to the individual for assessing the extent of the impact.

There must be some degree to which the subjective understanding of the beneficiary is included in the assessment given that the sources of value we discussed earlier (experiences and purposes) have a subjective dimension. Thus, for instance, it makes sense that, in determining the impact on an individual of discrimination, the subjective harms experienced by that person are considered. At the same time, there may be all sorts of reasons why the impact on individuals may vary from a subjective point of view – it may not be reasonable to take account of some of these in determining the obligations of other agents. Free-spirited individuals may find it an egregious violation of their free speech that they cannot opine on the corporation's Facebook page. If they are able to express their point of view on their own Facebook page, it would be objectively unreasonable to regard the interference with their ability to express themselves as being at a severe level,

[71] See the discussion on necessity in the next chapter, section 7.3.4.

even if it is subjectively experienced as such.[72] Consequently, it is necessary to add an objective dimension to the assessment of degree of impact: that would involve understanding objectively the effect of a particular action on the fundamental interests of an individual and the extent to which it imperils the necessary conditions for their being able to live lives of value.

A further important dimension of the impact enquiry is that an impact can be more or less severe depending on the agent that has the concrete effect on an individual's interests. To illustrate this point, consider Vusi's dignity interest in his reputation. After a drunken night out, his parents come to know of his bad behaviour and criticise him for it; yet, given he is a celebrity, the events of the night are publicised in a national newspaper where his behaviour is roundly condemned. An assessment of the situation would reasonably conclude that there was a lesser impact on his dignity interests when only his parents came to know about his conduct than when it was publicised more widely. This assessment is not simply based on the fact that the reporting in the newspaper meant that more people knew about the incident and, thus, objectively, his reputation was affected more extensively. It is also because the relationship with one's parents makes it easier to bear their learning negative facts about one's behaviour and criticising one for it than when that occurs in relation to an entity with which one has, at most, a distant relationship. Similarly, disciplinary proceedings conducted by a corporation against employees whose identities are bound up with it and have devoted years of loyal service to advancing its purposes will likely have a grievous effect on their self-esteem compared to a charity from which they are forced to resign but have only volunteered for two hours a month. These examples illustrate that relational factors such as the nature and character of an agent and the rights-holder's relationship with it need to be taken into account in assessing the impact of actions by that agent in relation to a specific beneficiary.[73]

Importantly, the fact that an agent has an impact on a right is not sufficient alone to impose obligations on it or determine their substantive content.[74] In relation to negative impacts, the question still arises as to

[72] This is why causing subjective offence, for instance, is not a sufficient ground to find a violation of the right to free speech: see *Handyside* v. *United Kingdom* para 49. The adaptive preference problem discussed at notes 30 and 31 earlier could also rear its head in this context, supporting a move away from a purely subjective assessment.

[73] As Fineman, 2013: 22 points out, these impacts arise because of the embeddedness of individuals within societal institutions and relationships.

[74] In fact, as Birchall, 2019: 137–139 argues, the notion of impact goes beyond the realm of legal liability.

whether such an impact is justifiable or not (see more on this in section 6.3.2). We can nevertheless recognise a number of important principles in this regard. Firstly, impact must be ascertained in the concrete circumstances of a case and determined with due regard to the degree of harm, the nature of the agent, and the relationship between the beneficiary and the agent. Secondly, once an impact is determined in relation to a specific agent, **there will be a prima facie obligation to avoid any negative impact** (and, remedial responsibility if it has already occurred).[75] Thirdly, in any balancing enquiry, the greater the impact an agent has on fundamental rights, the greater will be the weight attached to the interests underlying the right and the consequent burden to justify such an impact on those interests.

6.3.2 *Agent-Relative Factors*

The principles discussed thus far flow from factors relating to the rights-holder or beneficiary and create a prima facie case for the imposition of obligations on agents that can have an impact on a right. They are not sufficient, however, to determine the substantive content of those obligations – in other words, what must be done by particular agents. In determining the allocation and nature of the obligations of particular entities, we need to consider a series of factors that are connected with the agents themselves – what I term 'agent-relative factors'. Drawing on the analysis of the case law in the previous four chapters, I suggest three critical agent-relative factors have emerged: capacity, function, and autonomy. I now elaborate on each of these and how they condition the obligations of corporations.

6.3.2.1 Capacity

One of the most commonly utilised agent-relative factors is the capacity of a non-state actor either to harm or positively contribute towards the realisation of a fundamental right. As we saw, the South African Constitutional Court in *Khumalo* found that a central feature in determining the application of a right to non-state actors was 'the potential invasion of that right which could be occasioned by persons other than the state or organs of state'.[76] Similarly, in the *Stadium Ban* case, we saw the German Constitutional Court recognise that an important factor in

[75] Chapter 8 will discuss the relationship between impact and positive obligations.
[76] *Khumalo*: para 33.

its deliberations concerning the obligations of football clubs was the fact that 'this ban has a considerable impact on the ability of the persons concerned to participate in social life'.[77]

These are only two examples, but this factor was present in all of the cases discussed either expressly or implicitly and its relevance has also been recognised in academic literature in both law and philosophy.[78] The capacity to affect fundamental rights is thus central to the imposition of obligations upon non-state actors and the reason for this is clear. The capacity to affect a right is the flip side of vulnerability: the former concerns the power of an agent to affect the fundamental interests of an individual and the latter involves the susceptibility of the individual to the exercise of such power. These dimensions will often be closely related but they should, nevertheless, be considered separately: firstly, they address matters from two different perspectives – namely, the beneficiary and the agent; and secondly, in real-life, they can come apart.

To understand the latter point, let us consider a corporation which has a large potential capacity to pollute the environment and thus harm the fundamental rights of many individuals. In purely theoretical terms, the vulnerability of individuals is co-extensive with the potential to harm. However, in real-life situations, let us imagine there are several active civil society groupings which defend the rights of surrounding communities and have an influence on political leaders. In this scenario, rights-holders may in actual fact be less vulnerable given the corporation is under social and political constraints not to exercise its harmful capacity. In a different scenario, where no such influential groupings exist, vulnerability may track the capacity of the corporation to inflict harm. The obligations of a corporation in the latter circumstances may also be greater given the lack of adequate social structures, regulations, and controls.[79]

Thus, the 'capacity' factor involves considering from the perspective of the agent what ability they have to impact upon fundamental rights of individuals. Engaging with capacity starts with an investigation into the *potential* ability of such an agent to impact on fundamental rights. Potential capacity, however, will not always translate into actual capacity if there are social measures or limitations on the exercise of the agent's power.[80]

[77] *Stadium Ban*: 283, 284.

[78] See, for instance, Ratner, 2001: 524; Kinley and Tadaki, 2004: 933; Wood, 2012: 65, Wettstein, 2012: 753–754.

[79] Karp, 2014: 94–99.

[80] Wettstein, 2009: 147–148.

What then is the relationship between the capacity of an agent and their obligations? Let us consider an argument of the form: 'X' has a right; 'Y' has the capacity to harm the right; therefore, 'Y' has an obligation not to harm the right.[81] We could state the principle as follows: **where a non-state actor has the capacity to harm a right, it has an obligation to desist from actually harming that right.** This formula of course provides some guidance but, whilst it appears attractive and seemingly easy to apply, it is only in fact a prima facie principle and is not adequate to determine the final obligations of a non-state actor. Why?

The main problem relates to what is included in the notion of 'capacity to harm'. The phrase itself hides an important issue we have already had to engage with in Chapter 5[82] – a non-state actor may have the capacity to impact negatively on a right; yet, not every exercise of such an ability is automatically impermissible.[83] It is only when that ability translates into impermissible harm that an action is proscribed. In other words, the fact that a non-state actor has an ability to impact negatively on a right does not automatically translate into an obligation not to cause that impact.

An example can help clarify this point. In *Khumalo*, the newspaper in question had a significant ability to affect the reputation (and thus the dignity) of an individual through publishing information about him. Yet, that ability does not automatically translate into an obligation not to publish that information. Whether such an obligation exists will depend on a range of factors which include, for instance, the reasons for the publication of the information, the vulnerability of the individual, and the role of the publishing companies in society. The capacity to impact does not automatically translate into an obligation to desist from causing the impact without considering additional factors that are at play and balancing these all together.

At the same time, a capacity to impact is of course a central consideration in determining whether an obligation of a non-state actor exists. If there is no ability to affect a fundamental interest underlying a right, then there seems to be no point in holding an entitlement against such an agent. Capacity to impact is thus a necessary but not a sufficient condition for any resulting obligation. The point here is that the capacity to impact actually overstates a defensible account of the extent of the obligations of non-state

[81] Karp, 2014: 89, similarly, formulates a 'capacity principle' – which he critiques – where obligations track capacity.

[82] See section 5.3.2.

[83] Ratner, 2001: 514.

actors.[84] That is as true in the context of negative obligations to avoid harm as in relation to positive obligations, which will be addressed in Chapter 8.

How does this all bear on corporations specifically? Capacity, importantly, requires a factual investigation of what exactly the corporation can do in a particular circumstance given that corporations may have variable abilities to affect fundamental rights. Their operations or function (as discussed further below) may provide them with special abilities to affect rights. Capacity will also often emerge from particular relationships that the corporation has with individuals which can affect the nature of the obligations that it has. It is important in this context to recognise the implications of the point made in Chapter 1, namely, that corporations are not simply reducible to the individuals underlying them but supervenient upon them. The capacity of the corporation thus must take account of the capacity of the individuals underlying the corporation (upon which its actions are supervenient) plus the effects of its separate legal personality. For instance, a defamatory statement about an individual by a respected corporation may cause more harm than if it were issued simply by an individual. The dismissal of an employee whose identity has been tied up with a corporation may be felt more acutely than if she were dismissed by an individual sole proprietor. A clear-headed understanding of a corporation's capacity to affect fundamental rights negatively provides us with a starting point for determining obligations though, as we have seen, that is not sufficient. We could thus arrive at the following presumption that can aid decision-making: it is presumed **that a corporation has a prima facie obligation to avoid causing any negative impact upon fundamental rights that it is capable of causing**.

This presumption only provides part of the picture surrounding capacity. Indeed, I will now briefly discuss three additional dimensions to the capacity criterion which are important in developing a holistic understanding thereof even though they cannot be addressed in detail here.

6.3.2.1.1 Probability Determining the capacity to affect rights raises the question not just of the potential ability of an entity to affect fundamental rights but also of the probability that such a potentiality will be actualised. Let us imagine an example where a cosmetics corporation is the largest employer in a region of Mali. Its factory is set up in an environmentally responsible way: the waste products of the manufacturing process produce a chemical that is placed in an adjacent waste-storage

[84] Wettstein, 2012: 754–755; Karp, 2014: 115.

facility specially built so that it quickly breaks down and does not contaminate any water sources. There is a slight risk, however, that, if there is a large amount of rain, the storage facility will be flooded and the chemical will pollute the main water sources. Mali has not had such a large amount of rain in 100 years and its climate usually poses very little risk in this regard. Transportation of the chemical to a site with no risk of flooding raises additional safety hazards. In order to eliminate any risk, the plant would need to close down with a severe effect on employment in the region.

In this example, the cosmetics company clearly has the potential capacity severely to impact on the right to water of individuals yet the likelihood of such a capacity being actualised is very low. This example is designed to show that the probability of risks being realised needs to be taken into account in determining an agent's obligations.[85] This does not mean that remote risks with high costs to fundamental rights should readily be accepted but, given that there is uncertainty in life around impacts, it seems reasonable that decision-making surrounding duties must take into consideration the degree of risk. In environmental law, a precautionary principle has been developed precisely to take account of probabilistic harms.[86] This dimension is also of relevance to the proportionality enquiry discussed in the next chapter, where the likelihood of harm will affect the balancing process and thus the final obligations of non-state actors.[87]

6.3.2.1.2 Intention Capacity to affect rights is ultimately a consequentialist criterion for determining obligations: it relates to the consequences an agent can bring about in relation to fundamental rights. The question, however, arises as to what the role of intention is in determining the obligations of an entity and any concomitant accountability. The logic of utilising the language of obligations, as we have seen, requires that there be an agent that can act through considering reasons and being responsive to them. This issue becomes much more complicated when we are dealing with corporations where there are complexities in determining what constitutes its intention.[88] A full examination of this question would require a detailed treatment and cannot be conducted here: for our

85 When assessing capacity, the probability will need to be broadly determined, which will then, in turn, impact upon the balancing process.
86 See, for instance, Sandin, 1999: 898.
87 See Alexy, 2002: 418–19 and the 'Second Law of Balancing'.
88 Simester, 2005: 27–28.

purposes, it is important to recognise that the pursuit of fundamental rights claims usually takes place through tort law, which effectively imposes an objective negligence standard for intention in one's conduct towards others.[89] That essentially requires the adoption of a 'reasonable foreseeability' standard for determining intention in the behaviour of corporations towards individuals. The notion of due diligence in the UNGPs could be understood to involve a proactive development on the classic negligence test: it requires reasonable steps to be taken by the corporation to inform itself of its potential and actual impacts on individuals in order to prevent a form of wilful ignorance being claimed, and providing a basis for denying responsibility.[90]

It remains important, however, to distinguish the substantive obligations of corporations from the standard of intention for their expected behaviour (the 'intention' element), as we saw in Chapter 5.[91] A simple example can illustrate this distinction: the law clearly creates a substantive obligation not to harm others through crashing one's motor vehicle into another's; in the pursuit of this obligation, it would be safer to stay at home when the roads are wet, yet the law permits one to drive in such conditions but in a careful manner. If one had an accident, it would not be sufficient for liability that one caused harm to someone else's vehicle – it would also have to be proved that one's driving behaviour was 'negligent' in the circumstances. My focus in this book is on creating a legal analytical framework for determining the substantive obligations of corporations and not on the 'intention' requirement. Nevertheless, it is important to point out that, in determining liability for a failure to perform substantive obligations by corporations, it will be necessary to consider whether it acted with the requisite negligence in performing its obligations (the intention dimension) and, therefore, can be held responsible for any actual exercise of its capacity to impact upon fundamental rights.

6.3.2.1.3 Contribution This dimension of capacity involves considering the relationship between impacts on rights caused by one entity and those caused by others. The capacity of one entity to harm rights, for instance, may be weak by itself but, together with others, increases significantly. When understanding capacity and the obligations it imposes, it is thus necessary to take into account the possibility that individuals or entities

89 Meeran, 2011: 3–10.

90 Muchlinski, 2012: 157.

91 I argued at Chapter 5, section 5.3.2, that due diligence is not a complete obligation given we have to understand in relation to *what* one must exercise due diligence.

may join together in ways which increase their impacts on fundamental rights. One corporation, for instance, may also have an indirect impact on another corporation, which then directly harms an individual's fundamental rights.[92] Determining capacity thus requires charting the web of relationships in which an individual corporation finds itself as well as its modes of participation in a harm. A range of legal issues discussed in recent times fall under this heading, which require specific treatment: these include various forms of complicity of corporations in harms committed by others[93] as well as the capacity to influence whether harms eventuate.[94] Whilst a specific treatment of these subjects lies beyond the scope of this book, I note here the importance of these issues in developing a full picture of corporate obligations. At the same time, one cannot be complicit in a rights violation without understanding whether there was a primary obligation not to violate the right in the first place – the latter substantive obligations are the focus of this book.

6.3.2.2 Function

A number of the cases that were considered in previous chapters reference a second important agent-relative factor – namely, the function of a non-state entity in determining its obligations.[95] *Khumalo*, as we saw, involved the court considering the important role of the media in a democracy as did *Blinkfüer*. *AllPay* considered the function of paying subsistence social grants to individuals. Other cases from the United States, Germany, and Colombia considered the function of specific spaces: *Marsh* (a town-centre), *Evans* (a park), and *Logan Valley* (a shopping-centre parking lot), T-909 of 2011 (a shopping centre), *Fraport* (an airport), and *Stadium Ban* (a sports stadium).

There are a number of issues that need to be disentangled in making sense of this criterion, which I shall seek to analyse in what follows. Firstly, we need to consider determining the general function of entities of a particular type – such as the corporation – in society. I have addressed this question in Chapter 1 and so will only briefly discuss it here. Secondly, we need to consider how to determine the specific

92 Tófalo, 2006: 344–346.

93 Tófalo, ibid: 336–337 attempts to explore various forms of complicity that exist. See also the ICJ Complicity Report, 2008.

94 The capacity of corporations to influence social conditions relevant to fundamental rights is a starting point for leverage-based responsibility: see Wood, 2012: 76.

95 See Dafel, 2015: 65.

function of particular entities and how that affects their obligations. Finally, we need to consider the relationship between function and capacity.

6.3.2.2.1 The Corporate Function The issue of function can take us all the way back to ancient Greek philosophy where Aristotle famously recognised that, in general, 'for all things that have a function or activity, the good and the 'well' is thought to reside in the function'.[96] Once we have a conception of the function of an entity or object we can understand what it is supposed to achieve. The function of a food-blender, for instance, is clear in that it was specifically designed and created for purposes of assisting people to blend food. Whether it is a good food-blender can be judged by how well it performs its function. Determining a function is not always as readily obvious as this example suggests but for entities or objects that are formed by humans, these can readily be ascertained by reference to the reasons for creating those entities or objects.

In Chapter 1, I sought to address the purpose (and thus function) of the corporation, generally, in society. I argued there that the corporation must be understood to have a complex aim: 'its ultimate goal is the enhancement of overall well-being adjudged from an impartial perspective but the achievement of this goal is designed to occur through a structure that enables individuals to advance their own interests through it'.[97] This entity thus is designed to achieve social benefits through harnessing individual self-interest. A good corporation would thus be an entity that achieves significant social benefits and, in doing so, it may not create significant social harms. It, nevertheless, need not in all it does aim directly to achieve these benefits. Nevertheless, what is clear is that the function of the corporation, generally, supports the prima facie conclusion that, **in conducting their activities, corporations have obligations not to cause social harms pursuant to advancing their goals.**[98]

The corporate function thus far is stated at a high level of abstraction and so is the consequent principle concerning obligations. Corporations function in specific contexts and take on particular social functions that have specific implications for their obligations. Consequently, when determining their obligations, we must not only consider their generalised function but also their specific one.

96 Aristotle book 1 part 7.
97 See Chapter 1, section 1.4.3.
98 I shall consider its positive duties in Chapter 8.

6.3.2.2.2 Specifying the Function of Particular Entities Obligations, importantly, can flow from a specific function that a body has. The Constitutional Court of South Africa in *Khumalo*, for instance, considered the role played by media publishing houses as an important factor in determining the nature and limits of their obligations.[99] In modern societies, the media plays an important role in enabling individuals to participate politically; to understand what is happening around them; to share and form their opinions; and to express themselves. This role is central to the exercise of freedom of expression and political rights but, as such, also empowers the media with a large capacity to harm these rights and others, such as the right to reputation and dignity. The function of the media in society thus leads it to affect fundamental rights both positively and negatively and, consequently, places particular obligations upon it to exercise its function responsibly.[100] It thus may not deliberately peddle false information as doing so may harm the ability of individuals to exercise their civil and political rights adequately. The publication of false accusations may seriously harm an individual's dignity. The specific function of an entity can thus grant it the capacity negatively to harm the fundamental interests of individuals in a particular way, which, in turn, generates specific obligations. The following presumptive principle could thus follow from this discussion: **where the specific function of an entity grants it a particular power to harm fundamental rights in a particular way, it will have a prima facie obligation to avoid harming such rights in that way.**

An interesting question arises concerning whether a function is inherent in the nature of a corporation based on how it is formed or whether it can be assumed. For instance, let us consider a corporation that sells jewellery whose specific activities do not immediately and obviously relate to any major public function. Instead, its social dimension would only relate to the general function it has to create social benefits which could include the generation of employment, and the creation of products that enhance individual happiness. Let us imagine, however, that this company is contracted by the state to provide all the clocks in hospitals across a particular country. Its role now becomes one with a major public impact given that clocks affect patient-waiting times, operations, and the entire activities of a hospital.[101] Whilst the company has obligations simply as a private jewellery company, these can increase significantly when its activities can have

[99] *Khumalo*: paras 22–24.

[100] Ibid: para 24.

[101] See Karp, 2014: 120–125 on providing collective goods and thus taking on a 'public' character.

a major public impact on the healthcare rights of individuals. There may thus be a difference between the function a company is established to perform and the role that it assumes.[102] A real-life scenario where this occurred is in the *AllPay* case discussed in Chapter 5 where the company concerned assumed the responsibility for paying social grants across South Africa.

The question of function (and its relationship with obligations) has often been discussed in courts through determining whether the function that is performed is public or private. The principle that has been adopted in many jurisdictions (some of which were discussed in Chapter 4) and some philosophical literature has been that the more public the function, the greater the justification there is for imposing more onerous obligations upon an entity.[103] Such a principle, of course, raises the question as to what is conceived of as a public or private function.[104] The analysis in Chapter 4 considered some of the comparative jurisprudence in this regard, which referenced a number of dimensions. Source-based factors involved determining whether the power emerged from the constitution or legislation, and whether the state had a controlling influence in the entity. Substantive factors included the degree to which an entity possesses asymmetrical power in relation to an individual, the impact an entity can have on fundamental rights, and whether the performance of the particular function was usually understood to be a responsibility of the state. These dimensions – whilst, in some respects, overlapping with other factors that have been analysed – are no doubt helpful in contributing to an assessment of the obligations of a non-state actor.

Yet, as I argued in Chapter 4, the focus on whether a function is 'public' or 'private' places the emphasis in the wrong place – the question really should be about whether the features of an entity support its bearing particular obligations rather than on an act of classification. Moreover, I contended that this reasoning also suggests a strict binary opposition between the public and the private domains – yet, there is actually a continuum between them. In determining obligations, there may be a balance to achieve between

[102] For a discussion, see ibid: 145–146.

[103] Ibid: 116, where Karp defines the publicness approach to responsibility as involving the claim that 'relevantly public but not relevantly private agents can justifiably be assigned human rights responsibility'. See also Valentini, 2017: 179–180.

[104] Karp, ibid: 117ff examines, philosophically, various criteria for conceiving of an entity as public or private. As we saw, courts have also, in many cases, sought to provide a basis for carving out that distinction. It should be evident from the argument that I do not endorse placing the public/private distinction at the centre of a determination of corporate obligations.

the public and private dimensions of an entity. It is also possible that an entity generally functions in the private sphere but, in a particular respect, exercises public power. Thus, it would be better for courts and other decision-making bodies to move away from simple classifications to an assessment of the features of these bodies which support particular obligations. What is ultimately important is to track how the function of an entity in society grants it the power to affect the fundamental rights of individuals. Its function may, in some cases, reduce its obligations and, in others, enable it to cause specific harms that increase its obligations.

6.3.2.2.3 The Relationship between Function and Capacity In the aforementioned analysis, what we saw is that aspects of the function of an entity can lead to obligations but these often relate to their capacity to affect the fundamental interests of individuals. Indeed, we can analyse some of the criteria courts utilise for determining what constitutes a public function as also including the dimension of capacity. In relation to source-based criteria, whether a function derives from the constitution relates to whether an agent has the capacity to impact on important interests that are deemed worthy of constitutional protection. Similarly, whether a function flows from a statutory power relates to whether there is a capacity of an agent to affect an interest that parliament has deemed necessary to pronounce on as important to its people. In relation to substantive criteria, the dimension of asymmetrical power specifically concerns the capacity of an agent to impact upon other individuals in a manner they cannot similarly affect that agent. Courts have also directly invoked the capacity to affect fundamental rights as a basis for determining what constitutes a public function. The question thus arises as to whether the 'function' criterion in fact is reducible to the 'capacity' criterion for determining obligations.

In my view, despite the close relationship between them, the answer to this question should be in the negative. Determining the function of an entity requires an examination of questions of source and teleology: the question of who founded it and for what purpose. It requires us to investigate both a priori and empirically what role it plays in society and, consequently, build a picture concerning its actual power to affect individual interests. As we have seen, the question of function may be a complex one and involve tensions between different aspects of an entity – how those are resolved can then affect its capacity. The question of 'capacity' involves an enquiry simply into the ability or power of an entity to affect rights but does not engage how or why that arises.

An example may help to sharpen this difference. Let us imagine there is a very popular individual, Manuel, who has the capacity to make negative comments about a colleague and, significantly, harm her reputation. This person has significant power to harm an important fundamental interest of another. Yet, he lacks any specific social function and his status simply emerges from his popularity. Consider, in contrast, a newspaper with a high circulation that has the capacity to harm the same person's reputation. The newspaper forms part of the media which has a particular social role that conditions how the content it produces is perceived and, consequently, affects the capacity that it has. Where there is a high level of trust in the media, for instance, any allegations it makes are likely to be treated as having more weight than a comment simply by an individual such as Manuel. Given the function of the media in society, it would be reasonable to contend that it has stronger obligations to ensure the veracity of any reports it releases than an individual does when making a statement or expressing an opinion.

The function of an entity thus can grant it certain capacities which play an important role in determining its obligations. Importantly, this point is analogous to one already made about the relational harms flowing from vulnerability: the function of an agent in society may well affect the impact it can have on a right. The social function of an agent grants it the capacity to harm in a way that it would lack without that role. Function and capacity are not identical although there is an important relationship between them. We may thus develop the following presumptive principles in this regard: **when the function of an entity involves its ability to exercise power over individuals in ways that affect their fundamental rights, it will have a prima facie obligation not to exercise that power in ways that harm those rights. Following from this, to the extent that the function of an entity grants it an increased ability to affect the fundamental rights of individuals, the extent of its obligations in relation to fundamental rights will increase.**

6.3.2.3 Autonomy

The last agent-relative factor that I will analyse and is of critical importance are concerns that fall under the notion of 'autonomy'. This factor often pulls in a different direction to the others that have been considered: there is a clear presumptive principle that **the autonomy of an individual (or entity) to make decisions in their own domain would tend to reduce the extent of what they are required to do in relation to**

others. The autonomy dimension often surfaces in the case law as a countervailing factor that requires balancing against the other factors.

What exactly does this factor involve? There is a large literature on the notion of autonomy and what it means to determine one's actions freely and act out of free will.[105] For our purposes here, we are concerned with its normative dimension. In relation to individuals, there are two important normative components to this idea which I shall focus on: the first is dignity, and the second is freedom. As we saw in Chapter 2 and earlier in this chapter, individuals who have dignity are regarded as having intrinsic value and must be accorded respect for their fundamental interests. They cannot also be treated merely as a means to the ends of other individuals or simply be treated instrumentally for achieving particular social purposes.[106] Freedom relates to the fundamental interest of sentient creatures to be able to realise their own goods and achieve their purposes.[107] For adult human individuals, freedom involves being able to choose freely the path of life one wishes to lead for oneself, alter it if needs be, and to exercise rational agency in one's daily life.[108]

These features condition the obligations that we have. The conception of obligations that we develop cannot ignore the dignity and freedom of individuals without failing to capture the range of normative considerations at issue. This claim does not entail that the dignity or freedom of an individual allows absolute freedom of action in relation to other individuals: living in society means interacting with others – who also have such dignity and freedom – and, consequently, must involve, at least, a curtailment of one's freedom to act when that imperils the fundamental interests of others.[109] Dignity and freedom thus do not prevent obligations to others from arising and in fact can form the foundation thereof. Nevertheless, they also place limits on the extent of such obligations.

[105] For some of the literature, see Bratman, 2003: 156.

[106] Kant, 2017: 29. Kant, 2017: 32–34 also sees the foundation of dignity as lying in autonomy though these concepts are distinct and other accounts are possible: see Nussbaum, 2005: 305–307.

[107] I connect freedom with the account of value discussed earlier in section 6.3.1.1.

[108] Rawls, 1993: 19 sees freedom as consisting in the capacity to form, revise, and to pursue a 'conception of the good' and to do so through the exercise of one's reasoning powers. Dworkin, 1988: 20 sees autonomy as involving a second-order capacity to reflect on one's desires and alter them in light of higher-order preferences or values.

[109] Mill, 1859 famously defends the 'harm principle' to this effect; see also Rawls' first principle of justice: Rawls, 1993: 291.

It is important, however, to appreciate that dignity and freedom apply most clearly in relation to natural individuals. International human rights covenants and many constitutions recognise the inherent dignity of the human individual. It is readily understandable why adult human beings wish to have the freedom to determine their own way of life. Some of the cases we considered recognise these autonomy interests such as Harlan's artistic freedom and ability to work in the *Lüth* case or freedom of testation in *Evans* v. *Newton*. How then can these ideas apply in the context of an entity such as the corporation?

Once again, it is important to refer back to the discussion in Chapter 1 concerning the nature of the corporate agent. As we saw there, the law conceives of a corporation as distinct from the individuals who, for instance, invest in it and work for it. It was suggested that the corporation can be understood to be 'supervenient' on the individuals underlying it: the corporation is non-reducible to those individuals but dependent upon them. Its corporate personality is conferred by the law for purposes of obtaining social advantages; at the same time, the corporation is designed to achieve these social gains by being a vehicle through which individuals can pursue their economic projects and self-interest. The social goals of the corporation would tend to de-emphasise the autonomy of the individuals underlying it. On the other hand, the fact that it is a vehicle designed to enable individuals to pursue their own economic goals clearly implicates the dignity and freedom interests of those individuals. In relation to the corporate entity itself, it is hard to see any sense in which it is itself a bearer of dignity[110] – and it appears to be a form that is set up entirely for human instrumental purposes. Nevertheless, if we are to conceive of it as an agent in its own right,[111] then it must have the freedom to realise the purposes for which it was set up.[112] We thus need to specify, in the particular circumstances of a case, what facets of autonomy are implicated and how they affect its obligations. It is necessary to be alert to the tendency – often encouraged by corporations – to overemphasise the autonomy interests at stake and the weighting to be accorded to it in any balancing enquiry (a matter for the next chapter).

When we look more closely at the case law that has been analysed, the autonomy dimension can be seen to cover a number of facets of the corporation. Certain cases relate to dimensions at the heart of

[110] *Hyundai*: para 18.
[111] See Chapter 1 fn 41.
[112] Ratner, 2001: 513; Kinley and Tadaki, 2004: 968. See Karp, 2014: 138–142 for a different way of arriving at a similar conclusion.

the corporation's economic activity: T-694 of 2013 dealt with the autonomy of corporations to choose their own employees; *Barkhuisen* involved the freedom to contract; and *Eweida* related to the freedom to protect its brand image. Other cases related to the extent of autonomy that flows directly from the corporation's property rights: *Marsh* (ownership of a town); *Logan Valley* (a shopping centre); *T-909/2011* (a shopping centre); *Fraport* (an airport); and *Stadium Ban* (a stadium). There were also facets of autonomy flowing from important social functions performed by corporations such as in relation to the media: see, for instance, *Von Hannover*, *Blinkfüer*, and *Khumalo*.

Taking into account this normative discussion about autonomy, we can develop certain presumptive principles. Certain of these interact with the other factors discussed earlier. Thus, where a non-state actor such as a corporation is involved, **their autonomy interests in a particular circumstance must be considered (though they will not be absolute)**. The weight accorded to such interests will be affected by how centrally they are implicated in a case. The nature of the entity will affect the weight to be accorded to these interests: given the fact that they do not have dignity, **the autonomy interests of corporations will never be as strong as those relating to individual human beings.**[113] **Moreover, the greater the power of an entity to affect the fundamental interests of another, the greater will be the justification for restricting its autonomy interests. Conversely, where a vital autonomy interest is affected and there is limited interference with the right of a beneficiary, there is a stronger justification for limiting that right.**

6.4 Conclusion

This chapter began the work of outlining an analytical legal framework for determining the obligations of non-state actors – and corporations in particular – in relation to fundamental rights. We had already seen in the case law of the previous four chapters how courts have referenced various factors in determining corporate obligations. Drawing on this foundation, I attempt to describe, systematise, and defend a generalised 'multi-factoral approach' for determining corporate obligations. An optimal articulation of this approach, I argued, requires a series of steps, three of which I sought to accomplish in this chapter: namely, identifying the various normatively relevant factors at play in a situation; examining

[113] See Fredman, 2008: 58, who adopts a similar position.

their normative grounding and understanding their relevance to the substantive content of corporate obligations; and developing presumptive principles that help us understand their implications for corporate obligations and can guide decision-making in particular cases.

I identified and explored the relevance of three beneficiary-orientated factors (interests, vulnerability, and impact) as well as three agent-relative factors (capacity, function, and autonomy). This chapter has also sought to show that none of these factors is alone sufficient to determine corporate obligations. The normative relevance of each factor for obligations must be taken into account in the particular circumstances of the case. Understanding the relationship of these factors to the obligations of non-state actors – and corporations in particular – flowing from fundamental rights was part of the task of this chapter which, in addition, considered how to evaluate the weight that should be accorded to them.

Nevertheless, a multi-factoral approach to determining obligations cannot stop with identifying and examining the relevance of multiple factors. If more than one is germane in a particular circumstance, we need to understand how we can reach final conclusions about the obligations of the agents in question. Moreover, we saw that some of the factors can pull, normatively, in different directions. The capacity of a corporation to affect a beneficiary's interest may support imposing an onerous obligation; the autonomy interests of that corporation may weaken any such obligation or, perhaps, even support a position where no such obligation exists. How are we then to make a final determination of the substantive content of an agent's obligations given that multiple factors are at play? The next chapter tackles this problem.

7

A Balancing Act – Proportionality in the Corporate Sphere

7.1 A Problem of Balancing

Let us imagine the following scenario. Recently, an employee of Davis Ltd (henceforth 'Davis'), a public company based in South Africa which produces wine, has been arrested for the possession of child pornography on his computer. The computer belonged to Davis. In response, the directors of Davis decide to institute a new policy: all emails and content that is downloaded onto a work computer will be monitored. Work computers will also be subjected to random inspections. Should anyone be found with material on their computer that is unlawful, they will be subject to sanctions and, possibly, dismissal. A mid-level employee, named Maria, who has worked at Davis for five years is outraged at the violation of her privacy and attempts to resolve the matter internally. These efforts fail after the company informs Maria that they believe the existing legal framework supports the new policy. Maria launches a constitutional challenge to the existing law, claiming that it cannot permit Davis to violate employees' right to privacy in this way.

The case reaches the Constitutional Court, which places at the centre of its enquiry the obligations that Davis must bear which flow from the right to privacy. Davis makes the argument that its policy is designed to achieve two important purposes: firstly, to protect its reputation through ensuring its employees adhere to socially acceptable standards of morality; and, secondly, to comply with the law and to ensure its own property is not used for unlawful purposes. On the other hand, Maria argues that computers today are basic tools for the work of many human beings and through which much human engagement occurs. Since individuals spend so much time on their work computers, it is not possible or reasonable to expect them to avoid all personal tasks on those work computers. Individuals also have an interest in maintaining control over what they share with their employers. Moreover, many of Davis' employees are not wealthy and cannot afford second computers. Davis' measures, Maria argues, essentially obliterate any privacy interests of employees for a large portion of their lives.

Both these arguments are based on factors or principles which have persuasive force. Those principles can also be stated in terms of fundamental rights: Davis claims that its right to property grants it the autonomy to make decisions around the use of its own computers; Maria's argument is rooted in the capacity of the corporation to have a serious impact on the fundamental right of employees to privacy, and the vulnerability of employees to such an exercise of power. How are such normative conflicts to be resolved?

Though this question is central to fundamental rights discourse, little attention has been paid to it in the context of non-state actors. Case law and legal doctrine have largely developed in relation to another set of normative conflicts: namely, where fundamental rights are violated in pursuance of important state objectives (whether that occurs through legislation or executive action). In jurisdictions across the world, courts have recognised that there are circumstances in which the state may justifiably infringe rights: it may, for instance when it reasonably suspects a crime has been committed, enter someone's property, search it, and seize incriminating material. Fundamental rights have, however, placed limitations on such powers: amongst other restrictions, any search and seizure must usually be pre-authorised by a court on the presentation of some evidence; it must be targeted towards specific goals such as crime prevention; and, it must be conducted in a respectful way.[1]

In deciding what is or is not a permissible infringement of a right, courts around the world have developed what is known as the proportionality test. Proportionality involves a structured process of reasoning that has been developed to take account of competing normative principles and assist in reaching a final determination. This process of reasoning will often lead to a decision in which one principle will not completely dominate over another: search and seizure thus may be allowed for a set of important

[1] See, for instance, seminal cases such as in South Africa *Investigating Directorate: Serious Economic Offences* v. *Hyundai Motor Distributors* [2000] ZACC 12; in the United States, *Katz* v. *United States* 389 US 347 (1967); in Canada, *Mckinley Transport Ltd* v. *the Queen* [1990] 68 DLR (4th) 568.

purposes – such as criminal investigations – but also only take place under strict conditions designed to protect individuals' right to privacy.

As has emerged from the case law analysed in Chapters 2–5, it is clear that, in the context of non-state actors, there are also competing normative principles that arise. Specifically in the context of this book, the pursuit of corporate purposes may involve the infringement of fundamental rights. As was argued in Chapter 6, such infringements are not always impermissible – the autonomy of the corporation to pursue its own ends may provide a justification, for instance, for such an infringement. Courts, usually, resort to balancing the relevant principles against one another but, as we saw, this often occurs haphazardly without any clear structure to the reasoning. The question thus arises whether we can do better. Doing so is important for a variety of reasons: it can help guard against extensive unguided discretion being exercised by decision-makers and provide an agreed decision framework within which they must operate. In turn, that would allow for the review of any decisions they make against a familiar and structured reasoning process. In so doing, constraints would be placed on any justifications for infringing fundamental rights and so avoid weakening them irredeemably.

In the first part of this chapter, I consider the justification for applying the proportionality test – largely developed to adjudicate conflicting principles that arise in the relationship between public authorities and individuals – to reach final determinations where there are competing normative factors that arise between non-state actors and individuals with a specific focus upon the corporation. I also consider challenges to the application of proportionality reasoning to the context of non-state actors and argue that these arguments do not succeed at least where non-state actors are asymmetrically situated in relation to one another. The second part of this chapter provides an outline of the various stages of the proportionality analysis. It considers in detail how each stage can apply to corporations and the complexities involved in this regard. In doing so, I shall draw on the discussion from the previous chapter and consider where each factor fits in the overall analysis. The focus in this chapter is on the negative obligations of corporations to avoid harming the fundamental rights of individuals. Ultimately, I shall argue that proportionality can be applied successfully to balance the fundamental interests of individuals against the interests of the corporation and thus can provide a structured process of reasoning for determining the final negative obligations of corporations.

7.2 Proportionality and the Corporation

7.2.1 *A Brief Outline of the Proportionality Enquiry*

Given the normative importance of fundamental rights, both under international law and in most constitutional systems, there is a strong presumption that such rights can only be infringed where there is a strong justification for doing so.[2] Courts around the world have adopted a structured reasoning process known as the proportionality enquiry to determine when such a strong justification exists and it is permissible for rights to be limited.[3]

The enquiry involves reasoning in two stages. The first stage seeks to determine whether a right has been infringed. Doing so requires examining the interests that are protected by the right, and the impact of the activities of a particular agent on the interests of particular beneficiaries as well as their specific vulnerabilities to the exercise of power by that agent. This enquiry places the focus on the beneficiaries of the right and the harms done to them.

Courts then turn, in the second stage, to determining whether the infringement (or limitation) of a right is permissible: in order to reach a judgement in this regard, courts in various jurisdictions have developed a structured set of four sub-enquiries which must be engaged with.[4] The first sub-enquiry involves determining the purpose of the measure that limits a fundamental right in order to evaluate the competing normative principles involved. Jurisdictions around the world vary in how they characterise this stage: in Germany, for instance, the purpose must simply be a 'legitimate purpose';[5] in Canada, the objective must be of

[2] Meyerson, 2009: 812. This presumption and particular weight accorded to fundamental rights means that it is not correct to contend that rights are simply treated as one consideration amongst many in the proportionality analysis, a charge mistakenly made, for instance, in Tsakyrakis, 2009: 474.

[3] See, for instance, *R* v. *Oakes* (1986) 1 SCR 103; BVerfGE 90, 145 *(Cannabis decision)*; *S* v. *Makwanyane* [1995] ZACC 3; and CA 6821/93 *United Mizrahi Bank* v. *Migdal Cooperative Village*, 49(4) PD 221 (1995). A deeper justification for the proportionality enquiry is provided in Alexy, 2002. The enquiry is not only used by courts but also by legislatures: for a defence of the legislature taking the primary role in relation to the limitation of rights, see Webber, 2009: 149.

[4] This description of the elements of proportionality draws from the more detailed analysis provided in Bilchitz, 2014. For purposes of simplification, I have included the 'purpose' requirement as one of the sub-enquiries although, sometimes, only the subsequent three are regarded as strictly making up the test.

[5] Grimm, 2007: 388.

'sufficient importance to warrant overriding a constitutionally protected right or freedom'.[6]

The second sub-enquiry involves considering whether the infringing measures are 'rationally connected to the objective'.[7] I shall refer to this as the 'suitability requirement', which essentially tests the rationality of the relationship between the measure(s) adopted and the purpose sought to be achieved. The third part of the test requires that the means 'impair "as little as possible" the right or freedom in question'.[8] This evaluation requires considering whether there is an alternative possible means that can sufficiently achieve the purpose sought but have a lesser impact on the right in question.[9] I shall refer to this as the 'necessity' requirement. The fourth and final component of the test requires that there exists a proper relation of proportionality between the benefits of the infringing measure and the harm to fundamental rights.[10] This I term the 'balancing requirement'. At this stage, '[t]he more severe the deleterious effects of a measure, the more important the objective must be if the measure is to be reasonable and demonstrably justified in a free and democratic society.'[11] As can be seen from this description, the proportionality enquiry requires an examination of 'the relationship between the object and the means of realizing it. Both the object and the means must be proper. The relationship between them is an integral part of proportionality'.[12]

This brief outline of the proportionality enquiry highlights a number of its important features. The enquiry is applied in cases where there are two (or more) competing intrinsically valuable normative principles: neither principle is automatically subsumed by the other. The value of the test lies largely in the structured process of reasoning it requires and the culture of justification, transparency, and accountability it gives rise to.[13] As Möller writes, '[t]he added value is that the proportionality test provides a *structure* which guides judges through the reasoning process as to whether a policy is constitutionally legitimate'.[14] The test as such

[6] *R* v. *Big M Drug Mart Ltd* [1985] 1 SCR 295, 352.
[7] See *Oakes*: para 71.
[8] Ibid.
[9] See Bilchitz, 2014 for a detailed engagement with the necessity enquiry.
[10] Barak, 2012: 340.
[11] See *Oakes*: para 71.
[12] Barak, 2012: 317.
[13] Barak, 2012: 458–9, Mureinik, 1994; Cohen-Eliya and Porat, 2011.
[14] Möller, 2012: 179. Proportionality has though in recent times attracted criticism as to whether it provides an adequate reason-governed process of addressing norm conflicts

requires decision-makers to address its various component parts which focus their minds on relevant questions: that alone, however, will not lead to any particular result. To be meaningful, the enquiry requires there to be a substantive engagement with the particular normative principles that are at stake, and the extent to which they are abrogated in the particular circumstances of the case.[15] In doing so, the enquiry forces the decision-maker to determine the weight of competing normative principles in the reasoning process and evaluate them against one another. The proportionality reasoning process is also context-sensitive but provides guidance as to the relevant features of each situation that a decision-maker must pay attention to. This structured process culminates in an enquiry about the proportionality of benefits to costs, having clearly identified the extent to which any trade-off is required. It also requires a decision-maker to 'think analytically, not to skip over things which should be considered and to consider them in their time and place'.[16]

7.2.2 *The Justification for Proportionality in the Corporate Sphere*

Proportionality as a test in law has developed largely in relation to the laws, policies, and actions of public authorities. Its origins are usually traced to German administrative law, but over the last thirty years it has become '*the* central concept in contemporary constitutional rights law'[17] employed by courts across the world. Cohen-Eliya and Porat provide a range of possible explanations for the spread of proportionality: these include its flexibility, which is attractive in systems where the constitutional jurisprudence is still developing, and its possible role in mitigating conflicts in divided societies.[18] They, however, ultimately do not accept the adequacy of such instrumental justifications and focus on its role in

for a range of reasons: some claim the considerations involved are incommensurable; and others that it provides an illusory sense of structure where it in fact involves vague, intuitionist reasoning and allows too much discretion to judges: see, for example, Urbina, 2012: 49–80; Webber, 2010: 179–202; and Endicott, 2014: 311–342. A full response to these critiques lies beyond the scope of this chapter though some points in the text outline the contours of such a response.

15 The proportionality test is not a substitute for an engagement with substantive considerations: the critique thereof, for instance, by Tsakyrakis, 2009 fails properly to recognise this point.

16 Barak, 2012: 461.

17 Möller, 2012: 13.

18 Cohen-Eliya and Porat, 2011: 468–9.

promoting a culture of justification, a term initially coined by the South African academic, Etienne Mureinik. They write that '[t]he global move toward proportionality is therefore a global move toward justification: it responds to a widespread and basic intuition: we want government to justify all of its actions'.[19] The legitimacy of laws and actions emanating from state authorities on this view is not simply rooted in their authority being recognised in law: rather, it flows from the justification these authorities are able to provide for such laws and actions. Proportionality has been utilised as a key tool in developing such a culture of justification.

Given this normative basis, the focus of scholarly work has been on proportionality in the context of governmental action and its justification in light of public reason.[20] The question that arises is whether this structured process of reasoning can and should be applied beyond the public sphere? In considering this question, Stephen Gardbaum asks a number of central questions that we must grapple with if proportionality is to be applied to relationships between non-state actors:

> [H]ow would proportionality be expected to work when it is not government action that is challenged as violating constitutional rights? Can public reason be expected to apply to the actions of private individuals? What would count as a legitimate private reason for the limitation of a constitutional right by another individual? How could one attempt to weigh such a reason against a right?[21]

Gardbaum, however, appears to ask these as rhetorical questions for he immediately states: '[h]ere we seem to have reached both a conceptual and a practical limit to proportionality' and leaves it there without attempting to develop answers to these questions.[22] In this chapter, I hope to challenge this view that proportionality cannot be applied properly to the relations between non-state actors with a focus on corporate–individual relationships.[23] Before grappling with the mechanics and the particular stages of the test when applied to non-state actors, it is important to outline a case for applying proportionality to this realm at

[19] Ibid: 474.
[20] Kumm, 2010: 152.
[21] Gardbaum, 2017: 246.
[22] Ibid.
[23] The possibility of applying proportionality in the corporate sphere was first engaged in an article I co-authored with Laura Ausserladscheider Jonas on directors' duties, Bilchitz and Jonas, 2016. I am grateful to my co-author for her permission to draw on this prior work though this chapter is a significant development on that article.

all. I turn now to provide three arguments for its application in the context of non-state actors.[24]

7.2.2.1 Proportionality as a General Structured Reasoning Process

The first argument involves considering the nature of the proportionality test itself. The question raised is whether there is any reason why this structured process of reasoning should only be applicable to situations where governmental authority is being exercised. If this is in fact a process of reasoning applicable to situations of conflict between normative considerations generally, then it is entirely appropriate to utilise it in cases of normative conflict both in the private and public spheres.

Let us imagine a simple situation where Mandisa, who is a doctor, has to decide as a parent whether to insist on vaccinating her child against tetanus after she scratched herself with a rusty nail. Her child is ten years old, averse to needles and expresses the view that she does not want to have the injection – to insist would be to violate her child's right to bodily integrity. Yet, given the serious health risks to her child of contracting Tetanus, Mandisa is convinced her child's view cannot be determinative. In evaluating what she should do, she identifies the purpose of forcing her child to vaccinate as being to preserve the health of her child, prevent her suffering and potentially save her life. Doing so, moreover, is rationally related to this purpose and there is no other way to achieve it. After considering the alternatives, Mandisa accepts that she could apply topical anaesthetic before administering the injection to reduce the pain and provide her child with medication to relieve her anxiety. In thinking, finally, about the balance to be struck, Mandisa acknowledges that her child's exercise of autonomy is important and that her fear of needles is real. At the same time, she recognises that insisting her child has the vaccine could preserve her child's health (and life), the pain from a needle is short-lived, and her child's fears are irrational. When considering the relationship between harms and benefits, Mandisa concludes that the harms caused by insisting that her child has the injection (with the suggested pain relief) are proportional to the benefits of receiving the injection.

24 This is not merely theoretical but is beginning to happen in the express engagement of courts with corporate obligations: see, for instance, the express usage of proportionality in the ground-breaking judgment imposing an obligation on Shell to reduce its CO2 emissions by 45% by 2030: *Vereniging Milieudefensie* v. *Royal Dutch Shell Plc* para 4.4.54.

This simple example is designed to show that we often utilise proportionality-like reasoning in dealing with normative conflicts in our daily lives. Whilst we usually do not go mechanically through every stage of the reasoning process, it is applied much more widely than only in the realm of state–individual normative conflicts. Indeed, this argument flows naturally from the approach adopted by Robert Alexy to fundamental rights. Alexy understands such rights as principles which must be realised to the greatest possible extent – principles are thus, in his view, 'optimization requirements'.[25] Proportionality, he attempts to show, logically flows from conceiving of principles in this way.[26] There is no reason, however, why the test must essentially relate to matters involving the state–individual relationship. Proportionality would rather apply in all cases where principles are involved which need to be optimised. Since fundamental rights are principles, it would apply in all cases where they are involved.[27]

Indeed, even if we do not conceive of principles and rights in the way Alexy does, proportionality reasoning is applicable to a wide range of situations in which there are moral conflicts. Cohen-Eliya and Porat state that '[t]he concept of proportionality has existed in some form in all cultures and from the earliest times'.[28] The justification for this claim must be based upon the centrality the test and its components have in human practical reasoning. Proportionality reasoning has been central to cost–benefit analysis; it is used in relation to the doctrine of double effect,[29] and has been utilised, for instance, in just war theory in moral philosophy.[30] A recent example is provided by Prof Thaddeus Metz, who utilises all four dimensions of the proportionality enquiry to evaluate the justifiability of violent student protests for achieving fee-free higher education in South Africa.[31] His analysis is not a legal one, however, but drawn from moral theory. This is but one example where the various components of the proportionality enquiry are utilised in examining

[25] Alexy, 2002: 47–48. I have challenged this feature of Alexy's account in Bilchitz, 2014: 42.

[26] Alexy, ibid: 66–69.

[27] Of course, this argument assumes that rights can be applicable against non-state actors but I have already attempted to establish that point in Chapters 2 and 5.

[28] Cohen-Eliya and Porat, 2013: 24.

[29] See, for instance, Kockler, 2007, who outlines the application of proportionality reasoning in the doctrine of double effect in relation to issues arising in bio-ethics. For a general outline, see 'Doctrine of Double Effect' *Stanford Encyclopedia of Philosophy* available at https://plato.stanford.edu/entries/double-effect/.

[30] See, for instance, Brown, 2003.

[31] Metz, 2016.

a wider moral question. Importantly, the example relates not simply to state conduct but to how students should go about protesting in a morally justifiable manner for a widely recognised good of being able to access higher education. If proportionality is itself a general dimension of human practical reasoning to address normative conflicts, there is no good reason why its application should be confined to the realm of state–individual relations.

7.2.2.2 Expanding the Culture of Justification to Non-State Actors

A second and more ambitious argument I shall consider relates to the role of proportionality in advancing a culture of justification in a society. As Kumm understands it, the focus of proportionality is on subjecting public authorities to the rule of public reason.[32] Cohen-Eliya and Porat also seem to concur.[33] Yet, when we return to Mureinik's original conception of the culture of justification, there is no particular reason why it need be limited to public authorities – it rather offers a wider conception of when the exercise of authority is justified. Mureinik first outlines the contrasting notion of what he terms 'a culture of authority', which focuses on the 'source' of a decision. In a culture of authority, it is sufficient for the legitimacy or justification of a decision that it flows from a particular authority that is authorised to make that decision and can command obedience. In contrast, in a culture of justification, the fact that a decision emerges from an authority authorised to decide may be a necessary condition but it is not sufficient. What is needed for the exercise of legitimate authority in a culture of justification is a reasonable substantive justification for the decision.[34]

If a different understanding of the legitimacy of authoritative decision-making is to exist in a society, it seems strange to stop at the borders of the state. Mureinik was writing in the context of the transformation of South Africa from the system of apartheid to a constitutional democracy. The exercise of arbitrary authority and discriminatory practices under apartheid did not just occur within the public sphere: indeed, one core reason for the horizontal application of the South African Constitution was the

[32] Kumm, 2010: 152.

[33] Indeed, they trace its origins in Germany to a conception of how a state governed by law (the Rechtstaat) should behave: see Cohen-Eliya and Porat, 2013: 25.

[34] Mureinik, 1994: 32 sees this as creating a 'culture in which every exercise of power is expected to be justified' – his examples do focus on exercises of public power, yet there is no reason why his conception cannot be extended to forms of private power too.

fact that unacceptable racist behaviour became widespread throughout the private sector too.[35] If discriminatory practices were to be excised from South African society, it was necessary to reform both public and private power and embed in both a culture of justification.[36]

This point applies beyond the South African historical context: developing a culture of justification requires reconfiguring the way in which authority is exercised both in the public and the private sphere. Why, though, should we accept such a wider extension of the culture of justification? One answer flows from the analysis offered in Chapters 4 and 6 (and further below), which demonstrates that the public and private spheres are not hermetically sealed off from one another. Decision-makers move between both spheres and, indeed, we live our lives in both realms. If we wish to entrench a culture of justification in the public sphere, it would be necessary to ensure it is not wholly contradicted by a culture of authority in the private realm.

If we wish to go deeper into the justification for such an extension, the intriguing prospect is raised of developing a wider theory of authority rooted in a culture of justification. Since developing such a theory is not the primary aim of this book, here, I will provide only a brief account of its possible contours, which is rooted in the foundational dignity of individuals who have the ability to act on the basis of reasons. A culture of authority allows an individual authorised to act (or command) to require another individual to behave in ways for which the latter individual potentially can see no reason. We can imagine, at an extreme, a director in a large corporation in Malawi requiring an employee to count thousands of pages of documents (and repeat the counting over and over again) simply because he wishes to assert his power and subdue the employee. Whilst the director is authorised to act and command the employee's obedience, such an exercise of authority treats the employee merely as an instrument to be utilised by the director.[37] Taking account of real-life power dynamics – such as the limited availability of jobs in developing countries such as Malawi – allows us to recognise how vulnerable an employee would be to such an exercise of the director's authority. A culture of justification would, in contrast, require such a director to have a substantive justification for

[35] Mureinik, ibid.

[36] See *Du Plessis* v. *De Klerk* [1996] ZACC 10 para 163 and Friedman, 2014: 67.

[37] That would violate the central Kantian maxim to treat individuals who have dignity as ends and never merely as a means: see Kant, 2017: 29; Hill, 1980 provides a useful exploration of its meaning.

why he ordered such an activity. If no justification was forthcoming, then any such decision could be challenged, regarded as an unfair labour practice with the consequence that the director could be censured for his behaviour and the employees be within their rights to refuse to obey such orders without any concern about dismissal.

Requiring a substantive justification allows an employee to understand the reasons for a decision and, therefore, treats the employee as an individual deserving of respect. It does not, of course, automatically require the agreement of the person but, at the least, their ability to see the rationale behind a decision. The culture of justification can be seen to give expression to the important principle that, in morality, what we owe to each other is a duty to act in ways that others can reasonably accept.[38]

These ideas do not entail that the reasons which are persuasive within the context of the private sphere need to be identical to those within the public sphere. In the public sphere, justifications must be based on 'public reasons': these are reasons that flow from values and premises that all who are reasonable could accept.[39] In contrast, there may be reasons that individuals can acknowledge as being valid within the context of particular private associations – such as the church or corporation – even if they would not suffice in the public sphere.[40] Rawls writes that '[t]he criteria and methods of these nonpublic reasons depend in part on how the nature (the aim and point) of each association is understood and the conditions under which it pursues its ends'.[41] For instance, an employer may reference a potential increase in profitability as a reason for a certain decision: that seems wholly appropriate in the corporate sphere but may not be acceptable as a justification for state action. The variability of reasons and their nature, however, does not entail that any form of reason will be acceptable: indeed, non-public reasons may be evaluated as to whether they in fact are justifiable within the relevant private context. Moreover, the greater the involvement and engagement of an entity with the public sphere, the greater will be the requirement that the reasons it provides are truly 'public' in nature and thus can be justified more broadly to all other reasonable agents.

[38] This idea underlies the work of John Rawls and has also been developed in detail by Scanlon, 2000: 4.
[39] Rawls, 1993: 226.
[40] This point is inspired by John Rawls' impressive analysis of the difference between various forms of private reason and public reason: see ibid: 220.
[41] Ibid: 221.

Whilst this wider conception of authority is worth developing more broadly, for the purposes of this book, what is crucial is that the conception of legitimate authority encapsulated by the notion of a 'culture of justification' should apply where the fundamental rights of individuals are at stake. Indeed, as we have seen in Chapters 2 and 5, where fundamental rights are at stake, we most obviously have a situation in which the dignity of individuals may be compromised. If a non-state actor threatens fundamental rights, then it is crystal clear that they are taking upon themselves the ability to diminish another's foundational worth. It is not clear why it would be justifiable for any individual or entity to be able to exercise such a form of authority over another without clear reasons for doing so. Consequently, where fundamental rights are threatened or harmed, it is necessary to ensure that any exercise of private authority can be justified taking into account the particularly strong weights to be attached to the fundamental rights of individuals. Any justification will need to be reasonable and thus capable of being recognised and accepted by the individual whose rights are infringed.[42] The proportionality enquiry offers just such a structured and transparent reasoning process. If, as Cohen-Eliya and Porat suggest, the proportionality test is a central component of a culture of justification, any justification for infringing fundamental rights must be able to pass each stage of this structured reasoning process.

7.2.2.3 The Blurry Line between the State and Corporations

The last reason I wish to explore for applying proportionality beyond the public sphere connects with the fact, as was already discussed in Chapters 4 and 6, that the line between the public and private spheres is often blurred in reality. As we have seen, the traditional context in which proportionality has been applied is in relation to the vertical relationship between the individual and the state. Indeed, part of the very reason for the recognition of fundamental rights in law historically has been to serve as a means of protecting individuals against the power of the state to harm their fundamental interests.[43] The mechanics of the

[42] An interesting question here is whether or not only 'public reasons' are acceptable as a ground for limiting fundamental rights. Usually that will be the case where exercises of authority by non-state actors radiate beyond their spheres of operation. When confined to those spheres, it seems to me reasonable to conclude that such nonpublic reasons must be capable of being accepted by the individual whose rights are violated. For a discussion of these matters in the context of religious associations who wish to discriminate, see Bilchitz, 2011a: 233; 239–40.

[43] See the discussion in section 2.2 of Chapter 2 and sections 4.2.1 and 4.2.2 of Chapter 4.

proportionality enquiry were designed in some sense to take cognizance of this asymmetrical power dynamic. For this reason, there is effectively a presumption against infringing on individual rights built into the test (thus already assigning significant weight to the fundamental interests underlying rights) and the power asymmetry is captured by placing an obligation on the state to justify any action or law that causes such an infringement through a rigorous process.[44]

Things seem to become more complicated in the case of non-state actors. In this context, we do not automatically have a clear conflict between an individual and a very powerful entity which represents the overall political collective and has a monopoly on the use of violence.[45] The conflict is instead between one individual and another individual (or individuals) on a similar plane or between individuals and juristic persons with differing degrees of strength and power. The question thus arises as to whether the structure of the proportionality enquiry is apposite for this context. Two main circumstances appear to arise: the first concerns the applicability of proportionality in circumstances where there is an asymmetrical power relationship between the parties; the second concerns its applicability in situations where there is no clear disparity of power between the parties.

I shall focus on the first set of circumstances. The easiest cases concern situations in which a non-state actor exercises a function which is usually performed by the state or has been outsourced by it to the non-state actor. Thus, in *Allpay*[46] – the case concerning the payment of social grants which was dealt with in Chapter 4 – CPS was clearly performing a function that the state would otherwise have had to perform. Consequently, it wielded massive power in relation to the individuals who were reliant on the social grants it administered. Where a corporation exercises a clear public function usually performed by the state in such a way that it exercises significant power over individuals and can thus threaten a fundamental interest protected by a right, there is a strong justification for applying to it the same process of reasoning applicable to the state. In such circumstances, consequently, there do not

[44] Schauer, 2014: 178 sees this as an essential feature of proportionality: Schauer states that 'there is a presumption in favor of the right, or which is more or less the same thing, a burden of proof imposed on those who would restrict the right'. See also Mureinik's view (1994: 32–33) that this feature is central to the culture of justification mentioned earlier.

[45] Weber, 1919: 310–11 sees this as the central feature of the state.

[46] See *AllPay*, section 4.3.3.1 of Chapter 4.

appear to be any good reasons for departing from a proportionality analysis simply on the grounds that the public function is exercised by a non-state actor.

Asymmetries of power do not, however, only exist when a state function is performed by a non-state actor. They may arise from a range of sources: wealth, social function, social capital, and the widespread capacity to act and influence given abilities, size, control over resources, and much else. Such asymmetries render some individuals vulnerable to the exercise of power by other stronger entities or individuals. Where such circumstances exist and there is a threat to fundamental rights, it seems wholly justifiable to impose on those individuals or structures exercising such power an obligation to justify their infringement on the fundamental rights of others. We thus see, in a similar vein, in decisions such as *Stadium Ban* (Germany)[47] and *T-694 of 2013* (Colombia),[48] courts recognise that the asymmetrical power exercised by the non-state actors in these cases provides good reason for imposing requirements of procedural fairness on those actors which include, in some instances, a duty to provide reasons for a decision.

In relation to corporations, of course, there is a large degree of variability in their power to affect the fundamental interests of others. Some corporations rival states in their economic power[49] and others are much smaller in their capacities. Even so, I have already argued in the previous chapter that any corporate structure exhibits an asymmetry of power in its relationships with other individuals.[50] Consequently, it is justifiable to regard the very act of incorporation as an act of gaining power in such a way that the corporate structure itself must be considered to exist in an asymmetrical power relationship with individuals. The power it assumes and consequent vulnerability it creates provides a strong reason for requiring a corporation to provide a rigorous justification for any prima facie infringements of individual rights. The proportionality enquiry, as we saw, is specifically designed for this purpose: it includes a presumption in favour of fundamental rights and places a duty on the infringing party to provide a strong justification that responds to the various sub-enquiries. It therefore appears wholly justifiable to require an agent to satisfy the proportionality test where that agent prima facie

47 See Chapter 4.
48 See Chapter 5.
49 See Wettstein, 2009: 213–257, who focuses on such corporations.
50 See section 6.3.1.2, Chapter 6, on vulnerability where I make this argument.

infringes a right of an individual and exists in an asymmetrical power relationship with that individual.[51]

I have thus sought to provide three arguments why the proportionality test is in fact applicable beyond the sphere of the state in circumstances where non-state actors such as corporations infringe fundamental rights and exist in asymmetrical power relationships with individuals. However, as the earlier quote by Steven Gardbaum indicates, it is not the case that we can simply utilise proportionality in the corporate sphere without thinking through how its application differs in this changed context. In the next section, I turn to consider the various components of the test and how they would apply when corporations infringe fundamental rights.

7.3 Applying Proportionality to the Corporate Sphere – Examining the Components

7.3.1 *Infringement*

As was outlined earlier, the stage that takes place prior to the proportionality enquiry proper involves determining whether a fundamental right has been infringed. The focal point at this stage of the enquiry involves establishing whether a fundamental interest of an individual is imperilled that is protected by a fundamental right. This stage is vital in ascertaining, from the perspective of the rights-holder, the nature of the infringement and its seriousness. That will, in turn, impact later on the weight to be attached to these interests in any balancing enquiry. The key factors that will be of relevance at this stage are the beneficiary-orientated ones: interest, vulnerability, and impact. Ultimately, in the context of the corporation, the goal here will be to determine the nature and extent of any infringement and to chart the particular harms that flow from a corporate infringement of such rights.

[51] It remains an interesting question as to whether proportionality should apply where one individual/entity has no extra power in relation to another individual: in other words, where the individuals are symmetrically situated with respect to one another. A detailed treatment of this question cannot, for reasons of length, be provided nor is it necessary to answer it in relation to corporate obligations for the reasons detailed in the text. Proportionality reasoning may retain relevance even in such circumstances though, for purposes of this book, there is no need to defend its application beyond the realm of asymmetrical power relationships.

7.3.2 *Can Corporate Purposes Limit Fundamental Rights?*

The proportionality enquiry begins properly with a consideration of whether a purpose can be identified that is sufficiently strong to justify the infringement of a right. In the context of the state, the question usually concerns whether a *legitimate* purpose can be identified.[52] The state may, for instance, justify limited surveillance of citizens' emails on the grounds of national security and preventing terrorism. The state could not legitimately justify any action whose sole purpose were to discriminate unfairly between black people and white people or men and women. Determining what is a legitimate purpose, of course, requires a theory of the state itself, and understanding what kinds of goals it may or may not pursue. A purpose of discrimination, for instance, would be prohibited given that a central underlying justification for the state is that it is an entity that is designed to act impartially between people.[53] Courts have, however, tended to accept that most lawful purposes constitute legitimate purposes and the number of cases where there is a failure to identify such a purpose is the exception rather than the rule.[54]

Things appear to be more tricky when it comes to identifying purposes of non-state actors that would justify infringing fundamental rights. As we saw earlier, Gardbaum raises precisely this question as to '[w]hat would count as a legitimate private reason for the limitation of a constitutional right by another individual?'[55] In answering this question, it is important at the outset to recognise that proportionality applies to situations where there are conflicts of norms. Thus, a primary requirement for the application of the proportionality enquiry will be the need to identify a purpose which in some sense clashes with the fundamental right that has been infringed. That purpose must have a strong weight attached to it to trigger the application of the proportionality enquiry: if it is wholly trivial and cannot represent a counter-weight to a fundamental right, then there is no real norm conflict and the right will clearly prevail. Thus, given the fact that rights are already weighty normative considerations, only purposes of a similar level of normative import could justify the limitation of such rights. The terminology of legitimacy, however, is

[52] Klatt and Meister, 2012: 8.

[53] See the discussion of Locke in section 2.3.2.2.2 of Chapter 2.

[54] See Grimm, 2007: 388–389, who compares the German and Canadian jurisprudence in this regard.

[55] Gardbaum, 2017: 246.

awkward in the context of non-state actors as it is connected to a conception of when political authority may rightfully be exercised over individuals.[56] We may thus need to shift our terminology somewhat in the context of non-state actors. I would suggest that it may be better to speak of 'significant purposes' which capture the need for only weighty purposes to be considered. The question then becomes what constitutes a significant purpose in the corporate sphere that can be placed into the proportionality test. In addressing this, and to ensure the structure of the proportionality test is useful, it is important to identify a relatively wide range of purposes that would be included at this stage without it becoming a meaningless threshold criterion.

7.3.2.1 The Relationship between Significant Purposes and Social Function

At the outset, it is important to recognise that the purposes that may be significant for limiting a right are connected to the nature of particular agents and the function(s) they perform in society. At times, when individuals, for instance, perform a particular social function, there may be a greater justification for them to limit the rights of others than for the state to do so. Consider, for example, a parent who disciplines her child for the use of foul language: here the child's right to free speech is restricted but it is done for the purpose of educating the child in the proper norms of social intercourse. Usually, we would not allow one individual to restrict the right of another to express himself freely, yet the diligent performance of a parent's social role is critical in enabling the child to function adequately in society. That role and the motivation in question provide a strong justification for recognising the purpose of the parent as significant in this context. It would be unacceptable, however, for the state to intervene and impose some sort of criminal punishment on a child for the use of foul language. The significance of the purpose here is closely tied to the social role played by parents which is distinct from that of the state. Consequently, what is a significant justification on the basis of which a parent can limit the rights of their children does not constitute a significant justification for state intervention. The social function the agent plays is thus of importance in determining significance: in the example provided, this emerges from the special

[56] The term may be applicable in circumstances where a corporation clearly exercises functions peculiar to the state. I am concerned to articulate an analytical framework that can cover a wider set of cases than these.

relationship that exists between parents and children and the educative role of a parent.

Our focus in this book is not on individuals but the corporation – how then can we determine the significance of a purpose when confronted with corporate infringements of fundamental rights? There are a number of complexities in this regard upon which I will elaborate but it is important to note firstly that the significance of a purpose will depend on the nature of the social function a corporation performs within the particular sphere of activity in which it operates.

The social role or function of a corporation may be specified in the documents that make it up: a memorandum or articles of association. If it acts outside the bounds of its constituting documents, that may provide grounds to find that the purpose it seeks to achieve is not significant. Nevertheless, such a formalistic view of social function is too narrow: there needs to be an understanding garnered of the various social roles a particular corporation performs in actuality in a particular area. Comprehending its social function will thus require investigating the spheres of activity in which a corporation is involved: a corporation which runs educational institutions may have a different social function to one involved in diamond mining. The founding documents may suggest, however, that the corporation is solely concerned, for instance, with diamond mining but, in reality, it actually has taken on the function of providing healthcare services to the surrounding communities. Indeed, the social function of a particular corporation may also be affected by its scale: the same diamond company which is the only source of employment and services within a remote rural area will have a much more extensive social function than a small neighbourhood hardware store does. An understanding of the social function of an entity may thus help to determine what can and cannot be considered a significant purpose for a corporation.

A purpose will not pass the test of 'significance' if the corporation exceeds the boundaries of its social function. For instance, a corporation operating private schools may seek to become a leader in providing excellent education to the scholars that attend its schools. It may not, given its social role, aim to take over the determination of education policy in a country. The function of such a corporation is to be a provider of education according to publicly specified rules applicable to all. If it becomes the body that determines education policy, it moves into performing a state function which it was never designed to perform.

7.3.2.2 Determining Significant Purposes in Light of the Duality of the Corporation

We have seen the need for a consideration of the social context, the sphere of activity and scale of a corporation in determining what constitutes a significant purpose. However, in Chapter 1, I defended the 'socio-liberal' understanding of the purpose of a corporation that involves dual dimensions: on the one hand, the corporation is constructed for the purpose of achieving social benefits; yet it achieves those very benefits through being a vehicle for the realisation of the purposes of the individuals who are involved with it. Taking account of both these societal and individual dimensions raises complexity in terms of how we evaluate the significance of the purposes of a corporate agent and whether, in doing so, justification on one of these dimensions is sufficient. If these two dimensions would always pull in the same direction, that would not be a difficult question. Yet, there are many occasions where they seem to come apart.

Consider the following example. A corporation deliberately releases effluent into a river to avoid the costs of building an expensive recycling plant. A surrounding community which relies on the river for food and water complains that doing so is a violation of the rights of its individual members to food and water. The corporation claims that its purpose is to achieve profits for its shareholders and, doing so, requires it to take the most cost-effective measures. It raises an additional argument that such efficiencies would, in turn, enable it to expand and employ more people from the community. Yet, it seeks to achieve these goals in a manner that involves serious social harm and an infringement on the rights of individuals in the surrounding community. Does the advancement of profit alone constitute a significant purpose when evaluating a corporate infringement on the rights of individuals? Does the social purpose of expanding employment advance its justification?

The purpose of increasing profits gives expression to a key aspect of the individual dimension of the corporation: for individual investors or shareholders, it is important for the achievement of their purposes to be able to utilise the corporation as a vehicle for attaining sizeable profits. Yet, the corporation also has a societal dimension: in the given example, it is creating serious social harms for the surrounding community. It also argues, however, that it aims to create social benefits through the expansion of its activities, enabling greater employment. The question that this example underscores is how best to capture both the individual and societal dimension of the corporation in the proportionality enquiry and, particularly, how strictly to construct the notion of 'significant' purposes. There are two approaches that can be followed.

The first approach would create a strong threshold enquiry concerning what constitutes a significant purpose for a corporation. One natural starting point is that a corporation cannot negate either of its individual or societal dimensions. A corporation may therefore resist any attempt simply to render it part of the state and so ignore the individual dimension of its character (provided it has not itself sought to take over state functions). It may also, however, not prioritise its individual dimension to the extent that it ignores the social benefits it is designed to achieve. Thus, if an activity will create severe social harms, the corporation may not utilise the benefits for some individuals it achieves by increasing profits as a justification for those harms.

Thus, the social harms from the pollution of the river in the aforementioned example are clearly foreseeable and seriously undermine the well-being of individuals in the community. They cannot be regarded as significant, on this view, simply because of contributing to greater profits for the corporation. The promised social benefits are also not sufficient to outweigh their harms and in fact are contradictory: one cannot seek to advance people through employment and then undermine their very basic ability to acquire food (one of the reasons they wish to be employed). The self-interested individualised benefits of such a policy thus fundamentally undermine any social benefits that could be achieved and, consequently, the purpose would not be regarded as significant (in this particular sense).

The problem with this approach to 'significance' is that it already places an assessment of the conflict between the individual and societal dimensions of the corporation into the enquiry concerning what constitutes a significant purpose. This leads to two major issues. Firstly, this approach suggests that corporate activity can only be justified by reference both to the individual and societal dimensions of its nature. A justification simply rooted in advancing the profits or reputation of a company cannot be regarded as having significance alone. The benefit of always requiring reference to the social benefits of corporate behaviour in determining significance is that it renders them always of central importance to the corporation. However, the drawback of doing so is that it can also fail to give adequate weight to the individual dimension of the corporation and suggests that profit-making must always be considered as being directly instrumental to the achievement of social purposes. Whilst the corporate structure is created, ultimately, to achieve social benefits (as was argued in Chapter 1), it is not clear that decision-makers in corporations would always *directly* be required to aim at the achievement of social purposes. Instead, the corporation is commonly understood to be an entity designed as a means of harnessing self-interested behaviour by individuals for the achievement of social purposes.[57] Thus, the social benefits of the corporation are meant often to be achieved 'indirectly' rather than directly. Consequently, it would be permissible for decisions to be made without directly focusing on achieving social benefits and so the 'significance' enquiry should not always require that there be a direct reference to social purposes.

The second and perhaps bigger problem with this approach is that it already requires engaging in balancing when determining what constitutes a significant purpose. That would in turn render the last three stages of the proportionality enquiry meaningless and lose the benefits of the structured reasoning process proportionality introduces to balancing. The point of the proportionality enquiry is to balance the normative principles appealed to by the corporation against those that relate to the claims of the individuals concerned. If we seek to conduct such a balancing process within the enquiry concerning what constitutes a significant purpose, then the conflict is translated into an internal one between the individual and social dimension of the corporation. Whilst the conception of the corporation I have articulated allows for such an internal conflict, conceptualising matters in this way fails to offer us a structured method to adjudicate between the conflicting goals of the company.

It is better and analytically more rigorous, in my view, therefore to adopt a second approach. At the stage of determining the significance of the purposes involved in a rights-infringement, we rather should accept a wide array of purposes as significant[58] – emanating from either the individual or societal components of the corporation – provided they are advanced in good faith and are not trivial.[59] The only purposes excluded,

[57] See for instance, Keay, 2011: 65 and section 1.4.3 of Chapter 1.

[58] Such an approach accords well with the wide approach adopted in most jurisdictions at this stage in relation to the purposes of the state as well where it is rare to exclude such purposes as not being 'legitimate': see Grimm, 2007: 388–389.

[59] Klatt and Meister, 2012: 23 attempt to address some of the criticisms of proportionality by developing a 'weak trump model': this involves the idea that the only justifiable purposes for limiting a right must be those which emerge from 'constitutional values'. The problem with this approach as a limiting condition, in this context, is that corporations can claim that realising their individualised purposes – such as profit-making and the protection of

at this stage, are what may be termed 'nefarious' ones which directly aim at harming the fundamental rights of other individuals. Such purposes need not be balanced against the fundamental interests of others: they are immediately excluded from the proportionality enquiry. Since fundamental rights represent foundational grundnorms of political communities, no corporation can claim to aim directly to harm these fundamental principles which bind it as much as any other entity in society. The individual dimension of the corporation, as we have seen in Chapter 1, also involves attaining fundamental rights for the individuals involved with it – such as property, work and autonomy – and thus there is no basis for any claim for it to be permitted to undermine the fundamental rights of others. An individual or entity may, therefore, in no way pursue a purpose that directly aims at harming the fundamental rights of others.

A complication is raised by the question of indirect harm: in our effluent example, the corporation claims that its direct goal is to continue its operations at the least cost – an unfortunate side effect involves releasing effluent into the river but it in no way directly wishes to harm any individual's fundamental rights. The approach I advocate does not require excluding the *good faith* purposes of a corporation from being regarded as 'significant' provided they do not directly aim at causing harm to fundamental rights. The justification for doing so is that the conflict in the aforementioned example is precisely what the proportionality enquiry aims to address and so it is best not to remove such forms of indirect harm from the enquiry at this point: the balancing of interests will take place later in the reasoning process.

This approach, therefore, entails that most purposes put forward by a corporation will pass the 'significance' test, which simply requires that its purposes must be in line with its social role and not be nefarious. In constructing whether they are nefarious and its claims are made in good faith, it will of course be necessary to consider all objective facts and not simply rely on the corporation's stated objective.

This approach allows the individual dimension of the corporation to be recognised as having significance given that the achievement of profit or protection of reputation will usually be put forward as the underlying general purposes behind most corporate actions. At the same time, in

their reputation – gives expression to fundamental rights that protect the autonomy of individuals. It is thus better at the outset (as argued in the text) to recognise the significance of these interests and then test them within the broader proportionality enquiry rather than to attempt to exclude certain purposes from the outset.

determining the weighting of the competing interests which is so central to the proportionality enquiry, such purposes will be understood only to be drawn from one dimension of the corporation.[60] The weight to be accorded to such a purpose will be reduced where the social and individual dimensions of the corporations are not in alignment. I will explore further below how the different dimensions of corporate activity and the social harms it creates play out in the different sub-tests of the proportionality enquiry. The social dimension of the corporation can, as we will see, also be given expression to in the rest of the enquiry. It is thus important not to allow the test for 'significant' purposes to subvert the operation of the rest of the enquiry: in this way, we are able to gain the benefits of the structured process of reasoning given expression to in the particular stages of a proportionality analysis.

7.3.2.3 Rights against Rights

It is worth considering an objection that could be made at this point when determining the significant purposes of a corporation. It can be argued, as we saw, that, traditionally, proportionality has been applied in law where the powerful actor is the state. In this context, the legitimate purpose of the state involves a collective or general interest which has to be evaluated against the rights of individuals. Karavias contends as follows:

> Proportionality measures whether the cost to the right is justified by the public interest. It is thus questionable whether it can provide clear guidance when a communal interest is lacking as is the case with restrictions arising from corporate conduct.[61]

This objection acknowledges correctly that the state itself cannot claim fundamental rights and so the purposes for which it restricts rights may not be its own claim to have such rights protected. The justifications it provides for limiting rights, however, are more complex than is suggested in this objection. Usually, the purposes sought to be achieved by the state are in fact of two kinds. The objection only deals with the first of these, namely, where the state may infringe rights in order to advance a pressing

[60] Often, these purposes will also only be expressed from the perspective of the managers or owners, yet they are not the only individuals whose perspectives matter in relation to the corporation, as was explicated in Chapter 1. The fact that other individuals with a stake in the corporation are not advantaged by the purpose put forward as a justification for a rights violation can also reduce the weight to be attached to the purpose.

[61] Karavias, 2013: 194.

normative goal: for example, it restricts the property rights of owners for the purposes of environmental protection. However, there is a second broad 'ground' of justification that the state may offer for infringing rights, which involves precisely limiting the rights of some in order to protect the rights of others. Thus, for example, the state may place restrictions on the freedom of speech of an individual to express hateful sentiments or incite violence in order to protect the rights to equality and security of the person of other vulnerable individuals in society. Protecting the rights of some individuals may require limiting the rights of others, and the state is precisely there to ensure a fair balance is achieved in society.[62]

The matter is different in the context of a clash of rights between individuals where we are directly concerned with the respective rights of both individuals. In situations where individuals are in symmetrical power relations, they too can claim that they wish to restrict the rights of others on two types of grounds: the first relates to advancing their individual goals; and the second relates to protecting their own rights. The first form of justification would only provide sufficient justification for intruding into the rights of other individuals if the individual goals claimed would involve protecting the rights of others. It thus seems that only one form of justification will broadly suffice in such cases.

In the context of corporations, matters become more complex. As we saw in Chapter 1, corporate agents are not simply reducible to the individuals who lie behind them though they give expression to many of their interests – particularly, their economic interests. Corporations are also constructions of law and not the original bearers of fundamental rights or dignity.[63] Any justification then that corporations provide for restricting rights are likely to be of two kinds: on the one hand, corporations could justify restricting rights to achieve the purposes that are at the core of their operations. There is of course a central question as to the value of such purposes and whether they are sufficient to override the fundamental rights of individuals. On the other hand, they could justify

[62] There is an interesting question whether the first type of justification is always a species of the second: for instance, whether the legitimacy of state purposes such as environmental protection actually can be reduced to claims about protecting the rights of others (say, for example, the right to live in a healthy environment). We might want to preserve the notion that there are important normative considerations that may not ultimately be expressed in terms of fundamental rights. Whether this is true and whether such considerations may outweigh fundamental rights is an important question but beyond the scope of this book to resolve.

[63] We already canvassed this point at section 5.2.3.1 of Chapter 5.

restricting rights on the grounds that such a course of action is necessary to give effect to the rights of individuals who have a 'stake' in the corporation: shareholders, employees, or customers, for instance.

Again, the crucial question arises as to whether normative purposes other than realising fundamental rights can justify infringing the rights of individuals. There is less justification for recognising wider normative purposes when dealing with non-state actors than in the case of the state: indeed, it appears to be more justifiable to allow the normative principles relating to the common good – whose advancement is a central goal of the state – to justify infringing individual rights than those that flow from the self-interest of particular individuals who lie behind a corporation. It is also questionable whether there would generally be strong social purposes lying at the core of for-profit corporate behaviour that could alone provide sufficient justification to override the rights of others. Generally, as a result, in relation to corporations, it would only be possible to infringe the fundamental rights of some individuals for reasons connected to advancing the fundamental rights of other individuals (who have a 'stake', for instance, in the corporation).

It is not clear that this restriction places too strong a constraint on the corporate infringement of rights though since much of what takes place under the guise of self-interest can be understood to be an expression of realising the property rights (or other autonomy rights) of the individuals underlying the corporation[64] or as having implications for the rights of others – the growth of a business, for instance, could be conceived of as advancing the rights of some individuals to a livelihood. Whilst corporate claims surrounding fundamental rights are not equivalent to those of the individuals underlying it, the rights of those individuals – which are mediated, in some respect, through the corporate form – need some consideration. Thus, the justification provided by the corporation for infringing rights must usually reference the rights of some (or all) of the individuals lying behind it.[65]

64 Here the supervenience of the corporate form upon individuals is important as was articulated in Chapter 1. We cannot reduce corporate interests to those of the individuals underlying them but we need to recognise its relationship to them and the effect of any restrictions on its behaviour on them.

65 Karavias, 2013: 194 states that 'balancing corporate and individual rights differs from the existing modes of balancing under international law, in the sense that in the first situation international law will be employed with a view to striking a balance between two human rights invoked simultaneously by their respective rights holders'. It is important as I argue in the text to recognise that corporate claims to fundamental rights are not equivalent to individual claims and are inherently weaker given they emerge from an entity that lacks

The proportionality enquiry thus remains apposite both to situations where the purpose for an infringement is a normative social goal as well as where it focuses on the advancement of a fundamental right. Both circumstances apply in the case of the state whilst only the latter is generally applicable in the context of non-state actors in asymmetrical relationships with other individuals. Either way, it will be necessary to understand the normative weight of the underlying purpose of the more powerful actor and the degree to which it can justify infringing upon the interests protected by the fundamental right of the more vulnerable individual. The point here is that whilst there may be some differences between the context of the state and corporations in terms of the nature of the purpose that could justify infringing a fundamental right, this stage of the proportionality test remains apposite in relation to both sets of actors.

7.3.3 Suitability

The second stage of the proportionality enquiry – the suitability test – requires an understanding of whether the measures taken which infringe upon fundamental rights are suitable to achieving the purpose that has been identified in the first stage. This test requires a transparent investigation of whether in fact there is a rational relationship between means and ends: it is possible – and perhaps a frequent occurrence – that insufficient attention is paid to the means that are adopted which infringe rights which, in many cases, do not actually achieve the purposes they aim to realise. If that is so, then there are no good grounds for infringing rights through the use of such means – even if the purpose is significant.[66]

In the context of corporations, this sub-test can force them to consider carefully whether the means they are adopting – which infringe rights – are in fact suitable for achieving the purposes they seek to achieve. Yet, interestingly, this enquiry can also add a particular substantive dimension in the case of corporations. Consider the aforementioned example where a corporation releases effluent into a river and thus infringes on the right to food and water of the individuals in the surrounding community. This measure is justified partially by the corporation, as we saw, in terms of being designed to execute its operations on a profitable basis.

dignity in its own right and are not reducible simply to the entitlements of the individuals lying behind it.

66 Alexy, 2002: 68–69 provides a more technical justification for the suitability test which gives expression in symbolic notation to this argument.

Yet, such a measure, whilst facially achieving the purpose of the company, may well be harming its relationship with the people in that community. As such, it could be undermining its own interests in being able to continue operations and making profits in the area in the medium to long run.

The United Nations 'Protect, Respect and Remedy' Framework for Business and Human Rights makes reference to the fact that corporations require a 'social license to operate'.[67] If a corporation harms a community in such a way that undermines its ability to operate its business in the future, then the relationship between its polluting actions – for instance – and its ability to make profits is placed in doubt. In the extreme case, the relationship between means and ends may be completely severed by the social harms that are created: where, for instance, strong social action leads to the shutting down of corporate activities.[68] Measures that infringe rights thus may fail to achieve the corporation's very own purposes in enhancing its reputation or making profits. Where the evidence is mixed concerning a measure's contribution to profitability, such social harms may also undermine the weight to be attached to the corporate justification for infringing rights.

Indeed, when profit is placed as a central motivation for a measure that infringes rights, the question arises whether the corporation is conceiving of its purposes too narrowly: its profits may increase this quarter but its activities create the seeds for a long-term collapse. Many features of what are often referred to as the 'business case for human rights' could thus be considered in relation to this sub-test.[69] Failing to treat workers with respect through poor working conditions may well seem to advance short-term corporate purposes; but doing so may well harm the corporation in both its productivity and its capacity to attract excellent new employees. In addition, rights violations may in fact severely harm the reputation of the company as well as its financial bottom line through

[67] UN Framework 2008: para 54.

[68] These are not merely theoretical claims and have happened in places across the world: see, for instance, the cessation of operations of the copper mine in Bouganville described in Bilchitz, 2017a. Similarly, there have been severe disruptions in mining operations in Latin America: see, for instance on the latter, NT Flannery 'Protests in Peru Scaring Off Mining Investment, Government Responds with Social Programs' Forbes (Oct 29, 2012) available at www.forbes.com/sites/nathanielparishflannery/2012/10/29/protests-in-peru-scaring-off-mining-investment-government-responds-with-social-programs/#528eca7f102b.

[69] See, for example, Morrison, 2011 available at www.ihrb.org/pdf/IHRB_Speech_2011_04_28_John_Morrison_The_Business_Case_for_Human_Rights.pdf.

multiple legal claims. The suitability test may thus, interestingly, highlight situations where the failure to address the social harms of corporate activity in fact undermines the corporation's reputation and its ability to make profits. In so doing, this test thus may offer more opportunity for challenging harmful behaviour by corporations than is often thought.

7.3.4 Necessity

The third stage of the proportionality enquiry – the necessity test – requires an understanding of whether there is an alternative measure which sufficiently realises the purpose identified by the corporation but has a lesser impact on the right.[70] If such an alternative can be identified, then it means that there is no justification for infringing a right more than is required.[71] Similar reasoning is often used when attempting to achieve a fair balance between competing private interests: such reasoning, for instance, was in evidence in some of the cases already discussed, such as *Khumalo, Fraport,* and *Eweida.*

In the context of corporate behaviour, this enquiry forces an examination of alternatives to the current modus operandi of the corporation. It can help disrupt a casual sense that certain harms to fundamental rights are inevitable by forcing a consideration of which alternatives could minimise any such harms. It could also in fact stimulate the development of alternative technologies, for instance, to minimise any negative human rights impacts.

As with the suitability enquiry, the complex nature of a corporation will play an important role in the way in which the necessity enquiry is conducted. The necessity test can be broken down into various steps: it requires an understanding of the range of alternative measures that are possible; the degree to which they realise the purposes that have been identified; the differing impacts of these different alternatives on the right in question; and finally a comparison between which alternative is the best from the perspective of both realising the purpose and minimising the impact on the right.[72] The final comparison inevitably involves some degree of balancing: there will always need to be an evaluation of the

[70] See Bilchitz, 2014: 61, where I explain why it is important to formulate the test in this way. The Indian Supreme Court adopted this formulation in *Justice K.S. Putaswamy* v. *Union of India* https://indiankanoon.org/doc/127517806/.

[71] Once again, this provides a basic explanation of the technical argument justifying the necessity test made by Alexy, 2002: 67–68.

[72] I explore these elements in more detail in Bilchitz, 2014: 51–57.

justifiability of utilising a means that has a lesser impact on a right but is slightly worse in achieving the purposes of a corporation.[73]

As we saw in relation to suitability, however, those purposes might be specified, for instance, in relation to short-term or long-term profitability of the corporation. Where the gain in efficiency for enhancing profits is in relation to a short-term purpose but not in relation to a long-term purpose, there will be an inevitable degree of balancing when considering two alternative measures. Nevertheless, it is likely that, in such circumstances, it will be unacceptable to impose a greater harm to a right for short-term gain where the longer-term goals of a corporation can be achieved by a measure that has a lesser impact on the right.

Let us go back to the environmental pollution case we have discussed. Clearly, there is an alternative that could be identified which has a lesser impact on the right: namely, the building of a recycling plant.[74] The reason the corporation has not done so is that the building of such a plant would be expensive and reduce short-term profits. Two scenarios can be identified: the first is where the cost of recycling reduces the profits of the corporation; the second is where the cost is so high that it prevents any future profit-making by the corporation at all. Importantly, the necessity test is of application in the first scenario, but not the second. In the second scenario, the purpose identified by the corporation is not achieved at all and so, ultimately, the question becomes about whether the purposes of the corporation are normatively strong enough to justify the limitation on the rights of individuals in the community – which is a matter of balancing and thus addressed in the final stage of the proportionality enquiry. The first scenario, however, is different: in this situation, the corporation can in fact achieve its purpose but to a lesser degree. The corporation can make profits but must bear the burden of the additional cost of building a recycling plant to lessen the impact on fundamental rights. In such circumstances, the necessity test will generally not be passed if it continues to pollute without building the plant. The reason is that the purpose of making profits can still be achieved to a sufficient degree – profit expectations may simply have to be reduced to avoid fundamental rights violations. Consequently, alternatives that enable a corporation to remain profitable but reduce the impact on fundamental rights must generally be adopted. Achieving *maximum*

[73] Ibid: 56–57.

[74] I assume this is the only alternative for purposes of the example.

profits cannot provide an adequate justification for overriding the significant weight attached to fundamental rights.

7.3.5 Balancing

The last stage of the proportionality enquiry involves balancing and determining whether the harms to the rights of individuals are proportional to the benefits to be achieved by the corporation. Clearly, this enquiry involves a value-laden judgement.[75] It will involve an assessment of the relative weight of the interests of the company vis-à-vis the interests of the individual in the particular circumstances. That, in turn, will require assessing the importance of the purpose of a proposed measure by a corporation that limits rights (and the probability it will be achieved) against the importance of the right that is infringed, and the degree of impact on the right (and the probability that the infringement will occur).[76] This enquiry means, for instance, that a massive harm to fundamental rights cannot be justified by a minimal or even moderate benefit to the corporation; a limited restriction on such rights may be justified, however, if connected to a strong benefit for the corporation.

The *Von Hannover* case in the ECHR can provide a clear illustration of how this stage of the enquiry works. On the one hand, the court there recognised the value of freedom of expression and the press; yet it only accorded a limited weight to satisfying the prurient interest of the public in Princess Caroline's private life and, in so doing, increasing the sales of the publication in question. On the other hand, the intrusion into the most intimate sphere of Princess Caroline's life involved a serious infringement on her privacy interests. In balancing, the court found that the weak commercial and prurient interests could not outweigh Princess Caroline's strong claim to enjoy a private life away from the cameras.

7.3.5.1 Profit and Balancing

The discomfort many people feel with applying proportionality in this context may arise from the sense that certain harms need to be recognised as unjustifiable no matter the purposes of the corporation. No matter how profitable it is, for instance, many would argue that the release of effluent into a river that imperils the rights to food, water and health of

[75] Barak, 2012: 342.

[76] Ibid: 369–62. I cannot discuss the issue of probability further here but it was briefly addressed in section 6.3.2.1.1 of Chapter 6 and relates to the 'Second Law of Balancing' of Alexy, 2002: 418–19.

individuals in a community can never be justified. The proportionality enquiry, it could be claimed, does not adequately give expression to this intuition. Put differently, we could imagine an interlocutor raising a seemingly obvious objection: how can profit ever be used as a justification for violating fundamental rights?

Though the intuition is rhetorically effective, it is necessary to think more carefully and deeply about this challenge. The first issue concerns whether or not there are harms that are too severe ever to be justified by corporate purposes such as profit-making or protecting its reputation. The proportionality enquiry, however, accepts the existence of such scenarios: the key question, ultimately, comes down to the weighting of the normative considerations.[77] The severity of the harms may be weighted so heavily in any balancing enquiry that it becomes impossible to justify any corporate activity that inflicts those harms no matter the impact on the profitability of the enterprise. Indeed, this point is also applicable to the state and is often made in relation to the 'core' of fundamental rights where it is particularly difficult to justify any interference. Thus, it may be that the release of effluent which poses severe threats to the health of a community could never be justified by operational and profit-making considerations. In circumstances where the environmental harms are extremely severe, if the company is not able to avert those harms, the only choice is for it to stop operating.

A second issue that arises from the aforementioned objection is whether achieving profits can ever be an adequate justification for restricting fundamental rights. The answer to this question must, in my view, be clearly in the affirmative. Consider, for instance, the modern workplace which by its very nature requires certain limitations on individual rights: individuals may need to tolerate restrictions on their movement (during work hours); speech (in corporate contexts); privacy (on their computers); and much else. In some industries – such as mining and manufacturing – there is an inevitable degree of negative environmental impact which may affect fundamental rights. It thus cannot be that any negative impact on rights will in all cases be unjustifiable and prevent the achievement of corporate purposes such as profit-making: the question rather must be the justification for any such impacts, the degree thereof, and their proportionality in relation to the objectives sought to be achieved.

[77] Klatt and Meister, 2012: 38.

There is also an interesting aspect to add in relation to the social dimension of a corporation. I argued in section 7.3.2.2 that enhancing profit or reputation should be considered a 'significant' purpose that can be factored into the proportionality enquiry. Yet, doing so may not adequately do justice to the social dimension of the corporation that involves achieving social benefits: in what way can that facet of its nature be given expression to? The balancing enquiry necessitates quantifying the harms that are created by the corporation and, in doing so, also requires us to engage with the nature and function of the agent that commits the rights infringement. The fact that a corporation, as part of its general societal function, is designed to achieve social benefits has relevance to the relative weights to be attached to its purposes and the harms that it causes. As a result, where a corporation creates social harms in the process of achieving purposes designed to advance the self-interest of individuals underlying it, less weight is attached to those purposes. The social dimension of a corporation thus helps to condition the weights that are assigned in the balancing enquiry and, also, to place an extra degree of emphasis on the social nature of the corporation itself. Thus, in the example of the corporation causing serious environmental pollution to the river, the corporation's interest in achieving profit – derived from its individual dimension – will have a lesser weight attached to it because it creates a massive social harm: indeed, the corporation is going against part of its very existential purpose and so its interest in causing such harm is limited. The scales will thus strongly tip in favour of proscribing such harm.

In this way, the balancing process allows us to factor in the social nature of the corporation. The implication of this reasoning is that the function or social role of an agent that imperils a right is an important factor to be taken into account in any balancing process. With this recognition, therefore, it should be clear that very severe harms to individual rights will clearly not pass the balancing test both because of their impact on fundamental rights and because they contradict an important part of the very function of corporations in society. That, in itself, should provide significant guidance to decision-makers about which harms are clearly proscribed. Limited and moderate infringements of rights will, however, be capable of being justified in terms of the proportionality enquiry through following the various steps I have outlined earlier. When doing so, both the social and individual dimension of the corporation will also need to be considered in the weightings accorded to the relative interests.

7.3.5.2 The Overarching Evaluation

One difficulty in applying proportionality to the corporate sphere concerns the nature of the overarching question dealt with at the balancing stage. In the context of states, ultimately, one needs to consider a dimension in which harms and benefits can be compared.[78] I have in past work suggested that the overarching enquiry concerns determining which courses of action 'best respect the equal value of individual lives'.[79] Can such a standard apply in circumstances relating to corporate infringements of fundamental rights?

Unlike the state, the corporation is not itself bound always to advance the equal importance of individuals and may act out of a sense of partiality for its own interests – that flows from the dimension of autonomy, which is an important factor applicable to determining its obligations and the justifiability of its behaviour. Yet, in circumstances where it infringes on the fundamental rights of individuals – which are of central importance both to individuals and the society in which they operate – its justification must ultimately be one that can stand up to public scrutiny, which includes taking into account the particular nature of its own activities. The perspective from which judgements are ultimately made must then be capable of being justified on an impartial consideration of the relevant interests at stake. Equal importance is a standard that flows from such impartial consideration: consequently, where a corporation wishes to interfere with fundamental rights, ultimately, the common perspective that can be used in evaluating harms and benefits must be the goal of achieving a state of affairs where the equal importance of persons is maximised.[80] That requires evaluating which state of affairs can best do justice both to the crucial importance of the interests underlying the beneficiary's fundamental rights and the function of a corporation and its autonomy to pursue its own goals.

7.3.6 Application to Davis Example

Let us return to the Davis Ltd case with which we began this chapter to see how the proportionality analysis would be applied to a specific example. We must first chart the interests of the rights-holders, their

[78] The problem often raised is that the benefits and harms are 'incommensurable': see, for instance, Da Silva, 2011: 273–301 for a response to this objection.

[79] Bilchitz, 2007: 100.

[80] This test essentially tries to balance consequentialist and deontological dimensions: I have written more on this in ibid: 98–100.

vulnerability, and the impact of Davis' policy on their lives. At stake are privacy interests which relate to the ability to retain an intimate private sphere of one's life and to control what information about one is released. Individual employees are vulnerable to the decision by Davis' executives and, in a constrained job market, are often unable simply to leave their jobs where they may be unhappy. The impact of Davis' intrusive policy would be seriously to undermine the privacy interests of employees: they would lose the ability to control what information their employer knows about them even in relation to the most intimate spaces of their lives. Maria makes a compelling argument about the role such machines play today for individuals and the inability strictly to separate personal and work-related matters. We can thus accept that the right to privacy of employees in Davis has been infringed. The next step in the reasoning involves conducting a proportionality analysis to determine whether the infringement is justifiable.

The purposes of the corporation first need to be identified and they are clearly significant: to protect its reputation (which relates to advancing its property interests and rights) and to comply with the law. The corporation here is acting in a way in which its social and individual dimensions are harmonised: its self-interest coincides with avoiding a serious social harm. In relation to the next prong of proportionality – the suitability test – the monitoring measures it has taken appear clearly to be rationally related to achieving its purpose. Yet, by instituting such a strong policy, Davis may be harming its own longer-term operational goals through alienating some of its employees.

The third stage of the proportionality enquiry requires a consideration of the necessity of the proposed measures. It does seem to be true that without some monitoring of the content on its computers, it will be impossible for Davis to guarantee the lawfulness of its employees' activities and to protect its reputation. Davis could though adopt measures which are less draconian: it could make clear policy statements that it is a corporation which expects its employees to abide by the law and that employees who fail to do so will be subject to disciplinary consequences. Moreover, it could institute a system of random checks once every six months only within a specified window period. Such an alternative approach would create more predictability and control for employees and so involve a lesser violation of their privacy; at the same time, it is significantly less effective, of course, for Davis to achieve its purposes. We therefore may accept that its proposed measures meet the necessity test but seek to evaluate the alternatives at the last stage of the proportionality enquiry.

To do so, we need to decide whether the harms to employees like Maria are outweighed by the benefits that can be achieved in the pursuit of the corporation's purposes. The harms to the privacy rights of employees are quite significant in this scenario: employees, of course, can have personal computers but given the length of time they spend at work, they may well need to conduct certain personal affairs on their work computers. The policy of Davis leaves them little or no control over what their employer sees and learns about them. On the other side of the equation, Davis itself has an interest in protecting its reputation (which directly affects its property rights) and ensuring compliance with the law. Its social function here works in two ways: on the one hand, its attempt to ensure compliance with the law strengthens the weighting of its own interests; on the other hand, the harshness of the measures it has adopted causes a social harm to the right to privacy of employees. Though the alternative measures suggested may reduce the effectiveness of its surveillance in achieving its purposes, it seems that they could provide a better balance between the interests of individual employees in privacy and the significant purposes of the corporation. Consequently, Davis could justify some measures to restrict the privacy of employees to achieve its purposes but not as wide-ranging an infringement of rights as its initial proposals would have effected.

7.4 Conclusion

This chapter has sought to consider how we determine the final obligations of a corporation where its actions or policies infringe upon fundamental rights. Doing so requires a balancing of different interests, and this chapter argued for the utilisation of the proportionality enquiry to determine whether an infringement of a right by a corporation is justifiable or not. In doing so, I sought to justify applying proportionality beyond the public sphere as well as to respond to the challenges involved in doing so. I then examined in some detail the various stages of the test and how they could be applied to corporate actors.

It is worth summarising here how I envisage the multi-factoral approach working and the relationship of the various factors to the stages of the proportionality analysis that have been discussed earlier.[81] Beneficiary-orientated factors will usually be considered at the prior

[81] It is useful for those concerned with understanding its application to consult the Davis example at section 7.3.6 of this chapter.

stage of the analysis where a decision-maker is required to assess whether there is an infringement of a right and the degree of seriousness thereof. The assessment here will involve understanding the interests underlying the right, the vulnerability of individuals to the corporation in relation to these interests, and the impact the corporate activities have on these individuals in the concrete circumstances of the case. In determining impact and vulnerability, agent-relative factors may be relevant: the capacity of the corporation to harm the rights of individuals and its social function may affect the conclusions that will be drawn.

Having found that there is an infringement, a decision-maker then needs to consider all four stages of the proportionality enquiry in determining whether the measure in question is justifiable. Determining the purposes of the corporation in effecting the measure will require understanding its general function – both social and individual dimensions, as well as its specific function – drawn from the particular sphere in which it operates (the press, for instance). It will also require understanding the reasons the corporation has for the measure and the value of its autonomy in being able to act in the way it wishes. As I argued, purposes drawn from the individual dimension of the corporation – profit-making or the protection of reputation – should be regarded as significant for purposes of this test. That then allows the harms to the fundamental rights of beneficiaries and also the social dimension of the corporation to be expressed through the other prongs of the enquiry.

The suitability test as we saw involves considering the relationship between means and ends, thus identifying possible irrationalities in the decision-making process of the corporation. It also can require a larger look at whether the measures actually achieve the purposes the corporation sets for itself both in the short and long term. The necessity test requires a search for alternatives and examining their relative efficiency in achieving corporate purposes as well as their impact on rights. Doing so involves considering both the function and capacity of the corporation. Finally, the balancing enquiry entails a weighting of the respective interests vis-à-vis one another. In particular, it will consider whether the weight accorded to the autonomy interests of the corporation in being able to achieve its purposes outweighs the weight accorded to the serious interests of individuals in relation to their fundamental rights.

Proportionality, thus, I contend can provide a reasoning structure for determining the final negative obligations of corporations in the face of conflicting rights or interests. Nevertheless, it is clear that its application to concrete cases involves a significant degree of judgement being exercised. This raises a major question: since fundamental rights are at stake, who should be entitled to make such judgements? How can decent, good-faith decision-making in this regard be fostered? How can more concrete standards be developed? Chapters 9 and 10 of this book attempt to address these questions. Before doing so, it is necessary in the next chapter to consider whether corporations have positive obligations to realise fundamental rights and, if so, how to reach a final determination of their substantive content.

8

The Multi-Factoral Approach and Positive Obligations for Corporations

8.1 The Question of Positive Obligations

In the previous two chapters, I have considered an analytical framework for determining the negative obligations of corporations not to harm fundamental rights. Yet, corporations also have significant power actively to contribute to the realisation of fundamental rights – do they also have 'positive' obligations and, if they do, how do we determine the substantive content thereof? I have already provided a concrete example in the introduction of this book to concretise this question.[1] It related to the high pricing of the drug Herceptin, which is used to treat breast cancers that arise from over-expressing the HER-2 protein. Without access to this drug, many women who have breast cancer will die. Does the manufacturer of the drug, Roche, have a positive obligation actively to pursue the realisation of the right to healthcare for these women and, if so, how far do its obligations extend? Would it, for instance, be required to make the drug available for free or, rather, to price it at a rate that is affordable?[2]

This chapter aims to address the question of positive obligations in three parts. Firstly, I outline the contours of what I term the 'negative obligations model' ('NO model'), which utilises the negative/positive obligations distinction to distinguish between state and non-state actors' obligations.

[1] See section 1 of the Introduction.

[2] This question is more complex than it looks. Firstly, there is the question of whether the drug must be affordable to individuals or to the government of a country as a whole (taking into account its competing priorities). Secondly, what would constitute affordability? The latter question may also implicate interesting issues around prohibiting excessive pricing, a matter regulated in the Competition Law of some countries: see, for instance, section 8(a) of the Competition Act 89 of 1998 of South Africa.

I consider a number of justifications for this approach and seek to show that none are convincing. In so doing, I also outline a positive case for recognising that non-state actors have both positive and negative obligations and consider specifically the case for imposing positive obligations on corporations. Having established that such obligations exist, the second part of the chapter turns to determining their substantive content. I argue for the suitability of utilising the multi-factoral approach and proceed to examine the relevance of the particular factors discussed in Chapter 6. I also contend that, in the context of positive obligations, there is a crucial additional factor that must be considered, namely, the other agents that are capable of contributing positively to the realisation of fundamental rights. In reaching final determinations about a corporation's positive obligations, I argue that the proportionality enquiry is not as helpful as it can be in the case of negative obligations. Instead, I develop a seven-part test that can guide decision-makers in reaching final judgements about a corporation's positive obligations.

The last section of this chapter turns more concretely to two jurisdictions in which the question of positive obligations for non-state actors has been engaged in the law. I first consider the evolution that has taken place in the case law of the Constitutional Court of South Africa from effectively adopting the NO model to a limited recognition that non-state actors have positive obligations. The discussion of this jurisprudence highlights the confusion created by the negative/positive obligations distinction and why the multi-factoral approach is a much better guide to determining the substantive content of non-state actors' obligations flowing from fundamental rights. I then turn to India, where the legislature has imposed a strong positive obligation upon large corporations to contribute at least 2 per cent of their average net profits to corporate social responsibility projects. This legislation shows how positive obligations can be operationalised and I will aim to show how the multi-factoral approach can both help ground the Indian legislature's approach and also provide an understanding of the reforms required to enhance it in the future.

8.2 The Negative Obligations Model

8.2.1 The Contours of the Model

The NO model, in a sense, is compatible with various approaches to determining corporate obligations canvassed in Chapters 2–5. For simplification, we can consider it as a species of the direct obligations model discussed in Chapter 5. The NO model, however, asserts that non-state actors' obligations are only 'negative' in nature – in other words, they involve duties to avoid harming fundamental rights alone. This approach usually rests on two premises.

The first is that the obligations of non-state actors differ from those of the state. The plausible intuition, as has already been discussed in Chapter 6, is that the nature of the agent makes a difference to the obligations that it has. This core reasoning is, for instance, exemplified in the context of corporations in a report of the Special Representative of the Secretary General's (SRSG) mandate, which states that '[b]y their very nature, therefore, corporations do not have a general role in relation to human rights like states, but a specialized one'.[3] Similarly, Steven Ratner writes that 'simply extending the state's duties with respect to human rights to the business enterprise ignores the differences between the nature and functions of states and corporations'.[4]

The second step in the argument is the proposition that the distinction between negative and positive obligations can accurately capture the difference in the substantive content of the obligations of state and non-state actors. Thus, in the context of corporations, Ratner writes that 'the company will usually have only negative duties or those positive measures clearly necessary to effect them'.[5] He justifies this claim by arguing that 'to go further than this position would effectively ignore the functional differences between states and businesses'.[6] That view has been influential and effectively adopted in the UNGPs, which identify the main responsibility of businesses as being to respect fundamental rights. The responsibility to respect is essentially understood as a duty to avoid harming those rights.[7] Any positive actions required of businesses essentially are incidental to the duty to avoid harm.[8] Similarly, the important *Urbaser* arbitral decision found that corporations have duties to avoid harming fundamental rights directly under international law but not positive obligations to fulfil rights

[3] SRSG 2006 Interim Report: para. 66.
[4] Ratner, 2001: 493.
[5] Ibid: 517.
[6] Ibid.
[7] UNGPs: GPs 11 and 13.
[8] UNGPs: Commentary to GP 11 and see Bilchitz, 2010b: 207. That it includes some positive actions demonstrates that the distinction is not sharp enough simply to confine non-state actors to avoiding acting in harmful ways. The SRSG does restrict positive obligations actively to contribute to realising rights (the duty to fulfil) only to certain constrained circumstances – for instance, where there is a prior undertaking to provide through contracts or in emergencies: see SRSG 2010 Report: paras 63–64.

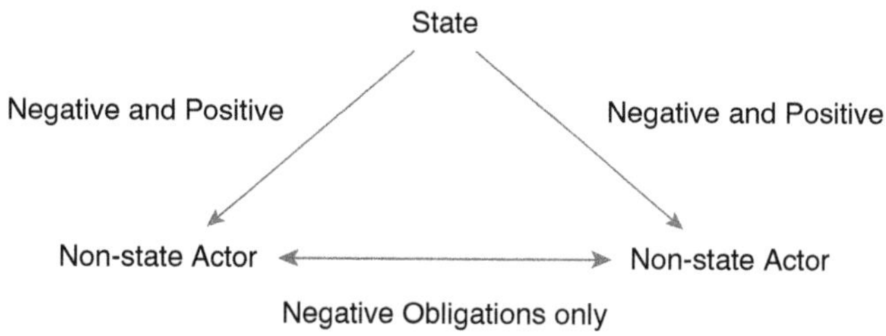

Figure 8.1 The negative obligations model.

such as actually to provide water to those who lack it.[9] At the national level, the initial approach of the South African Constitutional Court also sought to utilise the negative/positive obligations distinction as the basis to distinguish between the obligations of the state and those of non-state actors. As we will see later in this chapter, it has since modified its position.

The NO model is summarised diagrammatically in Figure 8.1.

8.2.2 *The Justification for the Negative Obligations Model*

The notion that the content of the obligations of state and non-state actors often differs is not generally controversial and, as is evident from the discussion in Chapters 6 and 7, I would accept that agent-relative factors play a role in determining obligations. However, there is a large gap between this claim and the proposition that non-state actors only have negative obligations. In this section, I will outline the key justifications for this second claim and, in the next, argue that they cannot be sustained.

8.2.2.1 Autonomy

Philosophically, the central idea behind the 'negative obligations' view seems to be based on the importance of autonomy to non-state actors, which is not, in the same way, relevant to the state.[10] The starting point for this argument would be that for every individual adult human being, there is an important interest in being able to decide on and follow their own course of life in whichever way they wish.[11] They, however, cannot seek to do so in ways that harm the ability of others similarly to pursue their own course of life. Consequently, there is a presumption in favour of the liberty

[9] *Urbaser* arbitral decision para 1199 – 1210.
[10] Ibid: para 58.
[11] Rawls, 1993: 19 and Raz, 1986: 204.

of individuals to do whatever they like provided they do not harm others in the process.[12] To place a duty on individuals to aid others in realising their fundamental rights would be too intrusive upon the autonomy of individuals to pursue their own course of life. Consequently, as a matter of course, individuals would only have negative duties and not positive duties towards others.[13] Clearly, such reasoning requires some adaptation for entities such as corporations: based on this rationale, proponents of the NO model would claim, for instance, that the corporation is simply a vehicle through which individual shareholders realise their economic goals and, as such, they should be left alone freely to maximise their profits.[14] In doing so, just as in the case of individuals, they must not harm others but need not actively contribute to advancing their rights.

8.2.2.2 The Social Function of the Entity

This argumentation can be supplemented by the claim that the social function of an entity is an important component in determining its obligations, which I accepted in Chapter 6. Those in favour of the NO model claim that the social function of certain non-state actors is incompatible with performing positive obligations. Thus, in defending the view that corporations generally have negative obligations only, the SRSG argues that wider social obligations upon corporations may undermine 'the company's own economic role and possibly its commercial viability'.[15] Clearly, the SRSG here has a conception of the economic role of a corporation as involving at least the advancement of its own business interests. Performing positive obligations for the realisation of fundamental rights would take it away from this primary role and require it to assume wider social functions. Ratner similarly argues that to impose positive obligations on a corporation would be to 'ask too much of the corporation, especially at this stage of the international legal process, when the broad notion of business duties in the human rights area is just emerging'.[16] Ratner's approach is more pragmatic and less dogmatic than the SRSG, but his statement also appears to assume the imposition of

[12] Mill, 1859: chapter 1. Interestingly, in that same chapter, Mill did not utilise this principle to deny the existence of some positive obligations upon individuals.

[13] An exemplification of this is the fact that many legal systems do not impose a duty to rescue strangers even if there is little risk to oneself: see, for instance, Ashton, 2009: 75–78.

[14] Friedman, 1970: 55.

[15] SRSG 2010 Report: para 64.

[16] Ratner, 2001: 517. Ratner goes on to say that to require proactive steps to promote human rights 'seems inconsistent with the reality of the corporate enterprise' (at 518).

positive obligations will automatically involve extensive duties which may conflict with the primary economic function of the corporation.

8.2.2.3 The Shirking of Responsibility by States[17]

The SRSG presents a series of practical objections against corporations assuming a wider role in advancing fundamental rights. He suggests that placing positive obligations on business can lead to 'diminishing the State's incentive to build sustainable capacity'.[18] He worries that 'a large and profitable company operating in a small and poor country could soon find itself called upon to perform ever-expanding social and even governance functions'.[19] Through assuming positive obligations, businesses essentially shoulder a burden that should be borne by states and thus allow states to shirk their obligations to address the deficits of fundamental rights realisation in their societies. That, in turn, he claims can 'undermine efforts ... to make governments more responsible to their own citizenry'.[20] The SRSG appears to be concerned that the existence of corporate positive obligations could lead to persistent attempts to shift responsibility for provisioning from the state on to businesses. Recognising the state as the sole locus of positive obligations would prevent such an undesirable shifting of burdens between different actors in the society.

8.2.3 The Inadequacy of the NO Model and the Case for Positive Obligations

I shall now argue that none of the justifications offered in the preceding section succeed in providing a justification for imposing only negative obligations on non-state actors (and corporations in particular). This critique also is conjoined with a number of arguments which provide a positive case for why non-state actors, and corporations, in particular, should also have positive obligations. The responses to the autonomy objection apply to all non-state actors, whereas the other responses focus on corporations more specifically.

[17] The discussion here draws on Bilchitz, 2013. There I also engage with the SRSG's objection that unelected corporations lack democratic legitimacy to perform wide-ranging governmental functions. I do not address this objection here as the response is less connected to the multi-factoral approach.

[18] SRSG 2010 Report: para 64.

[19] Ibid.

[20] SRSG 2006 Interim Report: para 68.

8.2.3.1 Why Autonomy Supports Positive Obligations

8.2.3.1.1 The Preconditions of Autonomy The claim that negative obligations flow from a concern to protect the autonomy of individuals fails to engage with the preconditions for individuals to be able to exercise their autonomy. For example, were an individual not provided with a basic amount of food as a child, she would die and never develop into an adult capable of exercising her autonomy. That same child may have been provided with enough food to survive but grew up in a state of constant malnourishment. That situation, in turn, may have compromised her mental development, thus impairing her ability to exercise her autonomy for the rest of her life. Consequently, if we value autonomy, we must value the conditions necessary for the development of those capacities which are central to the exercise of autonomy – I term these 'developmental conditions'.

A similar point can also be made about individuals who are already fully developed: they need certain conditions to obtain that enable them to continue to exercise their autonomy. These conditions do not just involve freedom from coercion but also, as biological beings, require having the necessary resources to be able to exercise their freedom. If individuals are so hungry that they are too weak to move around, then they lack certain necessary conditions for the exercise of their autonomy.[21] Thus, if we value autonomy, then we must also value what I term the 'maintenance conditions' for autonomy: the necessary conditions for individuals to *continue* to exercise their autonomy.[22]

Developmental and maintenance conditions thus require certain resources to be provided and active steps taken to enable individuals to exercise their autonomy.[23] The first justification for the NO model discussed earlier, however, could be taken to suggest that the state should bear the obligation for ensuring these conditions are met. Non-state actors, on the other hand, should be left alone to exercise their autonomy as they see fit and not be saddled with positive obligations.

There are three important responses to this argument. Firstly, it could be argued that the state must have the resources to meet its positive obligations to address the developmental and maintenance conditions for the autonomy of its people. Those resources are not magically

21 See Raz, 1986: 156 and 205. There are of course complexities in working out exactly what is required to meet this standard but, for our purposes, it is not necessary to clarify that.
22 Nedelsky, 1993: 8.
23 Rawls, 1993: 326 distinguishes between liberty and the worthy of liberty and recognises the need to guarantee certain all-purpose means to advance our ends.

obtained but rather come, largely, from taxation upon private individuals and corporations. As such, effectively the obligations of the state translate into obligations upon non-state actors to contribute towards ensuring the developmental and maintenance conditions of autonomy are fulfilled for all individuals. This point in itself provides a response to a pure libertarian philosophy that focuses on autonomy without recognising that this very value requires limits to be placed on it through the assumption of obligations by non-state actors.[24] Yet, this argument is limited because it addresses the obligations of non-state actors to fund the state's realisation of its own obligations rather than providing a case for the direct imposition of positive obligations on non-state actors themselves.

A second response builds on the latter point to recognise more generally the manner in which the state's own capacity to meet its positive obligations cannot be separated entirely from the actions of non-state actors. The private sector may, for instance, head-hunt senior capable professionals in the public sector and may thus affect the ability to recruit and retain capable officials through offering them, for instance, better salaries. Moreover, the ability to provide life-saving healthcare may be undermined by the high pricing of drugs such as Herceptin or machinery such as ventilators. At both a national level and internationally, there is an intertwining of state and private sector control over the vital resources necessary to realise rights.[25] Consequently, state capacity to meet its obligations cannot be considered wholly independently of private sector capacity.[26] As a result, the private sector may have positive obligations to assist the state to realise rights given that it affects the state's own capacity to meet its obligations. The inability strictly to separate the state and private sectors thus undermines the case for restricting the latter's obligations only to those of a negative character.

The last response challenges the NO model's assumption about the state always being capable alone of meeting its obligations to ensure the developmental and maintenance conditions for autonomy are realised. There are indeed many circumstances where the state lacks the capacity to do so. Such a situation can arise in countries where the state lacks the budgetary means or administrative capacity successfully to ensure these conditions are met. In yet other states, there may be the capacity but unwillingness to meet their obligations in this regard on behalf of the

[24] See, for instance, Cohen, 1995: 236–238.

[25] For instance, the relationship between public and private provision of healthcare arose in the Canadian case of *Chaoulli* v. *Quebec (Attorney General)*: see King, 2006: 637.

[26] Mass privatisation, for instance, in post-communist societies led to a decline in state capacity: see King and Hamm, 2005: 27.

political leaders. In these situations, there is no sense in allocating obligations to an entity that cannot meet them. It will thus be necessary then to consider enhanced positive obligations for non-state actors in such situations who do have the capacity to help ensure these conditions are met. Whilst it would be important to develop the capacities of the state – where that is possible – it would not be permissible to leave people in desperate circumstances during this process.

8.2.3.1.2 No Man or Woman Is an Island The NO model's autonomy rationale also gives expression to a very strong form of individualism which fails adequately to acknowledge the social dimension of human beings.[27] It suggests individuals are essentially 'islands unto themselves', who each restlessly pursue their own goods without a care or concern for others. There are a number of fundamental objections to such an approach.

Firstly, this approach does not capture the reality of human lives. If I do what I want with no care about or sense of duty towards others, they will treat me similarly. Given the fact that we are vulnerable creatures, in order to be fully functioning autonomous beings, we are often dependent on others for assistance: for example, we all have times when we become ill and need care. Indeed, this point is made by Kant in his famous argument for positive moral obligations: since an individual might need help, at times, she cannot in fact 'will' a situation where everyone operates on a universal principle that 'no one has an obligation to help another'.[28] Given that our own vulnerabilities and social natures render us, at times, in need of assistance, we cannot consistently defend a society in which no positive obligations of assistance exist. If that is so, then we must recognise the existence of certain positive obligations of each individual – and, by extension, of other non-state actors.

Secondly, there is a real question as to the desirability of a society that is based on the libertarian vision of rugged individualists exercising their autonomy without concern for others. A 'pure' NO model suggests the relations between individuals in society are simply the 'cold' ones of non-interference. Such a society is one where the bonds between individuals are weak and it is likely to contain a degree of heartlessness towards the suffering of others.[29] On the other hand, a society where individuals have obligations towards one another actively to care for each other's

[27] West, 2003: 86 argues it rests on a false conception of our nature.
[28] Kant, 2017: 25; see Herman, 1993: 55.
[29] Nedelsky, 1993: 17.

well-being is one where there is a sense of responsibility towards the other and the bonds of connectedness are stronger.[30] In such a society, individuals do not necessarily have to give up a large amount of their autonomy but they recognise that the welfare of others is something they need actively to be concerned about and contribute towards. Such a view gives better expression to the social dimension of human beings.[31]

8.2.3.1.3 The Incomplete and Harmful Effects of a Pure NO Model

The allocation of only negative obligations to non-state actors can also potentially undermine the achievement of the developmental and maintenance conditions of autonomy. Consider a supermarket chain heavily invested in a poor country such as Bangladesh which decides that it wishes scrupulously to avoid harming fundamental rights. Given the poor state of buildings in Bangladesh and the high rate of child labour, the chain decides that its best option is to leave Bangladesh. Pulling out of the country will result in thousands of people being without a job and unable to secure for themselves their basic means of subsistence which the state cannot provide to all.[32] If corporations only have negative obligations, the chain's decision to leave Bangladesh is rational – it can avoid any responsibility for harms to fundamental rights that may ensue.[33]

However, if it follows this path, it will seriously undermine the ability of individuals to access their basic socio-economic rights. If we recognise that the supermarket also has positive obligations to contribute towards the realisation of rights, then it could be obligated to remain in the country providing employment, and consider how to reduce the possibility of harming individuals as much as possible whilst seeking to improve their conditions of work. This example can help explain why an obligation to refrain from harming individuals is not sufficient and

30 There is both a sociological and normative dimension to these ideas: sociologically, see Putnam, 2000: 287–295, who outlines the benefits of social capital and provides empirical evidence of the negative effects associated with loosening bonds between people in the United States; normatively, see authors in diverse traditions such as Pally, 2016: 289–290; Gyekye, 1997: 65–66; Metz, 2011: 550–551.

31 West, 2003: 86.

32 This is not simply a theoretical example and one I have come across in engaging with businesses around their decision-making in this field.

33 Hsieh, 2009: 264. This is a potential problem with the UNGPs given the focus therein on negative obligations though the Commentary to GP 19 appears to recognise the need to exercise leverage in such circumstances: see Wood, 2012: 81.

can in fact undermine overall the realisation of rights if not conjoined with, at least, certain positive obligations.[34]

8.2.3.1.4 The Nature of the Positive Obligations The autonomy argument in favour of the NO model assumes that the imposition of positive obligations would intrude impermissibly – and potentially extensively – upon the autonomy of individuals. Yet, this assumption in itself needs challenging: it suggests that the mere fact that some positive action is required of an individual is automatically intrusive. Yet, even the negative duty to respect rights, at times, involves taking certain positive actions to avoid harming someone else.[35] If I do not want to harm someone through driving my car, I actively need to ensure it has been properly serviced and to drive carefully and within the speed limit. A corporation may be required to take positive steps such as through the adoption of a non-discrimination policy, for instance, to avoid harm to the equality of its employees.[36] Positive actions may thus be required by a duty to avoid harm (a negative obligation) and they may be quite extensive.

The fact that negative obligations can entail duties to act, in some sense, blurs the line between positive and negative obligations and demonstrates that the negative/positive distinction does not entirely overlap with the action/omission distinction.[37] As I utilise the distinction in this book, therefore, negative obligations are those which are *aimed* at avoiding harm to rights and positive obligations are *focused* on active contributions to realising rights. The line between these two is also not entirely rigid, as will emerge from the discussion of the South African case law below.

Importantly, positive obligations – as conceptualised in the last paragraph – also vary in their level of intrusiveness into the lives of individuals or activities of other non-state actors. A positive obligation can involve a corporation simply making an ordinary decision to source supplies from the local community rather than a large multi-national as part of its business operations. It could involve the regular obligation to pay tax. More intrusively, it could require leveraging its influence to advance rights[38] or ear-marking a percentage of its net profits to contribute towards the realisation of fundamental rights. Indeed, there is a live

34 Cragg, 2010: 290–291; Wettstein, 2012: 756.
35 Arnold, 2009: 65–66; Wood, 2012: 65.
36 UN Framework 2008: para 55.
37 Wood, 2012: 65.
38 Ibid: 76.

debate amongst philosophers about the nature and extent of positive obligations. Some, such as Peter Singer, argue that they involve significant sacrifice on the part of individuals[39] whereas others recognise those obligations exist but develop principles that more sharply seek to delineate their limits within manageable bounds.[40]

None of the arguments I have provided suggest that individuals or non-state actors must sacrifice their autonomy entirely in the service of others. Indeed, the greater the importance of autonomy to the agent in question, the more likely it will be to justify reducing the degree of intrusiveness of any positive obligations.[41] The value of autonomy may affect the extent of positive obligations but fails to provide a reason against non-state actors having positive obligations *tout court.*

8.2.3.2 Corporations and Positive Obligations

The objection that positive obligations are inconsistent with the corporate function rests upon a number of mistakes. Firstly, it is based upon a particular understanding of the corporation which, in Chapter 1, I have sought to show is mistaken. Secondly, it suggests that the negative and positive obligations of corporations can be neatly separated. Finally, it rests upon an assumption that positive obligations would require too much of corporations. I now elaborate upon these points and seek to provide four arguments for why they do in fact have positive obligations.

8.2.3.2.1 Compensating for the Harms of the Corporate Structure The NO model works with the notion that corporations have a duty to avoid harming fundamental rights. That obligation may initially appear only to involve a corporation conducting its ordinary activities without infringing on people's rights. Yet, I shall argue that this very duty can also provide a case for positive obligations on the part of corporations.[42]

In Chapter 1, I argued that from an individual perspective, one of the key reasons for creating a corporation is for purposes of economic gain

39 Singer, 1972: 238.

40 See, for instance, Murphy, 2000; Cullity, 2004.

41 Such a principle would be similar to that adopted in section 6.3.2.3 of Chapter 6 in the case of negative obligations.

42 This argument is drawn from and developed in more detail in Bilchitz, 2010a: 11–16. See also Hsieh, 2009: 256–264 for a similar attempt to ground certain positive duties in a negative obligation to avoid harm.

whilst limiting one's liabilities.[43] Thus, at its core, the corporation is deeply connected with the process of accumulating wealth and thus operates in the realm of acquiring and transferring property. Empirically, it is important to take note of the fact that corporations are the owners of some of the largest concentrations of wealth in the world.[44]

As it is currently instantiated in the world, the private property system, whilst clearly having many advantages, also creates a number of severe harms for individuals. In practice, this idea can be understood through considering the fact that a pharmaceutical company's patent over medicines prevents others from producing them and, usually, increases prices in a manner that can exclude individuals from being able to acquire them if they lack sufficient funds to do so. Ownership of land prevents other individuals from having access to that land without the owner's permission. Indeed, in a world where all property is owned (as is largely true of our world) and such ownership confers rights to exclude others from that property, individuals can be left in a position where all the resources necessary to meet their basic needs are owned and they have insufficient income to acquire such resources.

Locke famously defended private property rights. Yet, he placed a crucial qualification on the acquisition of such rights: it would only be fair to appropriate a resource and, consequently, for an acquisition to be legitimate where 'there is enough, and as good left in common for others'.[45] The Lockean proviso would effectively ensure that individuals are not left in a destitute position without any possibility of acquiring the crucial resources they need to live and exercise their autonomy. Robert Nozick too is famous for his modern-day development of a Lockean theory of property rights. Yet, he also accepts a proviso on the acquisition of property rights which, whilst weaker than that of Locke, still requires any just acquisition to leave 'enough and as good' for other people to use. For Nozick what is key is 'whether the appropriation of an unowned object worsens the situation of others'.[46] He provides an example to illustrate this point: an individual, he claims, could not appropriate the

[43] The relationship between limited liability and wealth accumulation is even admitted by strong defenders of corporate interests: see Epstein, 2011: 647.

[44] For a sense of how much wealth, see, for instance, the comparison of company market capitalisation versus the GDP of some countries at https://howmuch.net/articles/putting-companies-power-into-perspective.

[45] Locke, 1988: 288.

[46] Nozick, 1974: 175.

only water-hole in a desert and exclude all others from being able to drink the water in it (or charge whatever prices the individual wishes which others cannot afford).[47]

If one cannot legitimately own or purchase the only water-hole in a desert and thus exclude other needy individuals, then surely this implies more generally that individuals cannot be left in a position where all the resources necessary to meet their basic needs are owned and they have insufficient income to acquire such resources. Since the private property system as it currently exists prevents poor individuals from taking resources from others, the duty would have to be on the beneficiaries of the private property system – owners – to ensure that their holdings do not deprive individuals of access to such goods. To do so, they would need actively to ensure that individuals have at least the resources they require to realise their most basic needs.[48] Thus, owners of property have positive obligations which flow from the very conditions necessary to ensure that their entitlements are legitimate. Such obligations could also be founded in a duty to compensate individuals for the harms caused by the private property system within which owners are deeply embedded.[49]

The argument provided here has particular application in relation to corporations: for the economic focus of these entities embeds them in the process of acquiring resources and property rights and, since their inception, they have been the sites of accumulation of large amounts of wealth. Such an entity must thus have duties to ameliorate the harms caused by the very system of property rights that enables it – and the individuals underlying it – to achieve its economic purposes. Thus, the very economic purpose of corporations and their success in accumulating wealth highlights their crucial role in the property system and provides the basis for recognising a positive obligation upon them to help alleviate at the very least the worst effects of such a system: the exclusion of individuals from having the resources necessary to realise even their most fundamental interests.[50] In

47 Ibid: 179–180.

48 Flowing from the argument presented in Chapter 6, these involve at least the two thresholds identified in section 6.3.1.1 there.

49 I here extend to the property rights system as a whole a similar argument made by Pogge, 2002: 15–26 in relation to the duty to compensate for harms caused by the injustice attendant on current global institutional arrangements.

50 For some possible objections and my responses, see Bilchitz, 2010a. That exclusion has been particularly acutely felt during the COVID-19 pandemic in the deep asymmetry between developed and developing countries in relation to access to COVID-19 vaccinations, which arises partially from the ownership of those vaccines by pharmaceutical companies.

a world where everything is owned, there is a duty actively to contribute towards the fulfilment of those interests – the exact extent of this duty, however, is not specified by this argument and will be addressed in section 8.3 of this chapter.

8.2.3.2.2 Positive Obligations and the Societal Dimension of the Corporation The second argument I present goes more squarely to the question of the corporate function itself.[51] I argued in Chapter 1 that, in forming corporations, law-makers can only legitimately be motivated by an impartial societal perspective which recognises the equal importance of all individuals. As was argued in Chapter 6, that principle should plausibly be construed to entail individuals have fundamental rights that must be protected and realised by a society. As such, the societal perspective, as articulated above, requires us to assess the social advantages brought about by the corporate structure through considering its impact on fundamental rights.

At the same time, the corporation is not an organ of state and its method of achieving social advantages is through enabling individuals to pursue their economic goals. The corporate structure, it is claimed (as was discussed in Chapter 1), encourages entrepreneurial risk-taking and stimulates innovation which can lead to economic growth – these benefits may themselves have important implications for fundamental rights in society. If the corporate structure would, for instance, encourage greater employment, that would help realise the socio-economic rights of employees through enabling them to meet their own needs. Some innovations produced by corporations may also have implications for rights: for instance, a new medical treatment could help advance the right to healthcare of individuals. Part of the very underlying justification for a structure such as the corporation is thus the argument that it can help to harness the creativity and productivity of individuals in such a way as to have significant benefits for the realisation of fundamental rights.

However, the very indirect manner in which the corporation is meant to achieve these benefits also means that these consequences are not guaranteed. In fact, moral hazards can be created and actually inhibit the realisation of rights. Careful regulation will, therefore, be necessary to balance individual and societal perspectives and ensure that the corporation in fact achieves the wider social advantages for rights realisation it is

51 This argument was presented initially in Bilchitz, ibid: 19–23.

meant to achieve.[52] That balance can be attained by recognising positive obligations flowing from the societal perspective but limiting their extent such that they do not undermine the economic goals of individuals underlying the corporate entity.

This point can be illustrated by considering the patenting of a medication like Herceptin which allows the corporation that developed it a limited monopoly over its production for a fixed period of time. As a reward for developing a successful drug, such a corporation is effectively able to charge inflated prices for it, with access being confined to those who can afford the drug. One of the benefits of the corporate structure – enhanced risk-taking and innovation – would here only help a particular sector of society with many people being unable to enjoy those very benefits. Some may in fact die from not being able to gain access to such a new medication. Given that the corporate structure was in fact designed impartially to achieve social benefits – the most urgent of which involve realising the fundamental rights of individuals – there is a strong case for ensuring that the benefits emerging from such a structure (particularly in areas that impact upon fundamental rights such as in medicine development) must be made accessible to all.

The societal perspective would thus support the recognition of a positive obligation upon the pharmaceutical corporation to ensure that the benefits of its innovation are made accessible to those who cannot afford the medicine.[53] That, however, does not mean the corporation becomes a wholly nationalised entity or non-governmetal organisation working purely for social advancement. Instead a balance must be achieved between the individual and societal dimensions of the corporation: regulation – both national and international – would thus need to ensure that the medical innovations that result from corporate activity both create incentives for drug development but also contribute to the realisation of fundamental rights for all individuals. That could, for instance, be accomplished through a policy of differential pricing:[54] countries able to afford higher prices would effectively contribute to rewarding the corporation for its innovation whilst those that cannot do so would still be entitled to have access to the drug at a lower cost. Corporate profits would be reduced but not eliminated. Understanding

[52] The current libertarian perspective in many countries emphasises the individual perspective over the societal perspective: the argument I make is for a careful balancing to take place between them *not* for the wholesale nationalisation of business.

[53] Santoro and Shanklin, 2020: 561–562 root such obligations instead in a form of 'social contract'.

[54] See, for instance, Lee and Hunt, 2012: 225–226.

the implications of the societal dimension of the corporation thus provides a clear case for recognising that it has some positive obligations to contribute to the realisation of rights. The individual dimension supports there being a limit on the extent of those obligations.

8.2.3.2.3 Corporations Are Not Exceptional Structures Moreover, apart from the last argument, excluding corporations from having positive obligations would render them highly exceptional entities.[55] Both Kantian and utilitarian ethical theories recognise that individuals have, at least, some positive moral obligations: if this is so for individuals, it is hard to see why corporations – which are structures behind which usually lie conglomerations of individuals – should be exempted. In fact, there is a powerful case for imposing stronger positive obligations on corporations than on individuals given that the structure involves multiple individuals in corporate activities, confers the significant benefits of separate legal personality and facilitates the wielding of substantial economic power.[56] The way in which these considerations condition the obligations of corporations will be explored further below.

8.2.3.2.4 The Beneficial Consequences of Recognising Positive Obligations A final argument against the NO model considers the beneficial consequences of recognising that corporations have positive obligations. In the modern world, corporations are a central prong of the economy. They create and accumulate large amounts of social wealth and play a key role in affecting the well-being of many individuals who are reliant on them for employment. In short, corporations have the potential as well as the power to have a major positive impact on the advancement of fundamental rights.

It is thus disappointing and inaccurate to see the United Nations Working Group on Business and Human Rights making a statement that 'the most significant contribution most business enterprises can make towards sustainable development is to prevent and address adverse impacts on human rights through effective human rights due diligence'.[57] Corporate capacity to contribute towards the realisation of rights extends way beyond preventing harm to those rights. Moreover, as was discussed above, many states are also unable fully to achieve the realisation of

55 This argument and the next were initially written up in Bilchitz, 2017b: 202–206.
56 See also Bilchitz, 2013: 130–132.
57 Working Group HRDD Report, 2018: para 18.

fundamental rights and corporate activity, at times, can interfere with the state's ability to do so. As a result, in the struggle to realise rights, it is self-defeating simply to exclude such major economic actors from having any obligations positively to contribute towards their advancement.[58] Recognising the beneficial consequences of imposing *some* positive obligations upon corporations, once again, does not imply that they have unlimited obligations to address the lack of fundamental rights experienced by so many in the world.[59] The useful question is thus not whether corporations have such obligations but rather how to determine their substantive content, which I turn to consider in section 8.3 of this chapter.

8.2.3.3 Collaborative Responsibilities[60]

Would positive obligations for corporations shift the responsibility for realising fundamental rights from governments and allow them to shirk their duties? In circumstances of developed democracies, it seems unlikely that this would happen, given the wide-ranging mechanisms of accountability that exist. In the developing world, the positive obligations of corporations are likely to be more extensive given the high level of need and the breakdown in the capacity of governments to fulfil their duties. Yet, it is hard to see why the solution to possible shirking on the part of the state is to relieve business of its responsibilities. In such circumstances, denying that corporations have positive obligations will consign individuals to continuing desperate circumstances and does nothing to restore responsible and effective government. Corporate involvement – where there is such a breakdown in capacity – can rather help provide much needed services and be directed towards creating the conditions for the restoration of adequate governmental capacity,[61] which will be beneficial both for the corporation and other individuals.

Corporations, at times, also hinder the development of sustainable capacity in the government (particularly in developing countries) through, for instance, attracting highly skilled workers away from the public sector with large salaries. Placing positive obligations upon them can thus be essential to *ensure* that sustainable capacity is built in the public sector. Again, understanding the arguments for positive obligations means recognising that the state cannot seek to place all social provisioning obligations upon corporations. The SRSG makes the mistake of thinking that imposing *some* positive obligations on corporations requires them to take

58 See Wettstein, 2012: 759.
59 Ibid: 754–55.
60 This response is drawn from Bilchitz, 2013: 135–136.
61 See Hsieh, 2009: 262–264.

over *all* such obligations. Corporations and the business sector will always have limited positive obligations, but, nevertheless, remain capable of assisting the state in realising its own obligations. The state retains a crucial role in this regard; indeed, arguably, corporate involvement in the field of rights realisation may be hampered without planning and co-ordination, a role which the state is well-designed to perform.[62]

If we analyse the objection of the SRSG more deeply, it appears to articulate the idea that corporate positive obligations in some sense 'compete' with governmental duties in this area. Yet, the need for greater fundamental rights realisation is so extensive currently that it requires a range of actors to contribute towards alleviating the plight of the poor and vulnerable. It would thus be better instead to articulate a collaborative conception of how corporations can work together with the state to advance the realisation of fundamental rights.[63] Corporations could, importantly, be involved in enhancing the capacity of the state itself to deliver the services it is unable to provide.

8.3 Corporations and Positive Obligations

I have thus far sought to show that the distinction between negative and positive obligations should not be utilised to distinguish the obligations of corporations and the state. I have also sought to provide a positive case for recognizing that corporations have positive obligations in the process of critiquing the NO model. Throughout, I accepted the claim that the state and corporations are different actors and that agent-relative factors are relevant to determining their respective obligations. The question thus arises, how can we determine the substantive content of corporate positive obligations? I now turn to address that question.

Chapter 6 defended what I term a multi-factoral approach towards determining the substantive content of the obligations of corporations though the focus there was on negative obligations. The same justifications apply for adopting such an approach in relation to positive obligations: there is indeed much normative complexity, the need for

[62] See the examples of the pitfalls of implementing corporate social responsibility without proper planning and coordination detailed in Frynas, 2009: 116–130.

[63] More recently, there have been attempts to articulate collaborative conceptions of the separation of powers between various branches of government: see, for instance, Kavanagh, 2016: 238–239. The text suggests collaborative understandings may have a role to play in articulating the obligations of both state and non-state actors in respect of the realisation of fundamental rights: see also Wettstein, 2012: 757.

contextual sensitivity and incrementalism in developing our understanding of these obligations.[64] At the same time, such an approach is subject to similar drawbacks: there is a need for greater clarity in this area and corporations would have a particular incentive to minimise their positive obligations. The intermediate position I defended there thus commends itself: we need to identify the relevant factors for determining these obligations and understand how they individually condition such obligations. A crucial question will also be how to reach a final conclusion about the substantive content of these obligations. These questions will be addressed in this part of this chapter and the multi-factoral approach applied to positive obligations.

8.3.1 *Beneficiary-Orientated Factors*

From the perspective of individual rights-holders, there are strong prima facie reasons for imposing significant positive obligations upon corporations. As I argued in Chapter 6, however, a final determination of those obligations can only be arrived at after considering also agent-relative reasons which is the subject of section 8.3.2.

8.3.1.1 Interests

In Chapter 6, we saw that the starting point for a determination of obligations must be the fundamental interests of individuals. An articulation of these interests helps to determine which positive actions are required to ensure they are realised. The interests underlying rights can broadly be divided into two main dimensions: freedom and well-being. In relation to freedom, we already saw that individuals need to be provided with the developmental and maintenance conditions for the exercise of their autonomy. Moreover, many freedoms are facilitated through the existence of social institutions. The media, for instance, plays an important role in enabling individuals to become informed and engage with others: it has become highly significant in rendering freedom of expression meaningful. The media of course includes outlets owned or operated by both the state and private sector: the allocation of positive obligations, in this context, thus does not follow immediately from an analysis of the interest of individuals in free speech. Nevertheless, what the example indicates is

[64] See also Wood, 2012: 88 and Meyersfeld, 2020: 446–448, who also adopt multi-factoral approaches: the approach I propose would, to an extent, encompass their slightly different taxonomy of factors.

that to enable individuals to exercise their freedom effectively requires the existence of positive obligations which may fall not only on the state but also on various non-state actors. Rights relating to socio-economic well-being, similarly, may involve both negative and positive obligations: the interest in housing, for instance, may require that individuals not be evicted from the places where they live; in some cases, it could require that individuals actually be provided with homes. It is thus important to have an understanding of the obligations necessary to realise a right before it is possible fully to determine the allocation of those obligations.

In allocating obligations, we saw in Chapter 6 that the interests of an individual can be realised to a greater or lesser degree. Some failures to realise interests have a strong 'urgency' in that they threaten the very survival of individuals; others are not as urgent but nevertheless can hamper individuals in the realisation of their purposes. Once again, we can articulate a principle that **the greater the urgency of the need to realise an interest, the stronger will be the case for a positive obligation to be imposed upon an agent capable of realising that interest.**[65] **Greater urgency may also justify more extensive obligations.** Consider, for instance, the example of Herceptin and the position of poor women in South Africa with breast cancer. The interest at stake is their very survival as well as avoiding the suffering and decline attendant on a death by cancer. Herceptin is a treatment that can effectively remove this serious threat to their lives and well-being: they are thus in an urgent situation where they need the drug without having the ability to acquire it themselves. There is thus already a prima facie strength to any claim that the corporation has positive obligations to make the treatment available either for free or at an affordable rate. Determining which of these options should be adopted will require reference to agent-relative factors but the strength of the interests at stake would support imposing an extensive positive obligation on Roche.

8.3.1.2 Vulnerability

The principles articulated in Chapter 6 relating to vulnerability are applicable not only to negative obligations but also to positive obligations. As has been argued, corporations will always be regarded as being in an asymmetrical relationship with individuals and so, prima facie, there is a good case for imposing stronger positive obligations on corporations than individuals. In determining their obligations, it will be necessary to examine the

[65] Wood, 2012: 79 and 87 also recognises the relevance of urgency to certain positive obligations.

particular vulnerabilities of individuals in the concrete context that is being considered. We can also develop a principle in relation to positive obligations: **the greater the vulnerability to an omission by a corporation, the greater will be the justification for imposing a positive obligation to address that vulnerability. Greater vulnerability will also tend to support more extensive obligations on those with asymmetrical power over others.** Returning to the Herceptin example, poor women are extremely vulnerable to the pricing of the drug by the corporation. They lack the purchasing power to fund the drug themselves; and, often by virtue of being ill, are disempowered in their ability to organise politically to lobby for its provision in the public sector. High pricing may affect the ability of states to provide the drug to all the women who need it in light of the many pressing competing demands on the public purse. Given their high degree of vulnerability to corporate power in these circumstances, there is a strong prima facie case for imposing an extensive positive obligation on Roche to ensure the drug is accessible to them.

8.3.1.3 Impact

In deciding on the allocation of obligations, we will need to consider also concretely the impact upon the interests of individuals of a lack of action by a corporation. That requires a contextual determination, drawing on the other two beneficiary-orientated factors. As we saw, it is important to recognise that the nature of an agent may affect its impact upon a beneficiary. Given the role corporations play, for instance, in the lives of employees, their withdrawal of specific employment benefits for punitive reasons (for instance) may have a more significant impact on the life of an employee than if the state changes the terms of its unemployment benefits scheme (that affects everyone in the same way). Relational factors may thus reduce or exacerbate impact.[66] Once again we can develop a prima facie principle: **the greater the degree of impact on an individual's interests, the greater will be the case for and extent of the positive obligations of a corporation.**

8.3.2 *Agent-Relative Factors*

Certain agent-relative factors will count in favour of stronger positive obligations for corporations whilst others would support limiting the

[66] Metz, 2011: 538 provides a reason why this is so: individuals in corporations often identify with the corporation they work for and conceive of themselves as part of a collective enterprise.

extent of those obligations. I now consider the most significant of these in the following sections.

8.3.2.1 Capacity

As we saw in Chapter 6, a central factor in determining corporate obligations is their capacity to impact on rights – in the context of positive obligations, this would involve considering their capacity to contribute towards realising fundamental rights. The capacity of a corporation must be considered in light of the context in which it operates and any special or general relationships it has. In the context of positive obligations, the general principle derived from the capacity criterion could be expressed in a rather extreme form: where a corporation, for instance, has the capacity to advance the realisation of a right, it must use all available means at its disposal to do so.[67] The problems with this approach are two-fold: first, it seems to contradict the economic purpose of forming corporations by potentially placing unlimited obligations upon them to advance the realisation of rights;[68] and, secondly, in the context of positive obligations, there are multiple actors that can be involved in realising rights – this principle does not help us determine which actors, amongst those with capacity, have which positive obligations. I shall consider the latter problem in section 8.3.2.4 and address the first here.

Consider an example of Apple which, as a corporation, is now a massive behemoth with earnings in excess of the GDP of Mexico.[69] Apple, therefore, has resources that could enable it potentially to ensure every person in Mexico has access to decent healthcare services. The question then arises: does it have a duty to deploy its resources for this purpose? The pure capacity-based principle articulated above would suggest that it does but fails to specify any limits to its responsibility. Does Apple have to use all its earnings to do so, even if that entails ultimately affecting the very sustainability of the company? The principle appears to mistake Apple – a corporation that develops high-quality computers and phones – for the state and the objections to positive obligations discussed above have the strongest purchase in relation to such an extreme position.

[67] Karp, 2014: 89 articulates a similar principle.

[68] See the SRSG's objection to a pure capacity-based criterion that it would undermine 'the company's own economic role and possibly its commercial viability': see SRSG 2010 Report: para 64.

[69] Apple surpassed the GDP of Mexico at the end of 2019: see www.investopedia.com/news/apple-now-bigger-these-5-things/.

It is possible, however, to adopt a more moderate and convincing principle which recognises that **capacity to assist in the realisation of rights creates a prima facie obligation to contribute towards the realisation of those rights.**[70] Capacity becomes also a necessary condition for determining whether corporations have a positive obligation in a particular circumstance. It is not, however, sufficient and the full specification of corporate positive obligations will depend on the complete range of factors discussed in this chapter. In the above example, Apple would thus have a prima facie obligation to contribute towards the realisation of rights without having to expend all its capacity on that project. A further moderate principle can be drawn from the capacity criterion in relation to positive obligations, namely that **the greater the capacity, the stronger the obligations**. Consequently, it is quite clear that Apple will have stronger positive obligations to assist in the realisation of rights than a small technology company that has recently started its business.

8.3.2.2 Function

A second important factor in determining obligations is the function of the entity under consideration. As we saw in Chapter 6, function involves two components. The first concerns the general role of an entity such as the corporation: that involves a recognition that it is designed to create social benefits through harnessing the power of individual self-seeking behaviour. The second component involves considering the specific role of a particular corporation within a society which enables it to affect fundamental rights in specific ways. If the specific function of a corporation increases its power to impact on individual rights, that will have normative relevance for determining the extent of its obligations. The justification of this claim could be rooted in the fact that a specific function could create a special relationship between the corporation and the rights-holder(s).[71] Moreover, it appears justifiable to connect responsibility to the actual activities of the company and how they affect the fundamental interests of individuals.[72]

Consider, for instance, Roche, the manufacturer of the medicine Herceptin. Apart from its being constituted as a corporation and thus being designed to achieved social benefits more generally, it also operates within the pharmaceutical sector which produces goods that relate to the

[70] Wettstein, 2012: 758.
[71] See Wood, 2012: 82–83.
[72] Ibid: 83.

fundamental well-being of individuals. If the drug remains under patent, it is the sole producer thereof and thus can effectively determine whether a woman with breast cancer lives or dies. These features of a corporation and its role are of great importance in determining its obligations. They both clearly are relevant to and create a relationship with the individuals who require the drug.

We might thus develop the principle that a corporation with a function in a specific area that creates a relationship with individuals and thus grants it the capacity to have a positive impact on fundamental rights will have prima facie obligations to contribute towards the realisation of those rights. Its function does not necessarily impose an exclusive obligation to do so – but, the greater its control over an area that affects fundamental rights, the greater will be its obligations in this regard. Thus, a pharmaceutical company such as Roche has a very specific ability to help contribute towards improving the health and survival of women suffering from breast cancer.

Its obligations in this area can also be justified by virtue of the fact that its shareholders specifically decided to operate within a sphere of activity which relates to the most fundamental interests of individuals and, as a result, must expect to shoulder greater societal obligations. Indeed, arguably, those developing businesses in such an area expect greater rewards as a result of exploiting the fact that people need the drugs they produce and that governments have a duty to ensure they are provided to individuals. Where a company like Roche has a patent, granting it sole rights to manufacture particular drugs, its obligations will be much more extensive: they could include, for instance, ensuring it does not price those drugs out of the reach of any person or adopting a differential pricing model within or between societies.

The position of Roche can usefully be contrasted with that of a jewellery company. The business of the latter is about luxuries and less entwined with the fundamental needs of individuals. As such, its social role in regard to what it produces is less critical and, on this ground alone, it may only have the positive obligations flowing from its general duties to advance fundamental rights flowing from its corporate nature. At the same time, it is possible that such a company, for instance, is the sole employer in an area with a very depressed economy. In such circumstances, once again, its social role changes and its obligations to the local community increase.[73]

[73] It may, of course, also have concomitant negative obligations not to harm fundamental rights through sourcing minerals from zones in which armed conflicts are endemic.

I will in section 8.3.2.4 consider the role of other actors in a field in determining the extent of the positive obligations on a particular agent. Functional differentiation is extremely useful in helping to identify a sphere in which corporations can have a strong impact and where their expertise can be utilised to advance rights. We can thus develop the principle that **if corporations have a specific social function, and there is a need within the sphere in which they operate, they will have prima facie positive obligations to contribute towards the advancement of fundamental rights primarily within that sphere.**[74] Where there is no specific function performed by a corporation that relates to fundamental rights, then it will only have the more limited general obligations that all companies share to advance those rights. The exact contribution it is required to make will need to be determined by a co-ordinating agency.

8.3.2.3 Autonomy

Autonomy, as we saw in Chapter 6, can be understood to involve two components, namely, dignity and freedom. In the context of positive obligations, these interests too, of course, have primary application in relation to natural persons. As a result of the supervenience relationship between the corporation and individuals, the former agent retains some interest in autonomy though the interest is less significant in comparison with natural persons. Consequently, the autonomy of natural persons would be a strong reason to reduce the extent of their positive obligations; for a corporation, it remains a reason but is less weighty. Indeed, given the social dimension of a corporation, part of its very purpose involves advancing social benefits, the most important of which are the fundamental rights of individuals. Nevertheless, corporations, as has been argued, also have an individual dimension and their achievement of social benefits is usually to be attained through harnessing the self-interest of individuals underlying the formation and operation of the corporation. In determining obligations, the notion of 'autonomy' embraces this individual dimension of the corporation and requires that a space be left open for the corporation to fulfil the economic goals of the individuals who set it up and its very raison d'être.[75] Consequently, the positive obligations of the corporation cannot be so extensive as to render it a wholly 'public' entity (unless that is the voluntary will of the

[74] It should be evident though that the specific function and its relationship with rights-holders is only one factor in determining obligations and not determinative contra Wood, 2012: 92.

[75] Cragg, 2010: 287.

corporation's stakeholders) and thus reduce it to a loss-making entity. There are normative positions which would support the nationalisation of all private property and enterprises; my contention, here, is that fundamental rights do not require the adoption of such a position. Given the experience that such systems seriously violate individual autonomy, there is also a question mark as to whether fundamental rights can be rendered consistent with such a collectivist economic model.[76]

Positive obligations, however, vary in intensity and do not automatically lead corporations to become loss-making entities. They can include general duties simply to consider the potential positive impact corporations can have on fundamental rights through their activities and integrate these considerations into their operations and planning. They can involve a duty to utilise their power and influence to advance rights through economic pressure and leverage.[77] They can also, of course, entail duties for the provision of specific goods.

The autonomy dimension suggests the presumptive principle that **the greater the impact on corporate autonomy, the greater the justification will be for reducing the extent of positive obligations; the lesser the impact, the greater the case for imposing positive obligations.** There can thus be little objection to positive obligations which have very limited costs – for instance, tailoring a corporation's work to have the most beneficial impact on rights or developing policies for the advancement of rights in the workplace. As we move into more specific and intrusive duties, the countervailing considerations raised by the 'autonomy factor' become stronger. In this regard, it will be important to distinguish between a restriction on the autonomy of the corporation and the complete obliteration thereof. That distinction also, importantly, in an economic sense, gives rise to a recognition that it will often be permissible to impose positive obligations that reduce the profits of such an entity – even significantly depending on the urgency of the interests at stake if fundamental rights are not realised – but that such obligations, in general, should avoid rendering the corporation a loss-making entity.[78] Fundamental

[76] This point only establishes that some form of freedom for business activity would be required by fundamental rights; it does not assert that the corporate form must of necessity be created or that profit-making be allowed in all sectors.

[77] Wood 2012: 72–92 develops an account of the foundations and extent of such responsibility.

[78] Wood, 2012: 92 also recognises this restriction at least in relation to leverage-based responsibility.

rights may require a significant social contribution from corporations but must still respect their ability to pursue their economic goals.

Returning to our example of Roche, it is clear that this entity was created to advance the economic goals of its shareholders and to make money from its activities. If a conception of its legal obligations were to ignore such a goal, and require it to provide all its drugs for free around the world, that would nationalise the entity and render it wholly public in nature. There may be a good case for doing so in certain spheres such as healthcare which touch upon the most fundamental interests of individuals. Nevertheless, it is important to acknowledge that such an approach effectively does away with the notion of the private corporation we are dealing with in this book and renders it a part of the state. If a decision is made to retain the corporate form in a sector, then it is necessary to allow some space for the advancement of the economic interests of the individuals underlying the corporation.

There is indeed also an argument to be made that allowing private sector involvement in the pharmaceutical sphere can have social benefits: with the hope of profit-making, large amounts of private resources, for instance, could be marshalled in the service of developing new medicines that could potentially benefit everyone. That is no doubt part of the justification for the patent system: the challenge is trying to ensure an alignment of such profit-making with the objective of ensuring everyone can access the medicines developed through the private sector. As we have seen, this approach seeks to reward research and development expenditure, but also leads to the charging of exorbitant prices and placing drugs out of reach of those who are worst off – such as poor women with breast cancer in the case of Herceptin. The social benefits of such a system are thereby reduced and produce an obscene situation where individuals are dying where there are treatments available for their ailments.

8.3.2.4 The Role of Other Actors

Given that positive obligations require active steps to be taken to realise fundamental rights, it is clear that, in many contexts, there will be multiple actors who can perform them. I now consider two important sets of issues that arise in this regard: first, there is the conceptual question of how one actor's obligation affects another's – what I term the 'content' question; secondly, there is the important practical concern to ensure the efficient co-ordination of actions such that they actually help advance individual rights optimally – the 'pragmatic' question.

8.3.2.4.1 The Content Question Let us return to the example of Apple and its duties to improve the healthcare available to Mexico's residents. The first important question concerns whether Apple should be involved at all given the Mexican state has a clear obligation to provide decent healthcare to its residents. Despite that obligation, however, it is evident that the state lacks the capacity to provide such healthcare to all its residents. Initially, for simplicity sake, we can imagine a situation where we have two actors: the state and Apple. Given Apple is set up as a corporation that develops and sells electronic devices, it is not obvious that it has a clear social function in providing healthcare. The first step would thus be to determine what the capacity of the state is – through taxation and its own structures – to provide decent healthcare to Mexicans. With that understanding, it will be possible to evaluate where corporations have the ability to supplement that capacity. That gap will be the space in which the positive obligations of corporations will need to be allocated. There will need to be greater attention paid by economists and political scientists to understanding the nature of this gap.

Let us complicate the picture by recognising that there is a gap in which Apple can contribute in this sphere – namely, the development and provision of health technology – but also that there is another major corporation, Microsoft, that can also assist in a similar manner. It too has a market capitalisation that exceeds that of Mexico.[79] Both corporations also sell their products and make money in Mexico.[80] Does Microsoft then also have positive obligations to ensure the people of Mexico have decent healthcare services? If this question is answered in the affirmative, how much should each corporation contribute? Clearly, it cannot be the case that Microsoft and Apple must separately contribute everything necessary to provide decent healthcare technology in Mexico (beyond the realm of what is required of the state). That would be illogical and wasteful, essentially requiring each to double up on what is required to meet the needs in question and diverting resources away from other needs. This example also illustrates why the capacity to provide alone

[79] See www.investopedia.com/articles/markets/111015/apple-vs-microsoft-vs-google-how-their-business-models-compare.asp#:~:text=As%20of%20May%202020%2C%20AAPL,of%20its%20cloud%20computing%20business.

[80] There is an interesting question how far such obligations reach and whether a limiting factor concerns whether a corporation operates within a particular political community. For the relevance of promixity-type considerations, see Wood, 2012: 82–84.

cannot be the whole determinant of the positive obligations of corporations.[81]

Ultimately, then, an equitable approach would suggest that such obligations be shared – yet, it would be unfair to impose the same obligations on corporations with differential capacities. Thus, the size and capacity of corporations in relation to one another will be important which can be the basis of a presumptive principle: **the greater the size and capacity a corporation, the greater will be its positive obligations.** Their respective specific functions will also be relevant, as has already been discussed.

Of course, in a real-life situation, these two corporations would be only two amongst many operating within Mexico. In the space where the state is unable to provide adequately, the positive obligations involved would be shared and vary with capacity and function. As has been mentioned, the preference would be for corporations with expertise in healthcare to provide services. One would then consider specific contributions that can be made by other corporations such as what Apple and Microsoft could offer in terms of health technology. Where there remains a shortfall after all contributions are taken into account, large corporations such as Apple and Microsoft – and even a large jewellery company – could have residual general obligations to contribute to advancing healthcare more generally. The fact that there are multiple actors in a context with the capacity to assist can help render the burden on any particular corporation manageable and still enable it to achieve its economic goals.[82]

Given the range and variety of corporations, there is some difficulty in working out exactly the content of the positive obligations of each vis-à-vis one another. Indeed, the existence of multiple agents in the context of positive obligations is a matter on which there have been several complex philosophical treatments which require simplification for purposes of practically determining what corporations must do concretely in law.[83] I will in section 8.4.2 consider a model that was adopted in India for

[81] See Karp, 2014: 106 and the modified capacity principle he considers.

[82] Goodpaster, 2010: 147 recognises that even if a company 'does not have a *categorical* responsibility, a responsibility to resolve the moral challenge *on its own*, it can still have a *qualified* responsibility to make an effort – or to *participate* in the efforts of others in seeking a collaborative resolution'.

[83] See, for instance, Murphy, 2000; Cullity, 2004. These treatments generally deal with the positive obligations of *individuals* in the context of multiple agents but can be applied to corporations. The details of these discussions are very complex and the principles arrived at often fail to provide the clear practical guidance needed for legal obligations. My discussion has attempted to simplify but also to capture the relevant normative principles which can then be factored into the seven-step test I propose.

addressing this problem in a novel way through imposing a blanket positive obligation upon large corporations to contribute a fixed percentage of net profits as a broad measure of their positive obligations.

8.3.2.4.2 Co-ordination One major practical difficulty where multiple actors have positive obligations is the problem of co-ordination. Frynas, for instance, describes how the lack of engagement between two entities – an oil company and the Niger Delta Development Commission – led to the building of two parallel roads in a region where infrastructure was poor.[84] Such a duplication of efforts is wasteful given the large need and extremely inefficient: if these entities had worked together, the benefits could have been multiplied through roads being constructed in two under-serviced areas, rather than one, thus improving the lives of many more people. This example illustrates the practical need for coordinating the efforts of multiple actors when determining what they must do to advance rights. That can, in turn, affect the nature and extent of their obligations and successfully help to reduce the burden of positive obligations on each.

Consider, for instance, a situation where both Roche and another pharmaceutical company – for instance, Glaxo Smith-Kline – produce a drug like Herceptin that can be used to treat breast cancer. If the positive obligations are shared, a range of inefficiencies could arise in the absence of co-ordination: competition could mean, for instance, they each produce more drugs than are needed, vying for lucrative contracts. Instead, it would be sensible for each company to be responsible for providing half the required amount of the drug to each hospital or, possibly, dividing the provision amongst them to half the hospitals in a country.

What this example demonstrates is that, where there are multiple actors who have positive obligations, there is a need for co-ordination to achieve optimum results for realising rights. Practically, this would entail there being a co-ordinating body. The state – whose very function it is to be impartial and act in the public interest – would usually be best placed to perform this function and would need to establish specific co-ordinating agencies for this purpose.[85] Where the state is dysfunctional or incapable of performing this role, there would be a positive obligation on corporations to establish

[84] See Frynas, 2009: 130.

[85] In section 8.4.2, I discuss the example of India, which is grappling with how best to address this problem.

such a co-ordinating body to ensure their active contributions are efficient and help to realise the fundamental rights of individuals optimally.

8.3.3 The Process of Reaching Final Determinations

I have thus far outlined the central factors and their implications for determining the positive obligations of corporations. Given that some of these factors pull in opposing directions, how are we to arrive at a final assessment thereof? In relation to the Herceptin example, how can we determine what are the final obligations of Roche?

8.3.3.1 The Limits of the Proportionality Enquiry and Positive Obligations

I argued in Chapter 7 that, in the context of negative obligations, the proportionality enquiry could assist in providing a structured reasoning process to arrive at final obligations. Unfortunately, there are some conceptual difficulties with applying proportionality in the context of positive obligations. The central problem is that we are concerned with an omission to act which renders proportionality difficult to apply.[86] The test was developed to evaluate a set of concrete actions and whether they could be justified where they achieve significant purposes but harm fundamental rights. Once concrete actions are in view, it is possible to apply the various features of the test. Without this, the test becomes vague and inchoate.[87]

Let us consider each aspect of the proportionality enquiry. In relation to positive obligations, any infringement of a right would emerge from a failure to act and so a burden of justification would arise to justify such an omission. Assuming for purposes of argument that an omission gives rise to a prima facie infringement of a right, the first sub-enquiry is to determine whether there is a significant purpose for the omission to act. Yet, this sub-enquiry simply does not work well in the context of omissions: with actions there is usually a justification in mind for why an individual or entity behaves in the way it does; in relation to omissions, individuals or entities may simply lack a specific justification for why they failed to act. It

86 See Alexy, 2009: 5; Klatt, 2011: 694–695, who recognise this difficulty in the context of dealing with proportionality and a different type of positive obligation on states to protect individuals against harms. See also Gardbaum, 2017: 244, who states that 'proportionality is most essentially a condition for permitting limited exceptions to negative duties'.

87 I am not convinced Alexy and Klatt convincingly resolve the problems discussed in the text in relation to wider positive obligations to fulfil and that even on their version, in real-life contexts, proportionality helps provide much guidance for determining them.

may just be, for instance, that Apple never considered it had any duty to advance healthcare in Mexico. If that is so, then the proportionality enquiry cannot properly even get off the starting blocks: since Apple lacks any good reason for not acting, the significant purpose test is not met. There would be no justification for its omissions and it would have to realise the positive obligation to advance healthcare rights in Mexico to the extent that lies within its capability. Yet, the very question that needs to be determined is whether it has this positive obligation and the substantive content thereof.

There is also a significant problem in that when determining a purpose, it is also important to examine which course of action must be taken. In the Roche example, must the company simply supply Herceptin for free to the women who cannot access it or would a significant discount on the drug to the public healthcare system be sufficient? Would Roche also be responsible for ensuring the women are empowered with information about a healthy diet that might affect the success of their treatment? Given that positive obligations can be realised in multiple ways it becomes difficult to identify the exact action that is needed: in the absence of being able to do so, it becomes more difficult to determine the specific purpose of any inaction.

These problems also affect the ability to apply the rest of the test meaningfully. The suitability test would only properly be capable of being applied if it were possible to specify the exact omission to act and its relation to an identified purpose. The problem, again, is that it is not clear which omission is to be tested and, even if it were, omissions could be justified on multiple grounds. In a similar vein, it would usually be very difficult to determine that an omission was necessary for achieving a particular purpose. There will usually exist actions that could have taken place which would have realised the corporate purpose (whatever that is) and had a lesser impact on the right. The test will thus usually be failed, but that does not help to address the central question which is to identify which of multiple alternative courses of action should have been adopted by the corporation. Finally, at the balancing stage, we would need to ask whether the failure to assist in the realisation of rights – and the attendant harms caused – would be justified by the benefits of the omission in these circumstances. Given the lack of clarity involved in understanding the purpose behind an omission, this stage of the proportionality enquiry again appears difficult to render meaningful. The existence of other actors who can help realise the right will also present obstacles to demonstrating, in many instances, that the failure to act by a particular agent causes the particular harms to the beneficiary. Consequently, its failure to act may often be proportional given the fact that the harms in question may not necessarily arise due to the possible intervention by other actors.

8.3.3.2 A Multi-Pronged Test for Positive Obligations

As I have just argued, the proportionality enquiry is not well-suited to determine what agents must *do* to advance fundamental rights rather than what they must *not do*. In the context of positive obligations, there is a central competing normative tension: on the one hand, there is a serious need on the part of individuals for positive action to be taken to realise their fundamental rights; on the other hand, there is the legitimate desire of non-state actors to be able to advance their own projects and goals without constantly being required to act in the service of others. How are these to be reconciled?

Clearly, there is a balance to be achieved. In the context of the corporation, that balance is central to its very raison d'être which, as we saw in Chapter 1, encompasses the tension between the social and the individual. Overarchingly, the abstract question must again be – as in the case of negative obligations – what set of final positive obligations can best respect the equal importance of individual lives? That abstract question requires recognising and evaluating what state of affairs can best do justice both to those whose fundamental rights are imperilled – through a lack of resources and deprivation of their basic needs – but, also, to the function of a corporation and its autonomy to pursue its own goals. Whilst it is important to articulate the broad overarching enquiry, it is necessary in law to move beyond this level of abstraction – where in a sense the tension is simply re-stated – and to develop a test that can provide more concrete guidance.[88]

In determining what must be done, I here propose that a seven-step reasoning process should be followed. The goal of doing so is to create, once again, a structured reasoning process that can guide decision-making about the content of corporate obligations. The difficulties with applying proportionality in its pure form, nevertheless, do not entail that some of its components are irrelevant in articulating final positive obligations. Consequently, certain dimensions of this enquiry have similarities to facets of the proportionality enquiry but are adapted to the normative character of positive obligations. It is hoped future engagements with this proposal by academics, corporate decision-makers and judges can help refine the test further.

[88] Santoro and Shanklin, 2020: 564, as do many authors, re-state the normative tension and argue for balancing without indicating any method of doing so.

The first step would be the 'impact' stage: it would require – with reference to an individual's interests, vulnerabilities as well as the specific context – determining the extent to which a right of an individual is imperilled in the absence of positive action. That allows for ascertaining the need for positive obligations to be assumed by other agents as well as the urgency of any intervention that is required.

The second step is the 'action step' and will involve identifying the most significant positive actions or interventions that are required in order to realise the fundamental interests of the beneficiary. As has been discussed, positive obligations are multiply realisable: as a result, this step requires identifying several leading courses of action that can meet the needs identified in the first step.

The third 'state capacity' step would involve considering the capacity of the state to make the positive interventions identified in the last step. If the state is fully capable of addressing the need, there will be a question whether there is any justification for it not to bear the full burden in this regard. Its inability to meet other needs, for instance, if it pays the full price for a drug such as Herceptin, would be such a relevant justification. It would then be necessary to determine the extent to which the state can contribute without affecting its ability to meet the other fundamental rights of residents. If the state is not fully able to meet the identified need, then it is important to specify why and the extent to which it is unable to do so. Similarly, where corporate involvement in an area affects the state's ability to take all the required actions to realise fundamental rights, then that would also constitute an adequate justification for some positive obligations being placed on such corporations.

The fourth 'specific function' enquiry would consider whether the corporation has a specific function – for example, through operating in the healthcare sector – that enhances its capacity to help realise the fundamental rights of the beneficiary (the 'specific function' step). If it does, the extent of its obligations will be more onerous in proportion to its ability to contribute. It will also be necessary to specify broadly which other corporations have a similar specific function – if there are others, the extent of any obligations on each will be reduced and the burden of provision shared. If there is a specific function, the next step can be skipped. It is also possible that only corporations with these specific functions will have obligations depending upon the evaluation in steps 6 and 7.

The fifth 'general obligation' enquiry will consider, in the absence of corporations having specific functions in an area and the state having the ability to provide fully, the range of non-state actors that can contribute to advancing the realisation of rights. It will then seek to articulate what an equal burden would be for all these actors which will vary with size and capacity. Should there be corporations whose specific function grants them a particular capacity to assist in an area (identified in step 4) and the burden not be too onerous upon them, it is possible other corporations will lack any obligations in relation to this specific fundamental right. General obligations will only be activated where there are needs that cannot be met by those who perform specific functions or where the burdens upon the latter companies are too extensive, requiring them to be shared more widely.

The sixth 'alternatives' step will involve considering the positive interventions identified in step 2 and the alternative courses of action open to the corporation. This step will require an evaluation of the impact of each alternative course of action on the corporation (and the realisation of its specific individualised purposes) and upon the rights realisation of beneficiaries. It will seek to identify a course of action that can substantively realise the fundamental rights of individuals whilst having an impact on the corporation that is not too substantial – for instance, that reduces it to a loss-making entity.[89]

The final and seventh 'balancing' step will involve evaluating whether the course of action identified in the last step can be justified given the benefits to the beneficiary and the cost to the corporation (the 'balancing' step). That step will ultimately seek to evaluate whether there is a proportionality between the benefits sought to be achieved and the costs to the corporation. In specifying the costs to the corporation, the 'autonomy' factor will need to be considered and the extent to which it is affected by any such obligation. In doing so, any evaluation will have to consider whether the corporation still retains some ability to pursue its own goals.

In order to illustrate the application of this seven-part test, I return to the Roche example discussed earlier. In relation to the first step, it is clear that the women who are unable to afford Herceptin or receive it from the public sector health service are in a situation where there is a serious risk to their very lives (and, consequently, their right to life is imperilled). It is thus a need with a high level of urgency that would justify the imposition of significant obligations. The second step would involve identifying actions to address this serious need. Three possibilities emerge: first, direct provision by Roche to the women for free; secondly, provision at a price affordable to the women; and, finally, provision to the public

[89] This enquiry is the analogue of the necessity test in the proportionality enquiry.

sector at an affordable cost where it becomes available to the women for free.

The third step would recognise that the state has an obligation to provide life-saving medicines to its residents. Let us assume the issue arises in a country like South Africa: given its poor economic situation, it is clear that, at the original prices, provision by the government would undermine its delivery of other essential services. Moreover, Roche's pricing undermines the government's ability to provide this life-saving treatment and, therefore, there is a case for shared responsibility. Additional considerations such as failures of capacity in the public health system of South Africa would suggest a limited governmental ability to pay the prices demanded by Roche and, possibly, to deliver the drug efficiently.

In relation to the fourth step, the individuals who formed Roche have specifically chosen to enter into the pharmaceutical industry and to develop medications that are potentially life-saving. It has a specific ability to provide for the most urgent needs of women suffering from a particular form of breast cancer. No other corporation has the ability to provide Herceptin given it is still under patent and so there is no good case for the sharing of the burden of provision. If there were another pharmaceutical company with a similar drug, the burden of provision would be shared. Given Roche has specific obligations in this area, it is not necessary to consider in detail the fifth stage except to say that it bolsters the case for it to bear significant duties: Roche, after all, is a corporation under a general obligation to help ensure that society benefits from its activities.

In terms of the sixth stage, the first possibility would be for Roche to provide the drug to women for free – that would, however, be the most costly and intrusive approach for Roche. The second alternative course of action would be for it to reduce the price of the drug significantly: that would be less burdensome to Roche if it remains able to benefit financially from its innovative product. Both of these alternatives would be less intrusive if implemented through existing pharmacies; having to set up a distributional infrastructure would increase the burdens on Roche. A final alternative would be for it to sell the drug at a reduced cost to the public health system for distribution (assuming one exists with an adequate level of efficiency): that would entail the least cost to Roche in avoiding having to invest in much infrastructure for distribution though perhaps not fully address the problem of state incapacity. Thus the alternative that has the most potential for realising the right and the least impact on the company – where the state is not capable of distributing the medication – would be the second one.

The last step would involve balancing. The significant need of poor women for these drugs in order to survive would strongly justify the imposition of some obligation on Roche to make them available. Not doing so would lead to a situation in which they are treated with little respect for their worth. At the same time, Roche is a corporation that invested significantly in developing the drug and consequently can claim legitimately that it wishes to reap some financial rewards for having done so. It also is not a state agency but a corporation formed by its shareholders to make profits, whilst at the same time having to create social benefits. As a result, the positive obligations of Roche must involve making the drugs accessible without destroying its nature as a private corporation. Forcing it to provide the drugs for free would undermine general economic incentives to develop such drugs but, also, potentially harm its ability to continue. Therefore, the preferred option that should be considered (except in cases of extreme scarcity) would involve requiring it to provide these drugs at a reduced cost rather than for free. In circumstances where a functional public healthcare system exists, that would be the preferable route for distribution; where that does not exist, Roche would need to ensure the drug's accessibility through the private market (and, if that does not exist, to develop the infrastructure for distribution). The possibility of differential pricing should also be considered at this stage: allowing it to charge higher prices in wealthier markets and supply the drug more cheaply in poorer countries.

Consequently, this example highlights how one can use the seven-step enquiry I have articulated to reach an outcome about the concrete positive obligations of corporations. The test is by no means mechanical and the steps are evaluative and require the exercise of judgement. That is no different, however, from the application of proportionality in the context of negative obligations and in fundamental rights adjudication more generally. Given the significant amount of judgement involved, who makes these judgements and accountability for them becomes of great importance: Chapters 9 and 10 will engage with those questions. Clearly, the abstract model I have outlined needs to be applied in concrete cases and, over time, more specific understandings of the exact positive obligations of corporations will be developed without having to revert to the seven-step enquiry each time.

8.4 Positive Obligations in Law

Having outlined the case for imposing positive obligations and a proposed approach to determining their substantive content, I now turn to examine two jurisdictions which have grappled with whether and how to impose legally binding positive obligations on non-state actors: South Africa and India.

8.4.1 *Leaving behind the NO Model: The South African Experience*

We have encountered in Chapter 5 the relevant provision of the South African Constitution for determining the obligations of non-state actors. For convenience sake, I reproduce section 8(2) here: it reads 'a provision of the Bill of Rights binds a natural or juristic person if, and to the extent that, it is applicable, taking into account the nature of the right and the nature of any duty imposed by the right'. Here I focus on 'the nature of any duty' element which requires interpretation when considering its relevance for determining whether and to what extent non-state actors have obligations. This notion could refer to a number of dimensions already discussed including how onerous the duty is,[90] the extent to which the duty relates to the function of the non-state actor and how closely related it is to an urgent interest of rights-holders. However, the Constitutional Court in a series of cases has focused on the distinction between negative and positive obligations and remains divided as to its usefulness in determining the obligations of non-state actors.[91] I will chart this development in the case law, highlight the inadequacy of the distinction for capturing the obligations of non-state actors and instead analyse the factors that are relevant to an assessment of their obligations. Whilst the main cases have not generally focused on corporations, the reasoning, as will be seen, can *a fortiori* be applicable to them.

8.4.1.1 *Juma Masjid*: The Insufficiency of the NO Model

In *Juma Masjid*,[92] the government had established a school on the property of a private trust. The trust brought an application to evict the school from the premises which was opposed by the governing body of the school. The government had failed to pay the rent it owed the trust and the trust had decided to establish its own school on the property. The key question, for our purposes, concerned the obligations of the trust vis-à-vis the existing school and its learners.

[90] Madlanga, 2018: 373.
[91] For another related analysis of this trajectory, see Meyersfeld, 2020: 463–476.
[92] *Governing Body of the Juma Masjid Primary School* v. *Essay N.O.* [2011] ZACC 13.

The Constitutional Court reasoned that the state had the primary positive obligation to ensure the right to education of the learners was realised:[93] given its failure to make alternative arrangements for the learners of the school after receiving notice from the trust of its intentions to terminate the rental agreement, it had breached its obligations in this regard. The court then turns its focus to the trust and finds that section 8(2) does not seek to obstruct private autonomy or impose the obligations of the state on private parties. Nevertheless, the trust does have obligations towards the learners which are largely negative in nature: the trust's duty was to 'minimize the potential impairment of the learners' right to a basic education'.[94] The trust, however, lacked a continuing positive obligation to make its property available for use as a school.[95] The court found that the trust had behaved reasonably in meeting its obligations by seeking to engage with the relevant government department to arrange a smooth closure of the school. Since it had provided the government with an opportunity to place the remaining children in alternative schools, the court issued an eviction order in favour of the trust.

This case appears to be an exemplification of the NO model with the state having the full panoply of duties and non-state actors only having the negative obligation to avoid harming the rights of individuals.[96] Yet, upon closer analysis, the court's language is confusing and the supposedly clear distinction between negative and positive obligations is in fact muddled. In seeking to characterise the substantive content of the negative obligations of non-state actors, the court states:

> [b]reach of this obligation occurs directly when there is a failure to respect the right, or indirectly, when there is a failure to prevent the direct infringement of the right by another or a failure to respect the existing protection of the right by taking measures that diminish that protection.[97]

The reference to indirect breaches of this obligation, it is clear, includes an obligation upon non-state actors to avoid harm to individuals through the actions of others closely connected to them. Such an obligation does not involve simply omitting to harm rights themselves but would require taking positive action to ensure others do not commit this harm. Such an obligation is not purely negative in character but requires positive action.

93 Ibid: paras 45 and 57.
94 Ibid: para 62.
95 Ibid: para 57.
96 Meyersfeld, 2020: 467 sees the case in this way.
97 *Juma Masjid*: para 58.

In a similar vein, the SRSG points out in the UN Framework for Business and Human Rights that a duty to avoid discriminating may well mean very little without a corporation putting in place a policy against discrimination and educating its employees in this regard.[98]

The third category of negative obligation the court envisages involves avoiding taking measures that 'diminish' existing protections for a right. The problem here is that the obligation not to diminish may be dependent upon there being an obligation to continue to provide for the realisation of the right. Thus, what is stated as a negative obligation could in fact in essence involve performing a positive obligation. *Juma Masjid* is such a case: the court speaks of a duty not to impair the right to education of the children but, in essence, that would translate into at least a temporary positive duty on the trust to continue to provide the space and facilities for their education. The ambiguity surrounding the line between negative and positive obligations and the interrelationship between them suggests that this distinction is not adequate as a basis for determining the substantive content of the obligations of different non-state actors.

A better basis for understanding the obligations of the trust in this case would have been to reference the factors and reasoning process I have identified. In fact, the court does effectively engage substantively with many of them but in a haphazard way. It places great emphasis on the importance of the right to education to children, their vulnerability and the need to provide adequate facilities for their schooling. It recognises the primary role of the state in this regard but, given the existing arrangement, also acknowledges that the function of the trust had changed from simply enjoying private power to exercising a public function.[99] Through accepting a school on its property, it increased its capacity to affect the rights of learners. Consequently, it had additional duties to behave reasonably in relation to the department and could not seek to evict the school from the property with immediate effect.[100]

However, given it was not the only possible site for the provision of education, the department had to investigate alternative spaces in which to fulfil its duties to deliver education to the learners. The court found too that it was necessary to balance the property rights of the trust with the right to education of the learners. In doing so, it needed to take account of

[98] UN Framework 2008: para 55.
[99] *Juma Masjid*: para 55.
[100] Ibid: para 64.

the autonomy of the trust to determine how its property was to be used. In reaching its final conclusion, the court effectively found that the duty not to impede the right to education actually required positive action on the part of the trust: to engage with the department to address the backlog in certain payments and, in the event of an eviction, to provide some time in which the school could be relocated.[101] Yet, the trust's obligations did not extend to making its land available perpetually for the state school.

The multi-factoral approach I propose does not rigidly link negative obligations to non-state actors and positive obligations to the state: rather, it allows the relevant normative factors to determine the allocation of obligations amongst agents. As this case illustrates, the negative/positive distinction is neither sharp enough nor desirable as a basis to determine fully the content of the obligations held by non-state actors, a point accepted by the majority in the *Daniels* case to which I now turn.

8.4.1.2 *Daniels*:[102] Towards a Multi-Factoral Approach

Daniels dealt with a domestic worker – Ms Daniels – who inhabited a dwelling on the land of a farmer. The case emerges from the history of South Africa where black people were systematically dispossessed of their land and forced to live on the farms of white people with minimal security of tenure. With the advent of constitutional democracy, South Africa passed a number of laws including the Extension of Security of Tenure Act (ESTA) which sought to ensure individuals living in these conditions had security of tenure. Ms Daniels wanted to make some improvements to her property which were necessary – according to both parties – to render it habitable. However, the landowner sought to prevent her from renovating the property. The case revolved around whether she was entitled to make those improvements in terms of the ESTA. The court found that Ms Daniels was entitled to make the changes but also required her to engage meaningfully with the landowner around the details of how she would do so.

In reaching this conclusion, the court had to consider an argument by the landowner which implicated the negative/positive obligations distinction.

[101] The court, similarly, found that it may impose on a corporation a duty temporarily to accept the presence of occupiers on its premises pending the provision of alternative accommodation to avoid rendering people homeless: see *City of Johannesburg Metropolitan Municipality* v. *Blue Moonlight Properties 39 (Pty) Ltd* [2011] ZACC 33. As Madlanga, 2018: 371 points out, that was clearly a positive obligation. For reasons of length, I cannot expand upon this judgment.

[102] *Daniels* v. *Scribante* [2017] ZACC 13.

The statute itself provided that a landowner may, upon the eviction of an occupier, have to pay for the improvements made by that occupier.[103] The landowner argued that this provision entailed that, ultimately, he would have to pay for the improvements. That amounted indirectly to imposing a positive obligation on him to provide habitable housing to Ms Daniels.[104] In accordance with *Juma Masjid*, it was argued that an owner does not have positive obligations to ensure an occupier lives in dignified conditions.

The majority of the court rejected the notion that reference to the 'nature of the duty' in section 8(2) of the Constitution entails that a non-state actor would never have any positive obligations. The court recognises a difference in function between state and non-state actors: the latter, it claims, need not be focused on the well-being of society as a whole and they fund 'their conduct from their own pockets'.[105] Nevertheless, that difference, it finds, should not be reflected in limiting the obligations of non-state actors only to negative ones but rather must be given expression to in determining the substantive content of their positive obligations. The court here distinguishes the question of the existence of positive obligations from their nature and extent.

Determining that extent, it holds, will require reference to several factors: these include the nature of the right, the history behind the right, what the right seeks to achieve, the best manner in which it can be achieved, the potential invasion thereof by non-state actors, and whether absolving private persons from these obligations would negate the essential content of the right.[106] In applying these factors, the court finds ultimately that the landowner was duty-bound to allow the improvements to be made despite potentially having to compensate the occupier when she leaves.

This judgment represented a substantial development of the Constitutional Court's jurisprudence in this area, recognising for the first time clearly that non-state actors may have positive obligations and that their content was to be determined by a multi-factoral

[103] Section 13 of ESTA.

[104] *Daniels*: para 37. This argument was phrased in terms of section 25(6) of the Constitution but, it was argued, essentially amounts to a duty to provide habitable housing.

[105] Ibid: para 40.

[106] Ibid: para 39. In the context of discussing the *Baron* case dealing with an eviction from private land under ESTA, Van Der Sijde, 2020: 91 suggests that landowners may have positive obligations and be denied eviction orders if they wish to disturb the possession of individual occupiers simply for reasons relating to economically benefiting from the property or their own convenience.

enquiry.[107] The judgment too effectively acknowledges the inexact nature of the positive/negative obligations distinction. In referencing the duties imposed by the right to tenure security, the court suggests that the obligation imposed is, on the one hand, a positive one – namely, to accommodate someone on their land. Yet, on the other hand, it states that 'the obligation is also negative in the sense that the occupier's right should not be "improperly invaded"'.[108] Improper invasion though appears to arise from interfering with the right to occupy which, in turn, flows from the positive obligation to allow individuals to inhabit the land in the first place. By referencing the language in *Juma Masjid*, the court subtly recognises the point I made above about the easy slippage and the interrelationship between duties to avoid harming and duties to provide. On the facts of the case, the landowner did not have to provide anything but simply allow Ms Daniels to renovate her habitation. There was, however, the potential that eventually that would result in expenditure on the landowner's part. The line between the different types of obligation was difficult to draw.

Despite its recognition of the general insufficiency of the negative/positive obligations distinction, disappointingly, the court resurrects its importance in relation to socio-economic rights: it finds that only the state has positive obligations in relation to these rights. Its holding is based on a prior interpretation of these rights in the *Mazibuko* case[109] and a narrow reading of the constitutional text.[110] Its approach, however, is unconvincing: the fact that the Constitution has specific provisions for determining the state's positive obligations in the sections dealing with socio-economic rights (sections 26(2) and 27(2) of the Constitution) does not mean that *only* the state has such obligations. The obligations of non-state actors can be derived from the prior sections that give expression to the general rights to adequate housing, healthcare, food, water and social assistance.[111] To the extent its

[107] Madlanga, 2018: 373. For reasons of length, I cannot deal with the minority judgment of Jafta J, which objects to imposing any positive obligations on non-state actors for reasons largely dealt with in the discussion of the NO model above: for a critique, see Meyersfeld, 2020: 471–473. The court appeared to confirm its holding in *Daniels* that non-state actors may bear positive obligations and the application of a multi-factoral approach in *Baron* v. *Claytile* paras 36–37.

[108] *Daniels*: para 49.

[109] *Mazibuko* v. *City of Johannesburg* [2009] ZACC 28.

[110] In effect, the majority in *Daniels* paras 42–43 accepts the reasoning of the minority, at paras 187–189.

[111] These are contained in sections 26(1) and 27(1), respectively.

previous jurisprudence suggests otherwise, the court should have developed it.[112] As we will see, this holding creates problems in the *Pridwin* case below.

The facts of *Daniels* also suggest why the court's holding in relation to socio-economic rights is normatively mistaken and, substantively, inconsistent with its finding. Indeed, the court based its decision on section 25(6) which deals with the right of individuals to tenure security. It is unclear though why tenure security is not itself regarded as a social right. Moreover, it is deeply connected to the right to housing as is recognised by the 4th General Comment of the United Nations Committee on Economic, Social and Cultural Rights.[113] Indeed, whilst framed in terms of tenure security, the facts before the court dealt extensively with the right of Ms Daniels to make improvements to her home. In essence, the decision related to the adequacy of Ms Daniels' housing and could equally have been framed in terms of the right to have access to adequate housing which is a socio-economic right. The court's restriction of positive obligations for non-state actors to rights other than socio-economic rights thus appears arbitrary and artificial. A better holding would have been to recognise that positive obligations may flow from every right – no matter whether civil-political or socio-economic – and their substantive content depends on the multiple factors outlined by the court.

Indeed, those very factors provide grounds for the extension of positive obligations to non-state actors in relation to socio-economic rights. For instance, such agents have the potential to impact heavily on the socio-economic rights of individuals. They may also have had a history of interference with the right (particularly in the South African context) and the goal of realising those rights might not be capable of being achieved effectively without their involvement. Consequently, there is no good reason simply on the basis of categorising a right as 'socio-economic' to limit the obligations of non-state actors only to those which have a 'negative' character.

8.4.1.3 *Pridwin*: Resurrecting an Incoherent Distinction?

Sadly, the effect of keeping the negative/positive obligations distinction alive led to significant confusion in *Pridwin.*[114] The case dealt with a decision by a private school – that received no state funding – to terminate its contract with the parents and thus require them to place

[112] The problem began with a problematic interpretation of these rights that can be traced back to *Minister of Health* v. *Treatment Action Campaign* [2002] ZACC 15 para 39.

[113] See para 8(a) available at https://tbinternet.ohchr.org/_layouts/15/treatybodyexternal/Download.aspx?symbolno=INT%2fCESCR%2fGEC%2f4759&Lang=en.

[114] *AB* v. *Pridwin Preparatory School* [2020] ZACC 17.

their two boys in a different school. That decision was arrived at after extremely abusive behaviour by the father towards the school and its staff. The Constitutional Court had to decide whether the termination was constitutional – given the school was private, a central question concerned constructing its fundamental rights obligations.

The majority of the court viewed the matter as requiring a direct assessment of the conduct of the school against the relevant constitutional rights. These were identified as the requirement in section 28(2) that 'a child's best interests are of paramount importance in all matters concerning the child' and the right to education in section 29.[115] The court thus first had to evaluate whether the school had constitutional obligations flowing from these rights. The court found unequivocally that it did and recognised that '[c]hildren should not be excluded from this protection merely because parental choices or circumstances have placed them in independent schools'.[116] Moreover, the court referenced the growth in the number of children attending independent schools – their increasing power also provided important reasons for enhanced constitutional protection for children attending those schools.[117]

The court then had to determine the content of the school's obligations and to evaluate its conduct in light thereof. It first considered section 28(2) which it stated, in essence, 'recognises the vulnerability of children, their special importance in our society and the need for additional protection for them'.[118] The key question, it held, was whether the school had adequately considered the best interests of the children in deciding to end their sojourn there. In deciding that question, the court found that, at a minimum, the school had a duty to request representations – from both parents and the children concerned – regarding the best interests of the children and consider them before making a decision. The school's failure objectively to demonstrate that a fair process had been undertaken to engage with the best interests of the children constituted a violation of its obligations under this section.

[115] The main minority judgment by Nicholls AJ is not entirely clear but appears largely to construct the matter as one of 'indirect application' concerning the constitutionality of a clause of the contract between the parents and the school: see paras 60–61 though para 91 confuses matters as to whether this is so. The majority seeks to avoid the contractual question.

[116] Ibid: para 131.

[117] Ibid.

[118] Ibid: 142.

The majority of the court also engaged in some depth with two parts of the section 29 right: section 29(1)(a) which states that 'everyone has a right to basic education... ' and section 29(3)(c) which involves the right 'to establish and maintain, at their own expense, independent educational institutions that ... maintain standards that are not inferior to standards at comparable public educational institutions'. In relation to section 29(1)(a), the court found that an independent school such as Pridwin lacks a positive duty to provide education which falls on the state. However, if it does provide such education, it has a negative obligation not to impair or diminish that right. The court finds that basic education relates to the curriculum that must be taught and that, if a child goes to an independent school, the school must ensure that basic education is provided. This point was bolstered by section 29(3)(c) which it found imposed a positive obligation on independent schools to provide education that is at a standard not inferior to that offered in state schools. Terminating the children's schooling without a hearing, the court found, constituted a violation of its obligation not to impair their education. Since there was no 'appropriate justification' for doing so, it found the school's behaviour to have been unconstitutional.

Given *Daniels*, and the challenging of the negative/positive distinction as a basis for defining obligations, it could have been hoped that the court would have focused its analysis simply on the relevant factors for determining obligations. Instead, unfortunately, its usage of the distinction obfuscates more than it clarifies and further highlights the inadequacy thereof as a basis for determining the substantive content of the obligations of non-state actors.[119]

In relation to section 28(2), the court does not, ultimately, seek to classify what must be done as being of a negative or positive character. The construction the court places upon it, however, makes it clear that it ultimately imposes a positive obligation upon both state and non-state actors to give due consideration to the best interests of the child. That, in turn, implies concretely a proactive duty to ensure fair processes take place and all sides of a matter are heard when deciding questions relating to children. The NO model thus is simply not apposite in this context.

In relation to section 29, the court is correct that it involves the 'legal entitlement to having one's basic learning needs met'.[120] The problems begin to arise with the court's confusing usage of the negative/positive

[119] I agree here with Finn, 2020: 604.
[120] *Pridwin*: para 166.

obligations distinction. The court finds that Pridwin 'provides a basic education despite the fact that they do not bear a positive obligation to do so'.[121] Instead, it simply bears a negative obligation not to interfere with the right to basic education of the children. Its only positive obligation flows from section 29(3) which involves maintaining standards not inferior to public schools.[122]

The court seems to be worried about the notion, presented in argument, that independent schools do not in the abstract have a duty to provide education to everyone. Yet, this concern is in fact a red herring: no school – state or private – can accommodate every child and there must be a sharing of educational provision across various schools established in the society. Moreover, no one is under a general duty to set up an independent school: however, once one does so, the school operates within a context in which, in relation to the children enrolled in that school, it will be taking over the obligations of the state for the *provision* of basic education. It is thus difficult to understand why the court finds that 'Pridwin does not have to step into the shoes of the state in order to provide basic education'[123] – that is precisely what it is doing. It is illogical then to suggest that an independent school only has negative obligations to avoid, for instance, expelling children from the school. The reason it must not do so lies in the fact that it is duty-bound to fulfil the right to education for the children who attend it – expelling them would thus affect their rights precisely because of a prior assumption of a positive obligation.

The court's attempt to distinguish the *AllPay* case dealt with in Chapter 4 is also not convincing.[124] That case is in fact apposite as the constitutional obligations of the corporation there – Cash Paymaster Services – flowed directly from the constitutional right to social security through a prior assumption of a function that directly related to the fulfilment of this right. The court states that the two situations are distinct: 'Pridwin, whilst subject to a negative obligation, does not incur positive obligations under section 29(1)(a). Pridwin may perform a constitutional function, but, unlike Cash Paymaster Services, it does not fulfil a constitutional duty'.[125] It is hard to understand this reasoning: although there was no original contract between Pridwin and the state (unlike in the case of *AllPay*), through accepting students and offering to

121 Ibid: para 178.
122 Ibid: para 157.
123 Ibid: para 178.
124 My analysis here disagrees with Finn, 2020: 604 that the cases are in fact distinct.
125 *Pridwin*: para 179.

provide them with a basic education, the school assumes the responsibility for actively fulfilling these children's right to basic education (in the place of the state).[126] It is unclear why its assumption of this function is not a sufficient reason to recognise it has positive obligations to those children to continue to provide them with education. Indeed, the holding in the case seems premised on the notion that the school may have to continue to provide such education unless, through a proper process, it can establish there is a good justification for not doing so.

The court's failure to recognise a positive obligation here is also disappointing given the acknowledgement in the main minority judgment of the disparity between some world class, well-resourced independent schools and the poor education and facilities available in many state schools.[127] It is true that it would be impossible for the wealthy independent schools to enhance the educational opportunities for all those attending the poorer schools: but, positive obligations are not all-or-nothing matters. There is no reason why the wealthier schools could not, without the risk of impoverishing themselves, be under a positive obligation to provide scholarships for admission to some of those who cannot afford to attend them. Moreover, there could also be positive obligations short of that to make their facilities available on occasion to poorer schools, and, through partnerships, to contribute their expertise and resources to improving the education in less well-off schools. Many such programmes already exist as voluntary initiatives[128] but it is unclear why such measures could not also be regarded as a matter of constitutional duty.

The *Pridwin* case thus highlights the insufficiencies of the NO model: the obligations of non-state actors should not be conceived of as being simply negative in character. Instead of attempting rigid classifications that fail to capture the normative complexity involved, the court should draw on the promising strands in its jurisprudence which recognise the relevance of a range of factors as a basis for determining those obligations.[129] This chapter has sought to provide a more systematic

[126] The court seems to accept this at para 180.

[127] *Pridwin*: para 2. Meyersfeld, 2020: 452–454 argues that positive obligations should be recognised as they can help address the terrible inequalities in South Africa.

[128] See, for instance, examples of such initiatives: www.stmarysschool.co.za/bursaries-and-scholarships; and www.stjohnscollege.co.za/foundation/community-engagement/st-johns-college-academy.

[129] See its reference to the *Daniels*' enquiry at para 186 and approval by Meyersfeld, 2020: 47. For reasons of length, I have not analysed the balancing enquiry the court conducts in *Pridwin*, which also references multiple factors and a partial proportionality enquiry – see *Pridwin*: para 198. For a critique that this test lacks normative clarity, see Finn, 2020: 604–607.

analytical framework for determining those obligations which could perhaps be drawn on by the court in its future jurisprudence.

8.4.2 India: The Legislative Imposition of Positive Obligations

8.4.2.1 Key Facets of the Legislative Scheme

In 2013, the Indian legislature passed section 135 of the Companies Act, 2013. This section requires every large company – with either a net profit of 5 crore (50 million) rupees or more, a net worth of 500 crore (5 billion) rupees or more, or an annual turnover above 1000 (10 billion) crore rupees or more[130] – to establish a Corporate Social Responsibility Committee (CSRC) that consists of three or more directors, one of whom is an independent director.[131] The Committee is responsible for developing a Corporate Social Responsibility Policy (CSRP) related to specified areas where the company can make a social contribution, recommending the amount of expenditure to be spent in this regard and monitoring the policy.[132] The board must consider the recommendations of the CSRC and formally pass a CSRP. The CSRP must also be made publicly available in its annual report and on its web-site. The board is responsible for ensuring that the activities recommended in the CSRP are undertaken.[133]

The key ground-breaking provision is section 135(5) which states that the board is responsible for ensuring that 'the company spends, in every financial year, at least two percent of the average net profits of the company made during the three immediately preceding financial years, in pursuance of its Corporate Social Responsibility Policy'.[134] In relation to this provision, the Act prescribes that the company shall give preference to projects in the local area in which it operates; and, in the event it fails to spend the required amount, that it provides a justification for the shortfall in its annual report to the annual general meeting. The areas of social contribution on which a company may spend are outlined in Schedule 7 of the Act and include activities such as eradicating extreme hunger and poverty, the promotion of education, and combatting diseases.[135] Clearly, most of these areas involve contributions to realising fundamental rights such as the right to food, education, and healthcare amongst others. The Act can, therefore,

[130] A crore is ten million.
[131] Section 135(1).
[132] Section 135(3).
[133] Section 135(4).
[134] Section 135(5).
[135] Schedule 7 of the Act.

be seen to impose a positive obligation on large corporations to spend a minimum percentage of their net profits in helping to advance and realise the fundamental rights of individuals who are badly off in India.

Before engaging in more detail with the extent of the obligations outlined in this scheme, it is useful to examine the contours of the model that was adopted in this novel legislative schema. Firstly, a requirement was imposed to form a committee made up of senior decision-makers in the corporation to develop the CSRP. The board is then required to take ownership of the policy by adopting it and devoting resources to its implementation. As Chatterjee, one of the key architects of the scheme, explains, corporate social responsibility (CSR) is now placed at the forefront of decision-making and moved 'from the backroom to the boardroom'.[136] Secondly, the money must be spent on specific projects adopted by the company. Informal CSR is not enough: rather, the corporation is required to develop a strategy around specific projects which includes goals, milestones and monitoring.[137] Thirdly, instead of prescribing specific projects, the legal schema allows companies the discretion to decide on areas in which they wish to contribute – within the range outlined in Schedule 7 – and the projects they wish to undertake. The focus is on developing an inclusive social development agenda, many planks of which relate to fundamental rights,[138] but also harnessing the creativity that emanates from the particular interests and passions of the decision-makers within a corporation.

Fourthly, once a project is decided upon, there is a need to ensure it has sufficient financial resources available to it. A key component of the schema is the quantification of CSR expenditure to a percentage of net profit. Finally, a major question arose surrounding human resources and who would implement the projects decided upon by corporations. Corporations do not automatically have the capability to do so and, thus, the scheme allows them to provide funds to non-governmental organisations who have the capacity and expertise in, for instance, reducing hunger and improving education. There also is an option to contribute to a government fund that would then spend the money on social upliftment projects. However, Chatterjee explains that the scheme attempts to avoid simply providing an extra source of revenue to the government but seeks to harness the many strengths corporations have in

[136] Chatterjee and Mitra, 2017: 14. The language utilised is perhaps not ideal and outdated by focusing on the notion of corporate social responsibility (CSR) rather than fundamental rights.

[137] Ibid.

[138] Ibid: 15.

the service of social development.[139] The private sector, he states, 'has many strengths, efficiency, lean and mean, bang for the buck, innovation, quickness to respond, which are some of the things that the Government is sometimes limited with, by the very nature in which they are structured'.[140] In this model, he claims, 'the strengths of the private sector are used to complement or supplement what the Government is doing, not to duplicate it'.[141] The model is thus based on a collaborative ethos and provides a response to the charge that corporate positive obligations will simply allow the government to shirk its own responsibilities.

8.4.2.2 An Evaluation of the Legislative Scheme

At the time of writing, the Indian model is relatively new and its success will only be capable of being evaluated fully after a significant amount of time has passed. The Indian Institute of Corporate Affairs estimated that it could affect over 16,000 companies and generate annual revenue of around INR 200 billion or 2.6 billion Euros.[142] What is clear already is that corporate spending has increased on social causes as a result: according to a Guardian report in 2016, corporate spend grew almost 8 times from 33.67 billion rupees to 250 billion rupees.[143] This involves a significant expansion in the resources available for important social projects. 2015 data released by the Ministry of Corporate Affairs shows that about 70 per cent of 10,500 eligible companies reported on their CSR spend and only 30 per cent had made some expenditure on CSR. 74 per cent of the money that was supposed to be spent was actually disbursed. The top 10 companies spent about 32 per cent of the total CSR that was required.[144] It is thus clearly taking time for all companies to increase their CSR expenditure though figures show a year-on-year increase in compliance.[145]

The Indian model itself is a fascinating one and the first globally to place a binding legal obligation on corporations to contribute actively to

[139] See also Meyersfeld, 2020: 453–454 on the difference between an additional tax and a positive obligation pursuant to fundamental rights.

[140] Chatterjee and Mitra, 2017: 16.

[141] Ibid: 17.

[142] Rueth, 2017: 26. See also, Singh, 2018: 206.

[143] See www.theguardian.com/sustainable-business/2016/apr/05/india-csr-law-requires-companies-profits-to-charity-is-it-working.

[144] Ministry of Corporate Affairs Snapshot of CSR Spent for 7334 Companies in FY2014-15 available at www.mca.gov.in/MinistryV2/csrdatasummary.html.

[145] See https://thewire.in/business/five-years-after-csr-became-mandatory-what-has-it-really-achieved. See also the KPMG CSR Reporting Survey 2019 available at https://home.kpmg/in/en/home/insights/2020/02/india-s-csr-reporting-survey-2019.html

addressing social problems, including the realisation of fundamental rights. There are many of its aspects that can be evaluated but, of relevance to this chapter, is particularly the concrete obligation to spend 2 per cent of net profits on particular social projects of the companies choosing within a specified list of social contribution possibilities. Without a proper justification, the percentage seems arbitrary. It is thus useful to consider this obligation in light of the multi-factoral model and seven-step test I have proposed – that engagement can, I suggest, provide not only a justification but also ideas of how to improve the Indian model.

The starting point for determining positive obligations, I have argued, lies in identifying the impact of a lack of action to advance fundamental rights – that requires an understanding of the needs of individuals. I take it as well-established that in India, the needs are vast for realising all fundamental socio-economic rights such as housing, food, healthcare and education. Clearly, a range of concrete actions must be identified which can successfully advance each of these entitlements. The state in India does not deny its obligations and the Supreme Court has affirmed that certain socio-economic rights constitute part of the right to life.[146] At the same time, the state has serious shortcomings in its capacity to address these needs: often this has led the Supreme Court, for instance, in the right to food case, to appoint independent commissioners to supervise the implementation of its orders.[147] It is thus reasonable to conclude that the state alone cannot address all these needs.

Interestingly, the approach of the Indian legislature appears to jump over the next step in the enquiry I have proposed and simply articulates a general obligation upon all large corporations to contribute 2 per cent of their net profits to social projects. Doing so is important for equal treatment and, in a specific statute, it would have been difficult to articulate a more tailored approach. Moreover, given that it is a general obligation, the law essentially avoids having to address a diminishment or increase in obligations due to the particular activities, functions and capacities of other non-state actors by imposing a standardised percentage on everyone.

The statute, at the same time, allows for a discretion to be exercised about which projects will be supported by the CSR spending of particular companies. The specific function enquiry suggests a way of guiding this discretion – where a company exercises a specific function in relation to

[146] *Olga Tellis* v. *Bombay Municipal Corporation* (1985) 3 SCC 545, 572.

[147] *People's Union for Civil Liberties* v. *Union of India* (Civil Writ Petition 196 of 2001) – Interim Order (May 8, 2002).

one of the areas in which it may spend, it should seek to utilise its expertise to advance the realisation of fundamental rights in this area. The idea of harnessing the power of the private sector that is imbedded in the CSR model would be enhanced if capacities in specific sectors, where they exist, were utilised to improve fundamental rights in that sphere. Moreover, the activities of other actors in particular sectors would be an important consideration as to where companies should direct their spending.

The alternative step requires adopting a course of action that would contribute significantly towards realising the fundamental rights of individuals whilst having an impact on a corporation that is not too substantial. Given the general obligation imposed by the statute, there is at least a formally equal financial burden upon each corporation. The only aspect where this enquiry could be useful would be in relation to the human resources required of the corporation. That would again, in all likelihood, tend to favour contributions in sectors where the corporation already has a specific function or expertise.

Finally, in relation to balancing, the law can be understood to represent the outcome of a balancing process that the legislature has already undertaken. The legal obligation of large corporations is set at 2 per cent of net profit. That requires companies to make a social contribution but already includes an in-built recognition that corporate autonomy to achieve its economic goals must be preserved. Given the percentage comes from net profit and it is only a small percentage thereof, there is unlikely to be any substantial negative impact on the corporation's ability to pursue its economic aims and the major question becomes where the funds of the corporation can best be spent. Identifying a threshold such as 2 per cent will always be arbitrary, in some sense, but it will be justifiable as a matter of general law (or social policy) provided it is broadly a reasonable outcome of a normative evaluation of the competing considerations at play. Arguably, given we are considering net profit, this threshold perhaps has been set too low by the law: 5 per cent, for instance, would still have left 95 per cent of profits for shareholders. Nevertheless, given that this provision is already ground-breaking globally and generated much opposition, a conservative threshold could be justified.

I have thus sought to demonstrate how the multi-factoral model usefully helps to provide a grounding for the 2 per cent CSR obligation but also highlights two concerns about the manner in which it has been articulated: it may be too low and the legislative schema should direct (rather than simply permit) corporations performing specific functions to contribute within their areas of expertise. The factors I have outlined also suggest three further concerns.

First, the Indian approach at present is limited to very large corporations – clearly these entities have a high level of capacity and will not be severely affected by the spending requirement. At the same time, the law simply omits to place any obligations on small and medium enterprises to make social contributions. Arguably, many small and medium-sized enterprises have the capacity to make a significant contribution to the advancement of fundamental rights with even more minimal expenditure obligations – over time, therefore, it is arguable that the scheme should be extended to cover all enterprises.[148] That will of course have significant administrative implications and so perhaps could start out as an obligation to report on social spending without substantial monitoring.

Secondly, it is also important that the 2 per cent spending threshold is not regarded as being exhaustive of the positive obligations of corporations. Some have criticised the law for suggesting that all a corporation must do is contribute its 2 per cent of net profits and then it has made its social contribution.[149] That could be so even if it harms society in multiple respects. It should be clear that a corporation may have positive obligations to advance fundamental rights in the very business decisions it makes and specific obligations flow from that too. Spending money on social projects also does not compensate for harms to fundamental rights and, if any infringements are to be regarded as legitimate, they would have to be justified in terms of the proportionality enquiry discussed in the last chapter. The 2 per cent obligation is in addition to these other obligations it may have and, also, does not seek to set a maximum but a minimum spend on social projects.[150]

Thirdly, a serious problem with the scheme as it stands results from the rather decentralised approach it has embraced. The discretionary approach adopted has the up-side of placing emphasis on the autonomy of the decision-makers of a corporation to determine which projects they wish to support and also allows them to tailor their involvement to areas where they have a speciality or particular concern.

The down-side of this approach relates to the fact that it can lead to multiple disparate projects and thus can give rise to the co-ordination

[148] A recent report recommends in a limited way extending the CSR requirement to banks and certain other entities: see High-Level Committee Report 2018: 58–59.

[149] https://thewire.in/business/five-years-after-csr-became-mandatory-what-has-it-really-achieved

[150] See also Rueth, 2017: 27–28.

problems I raised above. The lack of central co-ordination can also lead to non-optimal outcomes with expenditure going to very similar projects or to those with a lesser priority. It does not allow for a focused approach to be adopted for areas where there are specific urgent needs. There have also been some reports, for instance, of technical compliance – such as building a hospital for high-paying patients – which subverts the point of the law.[151] The provision that encourages spending in areas close to the corporations has also led to a strong geographical imbalance in expenditure in India. More heavily industrialised states with stronger economies attract greater expenditure than those that are in fact the poorest.[152] There thus needs to be a consideration of how to improve co-ordination to ensure the benefits of the scheme are more widely and fairly distributed.[153]

India's legislative scheme gives effect powerfully to the social dimension of corporations and tries to balance it with the individualised dimension. The focus on a particular threshold has the strong benefit of providing a simple and quantifiable metric for determining the positive obligations of corporations. It can, with certain caveats, as I have suggested, be justified by reference to the multi-factoral approach I have developed and help provide a concrete instantiation of what is required – it should thus be commended to other countries. The multi-factoral approach also suggests areas for improvement in the legal schema which should be considered both in relation to the current law in India as well as other jurisdictions which might consider adopting it.

8.5 Conclusion

This chapter has sought to consider the question of whether corporations have positive obligations in relation to fundamental rights and, if so, how to determine the substantive content of those obligations. I first outlined the NO model which denies non-state actors have such obligations, and sought to argue why the negative/positive obligations distinction was not

[151] I was told of such anecdotal cases on a visit to the Ministry of Corporate Affairs in New Delhi.

[152] High-Level Committee Report 2018: 66.

[153] This point is recognised in the Report, ibid: 68 in its recommendation that companies should balance local area preference with national priorities – that relatively weak guidance hardly seems sufficient to address these co-ordination problems, which, to be dealt with adequately, probably require either a public or private co-ordinating agency. See also Rueth, 2017: 29.

an adequate basis for distinguishing the obligations of state and non-state actors. The discussion also sought to provide a justification for why non-state actors and, particularly, corporations do and should have such obligations. I then sought to show that the multi-factoral approach considered in Chapter 6 should also, suitably adapted, be adopted as a basis for determining the content of their positive obligations. A central additional factor is of relevance which involves considering the role and obligations of other non-state actors in contributing towards the realisation of rights. To reach a final determination of these obligations, I proposed a seven-step test that involves a structured reasoning process which takes account of the various factors and allows for a balancing of interests to take place. The last section of this chapter considered the legal instantiation of positive obligations through the courts in South Africa and the legislature in India. The multi-factoral approach, I suggested, could be helpful in systematising and guiding these developments.

As is evident from the multi-factoral approach both in relation to negative obligations and positive obligations, there is a significant amount of judgement involved in determining the substantive content of corporate obligations. Various factors are involved, and a balancing enquiry needs to be conducted before arriving at a conclusion about concretely what must be done in a particular circumstance. Whilst, over time, concrete rules and guidance will emerge, the ineliminability of judgement and discretion raises a number of questions: who makes these judgements and how can we improve the quality thereof? Addressing these questions is the subject of the next two chapters which focus on the institutional reforms – both at the national and international level – necessary to operationalise and implement the multi-factoral approach.

PART III

The Institutional Implications of the Multi-Factoral Approach

9

Embedding the Multi-Factoral Approach in Corporations: The Role of Corporate Law

9.1 Introduction

The multi-factoral approach clearly involves the exercise of judgement in determining the substantive content of corporate obligations in relation to fundamental rights. Such judgement arises from the normative complexity involved and precludes arriving at more specific, concrete rules without engaging reasoning processes such as the proportionality test – in the case of negative obligations – or the seven-step test I have proposed – in relation to positive obligations. The worry, however, is that a failure to provide concrete and specific rules governing corporate obligations opens the door for corporate decision-makers to avoid seeing them as binding requirements at all. It also opens the possibility for corporations to use normative complexity and context sensitivity as a fig-leaf behind which to avoid any onerous obligations and claim that they simply adopt a different view of what their obligations are. Given we are dealing with an entity that is partially constructed to realise individual economic purposes, it is possible and perhaps likely that narrow self-interest will be placed ahead of any sense of social obligation in relation to fundamental rights.

This challenge raises squarely the need to focus not simply on the factors and reasoning processes involved in defining the substantive content of corporate obligations but also on the manner in which any determinations surrounding such obligations are made. Questions concerning who has the responsibility for such decision-making and their accountability for such decisions become critical. In this way, an approach to substantive obligations has important institutional implications. In this chapter, I will focus on decision-making within the corporate structure itself concerning fundamental rights obligations.

In section 9.2, I contrast two different models for institutionalising corporate obligations relating to fundamental rights. A 'compliance-based' model simply imposes external rules on corporate actors that must be followed, whilst a 'voluntarist' model relies on corporations freely to assume responsibilities. After discussing the weaknesses of both, I argue for a third way, which I term the 'guided discretion model': it seeks to utilise a mix of regulatory measures to enhance the quality of decision-making within the corporation surrounding fundamental rights. This approach, when properly executed, reinforces the multi-factoral approach and offers the real opportunity to embed a commitment to fundamental rights within the corporate structure itself.

Section 9.3, the heart of this chapter, considers the elements necessary to give effect to this model with the focus being on enhancing decision-making surrounding fundamental rights. It is recognised that there is a role to be played by voluntary initiatives and incentive-based approaches which are complementary to the proposals made. However, the focus of this chapter – following the theme of this book – is on reforms to corporate law that can help embed fundamental rights within the basic legal structure of the corporation itself. In doing so, it is necessary to attend to a number of dimensions.

Firstly, I consider *who* are the decision-makers in corporations surrounding fundamental rights and argue for the need to provide a wider set of stakeholders with a voice. The focus is largely on expanding the diversity and expertise of directors who are ultimately responsible for the day-to-day operations of the corporation. Secondly, I consider *what* the obligations of those decision-makers are, with a particular focus, once again, on the directors. I argue for the recognition of a specific fiduciary duty on directors to consider the impact of the corporation on fundamental rights, to exercise demonstrably a high degree of care in deliberating about and reaching judgements about the substantive content of corporate obligations and to ensure compliance with those obligations. Such a duty would, of necessity, require that directors take a view on the substantive content of a corporation's obligations.

Thirdly, I consider the forms of accountability of decision-makers with a focus on the directors. In doing so, I consider measures ranging from transparency requirements to extending the actions available to victims of rights violations to directors in their personal capacity where they are negligent. Finally, I consider *to whom* directors are accountable. In doing so, I first consider the residual responsibility of shareholders and how their obligations in relation to fundamental rights should be understood. I then argue for the importance of review by external bodies of internal decisions relating to corporate fundamental rights obligations and focus on the role of courts. Enhancing accountability to courts, I argue, requires limiting the application of the business judgement rule in cases concerning fundamental rights. Apart from the courts needing to be prepared to develop the substantive content of corporate obligations, I contend that they should also utilise creative remedies in order to help embed a commitment to fundamental rights within the corporate structure.

9.2 Embedding Fundamental Rights in the Corporate Form: Making a Virtue Out of Necessity

9.2.1 Between Compliance and Voluntarist Models

Given that determining corporate obligations involves the exercise of significant judgement, it is of vital importance to pay attention to who is responsible for making these judgements. The first set of decision-makers who will make decisions with an impact on fundamental rights will be those internal to the corporation itself. As was discussed in Chapter 1, the corporate entity itself is dependent upon individual human decision-makers even though sometimes particular decisions may be difficult to trace to specific persons.

The corporate structure is itself usually set up by individuals as a vehicle through which they further their economic goals. Given the complexity of modern-day corporations, these shareholders generally do not run the business and appoint a board of directors that is, ultimately, responsible for its overarching strategy, operations and its key decisions.[1] The directors in turn often delegate day-to-day decisions to operational managers and, sometimes, individual employees lower down the hierarchy.[2] The directors are usually required by law, annually, to report to the shareholders on their activities.[3] Clearly, in terms of operations, the directors (and those to whom they delegate responsibility) are the decision-makers about the activities of the corporation which will affect

1 Armour et al., 2017a: 12.

2 Ibid.

3 The feature of the corporation whereby directors run the operations and shareholders own the stock is known as the separation of ownership and control: see, for instance, Hannigan, 2018: 105.

fundamental rights – consequently, much of the focus must be on their decision-making.[4] They are though accountable to shareholders who have some power and their obligations are also important to consider. If corporations are to realise their fundamental rights obligations, all the individuals who constitute the decision-making structure of the corporation must understand this to be one of their central responsibilities which they must exercise diligently. How can this best be accomplished?

The first approach I will consider is often termed a 'command and control' approach: this would involve having very specific fine-grained legal rules with particular understandings of corporate obligations and requiring the company to comply with these on pain of administrative, civil or criminal penalties.[5] This approach is based upon a scepticism that corporate decision-makers will themselves take fundamental rights concerns seriously given the prevailing ideology that the core focus of their attention should be on profit-maximisation and, thus, the economic goals of corporate activity. That scepticism is warranted yet responding to it simply with a plethora of further legal rules is problematic for several reasons.[6]

Firstly, it is very difficult for statutory law to provide for every concrete circumstance that will arise concerning fundamental rights. The advantage of doing so is that the legislature would itself conduct the balancing exercises required and there would be little for corporate decision-makers to decide. Yet, legal rules will always struggle to address concrete circumstances which do not exactly replicate what the legislature contemplated.[7] Many day-to-day decisions that have implications for rights will involve a significant amount of discretion being exercised.[8] Moreover, there will be new developments – particularly, in recent years, in the sphere of technology – and law will always in some sense be

4 It is also important to consider the obligations of and accountability of other decision-makers in the corporation; for a promising initiative, see the Senior Management Regime relating to banking and insurance in the United Kingdom (www.bankofengland.co.uk/prudential-regulation/authorisations/senior-managers-regime-approvals). For reasons of length, I focus primarily on directors.

5 Hodges, 2015: 162 explains that command and control regulation involves the state prescribing 'specific ways of doing, or not doing, something and may authorize or prohibit certain activities, breach of which will render the infringer liable to a sanction or sanctions'.

6 See Teubner, 1985 for further critiques.

7 Law is expressed in language which is always subject to interpretation: Hart, 1958: 607 sought to show that even a seemingly simple rule such as 'no vehicles in the park' may raise interpretive questions concerning its range of application.

8 Mares, 2010: 240 emphasises that the existence and management of discretion is key in enhancing responsible business practices.

catching up with reality. The law may also not always be flexible enough to deal with changing social circumstances.[9]

A second set of problems relates to the fact that the model often elicits a technical response of complying with an external constraint without shifting any of the internal norms within a corporation. The lack of change in the internal norms can result in serious harms where, for instance, the law is insufficiently precise. There is indeed also a phenomenon known as 'malicious compliance' where the letter of the law is followed but in a way that often violates its spirit.[10] There are also major questions about the effectiveness of this approach and the resources required to give effect to it.[11]

On the other side of the spectrum is the *voluntary* approach to the responsibilities of corporations for fundamental rights.[12] The UN Global Compact, for instance, contains a list of ten principles to which companies sign up voluntarily.[13] The idea behind it was articulated by its executive head as being 'an experiment in cooperation based on market mechanisms that would allow the catalytic effects of critical masses, collective action, transparency and front-runner behaviour to set examples and ultimately create behavioral norms'.[14] Underpinning these claims is the assumption that a collective decision by many corporations to join the Global Compact encourages the voluntary acceptance by corporations that they have responsibilities for fundamental rights (and other social concerns). Doing so demonstrates an internal decision to commit to the principles they have signed up to which can change corporate behaviour and thus move beyond simple box-ticking compliance with external constraints. The widespread acceptance today of the notion that corporations bear some responsibilities in relation to fundamental rights may be seen to be a sign of success of the voluntary approaches[15] yet they too have significant drawbacks.

[9] These problems are not unique to the realm of fundamental rights: see Ayers and Braithwaite, 1992: 110–111.

[10] See, for instance, McBarnet and Whelan, 1991: 849, who refer to this as 'creative compliance', and Mares, 2010: 251.

[11] Deva, 2012: 201; Hodges, 2015: 166–167.

[12] Such approaches originated with the concept of 'corporate social responsibility', which has evolved to include a component relating to fundamental rights: see Ramasastry, 2015: 239–240.

[13] See www.unglobalcompact.org/what-is-gc/mission/principles. Principles 1 and 2 deal with fundamental rights.

[14] Kell, 2005: 72.

[15] The Global Compact now has over 12,000 signatories; see www.unglobalcompact.org/participation#:~:text=12%2C000%2B%20signatories%20in%20over%20160,nearly%20every%20sector%20and%20size. See also Nolan, 2013: 154.

Firstly, there is the conceptual problem involved in suggesting that responsibilities flowing from fundamental rights are in some sense voluntary. The very logic and underpinnings of fundamental rights I have outlined in Chapter 2 indicate that they impose binding obligations which cannot in any sense be understood to be voluntarily assumed.[16] The second problem is the converse of the advantage claimed for the compliance-based model: if the assumption of such responsibilities is voluntary, are corporate decision-makers entitled to take them on? Those defending a libertarian model of the corporation – such as Milton Friedman – have famously argued that corporate decision-makers are duty-bound to act to advance the interests of shareholders. Taking on wider social obligations violates their obligations to shareholders.[17] The widespread recognition of some corporate social responsibilities suggests decision-makers widely adopt a less extreme perspective. Yet, even then, accepting that a corporation's responsibilities for fundamental rights are voluntary renders its commitment precarious. When balancing social and individual economic imperatives, the latter will often take precedence.[18] Indeed, the voluntary codes adopted by corporations and instruments they have signed up to often are vague and lack specificity about their commitments.[19] They also lack adequate modalities to monitor and ensure compliance – both internally and externally.[20] The serious harms that have often resulted from corporate behaviour suggest that a purely voluntarist approach is too sanguine and cannot develop the required seriousness of purpose surrounding fundamental rights.

9.2.2 A Hybrid 'Guided Discretion Approach'

How then can we try and adopt a model that draws on the insights of both these approaches without leading to the drawbacks of each? I would propose considering an alternative hybrid model that focuses on the importance of discretion or judgement in corporate decision-making surrounding fundamental rights.[21] The starting point, as has been argued, is the acknowledgment that it is both unrealistic and undesirable

[16] Cragg, 2010: 283. This is also the reason why CSR often excluded discussion of fundamental rights: see Wettstein, 2012: 748–749; Smith, 2013: 8.
[17] Friedman, 1970: 52.
[18] Macek, 2002: 124.
[19] Simons, 2004: paras 13–28.
[20] Ibid: paras 29–36.
[21] See also Mares, 2010.

for law fully to replace such discretion. As such, it is important to recast the role of law differently. In doing so, inspiration can be gained from several different sources.[22]

One of these is an approach developed based upon the notion of 'reflexive law'. This idea has its origins in Luhmann's systems theory, which perceives society as functionally differentiated into various autonomous and closed social systems such as the political system, economic system and legal system.[23] Central to Luhmann's theory is the notion that society in some sense involves differentiated systems of communication.[24] Each of the autonomous systems has its own 'logic', so to speak, and reflexivity refers to its ability to reflect on its own norms within the system. Reflexive aspects of legal systems include rules surrounding how decision-making within the system is made.[25]

The question of course arises concerning the relationship between each of these autonomous systems and other systems. Gunther Teubner considers the relationship between external norms and internal processes in particular systems.[26] He argues that, given society is differentiated into different systems, it is not possible for law to have an effect simply by imposing its own norms directly.[27] Law, in some senses, needs to draw on the resources of the various other systems and sub-systems to achieve its own ends. Thus, '[l]egal intervention is dependent for its effects on self-regulation within the systems, which are the target of legal initiatives'.[28]

What regulation aims at is thus not simply to prescribe compliance with fine-grained duties that are exhaustively laid out in the law – something that systems theory suggests is impossible to do but also, as we saw, faces serious practical hurdles.[29] Instead, the goal of regulation should be to mandate self-regulation: in other words, to enable and encourage the embedding of the norms underpinning the regulation within the 'system' to be regulated.[30] Rogowski, for instance, illustrates

[22] In what follows, I draw inspiration for an approach to corporate regulation from diverse bodies of literature without necessarily endorsing all the details of the accounts discussed.
[23] Luhmann, 1989: 138; Buhmann, 2013: 31. For a critique of the closure of such systems, see Braithwaite, 2006: 885.
[24] Herting and Stein, 2007: 11.
[25] Luhmann, 1989: 140–141.
[26] Teubner, 1985: 309–313.
[27] He explains why this is not possible or desirable by reference to a regulatory trilemma: see ibid: 311.
[28] Rogowski, 2015: 74.
[29] Teubner, 1985: 312.
[30] Ibid: 317.

this process through describing how the International Labour Organisation encouraged states to establish Decent Work Country Programmes and, thereby, nurtured their development of a plan of implementation for the decent work agenda.[31] In this way, an international regulatory regime demonstrated reflexivity through essentially encouraging self-regulation – and, thus, domestication of international standards – by states. Importantly, such a regulatory approach does not have to be simply voluntary or based on encouragement but can include the use of legal coercive measures: the entity or system subject to regulation may be obliged to institute the self-regulatory system.

These and other similar ideas have stimulated developments in regulatory theory such as the notion of 'regulated self-regulation', which is defined to involve 'a pattern in which outer boundaries of acceptable behaviour as well as stipulations of acceptable procedures for defining codes and standards are determined by public authorities, thus creating a space of variation in which state and non-state actors bargain and co-operate to set more detailed rules and standards'.[32] Similarly, Ayers and Braithwaite have articulated the notion of 'enforced self-regulation' in terms of which the government may itself impose duties on non-state actors to develop a set of rules tailored to their own unique circumstances, which the regulatory authorities then either approve or send back for revisions.[33] Much of the oversight would be outsourced to internal compliance groups with regulatory authorities having a residual role to play in monitoring these groups and taking punitive legal action against those who fail to comply with their own rules.[34] Such approaches have many important benefits but also drawbacks – for instance, there are significant costs to public authorities in scrutinising these rules, companies could write rules in ways that benefit them rather than society, and internal compliance groups may lack independence and thus fail adequately to monitor compliance.[35]

As a result of difficulties with any one particular regulatory strategy, the move has been to encourage the state to 'have recourse to a range of regulatory options'.[36] Ayers and Braithwaite, for instance, have developed an influential approach known as 'responsive regulation'.[37] They

[31] Rogowski, 2015: 76–78.
[32] Ougaard, 2004: 142.
[33] Ayers and Braithwaite, 1992: 106.
[34] Ibid. See also Baldwin, Cave and Lodge, 2011: 146–147.
[35] For these and other drawbacks, see Ayers and Braithwaite, 1992: 120–128.
[36] Ibid: 128.
[37] Ibid: chapter 2.

contend that when enforcing regulation, there is a spectrum of responses:[38] regulatory authorities should begin with softer forms of persuasion, and only in response to poor behaviour of organisations (or individuals) should they move to more coercive sanctions.[39] The existence of harder, coercive measures is, nevertheless, important and helps make softer measures more effective.[40] Harder law can thus play a role too in generating social pressures upon corporate decision-makers to comply with their obligations.[41] Building on these approaches, and in the context of addressing fundamental rights violations specifically, Deva challenges the presumption in favour of softer measures and the idea that harder measures should only be introduced subsequent to their failure. Instead, he puts forward an 'integrated theory of regulation' which proposes that 'depending upon the need and nature as well as the conduct of a regulated actor, all or some of the available strategies and sanctions may be invoked at the same time, if needed'.[42]

In the context of this book, it is important to understand the implications of this discussion for decision-making surrounding fundamental rights. As we have seen, the multi-factoral approach requires an exercise of judgement by decision-makers which has the important advantage of requiring their engagement with questions surrounding fundamental rights obligations rather than purely imposing an external set of constraints in this regard.[43] I would suggest, in light of this discussion, that the role the law can play needs to be conceptualised differently and be focused on ensuring that any discretion is exercised carefully and responsibly. In so doing, the role of law is not simply to command compliance with established rules but to develop a legal framework that involves setting expectations and principles in relation to which decision-making occurs and developing accountability mechanisms.[44] In a sense, this is akin to the role a constitution plays, in general, in relation to public power. In a similar vein, in setting this governance framework for corporations, the goal must be, as Muchlinski puts it, 'to "constitutionalise" concern over human rights impacts in the corporate psyche and

38 Ibid: 35–36.
39 Ibid: 48–49.
40 Hodges, 2015: 252.
41 Kampourakis, 2019: 560.
42 Deva, 2012: 194.
43 In so doing, it treats them as moral agents with moral responsibility: see Deva, ibid: 208.
44 This is perhaps akin to what Armour et al., 2017b: 31–32 refer to as a 'governance' rather than a 'regulatory' strategy.

culture'[45]. Doing so would involve internalising a commitment to fundamental rights within the corporate structure itself and penetrating 'deep into the organization in an attempt to make individuals within organisations act responsibly'.[46] Consequently, the focus of law reform must attend to the institutional structure and framework within which decisions are made by a corporation and these are set by corporate law.[47] In reforming corporate law, then, the goal must be to develop an institutional commitment and capacity within the corporation to take its fundamental rights obligations seriously.[48]

9.3 Corporate Law and Embedding Fundamental Rights within the Corporation

The Commentary to the UNGPs recognises how '[l]aws and policies that govern the creation and ongoing operation of business enterprises, such as corporate and securities laws, directly shape business behavior. Yet their implications for human rights remain poorly understood'.[49] It goes on to acknowledge that there is a lack of clarity as to what companies and their officers 'are permitted, let alone required, to do regarding human rights'[50] and that law and policies must provide guidance with specific attention being devoted to 'the role of existing governance structures such as corporate boards'.[51]

In giving effect to these pronouncements, there are many facets of corporate law that require consideration but I propose dividing the discussion into four main sets of issues that relate to improving decision-making by the decision-makers themselves. Firstly, I consider *who* the decision-makers are with a focus on the directors; secondly, I analyse *what* their fiduciary duties are and should be; thirdly, I investigate the *forms* of accountability for decision-makers with an emphasis on directors; and finally, I examine *to whom* directors are accountable. Some of the issues I raise have already been explored in corporate law but discussed, largely, in the context of the financial affairs of the company with an

[45] Muchlinski, 2012: 156.
[46] Hodges, 2015: 249.
[47] It is hard thus to understand the reticence to extend corporate law in this way expressed by authors such as Enriques et al., 2017: 108.
[48] See, generally, Teubner, 1985: 319; Cragg, 2010: 292–294.
[49] UNGPs: Commentary on GP 3.
[50] Ibid.
[51] Ibid.

emphasis on protecting shareholders. I will engage in the following sections with the potential for expanding the scope of options to enhance accountability for decision-making surrounding the fundamental rights of all *stakeholders*.

9.3.1 *The* Who *Question: Expanding the Range of Directors*

Corporate law enables shareholders to appoint directors to conduct the day-to-day affairs of the company. In doing so, the majority of shareholders is likely to appoint directors with a predilection to protect their interests. As a result, directors will have particular incentives to advance the interests of the majority of shareholders:[52] they ultimately can be dismissed by them and there may also be financial incentives created by these shareholders to do so. In making judgements concerning fundamental rights, there would therefore be an in-built bias by directors against other stakeholders. How could this be addressed?

One possibility that is being explored in some jurisdictions concerns reforming the composition of the board of directors in corporations to include directors who are structurally more inclined towards the interests of stakeholders other than shareholders.

Thus, to avoid the interests of minority shareholders being marginalised, some corporate law systems have allowed for the appointment of directors by minority shareholders with a certain percentage of shares.[53] To ensure the interests of employees are addressed, German law requires that, in large companies, employees (and, in some cases, unions) appoint directors in equal numbers to those appointed by other shareholders.[54] The idea behind this provision is that the interests of employees are represented at the board level and tensions that may exist – between, for instance, greater profits for shareholders and wage stagnation for employees – are debated between directors with different predilections. Employees also gain access to important information surrounding key decisions in the company.[55] The question then is whether this model could be adapted to take account of the interests of all those whose fundamental rights could be affected by corporate behaviour, such as members of a local community, who are not themselves in a direct contractual (or other legal) relationship with the company itself.

52 Enriques et al., 2017: 79.
53 Ibid: 80.
54 Sections 1 and 7 Mitbestimmungesetz.
55 Enriques et al., 2017: 91.

One possibility would be for corporate law to require the appointment to the board of directors of persons who represent constituencies in relation to which the corporation has a fundamental rights impact. It could be proposed, for instance, that there be representation on the board to address specific public concerns such as environmental matters, consumer interests and much else.[56] This idea has been taken up in a weaker form in South Africa, where most state-owned companies, listed public companies and companies above a certain size and turnover have to appoint a social and ethics committee.[57] This is a special institutional structure tasked with monitoring the company's activities in relation to a broad range of social matters such as its performance in relation to the UN Global Compact (which includes human rights principles) and the impact of the company's activities on the environment, health and safety.[58] The committee must include at least three directors, one of whom is a non-executive director not involved in the day-to-day management of the company.[59] It is empowered to draw matters that fall within its mandate to the attention of the board.[60] Apart from general monitoring, it has the right to report on matters within its mandate to the annual general meeting (AGM) of shareholders.[61]

The social and ethics committee thus is a special institutional structure that both places responsibility on certain existing directors for addressing the social obligations of business and effectively widens the pool of directors and increases their diversity.[62] Whilst innovative and promising, there are also several problems with relying on this kind of approach alone – which attends to *who* makes the decisions – as a basis to improve decision-making surrounding fundamental rights.

Firstly, the question arises as to how it would be possible for a limited number of directors to represent a range of different fundamental rights

56 See, for instance, Chayes, 1959: 41.

57 The social and ethics committee is constituted in terms of section 72 of the South African Companies Act and its functioning governed by Regulation 43 of the Companies Regulations, 2011.

58 Ibid: Regulation 43(5). Kloppers, 2013: 187 expresses disappointment about the vague remit of the Committee and lack of clarity surrounding what is expected of it. Particularly disappointing is the failure expressly to include reference to fundamental rights: see Havenga, 2015: 291.

59 Ibid: Regulation 43(4). See Kloppers, ibid: 170, who suggests this enhances transparency and is designed to counter 'corporate greenwash'.

60 Regulation 43(5)(b).

61 Regulation 43(5)(c).

62 Armour et al., 2020b: 1265–1266, similarly, propose adding independent directors to the board with expertise in 'compliance'.

concerns.[63] In Germany, for instance, workers' representatives are supposed to address the interests of a particular constituency on the board but, even there, there is no uniformity.[64] Moreover, workers' interests do not always overlap with protecting the fundamental rights of individuals or communities: some workers may seek to enhance the profitability of the company if they are promised better wages even if that causes wider environmental or social harms where they are not immediately affected.[65] Employees of Volkswagen famously were involved in its attempt to misrepresent the corporation's carbon emissions from the motor vehicles it produces.[66]

Importantly, there is no one constituency that can be identified as uniquely impacted on by corporate activities that relate to fundamental rights; rather, there is a range of different impacts on different individuals and groups. A company is not itself a legislative body which includes representatives that engage all the multiple interests in the society. It would thus be relatively absurd to expect the directors to represent all the different interests engaged by fundamental rights. Clearly, one could aim to appoint, for instance, experts in fundamental rights to boards which would be an improvement – but, even then, there is no person who is concerned about and would adequately give effect to every particular right of every stakeholder equally.

Secondly, there is a serious question concerning how the representatives of diverse stakeholders are chosen. The South African regulations require the board of directors to appoint the members of the social and ethics committee.[67] That, in turn, can allow the existing board to appoint persons who ostensibly are designed to protect other stakeholders but in fact are more concerned with the interests of certain shareholders or directors. Any appointment process by directors is likely to reflect their biases as would any such process run by shareholders.[68] The appointment by an external body such as the government would usually involve too much interference in the workings of a company. Thus, there are significant difficulties in designing

63 Nader et al., 1976: 124.

64 See the *AMCU* case, section 4.3.3.2 of chapter 4, which illustrates the conflicts that can arise between different unions claiming to represent workers' interests.

65 This is why I depart from Botha, 2017: 16–17, who appears to assume that enhancing worker participation on the social and ethics committee would lead to benefits for other stakeholders or the environment.

66 Enriques et al., 2017: 93.

67 Regulation 43(3) but see Havenga, 2015: 287–288 regarding some unfortunate ambiguity in the regulations in this regard.

68 The initial proposal in SA was to do this via the Annual General Meeting: see Draft Regulation 50(5), available at www.uct.ac.za/usr/companylaw/downloads/legislation/Companies_Regulations_%202010_draft.pdf.

an appointment process that can adequately correct for the bias towards shareholder interests.[69] Perhaps the best that can be achieved is to provide guidelines as to the kind of expertise required for appointees who represent fundamental rights concerns.[70] The appointment of a non-executive director is too weak a requirement as such a person could themselves be more sensitive to shareholder interests even if not involved in the day-to-day running of the company.[71] Moreover, if non-executive directors can easily be dismissed from their positions, there may be financial incentives, for instance, to toe the company line.

Thirdly, in South Africa, the social and ethics committee appears to operate outside the board – it is clearly a structure designed to identify the wider social impacts of corporations and draw the board's attention to such matters. Yet, there is no compulsion on the board to do anything about any report or recommendations of the committee.[72] Similarly, the committee has the significant power to report to shareholders,[73] yet again they are not required to act on the report. The idea behind these features of the committee's design appears to be to enable it to increase awareness of the social and environmental impact of a company and, through doing so, to encourage better behaviour. Yet, given its institutional placement and lack of any formal power, the structure is weak. Stronger approaches such as the 'co-determination model' in Germany do exist: yet, even there, the chairperson – who is a director appointed by shareholders – has a deciding vote:[74] shareholder primacy still remains entrenched even in this more progressive structure.[75]

Finally, one troubling aspect of the approach of expanding the range of decision-makers is that, as currently articulated, it assumes that

[69] An innovative advance, for instance, is the New York Stock Exchange requirement mandating a nominating committee made up of independent directors who must identify individuals to serve as board members: see Armour et al., 2020b: 1266.

[70] It was initially proposed that there would be a social and ethics advisory panel to advise the social and ethics committee. Criteria were developed concerning the expertise required for that panel: see Draft Regulation 50(7) (fn 68).

[71] The King IV Code, 2016 at recommended practice 70 proposes a majority of members of the committee be non-executive directors – presumably, this is meant to ensure distance from day-to-day operations and a wider perspective. Nevertheless, unless there is some specific expertise required, there is no good ground for thinking non-executive directors will necessarily be sensitive to fundamental rights: see Kloppers, 2013: 170.

[72] Botha, 2017: 15 recognises the need for more authority to be given to the committee.

[73] Kloppers, 2013: 186 sees this as the most effective tool of the committee.

[74] Section 29 Mitbestimmungsgesetz.

[75] It is though tempered and gives workers significant power: see Enriques et al., 2017: 90–91 and 105–6.

individuals are essentially tied to defending particular interests and are locked into specific identities: directors appointed by shareholders, it assumes, will be favourable towards shareholders and unlikely fairly to consider the interests of other stakeholders who will be represented by other sets of directors. There may be some truth in the existence of such structural biases: yet, at the same time, the very change required by a socio-liberal conception of the corporation is for all stakeholders to recognise and respect both the social and individualised dimension of the corporation. Directors have a fiduciary duty to act in the 'best interests of the company': if the company is conceived of as a socially embedded entity, then all directors – no matter who appoints them – must take seriously both the social and individual imperatives thereof. It is better thus not to conceive of directors as being locked into representing a particular constituency and rather encouraging a wider socially-responsible and holistic engagement from all directors. Such an approach is also important instrumentally: the fact is that even on the most extensive co-determination model discussed earlier, directors elected by shareholders will have the casting vote. Therefore, if we want the fundamental rights of individuals to be taken seriously, then it will be necessary for all directors to have to engage with these questions and not only specially appointed directors.

Having taken these drawbacks into account, it is clear that expanding the range and diversity of directors (or decision-makers more broadly) – and creating special institutional structures within the board – is not itself sufficient to correct for structural biases in favour of shareholders or for ensuring corporate decision-making takes the fundamental rights of all stakeholders seriously. Nevertheless, expanding the diversity of perspectives on the board would still be a helpful prong in a wider reform effort to ensure that decent decision-making relating to fundamental rights is embedded in the corporate structure.[76] Special institutional structures such as the social and ethics committee could provide specific fora for considered decision-making surrounding fundamental rights.[77] Such

[76] See also the proposal by Nader, 1976: 125 for there to be a variety of directors with specific oversight responsibilities and expertise (including those relating to social issues) but each still engaging with the overall success of the company.

[77] A fascinating new institutional structure driven by a massive corporation that seeks to draw in fundamental rights expertise is the Facebook Oversight Board: see https://oversightboard.com/. It has a very specific remit: to review Facebook's decisions relating to the removal of content from its social media platform based on their compatibility with the right to freedom expression and reasonable limitations thereon. Facebook has granted the Board binding powers and guarantees of independence. The multi-factoral approach

a structure could be enhanced in various ways, for instance, by requiring directors to respond to its concerns and, if they fail to do so, be potentially subject to various sanctions discussed further later in this chapter.[78] Clear evidence of engagement with the work of the committee could also provide important evidence of the degree to which they have complied with the expanded conception of fiduciary duties that I will now propose.

9.3.2 The What *Question: Directors' Fiduciary Duties and Fundamental Rights*[79]

Shareholder theory sees directors as themselves, ultimately, tasked with furthering the interests of the shareholders. Yet, directors have interests of their own which can, at times, conflict with those of the shareholders.[80] Moreover, if directors are accountable only once a year to shareholders, there is a great possibility that they may take decisions with which shareholders are unhappy but have no ability to control. When we add in the recognition that there are multiple shareholders, many problems arise concerning how to ensure directors do not only prioritise the interests of those with controlling stakes.

The very concept of the 'fiduciary duty' was developed in this context to articulate the obligations of directors and that they effectively hold the operation and management of the company in 'trust' for shareholders.[81] The fiduciary duties of directors usually include a number of components that set the standards for decision-making by directors.[82] The South African Companies Act, for instance, includes the following significant

could be helpful to the Oversight Board in helping to guide its decision-making on Facebook's obligations. The remit is currently more limited than the social and ethics committee discussed in the text and at present this is a voluntary initiative of one corporation. The fact that Facebook set it up, however, indicates the need for an independent body that can help enhance decision-making surrounding fundamental rights within corporations. This initiative could potentially be regarded as a pilot that, in time, catalyses law reform which mandates the creation of similar institutional structures across corporations (with the changes for context required by their size and capacity).

[78] Kloppers, 2013: 188 raises this as a possibility for future research. The time has come to make this a reality.

[79] This section draws on Bilchitz and Jonas, 2016. I am grateful to my co-author, Laura Ausserladscheider Jonas, for her contribution to developing these ideas on directors' duties.

[80] Armour et al., 2017b: 29–30.

[81] Berle, 1931: 1049.

[82] On the distinction between rules and standards in this context, see Armour et al., 2017b: 32–33.

fiduciary duties: directors must exercise their powers and functions 'in good faith and for a proper purpose'; they must act 'in the best interests of the company'; and they must act with the degree of skill, care and diligence that may reasonably be expected of a director in a company and who has the general knowledge, skill and experience of such a - director.[83] Similar duties are included in the corporate law of other jurisdictions.[84] These fiduciary duties are an important component of the institutional architecture of the corporation, indicating the expectations of directors. The key question in this chapter concerns in what way directors should exercise their discretion when fundamental rights are at stake and, in particular, whose interests they are required to take into account: is it, for instance, only the shareholders who should be the focus of attention or do other stakeholders also matter when discharging their duties?

In many parts of the world, corporate law has enshrined the approach that directors have duties to manage the corporation in the interests of shareholders.[85] This view flows from the libertarian conception of the corporation as an entity whose objective is ultimately to maximise economic value for shareholders. Friedman, for instance, argues that corporations do not have any wider social responsibility than the self-interested pursuit of profit: it is only individuals and the state that have such broader responsibilities.[86] Directors indeed may not use corporate funds to advance social responsibility projects and to do so is in fact a violation of their duties to shareholders.[87]

This theory has the benefit of relative simplicity: it is, supposedly, clear to whom the directors owe their duties and how their performance is to be measured.[88] The judgement about maximising shareholder value is

[83] These duties are outlined in section 76(3) of the Companies Act and partially codified previous common law duties.

[84] See, for instance, sections 170–177 of the UK Companies Act, 2005, and sections 180–184 of the Australian Corporations Act, 2001.

[85] Berle, 1931: 1074; Keay, 2007: 577–578; Armour et al., 2017a: 23. For a defence and strong attack on the alternative stakeholder approach, see Bebchuk and Tallarita, 2020 – this chapter and book offers responses to many of their critiques at least in relation to circumstances where the fundamental rights of a wider group of stakeholders are at issue.

[86] Friedman, 1970: 52 and 55 – he does qualify this statement by recognising they must do so within the confines of the law and ethical custom which opens the door to a minimal set of social obligations.

[87] Ibid: 52. See, famously, also *Dodge* v. *Ford Motor Co.* 170 N.W. 668 (Mich. 1919) 684.

[88] Jensen, 2001: 300–301 writes that it enables firms to have a 'single-valued objective'.

not an easy one in itself,[89] but it has the benefit of focusing the minds of directors on only one constituency within a corporation. The theory though is clearly inadequate once we recognise that corporations have obligations in relation to fundamental rights and their very purpose involves creating social benefits.

To understand why, it is important to consider certain key features of fundamental rights, many of which have already been discussed in Chapter 2. Fundamental rights, as we saw, constitute protections for the fundamental interests of individuals which are deeply connected to the recognition of their inherent dignity. Those rights place obligations on all actors – including non-state actors – who have the capacity to affect them. Since fundamental rights and the obligations they impose have a weighted normative priority over other matters, other branches of law – such as corporate law – must be harmonised with these important entitlements. The corporation cannot be understood as some exceptional entity that does not have to consider fundamental rights; rather, it is itself subject to duties that are derived from fundamental rights, and its activities must take place within the constraints imposed by them.

This reasoning has important implications too for the duties of directors. If corporations are themselves bound by fundamental rights, then directors are required to ensure that they comply with their obligations in this regard. Whilst directors must be responsive to shareholders, they must also consider all those whose fundamental rights may be affected by their decisions. The list of such individuals would include employees, customers, investors, suppliers, members of local communities and even distant persons.[90] As such, legal systems that accept the importance of fundamental rights must of necessity place duties on directors which move beyond a focus on shareholders alone.

This reasoning also flows from the socio-liberal conception of the corporation. Once we acknowledge that the corporation is itself set up to achieve social benefits, it is no longer possible to view directors as simply acting to advance the economic interests of shareholders. They

[89] For a detailed engagement, see Keay, 2011: 61–109.

[90] Some jurisdictions (such as the United Kingdom in section 172 of the Companies Act, 2006) expressly recognise duties upon directors to consider the interests of many of these groupings (as part of their duty to promote the success of the company) though, as yet, none expressly addresses fundamental rights. A positive step towards expressly including fundamental rights was the introduction of section 414C of the above-mentioned Companies Act which requires directors to prepare strategic reports which, in the case of quoted companies, must include information about social, community and human rights issues.

also need to ensure the corporation meets its social obligations, the most important of which relate to fundamental rights.

The interesting question is how far this reasoning takes us. In recent years, two alternative approaches to directors' duties have developed. The first is termed the 'enlightened shareholder value' approach ('the ESV approach'), and the second the 'stakeholder' approach ('the ST approach'). The former approach retains a focus on achieving maximum benefits for shareholders but considers what will be in the long-term best interests of an enlightened shareholder. As such, it requires decision-making by directors not only to focus on short-term financial results but also to take into account the importance of building longer-term relationships.[91] This can involve 'striking a balance between the competing interests of different stakeholders in order to benefit the shareholders in the long run'.[92] This approach ultimately adopts a more expansive vision as to what constitutes the interests of shareholders, accepting that 'we cannot maximise the long-term market value of an organisation if we ignore or mistreat any important constituency. We cannot create value without good relations with customers, employees, financial backers, suppliers, regulators, communities, and so on'.[93]

The ST approach, on the other hand, adopts a different approach to corporate decision-making (and the corporation itself). 'The primary responsibility of the executive is to create as much value as possible for stakeholders.'[94] A stakeholder is defined as 'any group or individual who can affect or is affected by the achievement of the organisation's objectives'.[95] In less academic parlance, it has come to mean 'all parties that have an interest, financial or otherwise, in a company'.[96] The main stakeholders of a corporation are usually taken to include at least

[91] Keay, 2007: 590. The tendency to short-term thinking by directors is a wider problem also affecting the long-term performance of corporations: the nature and the scope of the problem as well as certain recommendations are made in the 'Kay Review of UK Equity Markets and Long-term Decision-making'.

[92] Armour, Deakin and Konzelmann, 2003: 537. Section 172 of the United Kingdom's 2006 Companies Act is an exemplification of this approach: it requires that directors reference the interests of other *stakeholders* in understanding what constitutes the best interests of *shareholders*: see Keay, 2013: 85ff.

[93] Jensen, 2001: 309.

[94] Freeman et al., 2010: 28.

[95] Freeman, 2010: 46.

[96] See the definition of 'stakeholder' at 'The Economist A-Z Terms' (available at www.economist.com/economics-a-to-z/s#node-21529358).

employees, shareholders, suppliers, consumers and the local community.[97] In making decisions relating to the corporation, on this view then, directors must consider all stakeholders and seek to balance their interests.[98]

Both the ESV and ST approaches increase the range of stakeholders whom directors must consider when deliberating about and performing their duties. However, they differ on the manner in which the interests of non-shareholders are to be considered. In the ESV approach, the interests of non-shareholders are always to be evaluated in relation to the best interests of shareholders. As such, their interests are always considered in an instrumental or subordinate way, as a means to the best realisation of the shareholders' ends. The problem is that, in so doing, the ESV approach clashes profoundly with a key feature of fundamental rights that flows from their normative foundations.[99]

The dignity of individuals which is at the foundation of fundamental rights is understood to imply that individuals and their interests cannot simply be conceptualised as mere instruments for others' ends: the worth of individuals implies that they are intrinsically valuable and are deserving of consideration in their own right.[100] This idea may be grounded in diverse ethical theories[101] but is most often traced to the philosophy of Immanuel Kant, who, in his second formulation of the categorical imperative, wrote that one must act in such a way as to treat 'humanity, whether in your own person or in that of anyone else, always as an end and never merely as a means'.[102] Thomas Hill Jr, in elucidating this principle, contends that Kant here requires respect for the rationality of individuals and their power to set their own goals.[103] For Kant, these characteristics were central to having dignity and 'whatever has dignity has value, independently of any effects, profit or advantage which it might produce'.[104]

[97] Freeman et al., 2010: 24–26, who recognise though that there are other stakeholders beyond this group too.

[98] Hansmann, and Kraakman, 2000: 447.

[99] It also assumes alignment between the fundamental rights of individuals and the long-term interests of investors, which is far from clear: see Enriques et al., 2017: 94.

[100] See for instance, the South African Constitutional Court's statement in *S* v. *Dodo* [2001] ZACC 16 para 38 that '[h]uman beings are not commodities to which a price can be attached; they are creatures with inherent and infinite worth; they ought to be treated as ends in themselves, never merely as means to an end'.

[101] For a utilitarian grounding for fundamental rights, see Sumner, 1989.

[102] Kant, 2017: 29.

[103] Hill, 1980: 85–86. See also in this regard O'Neill, 1989: 137–140; Wood, 1999: 119.

[104] Hill, ibid: 91.

If we accept this reasoning, then the interests protected by fundamental rights must not function as reasons for directors in making their decisions only because they serve shareholder interests but precisely because they are reasons that have an independent standing and importance for the individuals concerned.[105] The ESV approach is therefore in direct conflict with this crucial feature of fundamental rights and must therefore be rejected in any system that recognises such rights as foundational, binding normative commitments on the legal system. This is not to deny that the ESV approach may improve outcomes for non-shareholders in certain instances; however, a legal system that takes fundamental rights seriously should not enshrine in its basic doctrines of corporate law – and the consequent corporate culture that the regulatory framework generates – an approach that directly contradicts the conception of individual dignity and value that these rights entail.[106] In light of the reflexive approach outlined earlier, that would also encourage the wrong sort of self-regulation by the corporate entity itself. It is plausible to contend that an instrumental approach to other stakeholders (which characterises the ESV approach) would influence not only their deliberative practices but also their ultimate actions.

The significant conclusion of this section is that both the shareholder value approach and the ESV approach to directors' duties must be rejected in legal systems with fundamental rights at their heart. The fundamental rights and interests of individual stakeholders are to be treated as independent ends (or reasons) that must be considered to be worthy of respect in their own right.[107] The ST approach accepts this insight as it requires directors to consider all stakeholders in the corporation as having independently valuable interests which must be balanced against one another.[108] This approach accepts that normative complexity

[105] See Korsgaard, 2009: 201–202. To put this more strongly in Kantian terms, each agent must be treated with respect for their agency rather than simply being considered as a means to achieve the subjective ends of corporate decision-makers.

[106] Muchlinski, 2012: 166 encapsulates the thrust of the model when he writes that it 'can allow for some room to make human rights oriented decisions provided that they do not weaken the success of the company'. The ESV approach is flawed not only because it encourages the wrong motivation amongst directors towards the interests of stakeholders other than shareholders but also because it mandates in its very conceptual underpinnings a particular deliberative process which is in conflict with the normative foundations of fundamental rights. As such, it would also not be conducive to developing a rights-respecting corporate culture.

[107] See Cassim, 2012: 520.

[108] Muchlinski, 2012: 165. For a defence that this is rational, see Rogge, 2020. I only here consider the ST approach in so far as it impacts on fundamental rights though the

and the weighing of independently valuable reasons cannot be avoided and are a central feature of decision-making in business.[109]

In general, rendering the corporate law surrounding directors' duties consistent with fundamental rights will require reform in almost all countries. The most far-reaching provision in conceptualising directors' duties differently has been enshrined in the Indian Companies Act of 2013.[110] Section 166(2) states as follows:

> A director of a company shall act in good faith in order to promote the objects of the company for the direct benefit of its members as a whole, and in the best interests of the company, its employees, the shareholders, the community and for the protection of the environment.[111]

This provision does not just focus upon the benefits accruing to members but also engages the best interests of a wide range of stakeholders. The language prima facie suggests that the interests of a wider set of stakeholders matter in their own right and appears to conform with the ST approach.[112] Yet, there still remain several criticisms that can be made of the Indian provision from a fundamental rights point of view.

Firstly, there is no express mention of fundamental rights. Given their normative priority, their inclusion should not be left in doubt; nor should they be regarded simply as one factor to be taken into account amongst others. Secondly, the Indian provision still separates out shareholders from other stakeholders, once again allowing for an interpretation that primacy is to be accorded to 'members'. Finally, it is necessary to consider the provision not simply on its face but also its relation to other components of corporate law and, in particular, how it is to be enforced. In this respect, Naniwadekar and Varottil argue that the Indian provision has in essence functioned very similarly to the ESV approach (which has been utilised in the United Kingdom).[113] Despite adopting a different approach on its face, the Indian legislature has failed to consider properly how to give this far-reaching fiduciary duty institutional legs. These authors highlight a clear

reasoning might be developed to support a wider ST approach to directors' duties. Bilchitz and Jonas, 2016 propose proportionality as the reasoning process through which the interests of different stakeholders should be balanced though the seven-step test proposed in this book would be better when dealing with positive obligations.

109 Rogge, 2020: 65.

110 There has also recently been a proposal by the EU to adopt a stakeholder approach to directors' duties: see Directors' Duties Study, 2020: 73.

111 Indian Companies Act, 2013.

112 Naniwadekar and Varottil, 2016: 102.

113 Ibid: 113.

enforcement gap: the lack of corresponding remedies that enable a wider group of stakeholders to hold directors to account. The class action remedies envisaged in the Companies Act only apply to shareholders and the derivative action remains a basis for shareholders to hold directors to account for harming their own interests.[114]

This discussion of the Indian provision thus suggests that part of the remedy for these defects requires imposing a *specific* and clear fiduciary duty on directors relating to fundamental rights. The recognition of such a duty would give fundamental rights the normative priority they deserve and enable directors to do so in their decision-making even where that may reduce the profits of the company. Such a duty could be formulated along the lines of the following proposal: 'A director of a corporation has a fiduciary duty to consider the impact of the corporation on the fundamental rights of all stakeholders, to exercise demonstrably reasonable care, skill and diligence in reaching judgements about the substantive content of corporate obligations in relation to fundamental rights, and to take all necessary action to ensure compliance with those obligations.'

The formulation of this duty, in some sense, tracks what would be required of a company through the human rights due diligence processes required by the UNGPs but seeks to correct for the serious normative gap thereof (discussed in Chapters 5 and 10). The various elements of the UNGPs – suitably complemented by the proposals I make in Chapter 10 – could also provide some guidance as to what is required of directors. For instance, in discharging their fiduciary duty, it would be useful if directors engaged meaningfully with potentially affected groups.[115] At the same time, importantly, the specific fiduciary duty I propose would become a personal requirement for each director rather than simply a collective responsibility.[116] That, in turn, would encourage the integration of fundamental rights considerations into all business decisions.[117] The multi-factoral approach could help guide directors' decision-making in this area. Failure to perform the duty diligently should open up the possibility of personal liability for breaches thereof. In the next section, I turn to consider some of the options for the accountability of directors and ensuring they meet their obligations in relation to fundamental rights.

[114] Ibid: 108–110.

[115] UNGPs: GP 18(b).

[116] Muchlinski, 2012: 161.

[117] That could include across corporate groups and supply chains, an issue, as mentioned, I do not focus on in this book though of much importance.

9.3.3 *Expanding the Forms of Accountability of Directors*

Once we recognise that directors have a fiduciary duty relating to fundamental rights as proposed, the question arises as to how to ensure they, in good faith, take their responsibilities in this regard seriously and make as optimal decisions as they can. Accountability can occur in multiple ways and, as was discussed in relation to the 'responsive' and 'integrated' regulatory approaches, there is an increasing scale of intensity that can be developed in this regard. Firstly, there are incentive-based structures that can be created that provide a degree of scrutiny over corporate activities and offer benefits for participating therein. Secondly, there can be a range of legal requirements – which are perhaps the least intensive regulatory measures in this area – that can require directors to disclose their decisions, and the information upon which they were based. A more onerous requirement would be to mandate the disclosure of the reasons for their decisions. Thirdly, there could be allowance made for challenging the decision of the director (either internally or to an external body). Finally, there are a range of penalties that could be considered for the failure to perform these duties adequately: these could include penalties for the company or director, personal liability for the director, removal of the director and disqualification from serving in future as a director.[118] Whilst there are a range of other innovative possibilities currently being proposed,[119] in the ensuing discussion, I will focus on two aspects that relate to the very architecture of corporate law: disclosure requirements and actions for victims of rights violations against directors. These possibilities draw, in the main, on already existing mechanisms in corporate law but extend them to embrace other stakeholders.[120]

[118] I have here sought to simplify the range of alternatives. Armour et al., 2017b: 31–45 relatedly identify a number of strategies that can be used in the law to limit agency costs.

[119] The discussion is not meant to be exhaustive and is open to other novel reforms. See, for instance, the proposal by Armour et al., 2020a: 50–52 for possible reductions in directors' share earnings for failures of 'compliance'.

[120] Given the limits of one chapter, I cannot engage in detail with all the approaches involved here but essentially provide illustrations of initiatives and provisions that lie along this scale of intensity. I, unfortunately, could not include a detailed engagement with the corporate governance codes that exist, for instance, in the United Kingdom and South Africa. They have also increasingly included requirements to explain how the board of directors has taken into account the impact of corporate activities on a wider set of stakeholders (for instance, UK Code: Part 1, Provision 5 at 5; SA code, Principle 16 at 71). In the case of South Africa, the code expressly includes reference to being a good corporate citizen and complying with the Bill of Rights (Principle 3, Practice 12 at 45).

9.3.3.1 Disclosure Requirements

In order to ensure a minimum level of accountability for decision-making, the most basic legal requirement is the need to disclose the decision that was made.[121] Of course, a decision can – to an extent – be inferred from the actions or behaviour of a corporation and the consequences it brings about. Yet, a crucial dimension in accountability is a 'publicity' requirement: knowing that the decision one makes will be publicised.

In addition to publicising a decision, enhanced accountability – in particular, for fulfilling the fiduciary duty proposed earlier relating to fundamental rights – would also require disclosure of the information utilised in making a decision and, potentially, the reasons for the decision. This would clearly be justifiable where fundamental rights are at stake, which involve important interests with a high degree of normative strength. A requirement to disclose reasons need not be overly onerous but simply entails outlining the key justifications for a decision concerning corporate obligations – the analytical framework proposed in this book could assist in identifying the main factors that would need to be engaged as well as the structure of any balancing process. That would allow for public accountability and also for further challenges in terms of the harder procedures discussed in more detail later. Thus, a requirement should be added to company law that where the directors make a decision that has a material impact on fundamental rights,[122] they must provide reasons that explain their understanding of the content of corporate obligations in this area and why their decision complies with those obligations. They should also be required to disclose the information upon which such a judgement is based.[123]

General company law already includes disclosure requirements relating to the economic performance of the corporation.[124] Each year companies are required to produce annual reports which are lodged with a registrar of companies.[125] More recently, there have been attempts to impose non-financial reporting requirements and to use disclosure

[121] Armour et al., 2017b: 38.

[122] To avoid such a requirement being too onerous, the focus of reporting should be on material impacts.

[123] In a sense, this allows for the development of what may be termed 'corporate case law', which can be used to guide similar cases that arise in future: see Ayers and Braithwaite, 1992: 129–131.

[124] Taylor, 2015: 202.

[125] In the United Kingdom, see for instance, section 441 of the Companies Act 2006; in South Africa, see section 33 of the Companies Act of 2008.

obligations to try and improve the behaviour of corporations towards stakeholders more generally.[126]

The United Kingdom, for instance, in 2013 introduced a requirement for companies over a certain size to produce a 'strategic report'. The strategic report is designed to 'inform members of the company and help them assess how the directors have performed their duty under section 172 (duty to promote the success of the company)'.[127] In relation to a company listed on a stock exchange, the report must contain information about its impact on the environment and relevant social, community and human rights issues.[128] Two provisos though are included: the first is that the disclosure of this non-financial information is required only 'to the extent necessary for an understanding of the development, performance and position of the company's business'.[129] The second proviso allows nothing to be disclosed if, in the opinion of the directors, it would be 'seriously prejudicial to the interests of the company'.[130] The strategic report must be approved by the board of directors.[131]

A requirement that has been added since 2017[132] is that the directors of large companies must issue a statement which indicates how, in the performance of their fiduciary duties, they have taken into account the specific matters required by the Companies Act which include the company's impact on wider stakeholders.[133] Certain non-listed larger companies are also required to issue a non-financial information statement. Such a statement must include, at a minimum, information relating to the impact of company activities on the environment, employees, social matters, respect for human rights and anti-corruption matters.[134] If the company does not pursue policies in relation to the above-mentioned categories of non-financial issues, it must explain why not.[135] The new provisions though retain two similar provisos (discussed in relation to

[126] Enriques et al., 2017: 94–95; Taylor, 2015: 202. The EU has, for instance, issued directive 2014/95/EU requiring large companies to provide a range of social and environmental disclosures.

[127] Section 414C (1) of the UK Companies Act, 2006.

[128] Section 414C(7).

[129] Ibid.

[130] Section 414C(14).

[131] Section 414D(1).

[132] These provisions were passed in order to comply with the EU Directive on non-financial information: see www.frc.org.uk/getattachment/3dfe0ac6-ac6d-41a0-91bf-df98cbba0ad6/Non-Financial-Reporting-Factsheet-Final.pdf.

[133] Section 414CZA.

[134] Section 414CB(1).

[135] Section 414CB(4).

the strategic report) that limit the circumstances in which disclosures are required.[136]

The Companies Act also requires the circulation of these reports to all members of the company.[137] In addition to this, for listed companies, the annual reports including the strategic report mentioned earlier must be available on the website.[138] For companies that must provide a non-financial information statement, it must also be available on the internet.[139] For each financial year, both quoted and unquoted companies must file their annual reports with the registrar of companies which include the strategic reports.[140]

The UK corporate law regime thus, importantly, imposes obligations upon corporations – upon the pain of financial penalties and committing a crime – to report on non-financial matters and, significantly, the impact of a company's activities on fundamental rights.[141] These disclosure obligations are essentially focused upon transparency and demonstrating the awareness corporations have of their impacts on fundamental rights and concomitant obligations. The regime requires companies to apply their minds to specific non-financial issues (including fundamental rights expressly) and thus could be understood to influence internal deliberations within a company and to encourage it to internalise its commitment to such rights. It also ensures that the non-financial statements and strategic report are widely accessible, which can contribute to public pressure on the corporation to improve its behaviour where that is found wanting.[142]

The regime has much to commend it but a number of weaknesses remain – I shall consider each in turn and the possibilities for reform. Firstly, the duties to report are very widely formulated and there is no clarity about exactly what must be reported on in relation to fundamental rights. Secondly, the provisos are particularly problematic. As with the

136 Ibid. and Section 414CB(9).
137 Section 423.
138 Section 430.
139 Section 426(B).
140 Section 441.
141 In relation to a narrower and extreme set of fundamental rights violations, the Modern Slavery Act of 2015 follows this approach and requires in section 45(1) an additional annual slavery and human trafficking statement to be provided by large corporations. The statement details the measures taken by a large corporation to ensure slavery and human trafficking are not taking place within its supply chains. Corporations must also publicise the statement on their website (section 54(7)).
142 Simons and Macklin, 2014: 212.

directors' duties, it appears that fundamental rights and other non-financial matters (in the strategic report) are included in a rather instrumental way, as being relevant to report only in so far as they relate to the company's general business activities. Thus, for instance, if protests by a local community are hampering a mining operation, then that would be a relevant matter to report; yet, if the same company pollutes a river but doing so has no impact on its operations, then it would not be necessary to disclose this environmentally-damaging activity. Once again, this approach suggests a priority for business considerations and fails to acknowledge the intrinsic value of individuals and the normative importance of fundamental rights. Furthermore, the second proviso that the company need not report on matters that, in the opinion of the directors, could harm the commercial interests of the company fundamentally undermines the wider non-financial reporting provisions and provides an escape clause for companies to avoid reporting matters that could harm the company's reputation. That significantly reduces the benefits of this disclosure regime.[143]

Clearly to render the current disclosure requirements meaningful, these provisos should be repealed and the reporting on fundamental rights issues be required irrespective of its effect on corporate activities or interests.[144] Even so, the general disclosure provisions relating to fundamental rights are too vague and the argument of this book is helpful in directing how such legal reporting requirements should be reformed. It is suggested firstly that corporations should be required to identify the main areas in which they impact upon specific rights. If they infringe any rights but regard such an infringement as acceptable, then they need to provide an explanation as to their reasoning concerning their obligations (which should broadly draw on the factors identified together with the proportionality enquiry I have outlined in Chapter 7). In determining their positive obligations and whether they fail to meet them, they also need to provide an explanation of their reasoning for not doing so (which should also draw on the factors and utilise the seven-step test I have outlined). Through transparently outlining the reasoning process

[143] Ibid: 216.

[144] I also believe the limitation of such reporting only to large companies should be removed. Whilst the content and stringency of the reports should vary with the size of the company, all companies, no matter their size, should be required to provide some non-financial reporting about their impact on fundamental rights and wider social and environmental matters.

involved in decision-making, it will also be rendered easier for external bodies to evaluate any company's approach to these matters.

A third major weakness of the UK regime is the fact that there are very limited external checks or reviews of what has been stated in the strategic reports. Auditors are required to state whether the information in these reports is consistent with the financial statements, is prepared in accordance with applicable legal requirements and contains any material misstatements.[145] The first two of these requirements do not engage in detail with the substance of the report, whilst the third alone engages with its content. The criterion itself, however, is relatively unclear and there is an important question of interpretation as to what constitutes a material misstatement in this sphere. The major question that arises concerns what kind of verification activities auditors must undertake to provide such an assurance. The training of auditors has generally focused upon financial matters, and it is unclear that they are well-suited to provide the verification of non-financial reporting.[146] Addressing this problem will involve improving their training surrounding fundamental rights. That, in turn, will need to allay concerns that auditing will distort corporate behaviour in this area by focusing on compliance with measurable standards that may not be appropriate when dealing with the complex issues that arise surrounding fundamental rights.[147] The duty on auditors it seems needs adaptation to address social concerns: for instance, the verification of non-financial reporting would be better expressed as requiring auditors to ascertain whether the strategic report provides a 'true and fair view' of the impacts of the corporation on fundamental rights and its obligations. That, in turn, could also encourage a dialogical process between the auditors and corporate decision-makers, thus deepening the engagement surrounding fundamental rights obligations.

Once submitted to the registrar of companies, there is also the further question as to what is done with these reports by the relevant authorities. There does not seem to be a process whereby there is any engagement in detail with the contents of the strategic report by the regulatory authorities. The focus seems to be upon reflexive regulation which seeks to encourage thinking within corporations surrounding their impact on

[145] See Financial Reporting Council 'Guidance on the Strategic Report' (July 2018) available at www.frc.org.uk/getattachment/fb05dd7b-c76c-424e-9daf-4293c9fa2d6a/Guidance-on-the-Strategic-Report-31-7-18.pdf at para 3.7.

[146] See Sarfaty, 2013: 610–611.

[147] See Sarfaty, ibid: 613–614; Sinkovics et al., 2016.

fundamental rights, the wider society and the environment. The regime appears to be based on the notion that disclosure will lead to market consequences for poor performance, which may or may not eventuate.[148] Regulatory authorities, arguably, also need to develop the capacity to engage in a review of the non-financial reports submitted. To avoid such a duty becoming overly burdensome, this need not be done every year for each company but could be staggered over time: the mere knowledge that the report may be reviewed could encourage a greater seriousness about its contents and generate better and more detailed reasoning relating to fundamental rights matters.[149]

Another example of a disclosures regime that relates specifically to concerns about fundamental rights violations is that which was instituted pursuant to section 1502 of the Dodd-Frank Act in the United States. The provisions and related regulations[150] require reporting relating to the provenance of conflict minerals that are derived from the Democratic Republic of the Congo (DRC). Importantly, as in the United Kingdom, the obligations placed on corporations are all informational: they relate to whether conflict minerals were used and to conducting due diligence enquiries about the source of the minerals. There are, however, no direct obligations upon the corporation to take specific actions to avoid using conflict minerals. The idea, common to such provisions, appears to be that by making companies aware of the source of their minerals and forcing them to disclose these to the public, market forces will place pressure on them to change their behaviour and avoid using conflict minerals that finance fundamental rights violations by armed groups.[151]

The Dodd-Frank Act does indeed appear to have been effective in impacting on the corporate willingness to utilise minerals sourced in the DRC.[152] Yet, it also highlights a serious problem with focusing on

[148] See Dhir, 2009: 62.

[149] The lodging of this information and rendering of it public, of course, does allow the report to be challenged by victims of fundamental rights violations and non-governmental organisations which can seek to show that the reporting is not accurate. That, in turn, could place some risk on the directors who could be liable for criminal convictions and penalties in terms of section 414D of the Act.

[150] Securities and Exchange Commission Release 34-67716 available at www.sec.gov/rules/final/2012/34-67716.pdf.

[151] Taylor, 2015: 208. See also Jägers, 2013: 306 on the importance of access to information in influencing corporate behaviour.

[152] See, for instance, Bafilemba et al., 2014: 8 and Matthysen and Zaragoza Montejano, 2013: 35, who indicate that many companies have stopped utilising minerals from the DRC. These authors differ on the social impact of their having done so.

disclosures alone: namely, that disclosures in and of themselves provide no guidance about what corporations must do after they have discovered the information that they are utilising conflict minerals. The most natural response is simply to desist from buying all minerals in the DRC and procure them elsewhere (where that is possible). Yet, that very response may actually harm the fundamental rights of individuals through removing a significant source of their livelihoods from mining activities.[153] It may also remove a significant source of pressure to end the conflict and prevent the use of minerals for the financing of war. This is precisely why an approach simply based on duties to avoid harm is not adequate: rather, there is a need to balance both the negative and positive obligations of corporations. In so doing, the corporation may need to continue to use minerals from the DRC and take strong steps to ensure they do not contribute towards financing armed groups. Thus, disclosure alone is a blunt tool and fails to indicate what the wider obligations of corporations are in relation to fundamental rights.

I have outlined thus far the power and limitations of disclosure requirements. They can and should be strengthened and the human rights due diligence approach discussed in the next chapter partially seeks to do so. Yet, ultimately, whilst they can encourage better decision-making, if matters stop at disclosure, directors may simply decide that the economic benefits for failing to comply with their fundamental rights obligations outweigh the negative reputational harms. To encourage decision-making by directors respectful of fundamental rights, there must, therefore, be strong consequences for failing to make good decisions and exercise their judgement adequately – that is the subject of the next section.

9.3.3.2 Legal Actions against Directors in Their Personal Capacity

As was mentioned earlier, making decisions in relation to the obligations of the corporation in relation to fundamental rights should be seen to be part of the fiduciary duties of directors. The director must consider the interests of all stakeholders in their own right and also exercise the degree of skill, care and diligence required by someone assuming this office.[154]

[153] See Matthysen and Zaragoza Montejano, ibid: 35 (who detail how this can also fuel desperation and so perpetuate conflict) and Simons and Macklin, 2014: 222.

[154] It is recognised that directors may lack expertise on fundamental rights. This can be addressed through training but also may be taken into account by courts when adjudicating on their culpability.

A failure to do so can be seen therefore to be a breach of their fiduciary duties. Company law and tort law already have a number of remedies for such breaches though the focus in the past has largely been on shareholders: the question is thus how to extend such accountability measures to all stakeholders.

Some studies show a very limited enforcement of directors' duties by shareholders, with very few directors ultimately being held personally liable for their decisions or facing out-of-pocket payments.[155] This raises the question of whether focusing on expanding the enforcement of fiduciary duties to a wider set of stakeholders can in fact make a difference to corporate decision-making. Whilst the studies support the need to utilise a suite of measures to hold directors to account for their decisions, I believe there are at least three reasons why it remains important to expand the possibilities for enforcing fiduciary duties to stakeholders – and, particularly, ensuring wider accountability for the specific fiduciary duty I have defended in relation to fundamental rights.

Firstly, it is vital that the institutional structure of the corporation be set up in such a way that indicates the key expectations of directors in respect of fundamental rights and provides for sanctions where they are not met. This is not only symbolically valuable but doing so helps to harmonise corporate law with fundamental rights, the most foundational legal commitments of decent societies. Secondly, wider fiduciary duties and enforcement actions have serious practical consequences: they always open up the possibility of liability for directors and will, at least to an extent, function as a deterrent. As such, they contribute to preventing fundamental rights violations before they occur. Finally, the studies on the enforcement of directors' duties relate mainly to breaches of their obligations to shareholders who may have limited incentives to bring such actions and have other modes of redress.[156] Mechanisms – such as those proposed later in this section – which allow external parties who are victims of rights violations to sue directors in their personal capacity have, in the main, not existed. The empirical studies are thus not clearly apposite to determining the uptake such actions would have by a wider set of stakeholders. The growth of litigation against companies in relation to the Alien Tort Claims Act in the United States (before it was

[155] See Armour et al., 2009: 696–701 (UK) and 701–710 (USA).

[156] See ibid: 692, who focus on the role of private enforcement in 'robust stock markets with dispersed share ownership'. They also indicate in relation to the United Kingdom that stronger shareholder governance rights enable shareholders to protect themselves without having to file suits (at 721).

eviscerated by the Supreme Court) provides an optimistic outlook that these new actions may well be utilised by victims of rights violations (and supporting NGOs) and not simply be idle threats. As such, they would constitute a deterrent for directors and encourage them to take their obligations in relation to fundamental rights seriously.

I now turn to consider possible enforcement actions. For any of these to be effective, of course, it is necessary to point out at the outset that the law clearly should exclude the possibility of any insurance being taken out by directors to cover the costs of any claims against them for breach of their fiduciary duty relating to fundamental rights.

The first key possibility concerns the ability to bring actions against directors in their personal capacity for the losses caused by their failure to exercise their fiduciary responsibilities properly. Section 77(2)(a) of the South African Companies Act provides such an example: it states that the director of a company may be held liable 'in accordance with the principles of the common law relating to breach of a fiduciary duty, for any loss, damages, or costs sustained by the company as a consequence of any breach by the director' of their fiduciary duties. A crucial aspect of this provision is the fact that it applies only to 'losses, damages or costs *sustained by the company*'. The question thus arises as to how this action could be adapted to hold directors to account for their decisions in relation to the fundamental rights of individuals. In principle, it seems possible for an individual or community whose rights are violated to sue the company in question for damages. If the company is ordered to pay such damages, that would constitute a loss to the company. If the loss results from a breach of the directors' fiduciary duties, then they could be sued to pay for this loss. Theoretically, thus, an action for the breach of fiduciary duties could impose liability on directors for harms caused to fundamental rights through their negligent decisions. Yet, there are a number of problems – both legal and practical – why this indirect approach to the personal liability of directors is unlikely to result in real accountability.

The first practical problem relates to the difficulty for victims of fundamental rights violations successfully to claim damages from a company. If directors see that they may be personally liable, they will use company resources to defend themselves. Given the usual asymmetry in financial resources between companies and victims of human rights violations, these actions will often not succeed and thus allow directors to escape liability. The pattern of unsuccessful damages claims arising from the Alien Tort Claims Act in the United States does not portend well for such actions.[157]

Secondly, it may be that the fundamental rights violation led to a damages award, but it also may have had commercial advantages for the company. It may thus be difficult when suing a director to show an overall loss to the company through the decision. Thirdly, there is also a problem concerning who would claim damages from the director(s): if the shareholders, for instance, were satisfied overall by the performance of the company, they may have little incentive to claim damages from the directors in their personal capacity. Employees may well be affected by losses to the company and might perhaps sue directors in some cases in this regard. However, individuals whose rights are violated but are not connected in any other way to the company would struggle to make out a case for why they should be allowed to sue to recoup the *company's own losses* from the directors. For the personal liability of directors to be effective, it will usually be necessary for one of the stakeholders with a direct stake in the company's losses to sue the directors for those losses. That would require a common cause between that stakeholder group and the individual or community who has been harmed due to the fundamental rights violation. It is not clear that there will always be such a connection: employees – perhaps the most likely group to have common cause with the affected individuals or communities – may themselves, for instance, have a different set of interests and so not be a reliable partner to claim for harms other than to their own fundamental rights.

A similar point can be made about the utility of the derivative action for addressing the harm to individuals or communities caused by a failure to fulfil fundamental rights obligations. In essence, it is an action that allows a person with an interest in the company to sue – on behalf of the company – for losses caused to the company. The need for the action arose as a result of situations where directors, for instance, collude with the majority shareholders to cause losses to the company for their own personal enrichment. Thus, Dine gives the example of a director who sells land to a company that is worth GBP 10,000. The company buys it for GBP 20,000. The director and majority shareholders pass a resolution that the company should not take any action to have the excess amount paid back to the company. In these circumstances, the minority

[157] Choudhury, 2005: 44 writes that 'no case concerning corporations has been determined on its merits' under ATCA. The situation has only become worse with the Supreme Court effectively closing this route with its judgment in *Jesner* v. *Arab Bank*.

shareholders see the value of the company and their shares diminished for no good reason with the directors clearly not acting in the best interests of the company.[158] The derivative action allows those minority shareholders to sue on behalf of the company for losses to the company. There are though a range of requirements for someone to be allowed to step in and sue for losses to the company.[159]

The question for our purposes is not a detailed analysis of this remedy but whether it can assist in creating accountability for harms to the fundamental rights of individual stakeholders. In some jurisdictions, the derivative action has been extended to a wider group of stakeholders. Thus, in South Africa, in addition to shareholders and directors, a registered trade union that represents employees of the company or a representative of such employees may institute legal proceedings to protect 'the legal interests of the company'.[160] In Canada, the provision appears to be wider and allows any 'complainant' to bring such an action provided it is in the interests of the corporation.[161] It is thus potentially possible for a wider group of stakeholders to be able to bring the derivative action.

Yet, there are several problems in rendering this remedy effective, which are similar to those discussed earlier in relation to personal actions against directors. Usually, there is a requirement that leave be granted to the stakeholder to intervene on behalf of the company. Satisfying this requirement may prove difficult for victims of fundamental rights violations who are unrelated to the company who must argue that they are acting in the best interests of the company itself. Furthermore, perhaps the biggest hurdle is that the derivative action is designed to address losses to the company itself and so raises all the problems of the indirect approach addressed earlier. The usual remedy would be, for instance, for the company to claim back money from the truant director for losses it incurred but this action is not designed to remediate individuals directly for their losses. In relation to fundamental rights matters, losses to the company are also likely to be seen in terms such as loss of reputation, which often will be difficult to quantify. Given the difficulties of bringing such an action for stakeholders outside the direct ambit of the company,

[158] Dine and Koutsias, 2005: 250.
[159] On the UK law, see Armour, 2019: 420–422.
[160] Section 165(2)(c) of the South African Companies Act, 2008.
[161] Section 239(1) and (2) of the Canadian Business Corporations Act of 1985. See also the analysis of Keay, 2013: 261–263.

it is unlikely that such an action will be able to hold directors to account adequately for their decision-making in relation to fundamental rights.

As we have seen, there are conceptual and practical problems with the remedies discussed for victims of fundamental rights violations which arise because fiduciary duties are conceived of as being owed to the company itself. They may be able to be extended to stakeholders who are directly connected to the fate of the company: these include shareholders, creditors, suppliers and employees. They are, however, not helpful in dealing with wider social harms caused to those not linked directly to the company: the most urgent and important of these harms are those relating to fundamental rights.

A more promising legal avenue is to explore the possibilities that exist in some jurisdictions such as the United Kingdom[162] and Canada, where particular members of a company may claim relief for situations in which the business affairs of a company have been carried out in a manner that is 'oppressive or unfairly prejudicial to or that unfairly disregards the interests of any security holder, creditor, director, or officer'.[163] The focus of this action has been largely on avoiding abuse of their position by those who control the company such that they harm the interests of those who have a financial interest in the corporation but do not control its actions.[164] Importantly, such an action is a personal action and thus allows for a remedy that addresses the wrong to the individual or group directly. The target of the action may well be the company as well as directors in their personal capacity.[165] Moreover, no leave is required of a court to pursue such an action. Currently, the limitation of such an action is that it has generally focused on the protection of minority shareholders and is limited to 'members' of a company[166] or a 'security holder, creditor, director or officer'.[167] As a result, it has not been considered as a mechanism to protect the fundamental rights of a wider set of stakeholders.[168] If extended to provide those stakeholders with a right to institute the action, it could potentially in the future

[162] Section 994 of the Companies Act, 2006.
[163] Section 241 (2) of the Canadian Business Corporation Act of 1985.
[164] Dine and Koutsias, 2005: 262.
[165] For the Canadian position, and criteria as to when it is appropriate to hold directors liable in their personal capacity, see *Wilson* v. *Alharayeri* 2017 SCC 39 paras 47–57.
[166] Section 994 of the UK Companies Act.
[167] Section 241(2) of the Canadian Business Corporation Act of 1985.
[168] Naniwadekar and Varottil, 2016: 110 also regard it as an open question whether this action can provide a proper avenue for redress by a wider group of stakeholders in India.

provide an accountability mechanism for directors to this wider constituency.

A preferable route to follow, however, would be explicitly to reform existing laws to recognise a specific new action that individuals whose rights have been infringed by a corporate decision can sue a director directly and in their personal capacity for making a decision that clearly violates the specific fiduciary duty I have proposed earlier relating to fundamental rights. To avoid too broad a liability that would be unfair to directors, this would need to be couched in a way that covers *significant* abuses of judgement or the failure to exercise their responsibility to address the corporation's obligations in respect of fundamental rights. It would also need to allow for a defence that enables directors to demonstrate reasonable measures have been taken to fulfil the corporation's obligations.

The possibility of personal liability against a director will encourage them to take their responsibilities in this regard seriously and also to be cautious in circumstances surrounding the violation of fundamental rights. Importantly, the compensation in question that was recouped could go to the victims of fundamental rights violations themselves. This action would essentially mean that directors could not hide behind the corporate veil to avoid responsibility for fundamental rights wrongs. Clearly, some would oppose this proposal because it would involve piercing the corporate veil for purposes of holding directors to account for poor decision-making surrounding fundamental rights. Such a veil, as has been mentioned, is already capable of being pierced in some jurisdictions such as Canada for oppressive conduct taken towards certain stakeholders.[169] A fortiori, in my view, the normative importance of fundamental rights can provide a good justification for setting aside the veil in these circumstances. Doing so, would also indicate to directors the critical significance of these rights and how they must be factored into all of their judgements.[170]

Other less radical approaches are also possible. Section 166(7) of the Indian Companies Act states that 'if a director of a company contravenes the provisions of this section such director shall be punishable with a fine which shall not be less than one lakh rupees but which may extend to five lakh rupees'.[171] The possible fine ranges translate to between USD1500

[169] See *Wilson* note 165 earlier.

[170] See Campbell, 2012: 56 on why rights provide 'a very effective basis for the articulation of morally acceptable boundaries for the imposition of intrinsic CSR'.

[171] A lakh is 100,000.

and 4500. The idea behind this provision is to impose a penalty on the directors in question for failing properly to exercise their functions (in addition to other remedies that are available). Such penalties may indeed encourage directors to exercise their functions diligently. If we add to these responsibilities the need to exercise their judgement with due care and skill surrounding fundamental rights, that could advance decent decision-making in this area.[172] The amounts though are relatively small and may not be sufficient truly to represent a deterrent to negligent decision-making by wealthy directors of large corporations. That of course could be fixed by increasing the amounts.[173] Rendering such penalties effective will also require external regulatory agencies to investigate and take breaches of these duties seriously. A broader problem with this remedy is that the fine would presumably be collected by the state rather than the concerned victims of the rights violations and thus it would not serve to provide a remedy to the victims. That problem too could be remedied by a state commitment to use the funds to help address the plight of victims and/or allowing them a civil action for damages against directors found guilty of contravening this kind of provision.

9.3.3.3 Removal and Disqualification of Directors

A further remedy which could be utilised to encourage strong directorial accountability is the removal of directors who fail adequately to exercise their judgement in relation to fundamental rights. Usually, directors are accountable directly to shareholders who may remove them from office if they so desire. Section 71 of the South African Companies Act, for instance, states that 'a director may be removed by an ordinary resolution adopted at a shareholders meeting by the persons entitled to exercise voting rights in an election of that director'.[174] Directors may also be removed by the board if they have 'neglected, or been derelict in the

[172] Such an action against directors in their personal capacity could be an extension of the idea proposed in the United Kingdom of creating a corporate crime/civil action of failing to prevent fundamental rights abuses: see JPCHR Report, 2017 and BIICL Report, 2020.

[173] See Armour, 2020a: 50. Significant fines imposed by external regulators on corporations (rather than directors) could also reduce corporate economic performance and thus, possibly, lead to shareholders taking action against the directors. I am indebted to John Armour for highlighting this possibility for indirect accountability though it would share some of the weaknesses of the indirect approaches discussed earlier. There is also a lack of an external regulator that would cover the full range of fundamental rights impacts of corporations, which may be another direction for institutional law reform.

[174] Section 71(1) of the Companies Act 2008.

performance of the functions of the director'.[175] The grounds for removal should perhaps be expanded to include circumstances where directors have been shown negligently to disregard the fundamental rights of persons in the exercise of their duties. Such a provision would focus the minds of directors on fundamental rights without being unfair to them in that only the negligent performance of their duties would count for purposes of removal.

There are also grounds in most Companies Acts for disqualifying directors from future appointments in companies. The focus in current provisions has been on whether the director has been convicted of criminal offences, been dismissed for reasons of dishonesty from a job, is insolvent or is too young for the job.[176] These provisions could be modified to disqualify directors from holding appointments in companies if their record discloses a history of negligently or intentionally violating the company's fundamental rights obligations. Such a provision would, importantly, entail that directors could not simply move from one company to another if they have been found to have disregarded fundamental rights concerns.

9.3.4 *The* 'Whom' *Question: Internal and External Accountability*

9.3.4.1 Internal Accountability to Shareholders

Since the removal of directors is primarily a matter for shareholders, it raises the very interesting question concerning the responsibilities of shareholders for the conduct of the corporation in relation to fundamental rights. I have focused on directors as being ultimately responsible for day-to-day decision-making; yet, the directors are, in the end, accountable to the shareholders who have a significant interest in the economic success of the company. Corporate law provides for a number of residual responsibilities for shareholders: there must, for instance, be an AGM and reports presented by the directors at that meeting to the shareholders. Shareholders also have the right to remove directors and, in extreme cases, to wind up and dissolve the company itself. Corporate law does not, in general, affirm the shareholders' right to supersede the ordinary day-to-day decisions of directors other than through special resolutions (which require super-majorities of shareholders).[177]

[175] Ibid: section 71(3)(b).
[176] Ibid: section 69, in particular section 69(7) or (8).
[177] See, on the UK position, Dine and Koutsias, 2005: 159–161.

Shareholding in large modern corporations, however, is very diffuse and constantly changing. Consequently, the possibility of interfering in particular decisions through special resolutions is relatively limited.

Shareholder obligations, in my view, should be conceived of as being consonant with their powers and have three main dimensions. The first duty concerns proactively setting up the framework of the corporation in a manner that expresses the recognition that it has and must realise its obligations in relation to fundamental rights. Institutionally, this could be accomplished by a statutory requirement to place in the Memorandum of Association a recognition that one of the central objectives of the corporation is, through its activities, to advance the fundamental rights of individuals and to realise its concomitant obligations in this regard. The Articles of Association – which set the rules that govern the corporation – should themselves indicate clearly the expectation that directors (and other decision-makers) must, at all times, be bound to exercise diligently any discretion that relates to determining the content of those obligations and that they shall be required to take all necessary measures to fulfil them.

The second duty should be to hold directors accountable for decision-making that fails to comply with the corporation's fundamental rights obligations. Accountability could be achieved in various ways: in many corporate regimes, there is a requirement that directors place a report before the AGM on the impact of the corporation's activities on fundamental rights (and wider social and environmental concerns). Shareholders would then have the right to interrogate directors on their performance in this regard. That could also provide another opportunity for deliberation on the judgements made by directors when applying the multi-factoral approach to determining the fundamental rights obligations of corporations. Corporate law could be reformed to require an AGM to consider any material impacts the corporation has on fundamental rights. Doing so could not guarantee the quality of any deliberation but would indicate the seriousness with which the directors need to regard corporate obligations with respect to fundamental rights.

The recent development of greater shareholder activism suggests the significant possibilities that exist for shareholders to set the tone for the corporation surrounding fundamental rights and to interrogate what is being done in its name.[178] Canada, for instance, empowers shareholders through enabling them to submit proposals for particular issues to be

[178] See Dhir, 2009: 73–74; Simons and Macklin, 2014: 232–233 for some examples.

discussed at the AGM which can then be deliberated about and voted upon.[179] For these proposals to be discussed, certain procedures must be complied with and the proposal must relate 'in a significant way to the business or affairs of the corporation'.[180] This language is broad enough to cover impacts the corporation has on fundamental rights – as well as wider social and environmental effects – and, indeed, this procedure has been utilised to raise such concerns.[181] Corporate law should be reformed to enable such proposals to be made in jurisdictions that lack such a procedure. For the scrutiny by shareholders to be meaningful, they should also be entitled to access all relevant information concerning the decisions taken by directors surrounding corporate obligations in this regard.[182] Moreover, in circumstances where it is disclosed that directors are clearly in breach of their duties and caused significant harm to the fundamental rights of individuals, the shareholders should have an obligation to remove the directors from their positions. Failure to do so should attract significant penalties against the corporation, thus reducing shareholder value.

The final duty upon shareholders that should be developed is to ensure that directors comply with their duties to provide remedies for harms caused to individuals through fundamental rights abuses committed effectively in their name. Shareholders should be required to pass resolutions – whether ordinary or special, if needed – halting any continuing violations and providing compensation to affected individuals for harms already caused. Failure to do so, once again, should attract financial penalties against the corporation and reduce shareholder value. In protecting their interests, shareholders could always bring a derivative action against the directors involved for harm caused to the company (which could constitute a deterrent for the director).

There is though a central tension for shareholders involved in the compliance with their duties in this regard: a duty of remediation, for instance, would reduce their share of the company's profits and thus conflict with their financial interests. Ensuring compliance with corporate fundamental rights obligations requires them to think beyond their

179 Shareholder proposals are regulated by section 137 of the Canadian Business Corporations Act.

180 Ibid: section 137(5)(b.1).

181 Dhir, 2012: 101–102. Dhir (at 106), though, points out that the language is sufficiently vague to allow directors to reject proposals on wider social issues unless they can be shown to have a pecuniary impact on the firm.

182 Simons and Macklin, 2014: 233.

narrow self-interest to the social effects of corporate activity. That is precisely the shift that is required if fundamental rights are to be taken seriously by corporate actors: yet, whilst some shareholders may be altruistically motivated and capable of more holistic thinking, there are likely to be many who focus largely or exclusively on their self-interest and the economic profitability of the corporation. For large publicly listed corporations, the shareholder base is also constantly changing, raising obstacles to collective action and rendering it practically difficult to enforce any obligations they bear.

To encourage shareholders to take their responsibility seriously, law reform thus needs to align the self-interested motives of many shareholders with the societal objectives of ensuring compliance with corporate fundamental rights obligations. In relation to shareholders, it is necessary to consider sanctions against the company itself – it is possible, for instance, to imagine legal provisions that impose large penalties on a corporation (perhaps that vary with the size of its profits) or increased damages awards for wilfully or negligently failing to realise its fundamental rights obligations. Such provisions would in and of themselves reduce the profits of shareholders and so help align self-interest with social responsibility, rendering them more likely to exercise their responsibilities surrounding the corporation's fundamental rights obligations.

Nevertheless, even with such provisions, many shareholders will always have a bias towards their economic self-interest. The expertise of directors and shareholders, moreover, usually relates to business rather than in relation to fundamental rights issues. Consequently, it is necessary to consider not only internal accountability but also accountability to other external mechanisms and fora to advance fundamental rights realisation by corporations. I have already considered the possibility of a more proactive role being adopted by the registrar of companies in relation to reporting on fundamental rights. Human Rights Commissions also have a mandate to adopt a proactive role in this regard, though I shall not investigate this further here. In the next section, I turn to explore the role of courts which is particularly significant where violations of fundamental rights obligations are concerned.

9.3.4.2 Accountability to Courts

I have already discussed the possibility of various legal actions being lodged against directors to hold them accountable for their decisions relating to the fundamental rights obligations of corporations. All such possibilities envisage a role for courts in examining the decisions taken by directors (and other corporate decision-makers) relating to fundamental rights. The possibility of such review in itself can encourage better decision-making and so help deepen a culture of fundamental rights realisation within a corporation. Through their decisions, courts can accomplish two additional aims. Firstly, they can provide authoritative interpretations of the substantive content of corporate fundamental rights obligations. Over time, the multi-factoral approach and balancing enquiries will crystallise into more concrete rules which will provide greater guidance and clarity about what is expected of corporations. Secondly, courts can, importantly, ensure there are binding and serious legal consequences for failing to abide by corporate obligations. A major stumbling block though to the courts performing their review function is the 'business judgement rule' that has been developed in the corporate law of many jurisdictions. I will now argue why it should not apply in relation to corporate decisions concerning fundamental rights.

9.3.4.2.1 Beyond the Business Judgement Rule The business judgement rule in essence provides that courts should display clear deference to the decision-making of directors in a corporation and not second-guess their 'business judgements'. The rule has, for instance, received clear expression in the Australian Corporations Act.[183] A business judgement is defined in section 180(3) as 'any decision to take or not take action in respect of a matter relevant to the business operations of a corporation'.[184] The rule is formulated in the context of the duty on directors to act in the best interests of the company and 'with the degree of care and diligence that a reasonable person would exercise'.[185] Section 180(2) encapsulates the essence of the rule when it states the following: '[t]he director's or officer's belief that the judgment is in the best interests of the corporation is a rational one unless the belief is one that no reasonable person in their position would hold'.[186]

This provision in the Australian Act is similar to earlier statements of the rule in United States Corporate Law[187] and subsequent expression

[183] No 50 of 2001.

[184] Section 180(3) of the Australian Corporations Act 2001.

[185] Ibid: section 180(1).

[186] Ibid: section 180(2).

[187] See the early and similar formulation by the American Law Institute 'Principles of Corporate Governance: Analysis and Recommendations' (1994) section 4.01 (c). Delaware courts formulated the business judgement rule as a presumption.

thereof, for instance, in the South African Companies Act.[188] Courts in the state of Delaware in the United States have approached the rule as a presumption 'that in making a business decision the directors of a corporation acted on an informed basis, in good faith and in the honest belief that the action taken was in the best interests of the company'.[189] Thus, the rule effectively encourages courts to defer to corporate decision-makers when dealing with business decisions.[190] The rule has been used in the commercial context to stop derivative actions against directors and to prevent reviews of decisions on takeover bids.[191]

What then is the normative justification for the rule? This may be understood from two perspectives. The first is that of the directors: there would be a major disincentive for individuals to agree to act as directors if their good-faith business decisions could easily be overturned and, on that basis, they could be held personally liable for any financial harms caused to shareholders. Moreover, without some protection for the business decisions of a director, they are likely to become extremely cautious and avoid taking risks.[192] That in a sense would counteract some of the very advantages of the corporate form itself which, as we saw in Chapter 1, is designed in part to facilitate the taking of those risks (which in turn may be socially beneficial).[193]

The second perspective would be that of the courts themselves. Courts may well often lack the expertise and also not be well-placed to second-guess directors on business decisions.[194] Branson writes, for instance, that 'those decisions often involve intangibles, intuitive insights or surmises as to business matters such as competitive outlook, cost structure, and economic and industry trends. Business decisions often come down to matters of touch and feel not susceptible to systematic analysis'.[195] By deferring to business executives, courts thus avoid substituting their judgements for those better placed to make them.

[188] See section 76(4) of the South African Companies Act, 2008.

[189] *Aronson* v. *Lewis* 473 A.2d 805, 812 (Del.1984).

[190] Whilst the doctrine does not formally exist in United Kingdom law, a similar level of deference is accorded by courts to business judgements: see the formulation of the section 172(1) fiduciary duty and, for example, *Birdi* v. *Specsavers Optical* para 62.

[191] There have been some refinements of the rule in each of these contexts: see Branson, 2002: 647–653.

[192] Armour, 2020a: 41.

[193] Armour et al., 2017c: 70.

[194] Ibid.

[195] Branson, 2002: 637.

This reasoning may be persuasive in relation to business decisions that solely relate to the economic operations of the business and its strategy. The rationales just articulated are not persuasive, I contend, in relation to those decisions of directors that concern or impact upon the fundamental rights obligations of corporations.

Firstly, from the perspective of directors, it is true that there may be some deterrent effect on individuals becoming directors if they know any decisions they make that relate to the fundamental rights impacts of a corporation will potentially be scrutinised closely by courts. Yet, arguably, those who would be deterred are precisely unethical business leaders for whom financial considerations are primary and fundamental rights of limited concern. Directors who would diligently exercise their judgements surrounding fundamental rights would have little to worry about. Moreover, it would in fact be desirable if the lack of deference by courts to directors where fundamental rights are concerned leads them to be more cautious and prudent in their decision-making in this domain. Indeed, as I have argued, that is entirely consistent with the reflexive approach discussed earlier in which one of the goals of corporate law reforms should be to encourage the embedding of fundamental rights considerations into the DNA of corporate decision-making. The fact that directors could potentially have to explain their decisions in relation to fundamental rights to a court is likely to encourage better decision-making in this area. It would also not undermine the ability of businesses to take risks with shareholder capital and innovate: they are simply not entitled to take unreasonable risks with the fundamental rights of other stakeholders.

From the perspective of courts, the expertise argument is much less persuasive in the context of business decisions that have an impact on or relate to fundamental rights.[196] Judges are precisely meant to have expertise and sensitivity in the area of fundamental rights. Decisions that affect those rights need to be made with a stronger justification than on the basis of a mere 'touch and feel'. The recognition that determining the substantive content of corporate obligations requires an ineliminable degree of judgement – which I have argued in this book – provides a strong argument for a neutral, impartial body to review first-order decisions made in this area by directors who are likely to have an institutional bias.[197] Judicial

[196] Armour, 2020a: 51.

[197] Fallon, 2008: 1695 argues for judicial review on the basis that it creates an extra layer of protection for these rights by ensuring that both the legislature and the judiciary have 'veto powers over legislation that might reasonably be thought to violate such rights'. A similar argument can be made for the importance of reviewing corporate decisions,

decisions in this area will also be helpful in guiding corporations about the substantive content of corporate obligations. Judicial review in this sphere is thus not really different than judicial review of decision-making by other organs of state: both seek to render these bodies more likely to make better decisions.[198]

Moreover, judicial decision-making can be defended as being part of the very function of courts which is to ensure that the fundamental rights of individuals are protected and to provide remedies where they are violated. By refusing to show deference, judges effectively assert the centrality of such rights for all entities in society and their normative priority even in the context of business activities.

The upshot is that there is little justification for the application of the business judgement rule to any decision – including one that has an economic motivation – where fundamental rights are at stake.[199] Deference should only be shown to business decisions that relate solely to the corporation's economic activities and the deployment of the capital of the shareholders to this effect. What will this mean in practice?

Clearly, the lack of application of the business judgement rule in this area does not mean that courts should ignore the reasoning of directors. In addressing cases where corporate decision-making has affected fundamental rights, court processes should require directors to lay out clearly the impact of corporate activities on fundamental rights and the reasons they have adopted for understanding the content of corporate obligations in a particular way. Courts should be entitled to take judicial notice of what has been stated by the corporation in its non-financial reports (if these are available) and whether there is a consistency between that information and what has been placed before the courts. Any human rights due diligence processes conducted must be outlined. Courts should, of course, also attempt to understand the perspective of rights-holders who claim a violation of corporate obligations in relation to their fundamental rights.

There is a valid concern that the 'reasonableness' component of the specific fiduciary duty relating to fundamental rights will still lead to a high level of deference being shown by courts to the

particularly given the strong institutional biases corporate decision-makers have currently towards shareholders' interests.

198 See Dworkin, 1996: 34.

199 It could also strongly be argued that decisions relating to matters that have a wider social and environmental impact should also not be afforded deference and be excluded from the application of the rule.

decisions of directors.[200] Consequently, in order to make judicial review meaningful and ensure directors take their responsibilities seriously, a high standard of information-gathering and deliberation should be required of directors to meet their fiduciary duties in this regard. To correct for the current institutional deferential tendencies of courts in this sphere, the burden of proof could be placed on directors to demonstrate that their decisions were indeed reasonable.

The legal analytical model outlined in this book can also help guide judicial decision-making in this area. In relation to any justification offered for an infringement of a right, courts must attempt to understand clearly why the directors reached the decision they did, in the context of corporate operations, and whether their reasoning can be justified by the relevant factors and the proportionality enquiry. Similarly, in any construction of a corporation's positive obligations and the failure to honour these, courts must consider the directors' reasoning in relation to the relevant factors and the extent to which it mirrors the seven-step process I have outlined. As we saw in Chapters 2–5, courts already engage with corporate obligations through a range of doctrines: they can utilise the multi-factoral approach developed in this book to refine the manner in which they apply those doctrines and bring more clarity to their reasoning process when determining corporate obligations in relation to fundamental rights. Given the fact that this is an area of fundamental rights law that is developing, courts should be mindful of the need to provide guidance concerning the ambit of corporate obligations in a way that can have useful precedential value.

9.3.4.2.2 The Exercise of Remedial Powers by the Courts Once a violation of an obligation has been found, it will be necessary for courts to decide on the appropriate remedies. Remedial orders too may have an impact on improving decision-making in the corporation surrounding fundamental rights. I shall focus on three types of remedies that may be granted: preventive remedies, responsive remedies and coercive remedies.

Firstly, it is clearly critical that a court attempts to avert violations of corporate fundamental rights obligations where it becomes aware that they may transpire or are occurring. There is consequently a need to ensure that there are adequate procedures in place for litigants to lodge actions to prevent those violations from occurring. Due diligence

200 I am indebted to Peter Muchlinski for pressing this point.

responsibilities (discussed in Chapters 5 and 10) can be understood to involve internal corporate processes to identify violations of fundamental rights obligations and to take measures to avert them. Yet, arguably, such processes should go along with duties upon senior decision-makers to break ranks from other leaders if they are of the view that an unjustifiable violation of fundamental rights obligations will take place. Corporate law should be reformed to create an easy remedy to enable a director (and potentially any employee) to approach a court in advance to prevent such violations from taking place and to be protected in their positions if they take such action.[201] Of course, individuals with knowledge of a potential violation of their rights should be entitled to approach a court for a declaration of their rights (and the corporation's obligations) as well as an interdict to prevent any violation from taking place (or to require certain actions by the corporation where positive obligations exist).

Secondly, remedies can also play a role in encouraging greater attention be paid to fundamental rights obligations within the corporate structure. To do so, courts may wish, at times, to consider the experimentalist and participatory approaches that have been developed in recent years surrounding state obligations in relation to fundamental rights.[202] Consider the remedy of the South African Constitutional Court in the *Olivia Road* case,[203] where the Johannesburg municipality sought to evict 400 occupiers from an inner city building that was in a woeful state of disrepair and posed significant dangers to those living in it. The city wished to move the occupiers to better lodgings but in a location that was far removed from the environment in which they earned a living. Instead of deciding one way or the other, the court ordered the occupiers and the city to engage meaningfully with one another to come up with a win-win solution to the problem. The court then reviewed the resulting settlement agreement and, finding it to be acceptable, made it an order of court.[204]

It is likely that corporate decision-making surrounding fundamental rights will also provide numerous circumstances like the *Olivia Road* case where the court is faced with strong competing contentions with no clear right answer. Consider a situation where half a community wants the new

201 This is similar to some of the provisions contained in whistle-blowing legislation in a number of countries but could have a particular relevance to due diligence processes.

202 Dorff and Sabel, 1998; Sabel and Simon, 2017.

203 *Occupiers of 51 Olivia Road, Berea Township and 197 Main Street Johannesburg* v. *City of Johannesburg* [2008] ZACC 1.

204 For a fuller engagement with experimentalism in the context of the decision-making of the South African Constitutional Court, see Woolman, 2013; Ray, 2016.

investment a mine will bring to their region whilst the other half is opposed to the mine due to concerns about its environmental effects. This classic tension between economic development and preserving the environment has often led to serious conflict between businesses and local communities. Drawing on the insights of experimentalism, courts in such circumstances could, for instance, order a meaningful engagement process to take place between the mine and representatives of both sides of the community. In such circumstances, it may not be desirable immediately for courts to make a binding order but, essentially, provide the corrective to the power imbalance between the parties by requiring a good-faith process of mediation. During that process, victims of any actual or potential rights violations could ensure decision-makers are aware of the human rights impacts of their decisions; that enables those decision-makers to gain a stronger understanding of these impacts which can in turn affect their behaviour. Courts should review any agreement ensuring it reflects processes that are truly inclusive, that the agreement reflects a true consensus and that the power of the business has not been used to browbeat the community into submission. Moreover, as in *Olivia Road*, courts should also review such agreements substantively to ensure they are consistent with their understanding of the fundamental rights obligations of those businesses.

Such remedies help combine 'local initiative with accountability'.[205] There is also an understanding that people on the ground have an expertise that should be reflected in any solution and that there is a need to give meaning to abstract rights in the particularity of complex circumstances.[206] These ideas suggest the need for courts to think through how their remedial orders can draw in the expertise of decision-makers in a corporation as well as other stakeholders to address fundamental rights challenges that may arise.

Responsive remedies of the experimentalist kind will also have their limits for a variety of reasons. There may be egregious violations of fundamental rights committed that simply require orders for damages to be paid and various forms of remediation to take place. Victims of rights violations may themselves agree on what is required and a corporation may be extremely uncooperative and unlikely to engage in good faith with other stakeholders. The rights violation may also be of a kind that does not involve a high level of complexity and is susceptible

[205] Sabel and Simon, 2017: 484.
[206] Ibid: 486.

to a simple coercive remedy. In such circumstances, courts should not hesitate to exercise their general coercive remedial powers which should be aimed at addressing the violation in the best way possible, to compensate individuals for harms and to prevent future violations.

In relation to coercive remedies, a particularly interesting possible order that includes some of the experimentalist insights discussed earlier is the supervisory interdict.[207] Such a remedy involves the court making an order that outlines the parameters of the actions required and then obliges the corporation (in this instance) to report back within a specified period as to what it has done to address the violation. That report then is the subject of a further court order and this process can be repeated until the court is satisfied that any violation of obligations has been addressed. The supervisory interdict has usually been used in cases where the court needs to supervise the implementation of an order directed at the state, for instance, in relation to the fulfilment of its obligations in relation to socio-economic rights.[208] Such an order has often been used in cases where there is a lack of capacity or unwillingness by the state to meet its obligations.[209]

Analogues of these types of situations may arise in the corporate context too. For instance, one of the major areas in which corporations have had a deleterious impact on fundamental rights has been in relation to pollution and environmental harm.[210] What is often needed in such circumstances would be for courts to retain jurisdiction over the case and require reporting from the corporation against measurable goals as to the advances in any clean-up operation which may be complex and take time. That would also allow victims of the rights violations to make submissions to the court as to whether the corporation is complying with its obligations and allow for flexibility and variation where needed. Of course, such an order would also be useful where a corporation fails to meet its positive obligations to enable courts, for instance, to supervise the implementation of a policy of non-discrimination in the company or a shift in its pricing policy towards vital medicines. These sorts of remedies may also develop a dialogical relationship between the decision-makers in the corporation and the courts, thus helping to

[207] Roach and Budlender, 2005: 325ff.

[208] *People's Union for Civil Liberties* v. *Union of India* (Civil Writ Petition 196 of 2001) and *Black Sash Trust* v. *Minister of Social Development* [2017] ZACC 8.

[209] Roach and Budlender, 2005: 345–351.

[210] For instance, the oil pollution of Ogoniland in Nigeria where Shell has been implicated and the collapse of the dam at Brumadinho in Brazil where the mining company Vale is implicated.

facilitate the internalisation of diligent decision-making in the corporation surrounding fundamental rights.[211] They may also encourage institutional learning as well as, in some instances, restorative justice mechanisms such as reconciliation processes.

This section has thus sought to highlight the fact that the exercise of court powers in this area also needs more attention. Courts have a critical role to play not only in giving substantive content to corporate obligations and standard-setting but also in a number of other respects. By virtue of having strong coercive powers, they can provide the ultimate check on corporate decision-making relating to fundamental rights. This section has argued, however, that they may wish to utilise their strongest powers judiciously and recognise that, in many situations, the resolution of rights conflicts may benefit from their encouraging of processes that can lead to input by and, at times, agreement amongst various stakeholders.

9.4 Conclusion

Given the ineliminable need for judgement to determine the substantive content of corporate obligations in relation to fundamental rights, this chapter has sought to consider who makes such decisions and how to ensure they are made with the requisite attention and skill. I argued for the need to adopt a regulatory approach that seeks to internalise fundamental rights norms within the corporation. Doing so requires attending to both who makes the decisions and what their duties are, as well as their accountability. This chapter, ultimately, has sought to show the importance of engaging with multiple processes and approaches that, in various ways, can embed a seriousness of purpose amongst corporate decision-makers in relation to fundamental rights.[212] We saw that these institutional processes vary from softer to more binding mechanisms and from incentives for good behaviour to punishment for non-compliance. I made a number of corporate law reform proposals at the national jurisdiction level, which I summarise in Table 9.1. In the next chapter, I consider the international level and the possibilities for reforming and creating global institutional mechanisms that can enhance decent decision-making surrounding fundamental rights by corporations and our understanding of the substantive content of their obligations.

[211] See Jhaveri, 2019: 814 for how dialogical remedies may 'facilitate a greater rights consciousness in political arms of government' (drawing on Gardbaum, 2013).

[212] In this sense, I agree with Deva, 2012: 195, who writes: 'no one single level of regulation, strategy or sanction is adequate to deal effectively with human rights violations by companies'.

Table 9.1 *A summary of key corporate law reform proposals*

1. Ensuring a diversity of experience amongst directors that involves a wider set of interests than purely economic ones being represented at board level, including specific sub-committees that focus on fundamental rights;
2. Recognising a new specific fiduciary duty on the part of directors: to consider the impact of the corporation on the fundamental rights of all stakeholders, to exercise demonstrably reasonable care, skill and diligence in reaching judgements about the substantive content of corporate obligations in relation to fundamental rights and taking all necessary actions to ensure compliance with those obligations;
3. Enhancing disclosure requirements where corporate activities impact on fundamental rights, including clarification about what must be reported on, improving the verification of the disclosed information and introducing the evaluation of such information by competent regulatory authorities;
4. A new enforcement action to be developed that allows directors to be sued in their personal capacity by anyone whose fundamental rights have been violated where it is shown that the directors breached their specific fiduciary duty (discussed in point 2 above) in that regard;
5. Creating regulatory fines for corporations which violate their fundamental rights obligations towards individuals as well as financial and other penalties for directors in their personal capacity – including removal and disqualification – in these circumstances;
6. An enhanced framework for a recognition of shareholder obligations – including the right to discuss the fundamental rights implications of business activities at the AGM – and developing penalties for the failure to fulfil them;
7. The express rejection (preferably through statute) of the business judgement rule and any deference to decisions made by directors where fundamental rights are concerned;
8. The utilisation by courts of responsive and dialogical remedies that can help deepen the culture of fundamental rights within corporations.

10

Corporate Obligations in a Global World: The Role of International Mechanisms

10.1 Introduction: Moving to the International Plane

In light of globalisation, the corporate law reforms discussed in the previous chapter are not sufficient to enhance corporate decision-making surrounding fundamental rights. It is also not enough to have national institutions such as courts having the power to review the internal decision-making of corporations surrounding their obligations and providing guidance on the substantive content thereof. It is necessary to move beyond the national sphere alone to consider the role of international mechanisms in this regard.

Section 10.2 considers the reasons why this is so through outlining enduring challenges posed by globalisation and how these demonstrate a close interrelationship between the national and international spheres. As such, attending to the latter is vital for integrating fundamental rights into corporate decision-making, advancing the understanding of corporate fundamental rights obligations and providing mechanisms for accountability.

Section 10.3 considers the role of the dominant 'softer' approaches – which include various initiatives by industry and multi-stakeholder initiatives – in enhancing corporate decision-making and elaborating upon the substantive content of corporate fundamental rights obligations. I then turn in section 10.4 to consider existing international mechanisms that could provide more authoritative guidance and critically evaluate their role thus far in advancing international standards relating to corporate fundamental rights obligations. Finally, section 10.5 looks to the future and, based on current weaknesses, considers possible ways in which the international system could be reformed to enhance corporate decision-making and our understanding of their fundamental rights obligations. In particular, it will consider fora that could utilise the multi-factoral approach to establish binding standards as well as make determinations in individual cases.

10.2 The Justification for Moving beyond the State

Why then is there a need to move beyond the nation state when seeking to enhance decision-making by corporate decision-makers relating to a corporation's fundamental rights obligations and when developing guidance about the substantive content of such obligations? Some of these reasons have already been alluded to in the introduction to this book as well as Chapters 2 and 5, but the focus here is more squarely on the ineliminability of discretion, which clearly emerged from the multi-factoral approach and the consequent twin goals of improving decision-making within the corporation and providing guidance on the substantive content of corporate obligations.

10.2.1 The Universality of Rights and Obligations

As we saw in Chapter 2, fundamental rights are in essence universal and apply to all who have dignity. The obligations they impose potentially apply to all agents and require allocation amongst them. The question then arises whether these facets of rights provide reasons for there to be international standards in regard to corporate obligations in particular and mechanisms to develop their content.

Given the fact that we remain at an early stage in the development of the substantive content of corporate obligations, the understanding thereof may well vary quite strongly between jurisdictions. Clearly, at times, such variation is desirable where it is necessary properly to give effect to fundamental rights within particular societies or cultures: a right to housing, for instance, will involve very different structures in countries where temperatures are freezing and those where they are sweltering. In relation to corporate obligations, however, there are reasons to be concerned that variations in understanding will not be driven by legitimate contextual differences – or even perhaps reasonable good-faith disagreement surrounding interpretation – but by a number of other more extraneous forces. These could include a desire on the part of some countries to attract businesses[1] – and thus reduce, for instance, what they require of them in their relations with

[1] Leader, 2017: 95.

individuals and communities – and what is sometimes referred to as 'corporate capture', namely, the ability of businesses in contexts where they have significant power to influence legislators (or regulators or other decision-makers) so that the rules in those societies are more favourable towards them (I will deal with this further in the next section).[2] Furthermore, there is also the well-known problem concerning a possible race-to-the-bottom, which will be discussed in section 10.2.2.2. To address these issues, it is important to have a common set of global standards emerging from fundamental rights as well as institutions to interpret these standards to ensure variation between countries does not result in downward trends in rights realisation eventuating.[3]

There is also a more positive argument for a move to the global level which focuses on the significant learnings that can take place between jurisdictions in advancing our understanding of the content of corporate fundamental rights obligations.[4] To gain these benefits, it is important that there are institutional structures capable of collating and analysing developments in different jurisdictions, which in turn can influence the setting of standards at the international level. Deliberative and adjudicatory fora at the international level can encourage engagement amongst experts and decision-makers, which in turn can bring the benefits of such cross-fertilisation to the global understanding of corporate obligations that emerges. Such a process should include an openness to the input of civil society organisations and thus draw on the richness and diversity of insights from people across the globe. Such approaches in turn, if genuinely adopted, can help give concrete expression to the very universality of rights themselves.

10.2.2 Weak State Governance

The weakness of states, in many instances, provides further reasons why there is a need for a move to the international level. There are different facets of this problem that need to be unpacked.

[2] See, for instance, Miller and Harkins, 2010: 568ff; Working Group Anti-Corruption Report, 2020: 72.

[3] Leader, 2017: 94 suggests this is one of the core reasons for a treaty on business and human rights.

[4] Besson, 2017: 237 recognises the dynamic and two-way relationship between the national and international spheres in this regard.

10.2.2.1 State Incapacity

There are many states across the world which lack the administrative capacity to develop regulations governing complex corporate activities and to implement such regulations. They are thus *unable* to determine, impose and implement adequate corporate standards relating to fundamental rights. This lack of capacity arises from a range of sources, including historical legacies of underdevelopment, ethnic division and civil war, a paucity of skills, poor training for officials, limited economic resources and much else. As a result, there is often a very weak regulatory infrastructure and very limited powers of enforcement.[5] Such circumstances can have a deleterious effect on internal corporate decision-making and provide excellent opportunities for sophisticated corporations to exploit these vulnerabilities for their financial benefit. In so doing, they may seek to avoid implementing even their most basic obligations relating to fundamental rights.[6]

A second source of systemic incapacity arises in states where corruption has become endemic.[7] Corrupt companies, for instance, may seek to influence public procurement processes in their favour, being awarded contracts where they lack the expertise to deliver vital services.[8] Where land title is not adequately recorded, corruption may enable businesses to have valuable land registered in their name, often entailing widespread land dispossession of local communities.[9] Moreover, corruption often leads to both a weakening of regulation – through corporate capture or other forces – and a failure adequately to implement or enforce existing regulations against powerful actors. For instance, manufacturing companies may seek to avoid vital health and safety checks,[10] whereas extractive industries are able to gain lucrative concessions in the absence of adequate social and environmental studies or the meaningful participation of local communities.[11]

[5] See Simons and Macklin, 2014: 7–8 and 16–17.

[6] Consider, for instance, the use of child labour in cobalt mining (used for mobile phone batteries) detailed at www.amnesty.org/en/latest/campaigns/2016/06/drc-cobalt-child-labour/

[7] Transparency International has developed a Corruption Perception Index available at www.transparency.org/en/cpi#, which outlines how corrupt the public sector of countries across the world are perceived to be.

[8] Working Group Anti-Corruption Report, 2020: para 12.

[9] Ibid: para 14.

[10] Ibid: para 16 and Evans, 2015: 603.

[11] Working Group Anti-Corruption Report, ibid: para 21.

The failures of regulation at the domestic level cry out for standards to be developed at the international level against which corporate behaviour can be measured. Such contexts also strongly indicate the need for mechanisms to hold corporations and their decision-makers to account beyond the nation state.

10.2.2.2 State Dereliction of Duty

A further set of problems relating to governance by states emerges from a reluctance or *unwillingness* to set standards surrounding corporate fundamental rights obligations and to hold those who violate them accountable. The first problem relates to the race-to-the-bottom mentioned earlier. Host states may well wish to limit the standards surrounding fundamental rights and the enforcement thereof as an incentive to encourage investment. Corporations may also clearly indicate that they will only invest in circumstances where the regulation of their activities is limited. Bilateral investment agreements may exacerbate this problem as corporations seek compensation for any interference with their investments. Home states may also contribute to the problem as they may be concerned that companies could relocate their headquarters if they impose stringent regulatory requirements relating to fundamental rights on what parent companies can do abroad – which in turn will lead to a loss of tax revenue and jobs in such jurisdictions.[12] International standards that cannot simply be waived by states would help address this problem.

The second problem relates to corporate capture that was raised briefly earlier and applies both in developing and developed states. Corporations often have sophisticated lobbying operations that enable them to affect the standards that are imposed upon them by legislative bodies. In authoritarian states, they may well be connected to the ruling elites, and, in democratic states, they may contribute towards political campaigns.[13] The standards developed by law-making bodies concerning the content of corporate obligations may thus reflect expedient rather than principled considerations. Thus, law-making bodies at the national level may well fail to offer an adequate understanding of the obligations of corporations in relation to fundamental rights.

[12] Leader, 2017: 96–97.

[13] See Klumpp et al., 2016 on the effects of the *Citizens United* decision on American democracy.

Moving to the international level can help mitigate the effects of this problem. The influence of a corporation on one country may be significant but it may lack similar influence in relation to other countries and so its power could become more diluted at the international level. This may be particularly so where it operates in several countries but has substantial influence only in some of these. Consequently, a move to the international level can help reduce the power of individual corporations to manipulate the standards developed surrounding the content of their obligations. The potential of corporate capture, of course, exists at the international level too.[14] It is for this reason that it is important that there be multiple diverse institutional structures which can address standard-setting in relation to corporate fundamental rights obligations. The likelihood of corporate capture of multiple institutions is reduced when compared with a situation where there is only one relevant structure.

The dual problems of state incapacity and dereliction of duty all point to the fact that there are major structural challenges to developing the optimal national institutional structures and legal framework argued for in the previous chapter. As such, it is necessary to consider supranational structures that can accomplish the twin goals of enhancing decision-making within the corporation surrounding fundamental rights and concretising the substantive content of their obligations.

10.2.3 Corporate Structures and Global Business

Corporations today often operate through complex group structures and create a range of subsidiaries in different states around the world. They also conduct businesses through long supply chains of contractors that perform different tasks in different jurisdictions. These features of international business allow a corporation headquartered in one country to argue that it is a separate legal entity from a subsidiary or sub-contractor in another country and thus cannot be held liable for its activities.[15] Corporations thus can deliberately structure their activities in such a way so as to avoid assuming responsibility for violations of fundamental rights by companies connected to them.

In such circumstances, national regulation is not sufficient unless it expressly addresses the liability of a corporation in one country (where it has its headquarters, for instance) for the activities of entities with which

14 See Seitz and Martens, 2017.
15 Simons and Macklin, 2014: 8–9.

it is connected in another. Even if it does so, there are significant legal difficulties that may arise: these include demonstrating the relationship between different legal entities such that liability ensues[16] and a range of practical evidentiary problems – as well as the cost – relating to bringing cases across borders. Relevant to the concerns of this book is the problem of determining which legal standards can be utilised to determine the obligations of corporations with respect to fundamental rights.

International standards would help in multiple ways. Firstly, in relation to social pressure, they would clearly aid international campaigning against corporate abuses across group structures and supply chains. Secondly, in national courts, the question often arises concerning the rules of which legal system to utilise to determine a violation of rights: are they, for instance, the standards of the country where the corporation is headquartered or where the actual violation occurred?[17] The issue would take on less importance if there were the development of clearer global legal principles not tied to any one jurisdiction and which states have a duty to incorporate in their domestic laws.[18] Even the existence of persuasive (rather than binding) international standards would have an influence on national jurisdictions and thus help align their laws more closely in relation to the fundamental rights obligations of corporations.

10.2.4 The Interaction of Different International Law Regimes

Today, there exist a number of international legal regimes dealing with economic matters. These include international trade regimes as well as bilateral and multi-lateral investment treaties. At times, these regimes may confer entitlements on corporations which can conflict with the fundamental rights of individuals.[19]

There is a serious problem in the lack of clarity about the relationship between fundamental rights and these international legal regimes.

[16] Few cases have succeeded in doing so and where they have, in general, the liability has been either of the parent for its own conduct – see *Chandler* v. *Cape* – or that of the subsidiary itself – see *Akpan* v. *Milieudefensie*.

[17] This has been framed as a question of private international law and, in particular, of 'applicable law'. In *Jabir* v. *Kik*, the application of Pakistani procedural law was fatal to the claim. A more successful result was obtained in the *Akpan* case ibid., which also utilised the law of the host state (Nigeria) to adjudicate the case. The problem is that the laws of the host state may be inhospitable to claims by victims of rights violations.

[18] The 2nd Revised Draft Treaty Article 11 attempts to address this problem.

[19] This arose, for instance, in *Piero Foresti, Laura de Carli* v. *Republic of South Africa* (ICSID).

Normatively, it is clear that the most foundational interests of individuals protected by fundamental rights should have priority over other considerations. However, the notion of a hierarchy in international law is itself controversial;[20] and, at present, the priority in fact lies with international economic law given the lack of widespread acceptance that corporations have legally binding fundamental rights obligations.[21] To address this problem, it is necessary to recognise that businesses are bound by fundamental rights under international law[22] and that there is an analytical framework – expressed by the multi-factoral approach proposed in this book – for determining the substantive content of their obligations that can provide guidance in cases where there is a conflict with the provisions of international economic law.

10.2.5 Access to Remedies

The problems I have thus far outlined often lead to a serious situation where individuals are unable to gain access to remedies at the national level where their fundamental rights are violated.[23] The state in which the violation of the right has taken place is inhospitable to the claim, but there are also insurmountable legal difficulties involved in bringing the claim in another jurisdiction.[24] Victims of rights violations are thus often unable to gain access to a remedy and corporations are able to act with impunity. To address this situation, it is necessary to create rules that enable victims of rights violations in one country to gain access to remedies for violations of corporate fundamental rights obligations in another jurisdiction.[25] Another possibility which will be explored later in this chapter is the development of a forum for victims to gain access to remedies at the international level. In both cases, international standards are of great importance in enabling fundamental rights claims. Such standards will help not only in providing guidance on the substantive content of corporate obligations (and the causes of action in such cases) but also in ensuring there are consequences for fundamental rights

[20] See, for instance, Koskenniemi, 1997; Shelton, 2006; De Wet and Vidmar, 2012.

[21] The UNGPs – which lacks binding legal status – cannot perform the role of counterbalancing hard law, something Ruggie, 2013: 184 recognises.

[22] The 'state duty to protect' model could also be utilised here.

[23] See the UNGPs: Commentary to GP 26 for some of the obstacles in this regard.

[24] See Choudhury, 2005: 45–56 for some of these difficulties.

[25] Simons and Macklin, 2014: 302–314; De Schutter, 2015: 54–55.

violations. Accountability, in turn, is likely to generate a greater seriousness surrounding decision-making in this area by corporate actors.

Having provided a case for international fora and standards, I now investigate existing possibilities, how they could be improved as well as innovative institutional possibilities.

10.3 Soft Standard-Setting Mechanisms

The lack of binding instruments relating to business and fundamental rights has led to the proliferation of a range of 'softer standard-setting mechanisms'. Given the wide range of initiatives, the discussion that follows is not meant to be exhaustive but to examine certain leading examples for their ability – or otherwise – to accomplish the twin goals discussed earlier: firstly, enhancing the seriousness with which corporate decision-makers render judgements concerning the fundamental rights obligations of corporations; and, secondly, their ability to clarify and develop our understanding of the substantive content of those obligations.

10.3.1 Multi-Stakeholder Industry Initiatives

Given the impetus sometimes brought about by a shocking case of a rights violation, a number of initiatives have been created – by groups of companies in particular sectors or between several stakeholders in an industry – to set standards relating to their fundamental rights obligations and enforce them. Clearly, any setting of standards through these schemes cannot be taken to be determinative of the obligations of corporations in these industries and, ultimately, they must be rooted in the multi-factoral approach identified in this book. I consider two examples of such initiatives in this section: one that deals with an agreement between businesses and unions, and another that deals with standard-setting within industries.

10.3.1.1 The Accord

On 24 April 2013, garment workers entered an eight-storey factory known as the Rana Plaza in Dhaka, Bangladesh. Clothes made in this factory were ordered by important multinational companies such as Benetton (Italy), Primark (UK) and Mango (Spain). Many workers were fearful to enter the building due to the visible cracks in it; yet, out of desperation, they went to work that day on pain of losing their wages or jobs. Tragically, the building collapsed upon them with 1,132 workers losing their lives and 2,500 being injured.[26] In the wake of this terrible disaster, there was a necessity to ensure that such a disaster did not take place again and that other buildings in Bangladesh were safe for workers.[27]

As a result, a number of global brands and retailers signed a legally binding agreement in May 2013 for five years with two global union conglomerations and their Bangladeshi affiliates. This agreement was known as the Accord on Fire and Building Safety in Bangladesh and sought to protect workers from fires or building collapses through taking reasonable health and safety precautions. The Accord involved an undertaking that there would be fire, electrical and structural inspections of over 2,000 factories. The findings were to be disclosed publicly and corrective action plans developed and implemented, with follow-up inspections to ascertain whether the improvements had been made. These measures resulted in 85% of the safety hazards being fixed with some buildings being evacuated where there was a high risk of collapse.[28] The Accord also involved safety training for workers and established a health and safety complaints mechanism.[29] Importantly, the Accord makes provision for binding arbitration to take place between unions and companies which can be enforced in the local courts of all participating retailers.[30]A further extension agreement known as the Transition Accord was signed in 2018 for a further three years.[31]

The Accord utilises a range of both proactive and reactive measures to address potential violations of health and safety best practices: independent inspections, public disclosure, the empowerment of workers and

[26] For a full account, see Evans, 2015: 603–604 and www.ilo.org/global/topics/geip/WCMS_614394/lang-en/index.htm.

[27] There was also the need to provide healthcare to the injured and to compensate them as well as those who lost vital breadwinners. The Rana Plaza Arrangement sought to accomplish these goals: see https://ranaplaza-arrangement.org/intro.

[28] Details on the 2013 Accord can be found at https://bangladeshaccord.org/2018/07/20/achievements-2013-accord/.

[29] See ibid.

[30] Evans, 2015: 607–608 notes that this in fact distinguishes the Accord from other agreements on improving industry safety. Blair et al., 2018: 393–397 note some of the limitations of these provisions.

[31] For a summary of details on the Transition Accord, see https://bangladeshaccord.org/about. The Accord has become mired in politics; after much wrangling, it was agreed that its activities and functions would be transferred to a body called the RMG Sustainability Council which is governed by representatives from the government, multinational corporations and trade unions.

complaint mechanisms. In the absence of strong government regulation, this approach helps to identify risky buildings and utilises the leverage of multinational companies on local manufacturers to ensure they adhere to basic health and safety measures.[32] It also 'represents a new model of accountability because it holds retailers, the biggest beneficiaries of the Bangladesh supply chain, jointly responsible for conditions of the actual manufacturers'.[33] Unions are recognised at the highest level of decision-making, and workers thus play an important role in drawing attention to unsafe buildings and also ensuring the commitments made by retailers are met.[34] These mechanisms all contribute to encouraging a seriousness of purpose within corporations when engaging with the health and safety of workers.

The Accord clearly also deals with critical fundamental rights surrounding life and health but involves an area where there is already significant agreement and relatively clear, concrete standards. Ultimately, it is about ensuring that buildings do not collapse and adequate fire safety measures are in place which, in both cases, involves objective standards with limited room for disagreement. Consensus between business and labour (and perhaps other stakeholders) is clearly easier to achieve where the nature of the obligations are relatively uncontroversial.[35] The lessons that can be learnt for other contexts are thus limited given that it does not venture into difficult areas where matters are less clear. The Accord also applies to a very specific set of circumstances in a particular country flowing from a particular incident. It may well be that the most concrete set of rules can be established in such circumstances. Where disputes arise, the degree to which any arbitral decisions will become public is also unclear given the tensions that have arisen in this context between confidentiality and transparency.[36]

The multi-factoral approach, nevertheless, remains of use as an analytical framework if we are to justify these more concrete obligations of

[32] Donaghey and Reinecke, 2018: 25.

[33] Evans, 2015: 620.

[34] Donaghey and Reinecke, 2018: 24–25.

[35] Even so, a number of US businesses were not happy with the binding elements and, out of concern for their own potential liability, refused to sign it. They created a much weaker 'Alliance for Bangladesh Worker Safety', which avoids any partnership with unions and involves largely self-policing with all its attendant flaws (see the discussion in Evans, 2015: 621–622). For a comparison of the underlying differences in approach, and also the mutually reinforcing dimensions, see Donaghey and Reinecke, 2018.

[36] See Blair et al., 2018: 399–400.

corporations – clearly, the interests of workers in safe buildings are of great urgency, and the potential impact the most severe possible. Workers in countries like Bangladesh are highly vulnerable given their desperate socio-economic circumstances and the unavailability of employment options. Corporations as a result have significant economic power that includes being able effectively to coerce workers against their better judgement to enter into unsafe conditions. In situations where there is widespread corruption and incapacity within the state, the function of corporations also can be understood to change – taking on a more public dimension. Indeed, part of the reason the Accord has become controversial with the Bangladeshi government is that it seeks to enable businesses and workers to take on the regulatory and monitoring roles in relation to health and safety that are usually the preserve of governments. Doing so is eminently justifiable in a context where the state is incapable of performing these tasks, placing workers at serious risk to their well-being. The lack of standards set by the state also illustrates why it is important to be able to have reference to global standards in this regard. It is also accepted by all parties that there are no real countervailing considerations as corporations cannot claim that their autonomy interests in any way allow them to place the lives and health of workers at risk by forcing them into unsafe buildings.

10.3.1.2 The International Council on Mining and Metals

The International Council on Mining and Metals (ICMM) describes itself as 'an international organisation dedicated to a safe, fair and sustainable mining and metals industry'.[37] It is comprised of twenty-eight major mining and metals companies and over thirty-five national, regional and commodities associations. The self-described vision of the association is to create a situation in which mining and metals are regarded as a 'respected industry, trusted to operate responsibly and contribute to sustainable development'.[38] The companies who belong to it have to commit themselves to ten principles which have been supplemented by a series of performance expectations. The latter are supposed to indicate 'how members should be expected to manage a broad range of sustainability issues at the corporate and operational levels'.[39] To belong, one has to comply with the requirements of an

[37] See www.icmm.com/en-gb/about-us.
[38] See www.icmm.com/en-gb/about-us/vision-and-values.
[39] Introduction of the Mining Principles available at www.icmm.com/website/publications/pdfs/mining-principles/mining-principles.pdf (henceforth 'Mining Principles').

admission process which involve providing information about the company, identifying gaps in compliance with its principles and undergoing independent verification of the company's performance. Every year, there is the need to obtain independent third-party assurance of their performance on the ICMM's sustainability criteria.

Principle 3 deals with fundamental rights expressly and requires member companies to 'respect human rights and the interests, cultures, customs and values of employees and communities affected by our activities'.[40] The eight performance expectations include such matters as support for the UNGPs and the undertaking of human rights due diligence processes; avoiding involuntary displacement of families and communities; and respecting the rights of workers.[41] In addition to the principles and performance expectations, the ICCM has also released a series of position statements which attempt to provide more detail on its approach to issues such as water stewardship and tailings management.

A framework like that of the ICMM can be regarded rather sceptically as an attempt by an industry which is notorious for causing serious harms to fundamental rights to project itself in a positive manner.[42] Indeed, this assessment is supported by its mission statement which makes specific reference to 'building recognition of its contribution to local communities and society at large'.[43] The focus here seems to be very much on *marketing* the benefits mining holds for society rather than the *making* of the contribution itself. The membership of the ICMM includes companies against which serious allegations have been made of causing fundamental rights violations and serious environmental harm – such as Vale and its responsibility for the collapse of the Brumadinho tailings dam in Brazil.[44]

From a positive point of view, this is an industry organisation that, on its face, is self-consciously committed to ensuring responsible mining. As such, it potentially may contribute towards internalising a seriousness surrounding fundamental rights obligations in the corporations concerned. Organisations like the ICMM, for instance, provide a forum for

[40] www.icmm.com/website/publications/pdfs/commitments/181126_performance-expectations.pdf.

[41] See ibid.

[42] See Fonseca, 2010: 358 on the 'greenwashing' charge.

[43] www.icmm.com/en-gb/about-us/vision-and-values.

[44] The Brumadinho tailings dam in Brazil collapsed in January 2019 and has caused untold damage to individuals and communities in that area: see www.bbc.com/news/business-47432134. Vale belongs to the ICMM.

companies to learn from one another in relation to their decision-making surrounding fundamental rights.[45] Furthermore, Principle 2 requires members to 'integrate sustainable development into corporate strategy and decision-making processes'[46]. The fact that reporting and external verification is required can also contribute to enhancing the attention corporate decision-makers devote to fundamental rights and wider social and environmental concerns.[47]

Such initiatives may also play a critical role in providing guidance on corporate fundamental rights obligations through their ability and power to consider specific issues and develop concrete standards. The performance expectations helpfully elaborate upon a number of the most pressing priorities in relation to fundamental rights that arise in the mining and metals industries. Moreover, the ICMM also develops specific guidance that deals with concrete violations: in relation to the Brazilian tailings dam disaster, for example, the ICMM recognised a responsibility to develop standards surrounding such dams.[48] Any standards developed by a body such as the ICMM are likely at least to receive widespread dissemination amongst companies that have signed up to it and, thus, may come to have an influence in this sphere. Indeed, the standards set may also extend their reach beyond members and represent industry best practice.

There are though a number of weaknesses in relation to this standard-setting function that require attention. Firstly, the performance expectations, at times, demonstrate a common weakness in multi-stakeholder initiatives, namely, the utilisation of malleable language which can be exploited to avoid compliance.[49] Consider, for instance, the vague phrasing that mining corporations must 'work' to obtain the free, prior and informed consent of indigenous peoples and 'support' diversity in the workplace.[50] Secondly, there is a worry that the performance expectations can come to be regarded as exhaustive of the fundamental rights obligations of corporations. It is important that it be clear that

[45] On the benefits and desire for a collective approach, see Mccorquodale et al., 2017b: 214–215.

[46] See Mining Principles in note 39 earlier.

[47] Fonseca, 2010: 364–366, however, highlights the limits of those assurance processes at the time of her research, including management capture thereof.

[48] www.icmm.com/en-gb/about-us/our-organisation/annual-reviews/2018.

[49] This is a common problem with multi-stakeholder initiatives of which this is one: see the discussion in the 'Not Fit for Purpose Report', 2020.

[50] Performance Expectations 3.7 and 3.8 referenced in note 40 earlier. See Fonseca, 2010: 358.

corporations have obligations in relation to all fundamental rights, including matters not covered explicitly by the ICMM principles such as freedom of expression, privacy or housing. Potentially, this concern can be mitigated by the commitment to develop human rights due diligence processes for each company. In light thereof (and as is elaborated upon later in this chapter), each company should be required to develop transparently a clear understanding of its obligations in relation to any area where it has a large impact on fundamental rights. The analytical framework developed in this book could be referenced and utilised to assist decision-making by corporations in this regard.

A third worry relates to the fact that the performance expectations simply re-state the content of existing initiatives on business and human rights and certain other international human rights standards relating to, for instance, the rights of indigenous peoples.[51] On the one hand, it could be argued that the streamlining of standards with other initiatives is in fact positive and represents a clear commitment on the part of these businesses to achieve them without reinventing the wheel. On the other hand, there is very limited normative development beyond these initiatives and any attempt to consider their concrete implications in the context of the industry.

Clearly, the approach adopted by the ICMM demonstrates the importance and usefulness of external standards and principles that are developed by international bodies such as the United Nations in providing guidance on corporate obligations. Yet, it is evident too that industry bodies have very little incentive to go beyond the existing normative frameworks created at the national and international levels.[52] Consequently, much attention needs to be paid to standard-setting under these existing frameworks considering their knock-on effects and the upward pressure they can place on industries – and associations like the ICMM – to internalise their standards governing fundamental rights. There is once again a complex interplay between externally-developed normative standards and advancing a culture shift within a company or collection of companies towards taking their fundamental rights obligations seriously and developing an accurate understanding of their content.

[51] See the Declaration on the Rights of Indigenous Peoples available at www.un.org/development/desa/indigenouspeoples/declaration-on-the-rights-of-indigenous-peoples.html.

[52] Indeed, the attempts to do so are often controversial: see Fonseca, 2010: 366. There are indeed important questions raised about their legitimacy to do so as well as the nature of any decision-making processes involved in setting such standards.

10.3.2 Reporting

We saw at the national level how enhancing reporting requirements surrounding fundamental rights can be an important method of ensuring decision-makers in corporations take those rights seriously. What then can the global level contribute? I suggest that it can help outline good practices relating to reporting, create learning opportunities and set global standards which credible reports must meet. Given that business takes place across borders, a global standard also enables comparison between different contexts. That can in turn enhance domestic reporting requirements. In the following section, I consider an attempt to accomplish these aims.

10.3.2.1 The Global Reporting Initiative

The Global Reporting Initiative (GRI) is an independent international organisation that has been involved with developing sustainability reporting since 1997. It aims to assist organisations across the globe to 'be transparent and take responsibility for their impacts so that we can create a sustainable future'.[53] It seeks to accomplish this goal through developing common standards for organisations around the world to report on their impacts on sustainability.[54]

The normative focal point of the GRI is the notion of 'sustainable development', which is defined as 'development which meets the needs of the present without compromising the ability of future generations to meet their own needs'.[55] Sustainability reporting concerns an organisation's public reporting practices on its economic, environmental and social impacts.[56]

Protecting fundamental rights is not mentioned directly as part of the goals of the initiative but is, importantly, clearly included within the social and environmental dimensions thereof. The GRI has adopted a specific standard on human rights assessment[57] which explicitly identifies the UNGPs as the 'international standard that establishes the expectations of responsible conduct for organizations with respect to human rights'.[58] Following the UNGPs, it requires organisations to take

[53] www.globalreporting.org/about-gri/mission-history/.
[54] Ibid.
[55] The definition is taken from the World Commission on Environment and Development, which is quoted in the opening document of the GRI standards available at www.globalreporting.org/standards/download-the-standards/.
[56] www.globalreporting.org/how-to-use-the-gri-standards/.
[57] GRI 412.
[58] Ibid: 4.

responsibility for their impacts on all internationally recognised fundamental rights which include, at a minimum, the International Bill of Rights as well as the International Labour Organisation's 'Declaration on Fundamental Principles and Rights at Work'.[59] The GRI standard requires reporting on the approach of the organisation towards fundamental rights assessments. It also mandates reporting on the number of operations that have been subject to a fundamental rights review as well as reporting on the training provided to employees on fundamental rights policies and procedures. There is also a requirement to report on the 'significant investment agreements' that include fundamental rights clauses. The explanation for this requirement is to provide a 'measure of the extent to which human rights considerations are integrated into an organization's economic decisions'.[60]

Apart from this general fundamental rights standard, there are a range of more specific standards that relate to rights: these include reporting on incidents of discrimination, areas where a corporation is at risk of utilising child labour and the human rights training of security personnel.

There are many good features of the GRI reporting framework which have achieved some measure of success in influencing governments 'to adopt binding and non-binding corporate disclosure standards based on its guidelines'.[61] It has also gained serious traction within the business world with a large proportion of large companies utilising its framework to report on 'sustainability' issues.[62] It is importantly designed in such a way so as to utilise reporting to develop a seriousness amongst decision-makers surrounding social responsibility within a corporate structure.[63] The most important tool it employs in this regard is what it terms 'management approach disclosures'.[64] These require the organisation to outline how its management 'identifies, analyzes and responds to its actual and potential impacts'.[65] The disclosures required are quite extensive. Firstly, the management needs to report on the impact of the corporation and how it causes the impact.[66] Secondly, with this picture in mind, it needs to explain its approach to managing the impact, the

[59] Ibid.
[60] Ibid: 9.
[61] Sarfaty, 2013: 592.
[62] Ibid: 596.
[63] As Sarfaty, ibid: 580 points out, the key goal is to change corporate behaviour.
[64] See GRI 103: Management Approach.
[65] Ibid: 4.
[66] GRI 103-1.

purpose of its management approach and the specific details of how it allocates responsibilities in this regard.[67] Lastly, it also needs to explain what processes it has in place to evaluate the management approach adopted.[68]

The management approach adopted is promising and the extensive reporting requirements – with some tweaks – could be understood to give effect to some of the arguments of this book. Indeed, decision-makers are required to disclose not only their impacts but also their response to them: properly understood, this indeed recognises that not every impact is impermissible. An approach fully in line with the argument of this book would require a specific statement about the management's understanding of and conclusions about its own obligations after having identified its impacts on fundamental rights. The multi-factoral approach could be utilised by the GRI to develop the guidelines for such a statement: reference to the interests, vulnerability and impact on potential victims as well as the organisation's capacity to impact on rights, its function in an area and autonomy interests at stake could provide a useful rubric to assist decision-makers to engage the relevant considerations in any judgements they make. The proportionality test in relation to negative obligations and the seven-step reasoning process in relation to positive obligations could assist with a useful framework for arriving at final decisions in this regard. Having such a statement would result in significant transparency surrounding decision-making relating to fundamental rights and thus offer both opportunities for other actors to engage with that reasoning and for external mechanisms such as courts to review it.

Despite the promise, there are some concerns. The first relates to the fact that some of the requirements are stated in a broad way and so could be satisfied at a high level of generality with decision-makers committing themselves to rather bland and vague statements in this regard. A related second major limitation of the GRI framework is the fact that it does very little to advance our understanding of the particular obligations of businesses in the context of fundamental rights. Consider the standard on human rights assessment. The focus thereof – as with the whole document – is very much on procedural and quantitative matters:[69] whether a human rights review has been conducted, whether

67 GRI 103-2.

68 GRI 103-3.

69 This is a general problem with the approach: see Sarfaty, 2013: 606–609; Simons and Macklin, 2014: 168–172.

employee human rights training has been conducted and whether human rights clauses have been included in investment agreements. If we delve a little deeper, we may want to ask, however, what exactly is the content of such a human rights review? The standard does not explain that which, in turn, opens the door for corporations to tick this box and claim to have conducted reviews which, ultimately, are shallow and fail to address its main impacts on fundamental rights. The reporting on employees concerns the number of hours devoted to training as well as the quantity of employees who have gone through such training. Yet, these quantitative features do not at all indicate anything about the content of such training: does it enable employees to understand their rights and obligations or address controversial questions surrounding the operations of the business?[70] The standard states that the training must be relevant to operations but, again, offers substantial discretion that may lead to an avoidance to deal with specific important topics.

Ultimately, the focus of the GRI is on reporting, but reporting must be conducted in relation to standards. The GRI, however, does not develop the standards; as with the ICMM, it relies on standards that exist outside the initiative such as the international bill of rights, and a range of other instruments listed at the end of the human rights assessment standard.[71] However, there is a mistaken assumption that the content of these instruments – with language mostly focused on state obligations – can simply be applied without modification to the activities of corporations. There is no effort to examine how to translate the implications of such international documents for the specific obligations of corporations.

This particular problem is compounded in the context of the generally promising recognition that external assurance concerning the report's contents is desirable (though not a requirement).[72] The difficulty arises because of the fact that those who conduct such verification processes – usually accountants and auditors – lack professional expertise in fundamental rights, yet are given the responsibility for making significant judgements about corporate obligations.[73] As I have argued in this book, one cannot simply read off the obligations of corporations from a list of rights and there is complexity in moving from state-based frameworks to those relating to corporations. Consequently, there is

[70] Sarfaty, ibid: 612.
[71] GRI 412 at 11–12.
[72] GRI 102: 41. There is also a concern about the lack of any uniform guidelines on the reliability of such verification processes – see Sarfaty, 2013: 597.
[73] Sarfaty, ibid: 610–611.

a major gap in the GRI which, in turn, could entail that corporations often fail adequately to report on their fundamental rights obligations.

There are two ways in which this situation can be rectified. The first would be to require corporations – in relation to fundamental rights that they can materially impact on – to reach judgements about their own obligations and transparently report their reasoning. As was argued already, the GRI could be developed to require more explicit reasoning by corporations in this regard. That would offer an opportunity for review at the national level by courts (and potentially human rights commissions) and at the global level by civil society organisations (pending more binding mechanisms). Such reviews could, in turn, generate discussion around these obligations and produce concrete guidance over time.

A second approach which is desirable for the future would be for bodies external to the corporation to fill the normative gap. The GRI could itself develop the content of the standards which govern corporate reporting – though it appears not to wish to do so and, of course, there is a question about its legitimacy to make such determinations. Achieving global standards for reporting clearly indicates the necessity of developing more authoritative standard-setting mechanisms at the international level – something I will argue for later. The problem, of course, thus far is that there is no such body. In the absence thereof, the GRI could draw on the analytical framework developed in this book to guide its approach to corporate obligations, which, as I have sought to show, in many ways tracks trends in the case law of many countries around the world and that of an important regional court (the ECHR). In doing so, it would need to move towards a more qualitative approach.[74] The inclusive stakeholder approach it identifies in its foundational principles also offers some possibilities:[75] if specific challenges arise – as they do – in areas such as privacy in the workplace, a convening of various stakeholders could take place to develop the content and implications of rights in that regard.[76]

10.4 Authoritative Guidance under International Law

The discussion thus far has indicated the degree to which global initiatives from industry and civil society draw on existing normative

[74] Ibid: 615–616.
[75] See GRI 101: 8.
[76] This would align with Sarfaty, 2013: 619–621, who contends that the GRI should expand participation beyond a narrow group of experts.

frameworks relating to fundamental rights. At the same time, they often fail to grapple with the challenge of translating the standards that have been developed in relation to states to the context of business. There is thus clearly a need for more authoritative guidance to be provided by external bodies which can then be utilised by industry bodies and reporting organisations to enhance decision-making within corporations relating to fundamental rights matters. The question then arises as to which structures are well-suited to accomplish such a task at the international level. Most of the existing initiatives have a number of weaknesses: they do not have clear processes to provide any authoritative guidance; they are non-binding in nature; they, at times, lack transparency; and, in fact, highlight the normative gap outlined earlier by failing to grapple with how to translate the content of fundamental rights developed in relation to states to the context of business.[77]

They have also sought to align themselves with a central document, the UNGPs, which was described by the UN High Commissioner for Human Rights as the 'global authoritative standard, providing a blueprint for the steps all states and businesses should take to uphold human rights'.[78] The UNGPs cannot be authoritative given their non-binding status in international law, but Chapter 5 has also shown clearly the normative gap surrounding the obligations of business at the heart of the UNGPs. Given their importance in the field, I will suggest an approach to remedying this gap within the due diligence process. Thereafter, I will consider the extent to which the Working Group that was set up to help implement the UNGPs has addressed the identified normative weaknesses. I then turn to the role of existing treaty mechanisms in providing guidance on the content of corporate obligations. Having found that none of these are adequate to address the normative gaps, I argue ultimately for the need

[77] For reasons of length, I have omitted a consideration of such influential non-binding initiatives such as the Global Compact and the OECD Guidelines on Multinational Enterprises. Each has improved its mechanisms over time but offers little value to generalised standard-setting at the international level. The latter has sought to align itself with the UNGPs and thus essentially reproduces the same mistakes. See Simons and Macklin, 2014: 101–122 for a fuller discussion of both these initiatives. A similar point can be made about the revised Tripartite Declaration on Multinational Enterprises and Social Policy of the International Labour Organisation (available at www.ilo.org/wcmsp5/groups/public/–ed_emp/–emp_ent/–multi/documents/publication/wcms_094386.pdf), which largely repeats the UNGPs and whose contribution lies particularly in the area of labour rights. Its follow-up mechanisms have largely been underutilised and relatively ineffective: see Shin-Ichi, 2018: 268–270.

[78] See Al Hussein, 2015.

for a new mechanism at the international level. In section 10.5, I will consider what that could and should look like.

10.4.1 *Strengthening the UNGPs*

The UNGPs have become a leading reference point in the field of business and fundamental rights probably due to their unanimous adoption in 2011 by the United Nations Human Rights Council. The document itself is said to aim at 'enhancing standards and practices with regard to business and human rights so as to achieve tangible results for affected individuals and communities, and thereby also contributing to a socially sustainable globalization'.[79] It is not itself a treaty, and explicitly states that it does not create any new international legally binding obligations.[80]

As we saw in Chapter 5, a key contribution of the UNGPs has been to require that, in fulfilling their responsibility to respect fundamental rights, businesses must conduct a human rights due diligence ('HRDD') process.[81] That involves investigating the impacts the corporation has on fundamental rights through its own activities and those with whom it has relationships.[82] Having done so, businesses are required to take steps to prevent harms from occurring, mitigate those that are already occurring, track and monitor what they are doing and remediate where necessary.[83]

The requirement to conduct an HRDD process appears to be designed to internalise a commitment to fundamental rights within corporations which, as I argued in the last chapter, should be one of the central goals of regulation in this sphere. Principle 16 requires a policy statement committing a business to respect fundamental rights which must be approved at the most senior level of the enterprise.[84] Principle 19 clearly addresses the need for any findings on human rights impacts and decisions about how to proceed to be integrated throughout the business. The commentary specifically states that '[t]he horizontal integration across the business enterprise of specific findings from assessing human rights impacts

[79] UNGPs at 1 available at www.ohchr.org/documents/publications/Guidingprinciples Businesshr_eN.pdf.
[80] Ibid.
[81] Mccorquodale and Smit, 2017a provide an analysis of the various dimensions of HRDD.
[82] UNGPs: GP 17.
[83] UNGPs: GPs 17–22.
[84] UNGPs: GP 16.

can only be effective if its human rights policy commitment has been embedded into all relevant business functions'.[85] Tracking the implementation of fundamental rights policies is also required by the UNGPs and must be 'integrated into relevant internal reporting processes'.[86] All these measures, if adopted, clearly would significantly help to improve the degree to which corporate decision-makers engage with fundamental rights and deliberate about their implications for enterprises.[87]

The discussion in Chapter 5, however, highlighted the normative gap at the heart of the HRDD process which simply assumes the ability to move from an identification of an impact on a fundamental right to an obligation.[88] As I argued, that is mistaken and, without an understanding of what determines when an impact is permissible or impermissible, it is impossible to reach a conclusion about what corporations must do – whether it be continuing with its actions, prevention, mitigation or remediation. This normative weakness thus affects the usefulness and clarity of the HRDD process and also demonstrates the lack of guidance provided by the UNGPs themselves about such obligations.[89] What then is needed to remedy this serious shortcoming?

[85] UNGPs: Commentary on GP 19.

[86] UNGPs: Commentary on GP 20.

[87] Mccorquodale et al., 2017b: 221–222 present empirical evidence, which demonstrates that corporations which conduct HRDD processes in fact appear to be more aware of the range of their fundamental rights impacts (and consider them) than those that do not.

[88] See Deva, 2013: 98. Mccorquodale and Smit, 2017a: 224 suggest impact should be read as violation: I disagree for a range of reasons – the notions themselves are distinct; the risk-based underpinning of HRDD suggests it is important to understand all 'risks' before deciding on a course of action which runs counter to reading 'impacts' as 'violations'; and, even on their reading, there is no explanation of how one determines what constitutes a violation by businesses (as opposed to states). Ultimately, there is no escaping thinking seriously about the obligations of corporations.

[89] The work by Mccorquodale et al., 2017b in fact bears out this point: unsurprisingly, they find that the focus of many companies is on easily recognisable violations such as the use of child labour, which are closely connected to their operations (208). They also find that 'there is a real risk that companies will neither identify the human rights impacts it or a third party makes, nor will they prioritise those human rights impacts which are most severe' (211). Arguably, this is partially because some impacts are considered permissible and there is no clear methodology for determining when they are impermissible. The authors also find that there is no 'consistent pattern of benchmarking and indicators' given by respondents (at 219). This focus on indicators and the heavy reliance on human rights impact assessments suggest the desire for criteria that can allow a box-ticking assessment. Whilst standards can be concretised over time, ultimately, a proper engagement with fundamental rights will require a process of deliberation and decision-making concerning corporate obligations drawing on the analytical framework proposed in this book.

The focus of the UNGPs initially on identifying impacts is to be welcomed because we can only determine what the obligations of a corporation are through, firstly, understanding the possible impacts it can have on the rights of beneficiaries and their vulnerability to the actions of the corporation. Having identified impacts, however, human rights due diligence requires an *extra* step: the corporation must transparently provide an understanding of its reasoning surrounding how it conceives of its obligations in relation to those specific impacts. That could be done through requiring decision-makers within a corporation to provide a statement that contains their reasoning that translates material impacts into obligations. Given the impacts of corporations will be varied and multiple, to render this obligation workable, it will be necessary to have some limit on their duty to give reasons concerning their obligations – hence, it is suggested that the duty focus on 'material' or 'significant' impacts (as the GRI recommends in relation to reporting).[90] The approach outlined in this book can help with identifying the relevant factors for making such a determination and the decision-making processes suggested – proportionality in relation to negative obligations and the seven-step process relating to positive obligations – would provide guidance about the steps required to reach a final conclusion. The proposed statement should also include how the corporation's understanding of its obligations leads to one of four possible courses of action: stopping its proposed activities to prevent any harm from occurring; continuing with its course of conduct; continuing with its actions but mitigating any harms; and, taking remedial measures to address harms that have already occurred.

This proposed additional dimension of the HRDD process need not be understood as a fundamental departure from the UNGPs but rather a development of its envisaged policy statement which is designed publicly to set out businesses' 'responsibilities, commitments and expectations'.[91] The policy statement, as I understand it, is a rather high-level commitment by a corporation to abide by fundamental rights and its relationship with the HRDD process is not entirely clear. My proposal would require such a statement to be supplemented by a valuable and necessary part of the HRDD process which would involve corporate decision-makers outlining how they conceive of the corporation's

[90] The Human Rights Translated Report, 2017: 4–6 uses the notion of 'salient human rights risks' as a basis to determine what should be the focus of the company although this may be too restrictive.

[91] UNGPs: Commentary on GP 16.

obligations in relation to the areas where it has a material impact. That, in turn, could be the basis for civil society engagement with the corporation as well as a review, for instance, by courts (or an international mechanism) in certain circumstances.

It is also vitally important that the HRDD process should be connected with the corporate law reforms discussed in the previous chapter.[92] One potential problem with the HRDD process is that it is a responsibility of the company and not directly of its office-bearers. Of course, indirectly, the office-bearers could be held to account for failing to ensure the company fulfils its HRDD obligations. Yet, as I argued in the previous chapter, it is also vital that decision-makers within the company – and, specifically, directors – have particular responsibilities for ensuring they exercise their judgement reasonably in relation to determining the fundamental rights obligations of corporations and that they ensure the corporation meets those obligations.[93] Apart from fundamental rights requiring a modification of their fiduciary duties, there need to be a range of accountability mechanisms for decision-makers, some of which were discussed there. The UNGPs hold out the promise – which, as yet, has not been fully realised – that they can create a widespread recognition of the law reforms that are necessary to ensure corporations take fundamental rights seriously.

10.4.2 Building on the UN Guiding Principles: The Working Group on Business and Human Rights

One of the difficulties with the UNGPs is that they are contained in a document that, on its face, lacks any international institutional mechanism to interpret it.[94] Given the normative gap contained therein, decision-makers in corporations would benefit from having guidance concerning the concrete content of their obligations flowing from fundamental rights which in turn could inform their HRDD processes. At the international level, there was indeed a major question about what to do after the release of the UNGPs concerning a mechanism to give effect to them.

In 2011, a Working Group on the issue of human rights and transnational corporations and other business enterprises ('Working Group') was set up by the United Nations Human Rights Council and its mandate has been renewed three times. It is comprised of five independent experts

92 I am grateful to Peter Muchlinski for emphasising the importance of this point.

93 Muchlinski, 2012: 161.

94 As Simons and Macklin, 2014: 101 point out, many NGOs supported a much stronger follow-up mechanism than eventuated.

from different regions of the world. The mandate of the Working Group includes the goal to 'promote the effective and comprehensive dissemination and implementation of the UNGPs' and also to assess and make recommendations in relation to the implementation of the UNGPs.[95] It is arguable that the terms of the mandate are wide enough to allow the Working Group to build on and develop the UNGPs in significant directions that are required for its implementation. Given the normative gap I have identified in the UNGPs, the success of the mandate could be understood to require it to recognise the gap, to try and plug it (through means such as the proposal in the last section) and to provide substantive content to the obligations of businesses in relation to fundamental rights, where the opportunity arises. An exhaustive analysis of its record cannot be conducted here, but I shall focus on two reports which demonstrate the need for it to adopt an analytical framework (such as is proposed in this book) relating to corporate obligations.

First, let us consider its reports on the HRDD process. These reports usefully seek to elaborate upon the process, identifying gaps and challenges, and good practices.[96] They are particularly good on the importance of deepening the commitment within a corporation to these processes.[97] Unfortunately, however, the Working Group has largely failed to recognise the normative gap I identified in Chapter 5 between impacts and violations and the effects of not doing so. As a result, it has also not expressly sought to adopt any systematic methodology in relation to determining the substantive content of corporate obligations.

Consider its statements after describing what corporations must do once they have identified actual or potential impacts (which is the critical step in determining corporate obligations): 'if the enterprise is causing the impact, it should take steps to cease or prevent it; if it is contributing to the impact, it should take steps to cease or prevent its contribution and use leverage to mitigate the remaining impact . . . '.[98] In a companion report, it states that 'every actual impact identified will need to be addressed'.[99] Clearly, this statement assumes that impacts simply can be translated into violations and lead to an automatic assumption of corporate obligations. Given that this cannot be the case in all

95 See A/HRC/RES/17/4 available at https://documents-dds-ny.un.org/doc/RESOLUTION/GEN/G11/144/71/PDF/G1114471.pdf?OpenElement.
96 Working Group HRDD Report, 2018: para 4.
97 Ibid: paras 11, 39 and 43.
98 Ibid: para 10(b).
99 Working Group Companion Report 2, 2018: 2.

circumstances where there are impacts (as has been explained in Chapter 5), it is likely to lead to corporations 'under-performing' – by simply not acting on many of the impacts they discover which, in some circumstances, would negatively affect rights-holders. A less likely scenario is 'over-performing' – by taking action to prevent or mitigate impacts that are justifiable, though that also will, in some sense, be unfair to the corporation in pursuing its own projects. The Working Group makes very little effort to analyse why performance is weak in relation to 'taking action' and 'tracking responses' in relation to impacts[100] – one partial explanation would be the failure to distinguish permissible from impermissible impacts.

Whilst the Working Group's reports never explicitly recognise the normative gap, it, perhaps unavoidably, proposes some measures that would be relevant to a determination of obligations. It suggests, for instance, considering the impacts on a local level, prioritising severe impacts and understanding how the company is involved in an impact[101] – yet, it still does not acknowledge the need for a judgement to be made about what corporate obligations substantively are. Its most promising statements are vague but relate to 'tracking performance' where it acknowledges that doing so involves qualitative dimensions and that the company must develop company-specific indicators.[102] In one report, almost as an afterthought, it mentions that good practice involves 'clear statements on how business enterprises understand their responsibility, as opposed to trying to shift responsibilities'.[103] This is encouraging but only referenced in the context of reporting and does not expressly mention any of the complexity involved in translating impacts into obligations. Its only indication of any gap is in a footnote to the Human Rights Translated Report which, whilst helpful, also fails to disclose a clear analytical framework for determining corporate obligations (as was explained in Chapter 5).[104] The initial flaws in the UNGPs thus appear to have been largely replicated by the Working Group though, as a continuing mechanism, it has the ability to self-correct in future.

A more recent context where the Working Group attempts to grapple with corporate obligations is its report on Gender Dimensions of the

[100] Ibid: para 26.
[101] Working Group Companion Report 1, 2018: 3.
[102] Ibid: 4.
[103] Working Group Companion Report 2, 2018: 13.
[104] Ibid: 3.

UNGPs.[105] The report essentially aims to provide 'specific and practical gender guidance in implementing the Guiding Principles'[106] and what integrating a gender perspective means in this regard. In doing so, it attempts to provide an understanding of the obligations of businesses in relation to women specifically. For instance, it outlines some of the core provisions of the Convention on the Elimination of Discrimination Against Women (CEDAW) and then states that '[t]he standards contained in the Convention apply to all businesses as part of their responsibility to respect human rights under the Guiding Principles'.[107]

The report is, in many ways, impressive and highlights the contribution a body such as the Working Group can make towards developing standards relating to business obligations with respect to fundamental rights. However, the report also exemplifies the normative gap I have identified: there is no clarity about the methodology of how the Working Group moves from the obligations of states to the obligations of businesses and little time spent grappling with this question.

For instance, to avoid infringing article 5 of CEDAW (which relates to addressing social and cultural patterns of behaviour which exemplify and entrench prejudices about male superiority and stereotyping), the report provides that 'corporate advertisements should avoid promoting sexual stereotyping'.[108] This claim seems simplistic: article 5 is a broad and important clause that requires a much deeper engagement with factors such as the vulnerability of women within the context in which the corporation operates; the capacity of the corporation to impact upon prejudices and stereotyping surrounding gender; and the function of the specific corporation in the relevant social context. These dimensions could be included in any HRDD process and, if the recommendation above is accepted, require corporations to outline their understanding of their own obligations to address the multi-faceted dimensions of article 5.

Similarly, the report states that to avoid infringing article 10 of CEDAW (which deals with eliminating discrimination in the field of education), 'private education providers should ensure that women have equal access to education and vocational training'.[109] Now, the Working Group should be congratulated for extending the responsibilities of corporations beyond negative obligations alone. Yet, to be persuasive,

[105] Working Group Gender Dimensions Report, 2019.
[106] Ibid: para 3.
[107] Ibid: para 24.
[108] Ibid.
[109] Ibid.

there is a need for an analytical framework to guide how it conceptualises their positive obligations. Its current statement does not appear to be reasonable: can private educational providers really be required to ensure women across society have access to equal education and vocational training? A proper engagement with corporate obligations in this regard would have required taking into account the factors I have identified: these include understanding the needs and vulnerabilities of women in the context of a corporation's operations; understanding its capacity to assist; its specific function in the realm of education; its autonomy interests to pursue its own goals; and the capacity of other relevant actors in the area of education. A deeper reflection on these factors together with the seven-step test I have proposed in Chapter 8 is likely to lead to a more nuanced set of obligations:[110] as an illustration, in their sphere of operations, private educational providers should ensure there are no barriers to female advancement. Moreover, in circumstances where women face systemic barriers to education in the public sphere, it is reasonable to expect that private providers have an obligation specifically to ensure that their student body comprises a significant percentage of women. To this effect, they may also have obligations to provide scholarships specifically to women where there are high levels of discrimination against women, female poverty and the inability of female children to gain access to a decent education.

A further significant limitation of the Working Group's work relates to the status of its reports and the guidance it offers. Its reports clearly emanate from a committee established by the Human Rights Council and many of its members are experts in the field – they are thus likely to have persuasive value. At the same time, unfortunately, the Working Group interprets and implements the UNGPs that already have a very weak normative status at the international level: its guidance may therefore be of interest to corporations seeking to comply with the UNGPs but lacks any real authority. The case is different in relation to committees established pursuant to binding international human rights treaties, to which I now turn.

[110] I also lack space here to provide a detailed engagement but suggest, for illustrative purposes, what the possible practical effects would be of utilising the analytical framework I have proposed.

10.4.3 UN Treaty Bodies and their General Comments

Expert committees have been established in relation to a number of core international human rights treaties to consider reports by states and, also, often, to issue 'General Comments' that provide interpretations of their particular provisions. These General Comments are not themselves binding in the same way that the provisions of the treaties are but are widely regarded as providing strongly persuasive guidance on the meaning of the articles and the obligations they impose.[111] A few of the UN Treaty bodies have, in recent years, considered the implications of certain treaty provisions for businesses. I will focus on two of the most prominent General Comments and the extent to which they assist in guiding our understanding of corporate obligations.

10.4.3.1 Committee on the Rights of the Child

In 2013, the Committee on the Rights of the Child released General Comment no 16 on 'State obligations regarding the impact of the business sector on children's rights'.[112] This General Comment seeks to provide states with a framework for implementing the Convention on the Rights of Child with regard to the business sector.[113] Clearly, as its name suggests, it principally seeks to address states' obligations under the Convention.[114] In an important statement, however, it recognises that 'duties and responsibilities to respect the rights of children extend in practice beyond the State … and apply to private actors and business enterprises'.[115] As a consequence, it finds that businesses are required to meet their responsibilities regarding children's rights, and states must ensure that they do so. Significantly, these statements represent a recognition by an influential committee that effectively businesses do have international obligations flowing from fundamental rights.

That recognition, however, does not lead to a detailed consideration of businesses' direct obligations. However, as was argued in Chapters 2 and 3, in providing an understanding of what the state duty to protect involves, there is an inevitable need to develop an understanding of corporate obligations in that sphere. In paragraph 28, for instance, the

[111] 2004 Treaty Bodies Report at 5. For an overview of the different views on their legal significance, see Keller and Grover, 2012: 128–133.

[112] The General Comment no 16 (2013) is available at www.refworld.org/docid/51ef9cd24.html.

[113] Ibid: paras 1 and 5.

[114] See ibid: para 8.

[115] Ibid: para 8.

committee recognises that state obligations include a duty to pass laws and regulations that 'frame how business enterprises can impact on children's rights. States must investigate, adjudicate and redress violations of children's rights caused or contributed to by a business enterprise'.[116] These two sentences highlight how state action is contingent upon having an understanding of what constitutes a violation by a business. Sadly, the committee here also suggests the normative gap evident in the UNGPs: it does not explain how a statement about the impact of a corporation on children's rights translates into an understanding of the violations it commits. Without such a step, which requires thinking carefully about corporate obligations, it will not be clear what actions the state must take in the fulfilment of its own obligations to respond to any violations.[117]

A further example of the committee's jump from impacts to violations is evident when it deals with specific rights, including the right to life, survival and development (article 6). In elaborating on the impacts of businesses, it states that 'selling or leasing land to investors can deprive local populations of access to natural resources linked to their subsistence and cultural heritage: the rights of indigenous children may be particularly at risk in this context'.[118] This statement addresses an important concern, but it fails to offer any guidance on what either businesses or states are obligated to do: must the state ban the sale or lease of such land to businesses? Are businesses obligated not to buy land in areas where indigenous peoples reside? Businesses' impacts on such communities can be severe but also in some cases bring benefits such as economic possibilities for adults and educational opportunities for children. Without engaging with the multiple relevant factors and structured reasoning processes identified in this book, it is not clear how one can specify corporate obligations (rather than simply identify impacts). This problem is evident in many statements in this General Comment and indicative of the need for such a treaty body to devote more attention to corporate obligations – rather than simply state obligations – and utilise a clear analytical framework to determine their substantive content.

116 Ibid: para 28.

117 The jump (and seeming interchangeability) between impact and violation is also evident in paras 62–65 of the General Comment, which deal with HRDD relating to children in particular.

118 General Comment 16: para 19.

10.4.3.2 UN Committee on Economic, Social and Cultural Rights

In 2017, a second important and useful General Comment on 'State Obligations under the International Covenant on Economic, Social and Cultural Rights in the Context of Business Activities' was released by the UN Committee on Economic, Social and Cultural Rights.[119] The General Comment, interestingly, at the outset makes a nod towards recognising direct obligations of businesses under international human rights law.[120] Apart from mentioning that, in some jurisdictions, such a direct approach exists, it also, interestingly, affirms that 'under international standards, business entities are expected to respect Covenant rights regardless of whether domestic laws exist or are fully enforced in practice'.[121] The General Comment then states that it expressly aims to assist businesses in discharging their 'human rights obligations and assuming their responsibilities'.[122] This paragraph initially appears to be cautious by referencing the UNGPs and 'international standards'. Yet, it expressly uses the word 'obligations' – which has come to have a legally binding connotation – rather than the weaker notion of 'responsibilities' employed in the UNGPs.[123] The focus, however, turns thereafter quickly to state obligations though, refreshingly, it acknowledges that 'it only deals with the conduct of private actors – including business entities – indirectly'.[124]

As before, when adopting an indirect approach, the duty to protect becomes of central significance.[125] A crucial question here is which obligations must state parties impose on corporations in giving effect to their duty to protect. Sadly, the General Comment also offers no clear methodology for answering this question. As a result, we see a range of important yet miscellaneous issues being addressed.[126] In outlining that the obligation to protect entails mandatory HRDD

[119] The General Comment no 24 (2017) is available at www.refworld.org/docid/5beaecba4.html.

[120] In ibid: para 51, it also recognises the importance of states allowing for remedies directly against businesses on the basis of covenant rights.

[121] Ibid: para 5.

[122] Ibid.

[123] This distinction flows from the language in the UNGPs which distinguish between 'obligations' of states that are legally binding and 'responsibilities' of businesses which are not.

[124] General Comment no 24: para 11.

[125] Ibid: paras 10 and 14.

[126] See, for instance, the range of issues mentioned briefly in paras 18 and 19.

processes,[127] the General Comment uses the words 'violations', abuses' and 'impacts' altogether in one paragraph without delineating the relationship between them.[128] Apart from a few examples it gives, it provides no framework for clarifying how states should approach determining the obligations of businesses in relation to economic, social and cultural rights specifically. At times, it makes reference to one or two of the factors I have identified, such as vulnerability[129] and function[130] but it does not develop any overarching decision-making procedure. Moreover, whilst negative obligations are of course important in this area, it is clear that socio-economic rights often require positive obligations to be assumed. The committee, to its credit, recognises the importance of business co-operation in assisting the state to realise its obligations to fulfil these rights.[131] Yet, the General Comment does not take us much further than that in determining the substantive content of businesses' positive obligations.

In summary, treaty committees such as the two engaged in this chapter can play an important role in providing guidance to states and the private sector concerning the substantive content of the obligations of businesses. They have a status and authority that enable them to issue normative guidance and lead their pronouncements to be taken seriously by important decision-makers even if they are not strictly legally binding.[132] As such, these committees could help advance our understanding of corporate obligations in the future.

At present, whilst the two committees have sought to press the boundaries to some extent, they are also constrained by a traditional and rather conservative understanding of their role. Indeed, thus far, these bodies expressly have regarded themselves as clarifying state obligations to prevent fundamental rights violations by businesses. They could have recognised that this task inevitably – as was argued in Chapter 2 – requires an understanding of the obligations of businesses but they have not done so. As such, they have not adopted any systematic approach to this question and, as a result, failed to offer sufficient guidance for the development of states' laws and regulations in this area. There are, instead, rather vague exhortations to enact 'measures', together with the non-sequitur of moving

127 Ibid: para 16.
128 Ibid.
129 Ibid: paras 8–9 and disability, for instance, is expressly mentioned in para 22.
130 Ibid: para 21.
131 Ibid: paras 23–24.
132 See Keller and Grover, 2012: 117–119; Van Alebeek and Nollkaempfer, 2012: 412.

from 'impact' immediately to obligations. Their current contribution towards the understanding of corporate obligations in relation to fundamental rights is thus limited. Given both committees have both recently adopted General Comments in relation to business, it is unlikely in the near future that we will see further developments emerging from them on these issues. As such, for further normative guidance, it seems that we need to look elsewhere. Section 10.5 considers the possibilities of new institutional mechanisms and the relative advantages and disadvantages thereof.

10.5 New Institutional Possibilities at the International Level

What emerges from the aforementioned analysis is that there is a lack of any mechanism at the international level that focuses on determining (or providing guidance about) the obligations of corporations in relation to fundamental rights. In proposing new mechanisms, it is important to have in mind the difficulties and limitations of existing structures and, thus, the goal of constructing them. The focus here is on an international mechanism that could help ensure greater clarity about the substantive content of corporate obligations. Such a mechanism would require a number of key features to achieve that goal.

Firstly, any such mechanism would need to have a degree of authoritative power such that its guidance has weight for both corporations and state-based institutions alike (henceforth, 'bindingness'). Secondly, the legitimacy of the mechanism would be enhanced if it could enable participation and inputs by non-governmental organisations and others concerned with the protection of fundamental rights in the formulation of standards ('participation'). Thirdly, it is of importance that its decisions are issued publicly rather than only to specific parties such that transparent and generally applicable standards can emerge in this area ('publicity'). Fourthly, it would need to have decision-making power over a range of fundamental rights (rather than simply a narrow area such as health and safety) that apply to corporations ('wide scope'). Finally, its rulings would need to be capable of establishing general principles that apply beyond particular cases ('generality').

What kind of mechanism could be developed that has these features? I shall consider four possibilities against these criteria.[133]

[133] These mechanisms could be complementary with one another and a choice need not necessarily be made between them.

10.5.1 *Business and Human Rights Arbitration*

In 2017, international law experts began to discuss the possibility of special rules to deal with arbitrations at an international level that involved business and human rights disputes. A drafting team was set up and a document composed which outlined some of the central issues.[134] At the time of writing, a draft set of rules has been released known as the 'Hague Rules on Business and Human Rights Arbitration'.[135] The goal was to consider the 'possibility of international arbitration as a method of resolving disputes over obligations and commitments arising out of human rights violations on the part of business'.[136] The idea here would be for businesses and victims of fundamental rights violations to agree to a private judicial process 'in which expert arbitrators chosen by the parties would be able to ascertain the violation of business and human rights obligations and offer due relief'.[137] The current rules attempt to adapt some of the existing frameworks around arbitration[138] to the business and human rights context. The draft rules provide guidance on issues such as the composition of the arbitral tribunal, details of how the proceedings are to be conducted and the nature of the award. Could such arbitrations help provide guidance concerning the obligations of businesses with respect to fundamental rights?

Importantly, any such arbitration process would of necessity be consensual as the draft rules admit that '[c]onsent remains the cornerstone of business and human rights arbitration'.[139] Businesses could thus refuse to accept such a process when they clearly recognise they have violated their obligations. If they do, it is clear that once the parties consent to the process, the determination by arbitrators is binding. That provides opportunities for the elaboration in concrete circumstances on the fundamental rights obligations of businesses.[140]

[134] The 'Elements Papers' is available at www.cilc.nl/cms/wp-content/uploads/2019/01/Elements-Paper_INTERNATIONAL-ARBITRATION-OF-BUSINESS-AND-HUMAN-RIGHTS-DISPUTE.font12.pdf.

[135] The 'Draft Hague Rules' are available at www.cilc.nl/cms/wp-content/uploads/2019/06/Draft-BHR-Rules-Final-version-for-Public-consultation.pdf.

[136] Elements Paper (note 134 earlier) at 3.

[137] Ibid.

[138] In particular, the UNCITRAL Arbitration Rules which are available at https://uncitral.un.org/sites/uncitral.un.org/files/media-documents/uncitral/en/uncitral-arbitration-rules-2013-e.pdf.

[139] Draft Hague Rules (note 135 earlier) 1.

[140] Blair et al., 2018: 412 see international arbitration as a promising avenue for not only 'enforcing, but also evolving the content of substantive rights and obligations'.

However, there are a number of limitations with arbitration in this regard: the binding effect, of course, only extends to the particular case and to the parties in question. An arbitral award would also, generally, lack any precedent-setting capacity other than to indicate, perhaps persuasively, how a particular matter has been resolved. The scope of any determination would also generally be narrow and focus on the particular dispute between the parties. Encouragingly, the current rules also provide for third persons who are not the subject of the dispute – such as non-governmental organisations – to make submissions to the tribunal. The provision, however, states that such participation will be allowed 'after consultation with the parties':[141] it is thus sadly conceivable that the parties to the dispute may veto such participation.

In relation to publicity, the current draft rules recognise the importance of a high degree of transparency of the proceedings.[142] They, however, attempt to leave determinations in this regard to the tribunal which must balance a number of factors.[143] The drafters, however, recognise in their commentary that whilst they counsel against this, the parties can choose to derogate from the transparency provisions.[144] Businesses will have a strong reason to do so and agree to arbitration only on the basis of the confidentiality of the proceedings.[145] If awards are kept secret, very limited benefits will be gleaned from such processes for the clarification and development of the substantive content of corporate obligations.

Thus, the new rules on international arbitration are an important proposal for settling disputes between parties and potentially for providing remedies to victims of fundamental rights violations by businesses. Yet, for the reasons provided, this initiative does not hold out much hope of developing a mechanism for providing greater and more authoritative guidance concerning corporate obligations with respect to fundamental rights.[146]

[141] Draft Hague Rules (note 135 earlier) section 24 bis.
[142] Ibid: Preamble para 6(d).
[143] Ibid: article 33.
[144] Ibid: Commentary on Article 33.
[145] See Blair et al., 2018: 399–400 concerning how this issue arose in arbitrations concerning the Accord in Bangladesh discussed earlier.
[146] A good example where some helpful guidance was provided – though of course being non-binding on future cases – was in the *Urbaser* arbitral decision concerning an investor–state dispute which recognised directly applicable negative obligations upon corporations in international law.

10.5.2 A Treaty Committee

The creation of an international mechanism for providing normative guidance on the substantive content of corporate obligations is one of the key arguments for a new treaty on business and human rights, which has been the subject of discussion in Geneva since 2014.[147] The 2nd Revised Draft Treaty (henceforth, 'Draft Treaty') on the table at the time of writing this book proposes the establishment of a committee similar to other UN Human Rights Treaty Bodies.[148] Apart from considering and providing concluding observations on reports issued by the states,[149] it is proposed in this draft that the committee has the key function to make 'general comments and normative recommendations on the understanding and implementation' of the treaty.[150]

As we have seen, General Comments have offered other treaty bodies the opportunity to issue guidance on the substantive content of fundamental rights obligations. In terms of bindingness, the exact status of committee decisions as legally binding is disputed – but most agree that they do possess a very strong degree of persuasiveness.[151] Short of the decisions of a court (which will be discussed later in the chapter), they are the most authoritative normative guidance that could be hoped for at the international level. In addition, General Comments and the interpretation provided therein by treaty bodies are often taken account of and influence domestic court decisions.[152] By their nature, General Comments also meet the criteria of applying generally and being issued publicly and so can be useful in advancing the understanding of international fundamental rights norms and their concomitant obligations. In developing General Comments, the UN Committee on Economic and Social Rights has also demonstrated the possibility of allowing participation from a wide range of interested parties. As a matter of course, it convenes a day of general discussion in which interested parties are invited to engage publicly with the committee concerning the proposed content of the General Comment and make relevant submissions.[153]

[147] See Bilchitz, 2016b: 212–214.
[148] 2nd Revised Draft Treaty, 2020, article 15.
[149] Ibid: article 15(b).
[150] Ibid: article 15(a).
[151] See Keller and Grover, 2012: 128–133.
[152] For a detailed discussion and examples, see Van Alebeek and Nollkaemper, 2012: 397–411.
[153] Keller and Grover, 2012: 177–178.

The major difficulty concerning the committee's power to issue General Comments is that it will be bound by the final scope of any treaty on business and human rights. A range of controversial issues have arisen in this regard[154] but, for our purposes, the major problem with the current draft is the fact that it focuses mainly on the obligations of states and hardly mentions corporate obligations in their own right. The current draft, importantly, moves beyond the language of impact to place the notion of 'human rights abuse' by corporations at its core. In the definition of this notion, however, the Draft Treaty does not expressly address the normative gap identified earlier and, arguably, suggests that any 'harm' to a right constitutes an abuse. The notion of 'harm' could allow for a distinguishing between permissible and impermissible impacts but the draft provides no express indication that this is its intention or any conceptual framework for how to approach this question. These gaps may provide an opportunity for the committee to advance our understanding of corporate obligations. At the same time, given that the focus of the text is on state obligations, the committee may face both internal and external disputes on how far it can go in interpreting corporate obligations themselves. As such, it is unclear how useful the current draft, if adopted, would be for the normative clarification of corporate obligations.

Currently, the contours of the new treaty are being established and appear to be unfavourable to the treaty itself including direct obligations for corporations. In my view, it would be desirable to include a recognition of such obligations and allow the committee scope to interpret them. However, even if this route is not adopted (which seems likely), there remains an opportunity to negotiate a text that allows for determinations by the committee of the substantive content of corporate obligations when delineating the nature of state obligations in this area, which, as we saw, is in fact a conceptual necessity.[155] The current draft would be greatly improved by enabling such determinations to be made expressly in perhaps the article on the committee's functions. If that is done, the committee would constitute a particularly significant addition to the institutional architecture surrounding fundamental rights at the international level.

[154] For an outline of the issues, see Bilchitz, 2016b: 220–221; Deva, 2017: 167–178 and recent state comments, in the Draft Sixth Session Report, 2020 para 24.

[155] See section 2.3 of Chapter 2.

10.5.3 An Individual Complaints Mechanism

One of the key points of criticism that can be made of the 2nd Revised Draft Treaty as it stands is the fact that it lacks a complaint mechanism for individuals at the international level where they are victims of fundamental rights violations by corporations. This situation is similar to what transpired in relation to the ICESCR prior to the coming into force of its Optional Protocol in 2013. In a recent article, Liebenberg argues for the importance of such an individual complaints procedure in providing concrete remedies to victims of violations. Importantly, for our purposes, she also contends that such procedures have a 'special role to play in developing the normative content and obligations imposed by the relevant rights in the context of complex factual scenarios'.[156] She maintains too that the lack of such a procedure contributed to domestic courts being reluctant to recognise economic, social and cultural rights as being fully justiciable.[157]

Such outcomes for a future treaty on business and human rights would be undesirable. The current model in the Draft Treaty seeks to rely on extraterritorial domestic enforcement rather than any international mechanism: in other words, it seeks to facilitate the bringing of actions in one state for violations that take place in another where victims cannot gain access to remedies in the latter.[158] Yet, despite the improvements in the Draft Treaty, victims may find it difficult to bring cases in another jurisdiction. Indeed, despite the obligations contained in the Draft Treaty surrounding mutual legal assistance and international co-operation,[159] states are unlikely to welcome investigations taking place about fundamental rights violations on their territory for purposes of furthering legal actions in another jurisdiction and may well see these as constituting interferences with their internal affairs. They could, as a result, place obstacles in the path of such investigations and the collection of evidence. Even if they do not, navigating the complexities of bringing a case in another jurisdiction may well be unrealistic for most victims of rights violations by corporations. From a perspective of normative guidance, judgments in particular national jurisdictions may have authoritative force nationally, but the degree to

[156] Liebenberg, 2020: 50.
[157] Ibid.
[158] Provisions such as article 9 (Jurisdiction) and article 11 (Applicable law) assist in this regard.
[159] 2nd Revised Draft Treaty Article 12.

which they have persuasive force in other jurisdictions is limited and will vary with legal doctrines and the openness of judges.[160] There may also be a lack of consistency surrounding decision-making relating to corporate obligations (and resultant remedies) that flow from the particularities of differing legal systems.[161]

Consequently, from the perspective of both enhancing normative guidance and access to remedies, it would be useful for the Draft Treaty to create an international mechanism not based in any state where individual complaints could be heard should they be unable to find any relief elsewhere. The most ambitious proposal would be to create a new international court to address corporate violations in relation to fundamental rights (a matter considered next in this chapter). Short of such an outcome, in line with other international fundamental rights instruments (such as the ICCPR and ICESCR), the proposed committee established in terms of the 2nd Revised Draft could be given jurisdiction to hear individual complaints.

Such a proposal was made when a Draft Optional Protocol (henceforth 'Draft OP') was released simultaneously with the Zero Draft of the Treaty.[162] Article 8 of the Draft OP provides that a State Party may recognise the competence of the committee 'to receive and consider communications from or on behalf of individuals or groups of individuals' with regard to violations of fundamental rights by businesses that fall within the scope of the Zero Draft.[163] As with other complaints mechanisms, all available domestic remedies must be exhausted.[164] Upon receipt of the complaint, the committee must then confidentially bring the complaint to the attention of the state and the business concerned and invite, within six months, a written response and details of any measures taken to address the matter.[165] It may then also request a confidential inquiry and report by one or more of its members about the complaint. After completing the inquiry, it must transmit the findings together with 'any comments or suggestions which seem appropriate in view of the situation' to the state or business

[160] The South African Constitution famously allows for consulting foreign case law in interpreting its Bill of Rights. In the United States, this is a highly controversial question: see Parrish, 2007: 642–652.

[161] Choudhury, 2005: 71.

[162] The Draft OP is available at www.ohchr.org/Documents/HRBodies/HRCouncil/WGTransCorp/Session4/ZeroDraftOPLegally.PDF.

[163] Ibid: article 8.

[164] Ibid: article 9.

[165] Ibid: article 10.

concerned.[166] It may finally include a summary of the inquiry it conducted in its annual report to the General Assembly of the United Nations.[167]

The Draft OP thus attempts to create an individual complaints mechanism that is similar in many respects to the dialogical approach adopted in other international fundamental rights instruments. Clearly, decision-making in individual cases allows for an examination of the content of corporate obligations in particular circumstances. As with other case law, decisions by the committee would not set general norms in the abstract but provide guidance as to how to approach similar cases in the future. An individual complaints mechanism is thus likely to offer significant normative guidance and would practically assist corporations in understanding their obligations in concrete settings. The problem mentioned in relation to General Comments though resurfaces: the current Draft Treaty focuses on state obligations which may affect the usefulness of the guidance the committee is able to provide on corporate obligations. It is not clear, for instance, whether complaints will be against a state's failure to protect individuals from corporate harms or directly against corporations themselves. It is though promising that the envisaged procedure includes communications with the business and invites written responses from them, which would, in itself, stimulate a deliberative process within the corporation surrounding the complaint.

Beyond the state, business and victims, at present the current provisions of the Draft OP do not envisage any wider participation of stakeholders such as non-governmental organisations or submissions from similarly affected communities. Hopefully, the inquiry provisions could be broadened to allow for such inputs into the committee's decision-making processes. On bindingness, it is clear that the committee does not have the same authoritative powers as courts do and so its decisions would have persuasive value only – even so, its findings will be significant in advancing an understanding of how the treaty is to be interpreted. The committee would also lack full powers of enforcement and rely on the goodwill of states to implement its decisions, which may explain the softer approach that is adopted in the Draft OP.

A final problem with the provisions as currently drafted is that they allow for maintaining the confidentiality of the process of investigation and the findings of the committee. These provisions can be defended as

166 Ibid: article 11(2).
167 Ibid: article 11(3).

seeking to encourage consensual solutions to be found; at the same time, they remove a major driver that spurs businesses to address the wrongs they commit relating to fundamental rights, namely, negative publicity. The current draft provisions do allow for a summary of any inquiry to be released publicly – which perhaps could include normative guidance on the content of corporate obligations useful for future cases – but they could be improved by making explicit the right of the committee to release all its findings if it deems this appropriate.

10.5.4 An International Court

The most ambitious proposal for a mechanism to provide authoritative guidance on the obligations of businesses with respect to fundamental rights would be the establishment of a World Court on Business and Human Rights (WCBHR).[168] Clearly the powers of any such institution would depend on the treaty setting it up.[169] It would be ideal if such a court would have the ability to hear cases concerning the failure by businesses to meet their obligations in relation to fundamental rights.[170] Clearly, to render the case load workable, this could not, in general, be a court of first instance – there would need, for example, to be the exhaustion of domestic remedies[171] or the inability of a victim to apply for such remedies because of some existing legal gap. There could also be principles according to which the court could control its jurisdiction to hear appeals from national jurisdictions in cases, for instance, that merit the clarification of corporate obligations in relation to fundamental rights. Arguably, like other international courts, it could be granted the power to issue advisory opinions that would help address a number of issues, including to clarify corporate obligations.

A dedicated court would have the benefit of being a mechanism with the highest degree of binding authority in international law – at least for the states signing up to the treaty.[172] It is likely too over time that its judgments would become highly persuasive even for those who have not signed the treaty. Its rulings would be focused on particular cases (apart

[168] See, for instance, Choudhury, 2005: 69–73; Bilchitz, 2016b: 219; Gallegos and Uribe, 2016.
[169] Choudhury, ibid: 70.
[170] This seems to be what Gallegos and Uribe, 2016: 7 and Choudhury, 2005: 71 envisage.
[171] Ibid.
[172] As Choudhury, 2005: 72 points out, it would be vital to have significant state participation for the legitimacy of this model.

from advisory opinions), but, once again, the general legal principles and doctrines it utilises could help provide more widespread normative guidance. Court judgments would also usually be public. Like other courts, it could have a procedure allowing for the intervention of amici curiae (friends of the court) which could expand participation in proceedings beyond the parties to a dispute. The scope of its powers would again depend on the treaty in terms of which it is constituted but should, ideally, allow it to make decisions concerning the full range of fundamental rights that can be impacted upon by business. Whether it is able to rule on the obligations of corporations directly will again be dependent on the terms of the treaty though, as has been argued, even an indirect model would require it to engage with corporate obligations. The analytical framework proposed in this book could be applied by the court and help to provide guidance on the substantive content of corporate obligations.

Consequently, this analysis suggests that an international court dedicated to making judgments concerning the obligations of businesses with respect to fundamental rights would be the best institutional solution to the current gap at the international level in this regard. These considerations should provide states with good reasons to consider such a mechanism. Yet, at present, even countries supportive of a treaty on business and human rights are reluctant to establish a court. The 2nd Revised Draft Treaty does not include any such proposal. The likely reason for this reticence relates to the large institutional costs of funding such a mechanism[173] and, perhaps, a lack of political will to create a mechanism with such binding authority which is harder to subvert.

Of course, there are existing international human rights courts which may, in the absence of creating such a new mechanism, be able to help provide greater normative guidance on the content of corporate obligations in relation to fundamental rights. The Rome Statute could be amended to allow juristic persons to be brought before the International Criminal Court.[174] Regional courts such as the European Court of Human Rights and the Inter-American Court of Human Rights are no substitute for a truly international mechanism given that they have a limited mandate and only provide authoritative guidance within the framework of the

[173] This is only briefly referenced by Gallegos and Uribe, 2016: 7.

[174] See, for instance, Kremnitzer, 2010: 917 though the history (described by Choudhury, 2005: 58–61) suggests this may also be unlikely. Such an extension would also only address the domain of egregious fundamental rights violations that constitute international crimes.

treaties with which they are concerned that only address a particular region of the world. The decisions of those courts, nevertheless, are often strongly persuasive in other regions and where they are well-reasoned can provide strong guidance on corporate obligations. As we saw in Chapter 2, however, the dominant paradigm utilised by the European Court of Human Rights (and this is replicated in the other systems too) is state-based and does not engage directly with the obligations of corporations. As I argued, such a state-based approach does inevitably require a construction of corporate obligations: as such, if these courts are prepared to recognise what is a conceptual necessity, they could play a much greater role in providing guidance on the substantive content of corporate obligations. The arguments provided in this book could assist such courts in the task of developing an analytical legal framework for determining the fundamental rights obligations of corporations. The possibilities for existing court mechanisms to provide greater substance to corporate obligations should thus be considered and realised.

10.6 Conclusion: Substance and Process in Developing Corporate Obligations

I have considered in this chapter a number of institutional possibilities at the international level in relation to how they achieve two goals: improving decision-making within corporations surrounding their fundamental rights obligations; and providing greater guidance concerning the substantive content of those obligations. We saw how most of the current approaches that have been adopted do not, in general, directly address the substantive content of corporate obligations. Where they do, they tend incorrectly either to read off corporate obligations from state obligations or to conflate impacts with violations. Apart from these flaws, most of the current structures are 'soft' and rather weak in terms of the authority they have to issue guidance. I made proposals in light of this analysis for reforms to existing structures and initiatives but also for developing new institutional mechanisms that would be capable of providing relatively authoritative guidance in relation to corporate obligations. Both existing and potential mechanisms could benefit from thinking deeply about corporate obligations; the analytical framework proposed in this book, I suggest, could help structure the reasoning process they utilise.

Doing so does not represent a radical departure but rather is actually a development of what already exists: a remarkable convergence by courts – at different levels and in different jurisdictions – on a range of relevant factors and the necessity of balancing different normative considerations when determining corporate obligations. I have sought in this book both to identify this nascent paradigm and then to systematise and develop it into the multi-factoral approach which I defend. Doing so involved analysing the most significant factors – which include vulnerability, capacity, function and autonomy – whilst also proposing structured reasoning processes through which they are to be balanced. Adopting this approach can help guide decision-makers – both within and outside the corporation – at both national and international levels when they make judgements concerning corporate obligations. There is indeed an interaction and mutually reinforcing relationship between the national and international domains and the need for institutional reforms in both to ensure the optimal implementation of the proposed analytical framework. With more judgements being made, the concrete implications of employing this framework for the negative and positive obligations of corporations will, ultimately, become clearer and, over time, potentially harden into certain rules. Understanding the deeper normative structures of reasoning that give rise to such rules will though, even then, help determine when it is necessary to consider exceptions to these rules.

This book thus builds on what is already recognised in many courts to lay out a blueprint for the future. Corporations have always had significant impacts on fundamental rights, yet they have often resisted recognition of their obligations. The time has come expressly to take their obligations seriously and attend to two critical matters: developing their substantive content and ensuring decision-makers are diligent in the judgements they make concerning them. I have proposed an analytical framework for the former and proposed various changes to the existing legal framework – both nationally and internationally – to accomplish the latter. There is here an important connection between substantive obligations and the processes necessary to ensure they are adequately delineated and realised. These proposals, it is hoped, will contribute to enhancing the global framework for fundamental rights protection – as well as our understanding of the social embeddedness of the corporation itself – to ensure not only that corporations do not harm our fundamental rights but also that they actively play a part in contributing towards their realisation.

BIBLIOGRAPHY

Addo, M. 1999. 'The Corporation as a Victim of Human Rights Violations'. In M. Addo (ed.).

Addo, M. (ed.). 1999. *Human Rights Standards and the Responsibility of Transnational Corporations*. The Hague: Kluwer Law International.

Alexy, R. 2002. *A Theory of Constitutional Rights* (trans. J. Rivers). Oxford: Oxford University Press.

Alexy, R. 2009. 'On Constitutional Rights to Protection'. *Legisprudence* 3: 1–17.

Alston, P. 2005. 'The "Not-a-Cat" Syndrome: Can the International Human Rights Regime Accommodate Non-state Actors?'. In P. Alston (ed.).

Alston, P. (ed.). 2005. *Non-state Actors and Human Rights*. Oxford: Oxford University Press.

Alvarez, J. E. 2011. 'Are Corporations Subjects of International Law?'. *Santa Clara Journal of International Law* 9: 1–35.

Amao, O. 2011. *Corporate Social Responsibility, Human Rights and the Law: Multinational Corporations in Developing Countries*. London: Routledge.

American Law Institute. 1994. *Principles of Corporate Governance: Analysis and Recommendations*. Washington: American Law Institute.

Aristotle. *Nicomachean Ethics* (trans. W. D. Ross) available at http://classics.mit.edu/Aristotle/nicomachaen.1.i.html.

Ariza, L. J. 2013. 'The Economic and Social Rights of Prisoners and Constitutional Court Intervention in the Penitentiary System in Colombia'. In D. Bonilla (ed.).

Armour, J. 2019. 'Derivative Actions: A Framework for Decisions'. *Law Quarterly Review* 135: 412–435.

Armour, J., Deakin, S. and Konzelmann, S. 2003. 'Shareholder Primacy and the Trajectory of UK Corporate Governance'. *British Journal of Industrial Relations* 41: 531–555.

Armour, J., Black, B., Cheffins, B. and Nolan, R. 2009. 'Private Enforcement of Corporate Law: An Empirical Comparison of the United Kingdom and the United States'. *Journal of Empirical Legal Studies* 6: 687–722.

Armour, J., Hansmann, H., Kraakman, R. and Pargendler, M. 2017a. 'What Is Corporate Law?'. In R. Kraakman et al. (eds.).

Armour, J., Hansmann, H. and Kraakman, R. 2017b. 'Agency Problems and Legal Strategies'. In R. Kraakman et al. (eds.).

Armour, J., Enriques, L., Hansmann, H. and Kraakman, R. 2017c. 'The Basic Governance Structure: The Interests of Shareholders as a Class'. In R. Kraakman et al. (eds.).

Armour, J., Gordon, J. and Min, G. 2020a. 'Taking Compliance Seriously'. *Yale Journal of Regulation* 37: 1–66.

Armour, J., Garrett, B., Gordon, J. and Min, G. 2020b. 'Board Compliance'. *Minnesota Law Review* 104: 1191–1273.

Arnold, D. 2006. 'Corporate Moral Agency'. *Midwest Studies in Philosophy* 30: 279–291.

Arnold, D. 2009. 'The Human Rights Obligations of Multinational Corporations'. In J. D. Smith (ed.).

Arnold, D. 2010. 'Transnational Corporations and the Duty to Respect Basic Human Rights'. *Business Ethics Quarterly* 20: 371–399.

Ashcraft, R. 1994. 'Locke's Political Philosophy'. In V. Chappell (ed.).

Ashton, A. 2009. 'Rescuing the Hero: The Ramifications of Expanding the Duty to Rescue on Society and the Law'. *Duke Law Journal* 59: 69–107.

Ayers, I. and Braithwaite, J. 1992. *Responsive Regulation: Transcending the Deregulation Debate.* Oxford: Oxford University Press.

Backer, L. C. 2017. 'The Human Rights Obligations of State-Owned Enterprises: Emerging Conceptual Structures and Principles in National and International Law and Policy'. *Vanderbilt Journal of Transnational Law* 50: 827–888.

Bakan, J. 2004. *The Corporation: The Pathological Pursuit of Profit and Power.* New York: Free Press.

Baldwin, R., Cave, M. and Lodge, M. 2011. *Understanding Regulation: Theory, Strategy and Practice.* Oxford: Oxford University Press.

Balkin, J. M. and Siegel, R. B. (eds.). 2009. *The Constitution in 2020.* New York: Oxford University Press.

Barak, A. 2001. 'Constitutional Human Rights and Private Law'. In D. Friedmann and D. Barak-Erez (eds.).

Barak, A. 2012. *Proportionality: Constitutional Rights and Their Limitations.* Cambridge: Cambridge University Press.

Barczak, T. 2017. 'Konstitutionalisierung der Privatrechtsordnung'. In F. Scheffczyk and Y. Fabian-Wolter (eds.).

Barnes, M. 2018. *State-Owned Entities in International Law.* Geneva: Graduate Institute of International and Development Studies.

Baskin, J. B. and Miranti, P. J. 1997. *A History of Corporate Finance.* Cambridge: Cambridge University Press.

Beale, S. 2009. 'A Response to the Critics of Corporate Criminal Liability'. *American Criminal Law Review* 46: 1481–1505.

Beauchamp, T., Bowie, N., and Arnold, D. (eds.). 2008. *Ethical Theory and Business* 8th ed. Englewood Cliffs, NJ: Prentice Hall.

Bebchuk, L. A. and Tallarita, R. 2020. 'The Illusory Promise of Stakeholder Governance' *Cornell Law Review* 106: 91–178.

Becker, Y. and Lange, F. 2014. *Linien der Rechtsprechung des Bundesverfassungsgerichts – erörtert von den wissenschaftlichen Mitarbeitern und Mitarbeiterinnen*. Berlin: De Gruyter.

Beever, A. 2011. 'Our Most Fundamental Rights'. In A. Robertson and D. Nolan (eds.).

Begg, D., Fischer, S. and Dornbusch, R. 2005. *Economics*. Columbus: McGraw Hill Education.

Beitz, C. 2009. *The Idea of Human Rights*. Oxford: Oxford University Press.

Bentham, J. 1987. 'Anarchical Fallacies'. In J. Waldron (ed.).

Berle, A. 1931. 'Corporate Powers as Powers in Trust'. *Harvard Law Review* 44: 1049–1074.

Berle, A. A. and Means, G. C. 1932. *The Modern Corporation and Private Property*. New York: Macmillan.

Besson, S. 2017. 'Human Rights as Transnational Constitutional Law'. In A. F. Lang and A. Wiener (eds.).

Beyleveld, D. and Brownsword, R. 2001. *Human Dignity in Bioethics and Biolaw*. Oxford: Oxford University Press.

Bilchitz, D. I. 2007. *Poverty and Fundamental Rights*. Oxford: Oxford University Press.

Bilchitz, D. I. 2008. 'Corporate Law and the Constitution: Towards Binding Human Rights Responsibilities for Corporations'. *South African Law Journal* 124: 754–789.

Bilchitz, D. I. 2009. 'Moving Beyond Arbitrariness: The Legal Personhood and Dignity of Non-Human Animals'. *South African Journal on Human Rights* 25: 38–72.

Bilchitz, D. I. 2010a. 'Do Corporations Have Positive Fundamental Rights Obligations?'. *Theoria* 125: 1–35.

Bilchitz, D. I. 2010b. 'The Ruggie Framework: An Adequate Rubric for Corporate Human Rights Obligations?'. *SUR International Journal on Human Rights* 12: 199–229.

Bilchitz, D. I. 2011a. 'Should Religious Associations Be Allowed to Discriminate?'. *South African Journal on Human Rights* 27: 219–248.

Bilchitz, D. I. 2011b. 'Does Balancing Adequately Capture the Nature of Rights?'. *Southern African Public Law* 25: 423–444.

Bilchitz, D. I. 2013. 'A Chasm between "Is" and "Ought"? A Critique of the Normative Foundations of the SRSG's Framework and the Guiding Principles'. In S. Deva and D. Bilchitz (eds.).

Bilchitz, D. I. 2014. 'Necessity and Proportionality: Towards a Balanced Approach'. In L. Lazarus, C. McCrudden and N. Bowles (eds.).

Bilchitz, D. I. 2016a. 'Corporations and the Limits of State-Based Models for Protecting Fundamental Rights in International Law'. *Indiana Journal of Global Legal Studies* 23: 143–170.

Bilchitz, D. I. 2016b. 'The Necessity for a Business and Human Rights Treaty'. *Business and Human Rights Journal* 1: 203–227.

Bilchitz, D. I. 2017a. 'Putting Flesh on the Bone: What Should a Business and Human Rights Treaty Look Like?'. In S. Deva and D. Bilchitz (eds.).

Bilchitz, D. I. 2017b. 'Corporate Obligations and a Business and Human Rights Treaty: a Constitutional Law Model?'. In S. Deva and D. Bilchitz (eds.).

Bilchitz, D.I. 2018. 'Fundamental Rights as Bridging Concepts: Straddling the Boundary Between Ideal Justice and an Imperfect Reality'. *Human Rights Quarterly* 40: 119–143

Bilchitz, D. 2021. 'How can Rights be Individuated?' In A. Linares-Cantillo (ed.).

Bilchitz, D. I. and Ausserladscheider Jonas, L. 2016. 'Proportionality, Fundamental Rights and the Duties of Directors'. *Oxford Journal of Legal Studies* 36: 828–854.

Bilchitz, D. I. and Deva, S. 2013. 'The Human Rights Obligations of Business: A Critical Framework for the Future'. In S. Deva and D. Bilchitz (eds.).

Bilchitz, D. I., Metz, T. and Oyowe, O. 2017. *Jurisprudence in an African Context*. Cape Town: Oxford University Press.

Birchall, D. 2019. 'Any Act, Any Harm, To Anyone: The Transformative Potential of "Human Rights Impacts" under the UN Guiding Principles on Business and Human Rights'. *University of Oxford Human Rights Hub Journal* 1: 120–147.

Black, C. 1967. 'The Supreme Court 1966 Term – Foreword: "State Action," Equal Protection, and California's Proposition 14'. *Harvard Law Review* 81: 69–109.

Black, E. 2009. *Nazi Nexus: America's Corporate Connections to the Nazi Holocaust*. Washington: Dialog Press.

Black, E. 2012. *IBM and the Holocaust: The Strategic Alliance between Nazi Germany and America's Most Powerful Corporation*. Washington: Dialog Press.

Blair, M. 2003. 'Locking in Capital: What Corporate Law Achieved for Business Organizers in the Nineteenth Century'. *UCLA Law Review* 51: 387–456.

Blair, M. M. and Stout, L. A. 1999. 'A Team Production Theory of Corporate Law'. *Virginia Law Review* 85: 247–328.

Blair, C., Vidak-Gojkovic, E. and Meudic-Role, M.-A. 2018. 'The Medium Is the Message: Establishing a System of Business and Human Rights Through Contract Law and Arbitration'. *Journal of International Arbitration* 35: 379–412.

Bonilla, D. 2013a. 'Toward a Constitutionalism of the Global South'. In D. Bonilla (ed.).

Bonilla, D. (ed.). 2013b. *Constitutionalism of the Global South: the Activist Tribunals of India, South Africa and Colombia*. Cambridge: Cambridge University Press.

Booysen, S (ed.). 2016. *Fees Must Fall: Student Revolt, Decolonisation and Governance in South Africa*. Johannesburg: Wits University Press.

Botha, M. M. 2016. 'Evaluating the Social and Ethics Committee: Is Labour the Missing Link?' (Part 1) *Tydskrif vir Hedendaagse Romeins-Hollandse Reg* 79: 580–593.

Botha, M. M. 2017. 'Evaluating the Social and Ethics Committee: Is Labour the Missing Link' (Part 2) *Tydskrif vir Hedendaagse Romeins-Hollandse Reg* 80: 1–17.

Bottomley, S. 2007. *The Constitutional Corporation: Rethinking Corporate Governance*. Ashgate: New York.

Bowie, N. E. 2017. *Business Ethics: A Kantian Perspective* 2nd ed. Cambridge: Cambridge University Press.

Braithwaite, J. 2006. 'Responsive Regulation and Developing Economies'. *World Development* 34: 884–898.

Branson, D. M. 2002. 'The Rule That Isn't a Rule – The Business Judgment Rule'. *Valparaiso University Law Review* 36: 631–654.

Bratman, M. 2003. 'Autonomy and Hierarchy'. *Social Philosophy and Policy* 20: 156–176.

Bratton, W. 1989. 'Nexus of Contracts Corporation: a Critical Appraisal'. *Cornell Law Review* 74: 407–465.

Brenkert, G. and Beauchamp, T. (eds.). 2010. *The Oxford Handbook of Business Ethics*. Oxford: Oxford University Press.

Brinktrine, R. 2001. 'The horizontal effect of human rights in German constitutional law: the British debate on horizontality and the possible role model of the German doctrine of "mittelbare Drittwirkung der Grundrechte"'. *European Human Rights Law Review* 4: 421–432.

Brown, G. 2003. 'Proportionality and Just War'. *Journal of Military Ethics* 2: 171–185.

Brownsword, R., Micklitz, H., Niglia, L. and Weatherill, S. 2011. *The Foundations of European Private Law*. Oxford: Hart Publishing.

Buchanan, G. S. 1997. 'State Action and the Public/Private Distinction'. *Harvard Law Review* 123: 1248–1313.

Buhmann, K. 2013. 'Navigating from 'train wreck' to being 'welcomed': negotiation strategies and argumentative patterns in the development of the UN Framework'. In S. Deva and D. Bilchitz (eds.).

Burkiczak, C. 2014. 'Grundrechtswirkung zwischen Privaten' in Y. Becker and F. Lange (eds.).

Campbell, T. 2012. 'Corporate Social Responsibility: Beyond the Business Case to Human Rights'. In W. Cragg (ed.).

Campbell, T. and Bourne, K. (eds.). 2017. *Political and Legal Approaches to Human Rights*. Abingdon: Routledge.

Carnwath, R. 2014. 'From Rationality to Proportionality in the Modern Law'. *Hong Kong Law Journal* 44: 447–58.

Carrillo-Santarelli, N. 2018. 'A Defence of Direct International Human Rights Obligations of (All) Corporations'. In J. L. Černič and N. Carrillo-Santarelli (eds).

Carroll, A. (ed.). 1977. *Managing Corporate Social Responsibility*. Boston: Little, Brown and Company.

Cassim, F. H. 2012. 'The Duties and the Liability of Directors' in F.H. Cassim (eds.).

Cassim, F. H., Cassim, M., Cassim, R., Jooste, R., Shev, J. and Yeats, J. (eds.). 2012. *Contemporary Company Law* 2nd ed. Cape Town: Juta.

Cepeda-Espinosa, M. 2004. 'Judicial Activism in a Violent Context: The Origin, Role and Impact of the Colombian Constitutional Court'. *Washington University Global Studies Law Review* 3: 529–700.

Cepeda-Espinoza, M. and Landau, D. 2017. *Colombian Constitutional Law: Leading Cases*. New York: Oxford University Press.

Černič, J. L. 2010. *Human Rights Law and Business: Corporate Responsibility for Fundamental Human Rights*. Amsterdam: Europa Law Publishing.

Černič, J. L. and Carrillo-Santarelli, N. 2018. *The Future of Business and Human Rights: Theoretical and Practical Considerations for a UN Treaty*. Cambridge: Intersentia.

Chappell, V. (ed.). 1994. *Locke*. Cambridge: Cambridge University Press.

Chatterjee, B. and Mitra, N. 2017. 'The Genesis of the CSR Mandate in India: Demystifying the "Chatterjee Model"'. In N. Mitra and R. Schmidpeter (eds.).

Chatterjee, D. K. (ed.). 2004. *The Ethics of Assistance: Morality and the Distant Needy*. Cambridge: Cambridge University Press.

Chayes, A. 1959. 'The Modern Corporation and the Rule of Law'. In E. S. Mason (ed.).

Chemerinsky, E. 1985. 'Rethinking State Action'. *Northwestern University Law Review* 80: 503–557.

Chirwa, D. 2006. 'The Horizontal Application of Constitutional Rights in a Comparative Perspective'. *Law Democracy and Development* 10: 21–48.

Choudhury, B. 2005. 'Beyond the Alien Tort Claims Act: Alternative Approaches to Attributing Liability to Corporations for Extraterritorial Abuses'. *Northwestern Journal of International Law and Business* 26: 43–75.

Ciepley, D. 2013. 'Beyond Public and Private: Toward a Political Theory of the Corporation'. *American Political Science Review* 107: 139–158.

Clapham, Andrew. 2006. *Human Rights Obligations of Non-State Actors*. Oxford: Oxford University Press.

Coase, R. H. 1937. 'The Nature of the Firm'. *Economica* 4: 386–405.

Coase, R. H. 1988. *The Firm, the Market and the Law*. Chicago and London: University of Chicago Press.

Cohen, G. 1995. *Self-ownership, Freedom and Equality*. Cambridge: Cambridge University Press.

Cohen-Eliya, M. and Porat, I. 2011. 'Proportionality and the Culture of Justification'. *American Journal of Comparative Law* 59: 463–490.

Cohen-Eliya, M. and Porat, I. 2013. *Proportionality and Constitutional Culture*. Cambridge: Cambridge University Press.

Coleman, B. 1975. 'Is Corporate Criminal Liability Really Necessary'. *Southwestern Law Journal* 29: 908–927.

Cragg, W. 2010. 'Business and Human Rights: A Principle and Value-Based Analysis'. In G. Brenkert (ed.).

Cragg, W. (ed.). 2012. *Business and Human Rights*. Cheltenham: Edward Elgar.

Craig, P. 2010. 'Proportionality, Rationality and Review'. *New Zealand Law Review* 265–301.

Cranston, M. 1967. 'Human Rights: Real and Supposed'. In D. D. Raphael (ed.).

Cruft, R., Liao, S. M., and Renzo, M. (eds.). 2015. *Philosophical Foundations of Human Rights*. Oxford: Oxford University Press.

Cruft, R., Liao, S. M., and Renzo, M. 2015. 'The Philosophical Foundations of Human Rights: An Overview'. In R. Cruft., S. M. Liao., and M. Renzo (eds.).

Cullity, G. 2004. *The Moral Demands of Affluence*. Oxford: Oxford University Press.

Currie, I. and De Waal, J. (eds.). 2013. *The Bill of Rights Handbook* 6th ed. Cape Town: Juta.

Da Silva, V. A. 2011. 'Comparing the Incommensurable: Constitutional Principles, Balancing and Rational Decision'. *Oxford Journal of Legal Studies* 31: 273–301.

Dafel, M. 2015. 'The Directly Enforceable Constitution: Political Parties and the Horizontal Application of the Bill of Rights'. *South African Journal on Human Rights* 31: 56–85.

Dahan, Y., Lerner, H. and Milman-Sivan, F. 2011. 'Global Justice, Labour Standards and Responsibility'. *Theoretical Enquiries in Law* 12: 117–142.

Davis, D., Geach, W. Loubser, A., Buba, Z., Burdette, D., Butler, D., Coetzee, L. and Mongalo, T. (eds.). 2019. *Companies and Other Business Structures in South Africa* 4th ed. Cape Town: Oxford University Press.

Davis, K. 1977. 'The Case for and Against Business Assumption of Social Responsibilities'. In A. Carroll (ed.).

De Schutter, O. 2015. 'Towards a New Treaty on Business and Human Rights'. *Business and Human Rights Journal* 1: 41–67.

De Schutter, O. (ed.). 2006. *Transnational Corporations and Human Rights*. Oxford: Hart.

De Wet, E. and Vidmar, J. 2012. *Hierarchy in International Law: The Place of Human Rights*. Oxford: Oxford University Press.

Desautels-Stein, J. and Tomlins, C. (eds.). 2017. *Searching for Contemporary Legal Thought*. Cambridge: Cambridge University Press.

Deva, S. 2012. *Regulating Corporate Human Rights Violations: Humanizing Business*. London and New York: Routledge.

Deva, S. 2013. 'Treating Human Rights Lightly: a Critique of the Consensus Rhetoric and the Language Employed by the Guiding Principles'. In S. Deva and D. Bilchitz (eds.).

Deva, S. 2017. 'Scope of the Proposed Business and Human Rights Treaty: Navigating Through Normativity, Law and Politics'. In S. Deva and D. Bilchitz (eds.).

Deva, S. and Bilchitz, D. (eds.). 2013. *Human Rights Obligations of Business: Beyond the Corporate Responsibility to Respect?* Cambridge: Cambridge University Press.

Deva, S. and Bilchitz, D. (eds.). 2017. *Building a Treaty on Business and Human Rights: Context and Contours*. Cambridge: Cambridge University Press.

Dhir, A. 2006. 'Realigning the Corporate Building Blocks: Shareholder Proposals as a Vehicle for Achieving Corporate Social and Human Rights Accountability'. *American Business Law Journal* 43: 365–412.

Dhir, A. 2009. 'Politics of Knowledge Dissemination: Corporate Reporting, Shareholder Voice and Human Rights'. *Osgood Hall Law Journal* 47: 47–82.

Dhir, A. 2012. 'Shareholder Engagement in the Embedded Business Corporation: Investment Activism, Human Rights and TWAIL Discourse'. *Business Ethics Quarterly* 22: 99–118.

Dicke, K. 2002. 'The Founding Function of Human Dignity in the Universal Declaration of Human Rights'. In D. Kretzmer and E. Klein (eds.).

Dine, J. and Koutsias, M. 2005. *Company Law* 6th ed. Hampshire: Palgrave Macmillan.

Donaghey, J. and Reinecke, J. 2018. 'When Industrial Democracy Meets Corporate Social Responsibility – a Comparison of the Bangladesh Accord and Alliance as Responses to the Rana Plaza Disaster'. *British Journal of Industrial Relations* 56: 14–42.

Donaldson, T. 1989. *The Ethics of International Business*. Oxford: Oxford University Press.

Donnelly, J. 1998. *International Human Rights* 2nd ed. New York: Taylor and Francis.

Dorff, M. C. and Sabel, C. F. 1998. 'A Constitution of Democratic Experimentalism'. *Columbia Law Review* 98: 267–473.

Dusza, K. 1989. 'Max Weber's Conception of the State'. *International Journal of Politics, Culture and Society* 3: 71–105.

Dworkin, G. 1988. *The Theory and Practice of Autonomy*. Cambridge: Cambridge University Press.

Dworkin, R. 1977. *Taking Rights Seriously*. Massachusetts: Harvard University Press.

Dworkin, R. 1986. *Law's Empire*. Cambridge: The Belknap Press.

Dworkin, R. 1996. *Freedom's Law: the Moral Reading of the American Constitution*. Oxford: Oxford University Press.

Dworkin, R. 2000. *Sovereign Virtue: The Theory and Practice of Equality*. London: Harvard University Press.

Dyzenhaus, D. and Thorburn, M. (eds.). 2016. *Philosophical Foundations of Constitutional Law*. Oxford: Oxford University Press.

Easterbrook, F. H. and Fischel, D. R. 1985. 'Limited Liability and the Corporation'. *University of Chicago Law Review* 52: 89–117.

Easterbrook, F. H. and Fischel, D. R. 1991. *The Economic Structure of Corporate Law*. Cambridge: Harvard University Press.

Elkins, Z., Ginsburg, T. and Simmons, B. 2013. 'Getting to Rights: Treaty Ratification, Constitutional Convergence, and Human Rights Practice'. *Harvard International Law Journal* 54: 61–95.

Elliott, M., Varuhas, J. N. E. and Wilson Stark, S. (eds.). 2018. *The Unity of Public Law? Doctrinal, Theoretical and Comparative Perspectives*. Oxford: Hart.

Elster, J. 1982. 'Sour Grapes – Utilitarianism and the Genesis of Wants'. In A.K. Sen and B. Williams (eds.).

Emedi, S. J. 2011. 'Utilizing Existing Mechanisms of International Law to Implement Human Rights Standards: States and Multinational Corporations'. *Arizona Journal of International and Comparative Law* 28: 629–658.

Endicott, T. 2014. 'Proportionality and Incommensurability'. In G. Huscroft et al. (eds.).

Enriques, L. Hansmann, H., Kraakman, R. and Pargendler, M. 2017. 'The Basic Governance Structure: Minority Shareholders and Non-Shareholder Constituencies'. In R. Kraakman et al. (eds.).

Epstein, R. 2011. 'Citizens United v. FEC: The Constitutional Rights that Big Corporations Should Have but Do Not Want'. *Harvard Journal of Law and Public Policy* 34: 639–661.

Evans, B. A. 2015. 'Accord on Fire and Building Safety in Bangladesh: An International Response to Bangladesh Labor Conditions'. *North Carolina Journal of International Law and Commercial Regulation* 40: 597–626.

Fagan, A. 2013. 'Causation in the Constitutional Court: *Lee v. Minister of Correctional Services*'. *Constitutional Court Review* 5: 104–134.

Fallon, R. H. 2008. 'The Core of an Uneasy Case for Judicial Review'. *Harvard Law Review* 121: 1693–1736.

Feinberg, J. 1980. *Rights, Justice and the Bounds of Liberty*. Princeton: Princeton University Press.

Ferreras, I. 2017. *Firms as Political Entities: Saving Democracy through Economic Bicameralism*. Cambridge: Cambridge University Press.

Fineman, M. A. 2013. 'Equality, Autonomy and the Vulnerable Subject in Law and Politics'. In M. A. Fineman and A. Grear (eds.).

Fineman, M. A. and Grear, A. (eds.). 2013. *Vulnerability: Reflections on a New Ethical Foundation for Law and Politics*. London and New York: Routledge.

Finn, M. 2015a. 'Organs of State: an Anatomy'. *South African Journal on Human Rights* 31: 631–654.

Finn, M. 2015b. 'Allpay Remedy: Dissecting the Constitutional Court's Approach to Organs of State'. *Constitutional Court Review* 6: 258–272.

Finn, M. 2020. 'Befriending the Bogeyman: Direct Horizontal Application in *AB* v. *Pridwin*'. *South African Law Journal* 137: 591–607.

Fletcher, G. P. 1987. 'Law and Morality: a Kantian Perspective'. *Columbia Law Review* 87: 533–558.

Fonseca, A. 2010. 'How Credible Are Mining Corporations' Sustainability Reports? A Critical Analysis of External Assurance under the Requirements of the International Council on Mining and Minerals'. *Corporate Social Responsibility and Environmental Management* 17: 355–370.

Fredman, S. 2008. *Human Rights Transformed: Positive Rights and Positive Duties*. Oxford: Oxford University Press.

Freeman, R. E. 2010. *Strategic Management: A Stakeholder Approach*. Cambridge: Cambridge University Press.

Freeman, R. E., Harrison, J. S., Wicks, A. C., Parmar, B. L. and de Colle, S. 2010. *Stakeholder Theory: The State of the Art*. Cambridge: Cambridge University Press.

French, P. A. 1979. 'The Corporation as a Moral Person'. *American Philosophical Quarterly* 16: 207–215.

French, P. A. 1995. *Corporate Ethics*. Dallas: Harcourt Brace.

French, P. A. 1996. 'Integrity, Intentions and Corporations'. *American Business Law Journal* 34: 141–156.

Friedman, M. 1962. *Capitalism and Freedom*. Chicago: University of Chicago Press.

Friedman, M. 1970. 'The Social Responsibility of Business is to Increase its Profits'. In T. Beauchamp et al. (eds.).

Friedman, N. 2014. 'The South African Common Law and the Constitution: Revisiting Horizonality'. *South African Journal on Human Rights* 30: 63–88.

Friedman, N. 2020. 'Corporations as Moral Agents: Trade-offs in Criminal Liability and Human Rights for Corporations'. *The Modern Law Review* 83: 255–284.

Friedmann, D. and Barak-Erez, D. (eds.). 2001. *Human Rights in Private Law*. Oxford: Hart.

Frynas, J. 2009. *Beyond Corporate Social Responsibility: Oil, Multinationals and Social Challenges*. Cambridge: Cambridge University Press.

Gallegos, L. and Uribe, D. 2016. 'The Next Step against Corporate Impunity: A World Court of Business and Human Rights?' *Harvard International Law Journal Online Symposium* 57: 7–10.

Gardbaum, S. 2003. 'The "Horizontal Effect of Constitutional Rights"'. *Michigan Law Review* 102: 388–459.

Gardbaum, S. 2008. 'Human Rights as International Constitutional Rights'. *European Journal of International Law* 19: 749–768.

Gardbaum, S. 2013. *The New Commonwealth Model of Constitutionalism: Theory and Practice*. Cambridge: Cambridge University Press.

Gardbaum, S. 2017. 'Positive and Horizontal Rights: Proportionality's Next Frontier or a Bridge too Far?' In V. Jackson and M. Tushnet (eds.).

Garrett, J. E. 1989. 'Unredistributable Corporate Moral Responsibility'. *Journal of Business Ethics* 8: 535–545.
Gatto, A. 2011. *Multinational Enterprises and Human Rights*. Cheltenham: Edward Elgar.
Gert, B. 2010. *Hobbes*. Cambridge: Polity Press.
Gewirth, A. 1978. *Reason and Morality*. Chicago: University of Chicago Press.
Goldsmith, M. M. 1966. *Hobbes' Science of Politics*. New York: Columbia University Press.
Goodin, R. 1985. *Protecting the Vulnerable: A Re-analysis of Our Social Responsibilities*. Chicago: University of Chicago Press.
Goodpaster, K. 2010. 'Corporate Responsibility and Its Constituents'. In G. Brenkert and T. Beauchamp (eds.).
Grear, A. 2010. *Redirecting Human Rights: Facing the Challenge of Corporate Legal Humanity*. Basingstoke: Palgrave Macmillan.
Grear, A. 2013. 'Vulnerability, Advanced Global Capitalism and Co-Symptomatic Injustice: Locating the Vulnerable Subject'. In M. A. Fineman and A. Grear (eds.).
Greenberg, J. D. and Brotman, E. C. 2014. 'Strict Vicarious Criminal Liability for Corporations and Corporate Executives: Stretching the Boundaries of Criminalization'. *American Criminal Law Review* 51: 79–98.
Griffin, J. 2008. *On Human Rights*. Oxford: Oxford University Press.
Grimm, D. 2007. 'Proportionality in Canadian and German Constitutional Jurisprudence'. *The University of Toronto Law Journal* 57: 383–397.
Gyekye, K. 1997. *Tradition and Modernity: Philosophical Reflections on the African Experience*. New York: Oxford University Press.
Hannigan, B. 2018. *Company Law* 5th ed. Oxford: Oxford University Press.
Hansmann, H. and Kraakman, R. 2000. 'The End of History for Corporate Law'. *Georgetown Law Journal* 89: 439–468.
Hariri, Y. N. 2015. *Sapiens: a Brief History of Humankind*. New York: HarperCollins.
Hart, H. 1958. 'Positivism and the Separation of Law and Morals'. *Harvard Law Review* 71: 593–629.
Hart, H. 1997. *The Concept of Law*. Oxford: Clarendon Press.
Harvard Law Review. 2010. 'State Action and the Public/Private Distinction'. *Harvard Law Review* 123: 1248–1314.
Havenga, M. 2015. 'The Social and Ethics Committee in South African Company Law'. *Tydskrif vir Hedendaagse Romeins-Hollandse Reg* 78: 285–292.
Henkin, L. 1962. '*Shelley v Kraemer*: Notes for a Revised Opinion'. *University of Pennsylvania Law Review* 110: 473–505.
Herman, B. 1993. *The Practice of Moral Judgment*. Cambridge: Harvard University Press.
Herting, S. and Stein, L. 2007. 'The Evolution of Luhmann's Systems Theory with Focus On the Constructivist Influence'. *International Journal of General Systems* 36: 1–17.

Hideg, I., Krstic, A., Trau, R. N. C. and Zarina, T. 2018. 'The Unintended Consequences of Maternity Leaves: How Agency Interventions Mitigate the Negative Effects of Longer Legislated Maternity Leaves'. *Journal of Applied Psychology* 103: 1155–1164.

Hill, T. E. 1980. 'Humanity as an End in Itself'. *Ethics* 91: 84–99.

Hobbes, T. 1996. *Leviathan* (ed. R. Tuck). Cambridge: Cambridge University Press.

Hodges, C. 2015. *Law and Corporate Behaviour: Integrating Theories of Regulation, Enforcement, Compliance and Ethics*. Oxford: Hart Publishing.

Hoexter, C. 2018. 'A Matter of Feel? Public Powers and Functions in South Africa'. In M. Elliott, J. N. E. Varuhas and S. Wilson Stark (eds.).

Hsieh, N. H. 2004. The Obligations of Transnational Corporations: Rawlsian Justice and the Duty of Assistance. *Business Ethics Quarterly* 14: 643–661.

Hsieh, N. H. 2009. 'Does Global Business Have a Responsibility to Promote Just Institutions?' *Business Ethics Quarterly* 19: 251–273.

Hudson, A. 2017. *Understanding Company Law* 2nd ed. London: Routledge.

Hugo, V. 1892. *Les Miserables* (trans. N. Denny). London: Penguin.

Hunt, M. 1998. 'The Horizontal Effect of the Human Rights Act'. *Public Law* 423–443.

Huscroft, G., Miller, B. W. and Webber, G. 2014. *Proportionality and the Rule of Law: Rights, Justification and Reasoning*. Cambridge: Cambridge University Press.

Ishay, M. 2004. *The History of Human Rights: From Ancient Times to the Globalization Era*. Berkeley and Los Angeles: University of California Press.

Itturalde, M. 2013. 'Access to Constitutional Justice in Colombia: Opportunities and Challenges for Social and Political Change'. In D. Bonilla (ed.).

Jackson, V. and Tushnet, M. (eds.). 2017. *Proportionality: New Frontiers, New Challenges*. Cambridge: Cambridge University Press.

Jägers, N. 2013. 'Will Transnational Private Regulation Close the Governance Gap?'. In S. Deva and D. Bilchitz (eds.).

Jensen, M. 2001. 'Value Maximisation, Stakeholder Theory and the Corporate Objective Function'. *European Financial Management* 7: 297–317.

Jensen, M. and Meckling, W. H. 1976. 'Theory of the Firm: Managerial Behavior, Agency Costs and Ownership Structure'. *Journal of Financial Economics* 3: 305–360.

Jhaveri, S. 2019. 'Interrogating Dialogic Theories of Judicial Review'. *International Journal of Constitutional Law* 17: 811–835.

Joseph, S. 2004. *Corporations and Transnational Human Rights Litigation*. Oxford: Hart.

Kahl, W. (ed.). 2018. *Bonner Kommentar zum Grundgesetz*. Munich: C.H. Beck.

Kampourakis, I. 2019. 'CSR and Social Rights: Juxtaposing Societal Constitutionalism and Rights-Based Approaches Imposing Human Rights Obligations on Corporations'. *Goettingen Journal of International Law* 9: 537–569.

Kant, I. 2017. *Groundwork for the Metaphysic of Morals* (ed. J. Bennett) available at www.earlymoderntexts.com/assets/pdfs/kant1785.pdf

Karavias, M. 2013. *Corporate Obligations under International Law*. Oxford: Oxford University Press.

Karp, D. 2014. *Responsibility for Human Rights: Transnational Corporations in Imperfect States*. Cambridge: Cambridge University Press.

Kater, J. 2016. *Grundrechtsbindung und Grundrechtsfähigkeit gemischtwirtschaftlicher Aktiengesellschaften*. Stuttgart: Mohr Siebeck.

Kavanagh, A. 2016. 'The Constitutional Separation of Powers'. In D. Dyzenhaus and M. Thorburn (eds.).

Keay, A. 2007. 'Tackling the Issue of the Corporate Objective: An Analysis of the United Kingdom's Enlightened Shareholder Value Approach'. *Sydney Law Review* 29: 577–612.

Keay, A. 2011. *The Corporate Objective*. Cheltenham: Edward Elgar.

Keay, A. 2013. *The Enlightened Shareholder Value Principle and Corporate Governance*. London: Routledge.

Keitner, C. 2011. 'Rights beyond Borders'. *Yale Journal of International Law* 36: 55–114.

Kell, G. 2005. 'The Global Compact: Selected Experiences and Reflections'. *Journal of Business Ethics* 59: 69–79.

Keller, H. and Grover, L. 2012. 'General Comments of the Human Rights Committee and their Legitimacy'. In H. Keller and G. Ulfstein (eds.).

Keller, H. and Ulfstein, G. (eds.). 2012. *UN Human Rights Treaty Bodies: Law and Legitimacy*. Cambridge: Cambridge University Press.

Kelly, D. 2003. *The State of the Political: Conceptions of Politics and the State in the Thought of Max Weber, Carl Schmitt and Franz Neumann*. Oxford: Oxford University Press.

Kennedy, D. 2011. 'A Transnational Genealogy of Proportionality in Private Law'. In R. Brownsword, et al. (eds.).

Kim, J. 1984. 'Concepts of Supervenience'. *Philosophy and Phenomelogical Research* 45: 153–176.

King, J. 2006. 'Constitutional Rights and Social Welfare: A Comment on the Canadian *Chaoulli* Health Care Decision'. *Modern Law Review* 69: 631–643.

King, J. 2012. *Judging Social Rights*. Cambridge: Cambridge University Press.

King, L. and Hamm, P. 2005. 'Privatisation and State Capacity in Post-Communist Society'. William Davidson Institute Working Paper no 806 available at https://deepblue.lib.umich.edu/bitstream/handle/2027.42/40192/wp806.pdf;sequence=3

Kinley, D. and Tadaki, J. 2004. 'From Talk to Walk: the Emergence of Human Rights Responsibilities for Corporations at International Law'. *Virginia Journal of International Law* 44: 931–1023.

Klare, K. and Davis, D. 2010. 'Transformative Constitutionalism and the Common and Customary Law'. *South African Journal on Human Rights* 26: 403–509.

Klatt, M. 2011. 'Positive Obligations under the European Convention on Human Rights'. *Heidelberg Journal of International Law* 71: 691–718.

Klatt, M. and Meister, M. 2012. *The Constitutional Structure of Proportionality.* Oxford: Oxford University Press.

Kloppers, H. J. 2013. 'Driving Corporate Social Responsibility through the Companies Act: An Overview of the Role of the Social and Ethics Committee'. *Potchefstroom Electronic Law Journal* 16: 166–199.

Klumpp, T., Mialon, H. and Williams, M. 2016. 'The Business of American Democracy: *Citizens United,* Independent Spending and Elections'. *The Journal of Law and Economics* 59: 1–43.

Kockler, N. 2007. 'The Principle of Double Effect and Proportionate Reason'. *Virtual Mentor* 9: 369–374.

Korsgaard, C. 2009. *Self-Constitution: Agency, Identity, and Integrity.* Oxford: Oxford University Press.

Koskenniemi, M. 1997. 'Hierarchy in International Law: A Sketch'. *European Journal of International Law* 8: 566–582.

Kraakman, R., Armour, J., Davies, P., Enriques, L., Hansmann, H., Gertig, H., Hopt, K., Kanda, H., Pargendler, M., Ringer, W.-G. and Rock, E. 2017. *The Anatomy of Corporate Law: A Comparative and Functional Approach.* Oxford: Oxford University Press.

Kremnitzer, M. 2010. 'A Possible Case for Imposing Criminal Liability on Corporations in International Criminal Law'. *Journal of International Criminal Justice* 8: 909–918.

Kretzmer, D. and Klein, E. (eds.). 2002. *The Concept of Human Dignity in Human Rights Discourse.* The Hague: Kluwer Law International.

Kumm, M. 2010. 'The Idea of Socratic Contestation and the Right to Justification: The Point of Rights-based Proportionality Review'. *Law and Ethics of Human Rights* 4: 142–175.

Kumm, M. and Comella, V. F. 2005. 'What Is So Special about Constitutional Rights in Private Litigation? A Comparative Analysis of the Function of the State Action Requirements and Indirect Horizontal Effect'. In A. Sajo and R. Uitz (eds.).

Kuper, A. (ed.). 2005. *Global Responsibilities: Who Must Deliver on Human Rights?* New York and London: Routledge.

Landau, D. 2012. 'The Reality of Social Rights Enforcement'. *Harvard International Law Journal* 53: 190–247.

Lang, A. F. and Wiener, A. 2017. *Handbook on Global Constitutionalism.* Cheltenham: Edward Elgar.

Laslett, K. 2012. 'State Crime by Proxy: Australia and the Bougainville Conflict'. *British Journal of Criminology* 52: 705–723.

Lassman, P. and Spiers, R. (eds.). 1994. *Weber: Political Writings.* Cambridge: Cambridge University Press.

Lazarus, L. McCrudden, C. and Bowles, N. (eds.). 2014. *Reasoning Rights* Oxford: Hart.

Leader, S. 2017. 'Coherence, Mutual Assurance and the Rationale for a Treaty'. In S. Deva and D. Bilchitz (eds.).

Lee, I. 2009. 'Citizenship and the Corporation'. *Law and Social Inquiry* 34: 129–168.

Lee, J. Y. and Hunt, P. 2012. 'Human Rights Responsibilities of Pharmaceutical Companies in Relation to Access to Medicines'. *Journal of Law, Medicine and Ethics* 40: 220–233.

Lehr, A. and Jenkins, B. 2007. 'Business and Human Rights – Beyond corporate spheres of influence' (12 November 2007) available at https://business-humanrights.org/en/business-and-human-rights-%E2%80%93-beyond-corporate-spheres-of-influence (last accessed 11 May 2020).

Leisner, W. 1960. *Grundrechte und Privatrecht.* Munich, C.H. Beck.

Liebenberg, 2010. *Socio-Economic Rights: Adjudication under a Transformative Constitution.* Cape Town: Juta.

Liebenberg, S. 2020. 'Between Sovereignty and Accountability: The Emerging Jurisprudence of the United Nations Committee on Economic, Social and Cultural Rights under the Optional Protocol'. *Human Rights Quarterly* 42: 48–84.

Linares-Cantillo, A. (ed.). 2021. *Constitutionalism: Old Dilemmas, New Insights.* Oxford: Oxford University Press.

Locke, J. 1988. *Two Treatises of Government* (ed. P. Laslett). Cambridge: Cambridge University Press.

Lopata, B. 1973. 'Property Theory in Hobbes'. *Political Theory* 1: 203–218.

López Latorre, A. F. 2020. 'In Defence of Direct Obligations for Businesses under International Human Rights Law'. *Business and Human Rights Journal* 5: 56–83.

Lübbe-Wolf, G. 1988. *Die Grundrechte als Eingriffsabwehrrechte.* Nomos: Baden-Baden.

Luhmann, N. 1989. 'Law as a Society System'. *Northwestern University Law Review* 83: 136–150.

Luhmann, N. 1997. 'Limits of Steering'. *Theory, Culture & Society* 14: 41–57.

Lustig, D. 2020. *Veiled Power: International Law and the Private Corporation 1886 – 1981.* Oxford: Oxford University Press.

Macdonald, K. 2011. 'Rethinking "Spheres of Responsibility": Business Responsibility for Indirect Harm'. *Journal of Business Ethics* 99: 549–563.

Macek, E. E. 2002. 'Scratching the Corporate Back: Why Corporations Have No Incentive to Define Human Rights'. *Minnesota Journal of Global Trade* 11: 101–124.

Madlanga, M. 2018. 'The Human Rights Duties of Companies and Other Private Actors in South Africa' *Stellenbosch Law Review* 29: 359–378.

Mares, R. 2010. 'Global Corporate Social Responsibility, Human Rights and Law: An Interactive Regulatory Perspective on the Voluntary-Mandatory Dichotomy'. *Transnational Legal Theory* 1: 221–285.
Mason, E. S. (ed.). 1959. *The Corporation in Modern Society*. Cambridge: Harvard University Press.
May, R. J. 1990. 'Papua New Guinea's Bougainville Crisis'. *The Pacific Review* 3: 174–177.
McBarnet, D. and Whelan, C. 1991. 'The Elusive Spirit of the Law: Formalism and the Struggle for Legal Control'. *Modern Law Review* 54: 848–873.
Mccorquodale, R. and Smit, L. 2017a. 'Human Rights, Responsibilities and Due Diligence'. In S. Deva and D. Bilchitz (eds.).
Mccorquodale R., Smit, L., Neely, S. and Brooks, R. 2017b. 'Human Rights Due Diligence in Law and Practice: Good Practices and Challenges for Business Enterprises'. *Business and Human Rights Journal* 2: 195–224.
Mdumbe, F. 2005. 'The Meaning of "Organ of State" in the South African Constitution'. *Southern African Public Law* 20: 1–28.
Meeran, R. 2011. 'Tort Litigation against Multinational Corporations for Violation of Human Rights: An Overview of the Position Outside the United States'. *City University of Hong Kong Law Review* 3: 1–41.
Menzel, J. and Müller-Terpitz, R. (ed.). 2017. *Verfassungsrechtsprechung*, 3rd ed. Tübingen: Mohr Siebeck.
Merhof, K. 2015. 'Building a Bridge between Reality and the Constitution: The Establishment and Development of the Colombian Constitutional Court'. *International Journal of Constitutional Law* 13: 714–732.
Metz, T. 2010. 'For the Sake of Friendship: Relationality and Relationship as Grounds of Beneficence'. *Theoria* 57: 54–76.
Metz, T. 2011. 'Ubuntu as a Moral Theory and Human Rights in South Africa'. *African Human Rights Law Journal* 11: 532–559.
Metz, T. 2016. 'The South African Student/Worker Protests in Light of Just War Theory'. In S. Booysen (ed.).
Meyersfeld, B. 2020. 'The South African Constitution and the Human-Rights Obligations of Juristic Persons'. *South African Law Journal* 137: 439–478.
Meyerson, D. 2007. 'Why Courts Should Not Balance Rights against the Public Interest'. *Melbourne University Law Review* 31: 801–830.
Meyerson, D. 2015. 'The Moral Justification for the Right to Make Full Answer and Defense'. *Oxford Journal of Legal Studies* 35: 237–265.
Michelman, F. 2008a. 'On the Uses of Interpretive 'Charity': Some Notes on Application, Avoidance, Equality and Objective Unconstitutionality from the 2007 Term of the Constitutional Court of South Africa'. *Constitutional Court Review* 1: 1–61.
Michelman, F. I. 2008b. 'Socioeconomic Rights in Constitutional Law: Explaining America Away'. *International Journal of Constitutional Law* 6: 663–686.

Mill, J. S. 1859. *On Liberty*. Available at www.utilitarianism.com/ol/one.html

Mill, J. S. 1863. *Utilitarianism*. Available at www.utilitarianism.com/mill2.htm

Miller, D. and Harkins, C. 2010. 'Corporate Strategy, Corporate Capture: Food and Alcohol Industry Lobbying and Public Health'. *Critical Social Policy* 30: 564–589.

Mitra, N. and Schmidpeter, R. 2017. *Corporate Social Responsibility in India: Cases and Developments after the Legal Mandate*. Switzerland: Springer.

Mokgoro, Y. 1998. '*Ubuntu* and the Law in South Africa'. *Potchefstroom Electronic Law Journal* 1: 17–32.

Möller, K. 2012. *The Global Model of Constitutional Rights*. Oxford: Oxford University Press.

Moore, G. 1999. 'Corporate Moral Agency: Review and Implications'. *Journal of Business Ethics* 21: 329–343.

Moseneke, D. 2009. 'Transformative Constitutionalism: Its Implications for the Law of Contract'. *Stellenbosch Law Review* 20: 3–13.

Moyn, S. 2010. *The Last Utopia: Human Rights in History*. Cambridge: Harvard University Press.

Muchlinski, P. 2010. *Multinational Enterprises and the Law* 2nd ed. Oxford: Oxford University Press.

Muchlinski, P. 2012. 'Implementing the new UN Corporate Human Rights Framework: Implications for Corporate Law, Governance and Regulation'. *Business Ethics Quarterly* 22: 145–177.

Muchlinksi, P. 2017. 'The Impact of a Business and Human Rights Treaty on Investment Law and Arbitration'. In S. Deva and D. Bilchitz (eds.).

Mulgan, T. 2001. *The Demands of Consequentialism*. Oxford: Oxford University Press.

Müller-Hoff, C. 2012. 'How Does the New Constitutionalism Respond to the Human Rights Challenges Posed by Transnational Corporations?'. In Nolte, D. and Schilling-Vacaflor, A. (eds.).

Mureinik, E. 1994. 'A Bridge to Where? Introducing the Interim Bill of Rights'. *South African Journal on Human Rights* 10: 31–48.

Murphy, L. 2000. *Moral Demands in Non-ideal Theory*. Oxford: Oxford University Press.

Nader, R., Green, M. and Seligman, J. 1976. *Taming the Giant Corporation*. New York: Norton & Company.

Naniwadekar, M. and Varottil, U. 2016. The Stakeholder Approach toward Directors' Duties under Indian Company Law: A Comparative Analysis. In M. Singh (ed.).

Nedelsky, J. 1993. 'Reconceiving Rights as Relationships'. *Review of Constitutional Studies* 1: 1–26.

Ng, Y. F. 2019. 'In the Moonlight? The Control and Accountability of Government Corporations in Australia'. *Melbourne University Law Review* 43: 303–336.

Nicholls, C. 2005. *Corporate Law*. Toronto: Emond Montgomery.

Nipperdey, H. C. 1962. 'Grundrechte und Privatrecht' In H. C. Nipperdey (ed.).

Nipperdey, H. C. (ed.). 1962. *Festschrift für Erich Molitor*. Munich and Berlin: C.H. Beck.

Nolan, A. 2009. 'Addressing Economic and Social Rights Violations by Nonstate Actors through the Role of the State: A Comparison of Regional Approaches to the 'Obligation to Protect'. *Human Rights Law Review* 9: 225–255.

Nolan, A. 2014. 'Holding Non-State Actors to Account for Constitutional Economic and Social Rights Violations: Experiences and Lessons from South Africa and Ireland'. *International Journal of Constitutional Law* 12: 61–93.

Nolan, J. 2005. 'With Power Comes Responsibility: Human Rights and Corporate Accountability'. *University of New South Wales Law Journal* 28: 581–613.

Nolan, J. 2013. 'The Corporate Responsibility to Respect Human Rights: Soft Law or Not Law?'. In S. Deva and D. Bilchitz (eds.).

Nolan, J. 2017. 'Human Rights and Global Corporate Supply Chains: Is Effective Supply Chain Accountability Possible?'. In S. Deva and D. Bilchitz (eds.).

Nolte, D. and Schilling-Vacaflor, A. (eds.). 2012. *New Constitutionalism in Latin America: Promises and Practices*. London: Routledge.

Noortmann, M., Reinisch, A. and Ryngaert, C. (eds.). 2015. *Non-state Actors in International Law*. Oxford: Hart.

Nozick, R. 1974. *Anarchy, State, and Utopia*. Oxford: Basil Blackwell.

Nussbaum, M. 2000. *Women and Human Development*. Cambridge: Cambridge University Press.

Nussbaum, M. 2005. 'Beyond "Compassion and Humanity": Justice for Nonhuman Animals'. In C. Sunstein and M. Nussbaum (eds.).

Nussbaum, M. 2007. *Frontiers of Justice*. Cambridge: Harvard University Press.

Oliver, D. and Fedtke, J. 2007. *Human Rights and the Private Sphere: A Comparative Study*. London and New York: Routledge and Cavendish.

O'Neill, O. 1989. *Constructions of Reason: Exploration of Kant's Practical Philosophy*. Cambridge: Cambridge University Press.

O'Neill, O. 1996. *Towards Justice and Virtue*. Cambridge: Cambridge University Press.

O'Neill, O. 2001.'Agents of Justice'. *Metaphilosophy* 32: 180–195.

O'Neill, O. 2004. 'Global Justice: Whose Obligations?' In D.K. Chatterjee (ed.).

Ougaard, M. 2004. 'The CSR Movement and Global Governance'. In S. Singh-Sengupta (ed.).

Oyowe, O. A. 2014. 'An African Conception of Human Rights? Comments on the Challenges of Relativism'. *Human Rights Review* 15: 329–347.

Pahuja, S. and Saunders, A. 2019. 'Rival Worlds and the Place of the Corporation in International Law'. In J. von Bernstorff and P. Dann (eds.).

Palacios, M. 2006. *Between Legitimacy and Violence: A History of Colombia 1975–2002* 2nd ed. (trans. R. Stoller). Durham: Duke University Press.

Pally, M. 2016. *Commonwealth and Covenant*. Michigan: Williams B. Eerdmans.

Parker, C. 2002. *The Open Corporation: Effective Self-regulation and Democracy*. Cambridge: Cambridge University Press.

Parkinson, J. 1993. *Corporate Power and Responsibility: Issues in the Theory of Company Law*. Oxford: Clarendon Press.

Parrish, A. L. 2007. 'Storm in a Teacup: The US Supreme Court's Use of Foreign Law'. *University of Illinois Law Review* 2007: 637–680.

Peretti, T. 2010. 'Constructing the State Action Doctrine, 1940–1990'. *Law & Social Inquiry* 35: 273–310.

Pérez, J. F. J. 2012. 'Colombia's 1991 Constitution: A Right's Revolution'. In Nolte, D. and Schilling-Vacaflor, A. (eds.).

Perez, O. 2016. 'The Green Economy Paradox: A Critical Inquiry into Sustainability Indices'. *Minnesota Journal of Law, Science and Technology* 17: 153–219.

Peritz, R. J. R. 1996. *Competition Policy in America: History, Rhetoric, Law* Rev. Ed. Oxford: Oxford University Press.

Peroni, L. and Timmer, A. 2013. 'Vulnerable Groups: The Promise of an Emerging Concept in European Human Rights Convention Law'. *International Journal of Constitutional Law* 11: 1056–1085.

Perry, M. 2007. *Towards a Theory of Human Rights*. Cambridge: Cambridge University Press.

Pogge, T. 2002. *World Poverty and Human Rights: Cosmopolitan Responsibilities and Reforms*. Cambridge: Polity Press.

Poscher, R. 2003. *Grundrechte als Abwehrrechte*. Tübingen: Mohr Siebeck.

Putnam, R. 2000. *Bowling Alone: The Collapse and Revival of American Community*. New York: Simon and Schuster.

Pyle, A.J. 2013. *Locke*. Cambridge: Polity Press.

Quint, P. 1989. 'Free Speech and Private Law in German Constitutional Theory'. *Maryland Law Review* 48: 247–349.

Ramasastry, A. 2015. 'Corporate Social Responsibility versus Business and Human Rights: Bridging the Gap between Responsibility and Accountability'. *Journal of Human Rights* 14: 237–259.

Ramose, M. 1999. *African Philosophy Through Ubuntu*. Harare: Mond Books.

Randall, P. 1972. *Apartheid and the Church: Report of the Church Commission of the Study Project on Christianity in Apartheid Society*. Johannesburg: Christian Institute of Southern Africa.

Raphael, D. D. (ed.). 1967. *Political Theory and the Rights of Man*. London: Macmillan.

Ratner, S. 2001. 'Corporations and Human Rights: A Theory of Legal Responsibility'. *Yale Law Journal* 111: 443–545.

Rawls, J. 1993. *Political Liberalism*. New York: Colombia University Press.

Rawls, J. 1999. *A Theory of Justice* Rev. ed. Cambridge: Belknap Press.

Ray, B. 2016. *Engaging with Social Rights: Procedure, Participation and Democracy in South Africa's Second Wave*. Cambridge: Cambridge University Press.

Raz, J. 1986. *The Morality of Freedom*. Oxford: Clarendon Press.

Regan, A. 1998. 'Causes and Course of the Bougainville Conflict'. *Journal of Pacific History* 33: 269–285.

Rios-Figueroa, J. A. 2012. 'Institutional Design and Judicial Behaviour: Constitutional Interpretation of Criminal Due Process Rights in Latin America'. In Nolte, D. and Schilling-Vacaflor, A. (eds.).

Ritz, D. 2001. *Defying Corporations, Defining Democracy: A Book of History and Strategy*. New York: Apex Press.

Rivers, J. 2006. 'Proportionality and Variable Intensity of Review'. *Cambridge Law Journal* 65: 174–207.

Roach, K. and Budlender, G. 2005. 'Mandatory relief and Supervisory Jurisdiction: When Is It Appropriate, Just and Equitable?' *South African Law Journal* 122: 325–351.

Robertson, A. and Nolan, D. (eds.). 2011. *Rights and Private Law*. Oxford: Hart.

Robins, N. 2006. *The Corporation That Changed the World: How the East India Company Shaped the Modern Multinational*. London: Pluto Press.

Rogge, M. 2020. 'Bringing Corporate Governance Down to Earth: From Culmination Outcomes to Comprehensive Outcomes in Shareholder and Stakeholder Capitalism'. *Notre Dame Journal of Law, Ethics and Public Policy* (forthcoming) available at https://papers.ssrn.com/sol3/papers.cfm?abstract_id=3572765.

Rogowski, R. 2013. *Reflexive Labour Law in World Society*. Cheltenham: Edward Elgar.

Rogowski, R. 2015. 'The Emergence of Reflexive Global Labour Law'. *The German Journal of Industrial Relations* 22: 27–90.

Rosenfeld, M. 2002. 'Hate Speech in Constitutional Jurisprudence: A Comparative Analysis'. *Cardozo Law Review* 24: 1523–1567.

Rousseau, J. J. 1947. *The Social Contract* (trans. C. Frankel). New York: Hafner.

Roux, T. 2009. 'Principle and Pragmatism on the Constitutional Court of South Africa'. *International Journal of Constitutional Law* 7: 106–138.

Rueth, R. 2017. 'Between Tradition, Cultural Influence, Social Structure, and Economic Growth: A Status Quo Analysis on CSR Engagement in India and a Critical Evaluation of the New CSR Law'. In N. Mitra and R. Schmidpeter (eds.).

Ruffert, M. 2001. *Vorrang der Verfassung und Eigenständigkeit des Privatrechts. Eine verfassungsrechtliche Untersuchung zur Privatrechtswirkung des Grundgesetzes*. Tübingen: Mohr Siebeck.

Ruggie, J. 2011. 'The Construction of the UN "Protect, Respect and Remedy" Framework for Business and Human Rights: The True Confessions of a Principled Pragmatist'. *European Human Rights Law Review* 2: 127–133.

Ruggie, J. 2013. *Just Business: Multinational Corporations and Human Rights*. New York: W. W. Norton.

Ryan, A. 1999. 'Hobbes' Political Philosophy'. In T. Sorrell (ed.).

Sabel, C. F. and Simon, W. H. 2017. 'Democratic Experimentalism'. In J. Desautels-Stein and C. Tomlins (eds.).

Sajo, A. and Uitz, R. (eds.). 2005. *The Constitution in Private Relations: Expanding Constitutionalism*. Utrecht: Eleven International Publishing.

Salomon, M. E. 2007. *Global Responsibility for Human Rights: World Poverty and the Development of International Law*. Oxford: Oxford University Press.

Sandin, P. 1999. 'Dimensions of the Precautionary Principle'. *Human and Ecological Risk Assessment* 5: 889–907.

Santoro, M. 2010. 'Post-Westphalia and Its Discontents: Business, Globalization and Human Rights in Political and Moral Perspective'. *Business Ethics Quarterly* 20: 285–297.

Santoro, M. and Shanklin, R. 2020. 'Human Rights Obligations of Drug Companies'. *Journal of Human Rights* 19: 557–567.

Sarfaty, G. 2013. 'Regulating Through Numbers: A Case Study of Corporate Sustainability Reporting'. *Virginia Journal of International Law* 53: 575–622.

Sarfaty, G. 2015. 'Shining Light on Global Supply Chains'. *Harvard International Law Journal* 56: 419–464.

Scanlon, T. 1972. 'A Theory of Freedom of Expression'. *Philosophy and Public Affairs* 1: 204–226.

Scanlon, T. 1975. 'Preference and Urgency'. *Journal of Philosophy* 72: 655–669.

Scanlon, T. 2000. *What We Owe to Each Other*. Cambridge: Harvard University Press.

Schaefer, J. P. 2012. 'Neues vom Strukturwandel der Öffentichkeit'. *Der Staat* 51: 251–277.

Schauer, F. 2014. 'Proportionality and the Question of Weight'. In G. Huscroft, B. W. Miller and G. Webber (eds.).

Scheffczyk, F. and Fabian-Wolter, Y. (eds.). 2017. *Linien der Rechtsprechung des Bundesverfassungsgerichts* vol. 4. Berlin: De Gruyter.

Schiff, D. and Nobles, R. (eds.). 2003. *Jurisprudence*. London: Butterworth.

Schlaich, K. and Korioth, W. 2015. *Das Bundesverfassungsgericht* 10th ed. Munich: C.H. Beck.

Schwabe, J. 1971. *Die Sogennante Drittwirkung der Grudrechte*. Munich: Goldman Wilhelm.

Seitz, K. and Martens, J. 2017. 'Philanthrolateralism: Private Funding and Corporate Influence in the United Nations'. *Global Policy* 8: 46–50.

Sen, A. 2004. 'Elements of a Theory of Human Rights'. *Philosophy and Public Affairs* 32: 315–356.

Sen, A. and Williams, B. (eds.). 1982. *Utilitarianism and Beyond*. Cambridge: Cambridge University Press.

Shelton, D. 2006. 'Normative Hierarchy in International Law'. *American Journal of International Law* 100: 291–323.

Shin-Ichi, A. 2018. 'A Convention or a Recommendation? The Experience of International Labour Legislation'. In J. L. Černič and N. Carrillo-Santarelli (eds.).

Shue, H. 1980. *Basic Rights*. Princeton: Princeton University Press.

Simester, A. 2005. 'Is Strict Liability Always Wrong?'. In A. Simester (ed.).

Simester, A. (ed.). 2005. *Appraising Strict Liability*. Oxford: Oxford University Press.

Simons, P. 2004. 'Corporate Voluntarism and Human Rights: The Adequacy and Effectiveness of Voluntary Self-Regulation'. *Industrial Relations* 59: 101–141.

Simons, P. and Macklin, A. 2014. *The Governance Gap: Extractive Industries, Human Rights and the Home State Advantage*. London: Routledge.

Singer, P. 1972. 'Famine, Affluence, and Morality'. *Philosophy and Public Affairs* 1: 229–243.

Singh, M. (ed.). 2016. *The Indian Yearbook of Comparative Law*. India: Oxford University Press.

Singh-Sengupta, S. (ed.). 2004. *Business-Social Partnership: an International Perspective*. Jaipur: Aalekh.

Sinha, M. K. 2018. 'The Applicability of Human Rights Treaties to Business Enterprises: A Case Study of India'. In J. L. Černič and N. Carrillo-Santarelli (eds.).

Sinkovits, N., Hoque, S. F. and Sinkovics, R. R. 2016. 'Rana Plaza Collapse Aftermath: Are CSR Compliance and Auditing Pressures Effective?' *Accounting, Auditing & Accountability Journal* 49: 617–649.

Skogly, S. 2017. 'Regulatory Obligations in a Complex World: States' Extraterritorial Obligations Relating to Business and Human Rights'. In S. Deva and D. Bilchitz (eds.).

Slye, R. C. 2008. 'Corporations, Veils, and International Criminal Liability'. *Brooklyn Journal of International Law* 33: 955–973.

Smet, S. 2017. 'Conflicts between Human Rights and the ECtHR: Towards a Structured Balancing Test'. In S. Smet and E. Brems (eds.).

Smet, S. and Brems, E. (eds.). 2017. *When Human Rights Clash at the European Court of Human Rights: Conflict or Harmony?* Oxford: Oxford University Press.

Smith, J. 2013. 'Corporate Human Rights Obligations: Moral or Political?' *Business Ethics Journal Review* 1: 7–13.

Smith, J. D. (ed.). 2009. *Normative Theory and Business Ethics*. Lanham: Rowman & Littlefield.

Sorrell, T. (ed.). 1999. *The Cambridge Companion to Hobbes*. Cambridge: Cambridge University Press.

Steinhardt, R. H. 2005. 'Corporate Responsibility and the International Law of Human Rights: The new Lex Mercatoria' in P. Alston (ed.).

Stephens, B. 2002. 'The Amorality of Profit: Transnational Corporations and Human Rights' *Berkeley Journal of International Law* 20: 45–90.

Stone, C. 1975. *Where the Law Ends: The Social Control of Corporate Behaviour.* New York: Harper & Row.

Stone, R. and Devenney, J. 2013. *The Modern Law of Contract* 10th ed. Oxford: Routledge.

Stout, L. 2012. *The Shareholder Value Myth: How Putting Shareholders First Harms Investors, Corporations and the Public.* San Francisco: Berrett-Koehler Publishers.

Sumner, L. W. 1989. *The Moral Foundation of Rights.* Oxford: Oxford University Press.

Sundaram, J. 2018. *Pharmaceutical Patent Protection and World Trade Law: The Unresolved Problem of Access to Medicines.* Abingdon: Routledge.

Sunstein, C. 1996a. 'Foreword: Leaving Things Undecided'. *Harvard Law Review* 110: 4–101.

Sunstein, C. 1996b. 'On the Expressive Function of Law'. *University of Pennsylvania Law Review* 144: 2021–2053.

Sunstein, C. and Nussbaum, M. (eds.). 2005. *Animal Rights: Current Debates and New Directions.* Oxford: Oxford University Press.

Taylor, C. 2015. 'Using Securities Disclosures to Advance Human Rights: A Consideration of Dodd-Frank Section 1502 and the Securities and Exchange Commission Conflict Minerals Rule'. *Journal of Human Rights* 14: 201–217.

Taylor, G. 2002. 'The Horizontal Effect of Human Rights Provisions, the German Model and its Applicability to Common-Law Jurisdictions'. *King's Law Journal* 13: 187–218.

Teubner, G. 1985. 'After Legal Instrumentalism? Strategic Models of Post-Regulatory Law'. In G. Teubner (ed.).

Teubner, G. (ed.). 1985. *Dilemmas of Law in the Welfare State.* Berlin: De Gruyter.

Teubner, G., Nobles, R. and Schiff, D. 2003. 'The Autonomy of Law: An Introduction to Legal Autopoiesis' in D. Schiff and R. Nobles (eds.).

Thompson, H. 1991. 'The Economic Causes and Consequences of the Bougainville Crisis'. *Resources Policy* 17: 69–85.

Timmer, A. 2013. 'A Quiet Revolution: Vulnerability in the European Court of Human Rights'. In Fineman, M. A. and Grear, A. (eds.).

Tófalo, I. 2006. 'Overt and Hidden Accomplices: Transnational Corporations' Range of Complicity for Human Rights Violations'. In De Schutter, O. (ed.).

Tsakyrakis, S. 2009. 'Proportionality: An Assault on Human Rights?'. *International Journal of Constitutional Law* 7: 468–493.

Tushnet, M. 2003. 'The Issue of State Action/Horizontal Effect in Comparative Constitutional Law'. *International Journal of Constitutional Law* 1: 79–98.

Tushnet, M. 2009. 'State Action in 2020'. In J. M. Balkin and R. B. Siegel (eds.).

Urbina, F. 2012. 'A Critique of Proportionality'. *American Journal of Jurisprudence* 57: 49–80.

Valentini, L. 2017. 'Human Rights, the Political View and Transnational Corporations: An Exploration'. In T. Campbell and K. Bourne (eds.).

Van Alebeek, R. and Nollkaemper, A. 2012. 'The Legal Status of Decisions by Human Rights Treaty Bodies in National Law'. In H. Keller and G. Ulfstein (eds.).

Van Alstine, M. 2009. 'The Universal Declaration and Developments in the Enforcement of International Human Rights in Domestic Law'. *Maryland Journal of International Law* 24: 63–74.

Van Der Sijde, E. 2020. 'Tenure Security for ESTA Occupiers: Building on the Obiter Remarks in *Baron* v. *Claytile Limited*". *South African Journal on Human Rights* 36: 74–92.

Van Ho, T. 2018. 'Band-Aids Don't Fix Bullet Holes: In Defence of a Traditional State-Centric Approach'. In J.L. Černič and N. Carrillo-Santarelli (eds.).

Vázquez, C. M. 2005. 'Direct versus Indirect Obligations of Corporations under International Law'. *Columbia Journal of Transnational Law* 43: 927–959.

Von Bernstorff, J. and Dann, P. (eds.). 2019. *The Battle for International Law: South–North Perspectives on the Decolonization Era*. Oxford: Oxford University Press.

Voorhoof, D. 2017. 'Freedom of Expression versus Privacy and the Right to Reputation'. In S. Smet and E. Brems (eds.).

Waldron, J. 1987. 'Jeremy Bentham's Anarchical Fallacies'. In J. Waldron (ed.).

Waldron, J. (ed.). 1987. *Nonsense upon Stilts: Bentham, Burke and Marx on the Rights of Man*. Abingdon: Routledge.

Waldron, J. 1993. *Liberal Rights: Collected Papers 1981–1991*. Cambridge: Cambridge University Press.

Waldron, J. 2002. *God, Locke and Equality: Christian Foundations in Locke's Political Thought*. Cambridge: Cambridge University Press.

Webber, G. 2009. *The Negotiable Constitution: On the Limitation of Rights*. Cambridge: Cambridge University Press.

Webber, G. 2010. 'Proportionality, Balancing, and the Cult of Constitutional Rights scholarship'. *Canadian Journal of Law and Jurisprudence* 23: 179–202.

Weber, M. 1919. 'The Profession and Vocation of Politics'. In P. Lassman and R. Spiers (eds.).

Weber, M. 1978. *Economy and Society* (trans. C. Wittich and G. Roth). Berkeley: University of California Press.

Wechsler, H. 1959. 'Toward Neutral Principles of Constitutional Law'. *Harvard Law Review* 73: 1–35.

Werhane, P. 1985. *Persons, Rights and Corporations*. Prentice Hall: Englewood Cliffs.

Werhane, P. 2016. 'Corporate Moral Agency and the Responsibility to Respect Rights in the UN Guiding Principles: Do Corporations Have Moral Rights?'. *Business and Human Rights Journal* 1: 5–20.

West, R. L. 1990. 'Equality Theory, Marital Rape and the Promise of the Fourteenth Amendment'. *Florida Law Review* 42: 45–79.

West, R. L. 2003. *Re-Imagining Justice: Progressive Interpretations of Formal Equality, Rights, and the Rule of Law*. Aldershot: Ashgate.

Wettstein, F. 2009. *Multinational Corporations and Global Justice: Human Rights Obligations of a Quasi-Governmental Institution*. Stanford: Stanford University Press.

Wettstein, F. 2010. 'For Better or for Worse: Corporate Responsibility beyond "Do No Harm"'. *Business Ethics Quarterly* 20: 275–283.

Wettstein, F. 2012. 'CSR and the Debate on Business and Human Rights: Bridging the Great Divide'. *Business Ethics Quarterly* 22: 739–770.

Whitney, T. 2015. 'Conflict Minerals, Black Markets and Transparency: The Legislative Background of Dodd-Frank Section 1502 and Its Historical Lessons'. *Journal of Human Rights* 14: 183–200.

Winfield, T. H. 1926. 'The History of Negligence in the Law of Torts'. *Law Quarterly Review* 42: 184–201.

Wood, A. 1999. *Kant's Ethical Thought*. Cambridge: Cambridge University Press.

Wood, S. 2012. 'The Case for Leverage-Based Corporate Human Rights Responsibility'. *Business Ethics Quarterly* 22: 63–98.

Woolman, S. 2006. 'Application'. In S. Woolman et al. (eds.).

Woolman, S. 2007. 'The Amazing, Vanishing Bill of Rights'. *South African Law Journal* 124: 762–794.

Woolman, S. 2013. *The Selfless Constitution: Experimentalism and Flourishing as Foundations of South Africa's Basic Law*. Cape Town: Juta.

Woolman, S. and Bishop, M. (eds.). 2006. *Constitutional Law of South Africa*. Cape Town: Juta.

Woolman, S. and Botha, H. 2006. 'Limitations'. In S. Woolman et al. (eds.).

Woolman, S. and Davis, D. 1996. 'The Last Laugh: Du Plessis v. De Klerk, Classical Liberalism, Creole Liberalism and the Application of Fundamental Rights under the Interim and Final Constitutions'. *South African Journal on Human Rights* 12: 361–404.

Yeh, J (ed.). 2015. *The Functional Transformation of Courts: Taiwan and Korea in Comparison*. Taiwan: National Taiwan University Press.

Young, I. M. 2006. 'Responsibility and Global Justice: A Social Connection Model'. *Social Philosophy and Policy* 23: 102–130.

Yune, J. 2015. 'Judicial Activism and the Constitutional Reasoning of the Korean Supreme Court in the Field of Civil Law'. In J. Yeh (ed.).

Zerk, J. 2006. *Multinationals and Corporate Social Responsibility: Limitations and Opportunities in International Law*. Cambridge: Cambridge University Press.

Zippelius, R. 2018. 'Art. 1 Abs. 1 u. 2'. in W. Kahl et al. (ed.).

Zuck, R. 2017. *Das Recht der Verfassungsbeschwerde*, 5th ed. Munich: C.H. Beck.

International Instruments, Reports and Internet Sources

Al Hussein, Z. R. 'Ethical Pursuit of Prosperity' (23 March 2015) available at www.lawgazette.co.uk/commentary-and-opinion/ethical-pursuit-of-prosperity/5047796.article

Bafilemba, F., Mueller, T. and Lezhnev, S. 'The Impact of Dodd-Frank and Conflict Minerals Reforms on Eastern Congo's Conflict' (2014) available at https://enoughproject.org/files/Enough%20Project%20-%20The%20Impact%20of%20Dodd-Frank%20and%20Conflict%20Minerals%20Reforms%20on%20Eastern%20Congo%E2%80%99s%20Conflict%2010June2014.pdf

British Institute of International and Comparative Law 'A UK Failure to Prevent Mechanism for Corporate Human Rights' (February 2020) available at www.biicl.org/publications/a-uk-failure-to-prevent-mechanism-for-corporate-human-rights-harms ('BIICL Report, 2020').

Castan Centre for Human Rights Law Monash University 'Human Rights Translated 2.0: a Business Reference Guide' (2017) available at www.ohchr.org/documents/publications/HRT_2_0_EN.pdf ('The Human Rights Translated Report, 2017').

Commission on Human Rights 'Responsibilities of Transnational Corporations and Related Business Enterprises With Respect to Human Rights' E/CN.4/2004/L.73/Rev.1(2004) available at www.refworld.org/pdfid/415298c04.pdf

Commission on Human Rights, 'Interim Report of the Special Representative of the Secretary-General on the Issue of Human Rights and Transnational Corporations and Other Business Enterprises', E/CN.4/2006/97 (2006) available at http://hrlibrary.umn.edu/business/RuggieReport2006.html ('SRSG 2006 Interim Report').

Committee on Economic, Social and Cultural Rights, General Comment 3 on 'the Nature of State Parties' Obligations', E/1991/23 (1990) available at www.refworld.org/pdfid/4538838e10.pdf

Committee on Economic, Social and Cultural Rights, General Comment 4 on 'The Right to Adequate Housing', E/1992/23 (1991) available at www.refworld.org/docid/47a7079a1.html

Committee on Economic, Social and Cultural Rights, General Comment 14 on 'The Right to the Highest Attainable Standard of Health', E/C.12/2000/4 (2000) available at www.refworld.org/pdfid/4538838d0.pdf

Committee on Economic, Social and Cultural Rights, General Comment 15 on 'The Right to Water', E/C.12/2002/11 (2003) available at www.refworld.org/pdfid/4538838d11.pdf

Committee on Economic, Social and Cultural Rights, General Comment No.24 on 'State Obligations under the International Covenant on Economic, Social and Cultural Rights in the Context of Business Activities', E/C.12/GC/24 (2017) available at www.refworld.org/docid/5beaecba4.html

Committee on the Rights of the Child, General Comment No.16 on 'State Obligations Regarding the Impact of the Business Sector on Children's Rights', CRC/C/GC/16 (2013) available at www.refworld.org/docid/51ef9cd24.html

Declaration of the Rights of Man and of the Citizen (1789) available at http://avalon.law.yale.edu/18th_century/rightsof.asp

Declaration on the Rights of Indigenous Peoples (2007) available at www.un.org/development/desa/indigenouspeoples/declaration-on-the-rights-of-indigenous-peoples.html

Draft Norms on the Responsibilities of Transnational Corporations and Other Business Enterprises with Regard to Human Rights E/CN.4/Sub.2/2003/12 (2003) available at http://hrlibrary.umn.edu/links/NormsApril2003.html ('Draft Norms, 2003').

European Commission 'Study on Directors' Duties and Sustainable Corporate Governance' (2020) available at https://op.europa.eu/en/publication-detail/-/publication/e47928a2-d20b-11ea-adf7-01aa75ed71a1/language-en ('Directors' Duties Study, 2020').

European Convention on Human Rights (1950) available at www.echr.coe.int/documents/convention_eng.pdf

Financial Reporting Council 'The UK Corporate Governance Code' (2018) available at www.frc.org.uk/getattachment/88bd8c45-50ea-4841-95b0-d2f4f48069a2/2018-UK-Corporate-Governance-Code-FINAL.pdf

Human Rights Council 'Clarifying the Concepts of "Sphere of Influence" and "Complicity"', A/HRC/8/16 (2008) available at https://www.refworld.org/docid/484d1fe12.html ('Sphere of Influence Report', 2008).

Human Rights Council, 'Protect, Respect and Remedy: a Framework for Business and Human Rights' A/HRC/8/5 (2008) available at https://digitallibrary.un.org/record/625292?ln=en ('UN Framework 2008').

Human Rights Council, 'Report of the Special Representative of the Secretary-General on the Issue of Human Rights and Transnational Corporations and Other Business Enterprises' A/HRC/14/27 (2010) available at www.refworld.org/docid/4c0759832.html ('SRSG 2010 Report').

Human Rights Council, 'Guiding Principles on Business and Human Rights: Implementing the United Nations "Protect, Respect and Remedy"

Framework' A/HRC/17/31 (2011) available at www.ohchr.org/documents/publications/guidingprinciplesbusinesshr_en.pdf ('UNGPs').

Human Rights Council, 'Report on the Sixth Session of the Open-ended Intergovernmental Working Group on Transnational Corporations and Other Business Enterprises with Respect to Human Rights' A/HRC/46/XX (2020) available at www.ohchr.org/EN/HRBodies/HRC/WGTransCorp/Session6/Pages/Session6.aspx ('Draft Sixth Session Report 2020').

International Covenant on Civil and Political Rights available at www.ohchr.org/en/professionalinterest/pages/ccpr.aspx ('ICCPR').

International Covenant on Economic, Social and Cultural Rights available at www.ohchr.org/EN/ProfessionalInterest/Pages/CESCR.aspx ('ICESCR').

International Commission of Jurists 'Corporate Complicity and Legal Accountability' (2008) available at www.icj.org/report-of-the-international-commission-of-jurists-expert-legal-panel-on-corporate-complicity-in-international-crimes/ ('ICJ Complicity Report, 2008').

International Law Association. 2004. 'Final Report on the Impact of Findings of the United Nations Human Rights Treaty Bodies'. *International Law Association Reports of Conferences* 71: 621–702 ('2004 Treaty Bodies Report').

Kay, J. 'The Kay Review of UK Equity Markets and Long-term Decision-making' (2012) available at https://assets.publishing.service.gov.uk/government/uploads/system/uploads/attachment_data/file/253454/bis-12-917-kay-review-of-equity-markets-final-report.pdf

Institute of Directors Southern Africa 'King IV Report on Corporate Governance for South Africa' (2016) available at https://cdn.ymaws.com/www.iodsa.co.za/resource/collection/684B68A7-B768-465C-8214-E3A007F15A5A/IoDSA_King_IV_Report_-_WebVersion.pdf ('King IV Code').

Matthysen, K. and Zaragoza Montejano, A. "Conflict Minerals' Initiatives in DR Congo: Perceptions of Local Mining Communities' (2013) available at http://afrikarabia.com/wordpress/wp-content/uploads/2014/01/IPIS-Conflict-minerals-local-perception-novembre-2013-.pdf

Ministry of Corporate Affairs, India 'Report of the High-Level Committee on Corporate Social Responsibility 2018' (Released 2019) available at www.mca.gov.in/Ministry/pdf/CSRHLC_13092019.pdf ('High-Level Committee Report 2018').

Morrison, J. 'the Business Case for Human Rights – Values, Expectations and Risk' (2011) available at www.ihrb.org/pdf/IHRB_Speech_2011_04_28_John_Morrison_The_Business_Case_for_Human_Rights.pdf

MSI Integrity 'Not Fit for Purpose: the Grand Experiment in Multi-Stakeholder Initiatives in Corporate Accountability, Human Rights and Global Governance' (2020) available at https://www.msi-integrity.org/not-fit-for-purpose/ ('Not Fit for Purpose Report').

Open-ended Inter-governmental Working Group Chairmanship 'Legally Binding Instrument to Regulate, in International Human Rights Law, the Activities of Transnational Corporations and Other Business Enterprises' (Second Revised Draft) (2020) available at https://media.business-humanrights.org/media/documents/7ebffa2b7510a719d61fdab83fd8b2c19de4c650.pdf ('The 2nd Revised Draft Treaty').

UK Joint Parliamentary Committee on Human Rights *Human Rights and Business 2017: Promoting responsibility and ensuring accountability* HL PAPER 153 HC 443 (5 April 2017) available at https://old.parliament.uk/business/committees/committees-a-z/joint-select/human-rights-committee/inquiries/parliament-2015/inquiry/ ('JPCHR Report, 2017').

United Nations Charter available at www.un.org/en/sections/un-charter/un-charter-full-text/

Universal Declaration on Human Rights available at www.un.org/en/universal-declaration-human-rights/ ('UDHR').

Working Group on Business and Human Rights on Corporate Human Rights Due Diligence, Report A/73/163 (2018) available at https://ap.ohchr.org/documents/dpage_e.aspx?si=A/73/163 ('Working Group HRDD Report, 2018').

Working Group on Business and Human Rights 'Companion Note 1 to the Working Group's 2018 Report to the General Assembly' (2018) available at www.ohchr.org/Documents/Issues/Business/Session18/CompanionNote1DiligenceReport.pdf ('Working Group Companion Report 1, 2018').

Working Group on Business and Human Rights 'Companion Note 2 to the Working Group's 2018 Report to the General Assembly' available at www.ohchr.org/Documents/Issues/Business/Session18/CompanionNote2DiligenceReport.pdf ('Working Group Companion Report 2, 2018').

Working Group on Business and Human Rights 'Gender Dimensions of the Guiding Principles on Business and Human Rights' A/HRC/41/43 (2019) available at https://documents-dds-ny.un.org/doc/UNDOC/GEN/G19/146/08/PDF/G1914608.pdf?OpenElement ('Working Group Gender Dimensions Report, 2019').

Working Group on Business and Human Rights 'Connecting the Business and Human Rights and the Anti-Corruption Agendas Report A/HRC/44/43 (2020) available at https://undocs.org/A/HRC/44/43 ('Working Group Anti-Corruption Report, 2020).

Wu, B. and Zheng, Y. 2008. 'A Long March to Improve Labour Standards in China: Chinese Debates on the New Labour Contract Law' (2008) available at https://www.nottingham.ac.uk/iaps/documents/cpi/briefings/briefing-39-china-new-labour-contract-law.pdf

INDEX

For EU product safety concerns, contact us at Calle de José Abascal, 56–1°, 28003 Madrid, Spain or eugpsr@cambridge.org.

www.ingramcontent.com/pod-product-compliance
Ingram Content Group UK Ltd.
Pitfield, Milton Keynes, MK11 3LW, UK
UKHW020404140625
459647UK00020B/2639
* 9 7 8 1 1 0 8 8 1 5 3 1 4 *